Psychological Warfai and the New World Order

Servando Gonzalez' exposé of the Alien Queen, also known as the CFR, could easily alter the future of Western civilization and America for the good. These are times when a single man may make great contributions to the cause of human dignity and freedom.

—Kevin E. Abrams, co-author with Scott Lively of *The Pink Swastika*.

Thoreau wrote, "There are a thousand hacking at the branches of evil to one who is striking at the root." Servando Gonzalez didn't waste any time hacking at the branches, and reveals the very crooked roots of evil. This is a most impressive book. A must read.

—G. Edward Griffin, author of *The Creature from Jekyll Island*.

Servando Gonzalez has studied in detail the men and organizations that rule the world. This book reveals the true story of how Fidel Castro came to power, and discusses the powerful group that has kept him in power for almost fifty years. It is one of the most important books of this decade. Read it and learn about the invisible forces that direct the course of world affairs.

—Stanley Monteith, author of *Brotherhood of Darkness*.

Read this book. Read it carefully. It not only tells you what's happening today but, with very well chosen historical perspective, it lets you look down the road of the recent past for proof of what it says. That is the best way to learn to look at the future in order to fathom what is coming your way. And what is coming our way in the U.S., Europe —the whole world— is riddled with grave dangers, pitfalls and perils.

—Adrian Salbuchi, author of *El cerebro del mundo*.

Edward Bernays wrote, "We are governed, our minds are molded, our tastes formed, our ideas suggested, largely by men we have never heard of." However, Servando Gonzalez, an astute researcher and author, masterly divulges the machinations behind many historical and contemporary events and reveals who is really managing the presidential puppet strings. As Servando maintains, the new American Revolution, using covert warfare, is a conflict without guns. Rather, the ammunition is lies and psychological warfare and every American citizen is a target. It is a fabulous book, a must-read!

—Deanna Spingola, author of *When the Power Elite Rules*.

Also by Servando Gonzalez

BOOKS

Arte: realismo o realidad
Historia de las artes visuales (with Armando Ledón)
Historia herética de la revolución fidelista
(published in Mexico as *Fidel Castro para herejes y otros invertebrados*)
Observando (Primera Edición)
Observando (Segunda Edición)
The Secret Fidel Castro: Deconstructing the Symbol
The Nuclear Deception: Nikita Khrushchev and the Cuban missile crisis
La madre de todas las conspiraciones: una novela de ideas subversivas

MULTIMEDIA

Real History of "The Horse": A HyperComic
How to Create Your Own Personal Intelligence Agency
The Riddle of the Swastika: A Study in Symbolism
Popol Vuh: An Interactive Educational Game
Hypertext for Beginners

DOCUMENTARIES

Treason in America: The Council on Foreign Relations
Partners in Treason: The CFR-CIA-Castro Connection

INTERNET SITES

Castromania: The Fidel Watch
Tyrant Aficionado
The Swastika and the Nazis

ELECTRONIC WORKS
(Amazon Kindle)

Obamania: The New Puppet and His Masters
Intelligence, Espionage, the 9/11 Events and the Cuban Missile Crisis

PERSONAL SITE

www.servandogonzalez.org

Psychological Warfare and the New World Order

The Secret War Against the American People

Servando Gonzalez

Spooks Books

Oakland, California

In Memoriam
Arthur B. Darling (1892-1971)

Cataloging-in-Publication Data

Gonzalez, Servando, 1935-

Psychological Warfare and the New World Order:
The Secret War Against the American People
p. cm.

Includes bibliographical references and index.

ISBN 978-0-932367-23-5 (soft cover)

1. United States—Politics and government—20th century. 2. Council on Foreign Relations.
3. United States—Central Intelligence Agency. I. Title. II. Gonzalez, Servando, 1935-

Cover illustration: Servando Gonzalez

First Printing, September 2010.
This book was printed in the United States of America.

www.psywarandnwo.com

Contents

PREFACE

It is natural for man to indulge in the illusions of hope. We are apt to shut our eyes against a painful truth, and listen to the song of that siren till she transforms us into beasts. Is this the part of wise men, engaged in a great and arduous struggle for liberty? Are we disposed to be of the number of those who having eyes see not, and having ears hear not, the things which so nearly concern their temporal salvation?

For my part, whatever anguish of spirit it may cost, I am willing to know the whole truth —to know the worst and to provide for it.

—Patrick Henry, Speech on the Stamp Act, Virginia Convention, March 23, 1775.

Let us never tolerate outrageous conspiracy theories concerning the attacks of September the 11th.

—President George W. Bush, November 10, 2001.

Apparently, "conspiracy stuff" is now shorthand for unspeakable truth.

— Gore Vidal.

This is a book about a conspiracy. It is not, however, about the imaginary "vast right-wing conspiracy" mentioned by Hillary Clinton.[1] Neither it is about the alleged "conspiracy of ideas" carried out by well-intentioned, honest people engaged in "an ideological battle," mentioned by Congressman Ron Paul.[2]

It is about a real vast right- left-wing conspiracy carried out by a group of criminal psychopaths without any ideology at all except maximum power and control. To carry out their plans, the conspirators usually resort to deception, coercion, extortion, usury, racketeering, Ponzi schemes, theft, torture, assassination and large-scale mass murder.

The ultimate goal of these conspirators is the total destruction of the American republic as we knew it[3] and the creation of a global communo-fascist feudal totalitarian society under their full control —a society they euphemistically call the New World Order.

The conspirators are a small group of Wall Street bankers, oil magnates and CEOs of transnational corporations, most of them senior members of the Council on Foreign Relations. Though their push for total control of the U.S. government began in 1913 during the Wilson administration, since the end of WWII it has become a fully developed psychological war of immense proportions secretly waged against the American people. Key elements in this secret war have been the Department of State, the National Security Council, the Central Intelligence Agency, as well as some of the conspirators' secret agents like Allen Dulles, Henry Kissinger, Zbigniew Brzezinski and Fidel Castro.

This conspiracy resembles a gigantic puzzle of which many pieces are missing or have been intentionally put in the wrong place in order to mislead. This explains why most analysts who have studied the phenomenon using the analytical method have failed to find the true source of the problem.

Consequently, I have used in this book the methodological instrument of synthesis rather than analysis to reassemble the puzzle in order to find meaning in it. The results, as you will see, are diametrically different from most studies about the subject.

One of the most fascinating features of intelligence work is that sometimes a single and apparently unimportant piece of information can set a whole bunch of seemingly unrelated facts into a meaningful pattern. Intelligence officers believe that if you can find that elusive piece of information you can rewrite large parts of history from a surprisingly different point of view.

In my research, I have not been able to find out that single piece of information that could instantly turn this undecipherable puzzle into a coherent picture. Nevertheless, I think I have done the second best thing. I have found that key piece of information for most of the single pieces of the puzzle. Once this was done, the whole picture, as if by magic, appeared clear and defined.

The main advantage of this methodology is that it provided me with a tool to discover that some occurrences are not the product of chance, or the effort of isolated individuals, as some people want us to believe, but the result of an intelligent design conceived by a group of well-organized conspirators. This sole conclusion made these incidents comprehensible, and renders them potentially controllable.

Dealing with an American conspiracy, I have dedicated much of it to the study of the Central Intelligence Agency, an organization many people see as the center of this conspiracy. Many books written about the CIA mention the Agency's inept attempts to assassinate Fidel Castro. Most of them, however, have failed to discover Castro's true role as an agent provocateur[4] working hard to help the very people he claims to hate.

Also, most books dealing with the CIA are either anti-CIA, written by authors who consider themselves progressive, liberal Democrats or outright leftists, or pro-CIA, written by authors who see themselves as conservative, Republicans, or outright rightists. I don't consider myself belonging to any of these two artificially created disinformational[5] categories, so this is a totally different kind of book, difficult to classify.

Some of the controversial ideas expressed in it will surely attach the label "conspiracy theorist" permanently to my lapel. I have no problem with that. But historical events are very rich and complex, and cannot be fully explained by labels alone. Therefore, my main objection is not that somebody may classify me as a "conspiracy theorist,"[6] but the use of the term "theory" to denote the type of knowledge I am trying to explain. The problem arises from the meaning of the word "theory."

Conspiracies and Conspiracy "Theories"

A scientific theory is just a temporary explanation of the causes of a phenomenon for which we still don't have all the data. Therefore, based on a few verifiable facts and a great deal of educated guessing, initially in the form of a hypothesis, eventually a theory is formulated. With the passage of time and continuous testing, the theory is either discarded, or fine-tuned until it is accepted as a scientifically proved fact.

In the case of conspiracies, however, most people, consciously or unconsciously, follow what is known as Shallit's Razor[7] advice: "Don't attribute to conspiracy what may be adequately explained by stupidity or incompetence." But, year after year, most of the people I will deal with in this book have consistently acted against the best interest of the American people.

Former Secretary of Defense James Forrestal once pointed out that the men conspiring to destroy this country are not incompetent fools. On the contrary, they are extremely crafty and intelligent. If they were merely stupid, every once in a while they would make a mistake in our favor, but they never do. They consistently and systematically work to destroy our country and freedoms.[8]

It is not far-fetched, though, to think that, on the contrary, what most people see as errors and failures are actually successes. The cause for this confusion is because the conspirator's true goals are not what they claim to be.

Consequently, to Shallit's Razor I oppose my Corollary to Shallit's Razor: Don't attribute to stupidity or incompetence what may be simply and adequately explained by a conspiracy. Moreover, I would like to advance what I would call Servando's Conspiracy Law:

> Human-caused events of a certain type —particularly the ones detrimental to a large segment of the population, but beneficial to a small, powerful clique — which are consistently repeated over and over, are most likely not the result of chance, stupidity, or incompetence, but of a well organized conspiracy.

A few years ago I was captivated by a radio program I discovered quite by chance late in the evening: Coast to Coast a.m. with George Noory. It grabbed my full attention until past 2:00 a.m. in the morning. The subject was Secret Societies, and consisted of a panel of experts composed by Linda Moulton Howe, Alex Jones, Steve Quayle and Jim Marrs, well-known researchers in the field of conspiracy theory.

One of the things they mentioned in the program, which aroused my curiosity, was a Report produced by the Project for the New American Century (PNAC), an organization formed mostly by so-called "neocons" supporters of the Bush administration. The 90-page Report, entitled "Rebuilding America's Defenses: Strategy, Forces and Resources For a New Century" was published in September 2000.

In synthesis, the Report called for an era of open, uncontested global American imperialism based on brute military force. Because of the openness and cynicism in the way it told the world the course of action the conspirators will follow, some of the panelists compared the PNAC Report to Hitler's *Mein Kampf.*

Being a skeptic, I didn't trust their words. So, next day, I searched the Internet and I found the Project's site, from which I downloaded a file with the Report. In it I verified that a paragraph quoted during the radio program by one of the panelists was actually there and it had been quoted literally.

In stark cynicism, the authors of the Report mention that, in order to transform the U.S. military for the new challenges it will face, the process of transformation, "... even if it brings revolutionary change, is likely to be a long one, absent some catastrophic and catalyzing event — *like a new Pearl Harbor.*"[9] (Emphasis added)

Notice that this report was written in September 2000, exactly a year before the September 11 events. But, as some of the panelists of the radio program expressed, the conspirators are so arrogant, confident and convinced that the rest of us are a bunch of ignorant fools who don't have the capacity to think for ourselves, that they didn't fear of openly talking about the evil plans they have for the rest of us.[10]

Further search in the Internet looking for critical opinions about the Project brought a series of articles, among them a revealing one by Alex Callinicos, a professor at the University of York, U.K., entitled "The Grand Strategy of the American Empire." In his article, professor Callinicos, who calls himself a Marxist, does a thorough analysis of the American actions since September 11, 2001, asserting, "the Marxist theory of imperialism provides the best framework for understanding the contemporary U.S. war drive."[11] The same theoretical Marxist framework is found in James Petras' recent book, *Rulers and Ruled in the U.S. Empire: Bankers, Zionists and Militants.*[12]

But just a cursory look at Callinicos' article and Petras' book, shows that, contrary to their claims, Marxist theory is *not* the right tool to understand what is currently going on in this chaotic post September 11 world. And the reason for this is not only because Marxism is a blunt, one-sided, biased tool for theoretical analysis, but also because it actually was developed by the conspirators themselves —Moses Mordecai Marx Levi, alias Karl Marx, was one of their secret agents[13] — as a disinformational device to avoid that the people focus in the right direction.

The fact may explain why American universities are full of Marxist professors fighting the evils of capitalism and imperialism, of which Noam Chomsky is perhaps the most notorious one, while getting financial support for their research from the tax-exempt "charitable" foundations controlled by the very imperialist conspirators they criticize. It also explains why, though Marxist Theory is widely studied in American campuses, Conspiracy Theory, a legitimate field of study for a growing sector of the population, is totally absent from the curricula, and when it is mentioned is only to ridicule its scholars, calling them kooks or worse.

But, contrary to Marx's claims, the true main motor of society has never been class struggle or capitalist greed and exploitation, but secret societies conspiring and fighting among each other for world control.[14] Explaining the current U.S. war drive as an imperialist fight for economic resources —the die hard leftist myth of "war for oil"— actually helps the conspirators' efforts in hiding their true current goals, which they have expressed on innumerable occasions: the elimination of at least 85 percent of the world's population and the destruction of industrial civilization. This will result in the reduction of the few survivors to pre-industrial, medieval levels of consumption in a communo-fascist totalitarian system they call the New World Order. Obviously, this has nothing to do with greed and exploitation, but with something much worse and evil.

A key component of the New World Order is population control and depopulation through eugenics. If one is to believe Jacques Cousteau, one of the conspirators' mouthpieces,

> The United Nations' goal is to reduce population selectively by encouraging abortion, forced sterilization, and control human reproduction, and regards two-thirds of the human population as excess baggage, with 350,000 people to be eliminated per day.[15]

Ted Turner, another strong depopulation advocate, donated in 1997 $1 billion to the UN, with the only condition that the money would be used for birth control. Some years ago Bill Gates, after the conspirators threatened him with dismembering his dear Microsoft, saw the message on the wall and, soon after, created the Gates Foundation. Its main goal, disguised under the banner of women's reproductive rights, is depopulation in Africa and other Third World countries.

Marxist analysis fails because it tries to provide rational explanations based just on economics to a fully irrational process closer to witchcraft and sorcery than science. The fact that some scholars still use Marxism as an analytical tool explains why the conspirators were instrumental in the creation of Marxism. Using smoke screens has always been one of their best tactics to keep their true goals in the dark.

Espionage and Skepticism

Most authors who have critically studied the CIA apparently have worked out of a sort of historical flat land, and their search for the Agency's roots rarely go beyond the Office of Strategic Services (OSS), which they see as the CIA's true and only ancestor. But, as I will show you in this book, the CIA's twisted roots go far deeper than that.

Despite their shortcomings, however, most academic studies about the CIA show a high level of scholarship. What they lack, though, is a healthy amount of skepticism. Despite the fact that they are dealing with spies, intelligence and espionage, the authors of these studies apparently ignore that a cardinal rule of the profession is that in the dark world of intelligence and espionage things are seldom what they seem. A curious characteristic of most of these books is that, though dealing with spies and espionage, their authors display not only a large amount of gullibility and naiveté, but also an almost total ignorance of even the most essential elements of the craft of intelligence and espionage.

I would dare say that, despite of their dealing with the subject of intelligence, most of these authors seem to ignore that in the field of intelligence and espionage the most accepted definition of intelligence is "information (raw data) that has been evaluated and validated." Given the fact that the information offered in most of these books has not been evaluated using the methodological tools of the trade, one has to conclude that most of the information these books provide don't have much value from the point of view of intelligence and fall into the category of misinformation or, even worse, disinformation.

Upon reading many of these works, one feels that their authors apparently have accepted at face value most of the (dis)information they have obtained in the form of declassified documents supplied by the CIA directly or through shady organizations like the National Security "Archive." They also seem to believe that most of the CIA officials they have interviewed for their books have either told them the truth or have just made a few honest mistakes. The authors of these studies seem to ignore that most of the people they have dealt with in these meetings are intelligence operatives (there is no such thing as a "former" intelligence officer. Once a spy, always a spy), that is, professional liars.

I am not using here the term "liar" in a pejorative sense, but just to indicate that, as it is expected from seasoned intelligence professionals, lies and disinformation are essential tools of their trade. As a matter of fact, learning how to lie convincingly is an important part of the training of intelligence officers all around the world. Some of them, like the Soviets and Cubans, made an art of beating the polygraph (commonly known as the lie detector).

Case officers' main job is recruiting and managing agents.[16] To do their job, they practice lying and deception as an art form and a way of life.[17] Early in their training, they learn how to convince others that they are something very different from what they really are.

Good deception combines the imagination of a fiction writer and the abilities of an actor. Intelligence agencies devote much of the training of their prospective case officers teaching them how to lie efficiently.[18] Once the officers have successfully operated in the field for some time, lying becomes second nature to them, to the point that most of them don't know any longer when they are telling the truth or not.

But most of the authors who have written books about the CIA[19] seem to ignore that espionage is a trade based on deception where cynicism and ruthlessness predominate. Nowhere in these works can one find a clear, unequivocal disclaimer alerting the reader about the potential disinformational value of the sources. A notable, and I would say unique exception, is Vladislav M. Zubok's paper "Spy vs. Spy: The KGB vs. the CIA." Showing an uncommon in-depth knowledge of the spy's work, and an admirable intellectual integrity, in the introduction to his paper Zubok warns his readers:

> For all their fascination, the internal KGB documents cited in this article should also be treated with a good deal of caution. They contain references to events, plans, individuals, and explicit or implicit relationships that are uncorroborated and should be carefully investigated and cross-checked with other evidence before their accuracy and significance can be confidently gauged. Many of the assertions contained in the documents will require, in particular, collation with relevant materials in the archives of other governments and intelligence agencies, especially the CIA, and analysis by specialists in the history of intelligence. . . . those who evaluate the documents that do become available must keep in mind that evidence of crucial matters may have been deliberately destroyed, distorted, fabricated, or simply never committed to paper.[20]

Actually, what Zubok is telling the readers is that documents and oral interviews provide information as well as disinformation. But, in order to transform that raw data into true intelligence —in the meaning of intelligence and espionage— it has to be corroborated and evaluated.[21]

Faithful to my methodology, I have not interviewed any ex-CIA officers for this book, nor have I used any source based on that aberration now in vogue called "oral history." Also, I have not had access to the secret archives of the CIA or other government agencies. Moreover, I have barely used heavily edited photocopies of declassified "documents" from the so-called National Security Archive.[22]

All the sources of information I have used in this book are in the public record. They are books, articles appeared in newspapers and periodicals, and U.S. Government official publications freely available in most libraries. In addition, I have used a very limited amount of information from the Internet, mostly only after I have confirmed it by other reliable sources. The same way the Internet is a wonderful tool for information, I am conscious that it can also be an excellent tool for disinformation —a fact known to intelligence agencies all around the world that currently use the Internet to inoculate their venom.

Historians and Intelligence Analysts

The goal of the historian and the intelligence analyst is basically the same: search for facts and establish the truth. Their approach, however, is totally different. Give a historian a document and he will do three things: check it for accuracy; evaluate its place in the context of his own knowledge of its subject matter; and try to exploit it for producing a finished paper or book.

Now give the same document to an intelligence officer. He will do four things, but quite different ones. First, he will examine it to verify that its source is the one it purports to be; second, he will try to know if its source has disseminated it wittingly or unwittingly, and, if unwittingly, if its source knows the fact that the document has been compromised; third, he will attempt to find, guess, or intuit the source's real motives for disseminating it; and, finally, he will try to use it —by divulging it, or by not divulging it— to influence somebody, either his employers, his employees, or his enemies.

In this sense, the historian is trained to react *ad causam*, the intelligence analyst to react *ad hominem*. The historian focuses on subject matter and its relevance to understanding recorded events, the intelligence analyst focuses on people and their motives. The tools of the historian are quite different from the tools of the intelligence analysts and, therefore, the results of their research will show considerable differences.

As a rule, intelligence analysts always keep in mind that some of their sources, particularly live ones, will try to intentionally deceive them. That is why, contrary to historians, intelligence analysts take vulnerability to deception into account, and do so explicitly. Therefore, one can conclude that intelligence analysts have better methodological tools than historians to successfully analyze intelligence operations, where deceit and disinformation play an important role.[23]

In the study of intelligence organizations, like the OSS, the Mossad, the MI6, the KGB, or the CIA, we must always keep in mind that we are not dealing with innocuous aspects of history like the origins of New Orleans Jazz, or Roman architecture during the Republic. On the contrary, this is recent history with a high content of intelligence and espionage and, therefore, deception. And, because the basic principles of tradecraft[24] don't change much over time among its different practitioners, intelligence services are reluctant to give their past, current, or potential opponents any feedback about the success or failure of their past operations. As a matter of fact, their goal is to disinform their opponents as much as they can by keeping them in the dark.

Most of what an intelligence service claims has been its successes are most likely its failures, and vice versa. As I already mentioned above, in intelligence and espionage things are seldom what they seem. No wonder Sun Tzu's main precept is "All warfare is based on deception."[25] Under this light, events like the Bogotazo riots, the Bay of Pigs invasion, and the September 11, 2001 events, just to mention three of the CIA's alleged greatest failures, need to be reevaluated.

Out of unavoidable oversimplification, most people, including myself, usually refer to actions taken by intelligence services as "the CIA knew," "the OSS thought," "the KGB acted," "the Mossad believed," etc., forgetting that intelligence services are not homogeneous entities. Due to the application of the need-to-know and compartmentalization principles,[26] a common characteristic of intelligence services is that the right hand doesn't know what the left hand is doing, and vice versa.

Therefore, when somebody says "the CIA knew," or mentions "a CIA Report," it actually means "some people at the CIA knew," or "some people at the CIA wrote a Report." In the case of critical operations, like assassination attempts on foreign leaders or using American citizens as unwilling guinea pigs to test psychedelic drugs, it is likely that most people at the CIA, including very senior officers, were left out in the dark about the operation.

The Art and Science of Historical Tradecraft

At some time, it was fashionable among historians to invoke some ethereal "spirit of history." Today, even after the natural death of communism in most of the world, there is a school of Marxist historians that invokes the equally ethereal "spirit of economic forces" to explain historical events.[27] Currently, however, many serious historians refuse to invoke none of these, and resolutely shun the temptation to impose upon their work an all-embracing theory of history. Instead, they choose to present us with the bare facts, and from these facts they draw logical conclusions. No one, consequently, may criticize their writing for being "unscientific." Nor is there present in their books any element that a rational mind would automatically question and reject.

Yet, as E. H. Carr has shown in his excellent *What is History?*,[28] the art of the historian does not merely consist of finding the facts, since everything that happens may be considered a fact, but in *selecting* the facts which, consciously or unconsciously, he believes are significant for his study.

In other words, historians emphasize the facts they believe are important, while neglecting the ones they feel are not. This emphasis may be consciously exerted, as in the case of Marxist historians, who fit history into the preconceived pattern of economic relations, or unconsciously, as in the case of historians who are determined by the conviction that history is a rational process. What looks to them like irrationalities and oddities, will be played down or forgotten. Therefore, everything depends on the facts which a historian selects from the infinite number that are available, and on the emphasis he gives to those facts, and the result is the pattern "seen" by the historian, which may be explicit or implicit in his narrative. Thus, there is no *objective* history; any more than there is no *objective* journalism.

I have a skeptic's attitude towards historical conclusions based on "facts." I firmly believe that there are no objective conclusions in history. All historical conclusions based on "facts" are impregnated with theories, which are contaminated with beliefs and political ideologies.

In the first place, historians usually differ about what they consider a fact. For example, most scholars of the Cuban missile crisis have accepted at face value the Kennedy administration's claims that the photographs provided by U-2 planes constituted hard, incontrovertible evidence that the Soviets were deploying strategic missiles in Cuba. But, as intelligence analysts know, photographic evidence alone is just an iconic sign pointing to a possible fact. In order for it to become true intelligence, that is, information that has been validated, it must be corroborated by information provided by other reliable sources, preferably by agents operating in the field and other independent sources.[29]

Second, conclusions based on facts can differ not only because of the selection of the facts but also because of the way they are analyzed. Third, many historians seem to ignore that, particularly in recent history, some of the "facts" have been left in for the sole purpose of disinformation. Finally, even though this book is full of new or less known facts about the CFR, the CIA, the OSS and Fidel

Castro, my major emphasis has been on the reinterpretation of the facts, including widely known ones.

Most intelligence services agree that the most difficult aspect of the intelligence business is not the collection of raw data, but its interpretation and transformation into usable intelligence. Many outsiders believe that intelligence consists mainly in stealing the bad guys' secrets. Most of the job of intelligence, however, consists in using your experience to evaluate the information you already know. Actually, not all intelligence involves cloak and dagger spooks[30] or high tech espionage. A vast amount of the information that later becomes intelligence proper comes from open sources —monitoring of foreign broadcasts, close reading of the press, attendance at commercial and scientific conferences, study of officially released statistics and, above all, books— all of which, added to the information obtained from secret sources, becomes raw material for the production of intelligence.

Contrary to intelligence analysts, most historians are wedded to the theory that "facts explain events" which, in the last resort, depends on the way in which you choose your facts. Even worse, historians try to reach conclusion based only on hard evidence. But they apparently ignore that the world of intelligence and espionage is built on lies and illusions, and most of the time what looks like evidence based on facts is actually cleverly designed disinformation planted to fool opponents. As Zubok pointed out in the quote above, facts are just information, and information is not true intelligence until it has been validated.

From the strict point of view of intelligence and espionage, only information that has been secretly taken from the enemy should be considered *bona fide* intelligence. But, if it is found out that the opposition has voluntarily turned it over, it automatically becomes suspect of being disinformation —a principle that automatically makes all books based on information provided by CIA's employees or ex-employees, as well as by CIA's declassified documents, potential sources of disinformation.

Intelligence officers believe that the best way to distinguish new intelligence from deception is by judging how well it fits in with the rest of the intelligence reports already at hand. If it neatly dovetails with other validated intelligence reports, it is assumed to be valid intelligence.

Therefore, let's analyze the CIA neither from the naive point of view of the true believers in honest mistakes and secret successes (the Right), nor from the point of view of the true believers in the CIA's evil intentions or stupidity (the Left), but from the skeptical, suspicious perspective of the conspiracy theorist. As I will show in this book, seeing from this perspective, things change considerably.

The implementation of a New World Order, openly advocated innumerable times by the CFR conspirators, is based on the success of several interrelated major psychological warfare operations[31] —an exercise in mass deception of gigantic proportions.

The deep secrecy surrounding this exercise explains why most of the authors who have studied the phenomenon have seen only part of a puzzle of which some of the pieces are missing and others have been intentionally placed in the wrong slots. Of lately, however, the conspirators have demonstrated a growing boldness and arrogance in showing openly their hand —an in-your-face technique author Michael A. Hoffman calls "the revelation of the method."[32] This is a sort of mental blitzkrieg to shock and awe the people by terrorizing and paralyzing them by fear, and making them unable to react. Moreover, Hoffman alerts,

> Exposure without action against the perpetrators of the crimes revealed devolves into a kind of perverse advertisement for the prowess of the cryptocrats, who are seen as having performed fantastic feats of criminal enterprise with a genius that renders them immune from the consequences.[33]

Still, it was not until recently that, thanks mostly to the Internet, some of the missing parts of this conspiratorial puzzle have begun to appear. And most of these new pieces perfectly fit together with the known ones, providing a better understanding of the whole picture of deception and treachery.

Currently, the evidence that there is a group of powerful people conspiring behind our backs to spoil our day it is not a theory anymore. The evidence proving that it exists is quite well documented and overwhelming.

Until a few years ago, the CIA, as a tool of the conspirators, had been an important element of this conspiracy. In this book I will show how the CIA has contributed to the success of this evil conspiracy, and why the Agency is fading into oblivion because the conspirators don't need it anymore.

Finally, I would like to make clear that I don't have a conservative, liberal, or any other type of secret agenda. Like Patrick Henry, my main motivation is just the pursuit to the best of my abilities of this elusive thing called truth. I have never been associated with or worked in any capacity for any intelligence service. I have never been a member of any pro-Castro or anti-Castro organization in the U.S. I have never been a member of any political party or any secret society.

Also, I would like to warn the readers that they will find some amount of cynicism throughout these pages. In the first place, because in writing this book I have used the approach of an intelligence analyst, and cynicism is endemic in the intelligence field —a sort of *déformation professionnelle*. Secondly, because cynicism is one of the main tools of the political satirist, and as a former writer of political satire I cannot take spies and conspirators, much less politicians, too seriously.

Servando Gonzalez,
Summer 2010.

Introduction

Out of these troubled times, our objective —a New World Order— can emerge. Today, that new world is struggling to be born, a world quite different from the one we have known.
—President George H.W. Bush.

In *American Government: The Rules of the Game*,[1] a college textbook published in 1984, professor David Schuman of the University of Massachusetts at Amherst wrote that, despite superficial differences, Americans of both main political parties were ideologically very similar. According to Schuman,

> In the final analysis, like it or not, people who live in the United States have a great deal in common: we speak the same language, watch the same television, wear the same kinds of clothes. Even given the regional differences, we are culturally a lot alike.
>
> In the classic sense, politically we are all liberals.[2] No matter which party you like, it is a pretty good guess that you believe in individualism, private property, capitalism, competition, limited government, free speech, and the like. On a different scale, we believe in democracy, the Constitution, the rule of law, and most of the First Amendment freedoms.[3]

I have no doubts that when professor Schuman wrote his observations in 1984, they were a quite accurate description of the American society at the time. But today, just a quarter of a century after, though it is obvious that the two main political parties are more similar than ever before, Americans cannot be more different. Lets take a closer look.

A Fractured America

According to Professor Schuman, in 1984,

1. Americans, "speak the same language."

But in 2010 Americans no longer speak the same language, and they don't want to. In cities like Los Angeles, San Jose, and Miami, and in most of urban California, the predominant language is rapidly becoming Spanish. In some other cities, Chinese is becoming another dominant language. A large segment of the residents of Oakland, California, speak an almost unintelligible native dialect called "Ebonics." The fact that even some government forms are printed in several foreign languages indicate that Americans don't speak the same language anymore.

On the other hand, the fact that Americans don't speak the same language is not as divisive as the "English only" crowd believe. Switzerland has four different official languages, and the country has not lost its identity. But multilingualism in America is actually the manifestation of deeper underlying divisions.

2. "Watch the same television."

Americans don't watch the same TV programs, nor read the same newspapers and magazines anymore. Following the growing foreign language audience, TV channels in foreign languages, on the air and on the Web, have proliferated. Most Latin Americans in the U.S. watch their soap operas in Spanish and are Soccer fans. Chinese films and soap operas are watched on Chinese channels. In the last decade, the vertiginous increase of Internet users has contributed to this informational fragmentation — which I think is more positive than negative, because it is the first step into breaking the mainstream media monopolistic control of information.

3. "Wear the same kinds of clothes."

Just a short stroll on San Francisco's streets show that we don't use the same clothes any more. The difference in the clothes we use is so different that some Americans could well be Martians, and nobody seems to care. Not only the clothes favored by young blacks and Hispanics are diametrically different from the ones sported by young Anglos, but also we now see more people wearing clothing favored in the Middle East countries. In the San Francisco Bay Area, it is not uncommon to see people sporting African-style clothes.

4. "Even given regional differences, we are culturally a lot alike."

Actually, we cannot be culturally more different. Southern Florida, Central California, Northern Arkansas, Southern Alabama and Northern Louisiana, just to mention the areas in which I have lived for some time, are so different culturally that it makes you think you are in different countries.

6. Americans, "Believe in individualism, private property, capitalism, competition, limited government, free speech, and the like. On a different scale, we believe in democracy, the Constitution, the rule of law, and most of the First Amendment freedoms."

Today, most Americans do not believe in individualism any more. Out of envy or ideology, most Americans have lost respect for other people's private property, capitalism has become a four letter word, big corporations' ultimate goal is destroying competition, limited government is only given lip service by so called "conservatives," and free speech is admitted by so called "progressive liberals" only when it does not oppose their ideas. Under the pretext of prohibiting "hate speech" —precisely the type of speech protected by the First Amendment to the Constitution— freedom of speech is under attack and in full retreat in America.

America is a country where the moral norms of civil society are systematically subverted. A country where, under the pretext of a fight against terrorism, citizens' rights guaranteed by the Constitution are disappearing at a fast rate.

Currently, most Americans have a low opinion of the republican form of government based on laws and would willingly change it for the government of the mob called democracy. They don't know and don't care about the Constitution. They think that the rule of law is a bad joke. They accept as normal to be governed by a gang of corrupt criminals and traitors, and have shown they can willingly renounce their First Amendment freedoms protected by the Constitution in exchange for promised security or government handouts.

The traditional interpretation of the U.S. Constitution was that maximum power resided in the people, not in the State, much less in the Federal government. Today's interpretation seems totally the opposite. A large segment of the American people apparently believe that it is okay if all powers reside in the Federal government, and that it is fully justified if the president takes any action whatsoever without consulting with the Congress, much less with the people.

The most divisive issue currently separating the American people into two factions is their view of the 9/11 events. While roughly half of Americans have accepted the official explanation offered by the government, the other half is firmly convinced that either the U.S. Government allowed the 9/11 events to happen, or the attacks were an inside job planned and carried out by people at the highest levels of the U.S. Government.

These two interpretations are diametrically opposed. Regardless of who is right or wrong about the interpretation of the 9/11 events, the sole fact that more than half of Americans believe that their own government conspired to allow the murder of 3,000 of its citizens, indicates the existence of a chasm dividing this nation.

Other issues violently dividing Americans are evolution, global warming, gay marriage, illegal immigration, socialized medicine, widespread pornography, abortion, and the current wars in Iraq and Afghanistan, just to mention a few.

The unavoidable fact is that we are living in a widely fractured America. The gap between the rich and the poor is growing, the middle class is in remission, ethnic and racial hatred is on the rise, and the ethics of the land is not Judeo-Christian anymore, but the intellectually dishonest situational ethics of political correctness.

A cursory look at America today shows that this country has shifted from a predominantly Christian worldview (even if not all Americans considered themselves Christians) toward a totally different one. Currently, the predominant worldview in America is one based on a materialistic, humanistic[4] religious worldview. Cardinal in the change of this worldview is the role played by the Supreme Court and other lesser courts in debasing the Constitution.

These two worldviews are so antithetically different that they cannot coexist together; at least not for a long time. Eventually one of them will eliminate the other. The fact that despite its dogmatism the Christian worldview has proved to be more tolerant of other worldviews than the materialistic, humanistic one indicates that the days of Christianity in the present Disunited States of America are numbered.

The Covert American Revolution

Normally, peoples and governments do not change their direction or policies drastically, or rapidly, or easily. Actually, when such drastic changes in a society occur in a short time, we call them "revolutionary."

The changes I mentioned above began sometime after WWII, but it was not until the late seventies when they became evident to keen observers. Today, it has become obvious for anyone with eyes to see that the 2010 America has not much to do with the America of the 1950s. The fact has been analyzed in some detail by Gertrude Himmelfarb in her book *One Nation, Two Cultures*,[5] and Robert Bork expressed it clearly in the title of a book he edited: *A Country I Do Not Recognize.*[6]

Between 1960 and 1995, violent crime has increased in the U.S. by 560 percent, single-mother births rose 419 percent, and both divorce rates and children living in single-parent homes increased by 300 percent. How come this country has changed so much in such a short period of time? Even more important, how come only a few Americans noticed this social phenomenon of radical transformation when it began two or three decades ago?

Only a revolution can produce such drastic changes in a country in such a short time. Therefore, I don't think it would be an exaggeration to say that this country has experienced a revolutionary change. But revolutions don't happen spontaneously or by chance. They are the direct result of the actions of professional revolutionaries who conspire in the shadows to overthrow the established system of society and replace it with a different one. Nevertheless, there was no revolution in the U.S. in the past fifty years —at least not an overt one. May it be that America has experienced a subtle, covert revolution?

In fact, it has, and it was forecasted in some detail by one of the main CFR conspirators, John D. Rockefeller III. In 1973 he described the coming "humanist revolution" in great detail in a book he titled *The Second American Revolution* in which he disparaged "old fashioned nationalism."[7] Following the progression of this plan, in 1974 a team of scholars at the Rockefeller Foundation produced the final draft for a new U.S. Constitution.

Finally, in 1987 Arthur S. Miller, sponsored by the Rockefeller Foundation, wrote *The Secret Constitution and the Need for Constitutional Change*,[8] in which he described in more detail about the new Constitution the conspirators have in mind. This new Constitution, which is nothing but a blueprint for a corporate take-over of America under a communo-fascist totalitarian dictatorship, seems too close for comfort to the new America we have seen vertiginously developing under the Bush and Obama regimes.

Contrary to the overt, violent communist revolution advocated by Marx and Lenin, or the coup d'ètats preferred by fascists, the new American Revolution has been a disguised, covert one. The new American Revolution has not used (at least, not yet) rifles and cannons to enforce its rule, but stealth, cunning, deception, lies and psychological warfare. The ideology of the new American revolutionaries who conspire behind our backs to impose it upon the rest of us is a mixture of fascism and communism, which they euphemistically call the New World Order. However, the techniques they are using to implement it are not the ones preferred by Fascists or Communists, but have been copied from the British Fabians and Italian Marxist intellectual Antonio Gramsci.

The British Fabians advocated communism as conceived by Karl Marx, but, contrary to Marx, Lenin, Trotsky and other Communist ideologues, they believed that the right way to do it was gradually, by infiltration, capturing the existing institutions from inside and putting them to work for their goals. No wonder the symbol of the Fabians is a wolf in sheep's clothing.[9]

Antonio Gramsci was an Italian Communist who lived in the early 20th century. After visiting the Soviet Union, he realized that the best way to implement communism was not by coercion or brute force, but by influencing and shaping the domain of ideas. He called his system "cultural hegemony." The main tool to change the prevailing ideas was by infiltrating the mainstream media, the schools and universities, in a way that is now known as the "culture wars."

As I mentioned above, the drastic changes experienced in America in such a short time cannot be the product of evolutionary change but of intelligent design. Therefore, who are the revolutionaries secretly pushing from behind the curtains this covert revolution down our throats?

They are not the typical communist or anarchist revolutionaries, dirty poor and angry against a society that has denied them everything. No. Actually, they are the most successful members of the very society they hate. They are the super rich. They are the ones pushing the so-called New World Order. They are the ones who, after creating an unequal world economic order, are now hypocritically pushing for a new, more equal world economic order.

Translated into plain English, the conspirators' alleged goal of creating "a new, more equal world economic order," actually means equality in poverty for the masses and unlimited richness and power for the dominant elite. The New World Order is a new form of slavery in the form of a communo-fascist, neo-medieval state mainly composed of dirty-poor serfs exploited by a small group of rich, all-powerful masters.

Apple Inc. making iPhones and iPods with children working under quasi-slave conditions in totalitarian Communist China[10] gives us a glimpse at this new type of society the conspirators envision. In contrast, Apple pioneered giving privileged rights to gay couples and environmental policies (did Apple ban smoking in its Chinese sweat shops?), to the point that convenient liar Al Gore now sits on its board of directors.

Who Are The New World Order Conspirators?

The conspirators who want to impose their New World Order upon us are mostly Wall Street bankers, oil magnates, CEOs of transnational corporations, and senior members of the military-industrial-academic complex. Even though they come in all sizes and colors, there is a link that unites them as a whole: most of them are members of the Council on Foreign Relations or some of its parasite organizations like the Trilateral Commission, the United Nations Organization, the World Bank and the International Monetary Fund, just to mention a few.

The Council on Foreign Relations (CFR) is a globalist organization founded in 1921 with headquarters at the Harold Pratt House in Manhattan. Currently several sub-Councils exist in main American cities, all of them loosely linked to the original one. Since its creation, it secret goal has been the elimination of U.S. national sovereignty, and the creation of a global government under their control.

Writing in *Foreign Affairs*, the Council on Foreign Relations' organ, CFR agent Richard N. Gardner clearly expressed the Council's ultimate goal, as well as the devious ways they will use to attain it,

> ... the "house of world order" would have to be built from the bottom up rather than from the top down. It will look like a great 'booming, buzzing confusion,' to use William James' famous description of reality, but an end run around national sovereignty, eroding it piece by piece, will accomplish much more than the old-fashioned frontal assault."[11]

In 1975, Admiral Chester Ward, a former Judge Advocate General of the U.S. Navy and a member of the CFR from 1959-1977 who broke with the organization, wrote that the CFR stated goal is the "submergence of U.S. sovereignty and national independence into an all-powerful, one-world government." Furthermore, Admiral Ward warned, "... this lust to surrender the sovereignty and independence of the United States is pervasive throughout most of the membership."[12]

Like the Wizard of Oz, the Council on Foreign Relations remained in the shadows for decades after its inception. This little-known, elitist organization has had among its members during the last 50 years at least 10 percent of senior government officials in active public service, during both Republican and Democrat administrations.

Surprisingly, and despite the fact that CFR members permeate the mainstream press, most Americans ignore the existence of this powerful organization. This invisibility, however, is not the product of chance, but of design. During one of the secret meetings of the Bilderberg Group —an international organization of globalist conspirators closely linked to the CFR— in Baden-Baden, Germany, 1991, David Rockefeller, chairman of the CFR from 1970-1985, thanked his friends in the press for keeping the CFR out of the American eye,

> We are grateful to the *Washington Post*, the *New York Times*, *Time* Magazine and other great publications whose directors have attended our meetings and respected their promises of discretion for almost forty years. It would have been impossible for us to develop our plan for the world if we had been subject to the bright lights of publicity during those years. But the world is now more sophisticated and prepared to march towards a world government. The supra-national sovereignty of an intellectual elite

> and world bankers is surely preferable to the national auto-determination practiced in past centuries.

But not all Americans have played the conspirators' game. In 1976, Congressman Larry P. McDonald pointed to the true source of the conspiracy,

> The drive of the Rockefellers and their allies [is] to create a one-world government combining super capitalism and Communism under the same tent, all under their control. . . . the Rockefellers and their allies have, for at least fifty years, been carefully following a plan to use their economic power to gain political control, first of America, and then the rest of the world.
>
> Do I mean conspiracy? Yes I do. I am convinced there is such a plot, international in scope, generations old in planning, and incredibly evil in intent."[13]

You don't need to be a "conspiracy theorist" to reach the conclusion that an internationalist organization, whose goal is the elimination of the U.S. national sovereignty as a first step to create a one-world government, has infiltrated and is now in control of the U.S. government.

As an American, you should be concerned after knowing that the CFR, an organization whose members have not been elected by the American people, has successfully penetrated the three branches of the American government, particularly the executive branch. The CFR penetrated since its creation the U.S. diplomatic corps and later the Department of State and the U.S. intelligence services. It is now in an accelerated process of penetrating the U.S. armed forces.

During the administration of George H. W. Bush, most Cabinet members were also CFR members. You should be even more concerned after knowing that the number of CFR members in the Clinton, W. Bush and Obama administrations is even higher. In these four administrations, most members of the powerful National Security Council have also been CFR members. It seems that the number of CFR members in the Obama administration will break all previous records.

Given the fact that, like horse whisperers, members of the Cabinet and the NSC are the ones who tell American presidents what to do, it happens that the list of the people who have had a cardinal role in the revolutionary changes I mentioned at the beginning of this Introduction, read like a membership roster of the Council on Foreign Relations. This cannot be the product of a coincidence.

Actually, behind every act of treason to the American people, and to the peoples of the world, you will find, hiding in the shadows, one or more members of the Council on Foreign Relations. (See Appendix I, A Chronology of Treason).

Granted, treason is a very strong word, and some readers may object my using the word treason when referring to most of the actions taken by CFR members over the years. Actually, according to Section 3, Article III of the U.S. Constitution, "Treason against the United States, shall consist only in levying War against them, or in adhering their enemies, giving them Aid and Comfort."

But, as I will show below in this book, this is precisely what the Council on Foreign Relations has been doing since its creation in 1921.

The Secret War Against the American People

This is a book about a long, protracted war against the American people. It began a century ago in Woodrow Wilson's era, or perhaps even before, when the *Maine* battleship was blown up at Havana's bay by a mysterious explosion, and it is still going on. It is not a conventional war waged with tanks, battleships and planes in conventional battlefields —at least not yet. It is a secret, insidious type of war whose main battleground is the people's minds. Its main weapons are propaganda and mass brainwashing mostly by using disinformation, deception, and lies in a large scale not used against the people of a nation since the end of Nazi Germany. Though important, those elements are just part of a series of carefully planned and executed long- and short-term psychological warfare operations. In synthesis, it is a psychological war.

The methodology used in this type of war is a variation of the Hegelian principle of thesis-antithesis-synthesis.[14] German philosopher Georg Wilhelm Friedrich Hegel (1770-1831) made change the cornerstone of his philosophical system, which he called Dialectics. According to Hegel, an idea or principle —which he called the thesis— is challenged by its opposite —the anti-thesis. Eventually, from this conflict emerges a new idea or principle that is a synthesis of both.

Though complex in its implementation —the variables are too many, and the results difficult to predict— the theory is very simple. I will give a simplified example.

Let's suppose some people have an animal in a cage and they open the door to send the animal to the slaughterhouse. But its instinct tells the animal not to try to escape through the door. So, they flash bright lights, make loud, frightening noises, and rattle the cage's walls, while fanning the smell of food through the door leading to the slaughterhouse. The result is what they expect: though reluctantly, the scared animal is fooled into choosing to get out of the cage as the lesser of two evils, and voluntarily goes right to the slaughterhouse.

A rough implementation of this type of psychological operation has been used by unethical politicians since early times: Nero's burning Rome as a pretext to persecute the Christians and Hitler burning the Reichstag to get dictatorial power over Germany are known examples. But the New World Order conspirators have used more sophisticated methods. For example, in early 1948, after the end of a long war, the people of the world wanted peace (thesis). So, the warmongering conspirators artificially created a crisis by instigating the assassination of Colombian leader Jorge Eliécer Gaitán and inciting the Bogotazo riots as a way to scare the American public with the fear of a larger artificial threat the conspirators already had created: Soviet Communism (antithesis). This artificially created fear allowed the conspirators to launch the highly profitable Cold War (synthesis), and convinced the people to accept it as the lesser of two evils.

More recently, after the unexpected fall of the Soviet Union and the end of the Cold War, the people of the world were happy at the beginning of what they saw as a new era of world peace and freedom (thesis) So, the conspirators instigated the 9/11 events to scare the American public with the fear of terrorism, an artificial threat they had created (antithesis). Then, they launched the war on terror and curtailed the people's freedoms (synthesis), which the people willingly accepted as the lesser of two evils.

But, contrary to what the conspirators and their professional disinformers want us to believe, the real enemy is not, and has never been, far away —in the Soviet Union, Central America, Asia or the Middle East. The enemy is inside the gates. The true haters of America, whose ultimate goal is to see it destroyed, are members of the U.S. ruling class. They are the ones who have been waging a protracted psychological warfare against us. They are the ones who have been conspiring behind the backs of the American people to destroy this country.

America is a country betrayed by its ruling class.

The leaders of the American ruling class don't see themselves as Americans any more but as internationalists and globalists. After having reached full oligarchic control of this country through a long process of gradual infiltration, the conspirators now want to control the whole world and establish a totalitarian communo-fascist dictatorship they euphemistically call the New World Order. But, unknowingly, the American people have become the main stumbling block in their path to world domination.

Americans, with their long tradition of representative self-government abhor totalitarianism. Even more important, contrary to other peoples of the world that have been enslaved, a large percentage of the American people own guns, know how to use them and would not hesitate to use them in the defense of their freedom. That is the reason why the CFR conspirators have resorted to defeat the American people using a much more devious form of war: a war in the people's minds; a psychological war, a PSYWAR.

According to the U.S. Army's Joint Strategic Plans Committee, August 2, 1948,

> Psychological warfare employs all moral and physical means, other than orthodox military operations, which tend to:
>
> destroy the will and the ability of the enemy to fight;
> deprive him of the support of his allies and neutrals;
> increase in our own troops and allies the will to victory.
>
> Psychological warfare employs any weapon to influence the mind of the enemy. The weapons are psychological only in the effect they produce and not because of the nature of the weapons themselves. In this light, overt (white), covert (black), and gray propaganda; subversion; sabotage; special operations; guerrilla warfare; espionage's political, cultural, economic, and racial pressures are all effective weapons. They are effec-

tive because they produce dissention, distrust, fear and hopelessness in the minds of the enemy, not because they originate in the psyche of propaganda or psychological warfare agencies.[15]

Of lately, particularly after the 9/11 events and even more after Barack Obama moved to the White House, the existence of this conspiracy has become more evident for anybody with eyes to see. This is only because the conspirators are so confident that they are close to their goal that, in their arrogance, they have become careless. They despise us so much that they don't care about what we can do to defend ourselves from their devious attack.

But, despite that the existence of this conspiracy has become obvious and most people suspect that something is very wrong, still a large percentage of the American people cannot pinpoint the true source of the conspiracy. Most of them have been brainwashed to believe that just by changing the treacherous rascals in Washington everything would be okay.

That was the mistake made by the Republicans in 2000, when they got rid of Clinton to have Bush, and by the Democrats in 2008, when they trashed Bush to get Obama. But, as the true liberals in the Democratic Party soon found out, just by changing the puppets and leaving the puppet-masters untouched would not solve the problem.

Currently, a powerful psychological warfare operation (PSYOP) is in place to convince diehard Republicans that getting rid of Obama will be the solution of the problem. I hope that when the true conservatives among the Republicans discover their mistake it will not be too late to correct it.

Walking Back the Cat

Walking back the cat is a counterintelligence[16] term born in a spy novel by Robert Littell. Like "mole,"[17] coined by John le Carré in one of his novels, it was later adopted by real-life spies.[18] Walking back the cat means taking a failed operation apart piece-by-piece looking for mistakes, leaks or enemy penetrations. Normally, the technique is applied to your own failed (or successful) operations, but it can also be applied to the analysis of an opponent's operations.

Walking back the cat is a sort of "acid test" used to determine retrospectively the loyalty or treachery of a particular agent, or, as I will do in this book, a whole government agency or policy organization.

Though complex and tiresome, the principle on which the method is based is relatively simple, and it is very similar to a profit and loss analysis of an account: all the cases in which the agent, or the agency, has participated, are totted up, by backtracking them and picking up all the pieces. Then, an opinion is formed about which side did best overall, the opposition or ours. Such an analysis sometimes produces surprising, unexpected results.

The purpose of this analysis is to determine if the successes of the agent or agency were the result of good performance and not because the enemy facilitated

them, as well as to determine if the failures were due to poor performance, not treason. Even more important is to determine if the people one suspects control the agent or the organization, benefited in any way with his/its supposed failures.
As author David Wise puts it,

> To the trained counterintelligence mind, every fragment, every detail, no matter how tiny or trivial, may have possible significance in unraveling a larger deception by the enemy.[19]

So, let's walk back the cat and, from the point of view of a counterintelligence officer's convoluted mind, take a close, critical look, beginning with its birth (or, even better, taking a close look at its conception and progenitors), at the monster itself, the Council on Foreign Relations. But, before getting into it, I would like to make a distinction.

According to the experts, the primary mission of counterintelligence is to "identify, neutralize and exploit the intelligence or secret infrastructures of the enemy." Though written from a point of view of counterintelligence, in this book I am limiting myself to identify the secret structure and goals of what I consider the enemy's key organization, the Council on Foreign Relations, as well as some of its main operational tools, the CIA and the National Security Council. I leave to the readers the job of neutralizing and eliminating them.

Chapter 1

Is There an Invisible Government of the United States?

> *Almost all people of all eras are hypnotics. Their beliefs are induced beliefs. The proper authorities saw to it that the proper belief should be induced, and people believed properly.*
>
> — Charles Fort.

Over the years, and particularly after the events of September 11, 2001, and the popularization of the Internet, even the most gullible American citizen has suspected that there must be a secret reason why more often than not our government acts against the best interests of the American people, as well as helps our enemies and betrays our friends. Just a handful of scholars, however, have seriously studied the phenomenon. The ones who have done it concluded that the U.S. Government has been hijacked by a group of rich, powerful individuals, who have been using it to advance their own private interests. This super-elite of a few hundred immensely wealthy and powerful individuals has been called different names: the Power Elite, the High Cabal, the Secret Team, the Secret Government, the Insiders, the Usurpers, the Invisible Government. I call them the Conspirators.

The CIA as Scapegoat

Probably the most known among the authors who have studied the problem are David Wise and Thomas B. Ross, whose book *The Invisible Government*[1] became a best seller in the early 1960s. Another attempt was Bill Moyers' documentary *The Secret Government*. But both works, mistakenly or intentionally, point to the Central Intelligence Agency as the source of this invisible or secret government of the United States.

For example, at the very beginning of his documentary, Moyers claims,

> The Secret Government is an interlocking network of official functionaries, spies, mercenaries, ex-generals, profiteers, and super-patriots who, for a variety of motives, operate outside of the legitimate institutions of government.

A little after, a picture of the CIA building at Langley, Virginia, fills the screen, and Moyers' voice off the screen affirms: "This is the house the Cold War built: The CIA, the core of the new Secret Government."

Joseph Trento made a similar mistake in his book *Prelude to Terror*. In it,

Trento expresses his conviction that,

> Since its creation in 1947, the CIA has been a service dominated by a handful of individuals who carried out their activities as they saw fit, some honestly trying to serve the national interest, others focusing enormous energy on personal political advantage, even personal profit.[2]

According to Trento, a group of unscrupulous, opportunistic CIA officers, lead by Theodore C. Shackley, created a secret splinter faction inside the CIA and put it to work for their personal gain.

More recently, even U.S. House Representative Ron Paul, a well-intentioned and otherwise incisive critic of the invisible government, fell into the trap of blaming the CIA for the current dismal state of events in this country. Speaking to an audience of like-minded Americans at a Campaign for Liberty regional conference in Atlanta on January 15-17, 2010, Paul said:

> There's been a coup, have you heard? It's the CIA coup. The CIA runs everything, they run the military. They're the ones who are over there lobbying missiles and bombs on countries. ... And of course the CIA is every bit as secretive as the Federal Reserve. ... And yet think of the harm they have done since they were established [after] World War II. They are a government unto themselves. They're in businesses, in drug businesses, they take out dictators ... We need to take out the CIA. [3]

Paul is right, but just on two counts. It is true that we need to get rid not only of the CIA, but also of the NSA and the rest of the alphabet soup of shady, unconstitutionally created agencies working hard to deprive us of our freedoms. He is also right that a silent coup has taken place in America. But, as I will show below in this book, the CIA is just a tool in the hands of the conspirators. Blaming the CIA for everything would be tantamount to believing that the small tail is wagging the big dog.

Granted, the CIA is in the drug and assassination business. It overthrows democratically elected leaders around the world and replaces them with corrupt, bloodthirsty dictators. But the CIA does all of this following orders from its true masters, the ones who created the Agency in 1947 for their own benefit. Currently, the CIA is fading into oblivion, because, now with almost full control of the U.S. military, the conspirators don't need the CIA anymore —except for using it as the fall guy in order to divert the attention from the true source of the problem.

The Council on What?

Probably the first author who rightly pointed to the Council on Foreign Relations as the true source of the invisible Government of the United States was Emanuel Josephson in his 1952 book *Rockefeller "Internationalist": The Man Who Misrules the World.*[4] Josephson titled Chapter XIII of his book, "The Council on Foreign Relations: "Foreign Office" of the Rockefeller Empire. The Invisible government."[5] A few pages later below he added,

> So consistently have high, policy-making positions in the government been filled from the ranks of the Rockefeller's Council that it can be called the invisible government of the United Sates.[6]

Another author who identified the CFR as the center of the invisible government of the United States was Dan Smoot in his 1962 book *The Invisible Government*.[7] Smoot, a former member of the FBI Headquarters staff in Washington, D.C., expressed his conviction,

> I am convinced that the Council on Foreign Relations, together with a great number of other associated tax-exempt organizations, constitutes the invisible government which set the major policies of the federal government; exercises controlling influence on government officials who implement the policies; and, through massive and skillful propaganda, influences Congress and the public to support the policies.
>
> I am convinced the objective of this invisible government is to convert America into a socialist state and make it a unit in a one-world socialist system.[8]

Later, John Stormer in his book *None Dare Call it Treason*,[9] Gary Allen in *None Dare Call it Conspiracy*,[10] and Phoebe Courtney in her *The CFR, Part II*,[11] further identified the CFR as the center of the invisible government.[12]

Like Ninja assassins, the main weapon used by the CFR conspirators to commit their crimes with impunity has been their invisibility.[13] Until recently, this group of rich, powerful people, who has an almost total control over the three branches of the U.S. government, the mainstream press, Hollywood's film industry,[14] the educational system, and currently is extending its tentacles to fully penetrate and control the U.S. armed forces, has been almost unknown to most of the American people.

But we should not blame the people. This group of powerful conspirators is very rarely mentioned in the mainstream press and is totally absent from textbooks.[15] Though their names are known, their ties to the CFR have been kept secret, and the conspirators have thanked the press for their good job on their behalf.

Speaking in 1991 at one of the secret Bilderberg meetings in Baden-Baden, Germany, David Rockefeller expressed his gratitude to a servile press for their "discretion" for almost 40 years of blackout. At the same time, he seized the opportunity to proselytize for his treasonous work undermining the constitutional principles of this country. According to David, a government run by an elite of bankers like him is much better than national sovereignty.[16]

But now, thanks mostly to the Internet, that has acted as an ultraviolet light revealing the harmful bacteria, the CFR conspirators are losing their powers of invisibility and more and more people are discovering who they are, how they operate, and what their plans are. I am talking about the Council on Foreign Relations (CFR), and a whole constellation of associated organizations in the U.S. and abroad, like the Royal Institute of International Affairs (Chatham House), the Bilderberg Group,[17] the Trilateral Commission,[18] the United Nations Organization, the World Forum, the Club of Rome, and others. Their ultimate goal is the establishment of a communo-fascist global government they disingenuously call the New World Order.

The Science of Historical Forensics

To the average person, forensics has to do with crime, autopsies, and the like. But, like Yahoŏ, Google, and other search engines in the Internet, forensic science mostly has to do with links. The basic principle of forensic science, as stated by Dr. Edmond Locard, one of the greatest experts in forensic science, is very simple: every contact leaves a trace.[19] Finding these traces in the scene of a crime and, through them, establishing the links to the criminal is what forensic science is all about.

When a criminal commits a crime, the first thing he does is to disguise, erase or destroy, all physical evidence linking him to the crime. These range from cleaning with a napkin all glass surfaces to erase thumbprints, to sending a person disguised as him to a party. Thus providing an alibi, backed by several witness, that he was in a different place when the crime was committed. Forensic science, however, has applicability beyond the area of law. Forensic science and history merge at the edges, for where one ends, the other begins.[20] Actually, conspiracy theory is an important tool of historical forensics.

The job of the forensic investigator consists in discovering these links, and revealing the links between the crime and the criminal. Unknowingly, the authors who first pointed to the CFR as the true seat of this anti-American conspiracy were practicing the science of historical forensics. And, despite the efforts of the criminal conspirators at the CFR to erase all traces linking them to their crimes against the American people, these authors discovered an amazing fact: behind every act of treason to this country and its people there is always one or more members of the Council on Foreign Relations or their parasite organizations working hard in the shadows against us.

The list of events in which they have conspired to destroy this country is very long, (See Appendix I, A Chronology of Treason) and even a non-exhaustive macro forensic historical analysis of the CFR treason can extend for dozens of pages. Nonetheless, just the examples I have compiled in the Appendix I are enough to prove beyond any reasonable doubt that what many people have suspected is true: a cabal of non-elected people is making the big decisions behind our backs and controlling our destinies.

Now, if it were discovered that all the persons mentioned in the Appendix I were members of the John Birch Society, riots would erupt in most American cities.[21] If all of them were Jews, everybody would be talking about a Jewish conspiracy. If all of them were Italians, we would be for sure dealing with an Italian conspiracy. If all of them were New York Yankees fans, or taxi drivers, I would be the first to talk about a baseball fan or taxi driver conspiracy. But there are several million Jews in America, and as many Italians, and probably even more NY Yankees fans and taxi drivers. In contrast, for many years the CFR has had less than a thousand members, and currently, with its largest membership of all times, it has a little more than four thousand members.

One can claim that the facts I mention in the Appendix I are not true, or difficult to confirm. Still, even if only half of them were true —and all of them are in the public domain and easy to verify— this should be a motive of concern for the American public.

Likewise, some may argue that my conclusions are fallacious, because this small group of people has joined the CFR only because of their prominence and money, and that is precisely what has made this organization so powerful. But, as in the cases of Dwight Eisenhower, Henry Kissinger, Jimmy Carter, Alexander Haig, Bill Clinton and Maurice Strong, just to mention a few, many of them reached prominence and fortune thanks to their membership to the CFR and not the other way around.

So, how to explain without resorting to conspiracy theories the fact that this small group of people control to such extent the foreign policy of the United States and of most countries in the world? How can one explain without resorting to conspiracy theories, the fact that, being so important and powerful, and having such control over the American mainstream media, the Council on Foreign Relations is almost unknown to the majority of the people in the United States and the world?

The Council claims that it has no affiliation with the U.S. government. Then, how can we explain these facts: Since the end of World War II, almost every Secretary of State, CIA Director, Secretary of Defense, Chairman of the Joint Chiefs of Staff, National Security Council member, Federal Reserve Bank Director, is or has been a CFR member. Currently, 124 high rank U.S. military officers and several U.S. senators and Supreme Court Justices are CFR members.

Actually, no other organization, not even any of the three branches of the U.S. government, exerts such control over this country.

Further proof that the Council on Foreign Relations is the true invisible government of the United States is the fact that in critical situations CFR agents infiltrated in the U.S. government bypass the legal government to report first to the invisible one. Examples of this are presidential adviser McGeorge Bundy (CFR) secretly informing the CFR about the missiles in Cuba before informing president Kennedy,[22] and CIA's Richard M. Bissell, Jr. (CFR), secretly reporting to the CFR about covert operations.[23]

When the chips are down, the conspirators' agents infiltrated in the U.S. government know perfectly well where the true center of power is located in this country —and it is not in Washington D.C.

Consequently, we have to conclude that there is an Invisible Government, a

High Cabal, a Power Elite, a Secret Team, a Secret Empire, a group of Conspirators, Infiltrators, Usurpers, Insiders, or whatever name you choose to call it, who, using Fabian[24] and Gramscian[25] gradual infiltration techniques, has penetrated the three branches of the U.S. Government as well as the Department of State, the CIA and the U.S. military, and currently has almost total control over them. It also controls the mainstream media and public education. Unfortunately, this group is currently working hard to take control of the governments of most countries in the world.

And this group of conspirators whose ultimate goal is the implementation of a New World Order resides at the Harold Pratt House in Manhattan, headquarters of the Council on Foreign Relations.

U.S. Presidents with Blinders On

Initially, not all American presidents were members of the Council on Foreign Relations. These were the cases of Truman, Kennedy, Johnson and Reagan. But, like carthorses wearing blinders, the CFR managed to surround U.S. presidents with a dark curtain of disinformation in the form of a large group of its secret agents, most of them grouped in the National Security Council.

The National Security Council is a key element in understanding how the CFR conspirators control the U.S. government. CFR secret agents in the U.S. government pushed the creation of the National Security Council and the CIA in 1947, allegedly as a tool to avoid events like Pearl Harbor and to manage the military, intelligence, and foreign policy areas of the U.S. government.

Soon after it was created, however, CFR agents in the National Security Council changed it into a tool to control the information reaching the eyes and ears of the Presidents, thus creating a smoke screen of disinformation around them. This guarantees that the policy decisions they take are the ones already made at the Harold Pratt House.[26] Fletcher Prouty best described this process in his book *The Secret Team* — which explains why the book was practically censored, and for many years was almost impossible to find.[27]

To make things even easier for them, the CFR conspirators created the concept of Presidents' plausible denial —a euphemism for Presidents' ignorance from which the conspirators highly benefited. Soon after, they expanded even further the concept of plausible denial with the notion that "what the President doesn't know can't hurt him politically." This meant that the CFR conspirators, through their agents infiltrated in the White House, gave themselves a free hand in planning and carrying out American foreign policy with as little consultation as possible with the incumbent President. This is exactly what they have been doing for more than half a century.

Since the Second World War, the CFR conspirators have been putting blinders on American Presidents and surrounding them with a curtain of disinformation. This explains why even the ones who were not CFR agents unknowingly advanced the goals of the CFR conspirators.

The CFR conspirators' total control over the American presidents explains the phenomenon known as the "imperial presidency," a term that became popular in the 1960s

One of the scholars who have studied in detail the phenomenon is CFR agent Arthur Schlesinger, Jr. In his book *The Imperial Presidency*,[28] Schlesinger shows the increasing role of the president in the U.S. Government and how by the early 1970s, when he wrote the book, American presidents already had become close to absolute monarchs. According to Schlesinger, the U.S. Presidency is out of control and it has exceeded by far its constitutional limits.

What Schlesinger conveniently didn't say, though, is why this has happened, much less who were the people behind the idea of an imperial presidency. By reading his book, one may reach the wrong conclusion that this has been a totally random process motivated by the craving for power of individual presidents. But this is not the case.

In their grab for power, the CFR conspirators faced a big obstacle: the separation of powers. Conscious of the politician's lust for power, the Founding Fathers created a form of government almost impossible to control, by avoiding the concentration of power in a single point. This was the idea behind the separation of power among the three branches of government: the executive, legislative and judicial powers. Eventually, the power of an independent press in the form of a watchdog to check on the other powers was considered itself a fourth power.

Nevertheless, as the conspirators have admitted, the Founding Fathers were too clever. The separation of powers created a strong barrier protecting the government from their attempts to control it. Granted, by the early 1930s they had a great control over the mainstream press and had effectively penetrated the State Department. But there were still many independent people they didn't control in the Congress and the judiciary. Consequently, they concluded that it would be a lot easier to control a single person than hundreds of them. The solution for this problem was the creation of the so-called "imperial presidency" —an emperor used as figurehead, but under their full control.

Until the mid 1930s, U.S. Presidents had a small staff, most of them located at the President's office in the U.S. Capitol. This, however, changed dramatically as soon as their secret agent Franklin D. Roosevelt took office. Using the Great Depression and World War II as pretexts, Roosevelt's Brain Trust of advisors, most of them CFR agents, implemented the New Deal and the creation in 1939 of the Executive Office of the President, a major step in the creation of the imperial presidency. Another major step was the implementation of the so called "executive orders," an unconstitutional power grab by which the president, bypassing Congress and behind the backs of the American people, wrote veritable *diktats*, more akin to dictators than to democratically elected presidents of a constitutional Republic.

Another big step was the creation of the CIA, allegedly as a President's tool. Though Truman was not a CFR member, he was an opportunistic individual, and soon became malleable material in the hands of the conspirators. The creation of the CIA and the National Security Council, two of the most touted achievements of his tenure, were actually conceived at the Harold Pratt House. At the end of his political career he had an uncommon moment of candor and expressed his concern about the monster he had helped to create,

> I think it has become necessary to take another look at the purpose and operations of our Central Intelligence Agency—CIA . . . for some time I have been disturbed by the way the CIA has been diverted from its original assignment. It has become an operational and at times a policy-making arm of the Government. This has led to trouble and may have compounded our difficulties in several explosive areas. We have grown up as a nation, respected for our free institutions and for our ability to maintain a free and open society. There is something about the CIA has been functioning that is casting a shadow over our historical position and I feel that we need to correct it. [29]

After Truman, the presidency went in 1952 to Dwight Eisenhower (CFR) who won against Adlai Stevenson (CFR). In 1956, Stevenson (CFR) challenged again Eisenhower (CFR). In 1960, Richard Nixon (CFR) ran against John F. Kennedy, but Kennedy's father pulled a fast one buying votes in Chicago and other cities, and his son was elected president by a small majority of 100,000 votes.

During the first months of Kennedy's presidency, the conspirators managed to have him under their control. But, particularly after the Bay of Pigs disaster, Kennedy discovered the ruse, stopped being malleable putty in the conspirators' hands, and began acting on his own. Even worse, he took some important measures without the approval of his CFR advisers. However, like many others before and after him, John F. Kennedy underestimated the evil nature of his CFR enemies, and paid dearly for his mistake.

After realizing that the U.S. Vietnam policy dictated by the CFR conspirators was wrong, Kennedy took measures to phase out direct U.S. military participation in the conflict. Despite strong dissent from CFR agents within his own administration, as well as from the military and the CIA, Kennedy initiated this U.S. withdrawal seven weeks before his death. Two days after the assassination, Johnson, following instructions from his CFR masters, reversed Kennedy's Vietnam policy and determined the course of action to follow —which paved the way to the Vietnam debacle. In addition to canceling the troop withdrawal and providing for troop increases, the policy shift resumed the program of covert action against North Vietnam.

After the resignation of President Richard Nixon in 1974, president Gerald Ford (CFR) appointed Nelson Rockefeller (CFR) as his vice-president. A year later, two assassination attempts on President Ford put Rockefeller just a heartbeat away from becoming the next president of the United States.

In 1968, Richard Nixon (CFR) won an easy victory over Hubert Humphrey (CFR). The 1972 election featured Nixon (CFR) against George McGovern (CFR). In 1980 Ronald Reagan (not a CFR member) was such a popular candidate that the conspirators had to accept his victory, but forced him to choose George H. W. Bush (CFR) as his vice-president. A few months later an assassination attempt on Reagan put Bush close to becoming president.

After Reagan, not only all American presidents have been CFR members, but also all the candidates running for both the Republican and Democratic factions of the Repucratic party.

When, for reasons one can only guess, the CFR conspirators decided that George H. W. Bush (CFR) would be a one-term president and the next president would be Bill Clinton (CFR), Bush ran such an uninspired campaign in 1992 that his running mate Dan Quayle (CFR) called it "The biggest presidential campaign that never was."

After eight disastrous years of the Clinton duo, the conspirators, now reassured that the gullible American voters would act again like sheeple, repeated the charade in the 2000 election, now using their agent Al Gore (CFR) to run a losing campaign against CFR agent George W. Bush.[30] In the 2004 presidential election, the charade was even more evident. Not only was John Kerry (CFR) part of it,[31] but American voters were given the choice of electing either a Yale graduate, member of the Skull and Bones secret society and a CFR agent, who had cheated on his military records, or a Yale graduate, member of the Skull and Bones secret society and a CFR agent, who had cheated on his military records. As expected, the election was stolen again from the naïve American voters.

The most recent act of this tragic comedy was the election of CFR-controlled puppet Barak Hussein Obama.[32] When the conspirators decided not to honor their promise, and instead of Hillary Clinton (CFR) gave the presidency to Obama, they assigned the role of pseudo-opponent to their trusted secret agent John McCain (CFR). The results were exactly what they expected.

If you are still not convinced that a group of conspirators is controlling the U.S. government, I'll give you further proof directly from the insiders: three CFR members who turned into whistle blowers. Rear Admiral Chester Ward, ex-Secretary of Defense James Forrestal, and former assistant secretary of state and U.S. Ambassador to Cuba Spruille Braden.

CFR's Inside Critics

At some time, Ward, Forrestal, and Braden reached the conclusion that they had been recruited by the CFR under the false flag[33] of that time: the fight against communism. Once they discovered the ruse, however, they turned against the conspirators and did whatever they could to expose the true purposes of the Council.

Admiral Chester Ward, a member of the CFR for over a decade, became one of its harshest critics, revealing its inner workings. In the 1975 book he co-authored with Phyllis Schlaffly, *Kissinger on the Couch*, Ward stated that the CFR has a goal:

> ... submergence of U.S. sovereignty and national independence into an all-powerful one-world government. ... this lust to surrender the sover-

> eignty and independence of the United States is pervasive throughout most of the membership.[34]

Another whistle blower was Admiral James Forrestal, America's first Secretary of Defense. Initially, Forrestal was one of the earliest and strongest promoters of what was soon to be known as the "Cold War." But eventually he became very dismayed when he witnessed the betrayal of American soldiers by the deliberate refusal of CFR members Generals Dwight D. Eisenhower and George C. Marshall, in complicit with President Roosevelt, to win World War II at least one full year before the hostilities ended.

Forrestal also saw how, as the result of a secret agreement between Roosevelt and Churchill, concocted by the CFR conspirators, the U.S. rearmed the Soviet Union with Lend-Lease war materials, and then waited until Russia marched into Berlin and captured all of Eastern Europe. Forrestal was so upset with these events that he stated,

> Consistency has never been a mark of stupidity. These men are not incompetent or stupid. If they were merely stupid, they would occasionally make a mistake in our favor.[35]

Soon after, Forrestal allegedly committed suicide under suspicious circumstances.

The third CFR whistle blower was Spruille Braden, former Assistant Secretary of State and ex-US Ambassador to Cuba. On April 5, 1954, Rene Wormser, general counsel for the U.S. House of Representatives Special Committee to Investigate Tax-Exempt Foundations, wrote to Spruille Braden concerning the activities of the Carnegie, Rockefeller, and Ford Foundations, and the Rhodes Scholarship Trust —all of them CFR-controlled. Braden's answer was clear and pointed right to the true source of the problem:

> I have the very definite feeling that these various foundations you mention very definitely do exercise both overt and covert influences on our foreign relations and that their influences are counter to the fundamental principles on which this nation was founded and which have made it great.[36]

But undoubtedly the most important CFR whistle blower of all time was Carroll Quigley, an obscure professor at Georgetown University. Not many Americans had heard about Quigley until Bill Clinton mentioned him in a speech at Georgetown when he launched his presidential campaign.[37] Clinton mentioned Quigley again during his acceptance speech to the 1992 Democratic National Convention.[38]

Carroll Quigley is a key element in proving the existence of this conspiracy, because he was a true insider who enjoyed the confidence of the conspirators to the point that they opened their secret archives to him, and wrote about the immense conspiracy he had discovered. But Quigley blew the whistle on the CFR conspirators not because he disagreed with their agenda. Contrary to Ward, Forrestal and Braden, the naïve professor believed that the conspirators' secret machinations only deserved praise, and should be made known to the American public.

In his book *Tragedy and Hope*, Quigley wrote about the existence of this conspiracy in friendly and praiseful terms:

> There does exist, and has existed for a generation, an international Anglophile network which operates, to some extent, in the way the radical Right believes the Communists act. In fact, this network, has no aversion to cooperating with the Communists, or any other groups, and frequently does so. . . .
>
> The Council on Foreign Relations is the American Branch of this network ... and ... believes national boundaries should be obliterated and one-world rule established.[39]

An objection could be made that, if this group of conspirators is so secret, how come they authorized Quigley to publish a book exposing its existence? Well, it seems that they didn't authorize it. But Quigley, who had no objections to their secret plans, took the liberty of publishing his book without their authorization.

Quigley's *Tragedy and Hope* was first published in 1966, but just a few weeks after it appeared in the bookstores, the remaining unsold copies were withdrawn and the publisher refused to do a new printing, allegedly because the plates had been destroyed.

Since the publication of the book, Quigley's fortunes quickly turned sour. Perhaps a key to the source of his misfortunes is the title of an article about Quigley *The Washington Post* published in March, 1975: "The Professor Who Knew Too Much." Two years later, Professor Quigley passed away in obscurity.

Need more proof? I have it for you. This is right from the horse's mouth, David Rockefeller himself. On page 405 of the paperback edition of his *Memoirs*, published in 2002, David wrote:

> For more than a century ideological extremists at either end of the political spectrum have seized upon well-publicized incidents such as my encounter with Castro to attack the Rockefeller family for the inordinate influence they claim we wield over American political and economic institutions. Some even believe we are part of a secret cabal working against the best interests of the United States, characterizing my family and me as 'internationalists' and of conspiring with others around the world to build a more integrated political and economic structure —one world, if you will.
>
> If that's the charge, I stand guilty, and I am proud of it.[40]

So, David Rockefeller himself, through his own words, confessed that,

–The Rockefeller family wields an inordinate influence over American political and economic institutions,

–He had a private encounter with Castro (actually he has had several),
–The Rockefellers are part of a secret cabal against the best interests of the United States,
–They are internationalists,
–They conspire with others around the world to build a one world government [also called the New World Order],
–He is guilty of all charges, and proud of it.

Of course, in his arrogance, David, like most tyrants and dictators, see himself as a benevolent father figure, a sort of Big Brother working behind the scenes to make a better world for the rest of us. This image, however, is highly disingenuous. And about his encounters with Fidel Castro, I will show you that there is more than meets the eye.

The CFR Octopus

Usually, when a revolution takes place in a country, the government in power, which I would call Government A, is quickly and violently substituted by the revolutionaries' Government B. This is what happened in Russia in 1917, in Italy in 1922, in Germany in 1939 and in Cuba in 1959, where legitimate governments A were quickly and violently substituted by communist or fascist governments B. Eventually, however, when most of the elements of the previous government have been eliminated, Government B, now in power, becomes the official, legitimate one, that is, Government A.

But the conspirators who planned to bring a revolutionary change of government in the United States to implement the communo-fascist regime they call the New World Order were a bunch of physical cowards, who didn't have the courage to risk their lives in a revolution by gun play. Consequently, despite the fact that the political system they wanted to implement was a mixture of communism and fascism, they neither adopted the revolutionary tactics of open insurrection favored by the Communists, nor the coup d'ètat techniques of the Fascists, but the evolutionary, infiltration techniques advocated by the British Fabians.

The Fabian Society was founded in 1884. Though their ultimate goal is not too different from the Communists or the Fascists, the British Fabians abhorred violence and believed that there was a third way to take control of a government: by gradual infiltration and pressure from inside. Appropriately, the coat-of-arms of the Fabian Society depicts a wolf in sheep's clothing.

A good description of the Fabian technique appeared in the November 1, 1930, edition of the British *Evening Standard*:

> The Fabian Society consists of Socialists. . . . They adjusted themselves to whatever was the creed or tenets of any camp they penetrated into, and by degrees converted its adherents to a turn of mind designed to procure the advancement of Fabian members into politi-

> cal, industrial or educational lines, with the final result that they secured "key positions."[41]

Further proof that this Fabian infiltration continues is an article by Richard Gardner (CFR) that appeared in April 1974 in *Foreign Affairs*, entitled "The Hard Road to World Order." In it, he made an explicit recommendation on how to carry out the world-government scheme of CFR founder Edward Mandell House. Gardner advises not to do it by violent means, communist or fascist style frontal attack, but in a Fabian way, making an end run around national sovereignty, and eroding it piece by piece.

The first successful attempt to infiltrate and control the U.S. Government was made by Col. Edward Mandell House, himself a Fabian, during the Wilson administration. But, as I mentioned above, the founding fathers of this country were visionaries with their feet on the ground, and to avoid the possibility of control by infiltration they divided the government's power into three different areas: the executive, the legislative, and the judicial powers.

Consequently, the conspirators found that, by controlling just the presidents, they didn't have full control of the U.S. Government. Therefore, their next step was infiltrating the two main political parties. Accordingly, they infiltrated and took control first of the Republican and, later, the Democratic Party.

In the late 1930's, they successfully infiltrated and got control over the U.S. Department of State. By that time they had already infiltrated what is known as the Fourth Power, the mainstream press, as well as the system of public education. Currently they also control the judicial system and the top echelons of the U.S. military.

As a result, even though we still have a U.S. Government A —the Main Street Government—, the one Americans see and, due to constant brainwashing, believe is the only and true one, it has become an empty shell. The government currently in power is Government B —the Wall Street Government—, fully under the control of the CFR conspirators. Until recently, U.S. Government B had been living a parasitical life of slow incubation, obtaining its nourishment out of the decaying body of U.S. Government A. Currently, however, everything indicates that the conspirators are ready for the final push to turn the illegitimate U.S. Government B into the legitimate government of the United States.

Nevertheless, despite all their power, the conspirators have not won the final battle —at least, not yet. The present economic crisis, which not only is economic, but also political, social and ethical, has occurred at a time when a new pervasive medium of communication they cannot control, the Internet, is threatening their monopoly on the press.

True American patriots are using the Internet to awake the American people to the fact that our supposedly "representative government," Government A, does not represent us anymore. It is evident that the Government in Washington D.C. is Government B, that is, the government representing the interests of Wall Street bankers, oil magnates, and CEOs of transnational corporations. And the true seat of Government B is not in Washington, D.C., but in the Harold Pratt House in Manhattan.

Like a malignant cancer, the Council on Foreign Relations has metastasized into a group of organizations; all of them created with the financial help of the Rockefellers and their Wall Street friends. Among the main ones are the Trilateral Commission, and the Bilderberg Group, as well as the United Nations Organizations and its dependent organizations like the UNESCO, the World Churches Organization, the World Health Organization, and the rest of the communo-fascist organizations they have created over the years with the pretext of protecting the environment, free trade, and third world women's reproductive health —a euphemism for Malthusian eugenics.

These people also control the main international financial organizations, like the International Monetary Fund, and the World Bank. The ultimate goal of these organizations is the creation of a New World Order, which is nothing but a communo-fascist totalitarian dictatorship under the control of Wall Street bankers and CEOs of transnational corporations — very similar to what Italian fascist dictator Benito Mussolini called "the corporate state."[42]

One may argue that one of the characteristics of fascism is its furious nationalism under the control of corporations, while the CFR conspirators champion globalization. Still, in a time of transnational corporations, it makes sense that the new fascism they envision will be global.

The CIA's True Bosses

Of the many books about the CIA, written by both apologists and critics, only a few authors have found the true key to decipher the mystery behind this secretive organization. One of them is Col. L. Fletcher Prouty, U.S. Air Force (Ret.), and the other is Ralph W. McGehee, a retired CIA officer.

In his excellent study of the CIA, *The CIA and Its Allies in Control of the United States and the World,* Fletcher Prouty explains how a group of CIA officers managed, through the administration of selective information to the President and other government leaders, to virtually control the U.S. Government. According to Prouty, "The CIA is a great, monstrous machine with tremendous and terrible power."

Prouty's book was initially published in New York by Prentice Hall in 1973, but the book was practically censored and disappeared from the bookstores. Then, new editions were printed in 1992 and 1997. In the Preface of the second edition of his book, published in 1992, Prouty affirms,

> I was the first author to point out that the CIA's most important "Cover Story" is that of an "Intelligence" agency. Of course the CIA does make use of "intelligence" and "intelligence gathering," but that is largely a front for its primary interest, "Fun and Games." Its allies, and its method of operation, are the principal subjects of this book.

In the Preface to the 1997 edition of his book, Prouty expanded even more on the subject,

> The CIA is the center of a vast, and amorphous mechanism that specializes in Covert Operations . . . or as Allen Dulles always called it, "Peacetime Operations." In this sense, the CIA is the willing tool of a higher level High Cabal, that may include representatives and highly skilled agents of the CIA and other instrumentality's of the government, certain cells of the business and professional world and, almost always, foreign participation. It is this ultimate Secret Team, its allies, and its method of operation that are the principal subject of this book.

But, contrary to other authors and perhaps conscious of the principle that in intelligence and espionage things are seldom what they seem, Prouty was not fooled by misleading appearances. At the very end of his book, he clearly states that, though the CIA is very powerful, ". . . in the majority of cases, the power behind it is big business, big banks, big law firms and big money. The Agency exists to be used by them."

Moreover, in an article Prouty wrote for the February 1986 issue of *Freedom* magazine, he clarifies even more the issue:

> The CIA is the best friend of the top executives of America's biggest business, and it works for them at home and abroad. It is always successful in the highest echelons of government and finance. . . . Translated into everyday terms, Casey's CIA, as was Allen Dulles' CIA, is one of the true bastions of power as a servant of the American and transnational business and financial community.

The other author who cut through the chase was Ralph W. McGehee, a former CIA officer. In the Introduction to his book *Deadly Deceits: My 25 Years in the CIA*[43] McGehee states,

> . . . the CIA is the covert action arm of the Presidency. Most of its money, manpower, and energy go into covert operations that, as we have seen over the years, include backing dictators and overthrowing democratically elected governments. The CIA is not an intelligence agency. In fact it is an anti-intelligence agency, producing only the information wanted by policymakers to support their plans and suppressing information that does not support those plans. As the covert action arm of the President, the CIA uses disinformation, much of it aimed at the U.S. public, to mold opinion. It employs the gamut of disinformation techniques from forging documents to planting and discovering "communist" weapons caches. But the major weapon in its arsenal of disinformation is the "intelligence" it feeds to policymakers.[44]

At the end of the book, however, McGehee gets even closer to the source of the problem when he modifies his previous statement that the CIA is the covert arm of the President, and changes it to affirm that actually it is the covert action arm *of the President's policy advisers*. And that simple modification makes a great difference, because in it resides the hidden truth of the matter. I am quoting below his statement in full:

> The CIA is not now nor has it ever been a central intelligence agency. It is the covert action arm of the President's foreign policy advisers. In that capacity it overthrows or supports foreign governments while reporting "intelligence" justifying those activities. It shapes its intelligence, even in such critical areas as Soviet nuclear weapon capability, to support presidential policy. Disinformation is a large part of its covert action responsibility, and the American people are the primary target audience of its lies.[45]

So, it is obvious that both Prouty and McGehee are convinced that, far from being the ultimate culprit, the CIA is just a tool. But, whose tool? Unfortunately, neither Prouty nor McGehee name names. But it is obvious that both authors are talking about the people behind the curtains who control our lives, the ones Prouty calls "The Secret Team," and others have called the invisible government of the United States of America.

More recently, a few more authors are reaching the same conclusion. For example, Paul David Collins is convinced that,

> The problematic intelligence organization seems to have been engaged in nefarious activity since its inception. What is the explanation for the Agency's seemingly systemic corruption? Anti-government writers claim that CIA corruption stems from the fact that the Agency is an organ of a corrupt government. However, this contention is a gross oversimplification. While the Agency does have a government charter, it can only be considered a quasi-governmental organization. For the most part, the Agency is the enforcement arm of its "founding fathers." While these "founding fathers" use national governments as their personal prostitutes, they inhabit a stratum that exists above governments. The "founding fathers" are the power elite.[46]

Another author who pointed exactly to the right direction is Henry Makow. According to Makow,

> Our main misconception about the CIA is that it serves U.S. interests. In fact, it has always been the instrument of a dynastic international banking and oil elite (Rothschild, Rockefeller, Morgan) coordinated by the Royal Institute of International Affairs[47] in London and their U.S. branch, the

Council on Foreign Relations.[48]

In an article entitled "Chinagate: The Third-Way Scandal," author Richard Poe reaches a similar conclusion. According to Poe, "When the Cold War ended, the CIA took on a new job —helping U.S. corporations compete in the global marketplace."[49]

Poe's assertion, however, is not fully true. The CIA didn't take a new job. Since its very creation — actually since its very conception in the minds of its true creators— the CIA's real, secret job has never been protecting and advancing the interests of the American people but of the invisible government of the United States: Wall Street international bankers, oil magnates, and CEOs of global corporations. The CIA's job is not new, the only difference is that the Agency is now doing it more openly, and the corporations the CIA is helping in their fight to destroy their competitors are transnational, not American.

As I will show below in this book, since its very creation the CIA has never been an intelligence agency, but an elaborate hoax, a subterfuge and a cover to justify and disguise the existence of the conspirators' secret military arm. It has also served as a sort of bullfighters' red coat to distract the American people's attention by focusing it on the puppet instead of the real source of the problem: the puppeteers who control the action behind the curtains.

"Did the CIA lie to Congress?"[50] This was the title of one of the latest psychological warfare fiction thrillers, starring Nancy Pelosi and developed by the conspirators in one of their think tanks, to keep the American people distracted and off the track. However, despite the eye-catching title, most likely the CIA didn't lie to the Congress. Actually, the ones who have been systematically lying to the American people are the CFR conspirators and their agents infiltrated in the media and the government, particularly in the bunch of corrupt politicians of the two branches of the Repucratic Party who control the U.S. Congress. The CIA just keeps faithfully playing its scripted role as the conspirators' mouthpiece providing the bogus intelligence they need to fool the American people. Sometimes, when the ruse is discovered, a limited hangout[51] operation is carried out and the CIA plays the role of the fall guy, keeping the American people looking in the wrong direction.

Chapter 2

Spying: The Rockefellers' True Passion

Competition is a sin.
—John D. Rockefeller.

We cannot depend on an alliance of angels to defend the free world.
—David Rockefeller.

Traditionally, the U.S. had no central intelligence agency. Usually, intelligence needs had been carried out by Military Intelligence, Naval Intelligence, the Secret Service, the Customs House, the Bureau of Investigation of the U.S. Department of Justice and the State Department. The first attempt to create a civilian, independent intelligence agency was made by a group of Wall Street bankers and oil magnates, particularly the Rockefellers.

Most books about the Central Intelligence Agency claim that the CIA was an offshoot of the Office of Strategic Services (OSS). What they don't mention, however, is that the OSS itself was an offshoot of a select group of scholars handpicked by powerful Wall Street bankers to act as spies and intelligence analysts allegedly to brief president Woodrow Wilson about the U.S. options for a postwar world,[1] which eventually turned into a veritable intelligence agency.

Throughout the winter of 1917-18, this group of intelligence analysts and would-be spies gathered secretly in a hideaway in Manhattan, interpreting and evaluating information and producing intelligence reports they thought were vital to making the world safe. Actually, they were working to keep safe the assets abroad of the Wall Street bankers and oil magnates who had recruited them. This secretive group was called the Inquiry.

The Inquiry: First U.S. Civilian Intelligence Agency

In the fall of 1917, Colonel Edward Mandell House, President Woodrow Wilson's confidential adviser, gathered about one hundred prominent men to discuss the postwar world. Dubbing themselves "the Inquiry," they made plans for a peace settlement, which eventually evolved into Wilson's famous "fourteen points" he presented to Congress on January 8, 1918.

Their plans advanced for the first time the idea of globalization, calling for the removal of "all economic barriers" between nations (now called "free trade"), equality of trade conditions, and the formation of "a general association of nations" —which later materialized in the short-lived League of Nations and later in the CFR-controlled United Nations Organization.

The idea of creating a private civilian intelligence agency —a concoction of a small group of Wall Street bankers and oil magnates conspiring to advance their interests, particularly the Rockefellers— was a meme,[2] implanted in Wilson's suggestive mind by an obscure, shady character and secret agent of the conspirators, "Colonel" Edward Mandell House, a sort of proto-National Security adviser. House had managed to recruit Wilson and, like most controllers,[3] psychologically manipulated the president until he became his most trusted aide. House developed the *modus operandi* later used by the conspirators through the National Security advisers to manage Americans presidents —which I call the "mushroom treatment": keeping them in the dark and feeding them manure.

The son of an English immigrant, Edward Mandell House grew up in Houston Texas. Like all agent controllers, House had a flair for making friends who appreciated his discretion, respected his views, and valued his counsel. This talent for winning friends and influencing people would remain the basis of his remarkable achievements in politics throughout his life.

After living in Austin since 1886, he moved to New York City in 1902. His biographer, Godfrey Hodgson describes how, soon after, his social connections, acquaintances and friendships among the rich and the powerful were extraordinary.[4] Most likely it was at that time when he associated himself with some Wall Street conspirators and became an agent for the Rothschild - Warburg - Rockefeller banking cartel.

The job of recruiting the scholars-cum-spies of the Inquiry was assigned to Walter Lippman, another trusted secret agent of the conspirators. Lippman recruited the initial group of spies and intelligence analysts and managed it. His job was not much different from any intelligence officer on the look to recruiting spies and intelligence analysts: "What we are on the lookout for is genius — sheer, startling genius, and nothing else will do,"[5] Lippman told some friends.

The initial group —which eventually grew up to 126 scholars— was composed mostly of American socialist-oriented intellectuals that formed the inner circle of the Intercollegiate Society. Under the direction of House's brother-in-law Sydney Mezes,[6] they worked in secrecy out of the American Geographical Society, doing historical research and writing position papers with plans for the upcoming peace settlement in Paris. The Inquiry was the *de facto* first formally sanctioned civilian U.S. Central Intelligence Agency.

Since its very creation, the Inquiry was organized and acted like an intelligence agency. In the first place, it was divided in several study groups. Some of these groups studied different geographic areas and countries: Africa, Austria-Hungary, Balkans, Far East, Italy, Latin America, Pacific islands, Russia, Western Asia and Western Europe. Other groups were devoted to study Diplomatic History, Economics, International Law and Cartography.[7] This division was quite similar to the "desks" later adopted by the CIA.

Secondly, the Inquiry's activities were surrounded in secrecy[8] Even its bland, disingenuous name, "the Inquiry," was adopted to hide the true purpose of the organization.[9]

In theory, the Inquiry was an autonomous organization responsible only to the President and secretly paid with funds controlled by him. Congress mostly ignored its existence. [10] It bypassed the State Department.[11] The Inquiry's work was kept secret from the American people. It was never mentioned in the mainstream press. Special armed guards patrolled its headquarters day and night.[12]

Thirdly, the Inquiry's activities were divided among four general categories: planning, collecting, digesting, and editing the raw data.[13] This roughly corresponds to the CIA's intelligence cycle: planning and direction, collection, processing, production and analysis, and dissemination.[14]

Finally, though the Inquiry's alleged sole purpose was to research and report to Wilson to prepare the U.S. case for the coming peace settlement, the fact that it had a Latin American study group indicates that its scope was much larger. Actually, the Inquiry was, among other things, the first step to systematically study Latin America's natural resources for the future exploitation of Wall Street bankers and oil corporations —a job later assumed by the Council on Foreign Relations.

In a short study about the Inquiry, CFR agent Peter Grose affirms:

> The vision that stirred the Inquiry became the work of the Council on Foreign relations over the better part of a century: a program of systematic study by groups of knowledgeable specialists of different ideological inclinations would stimulate a variety of papers and reports to guide the statecraft of policymakers. What began as an intellectual response to a juncture of history grew into an institution that would thrive through all the diplomacy of America's twentieth century."[15]

With a few exceptions, most of the Inquiry members later joined the CFR. Among the initial members of the Inquiry were Col. House himself (CFR), as well as George Louis Beer, Isaiah Bowman (CFR), Clive Day (CFR), Allen Dulles (CFR), John Foster Dulles (CFR), H. Haskins (CFR), Christian Herter (CFR), Mark Jefferson, Maj. Douglas W. Johnson (CFR), Walter Lippman (CFR), H. Lord (CFR), W. E. Lunt, Sidney E. Mezes (CFR), Charles Seymour (CFR), Whitney H. Shepardson (CFR), James Thomson Shotwell (CFR), Norman Thomas, W. L. Westermann, Allyn A. Young (CFR), Frank Aydelotte (CFR), Thomas W. Lamont (CFR), Jerome D. Greene (CFR), Archibald C. Coolidge (CFR), Gen. Tasker H. Bliss (CFR), Erwin D. Canham (CFR), W. Averell Harriman (CFR) and Herbert Hoover (CFR).[16]

There are good reasons for believing that most of them belonged to the American branch of the Rhodes' Round Table groups, a secret society devoted to advancing the British rule in the world.

In his 1877 *Confessions of Faith*, millionaire Cecil Rhodes exposed his idea of creating an organization to bring the whole world under British domination,

> Why should we not form a secret society with but one object, the furtherance of the British Empire, for the bringing of the whole uncivilized world under the British rule, for the recovery of the United States, for the making [of] the Anglo-Saxon race but one empire.[17]

To pursue his dream he established in 1891 a secret society made up of small cells called Round Table groups. At his death, Rhodes left his immense fortune to the Rhodes Trust, which funded his secret society as well as a Rhodes Scholarship Fund to propagate his ideas in pursuit of a British-controlled world government [18]

On November 1918, shortly before the armistice that would put an end to WWI, Colonel House sailed to Paris with a group of twenty Inquiry members and twenty military intelligence officers, now designated as the "Territorial, Economic and Military Intelligence Division."[19] To coordinate the conspirators' presence at the forthcoming Paris Peace Conference of 1919, bankers Paul Warburg and Bernard Baruch accompanied House in the trip.[20]

A month later, Wilson himself followed suit aboard his presidential cruiser to attend the Conference. He was accompanied in his trip by 20 of the Inquiry scholars now turned into spies.[21]

As soon as the Inquiry spies accommodated themselves at the Hotel Crillon, they engaged in their espionage activities. Grose describes these activities in some detail:

> The historical record of the Paris Peace Conference focuses on the meetings of the major powers: Britain, France, Italy, and the United States. To those of the Inquiry, however, and the colleagues they gathered among diplomatic and military officers in Europe, these plenary sessions mattered little. For them the daily teas at the Quai d'Orsay, the bridge games, the breakfast and dinner meetings of experts from a dozen countries gave enduring personal meaning to the peace conference.
>
> In congenial and civilized encounters, they floated ideas in the noncommittal style of the Oxford Common Room; they noted each other's expertise and forged livelong friendships without regard to age or nationality. In these unrecorded discussions the frontiers of central Europe were redrawn (subject, of course, to their principals' satisfaction), vast territories were assigned to one or another's jurisdiction, and economic arrangements were devised on seemingly rational principles.[22]

House and his Wall Street masters feared that the European monarchies might become an obstacle to their long-term plans of global domination. Consequently, they wanted the people to believe that, "the war [WWI] had been imposed on the peoples of Europe by the monarchies and their aristocracies,"[23] an idea House himself had already implanted in Wilson's mind. Therefore, Wilson became convinced that a postwar settlement should include the elimination of the Austro-

Hungarian and German empires and the creation of a number of new democratic states in central Europe.

It was to fulfill the details of this vision —which Wilson now was convinced it was his own idea— the argument House used to persuade Wilson to assemble this group of experts to study the problem and suggest solutions. The plan they created was the basis for Wilson's proposals at the Versailles peace conference — later known as Wilson's Fourteen Points.

Profiting form his almost total control over Wilson, House engaged actively in promoting the conspirators' interests. This ultimately led to the passage in 1913 of the illegal Federal Reserve Act that created the Federal Reserve Bank and the dreaded Internal Revenue Service, an old dream of the Wall Street bankers.[24] Both projects, wrongly attributed to Wilson, had actually been developed by one of the Wall Street conspirators, Nelson Aldrich.

House–Wilson: A Typical Case of Agent Recruitment

In 1911, Colonel House, one of the conspirators' main talent spotters,[25] detected what they considered a rising star, a man who, despite no previous political experience had just been elected the governor of New Jersey: Woodrow Wilson. Immediately Wilson became to them what in the intelligence field is known as a target or person of interest.[26] As such, they began researching his life and preparing a full intelligence dossier on him.

Knowing that after his election as governor he had manifested his intention of running for president, in the winter of 1910-1911 the conspirators sent their secret agent House to recruit Wilson. He was introduced to Wilson on November 24, 1911. House's recollection of the moment is highly revealing.

House recorded in his personal diaries that at that meeting, "a true marriage of minds took place."[27] Both of them had a remarkable congruence in their ideas about men and measures. After this first meeting, their friendship blossomed and continued for several years.

But House's recollection is highly misleading. Professor Lawrence Gelfand, one of the few scholars who has studied the Inquiry in detail, mentioned that the fact that this peculiar friendship lasted so long was remarkable,

> . . . for House and Wilson were quite different in temperament. Moreover, their backgrounds were quite dissimilar, and even their values, their ideals, their methods did not fundamentally coincide.[28]

What House does not mention, however, and apparently never crossed Gelfand's mind, is that this amazing coincidence of ideas was because, before attending the meeting, House had studied and memorized the main parts of Wilson's dossier —a standard operational procedure in agent recruitment.

Agent recruitment is basically based on the MICE principle —an acronym for money, ideology, compromise and ego. These are the basic human weaknesses exploited to convince or force an unwilling target for recruitment into treachery and espionage. Some tradecraft experts, however, argue that there is only a motivation that really matters, and that is ego. That is what ultimately leads someone to become a spy, to betray his country.

The target for recruitment may see himself as serving a higher cause, or may think he wants all the money he has been promised. But these are merely conscious expressions of something deeper, and that is ego. Woodrow Wilson's was a man dominated by a humongous ego and, therefore, easily manipulated by a trained intelligence officer.

Wilson was a man intoxicated with the sense of his own importance and historical relevance. On his thirty-third birthday, he wrote in his "confidential journal" the rhetorical question he already had answered in his mind: "Why may not the present generation write, through me, its political autobiography?"[29]

In a final analysis, Wilson, who before entering politics was just an obscure professor of international law at Princeton University, was a mediocre man, without any original ideas or imagination. As I mentioned above, none of the political ideas attributed to him were his own. His skillful controller, Edward Mandell House, had implanted all his ideas, including the fascist-like use of his Espionage Acts to repress opposition, in Wilson's mind.

The adjective "Wilsonian," commonly attributed to presidents who allegedly follow Wilson's ideas, is just a myth kept alive by the CFR's professional disinformers. Actually, there was nothing "Wilsonian" in most of Wilson's ideas. Actually, most of them were "Housian."

In the same fashion, none of the important U.S. documents about foreign policy by which American presidents are known — from the Cold War to the Alliance for Progress and the War on Terror[30]—, particularly the so-called presidential "doctrines," are their own. Actually, they have been conceived at the Harold Pratt House by the CFR conspirators and implanted in the presidents' minds by their CFR controllers or just placed on their desks for them to sign.

Of these, probably the most obvious is the U.S. policy document "National Security Strategy of the United States,"[31] also known as the Bush Doctrine, released in September 2002. Its most radical postulate is its new preemptive strikes policy, which is nothing but a more aggressive approach toward countries that get in the way of the CFR's Wall Street Mafia.

If ego is the main motivation for an individual to become a traitor, compromise is the tool used by a recruiter to firmly close the trap. One of the most common techniques used by recruiters to compromise an agent since the very first step of his recruitment process is to ask him to write a report about an innocuous subject, for which he is paid a modest sum. Unknown to the potential agent, the moment he gets his payment, even if it is in cash, is photographically recorded to be used later as a possible leverage tool if the need arises.[32]

But money is not the only compromising tool in the recruiter's toolkit. Sex, particularly homosexual sex, is another human weakness intelligence agencies use as a powerful recruitment tool. Was there a homoerotic element in the House-Wilson relationship? Despite the fact that it has never been mentioned I would not discount it.

FDR's son-in-law Curtis B. Dall, for one, seems to have sensed, if not suspected, that possibility. According to him,

> Both Howe [Roosevelt's controller] and House were rather delicate, physically, and were therefore inclined to collaborate with, and gravitate to those who were more physically active and aggressive.[33]

Following the conspirators' plan, House joined the group behind Wilson's campaign, "to do what I could to further Governor Wilson's fortunes."[34]

As Wilson's campaign strategist and intra-party peacemaker in 1911 and 1912, House played an important role, first, in getting Wilson first nominated as a presidential candidate for the Democratic Party and, later, to be elected president. Of course, Wilson would not have been elected if the conspirators had not helped him from the shadows. The main cause that determined Wilson's victory was that Theodore Roosevelt had bolted the Republican Party and ran as a candidate for the Progressive Party, thereby splitting the opposition to Wilson and ensuring a Democratic victory.

After Wilson's election, House played an even more important role. Soon after the election, the president-elect became engulfed in the cloud of his newly acquired position. Devoting most of his time to cultivating his enlarged ego, Wilson manifested little interest in the nuts and bolts of party politics, including the selection of men for cabinet and other high-level positions, and he left these decisions largely in House's hands. Wilson offered House himself any cabinet position he wanted, except secretary of state, which had been reserved for William Jennings Bryan. But, following the conspirators' orders, House declined, preferring to work behind the curtains as the president's most trusted advisor.

In this capacity, House quickly developed an extraordinarily intimate (homoerotic?) relationship with the president as political advisor, personal confidant, and frequent social companion. His psychological control over the President was so pervasive that, shamelessly, Wilson himself admitted: "Mr. House is my second personality. He is my independent self. His thoughts and mine are one."[35]

Another scholar described in some detail what he saw as a strange friendship,

> For seven long years, Colonel House was Woodrow Wilson's other self. For six long years he shared with him everything but the title of Chief Magistracy of the Republic. For six years, two rooms were at his disposal in the north wing of the White House. ... It was House who made the slate for the Cabinet, formulated the first policies of the Administration, and practically directed the foreign affairs of the United States. We had, indeed, two presidents for one![36]

As I will explain below, however, what seems to be a strange friendship of total psychological dependency may be easily explained as a typical controller-agent relationship.

Despite the alleged expertise of its members, however, the Inquiry didn't do a good job on behalf of the conspirators. It is true that some of them had substantial academic credentials, but none of them was a true expert in the convoluted field of European politics. This shortcoming was evidenced in Wilson's Fourteen Points, which proposed, among other things, major changes in the border of many European nations, as well as a general association of the nations —a multilateral international association of nations to enforce the peace later known as the League of Nations. But some important European leaders like David Lloyd George and Georges Clemenceau found them unacceptable.[37]

Convinced that "his" Fourteen Points would be accepted, Wilson departed from France in mid-February 1919, leaving House at the Conference "to act in his place and with full confidence."[38]

In the president's absence, however, House proceeded to do what he had been doing successfully for decades on behalf of his Wall Street masters: he made deals, compromising where necessary to gain the other parties' agreement and creating the best possible arrangements he could make in an extremely complex and challenging situation. Although House kept Wilson informed as he went along, the president seems not to have fully comprehended what House was agreeing to in France, much less who was House really working for.

When Wilson returned to France in mid-March and discovered the details of House's deals, he reacted with dismay to what he viewed as the betrayal of his high ideals for the settlement. His immense ego was deeply hurt and his relationship with House quickly dissolved.[39] Although he allowed House to continue negotiating specific matters at Versailles, he didn't allow him to act as the chief U.S. delegate, and the intimate relationship between the two men quickly dissolved:

> Their friendship never recovered from the events of February and March 1919. It ended in bitterness and mutual incomprehension, with grave consequences for both of them and ultimately—it really is no exaggeration to say—for the peace of the world.[40]

After the Germans signed the treaty in June, House saw the president just once before his return voyage to the United States. Their conversation on that occasion was short and cold, and it was the last they would ever have.

Wilson died a bitter man. At the end of his life, tortured by remorse, perhaps he remembered a confession he had made in 1913, the very same year he became President:

> Some of the biggest men in the United States, in the field of commerce and manufacture, are afraid of somebody, are afraid of something. They know there is a power somewhere so organized, so subtle, so watchful, so interlocked, so complete, so pervasive that they had better not speak above their breath when they speak in condemnation of it.[41]

The recruitment of Woodrow Wilson by the conspirators through their secret agent House was the first manifestation of a pattern that has repeated itself over and over, as evidenced in the cases of presidents Roosevelt, Eisenhower, Nixon, Carter, Reagan and Clinton, and now is becoming even more evident with Obama.[42]

In his book *F.D.R.: My Exploited Father in Law*[43] Curtis B. Dall explains how, closely following House's methodology, Louis McHenry Howe, another enigmatic character, infiltrated himself into Franklin D. Roosevelt's life. As his personal counselor, Howe eventually came to live with FDR and had a room on the top floor of Roosevelt's 49 E. 65th Street house in New York.[44]

Dall mentions that he never knew *who* and *what* Howe was, but he suspected that behind him were the "same 'influences' that put Col. Edward Mandell House *onto* Woodrow Wilson in 1912.[45] Dall's suspicions were correct. Most likely, Howe was FDR's case officer (controller) doing his job for his Wall Street masters.

After the creation of the National Security Council in 1947, the job of U.S. presidents' case officer became sort of institutionalized, when the CFR conspirators systematically assigned it to the president's National Security advisor. These were the true jobs of Zbigniew Brzezinski (CFR) during the Carter administration, Henry Kissinger (CFR) during the Nixon administration, and Alexander Haig (CFR) during the Reagan administration. They efficiently worked in the shadows controlling the puppet presidents on behalf of the CFR puppeteers.

Of lately, however, the conspirators' continued successes apparently have emboldened them, and the President's controllers are acting more openly. This was the case of Dick Cheney (CFR) acting as George W. Bush's controller. Currently, due to the fact that he is the one who initially spotted and cultivated Obama, it seems that Brzezinski is the case officer the CFR conspirators have assigned the job of controlling and managing Barack Obama. [46]

Wilson: The First Successful U.S. Puppet President

The strange relationship between an obscure man and the American President who became his lapdog has flabbergasted most of the scholars who have studied it and failed to find a satisfactory explanation to the mystery. One of them went to the point of calling this seemingly weird relationship "The strangest friendship in history."[47]

But, seen from the point of view of intelligence and espionage, this "strange" relationship loses its mystery and becomes easy to explain: Col. House was never Wilson's friend. House was actually a career intelligence officer at the service of some Wall Street bankers. As such, he was assigned the job of recruiting Wilson. After recruiting him, he became what in intelligence and espionage is known as his case officer (also known as controller).

Despite all the books and articles written by "serious" scholars, there was nothing "Wilsonian" in the Wilson administration. Wilson was an egotistical fool and an obedient puppet of his Wall Street masters. In a letter he sent to Col. House in 1933, President Roosevelt (a puppet himself), recognized the fact when he acknowledged,

> The real truth of the matter is, as you and I know, that a financial element in the larger centers have owned the Government ever since the days of Andrew Jackson —and I am not wholly excepting the Administration of W. W.[48] [Woodrow Wilson]

The main ideas that have been attributed to Wilson (Fourteen Points, League of Nations, Federal Reserve Bank, income tax and tax-free "charitable' foundations) were not his, but had been implanted in his suggestible mind by his skillful controller, Col. Edward Mandell House. The notion that Wilson was a successful president with original ideas is a myth created and reinforced *a posteriori* by CFR-controlled disinformers.

Wilson was an artificial product manufactured by the conspirators and field tested to evaluate its effectiveness. He was a key element in a new type of psychological warfare operation against the American people. Unfortunately for the American people, the Wilson PSYOP was a big success. Since then, the conspirators have been repeating it over and over, with slight variations, with extraordinary success.

The key steps followed in this type of PSYOP are:

Talent spotters working for the CFR conspirators detect potential candidates for puppet presidents and select them as persons of interest. A full background check is made of the targets, including a thorough psychological evaluation.

A few good prospects are found, tested and some of them are selected.

A case officer is assigned to each of them to begin the recruitment process.

With a few exceptions, all potential candidates are recruited as agents (that is traitors), and the training process begins. Afterwards, the conspirators use their influence to make them advance their careers in a sudden jump.

A final decision is made and then one of the newly recruited agents is selected by the conspirators to be next president of the U.S.

CFR conspirators use their influence in one of the two factions of the Repucratic Party to turn their agent into a viable presidential candidate.

Case officers, under the cover of political advisors, are assigned to surround the candidate with a curtain of disinformation.

The conspirators-controlled mainstream media begin a barrage of positive campaigning, disguised as independent reporting, to brainwash the American people on the virtues of the candidate.

The conspirators select a pseudo-opposing candidate under their control for the presidential campaign charade (i.e., Al Gore, John Kerry, John McCain, all of them CFR members).

If true independent opposing candidates appear, even in the far away horizon, they are either politically destroyed by the CFR-controlled media who ignore them (Ron Paul), paint them as madmen (Barry Goldwater), or make them look plain stupid (Sarah Palin). The most dangerous ones are terminated with extreme prejudice (Huey Long, Larry McDonald, Robert Kennedy, John F. Kennedy Jr.).

If the media brainwashing is not enough, widespread vote fraud is arranged (Jimmy Carter, Bill Clinton, George W. Bush, Barack Obama).

After resorting to all type of manipulations, including vote buying, tampering and outright fraud, the conspirators' candidate is elected.

As a way of payment for the conspirators' political support, the president-elect accepts that most of his cabinet members and advisers are CFR secret agents.

While the president is kept busy dealing with inconsequential issues, CFR agents in key positions control all foreign and domestic policies. The puppet president is brainwashed to make him believe that all these policies are his.

If, once in the White House, any of them make the mistake of believing that he is actually the president of the U.S. and begins acting independently, he is deposed through a coup d'état (Richard Nixon),[49] or terminated with extreme prejudice (John F. Kennedy).

Due to the fact that all the policies taken by the president are actually the conspirators', they logically benefit the CFR conspirators, not the American public. Consequently, sooner or later opposition to the incumbent president grows.

If the incumbent president is a member of the Republican faction of the Repucratic Party, critics on the left begin a campaign criticizing the failure of "his" policies. (i.e., Reagan's Evil Empire, W. Bush's War on Terror, etc.).

If he is Democrat, critics of the right do exactly the same. Hundreds of articles and dozens of books by serious, respectable journalists and scholars, most of them CFR members, are printed, and they circulate widely. All the blame is put on the incumbent president and "his" policies (i.e., Roosevelt's New Deal, Truman's Containment Doctrine, Johnson's Great Society, Obama's Health Care Reform, etc.).

The only solution offered by the CFR-controlled brainwashers is voting next time for the candidate of the other party. The alternative of electing a candidate of a third party is never given serious consideration. If a non-CFR-controlled candidate with possibilities appears (Barry Goldwater, Ron Paul), he is ignored by the mainstream media and ostracized by members of his own party.

The CFR conspirators detect another potential candidate for recruitment. The process begins again.

A few years later, serious, respectable historians, most of them CFR members, write books analyzing the policies of the past president, and his influence in American history. A myth of the president's independence and originality is created, and eventually written in textbooks and passed to students as true history.

If a big mess is made, (Pearl Harbor, Kennedy's assassination, CIA's domestic spying, 9/11 events) a CFR-controlled commission is created to investigate it. The commission's final report is a total whitewash.

This is the true process by which American presidents are actually elected; the rest is just smoke and mirrors.

The Council on Foreign Relations is a sort of new version on steroids of John D. Rockefeller's Standard Oil Company —which operated exactly like an intelligence and espionage agency. In fact, most of the illegal activities the CIA is known for were pioneered and field-tested by Standard Oil.

Since its very creation, the CFR reflected the psychology, mindset and interests of its creators, the Warburgs, the Rothschilds, the Rockefellers and other international bankers. The CFR's intelligence and espionage activities increased when Nelson and David Rockefeller took control over the organization. Like their grandparent John D., the Rockefellers, particularly David and Nelson, always have shown a special fascination for the activities of intelligence, espionage and covert action as a way to advance their business interests and engrossing their family's fortune.

The Family that Spies Together . . .

Histories of the Standard Oil written by most authors, pro or con, show that John D. Rockefeller, the originator of the family empire, was a person of a deeply conspiratorial, scheming nature. U.S. Senator Robert Lafollette went a step further, and called him "The greatest criminal of the age."[50] John D. himself would later in his life discover that his father's primary occupation had been pitchman and con artist.[51] "Cut from the same mold as the legendary P. T. Barnum, he was far from chagrined by his secret life. In fact, he seemed to revel in his petty larcenies." [52]

Since its very creation, John D. Rockefeller's Standard Oil Company —which other oil producers used to call "a gang of thieves"[53] —, worked like an intelligence and espionage organization. It had created a cult of silence and deception and enforced a policy of total secrecy.[54] It is known that some of the people who did business with John D. were forced to sign an oath of secrecy, promising to keep any deals strictly private.[55]

John D. pioneered the use of industrial espionage to advance his business interests.[56] According to author Gary Allen, the "Rockefeller's industrial espionage system was by far the most elaborate, most sophisticated and most successful that had been established."[57]

According to some witnesses, Rockefeller recruited agents everywhere, among competitors, politicians and in the media. In its continuous effort to monopolize the oil industry by eliminating all competition, Standard Oil employed spies who gathered information about foreign and American markets,[58] as well as analysts who evaluated the raw information and produced useful intelligence.[59]

In 1897, Rockefeller sent two of his secret agents on a mission to Asia, where they gathered information to asses a probable threat by the Royal Dutch oil company.[60] As one of Rockefeller's colleagues acknowledged at the time, "We have before us daily the best information obtainable from all the world's markets."[61]

In order to disguise the criminal activities of his Standard Oil in his effort to eliminate all competition, John D. Rockefeller and some of his co-conspirators created a fictitious organization under the innocuous name of South Improvement Company.[62] This was an early example of what the CIA later called a "proprietary," an ostensibly private business firm created and operated by the CIA as means of providing cover for large-scale secret operations.

Ida Tarbell, who wrote an authoritative study of the Standard Oil, called John D. Rockefeller, "a brooding, cautious, secretive man …"[63] Tarbell's research assistant wrote her: "I tell you this John D. Rockefeller is the strangest, most silent, most mysterious, and most interesting figure in America."[64] According to Tarbell, Mr. Rockefeller employed force, fraud and blackmailing to reach his ends.[65]

Matthew Josephson, another author who has studied the life of John D. Rockefeller, confirms Tarbell's vision. According to Josephson, "He was given to secrecy; he loathed all display. … His wife, Laura Spellman, proved an excellent mate. She encouraged his furtiveness, he relates, advising him always to be silent, to say as little as possible.[66] He also mentions how John D. Rockefeller customarily resorted to violence to destroy his competitors,

> But where the Standard Oil could not carry on its expansion by peaceful means, it was ready with violence; its faithful servants knew even how to apply the modern weapon of dynamite.[67]

Widespread opposition to what most people were convinced was a Rockefeller "conspiracy" grew to the point that, on April 29, 1879, a Grand Jury indicted John D. Rockefeller, William Rockefeller and other chieftains of Standard Oil for criminal conspiracy to "secure a monopoly of the oil industry, to oppress other refiners, to injure carrying trade, to extort unreasonable railroad rates, to fraudulent control prices," to use secret rates and deceiving their competitors as to what their rates were, etc.[68]

Even in a friendly article about the Rockefellers, author Lewis Galantière had to recognize the unscrupulous monopolistic principles on which he did business,

> The classic Standard Oil schemes were: (1) to get a lower shipping rate than rivals paid, and to get in addition, in cash from the roads, the difference between the two rates paid by the competitors; (2) to choke all crude supplies from competitors; (3) to force the transport companies to deny the competing refiners access to markets; (4) to work the fifth-column game by bribing servants of other companies, putting their own people into those companies, or secretly buying up a competitor and obtaining

> the trade secrets of rival groups through the officials of the company secretly acquired.[69]

In his book *The Rockefeller Syndrome*, Ferdinand Lundberg expands on John D. Rockefeller's abilities for intelligence and espionage. According to Lundberg,

> How, in a nutshell, cutting through volumes of apologetics, did the original Standard Oil operate? It operated in such a way as to be a model for any secret service operation such as the CIA or the GPU and KGB. Standard Oil had nothing to learn from them.
>
> In the first place, a large portion of Standard Oil's operations was illegal, as ascertained by the courts. The rule of secrecy was one constantly enjoined upon his associates by Rockefeller himself. As many of these were men of expansive temperament, they would have been, unless carefully coached, apt to tell anyone with pride what they were doing, thus showing what clever fellows they were.
>
> . . .
>
> In addition to using the aliases and disguises of satellite companies, the Standard Oil operated with a secret code and ciphers, lest anyone know what it was doing. It also had an efficient internal and external espionage system. It not only knew what everyone in its employ was doing (and internal pilferers and loafers were dropped at once), but it knew about the internal operations of those trying to compete. It not only had its paid informants planted in other companies, but through the handling of the shipments of others through apparently independent Standard-owed shipping agencies, it learned who rival's customers were, the quantities being shipped, and the prices paid. It used this information to the detriment of the competitor.[70]

In other part of his book Lundberg added,

> Standard Oil not only ladled out money to politicians, in and out of office, and to newspapers, and quickly hired for itself any specially bright lawyers it found acting for its competitors or hostile government agencies, but it had vast success in enlisting the aid of certified academicians. And here, in my opinion, was the worst subversion of all — the trammeling of the very citadel of truth.[71]

Author William Manchester seems to agree with Lundberg. According to Manchester,

> The trouble with fighting John D. was that you never knew where he was. He ran his company as though it were a branch of the C.I.A. All important messages were in code —Baltimore was "Droplet," Philadelphia

> "Druggewt," refiners were "Douters," the Standard itself "Doxy." Shadowy men came and went by his front door, shadowy companies used his back door as a mailing address. For a long time the public didn't realize how powerful he was because he kept insisting he was battling firms that he secretly owned outright. His real rivals were forever discovering that their most trusted officers were in his pocket. The tentacles of the octopus were everywhere.[72]

Eventually, the opposition to Rockefeller's unethical and criminal practices rose to a point that he was accused of conspiring against his business competitors. Writs were served against him and, on April 29, 1879, John D. Rockefeller and other senior executives of Standard Oil were indicted by a Grand Jury for a criminal conspiracy to secure a monopoly of the oil industry and other crimes,[73] but he managed to avoid being convicted.

In 1906, the accusations against John D. surfaced again when Theodore Roosevelt, an old Rockefeller critic, made public a report made by the Bureau of Corporations, revealing how Rockefeller had benefited enormously through the use of unethical business practices. At the same time, a lawsuit was initiated in the Federal Circuit Court in Eastern Missouri, with the goal of dissolving the Standard Oil as a conspiracy in restraint of trade. Nevertheless, John D. managed againt to escape the laws.

John D. Rockefeller was the inventor a new form of economic power —the corporate trust on which modern corporations are based.[74] Given the fact that Communism is a type of socialist government in which the state controls the corporations, and Fascism is a type of socialist government in which the corporations control the state, it makes sense that the New World Order the Rockefellers and their partners in crime envision will be a mixture of both types of totalitarian regimes.

John D. Rockefeller proudly affirmed: "I have never had a craving for anything."[75] As usual, he was disingenuous. Actually, he had a strong craving for lying, disinforming, obfuscating, scheming, duplicity, secrecy, betrayal and unfair play. He was also known for his systematic use of arson, murder, burglary, theft, extortion, swindling, blackmail, wholesale corruption of public officials, and gangsterism on a grandiose scale on his efforts to ruthlessly crush his competitors.[76] John D. was an early master in the use of the tricks of the trade of the great game of intelligence and espionage that have made the CIA infamous.

On one occasion John D. Rockefeller, an early promoter of social Darwinism, told a Sunday school class, "The growth of a large business class is merely a survival of the fittest."[77] The main reason for Rockefeller's love for Darwinism was because Darwin's theories not only provided him with a "scientific" ethical justification for his cutthroat business practices, but also because it supported his eugenic ideas of world depopulation.

According to one of his biographers, John D. inherited these personality traits from his father, who taught his son the tricks of doing business by a method he explained in these graphic words: "I cheat my boys every time I get a chance. I want to make 'em sharp. I trade with my boys and skin 'em and I just beat 'em every time I can. I want to make 'em sharp."[78]

Unfortunately for the rest of mankind, his son John D. passed these traits to his children augmented, and they eventually passed them on to the organizations they created, among them the Inquiry, the CFR, the OSS and the CIA. It is not by chance, though, that most of the evil traits critics blame on the CIA, are the same traits some critics blamed on the CIA's true creators and masters, the Rockefellers.

Nelson and David Inherit Their Grandpa's Passion for Spying

It seems that the passion for intelligence, espionage and intrigue runs deep in the Rockefeller family, and Nelson and David proudly continued the tradition that began with their grandfather John D. Rockefeller.

In the late 1930s, Nelson Rockefeller was appointed to oversee a secret U.S. government ideological and economic warfare offensive south of the border. In *American Propaganda Abroad*, former U.S. Information Agency official Fitzhugh Green states,

> In 1938 the United States government began its own modest cultural thrust among the Latin American republics, called the Office of Inter-American Affairs, under Nelson Rockefeller in the State Department."[79]

That innocuous name actually disguised the true job of the OIAA: waging psychological warfare against the Latin American peoples. Soon after it was created, a secret psychological warfare team was created at the OIAA.

The creation of the Office of Inter-American Affairs got strong support among politicians of both Rockefeller-controlled parties, who had been claiming for an agency to coordinate the U.S. defense activities in Latin America and to foster Latin American attitudes favorable to the conspirator's objectives, especially if its propaganda aspects were properly concealed.

As an undated and formerly classified White House memorandum relates, such "psychological" activities were then still too controversial with the American public to be discussed openly. "Propaganda was still a horrid word," says the document, a history of American propaganda efforts overseas, "and the national administration in 1940 could not hope to establish an admitted propaganda agency. American psychological operations or opinion-influencing activities had to be cloaked in the subterfuge of agency titles."

Two years later, in August 1940, Nelson A. Rockefeller was appointed as Coordinator of Commercial and Cultural Relations Among the Latin American Republics. At the time Nelson already had strong economic, financial and commercial ties in Latin America, and the primary covert function of his Office of Inter-American Affairs was to implement an extensive psychological warfare operation. This PSYWAR had been carefully planned to mold Latin American public opinion into accepting the CFR conspirators' plans of economic and ideological subjugation for the implementation of the coming New World Order.

Nelson served in different positions in the Roosevelt administration. But Truman was not a CFR member and he didn't see any need for Nelson's help in his administration. Under Dwight Eisenhower, however, Nelson's star briefly rose again. He served as the President's Special Assistant on Foreign Policy (1954-55) and as head of the secret "Forty Committee" charged with overseeing the CIA's covert operations —the fox in charge of protecting the hens.

Nelson favored the use of private organizations and foundations as government surrogates in the nation's psychological warfare effort. His idea was detailed in a secret June 4, 1952 memorandum titled "Cold War Resources of Private and Other Government Agencies," written by White House strategist William A. Korns and archived in the records of the old Psychological Strategy Board.

A condition for the deployment of "private resources," the memo advised, would be a determination on "the overt-covert issue." The document further explained that non-governmental actors should be used only when necessary to conceal the involvement of the U.S. government. "If there is reason to believe that the Made in America label may in some instances thwart the achievement of our long-range objectives, it would follow that private capabilities should be used on a highly selective basis," Korns wrote.

The same memo also hinted that such American business ventures could be of use in intelligence gathering because of their experience in dealing with local officials. It specifically referred to the Standard Oil Company's negotiations in India, at which time "the State Department [was] in close touch with the corporation," and mentioned Nelson Rockefeller's International Basic Economy Corporation as one organization regarded as "sensitive to political direction," a euphemism for spying and psychological warfare.

The Family Tradition Continues

In 1953, after an elected upstart named Dr. Mohammed Mossadegh nationalized Iran's oil business, a UK/US-backed coup returned the Shah to power. CIA Director Allen Dulles and his brother, Secretary of State John Foster Dulles, were instrumental in this coup. Previously, Iran's oil had been controlled by the Anglo-Persian Oil Co. (i.e., British Petroleum, BP) but after the U.S. role in this coup, U.S. companies got a 40% share and the top beneficiary was Standard Oil of New Jersey.

On December 1979, syndicated columnist Jack Anderson disclosed that the Rockefellers had helped to plan the August 1953 CIA coup in Iran. According to Anderson, a grateful Shah handsomely rewarded the Rockefellers by depositing huge sums of cash in Chase Manhattan Bank. He also consigned the construction of new housing to a Rockefeller firm.

The next year, the Rockefeller boys were at it again orchestrating a coup in Guatemala. This one ushered in decades of fascist military governments that killed hundreds of thousands of innocents. But it brought great profits for Rockefeller's

United Fruit Co., in which their secret agents, the Dulles brothers, had invested. CIA Director Allen Dulles had also been on the United Fruit Board of Trustees.

In 1964, one of Rockefeller's law firm's most important clients was the M. A. Hanna Mining Company. Hanna Mining was the largest producer of iron ore in Brazil. Soon after Joao Goulart was democratically elected president in 1961, he began to talk about nationalizing the Brazilian iron ore industry, and Hanna's executives were concerned about the company's investments in the country.

The CIA began to make plans for overthrowing Goulart. A psychological warfare program approved by CFR agent Henry Kissinger during his chair of the 40 Committee, sent U.S. PSYOPs disinformation teams to spread fabricated rumors concerning Goulart's Communist affiliations. Actually, Goulart was a wealthy landowner who was opposed to communism. But he was a nationalist who believed that Brazil's resources belonged to the Brazilian people, not to foreign interests.

In early 1964, CFR agent John J. McCloy opened a channel of communication between the CIA and Jack W. Burford, one of the senior executives of the Hanna Mining Company. On February 1964, McCloy traveled to Brazil and tried to convince Goulart not to go ahead with nationalizing the iron ore industry, but he rejected McCloy's arguments.

On the night of March 31, 1964, a CIA backed military-led coup overthrew Goulart.

Similar accusations have been made about a possible Rockefeller role in the 1973 coup that toppled Chile's Salvador Allende —actually a Castro-CIA joint operation.[80] The fact that Henry Kissinger, a well-known Rockefeller agent, played a key role in the overthrowing and killing of Chile's President Allende, points to a possible Rockefeller participation in the event.

Nelson Rockefeller's criminal activities around the world became so outrageous that by 1947 there was widespread suspicion about his treasonous activities in South America. At the same time he was in charge of Latin American intelligence, he turned a blind eye to Standard Oil's shipments of South American oil to the Nazis before and after the U.S. declared war against Nazi Germany.

Granted, Rockefeller was not the only major figure suspected of having engaged in treasonous acts during World War II. Others were Prescott Bush's attorney Allen Dulles, then-OSS Station Chief in Bern, Switzerland, and later Director of CIA. But it is not a coincidence that both were partners in Standard Oil Co. [81]

In his book *Trading with the Enemy*, Charles Higham offers ample proof of the Rockefellers' treasonous activities during the Second World War. [82] Germany lacked the oil needed to wage the war, but Nazi bombers were dropping bombs on London and other European cities thanks to the gasoline provided by the Rockefeller's Standard Oil.[83]

Nelson Rockefeller moved to Washington after the U.S. involvement in World War II, where Roosevelt named him Coordinator of Inter-American Affairs. Apparently, his principal task was to coordinate the refueling of German ships in South America from Standard Oil tanks. He also used that office to obtain important South American concessions for his private firm, International Basic Economy Corporation, including a corner on the Colombian coffee market. He immediately raised the price, a move that enabled him to buy several billion dollars worth of real estate in South America and also gave rise to the stereotype of "Yankee Imperialism." It also gave rise to several billion dollars worth of drug-growing real estate.

The Rockefellers have always used espionage as their main tool to advance their interests. For example, Stephen Schlesinger, a scholar with expertise in the field of cryptology, wrote an article in which he revealed some of the unethical espionage activities carried out by the CFR conspirators.

According to Schlesinger, before and during the San Francisco Conference of 1945 that created the United Nations Organizations, CIA officers, working on behalf of their CFR masters, spied on the delegates and intercepted their secret communications with their respective countries to know beforehand each country's negotiating positions. The knowledge of this private information allowed the CFR conspirators to have full control of the Conference, to the point that the UN Charter adopted by the delegates was the one the conspirators had already written at the Harold Pratt House in New York.[84]

Chapter 3

The Council on Foreign Relations: The Conspirators' Secret Intelligence Agency

The C.F.R. has come to be known as "the Establishment," "the invisible government" and "the Rockefeller foreign office." This semi-secret organization unquestionably has become the most influential group in America.

—Gary Allen, *None Dare Call It Conspiracy.*

The newly created intelligence agency the conspirators disingenuously called the Inquiry served the international bankers so well that they decided to make it permanent. A few days after the end of the conference, a group of conspirators from the U.S. and Britain Round Table Groups met at the Hotel Majestic, where the British delegation was staying, to talk about how to continue their intelligence and espionage experiment. To this effect, they planned the creation of a permanent espionage agency, with branches in London and New York, to continue serving their interests. As usual, they used an innocuous, disinforming name, Anglo-American Institute of International Affairs, as a cover to hide its real espionage and intelligence activities.

Just a few months later, however, the American branch of the conspirators decided to go independent, and created their own espionage agency. It was named the Council on Foreign Relations, and Colonel House was one of the founding fathers together with Elihu Root. The initial group of secret agents was augmented with the inclusion of promising new members anxious to get into the espionage business. Prominent among them were Herbert H. Lehman, W. Averell Harriman, and John Foster Dulles. The British conspirators changed the name of their own intelligence agency to Royal Institute of International Affairs.

The Conspirators Create an Anti-American Monster

Though the Council on Foreign relations describes itself as a non-partisan organization —in the conspirators' lingo, "non-partisan" actually means "CFR-controlled"— whose only goal is to promote international exchanges to reach a better understanding among countries, this is just what in intelligence and espionage is called a "cover story."[1] The CFR is actually an intelligence and espionage agency, and operates like one.

In his laudatory study about the Inquiry, CFR agent Peter Grose inadvertently exposed the true character and purpose of both the Inquiry and the CFR.

Both of them are veritable intelligence agencies at the service of the American plutocracy of Wall Street bankers, oil magnates and CEOs of transnational corporations.[2]

Like all intelligence agencies, the Council on Foreign Relations is a semi-secret society: although it is not secret where its headquarters is located, and who its senior executives are, nobody really knows what its secret activities are, much less its secret goals. Like all intelligence agencies, the CFR has listed members and secret ones.[3] Like all intelligence agencies, the CFR has a department specialized in information collection and analysis. But, contrary to conventional intelligence agencies, the intelligence analysts of this department do not work in-house, but live a parasitical life disseminated among other government and private institutions like the CIA, the NSC, the State and Defense departments, the Pentagon, the mainstream press, universities, think tanks and non-profit foundations.

As needed, the CFR intelligence analysts produce their own National Intelligence Estimates —they don't call them NIEs, but that is exactly what they are. Yet, because of the fact that they have been written from the point of view of the conspirators' interests, they greatly differ from the officially produced CIA NIEs written from the point of view of the U.S. interests. This explains why the NIEs produced by the CIA are largely ignored or forced to change according to the conspirators' political and propaganda needs.

Typical of these CFR NIEs are George Kennan's (CFR) 1947 article in *Foreign Affairs*, written under the pseudonym "X," explaining his —actually the conspirators'— theory of "containment." According to Kennan, the U.S. role in the coming Cold War should be limited to containing the expansion of Soviet Communism, not fighting to defeat it. Soon after, President Truman made Containment the core of "his" Truman Doctrine.

Another example of a CFR-created NIE is the infamous National Security Study Memorandum 200, allegedly written by CFR senior secret agent Henry Kissinger but actually a CFR product. NSC 200, kept secret for many years, delineated a genocidal policy of depopulating of much of the African continent, to allow U.S. transnational corporations, not the Africans, exploit the continent's natural resources. Nothing exemplifies better the implementation of NSC 200's genocidal plan than Castro's invasion of Angola in the fall of 1975.

Despite all the disinformation that appeared in the American mainstream media, the invasion was not a Soviet operation. It was planned and executed by Castro using the resources available in Cuba at the time. Actually, the Soviets let him go on with his plans because they were sure the operation was going to be a total failure. Only later, when to their utter surprise they realized that Castro was winning the war, they gave him some limited support.

What was the result of Castro's victory in Angola? A few months after Castro's troops took control of the country, Angola became one of the U.S.'s largest commercial partners in Africa. Chase Manhattan Bank, Bankers Trust, Citibank, and Morgan Guaranty, gave large loans to Angola. The business of General Motors,

General Tire, Caterpillar, Boeing, IBM, NCR, Pfizer, Xerox, and other American corporations, flourished in the country. 95 percent of Angolan oil was exported to Western countries. Castro's soldiers protected the refineries in Cabinda from "saboteurs," and Castro was paid in dollars for their services. Half of the production of Gulf Oil in Angola ended up in U.S. refineries. The consortium De Beers controlled diamond mines. So much for Castro's "anti-imperialist" and "anti-colonialist" policies.

A more recent example of CFR NIE is the September 2000 Report entitled "Rebuilding America's Defenses: Strategy, Forces and Resources For a New Century," published by the CFR-controlled neocon group Project for a New American [Imperialist] Century (PNAC).[4] The Report mentions that in order to transform the U.S. military for the new challenges it will face, the process of transformation, "... even if it brings revolutionary change, is likely to be a long one, absent some catastrophic and catalyzing event —*like a new Pearl Harbor*." [Emphasis mine] As if on cue, exactly a year later the 9/11 events provided on a silver plate the new Pearl Harbor the CFR conspirators were craving for.

Like all intelligence agencies, the CFR has a department specialized in psychological warfare, subversion, insurgency, and paramilitary operations —functions that, until very recently, had been mostly carried out by one of its branches: the CIA. Currently, however, after the conspirators gained more control over most key U.S. government areas, including a large segment of senior U.S. military officers, they don't need the CIA anymore and have transferred these functions directly to the U.S. military.

Like all intelligence agencies, the main job of some CFR members is to recruit spies and agents of influence, as a way to infiltrate other organizations they want to control, in the U.S. and abroad. In the case of ambitious and intelligent, but morally and ethically challenged young people, once the CFR recruiters find them and decide to proceed with their recruitment, the first step is usually granting them a Rhodes Scholarship. If they successfully pass this first step, they are offered a grant to study at the London School of Economics.

This was, for example, the case of Bill Clinton. Once Georgetown professor Carroll Quigley, a CFR recruiter, detected young Bill, and it was verified that he had the right stuff, he was offered a Rhodes Scholarship. Life proved that the selection was the right one.

Another successful CFR recruiter is Zbigniew Brzezinski. He was the hidden hand behind the recruitment of an unknown Georgia peanut farmer who had become interested in politics. He invited him to join the recently created Trilateral Commission and later his CFR masters pushed him into the White House.[5]

More recently, Brzezinski hit the jackpot again by bringing to the White House another potential CFR operative he had spotted. There are clues indicating that, while he was a professor at Columbia University in the early 1980s, Brzezinski recruited a young, ethically challenged, ambitious opportunistic student: Barack Hussein Obama. One of these clues is that when Obama was studying politics he wrote a paper whose main topic was Soviet nuclear disarmament. The paper was heavily influenced by Brzezinski's crazy ideas.[6]

As author Webster Griffin Tarpley pointed out, this may explain why Obama has been so secretive about his years at Columbia University, where all his records have been placed out of the scrutiny of researchers and the press. Evidently, there are things in Obama's past the conspirators don't want the American people to know about.[7]

The CFR: Second U.S. Civilian Intelligence Agency

The Council on Foreign Relations has become in practice the closest the U.S. has to a Communo-Fascist Party in power. Like the Communist Party of the Soviet Union or the Nazi Party in Germany used to be, CFR members have secret meetings where policies are discussed, and then they exert pressure on the government to guarantee that these policies are carried out. Like members of a Communist or Fascist party, they follow a strict party discipline: once a policy is approved in their secret councils, it becomes Party line and they push it with all their force. Like members of a Communist or Fascist party, they act in block, and no inner dissidence on key issues is allowed.

This block acting was experienced first-hand by President Lyndon Johnson. On November 1967, the group of presidential advisors called the Senior Advisory Group on Vietnam, Dean Acheson, Robert Lovett, John McCloy, McGeorge Bundy, Walt W. Rostow, Robert McNamara and Paul Nitze met with President Johnson, and all of them supported the continuation of the war.

In early 1968, however, the very same advisors who had been hawkishly pushing Johnson to continue and escalate the war, had a long meeting with the president, at which Johnson asked each of them to express his personal view about the conflict. All of them, without exception, suddenly manifested themselves against the war. The hawks had turned overnight into doves. It goes without saying that all them, without a single exception, were CFR members just following the Party line already decided at the Harold Pratt House.

According to a witness, Johnson was visibly shocked by the magnitude of the defection. A few days later, he went on television to announce the de-escalation of the war and his decision not to run for a new presidential term. According to the *New York Times*, the decision was a stunning surprise even to Johnson's close associates.

The Council on Foreign Relations is the aberrant creation of the Rockefellers and a group of wealthy international bankers. One of their pioneer secret agents was an enigmatic character: "Colonel" Edward Mandell House, President Wilson's controller and the true inventor of Fascism. In two insightful articles written in 1954, columnist Westbrook Pegler, an outspoken critic of Franklin Delano Roosevelt's fascist assault upon the American Constitution, compared Roosevelt's regime to Mussolini's. Moreover, he pointed to Col. House as the true creator of fascism. According to Pegler,

> Wilson's Rasputin, the most influential private citizen in America and

> indeed one of the most powerful human beings in all the world, copyrighted Fascism at a time when Mussolini was just a loud-mouthed, hand-to-mouth Communist in Milan, and Lenin and Trotsky were unknown vermin hiding in dark corners of Geneva and New York.[8]

A few weeks later, Pegler attacked again, this time right to the traitor's jugular:

> During all these years since 1911 or 1912, by the secret evil design of one man, the Government of this great republic has been corrupted and transformed into Fascism, which that man invented long before Benito Mussolini was heard of outside his native village. At that time Adolf Hitler was just another country boy in Austria."[9]

Even a perfunctory reading of Colonel House's novel *Philip Dru, Administrator*,[10] shows that Pegler was right on target. The ultimate goal of the CFR —which House helped to shape— is the complete takeover of America to change it into a socialist communo-fascist dictatorship. The last steps of the implementation of this plan are currently taking place under the evil eye[11] of the latest CFR puppet, Mr. Barry Soetoro (a.k.a. Barack Hussein Obama)

House's novel describes a conspiracy to infiltrate and capture from inside both political parties and use them to create a socialist world government. His plan included electing a president by using "deception regarding his real opinions and intentions."[12] The CFR's initial goal, similar to the one described by House in his novel, does not seem to have changed much over the years. To this day, the Rockefellers continue to be closely involved with the direction of this organization.

Founded in 1921, the CFR headquarters is located in the Pratt House, at 58 E. 68th Street, New York. Though in recent years it has opened its doors to a larger number of members (about 4,000), the few scholars who have studied the organization agree that the CFR is a Rockefeller front. Since its very creation, the CFR epitomizes all that is despicable, dirty, rotten and treasonous in the U.S. foreign policy and most of its domestic policy as well.

A Very Secretive Organization

If you don't know what the Council on Foreign Relations is, who its members are, what its role is in dictating the U.S. foreign and domestic policy, or what its ultimate goal is, you are not alone, because most Americans ignore it. Moreover, this ignorance is not by mistake, but by design, which explains why the CFR is not mentioned in U.S. History textbooks or barely mentioned by the mainstream press despite the fact that many editors of the most important American newspapers and magazines are CFR members.

CFR members exert an almost total control over the U.S. mainstream media

—actually they *own* most of it[13] — and use their power to avoid the limelight. The CFR publishes the influential *Foreign Affairs* magazine. If it happens that most of the predictions that appear in its pages soon after become reality, it is not because they have hired the best psychics money can buy, but because they actually make happen the events they have forecasted by virtually controlling not only all branches of the U.S. government, but also public opinion.

Though apparently just another club for the East Coast Establishment wealthy, particularly Wall Street bankers, the CFR is a very secretive organization. Since its creation, its activities have been private and confidential.[14] It is CFR policy not to publish the minutes of its proceedings.[15]

The CFR fully controls both the Democratic and Republican parties and, with a few exceptions, they are the ones who have placed most presidents in the White House. As Georgetown University professor and Bill Clinton's mentor Carroll Quigley, probably the scholar who most closely studied the CFR, pointed out, the idea that the two parties represent different, opposing ideas or policies is a foolish one. Both parties are identical, and no electoral change will lead to any true shift in policy because both parties actually pursue the same policies.[16]

Quigley's words are the best explanation for the existence of the Repucratic Party —which is nothing but another CFR cover front. The most recent replacement puppet is Barack Hussein Obama, who is seamlessly continuing the treacherous policies of his predecessors who, without an exception, only have advanced policies conceived at the Harold Pratt House.

Like a malignant cancer, the CFR has not only expanded by creating subsidiaries in key American cities, but also has metastasized into several important organizations, all of them created and funded mostly with Rockefeller money. Some of them are the Trilateral Commission, the Foreign Policy Association and its World Affairs Councils, the Brookings Institution, and the Carnegie Endowment for International Peace, just to mention a few. It also has close ties to international organizations like the Bilderberg group, the United Nations Organization, the World Economic Forum and the Club of Rome. The ultimate goal of these organizations, as openly expressed by their leaders, is none other than the creation of a New World Order —a sort of global communo-fascism controlled by transnational corporations in the hands of the Rockefellers and their Wall Street cronies.

A few political observers have pointed out that, of lately, the CFR has become a department of the U.S. government. They are wrong. Actually, the U.S. government is the one that has become a department of the CFR. The way the CFR folks have managed to get virtual control over the U.S. government has been by infiltrating it —a strategy most favored by intelligence services all around the world, which the CFR has refined into an art form. Currently most senior State Department and CIA senior officials, presidential advisors and Cabinet members, as well as U.S. senators and Supreme Court judges are CFR members.

The CFR conspirators have also managed to successfully infiltrate most American colleges and universities. The main tool for control used by the CFR is money, which they liberally distribute through the myriad of non-profit foundations they control. Cardinal among them are the Carnegie, Ford, MacArthur, Mellon, and Rockefeller Foundations, and a constellation of minor foundations who get most of their funds from the ones already mentioned. These minor foundations are used as cut-outs[17] by hiding the true sources of the money.

Am I implying that all the scholars who have received grants from these foundations to do research are told what they should write? Of course not. But, like mice in a psychologist's maze, scholars soon discover that some research conclusions guarantee a constant input of grant money, while others dry it.

Professor Antony Sutton, who found damaging information about some Wall Street bankers' collaboration with the Soviets and the Nazis, and wrote several extensively documented scholarly books about it, suffered the consequences. Soon after, he was fired from his senior research position at Stanford's Hoover Institution, and afterwards ostracized and harassed for life. More recently, University of Illinois political science professor Juan Lopez made the mistake of writing *Democracy Delayed: The Case of Castro's Cuba,*[18] a book in which he critically studied Castro's policies. Soon after the book was published, Lopez was denied tenure.

Since the end of WWII, CFR insiders have had total control over the State Department. Most Secretaries of State, both under Democratic and Republican administrations, have been CFR members. They own the Federal Reserve Bank—which, contrary to common belief, is not a U.S. government organization, but a privately owned corporation. In the case of the CIA, they didn't have to penetrate it because, since its very creation, the CIA has been totally under their control.

Enough proof of this is that, when President Truman disbanded the OSS at the end of WWII and refused to create a Central Intelligence Agency, CFR member Allen Dulles went freelance and created a private, secret one. It operated from a secret room at the Harold Pratt House in Manhattan. Finally Truman relented to the conspirators' pressure and created the CIA. A few years later, who was appointed CIA director? None other than Allen Dulles. After Dulles, all CIA directors have been CFR members, with the exception of the current one, for reasons I will explain below in this book.

The CFR: an Association of Criminal Traitors

Initially, the fortunes of most of the main conspirators —appropriately called the "robber barons," (Rockefeller, Carnegie, Morgan, Vanderbilt, *et. al.*) came out of the steel, railroads, and oil industries. But oil is a product difficult to find and costly to exploit, and building railroads and making steel are also arduous and time-consuming processes. So, late in the nineteenth century they discovered a new product as a better and more lucrative way to further engross their fortunes: selling thin air[19] in the form of fiat money. This explains why, without getting out of their traditional businesses, they began moving their fortunes into banking.

Banks are basically criminal enterprises that make money through a Ponzi scheme called "fractional banking," which essentially means using other people's money to make their own money without risking losing it. Currently, financial capital is the conspirators' main source of wealth.

To this effect they created the Federal Reserve Bank[20] and the Internal Revenue Service to steal from the American people the money they needed for their banks, as well as laws authorizing the creation of the so-called non-profit "charitable" foundations —a clever way to hide their money from the IRS thieves.

The business of lending money, particularly to governments, proved to be highly lucrative. But, in order to do this, they realized they needed to have, like traditional shark loan lenders, a strong arm to punish the few ones who dared to default on their loan payments.

Initially, the conspirators used the U.S. armed forces for this enforcement job. This was the true purpose of Teddy Roosevelt's "Great White Fleet," which he sent sailing all around the world showing the American flag (instead of the skull & bones flag of the Wall Street pirates) to scare potential troublemakers by reminding them of the military power of the Wall Street bankers. This was appropriately called "gunboat diplomacy."

Unfortunately, due to the fact that the conspirators were hiding their criminal activities under a cover of legality provided by the U.S. government, Marxists and other revolutionaries around the world began blaming the United States and its people for the criminal actions of the Wall Street Mafia. This was the true origin of the so-called "American imperialism," which is actually Wall Street imperialism. Therefore, it is not a coincidence that most of the main critics pointing to "American imperialism" as the main source of global evil have been directly or indirectly bankrolled by the Wall Street Mafia through their "charitable' foundations.

On the other hand, until recently the "conservative" intelligentsia strongly denied the existence of such thing as an "American imperialism." However, after the fall of the Soviet Union, the Wall Street Mafia moved quickly to surround Russia with unfriendly states as well as to enslave it economically to avoid its rebirth as a world power.

After accomplishing that, some secret CFR agents apparently saw their road to world power free of impediments and began talking openly of a new era of American imperialism —though a "benign" one. According to CFR agent Charles Krauthammer, American imperialism (actually Wall Street imperialism) had come out of the closet.[21] Another CFR agent who joined the new "empire" cacophony was Robert Kagan. Nevertheless, both Krauthammer and Kagan agreed that it was a "benign" empire.[22]

But the time of Wall Street's unopposed control of the world, which they termed the "unipolar era," proved to be short-lived. The Russians discovered the ruse, got a second air, managed to get out of the IMF trap, and quickly recovered economically and decided to restore their military power. Of lately, the callers for a new era of American "benevolent" imperialism seem to have lost some of their bravery.

Dozens of books, films and TV serials have been made depicting the criminal activities of the Italian Mafia —of which the novel and film *The Godfather* and the TV series *The Sopranos* are perhaps the most widely known—, to the point that the word "Mafia" has become a synonym for organized crime. Just a few have been made, however, about the Irish and Jewish Mafias, who also have played an important part in the criminal history of organized crime in America. In contrast, nothing has been ever said about the best organized, most powerful, most important, ruthless and successful of all American Mafias: the Wall Street Mafia.

Hiding behind an institutional cover of respectability, the Council on Foreign Relations is basically a criminal organization, the cover for a Mafia of Wall Street bankers, oil magnates and CEOs of transnational corporations, composed of ethically and morally challenged individuals, associated to carry out criminal activities. The criminal activities of this Wall Street Mafia have caused more death and suffering than the ones committed by all the other Mafias together. Why do the American people totally ignore the existence of this dangerous crime syndicate? Because, contrary to the other minor Mafias, the Wall Street Mafia exerts an almost total control over the mainstream media, particularly TV, national newspapers and magazines, and the book and film industries.[23]

Most officers of the Office of Special Services, the WWII intelligence agency, were Wall Street lawyers and bankers. There is abundant evidence proving that Wall Street bankers were instrumental in helping Hitler to grab power in Germany, and later did business with Nazi Germany before and during the war.[24] Therefore, it makes sense to think that the ones who joined the OSS didn't do it out of patriotism or altruism, to fight the Nazis or to protect the interests of the American people, but to protect their own niggardly interests. Actually, as I will show below in this book, one of the OSS's main secret mission during WWII was to help senior Nazi war criminals escape with their gold and to protect German corporations like the I.G. Farben, who had been collaborating with the Nazis while associated with Wall Street banks.

The CIA, as it was the OSS, has been for many years the hidden strong arm of the Wall Street Mafia. The bankers have used it to enforce their wishes upon non-compliant victims who have refused to accept their illegal rules imposed by criminal organizations like the International Monetary Fund, the World Bank and others they have created. To advance their criminal enterprises, the Wall Street Mafia normally resorts to extortion, threats, assassinations, economic aggression, and outright physical aggression of all types, including psychological warfare, covert military operations and conventional warfare.

Yet, despite all its negative connotations, even the word "Mafia" is inappropriate to describe the Wall Street criminal cabal, because the CFR conspirators are worse than the traditional Mafias. Despite their minor–scale criminal enterprises, the Italian Mafia loved this country, and they proved it during WWII by helping the U.S. military in several ways. On the contrary, the Wall Street Mafia viscerally hates this country, its Constitution, its laws, its institutions and its people, and has been working hard for almost a century to destroy America, as we know it.

The Council on Foreign Relations is basically a criminal organization.

Just a cursory view at the criminal activities of a few of the most prominent members of the Wall Street Mafia shows that perhaps it is easier to find more candor, honesty and purity at San Quentin than at the CFR:

Edward Mandell House – proto-fascist
Prescott Bush – Nazi collaborator
Alger Hiss – enemy spy
William Donovan – 5th columnist
Henry Kissinger – war criminal
Richard Nixon – crook
Sandy Berger – thief
Lewis "Scooter" Libby – perjurer
Sumner Welles – sexual maniac
George W. Bush – torturer-in-chief
Allen Dulles – Nazi rescuer
Dick Cheney – draft dodger
Franklin D. Roosevelt – fascist
Donald Rumsfeld – agent provocateur
Bill Clinton – serial killer
Hillary Clinton – psychopath
Timothy Geithner – tax cheat
John Kerry – mole
Zbigniew Brzezinski – neo-imperialist
Madeleine Albright – genocider
Daniel Ellsberg – fake leftist
Newt Gringich – fake conservative
Dianne Feinstein – corrupt politician
Alan Greenspan – bank robber
David Rockefeller – eugenicist
Nelson Rockefeller – enemy spymaster
Robert McNamara – democider (responsible for 58,000 American deaths)

The people I have mentioned above are not exceptions, but a true representation of the Wall Street Mafia. Actually, they are typical CFR members, that is, sociopaths totally lacking the ethical or moral restraints found in normal people.[25]

Acting on behalf of the conspirators, CFR members have committed massive genocide and assassination,[26] waged unprovoked wars, performed psychological warfare operations against the American and other peoples around the world, and overthrown legitimate government leaders through coups d'ètat and assassinations, including American presidents. They have systematically committed fraud and stolen money, property and natural resources from the American people and the peoples of the world. Their ultimate genocidal goal is the elimination of no less than 85 percent of the population of this planet —the "useless eaters" according to Bertrand Russell— and the reduction of the survivors to pre-industrial, feudal levels of consumption, after the implementation of a global totalitarian communo-fascist dictatorship they call the New World Order, which, of course, they plan to control.

The Council on Foreign Relations is the logical refuge for sociopaths with a criminal mind, where they can find their soul mates. As proof of it, I will provide three examples of the most notorious CFR criminals.

A man with a true criminal mind, Zbigniew Brzezinski (CFR) wrote a book[27] in which he advocated, among other nasty things, the use of bacteriological and climatological warfare against nations who refused to bend to the conspirators' will. And the beauty of it, he boasted, is that the targets could not prove that they had been under attack. In his arrogance, however, the psychopathic professor apparently never considered the possibility that other countries may use the same warfare techniques against the American people if they decide to retaliate.

The CFR conspirators loved Brzezinski's book so much that David Rockefeller himself made him the boss of his new pet project: the Trilateral Commission. My best hope is that the mad professor will not try to carry out his genocidal dreams through the new CFR puppet he now controls on behalf of his CFR masters: Barack Hussein Obama.

Another criminal who was recruited by the CFR conspirators was Herman Kahn (CFR), for many years the Director of the Hudson Institute, one of the many CFR-controlled think tanks. His book *On Thermonuclear War*[28] was such an obvious lucubration of a madman, that a true scientist, mathematician James R. Newman, rhetorically asked if there was really such a person as Herman Kahn, because no one could exist who thought like this.[29]

However, making use of their almost total control of the mainstream media, the conspirators defamed a true American patriot, General Curtis LeMay,[30] depicting him as the archetype of the madman that Herman Kahn really was. LeMay is one of the characters parodied in the film *Dr. Strangelove* as the mad general itching for a nuclear attack on the Soviet Union.[31]

Last, but not least, I will mention another psychopathic criminal and assassin who early in his career became a protégé of Nelson Rockefeller and, soon after, joined the conspirator's CFR Mafia: Henry Kissinger.

In the Preface of his book *The Trial of Henry Kissinger*,[32] Christopher Hitchens made a list of identifiable, provable crimes committed by Henry Kissinger for which he should be indicted. These are,

> The deliberate mass killing of civilian population in Indochina.
>
> Deliberate collusion in mass murder, and later assassination, in Bangladesh.
>
> The personal suborning and planning of murder, of a senior constitutional officer in a democratic nation —Chile— with which the United States was not at war.
>
> Personal involvement in a plan to murder the head of state in the democratic nation of Cyprus.
>
> The incitement and enabling of genocide in Timor.
>
> Personal involvement in a plan to kidnap and murder a journalist living in Washington, DC.[33]

Missing in the above list is Kissinger's key role in the assassination by the CIA-controlled Red Brigades of Italy's Prime Minister Aldo Moro.[34] Also conspicuously missing in Hitchen's book is the fact that Kissinger is a key CFR agent and that everything he did was with full support and following orders from his Wall Street masters.

Undoubtedly, even in an organization of corrupt, hard-core criminals which include people like Zbigniew Brzezinski, Robert McNamara, Maurice Strong, Bill Clinton, Dick Cheney and Donald Rumsfeld, just to mention a few of the most notorious ones, Kissinger stands alone above the crowd. But, like primitive people who believe the moon has its own light, Hitchens made the mistake of attributing to Kissinger alone all his criminal actions. Like the moon, however, Kissinger's evil is a reflected one. The true sun behind Kissinger and the rest of the criminals I mentioned above are the Rockefellers and a few powerful Wall Street bankers agglutinated at the CFR.

Further proof that Hitchens is pointing in the wrong direction —and, wittingly or unwittingly, distorting the truth— is that, in the page next to where he mentions Kissinger's crimes, he adds, "Many if not most of Kissinger's partners in crime are now in jail, or are awaiting trial, or have otherwise been punished or discredited."[11]

This assertion, however, is totally disingenuous. Kissinger's true partners in crime are not in jail or awaiting trial. None of them have been punished or discredited. Actually, they are revered in the pages of the American mainstream media[36] and their crooked faces frequently decorate the covers of the most important American magazines.

Moreover, it tells much about who really is in power in America, the fact that, adding insult to outrage, the conspirators ordered their puppet George W. Bush to appoint Henry Kissinger as head of the commission to investigate the 9/11 events. On the other hand, however, perhaps Kissinger was the right choice for the job. The whitewash to cover one of the greatest criminal actions committed by the CFR conspirators against the American people undoubtedly required the help of one of the conspirators' greatest criminal minds.

A possible explanation to why the CFR has become a sewer collecting the worst of the criminal dregs of American society is found in the field of intelligence and espionage itself. In a now declassified article originally published in 1986 in *Studies in Intelligence*, the CIA's secretive internal journal, Wilhelm Marbes, who identified himself as a psychologist, analyzed the psychology of treason.[37] According to Marbes,

> The agency[38] definition of a defector is an individual who has committed treason, a person who first accepted identification with a regime and then betrayed his allegiance to cooperate with a hostile foreign intelligence service.[39]

Senior CFR members have expressed on multiple occasions not only their contempt for the U.S. Constitution and sovereignty, but also their ultimate goal of creating a global communo-fascist government, which they call the New World Order. Therefore, unless they are totally naïve, people who voluntarily accept the invitation to become CFR members must know that, by joining this treasonous organization, they have defected their allegiance to the U.S. Constitution and are betraying their country.

Marbes examines what he considers the three main personality traits that characterize traitors. According to him, the first one is "immaturity or impulsivity," evidenced by a "lack of tolerance for frustration and/or an inability to defer gratification."

The second trait is sociopathy (also called psychopathy). Accordingly, most traitors are conscience and morally challenged. "They seldom hesitate to violate rights of others to serve their own ends. A lay definition might be a chronic 'son-of-a-bitch.'" Marbes adds that sociopaths are often referred to as people with "moth-eaten or Swiss cheese" consciences, and "what falls through the holes is a sense of loyalty to their country."[40]

Marbes is not alone in his evaluation. A Washington psychiatrist with a private practice that included many CIA officials learned enough about spies as to create a profile of them. Spies —she believes— fit the classic description of the antisocial personality, also known as sociopaths or psychopaths.

Sociopaths are people incapable of loyalty to individuals or groups. They are grossly selfish, narcissistic and egocentric. They are also callous, manipulative and contemptuous of others. Most of them are impulsive —with little long-term planning. They are unable to feel guilt, remorse, or shame, and are also unable to learn from experience or punishment. They show a low tolerance to frustration, and tend to blame others for their mistakes. Superficially charming, they are untruthful and insincere.

Moreover, sociopaths show poor judgment and have little insight. Most of them are incapable of feeling love at any level, and feel little anxiety or internal conflicts —as a rule, sociopaths act rather than feel. They have shallow interpersonal relations throughout their lives. They rarely commit suicide, because they have no sense of their own responsibility. They are dramatic, exhibitionistic, and often play the impostor. They are often involved in criminal acts.[41]

According to Marbes, the third trait traitors consistently show is narcissism. Narcissism has been described as a pathological self-absorption, a preoccupation of the self at the expense of all else. "Such individuals often posses a grandiose sense of their own importance."[42]

It seems that Marbes is on the right track. Just a cursory analysis of the personalities of most members of the CFR's nucleus and its two inner circles (see below), evidences the presence of most of the traits characterizing traitors —particularly their lack of loyalty to their country.

Like all secret societies, one of the methods the CFR uses to preserve its secrets is by applying the principle of common criminality. Actually, the principle is very old.

The cult of Isis flourished in ancient Greece, and its mysteries were protected by an oath of secrecy. But, in order to protect themselves from treason, the conspirators forced other members to commit a common crime. In this way they assured that if any member of the group were to betray the conspiracy, he would find himself charged with a crime with several witnesses testifying against him.

Recent examples of the principle of common criminality in action are Barack Obama appointing Timothy Geithner, a tax cheat, as Secretary of the Treasure and IRS chief. Another example is the conspirators appointing Obama as U.S. President.[43] Given the fact that nobody except the conspirators know where he was actually born, what his real name is, or even if he legally took the oath of office,[44] Obama is a malleable tool in the conspirators' hands.

If some day the conspirators decide that he is no longer useful, he would be discarded like a used Kleenex. If, like Nixon, he makes the mistake of refusing to be replaced, the conspirators can easily get rid of him just by releasing to the press the information about the crimes he has committed.

Granted, the CFR is not the only organization working hard in the shadows to establish a communo-fascist totalitarian dictatorship in America and the world. However, if one follows the money flowing in large quantities from CFR-controlled non-profit "philanthropic" foundations, it becomes evident that most of the lines point to Wall Street banks and oil and other transnational corporations.

The Invisible Government of the United States

The Council on Foreign Relations is not a homogeneous group. Like most secret societies, the CFR consists of a central nucleus and several concentric layers. The people in the nucleus are the brains behind the CFR, and the ones who actually control the organization and fully know its secret goals.[45] As some keen observer pointed out, "… few members of the CFR know the long-range plans of its small top management group."

I call these people the **planners**.

The CFR nucleus is formed by the Rockefellers, the Rothschilds, the Morgans, and a select group of oil magnates and Wall Street bankers. These people not only have immense fortunes, but also enormous power.

I don't discard the possibility, however, that, like Russian matrioshka dolls, the CFR's nucleus may itself be the cover of another, even more secret organization. Studying it, however, would fall far beyond the scope of this book. Therefore, at least for myself and for the time being, the buck stops here. On the other hand, if you want to get a short, but accurate look at the deeper sources of the CFR conspirators' evil, I suggest beginning by reading Dr. Stanley Montieth's *Brotherhood of Darkness*.

The nucleus is surrounded by a thin ring of select individuals who enjoy the total confidence of the planners —just to some extent, because the planners don't fully trust anybody. This group actively participates in the implementation of the plans emanating from the central nucleus.

They are the **implementers**.

Notable among the implementers are Henry Kissinger, Zbigniew Brzezinski, Maurice Strong, Jimmy Carter, John McCloy, Robert McNamara, and Dean Rusk. "Colonel" House, Sumner Welles, Prescott Bush, Averell Harriman, Charles Bohlen, Dean Acheson, George Kennan and the Dulles brothers also belonged to this group. To this circle also belong Bush father and son, as well as Bill and Hillary Clinton.

This internal ring is surrounded by another ring, a little more wider, formed by a large group of opportunistic and unscrupulous individuals, who have managed to infiltrate and control both the Republican and the Democratic parties. They have also infiltrated the executive branch of the U.S. government and most of the Congress, the judges, the mainstream media, the system of public education, the universities, and the armed forces of this country.

These are the **executors**.

Their role consists in executing the plans emanating from the central nucleus. Most of these people have gained their power and influence thanks to their membership to the Council. Typical examples of this type of executors are Colin Powell, David Petraeus, Stanley McChrystal, Paul Bremer, Timothy Geithner, Madeleine Albright and most of the so-called neocons. Their most recent acquisition to engross the executors' ring, even if he is not an overt CFR member, is Barack Hussein Obama.[46]

The Council on Foreign relations has infiltrated the United States government to the point that currently for all purposes the American government has become a branch of the CFR. In the past forty years, most of American presidents, vice-presidents, Secretaries of State, CIA Directors, Supreme Court judges, and high rank Pentagon officers, not to mention Federal Reserve Bank and IRS directors, belong to this group of CFR executors.

For many years, the Council was a relatively closed society, barely having a thousand members. However, about thirty years ago the CFR conspirators decided to add a wide outer circle, to which they attracted a large group of individuals from an ample spectrum of American society. As equal opportunity employers, a few of the people they have recruited for this outer circle they use as a convenient cover are women and dark-skinned minorities. But, like mount Everest, the higher you get in the CFR's hierarchy, the whiter it gets. The CFR's nucleus and the inner circle have always been mostly composed of old, white, rich males.

Nevertheless, the people in the outer circle have found in the Council an easy way to polish their enlarged egos[47] and advance their careers. Most likely, most of them have no real idea of what the Council's secret goals are, but they are part of a symbiotic relationship. They act as a smoke screen to hide the true goals of the Council while, because of the prestige of the institution, they benefit from the relationship.

This large group constitutes the **cover**.

The existence of this cover explains why a handful of honest, but disinformed people are Council members. They have been recruited under a false flag to form part of this outer ring. On the other hand, one can keep in mind that the best agent is the one who doesn't know —or doesn't want to know— that he has been recruited.

For all practical purposes, the CFR is a secret society. Like all secret societies, the CFR is well organized, its true activities and goals are secret, and is believed to be powerful. Moreover, while the true extent of its economic, political and social power remains carefully hidden to the public, its psychological influence is substantial.

If what I have described above seems like a conspiracy, it is because it *is* a conspiracy. And I am not talking about a "conspiracy theory," but of a proved, criminal conspiracy —a legal term clearly defined in the laws of this country:

> CONSPIRACY - 18 USC. 371 makes it a separate Federal crime or offense for anyone to conspire or agree with someone else to do something which, if actually carried out, would amount to another Federal crime or offense. So, under this law, a "conspiracy" is an agreement or a kind of "partnership" in criminal purposes in which each member becomes the agent or partner of every other member.

The CFR Conspirators Take Early Control of the Press

Very early in their criminal careers the Wall Street bankers realized that the best way to control people was by controlling their minds —what is now called "psychological warfare." So, using their money and power, they made a powerful grab to control the American free press. This maneuver was kept secret, and we know about it thanks to a patriotic politician, Congressman Oscar Callaway, whose statement was included in the *Congressional Record*. Congressman Callaway's statement is so important that I am quoting it in detail,

> On March, 1915, the J.P. Morgan interests, the steel, shipbuilding, and powder interests, and their subsidiary organizations, got together 12 men high up in the newspaper world and employed them to select the most influential newspapers in the United States and sufficient number of them to control generally the policy of the daily press of the United States.
>
> These 12 men worked the problem out by selecting 170 newspapers, and then began, by an elimination process, to retain only those necessary for the purpose of controlling the general policy of the daily press throughout the country. They found it was only necessary to purchase the control of 25 of the greatest newspapers. The 25 papers were agreed upon; emissaries were sent to purchase the policy, national and international, of these papers; an agreement was reached; the policy of the papers was bought, to be paid for by the month; an editor was furnished for each paper to properly supervise and edit information regarding the questions of preparedness, militarism, financial policies, and other things of national and international nature considered vital to the interest of the purchasers.
>
> This contract is in existence at the present time, and it accounts for the news columns of the daily press of the country being filled with all sorts of preparedness argument and misrepresentations as to the present

> condition of the United States Army and Navy and the possibility and probability of the United States being attacked by foreign foes.
>
> This policy also included the suppression of everything in opposition to the wishes of the interests served. The effectiveness of this scheme has been conclusively demonstrated by the character of stuff carried in the daily press throughout the country since March 1915. They have resorted to anything necessary to commercialize public sentiment and sandbag the national congress into making extravagant and wasteful appropriations for the Army and Navy under the false pretense that it was necessary. Their stock argument is that it is "patriotism." They are playing on every prejudice and passion of the American people.[48]

This almost total control of the U.S. mainstream press has continued almost uninterrupted to this day. Proof of it is that speaking at the Bilderberg meeting in Baden-Baden, Germany, June 5, 1991, CFR honcho David Rockefeller thanked the sycophantic press for doing a good job keeping the American people in the dark about the treasonous activities of the Wall Street bankers and other conspirators in the Council on Foreign relations.

In the same fashion, in the Introduction to a 1996 book by Carl Jensen, Walter Cronkite, a trusted secret CFR agent, wrote:

> A handful of us determine what will be on the evening news broadcasts, or, for that matter, in the *New York Times* or *Washington Post* or *Wall Street Journal*. . . . Indeed it is a handful of us with this awesome power. . . . a strongly editorial power. . . . we must decide which news items out of hundreds available we are going to expose that day. And those [news stories] available to us already have been culled and re-culled by persons far outside our control.[49]

As I mentioned above, the conspirators' control has continued *almost* uninterrupted to the present day. And I emphasized "almost," because since a few years ago a new, unexpected medium, the Internet, has been threatening their control. This informational (and disinformational) tool took them by surprise and, after many unsuccessful attempts to control and infiltrate it, apparently they have reached some conclusions. First, they have realized, first, that the internet is a medium too powerful to allow it to operate out of their control and, second, that, because of some intrinsic characteristics of the internet, it is almost impossible to control or censor it, therefore, they have to destroy it, at least in its present free, open form.[50]

Further proof that the conspirators fear the power of the Internet is that senators John Rockefeller (CFR) and Olympia Snowe (CFR) want to give the President the power to shut down domestic Internet traffic during a "state of emergency." Accordingly, they introduced a bill called the Cybersecurity Act of 2009. This Act establishes the Office of the National Cybersecurity Advisor —an arm of the executive branch that would have the power to monitor and control Internet traffic, allegedly to protect the country against threats to critical cyber infrastructure.

As expected, the Act does not define a critical information network or a cybersecurity emergency. That definition would be left to the president's interpretation.[51]

The Conspirators Extend Their Control Over the Press, The Arts and the Academia

Most brainwashed Americans still believe that we have a free press in this country, and that reporters and journalists provide them objective information based on facts. They ignore, however, that they get most of their news (actually carefully manufactured disinformation) from CFR-controlled television, newspapers and magazines.

On its part, the American left has accused the CIA of using the U.S. mainstream press in constant PSYOPs to mold public opinion. Having in mind, however, that the CIA is just an obedient servant of the CFR conspirators, the logic conclusion is that the Agency has just been doing its job on behalf of its masters.

Moreover, if the CIA has used the press to mold the opinion of the American public, the CFR conspirators themselves have consistently used their house organ, the prestigious scholarly quarterly *Foreign Affairs,* as their main tool in molding the opinion of the American ruling class.

But there is nothing new about this. Headed by Frank Wisner (CFR), with the support of Allen Dulles (CFR), Richard Helms (CFR) and Philip Graham (CFR), publisher of *The Washington Post*, the CIA began in 1949 the ultra secret Operation Mockingbird. Its goal was to recruit, under the false flag of fighting communism, American media news organizations and journalists as agents to disseminate CFR-generated disinformation.

Some years later, the CIA admitted having recruited more than 400 influential journalists who have secretly carried out assignments, from intelligence gathering to serving as go-betweens, inside at least 25 organizations of the U.S. mainstream media. Eventually, CIA assets in the American media included *CBS, NBC, ABC, CNN, Time, Newsweek, U.S. News and World Report, Reader's Digest, The Miami Herald, The Washington Post, The Los Angeles Times, The Wall Street Journal*, the Hearst Newspapers, news agencies *AP, UPI, Reuters,* and more. Since then, the conspirators' control over the U.S. mainstream media has increased.

Journalist Carl Bernstein mentioned that a senior CIA officer told him that between 1950 and 1966 the *NYT* provided cover for about ten CIA operatives.[52] According to other source, from around 1950 to 1975, some correspondents for the *New York Times*, *CBS News*, *Time* magazine, and many other press organizations, served as conduits for planted CIA stories, leaked information to the CIA, and in some cases even provided operational assistance. In addition, major news organizations such as the *NYT* wittingly allowed CIA operatives to pose as clerks or part-time correspondents and provided cover for others. Also, propaganda and disinformation disseminated abroad by the CIA was "blown back"[53] to the U.S. and reprinted as *bona fide* news by American newspapers.[54]

The CFR conspirators' push to control the press was so successful that they decided to expand it in other directions. Soon after, the CIA launched an offensive in the world of arts and letters, recruiting under a false flag, artists, writers, filmmakers, and other intellectuals. In her book, *The Cultural Cold War: The CIA and the World of Arts and Letters*,[55] Frances Stonor Saunders described in detail how the CIA massively funded cultural activities during the Cold War, including books, journals, magazines, films, international conferences, and even Abstract Expressionism.

At the same time, the CIA launched a propaganda offensive in the nation's most important universities, recruiting respected professors and promising students. In their effort, the Agency funded, through CFR-controlled foundations like Carnegie, Rockefeller, and Ford acting as covers, the first scholars who specialized in international studies. These unscrupulous scholars willingly turned themselves into agents of disinformation and prostituted their prestige by churning out book after book supporting, either by justifying or criticizing it, the artificially created Cold War against the Soviet Union. They are not too different from the present ones who now write book after book justifying the artificially created war against terrorism or the non-existing anthropogenic global warming.[56]

The Conspirators Infiltrate the Two Parties

Initially, the two-party system may not have seemed a bad idea. In a democratic society, most important political decisions are the result of a compromise of opposing factions, one slightly to the left, the other slightly to the right, competing for setting what they consider the best course the country they love should follow.

Early in the game, however, the conspirators who hate America and wanted to change it into a communo-fascist totalitarian society had a better idea. But, contrary to openly Fascists and Communists, who want to change society by fast, violent means, the conspirators chose slow, gradual infiltration techniques like the ones advocated by British Fabians and Gramscian communists. Consequently, they decided to infiltrate both main political parties to turn them into useful, secret tools to slowly advance their secret agenda.

Currently, the two main political parties are nothing but a fiction whose only purpose is to keep the voters confused. Both the Republican and the Democratic parties have become the two sides of the same coin, which I call the *Repucratic* Party. These two factions are fully under the control of the same oligarchy that has infiltrated their secret agents into almost every aspect of the life of this country. Due to the fact, however, that their Fabian methods of infiltration —if not their goals— differ from the ones employed by Communists and Fascists, they had to keep their treacherous activities hidden from the American people.

Once this initial infiltration step was achieved, and with almost total control of the mainstream media and the educational system, the conspirators began using sophisticated techniques of psychological manipulation to keep the American public under the impression that they were the ones electing their presidents running by the two contending parties. Nevertheless, the fact that in the last fifty years American presidents belonging to both parties have systematically trashed the Constitution and betrayed the people who voted for them is proof enough that the people's votes are irrelevant.

American voters don't elect American presidents anymore. Actually, with perhaps the exception of John F. Kennedy, would-be American presidents are tapped at the secret meetings of the Council of Foreign relations, the Bohemian Grove, the Bilderberg Group or the World Economic Forum. Once the CFR conspirators select them, the rest is just smoke and mirrors and psychological manipulation to make gullible American voters believe that they had been the ones who have elected the president.

Given the fact that psychological manipulation by the mainstream press alone doesn't fully accomplish the job, the conspirators support their brainwashing with vote tampering. Currently, the extended use of computerized vote machines have made vote fraud much more easier.[57]

When truly independent candidates threatening their control appear —even in the far away future—, they either eliminate them with extreme prejudice (Gen. George S. Patton, Robert Kennedy), threaten them (Ross Perot), mount defamatory campaigns to destroy them politically (Barry Goldwater, Sarah Palin),[58] ignore them (Chuck Baldwin), or ostracize them (Ron Paul).

The 2004 elections were just a remake of the previous one: both candidates, the Republican and the Democrat, were Yale graduates, members of the Skull & Bones and the Council on Foreign Relations, and both of them had cheated on their military records —not a wide selection of choices for the American voter, to say the least.

There is another bit of evidence pointing to the fact that Kerry was consciously playing his part in the charade that gave Bush the presidency for a second term. To the utter surprise of some of his brainwashed liberal and leftist supporters, it was obvious that Kerry didn't make any effort to win. As in the TV wrestling matches, the fight was a fake.

The 2008 elections brought to the White House another CFR-controlled puppet: Barack Hussein Obama. Even Louis Farrakhan has recognized that Obama is a puppet. During a Conference in Chicago on March 10, 2010, Minister Farrakhan cryptically mentioned that Obama had been selected before being elected. And added, "President Obama does not run the country."[59]

Some observers of the political scene noticed that Bush's neocons were delighted with the new man in the White House. An article by Stephen J. Sniegoski, published in the English-language edition of the Swiss newspaper *Zeit-Fragen*, reported that leading figures of the neocon/neo-Nazi cabal —David Brooks, Richard Perle, Max Boot, Mona Charen and others— were ecstatic over Obama's appointments. According to Sniegoski, the reason for their happiness was because they didn't see any difference between the Obama and the Bush administrations.[60]

But Mr. Sniegoski's conclusions are wrong. Actually, the true reason why the neo-cons were so enthused was because both Bush and Obama are puppets manipulated by the very same CFR puppet masters that control the neo-cons themselves.

Joining the neocon dissonant chorus, pseudo-conservative professional disinformer Rush Limbaugh highly praised the appointment of Hillary Clinton as secretary of state, and qualified Obama's decision as "brilliant." As a way of payment, Obama publicly criticized Limbaugh, in a subtle effort to strengthen his damaged bona fides vis-à-vis a growing number of his disenchanted listeners, who have growing suspicions that the radio host is not what he claims to be.

In the same fashion, faux-conservative David Horowitz scolded concerned conservative activists filing lawsuits regarding Obama's citizenship status. But it was not because he didn't believe the claims about Obama's illegitimacy, but rather because the new CFR puppet has shown his true hawkish nature —a fact he believes conservatives should appreciate.[61]

The Conspirators Infiltrate the State Department

The U.S. Department of State was for many years the focus of attention of many American patriots. Some of them, like Senator Joseph McCarthy[62] and Ambassador Earl T. Smith,[63] firmly believed that a Communist cabal had infiltrated the State Department and was using it to advance its treasonous agenda.

Senator Joseph McCarthy discovered that the State Department was teeming with individuals frantically working in the shadows to destroy this country by helping its enemies. During a speech at Wheeling, West Virginia, on February 9, 1950, he mentioned he had compiled a list of 205 State Department employees working hard against the best interests of the American people.

Unfortunately, McCarthy mistakenly concluded that the CFR agents he was fighting had to be Communists. Among them were State Department officials Alger Hiss (CFR), and Owen Lattimore (CFR), as well as Harry Hopkins and Laughlin Currie in Franklin Delano Roosevelt's White House and Harry Dexter White in the Treasury Department. He also accused General George Marshall (CFR) of treason.

As if on cue, President Eisenhower (CFR), Secretary of State Dean Acheson (CFR), John McCloy (CFR) and journalist Edward Murrow (CFR), joined forces in defending the traitors and vilifying McCarthy. The result was that, despite the fact that most of the people he accused eventually were proven traitors,[64] McCarthy's gross mistake cost him his career, and probably even his life.[65]

It would be unfair, however, to blame McCarthy for his mistake. As professor Carroll Quigley has explained, the CFR conspirators' *modus operandi* to some extent mimic the way the Communists act.[66]

Robert Welch made a similar mistake. In his book *The Politician*,[67] Welch accused both President Dwight Eisenhower and his brother Milton of being Communists,

In honor to truth, none of these people were Communists in the sense of being followers of the classic Marxist-Leninist doctrines, nor were they true secret agents of the Soviet Union. They were, though, at least half-Communists,[68] but only because they were secret agents of the true and only Communo-Fascist Party of the U.S.A.: the Council on Foreign Relations.

Actually, any effort to link the CFR conspirators to any known ideology is a waste of time.[69] The fact that they have supported fascist and communist regimes only mean that doing so has helped them advance their secret depopulation and deindustrialization agendas.

In the same fashion, the fact that they have supported some political groups like the gay movement or the New Age religion does not indicate that they share those beliefs. They have financed, promoted and supported these groups as fellow travelers, because some elements in these groups' agendas, i.e., eugenics, coincide with theirs. Nevertheless, they would not hesitate to get rid of or even destroy any of these groups as soon as they become a liability.

Proof of the above is that some of their most useful agents, like Kissinger, the Clintons, Brzezinski, the Bushes and Carter, just to mention the most notorious ones, are ideological prostitutes.

The first step the CFR conspirators took to achieve their goal of taking total control over the U.S. was to infiltrate, first, the Republican Party and, second, the Democratic party. Once they got control of the two parties, they were ready for the next step.

Though the CFR conspirators have always had several key agents in the State Department, it was not until late 1939, when they managed to fully infiltrate and establish their almost total control over State. For some time they had been waiting for a suitable excuse to justify their next pitch: full control of the U.S. Department of State. The opportunity presented itself with the outbreak of war in Europe in September 1939.

A second important step in the infiltration process was to offer their "help" by suggesting the creation of a group of "experts" in foreign policy to advise State Department officials. This was the true origin of the War and Peace Studies project, a clever scheme written by University of Chicago professor and CFR asset[70] Jacob Vinter. The project was financed with funds provided by the Rockefeller Foundation

Less than two weeks after the beginning of the war, the CFR conspirators sent to Washington D.C. two of their trusted secret agents, CFR executive director Walter H. Mallory, and Hamilton Fish Armstrong, editor of *Foreign Affairs*, to a meeting with assistance secretary of state George S. Messersmith, also a CFR member.

The distinguished visitors outlined a long-range plan to assure a closer collaboration between the CFR and the State Department. It consisted in the creation of several study groups composed of CFR intelligence analysts to study the problems created by the war, and to plan for the future peace. Based on results of their research, the groups would made recommendations to the State Department and President Franklin D. Roosevelt (CFR). However, due to the fact that the groups would not be government employees, their research would be kept hidden from Congress and the eyes of the American public.

Messersmith (CFR) approved Mallory (CFR) and Armstrong's (CFR) suggestions and that same day he met with Secretary of State Cordell Hull and undersecretary Sumner Welles (CFR) to outline the CFR's proposal. Both Hull and Welles found the proposal interesting. Soon afterward, CFR president Norman H. Davis, a close friend and adviser of Hull, took it to the secretary and received his verbal approval for the proposal.[71] In retrospect it seems clear that, way before Armstrong and Mallory visited Washington, all the deal had already been friendly closed at the Harold Pratt House in Manhattan.

On December 6, 1939, the Rockefeller Foundation granted the CFR $44,500 to finance the operation, which took the official name of War and Peace Studies Project.

Author James Perloff has described in some detail the CFR conspirators' infiltration into this key department of the U.S. Government:

> On September 1939, Hitler's troops invaded Poland. Britain and France declared war on Germany; World War II had begun.
>
> Less than two weeks later, Hamilton Fish Armstrong, editor of Foreign Affairs, and Walter Mallory, the CFR's executive director, met in Washington with Assistant Secretary of State George Messersmith. They proposed that the Council help the State Department formulate its wartime policy and postwar planning. The CFR would conduct study groups in coordination with State, making recommendations to the Department and President. Messersmith (a Council member himself) and his superiors agreed. The CFR thus succeeded, temporarily at least, in making itself an adjunct of the United States government. This undertaking became known as the War and Peace Studies Project; it worked in secret and was underwritten by the Rockefeller Foundation. It held 362 meetings and prepared 682 papers for FDR and the State Department.[72]

The CFR used its temporary position as a government adjunct as a way to spread its secret agents throughout the U.S. government. The State Department became particularly infested. In fact, the CFR's influence over State led to what can only be described as the privatization of foreign policy. Since then, American foreign policy became little more than a vehicle for advancing the agendas of Wall Street bankers, oil magnates, transnational corporations, globalists and elitists. After its creation in 1947, the CIA has provided this privatized foreign policy with its military muscle through covert action operations. This explains why the CIA has been called "the private army of the Fortune 500."

The myth of the State Department as the source of a treasonous conspiracy has persisted to our days. In a recent book, *Dangerous Diplomacy: How the State Department Threatens America's Security*, Joel Mowbray tells about many treasonous acts committed by State Department officials.[73] Granted, most of the facts Mr. Mowbray mentions are true. But, by failing to mention that the U.S. State Department has been for the last 50 years a tool of the Council on Foreign Relations, his book becomes disinformation.

For example, his depiction of how "State Department bureaucrats" mislead Colin Powell about the need to give Scud missiles to Yemen is totally misleading.

Both the "State Department bureaucrats" and Mr. Powell get their orders from the same source, the CFR.

Mowbray is a typical example of the "rightist" counterpart to "leftists" like Noam Chomsky, whose criticism of things bad in America never go beyond the CIA and the Pentagon —organizations also infiltrated and controlled by the CFR conspirators.

Apparently, both these "leftist" and "rightist" critics share the stochastic view of history, by which things just happen by chance. This is the view advanced by the mainstream media and hammered in the children's minds in the government's schools (the ones disingenuously called "public schools"). But, as I am showing in this book, the conspiratorial view of history offers a version of historical events much more closer to the truth.

Chapter 4

The OSS: of the Bankers, by the Bankers, for the Bankers

I know they are Communist; that's why I hired them.
—Gen. William Donovan, OSS chief.

Most books about the history of the U.S. intelligence services repeat over and over the story that the Office of Strategic Services (OSS) was the first central intelligence agency of this country. This is the case, i.e., of Christy Macy and Susan Kaplan's book *Documents*,[1] which they advertise on the book's cover as, "A shocking collection of memoranda, letters, and telexes from the secret files of the American Intelligence Community." According to them, "The CIA is the direct descendant of the Office of Strategic Services (OSS)."[2]

Jeffrey T. Richelson repeats the same piece of disinformation in his *A Century of Spies: Intelligence in the Twentieth Century*.[3] According to Richelson,

> In 1941 President Franklin Roosevelt established the first central intelligence agency of the United States, the Office of Coordination of Information. The man chosen to head the new office, which became the Office of Strategic Services (OSS) in June 1942, was William J. Donovan.[4]

Nevertheless, despite its intentionally misleading name, the Office of Coordination of Information (COI), was not a true intelligence agency. Its true role was not intelligence gathering and analysis, but covert military operations. It was the CFR conspirators' first incursion into "espionage, sabotage, 'black'[5] propaganda, guerrilla warfare, and other 'un-American' subversive practices."[6]

The creation of the Office of Coordination of Information, a veritable military arm directly serving the CFR conspirators, had enormous political significance. In the fist place because the U.S. had never before had a peacetime, civilian controlled, intelligence agency purely devoted to covert military operations. Secondly, because, being under the control of the executive power, the COI was an important unconstitutional expansion of presidential power which, given the fact that U.S. presidents are CFR puppets, actually meant a true power grab by the CFR conspirators.

The person who actually drew up the legal documents implementing the CFR conspirators' plan to create the COI was Benjamin Cohen, a trusted CFR agent. In violation of the U.S. Constitution, CFR agent Franklin D. Roosevelt signed it into law by executive fiat, ignoring the system of checks and balances among the executive, legislative, and judicial powers established by the Constitution. It was the start of the preeminence of the presidency as dictatorial government arm, a process that eventually became what CFR agent Arthur M. Schlesinger, Jr. called "the imperial presidency."[7]

American Intelligence Before and After WWI

Prior to the 1880s, U.S. intelligence activities were mostly centered in supporting military operations in time of war. This intelligence work was mostly tactical, like providing support to deployed forces, though some strategic intelligence was produced. It mostly consisted of intelligence on the strategic and geopolitical positions of other countries or their participation in a particular conflict.

On March 1882, however, the Office of Naval Intelligence was created within the Department of the Navy to collect intelligence on foreign navies both in peacetime and in war. This was the first permanent U.S. military intelligence organization. A similar organization was created within the Army three years later, the Military Intelligence Division. Its role was to collect foreign and domestic military data for the War Department and the Army.

It was not until the Administration of Theodore Roosevelt, however, that an American President systematically made active use of intelligence for foreign policy purposes. Roosevelt was also a pioneer in the used of covert action. He sent intelligence operatives to Panama to incite a revolution he would use as a pretext to justify before the American people and the world the annexing of the territory needed to dig the Panama Canal. In 1907, Teddy Roosevelt also relied on intelligence which indicated the growing military build-up in Japan as a justification to launch the worldwide cruise of the "Great White Fleet" whose main purpose was displaying the U.S. naval muscle to the world.

Despite these early attempts, most of the early part of the twentieth century didn't show an expanded use of intelligence for foreign policy purposes. It did show, however, an expansion of domestic intelligence capabilities. In 1908, the Justice Department established the Bureau of Investigation (the forerunner of the FBI) out of concern that Secret Service agents were spying on members of Congress. By 1916, the Bureau had grown from 34 agents focusing primarily on banking issues to 300 agents with an expanded charter that included internal security, Mexican border smuggling activities, neutrality violations in the Mexican revolution, and Central American unrest. After war broke out in Europe, but before the United States joined the Allied cause, the Bureau turned its attention to activities of German and British nationals within our borders.

At the time the United States entered the war, there was nothing close to a coordinated U.S. intelligence effort. President Woodrow Wilson, who considered himself a champion of open diplomacy, had always disdained the use of spies and never gave much credit to intelligence. However, perhaps as a result of his close association with the British intelligence chief in Washington, his views on the subject somehow changed to some extent.

Some historians have argued that British intelligence played a major role in pushing the United States into World War I. Public revelations by the British of German intelligence attempts to prevent U.S. industry and the financial sector from assisting Great Britain greatly angered the American public. Subsequently, British intelligence presented Wilson with the decryption of German diplomatic and naval traffic showing a German effort to entice the Mexican government into joining Germany against the United States in return for Texas, Arizona, and New Mexico if Germany won the war.

This intercepted communication, later declassified and disclosed to the public and known as the "Zimmerman Telegram," allegedly infuriated Wilson and added support to his address before a joint session of Congress in 1917 urging that the U.S. declare war on Germany. But, knowing the CFR conspirators' total control over Wilson, we may easily surmise that they played an important role in persuading Wilson to change his mind about the use of spies and intelligence.

As a result, in June of 1917 Wilson authorized the creation of the first U.S. signals intelligence agency within the Army. It was known as "MI-8," and was charged with decoding military communications and providing codes to be used by the U.S. military. When the war ended in 1921, the MI-8 was transferred to the State Department, and eventually became known as the "Black Chamber," where it focused more on diplomatic than military communications.

In 1921, with Herbert Hoover in the White House, the Black Chamber had one of its most significant successes by decrypting certain Japanese diplomatic traffic. The intelligence gained from this operation was used to support U.S. negotiators at a Washington conference on naval disarmament. Despite such successes, however, President Hoover decided that the State Department's interception of diplomatic cables and correspondence could not be tolerated. Apparently agreeing with the alleged, yet oft-quoted statement of his Secretary of State, Henry Stimson, "Gentlemen do not read each other's mail," Hoover returned the agency to a military orientation under the Army Signal Corps.

Other intelligence organizations remained in existence after the end of WWI but their resources were cut substantially. An exception to this general trend, however, was the Justice Department's Bureau of Investigation, which saw a marked expansion of its mission and workforce. In 1924, J. Edgar Hoover was named director of the Bureau (renamed the Federal Bureau of Investigation (FBI) in 1935).

In the years leading to World War II, the FBI's charter was broadened, particularly in areas dealing with U.S. internal security faced with growing concerns as a result of German aggression in Europe. Accordingly, the FBI was made responsible for investigating espionage, counterespionage, sabotage, and violations of the neutrality laws. It was also during this period that the first effort was made to coordinate the activities of the various intelligence elements of the Government. To this effect, an Interdepartmental Intelligence Coordinating Committee was created, but it had limited impact because it lacked a permanent chair and participating agencies were reluctant to share information with it.

Was the OSS an Intelligence Agency?

Most authors who attribute to President Roosevelt the creation of the OSS miss a very important point: like most American presidents before and after him, Franklin D. Roosevelt was a puppet put in the White House and closely manipulated by the CFR puppeteers.[8] Prominent in this group of close advisors, who FDR euphemistically called his "brain trust," were Harry Dexter White, Harry Hopkins, George Marshall and Henry Morgenthau, Jr., all of them CFR secret agents. They were an early version of today's National Security Council advisors surrounding Americans presidents.

Therefore, it makes sense to conclude that, like all important decisions taken by American presidents since Wilson, the creation of the OSS was an idea developed at the CFR and implanted in Roosevelt's brain by his CFR controllers. Moreover, given the fact that they already had their own intelligence agency, the CFR, the conspirators had no need for another one. Consequently, despite claims to the contrary the OSS was never a true intelligence agency, but just an undercover military arm of the CFR.

A widely accepted myth tells that, apart from being a brave soldier, General William "Wild Bill" Donovan was a man with great powers of persuasion, and he found a receptive ear in president Franklin D. Roosevelt. According to this rosy story, after discovering that president Roosevelt shared his passion for intelligence and espionage, Donovan managed to convince him that the U.S. needed an innovative intelligence organization to win the war: a civilian central intelligence agency independent from the intelligence services already existing in the different branches of the armed forces, who reported directly to the president. The result of Donovan's efforts was the creation in 1942 of the Office of Coordination of Information.

But, as I will show below, the true purpose of the OSS was not to defend the interests of the American people, but the interests of the Wall Street bankers, oil magnates, and owners of big corporations who had been doing good business arming the Nazi war machine. Contrary to what is written in most history books, the true goal of the CFR conspirators was not to defeat their Nazi partners, but to save them after Germany's catastrophic collapse —a job they accomplished to a great extent thanks to the OSS. This explains why they orchestrated the Pearl Harbor attack as a way to manipulate the American public into willingly accepting sending their sons to fight a foreign war Roosevelt himself had promised they would never be sent to.

Therefore, a more realistic story would be that, without denying Donovan's powers of persuasion, he had some help from his powerful CFR masters in convincing Roosevelt to create the OSS.

Many books and articles written about the OSS paint a romantic, heroic view of the OSS fighting the Nazis against all odds. But, contrary to the common myth, the OSS,[9] also known as the "Oh, So Social" in reference to the high social class origins of most of its members,[10] was a sort of a joke concocted by the children of the privileged who had discovered a way to avoid fighting the enemy face to face by entrenching themselves in the universities. Suddenly, they were offered a way to fight the war without getting involved in the messy and risky part of it.

Later studies by OSS critics show a very different story: most of the highly touted successes of Donovan's organization were highly exaggerated, and the U.S. military never had any respect for them. This explains why, when the OSS tried to expand their operations to the Japanese front, the Navy told them a polite "thanks, but no thanks." General Douglas MacArthur, for one, refused to allow the OSS to participate in war operations in the South Pacific.[11] Most members of the military high command, particularly the ones in G2 (military intelligence), were extremely dissatisfied with the work of this band of arrogant aficionados, with access to big amounts of cash and lacking in the most elementary techniques of intelligence and espionage.

A year after the OSS was created, G2's head General George Strong, denounced in the strongest terms the OSS and its "ambitious and imaginative Director" for being "constantly at war with other Government agencies" and seeking to reduce G2 and the Office of naval Intelligence "to the status of reporting agencies and research bureaus for the OSS."[12]

Moreover, since its very creation, the OSS acted like a magnet attracting psychopathic personalities. During his testimony as a defense witness in the 1950 trial of Alger Hiss, a senior CFR member and former State Department official accused of being a Soviet spy, OSS's psychological chief, Dr. Henry Murray of Harvard University stated,

> The whole nature of the functions of OSS was particularly inviting to psychopathic characters; it involved sensation, intrigue, the idea of being a mysterious man with secret knowledge.[13]

The OSS was never an intelligence agency in the true sense of the term for the simple reason that the conspirators already had one: the CFR. Actually, the record shows that the OSS never did any valuable job in the areas of information collection, much less in evaluation and analysis. Its main, and perhaps only activity was covert operations.

General William Donovan, the man who the Wall Street bankers and oil magnates selected to direct the OSS was a millionaire Wall Street corporate lawyer. In 1929 he created his own law firm, Donovan, Leisure, Newton and Lumbard.[14] .

His right hand, Allen Dulles, was a Wall Street lawyer and senior member of the Rockefellers' Council on Foreign Relations. Through his OSS office in Bern, Switzerland, Dulles kept an eye in the protection of the interests of CFR members. Sullivan & Cromwell, the law firm Dulles had worked for since 1926,[15] had strong business ties with the I.G. Farben, the chemical firm producer of Ziklon B, the lethal gas used to kill the Jews. It also represented the United Fruit Company and other Rockefeller interests. John Foster Dulles, Allen's brother and partner in Sullivan & Cromwell, had close ties to Carmel Offie, William Bullitt, George

Kennan, Paul Nitze and James Forrestal, all of them CFR agents or assets.

Most of the senior OSS members were secret CFR agents, and many of them had been part of the Inquiry. As such, they had played a key role in the behind-the-curtains machinations of the U.S. delegation to the Versailles negotiations. Most of them later played important roles in the development of U.S. intelligence and national security policy for many decades.

Less known, however, is the important role they had before, during and after World War II, in helping the development of international fascism. After Versailles, Inquiry member John Foster Dulles acted as a Special Counsel to the Dawes Committee, where he helped arrange the loans that re-capitalized Germany under the Dawes Plan.

The Wall Street law firm Sullivan & Cromwell to which John Foster and Allen Dulles were associated, profited enormously from those loans. The German firms capitalized under the Dawes plan were instrumental in promoting the rise of Adolf Hitler and the creation of his war machine. Other European fascists who benefited from the largesse of Wall Street banks were Italy's Mussolini, Spain's Franco and Poland's Pilsudski. It goes without saying that the money the bankers were giving to the European fascists was not theirs; the conspirators' IRS had stolen it from the pockets of the anti-fascist American people.

Frank Wisner, another OSS officer who later became CIA's chief of covert operations, had also been linked since 1934 to a powerful Wall Street law firm, Carter, Leyard, Milburn, which was the counsel for the New York Stock Exchange. Another CIA Deputy Director, Harding Jackson, was a former partner in Carter, Ledyard and Milburn, a Wall Street law firm.

William Colby, an OSS officer who eventually joined the CIA and became its Director, joined Donovan's law firm just out of law school. Other OSS Wall Street lawyers were William Jackson, Gordon Gray and Tracy Barnes.[16] All of them eventually joined the CIA.

At CIA, Gray became a psychological warfare expert, and Wisner had a cardinal role in helping Nazis escape from justice. One of them, Reinhard Gehlen, became an important CIA asset. Once in the CIA, both Dulles and Wisner worked closely with the Gehlen organization.

During WWII, Allen Dulles served as head of the OSS office in Berne, Switzerland. Under the cover of his OSS position, Dulles maintained close contacts with members of the German industrial and financial elite. Most of them he had known while working for Sullivan & Cromwell. After Germany's defeat, Dulles was instrumental in helping to preserve the Nazi elite. One of Dulles' principal contacts was Gero von Gaevernitz, who played an important role in introducing German spymaster Reinhard Gehlen to the U.S. intelligence operatives. Von Gaevernitz was instrumental in bringing the general and his organization into the American intelligence services.

But, despite the widespread criticism, one has to recognize that the OSS did a wonderful job. The only problem is that it was on behalf of its Wall Street masters.

It had nothing to do with their purported one, and its true goals had nothing to do with benefiting the interests of the United States or its citizens. Unfortunately, this was a vice inherited by the CIA.

OSS: The Gang That Couldn't Shoot Straight

In his book *OSS: The Secret History of America's First Intelligence Service*, by far the best study written on the subject,[17] author R. Harris Smith paints a picture of systemic chaos in the OSS organization. According to Smith, a Captain who had led an OSS team behind Japanese lines in China told him that, "All officers were quite junior, and as long as everybody did his work few of us bothered with military regulations. High brass was unlikely to inspect."[18]

It seems that Donovan's OSS men acted more like a band of brigands than military men. Insubordination was commonplace in the OSS, but, far from penalizing or criticizing it, Donovan seemed to encourage it. Confronted with cases of insubordination, he often commented: "I'd rather have a young lieutenant with guts enough to disobey an order than a colonel too regimented to think and act for himself."[19]

In what he erroneously qualifies as high-level "flaps,"[20] Smith mentions two occasions in which OSS officers acted apparently out of control and Donovan backed them,

> Donovan's men in Italy smuggled arms to Tito's Communist guerrillas in Yugoslavia without the approval of the British theater commander. And OSS men in Morocco sent Communist agents to Franco's Spain without notifying the American embassy in Madrid. In every case Donovan supported his officers. He had given his men their freedom of action and he would not allow them to be punished for exercising it with enthusiasm.[21]

In one case, Smith reports that, in China,

> … an OSS captain received an order to report on the attitude of the local populace in his operational area toward the contending Nationalist and Communist forces. He and his teammates suspected that the information was to be passed along to the Chinese government and they had no sympathy for the Chiang Kai-shek regime. Besides, they felt that the internal struggle in China should be just that, a domestic Chinese affair. "Let's put it to a vote," suggested the officer to his fellows. The order "lost" and was disregarded. That was the OSS way.[22]

In another case, OSS officers in Portugal broke into the Japanese embassy and stole a copy of the enemy's codebook unaware that a naval intelligence team had already broken the code and had been using it to tap into the Japanese coded traffic. But, after discovering the missing codebook, the Japanese promptly changed their code. Washington and the Joint Chiefs were incensed when they found the reason why they had been left without a vital source of information for several months until the new code was broken.[23]

In another incident following the establishment of a beachhead at Salerno, a group of OSS officers hatched a wild plot to reach the Italian Naval Command in hopes of convincing the Italian admirals to surrender their fleet to the allies. The officers apparently didn't know that the main body of the Italian fleet had already set sail from Genoa to Malta to surrender to the British.[24]

In yet another evidence of ineptitude, OSS agent Jane Foster obtained a large supply of condoms from a doctor in Ceylon (Sri Lanka). Foster and her team then stuffed the condoms with a message urging the residents of Indonesia to resist the Japanese invaders. They blew the condoms up and tied the ends shut; submarines then released hundreds of these condoms off the Indonesian coast. Nothing came out of the effort.

One of the main successes claimed by the OSS was its ability to parachute OSS officers behind enemy lines to join partisans to report enemy activities, destroy their communications and create havoc. The reality, however, is that of twenty-one OSS teams successfully parachuted into German occupied territory carrying radio transmitters, only one ever managed to establish communication. The Germans rapidly neutralized the rest.

The OSS commonly engaged in truly ludicrous operations. One of these involved a Hungarian astrologer the OSS recruited and sent to the United States to shake American public confidence in the invincibility of Hitler. After reading the Fuehrer's stars the astrologer predicted immediate doom for Hitler. The astrologer's report was carried from coast to coast in the media. No report was ever made about the success or failure of the operation.

If the Hungarian astrologer's operation bordered on the inane, another OSS operation stands out above all others as truly stupid. An OSS group based in London came to the conclusion that the Nazi state would self-destruct if only its leader could be demoralized. After conducting a long psychological profile of Hitler, the group concluded that Hitler could be unhinged by exposure to vast quantities of pornography. The OSS groups then proceeded to assemble the finest collection of pornography ever put together. The material was to be dropped by plane in the area around the Fuehrer's bunker under the assumption that Hitler would step outside and pick one up and immediately be thrown into a state of madness. The effort was in vain however, as the air force liaison officer stormed out of the first meeting with the OSS cursing them as maniacs and swearing he would not risk a single life for such an insane plan.

But perhaps the most farfetched plan among all the crazy ones carried out by the OSS was the idea of bombarding Japan with bats. According to the story, Roosevelt got a letter from an American citizen telling him about the Japanese mortal fear of bats. Accordingly, he mentioned the idea to Donovan and, soon after, some OSS officers began to experiment on how to bomb Japan with planeloads of American bats. But all attempts to find a way to dropping the bats from high-altitude planes failed when the animals froze to death before they landed.[25]

Probably the most serious allegation against the OSS, which coincided with Donovan's post-war attempts to create a permanent intelligence agency, was that it had been penetrated by British intelligence. John Franklin Smith, a journalist and friend of President Roosevelt who had been running a sort of private intelligence group for FDR since 1941, made the allegation.

As expected, Donovan emphatically denied the accusation, but there was some kernel of truth about it. Just a few months after the creation of the Office of Coordination of Information, it was revealed that British intelligence asset William Stephenson had given Donovan a map, allegedly taken from a German courier, showing Nazi plans for the reorganization of the Nazi movement in South America.

The captured documents helped Donovan build his prestige as a spymaster. Eventually, however, it was discovered that the map was a clever forgery made by the British intelligence, and Donovan had been the unwitting target used to convince Roosevelt about its veracity.[26] Roosevelt revealed the document to the American people in an address on October 27, 1941, in which he mentioned he had in his possession a map on Central and South America showing Nazi plans to Nazify the area.[27]

Stirred by the press, Americans were outraged. A few days later, the Senate repelled the Neutrality act, giving Roosevelt a free hand to begin waging a covert war on Britain's side against the Nazis. With the benefit of hindsight, however, we may safely surmise that both Donovan and Roosevelt knew that the map was faked, but used it to influence the American opinion in following a warpath already decided beforehand by the CFR conspirators.

In 1942 Hoover's FBI documented what they saw as a communist group inside the OSS. However, in his book *OSS*, R. Harris Smith mentions the fact that "In later life he [Donovan] developed an emotional hatred of Communism."[28] Yet, Smith ignored that, like most CFR members, Donovan's "emotional hatred of Communism" only appeared after his CFR masters had decided that Soviet Communism, a monster they had created, would be the appropriate replacement for Nazi Germany, another monster they also had created.

Actually, Donovan was not interested in ideologies. Like his CFR masters, he changed ideologies like snakes shed their skins: according to the needs of the moment.

OSS: The Conspirators' Fifth Column Inside the U.S. Armed Forces

Many books and articles about the OSS paint a picture of a chaotic, ineffective, though patriotic effort by well-intentioned aficionados in the arts of spying and subversion. According to Smith, safeguards in the OSS were virtually non-existent and there was little in its structure to promote respect for formal channels of authority. [29] OSS officers soon realized that disciplinary action would never be taken against them, even in cases of corruption or incompetence, and operational funds began disappearing to appear later in some officer's personal bank accounts.[30] This was mostly seen as the direct influence of its leader, General William Donovan himself. But there is at least a bit of information that contradicts that vision.

In a book he wrote after the war, senior OSS officer Allen Dulles, who later became CIA director, suggested,

> An intelligence officer in the field is supposed to keep his home office informed of what he is doing. That is quite true, but with some reservations, as he may overdue it. If, for example, he tells too much or asks too often for instructions, he is likely to get some he doesn't relish, and what is worse, he may well find headquarters trying to take over the whole conduct of the operation. Only a man on the spot can really pass judgment on the details as contrasted with the policy decisions which, of course, belong to the boss at headquarters.[31]

Smith, who quoted the paragraph above in his book, reaches the logical conclusion that the fact that such a "sedate and mature civilian intelligence operator like Allen Dulles" agreed with Donovan's style proves that the drive for operational autonomy in the OSS which created the organizational chaos, "was no fluke of erratical behavior, nor even a sign of youthful exuberance" but the "normal" way of doing things in the OSS.[32] Smith is quite right. Nonehteless, what he sees as organizational chaos was actually a disinformational smoke screen carefully conceived by Donovan, Dulles, and their CFR masters as a way to cover the true job of the OSS.

Contrary to the prevalent myth, the OSS was not an intelligence agency working for the benefit of the American public. Actually it was the conspirators' fifth column infiltrated into the U.S. armed forces to sabotage the efforts of true patriots like Patton to destroy the Nazi German war machine and win the war as soon as possible to save the lives of American soldiers.

Still, the CFR conspirators had other plans. Forced to fight the Nazi war machine because the monster they had contributed to create had turned into a Frankenstein's monster, their secret plan was to substitute it with another monster they also had created: Soviet Russia.

It seems that the OSS's main mission was to prevent the American military from winning the war too quickly and capture Nazi war criminals before the OSS provided ways for them to escape.[33] Their secondary mission was to make favorable conditions for the Soviets to get control over most of Eastern Europe. This perhaps explains why leftists and outright communist militants so extensively composed the OSS.

But there were some obstacles in the path of their plan. Despite the fact that the CFR conspirators controlled a few senior Army officers like Eisenhower, Marshall and Ridgway, most of them were true American patriots who firmly believed that their mission was defeating the Nazis. Unfortunately, they were wrong.

They ignored that the true goal of the war was protecting the conspirators' investments in Germany and allowing top Nazi criminals to escape justice.

At the time, not all ranking members of the U.S. military were under the control of the CFR conspirators, and Donovan immediately won several enemies, among them Major General George V. Strong, chief of the Army's G-2, who openly expressed his lack of confidence in the new organization and proceeded to set up his own competing clandestine intelligence service.[34] Another enemy, probably more powerful than Gen. Strong, was J. Edgar Hoover, the director of the Federal Bureau of Investigation. The FBI was the government agency responsible for counterespionage, and Hoover, who had been doing a good job, was protecting his turf.

While most of the American military men were risking their lives fighting what they considered a just war for the noble purpose of liberating Europe from the Nazi scourge, the conspirators' secret army, the OSS, was working in the shadows to protect the conspirators' interests in Germany and helping high rank Nazi leaders escape to South America with the help of the Vatican. And Donovan and his OSS men were there, not only to protect the Nazis, but also to keep an eye on loyal American officers to guarantee that they could not accomplish too early what they considered their main war mission: defeating the Nazis.

The fact that some OSS members were also true American patriots who firmly believed their main role was fighting the Nazis is irrelevant. They had been recruited under a false flag and, wittingly or unwittingly, were helping American pro-Nazis to help the Nazi thugs avoid paying for their war crimes.

Since the beginning of the war, the Rockefellers' Standard Oil had been supplying through North Africa the gasoline the Nazi war machine needed so badly. However, after the Allied invasion of North Africa, Standard Oil was no longer able to supply their Nazi friends with oil through that route. Standard Oil then began shipping oil to the Nazis through the neutral countries of Spain and Switzerland. Therefore, it is not a coincidence that most OSS officers in Spain and Switzerland had close links to Standard Oil.

A State Department memorandum dated August 1943 shows that trade had been authorized between a Standard Oil subsidiary in Venezuela, the Creole Petroleum Co., and a firm in Aruba. Eventually the Venezuelan oil was shipped to Spain and ended up in Germany.[35] The conspirators-controlled mainstream press willfully participated in the betrayal by keeping these transactions hidden from the American people who, at the time, were making long lines at the gas stations without complaining because they knew that American military men were in need of gas. They didn't know, however, that more gasoline was going to the Nazis via Spain and Switzerland than to the American troops.[36]

It is not a coincidence that secret CFR agent William Donovan had recruited most of his OSS officers from members of the very wealthy families whose companies were supplying the Nazis. Among the most notorious were Andrew Mellon's son Paul. Also, OSS chief in London, David Bruce, the son of a U.S. senator and millionaire, was married to Paul Mellon's sister, Aisla, herself a millionaire. The

Mellons' ties to the Nazis were well known.

J.P. Morgan's sons Junius and Henry also joined the OSS and had important positions in the organization. The Vanderbilts and the Duponts also allowed some of their scions to join the OSS to keep a protective eye on their family's businesses with the Nazis. Author Harris Smith mentions that only the Rockefellers were conspicuously absent from the OSS, but Nelson was already busy doing his own spy business in Latin America as Coordinator of Inter-American Affairs.[37] As a former Wall Street lawyer, Donovan himself had ties to I.G. Farben, one of the main German corporations linked to the Nazis.

Despite Donovan's apparent openness to fill the lower ranks of the OSS with lefties and communists, corporations like J. Walter Thompson, Paramount Pictures, and Goldman, Sachs had loaned many of its senior executive officers. And Standard Oil Company generously provided some of its trusted men, now transmogrified into OSS officers, to watch in Spain and Switzerland that gasoline shipments to Nazi Germany went unmolested. [38] On his part, Allen Dulles kept himself busy keeping hidden the close connections, up to shared ownership, between American and Nazi corporations.[39]

Since the very creation of the OSS, Donovan was criticized by his tendency to hire leftists, fellow travelers and outright militant communists. Donovan dismissed these criticisms by insisting that the sole objective of his organization was defeating the Axis powers. "I'd put Stalin on the OSS payroll if I thought it would help us defeat Hitler," he told one of his assistants.[40] The evidence, however, shows that, for some reason, the OSS seemed to have a soft spot for Communists. Donovan himself was known for saying that political leftists were among the most valiant OSS field officers in his espionage and sabotage branches.[41] His most trusted aide, Duncan Lee, was later found to have been a KGB spy all the time.[42]

On one occasion, FBI Director J. Edgar Hoover's presented Donovan with dossiers containing factual evidence showing that three OSS employees had fought with the Abraham Lincoln Brigade during the Spanish Civil war and were affiliated with the Communist Party. When Hoover demanded their separation from the organization, Donovan dismissed the issue by answering, "I know they are Communists; that's why I hired them."[43]

It would be a mistake, however, to conclude that Donovan himself had any sympathy for leftists or communists. Following a policy carefully planned at the Harold Pratt House, the General was using leftists and communists as unwitting tools in preparation for the coming Cold War. Though in theory the OSS was simply an intelligence agency, it played an important role in helping the CFR conspirators implement their foreign policy decisions. As author R. Harris Smith noticed, the OSS was fully under the control of the CFR conspirators,

> While Donovan diligently sought left-wing intellectuals and activists for the operational and research branches of the OSS, he saw no incongruity in appointing corporate attorneys and business executives as OSS administrators. [44]

The Assassination of General Patton

Donovan himself committed the final act of OSS treachery when, following the conspirators' orders, he ordered the assassination of a true war hero: General George S. Patton.[45]

General Patton died in a hospital in Heidelberg, Germany, on December 21, 1945, allegedly due to complications of a broken neck that he sustained eleven days earlier in a minor automobile accident near Mannheim. Immediately after his death, rumors of foul play and conspiracy surrounded the circumstances of the accident.

From the day of his death to the present, many have asked how a man of Patton's stature could die so commonly and uncharacteristically in an auto accident where both vehicles weren't moving faster than twenty miles per hour. Suspicion was cast on all those who Patton had offended, and there were many —among them generals Montgomery, Eisenhower and Bedell Smith, and even Presidents Roosevelt and Truman.

In his 2008 book *Target Patton*, author Robert Wilcox shows abundant circumstantial evidence indicating that an OSS officer following Donovan's direct orders assassinated Patton. Still, Wilcox expresses his belief that the officer who carried out the assassination orders apparently was not a traitor, but a war hero[46] who was convinced that he was following lawful orders in the benefit of his country.[47]

The first actions the CFR conspirators took against Patton began long before the end of the war, when he tried to accomplish what he thought was his main military mission: defeating the Nazis. Patton, perhaps without waiting for approval from the Allied command, pushed his victorious Third Army right up to the outskirts of Berlin, in an effort to take the city before the Soviets arrived. But the traitorous CFR conspirators already had decided to let Stalin take control of Eastern Europe. They had calculated that half of Europe under Soviet control would be a good pretext to justify their new upcoming strategic PSYOP: the Cold War.

Therefore, they paralyzed Patton's Third Army, cutting his fuel and ammo lines, and eventually ordering him to retreat a hundred miles to await the arrival of the Red Army. As expected, Patton was incensed, and complained forcefully about what he saw as actions bordering on treason.

Most likely, the pretext used by the conspirators to justify the assassination of General Patton was that after the end of the war he had turned pro-Nazi. After some off-hand remarks to a reporter —most likely a set-up— Patton had already began being branded pro-Nazi in the mainstream press.[48] This notion has been advanced in several books as well as in the 1986 film *The Last Days of Patton*, starring George C. Scott. Nevertheless, there is some circumstantial evidence that disproves that accusation.

Patton's war record could hardly be described as pro-Nazi. On the contrary, he was probably the American whose actions caused the death or the largest number of Nazis. Had he been a true pro-Nazi, the CFR conspirators would have welcomed him. There is abundant evidence showing that Wall Street bankers and oil corporations collaborated with the Nazis before, during, and after WWII. But there was not much love left between Patton and the conspirators, which he openly criticized in the strongest terms. Consequently, the facts don't add up.

After the end of the war, Secretary of the Treasure Henry Morgenthau (CFR) pushed his so-called "Morgenthau Plan" —actually conceived at the Harold Pratt House and penned by CFR's secret agent Harry Dexter White. According to the Morgenthau Plan, Germany would be divided down the middle into eastern and western zones, its industrial machinery should be destroyed, and the country turned into a strictly agrarian economy —not too different from what the CFR conspirators are now doing to the U.S. President Roosevelt agreed in principle, and in February 1945, at the Yalta Conference, strove to follow the Morgenthau Plan. Patton strongly disagreed.

A few months later, when Truman became president after Roosevelt's death, CFR agent General Dwight Eisenhower, as commander in chief of the European forces, took some measures to begin enforcing Morgenthau's plan. But Truman was not a CFR member and, therefore, not fully under the CFR conspirators' control, and he disagreed. He believed that turning Germany into an agrarian society would leave the country open for Soviet conquest. Patton agreed with Truman, and began putting back low-level Nazis in office after the war.[49] So, if Patton was not following Morgenthau's plan it was because he was following orders from his Commander-in-Chief.

But there is something even more difficult to explain.

As I have shown in this book, the CFR conspirators played a cardinal role in bringing the Nazis to power, and kept helping the Nazi war machine even after the U.S. had declared war against Germany. This has been documented in detail in books like Charles Higham's *Trading with the Enemy*,[50] Antony Sutton's *Wall Street and the Rise of Hitler*[51] and, more recently, in Jim Marrs' *The Rise of the Fourth Reich*.[52] Moreover, the CFR conspirators, mostly with the help of their secret agents William Donovan and Allen Dulles, were instrumental in helping many senior Nazi war criminals escape to South America. Trough Project PAPERCLIP, they brought ex-Nazi scientist to work in America as well as recruited Wehrmacht General Reinhard Gehlen and many of his SS thugs to work for the CIA.

Therefore, it makes no sense that the same traitors who had been cutting deals with the Nazis behind the backs of the American people had ordered Patton's assassination because he was pro-Nazi. Logic indicates that, on the contrary, had Patton being a true pro-Nazi, the CFR conspirators would have greeted him with open arms. On the contrary, the reasons why the conspirators ordered the assassination of General Patton were quite different.

After the D-Day invasion in Normandy, on June 6, 1944, Patton's Third Army cut through France like a hot knife through butter, covering almost five hundred miles, from Brest to Verdun. In a month, he had liberated most of France north of the Loire, and reached Metz, near the German border, in August. At that precise moment a group of German Army colonels, speaking on behalf of the Army Generals in charge of that sector of the front, came to Patton and offered his troops access through a bridge across the Rhine so that they could race to Berlin before the Red Army got there. According to the officers, the German army would not oppose Patton's advance.

Patton informed the Allied Command in London about the opportunity and prepared to move the Third Army across the Rhine up to Berlin. To this end, he asked the Allied Command to move all available troops in Normandy and England to start moving towards Metz as soon as possible. But, as soon as CFR secret agent General Dwight Eisenhower got the news, the Supreme Allied Command Headquarters ordered to stop all preparations and troop movements towards Metz and diverted the troops toward Paris, which had already fallen to the allies some weeks earlier.

When he got his new orders Patton got so furious that he said he would not stop the Third Army, and would go ahead with his plan. Moreover, smelling a rat, he demanded clarification of the new orders and their purpose. Then, to Patton's utter surprise, the Supreme Allied Command in London ordered the fuel and ammunition depots in Cherbourg and Normandy to stop all deliveries to Patton's Third Army, stopping it in its tracks.[53] The failure of Patton's Third Army to advance to Berlin resulted in prolonging the war for more than a year, which caused the U.S. Army the unnecessary deaths of many men.

Patton was enraged, because he believed Eisenhower's orders wrongly had prevented him from closing the so-called Falaise Gap in the autumn of 1944, allowing hundreds of thousands of German troops to escape and return to fight again. This led to the deaths of thousands of Americans during the German winter counter-offensive that became known as the Battle of the Bulge.[54] Of the close to a million casualties the Allied forces suffered in Europe, almost three-quarters happened after Patton's Third Army was stopped in its tracks.[55] Many millions more died as a result of military action and in the Nazi concentration camps in the last eight months of the war.[56]

If the Third Army had not being sabotaged by its own command, Patton would have taken Germany from the West earlier, and probably most of Eastern Europe. This would have drawn a different post-War map, without the Soviets projecting their sphere of influence so far into the heart of Europe. But the CFR agents in the U.S. military betrayed Patton and his courageous Third Army men.

Patton was furious and openly criticized his superiors for what he suspected was treason. After the end of the war, he expressed his intentions of using his political contacts and influence to push for the opening of an investigation of the events. Unfortunately, he died in an unexpected traffic accident in Germany, or so tells the official story. But many people suspected that Patton had been assassinated.

When Patton opposed the application of the Morgenthau Plan in his sector of occupation, he had a run-in with another general of higher rank, General Dwight Eisenhower. It is well known that they had heated debates about how the civilian population of Germany was to be treated. After realizing that they could not suborn, compromise or control him, the CFR conspirators sentenced Patton to death.

One day a military truck ran into Patton's car in what seemed like a very strange accident. General Patton's death, in any event, was extremely opportune. Patton had told some of his close friends that he was thinking of moving to the United States, where he was going to denounce publicly what was taking place in Germany. But he didn't have time. He had clashed with too many important people.

At Yalta, the CFR conspirators had agreed that the Soviets would be the first to enter the German capital. Patton wanted to prevent the Vandal-like entrance of the Red Army into the capital of the Reich, and made an enemy of Eisenhower. A month before, he could have entered Prague, but was also detained by Eisenhower, leaving him nailed to the ground by an order.

Patton's difficulties with his military commander over the occupation of Germany were so great that Eisenhower indecorously stripped him of his position as Commander of the Third Army, and stuck him with the command of a secondary unit. Patton knew he was in danger of being assassinated and confided as much to his family and close friends. The conspirators feared him because of his prestige —he was the most renowned American General, while Eisenhower was nothing more than a political general— and his words could alert the public and other honest Army officers to the reality of what was happening in Germany.

Thus, the accident was set up, which was not by any means the first. On the 21st of April 1945, Patton was flying to General Headquarters of the Third Army in Feldfield (England) when his airplane was attacked by what was assumed to be a German fighter-bomber, but it turned out to be a Spitfire piloted by an "inexpert" Polish pilot. Patton's plane was shot up, but was miraculously able to land. On May 3rd, some days before the end of the war, an ox-drawn cart charged Patton's jeep, and he suffered light injuries.

The collision with the truck occurred on October 13, 1945. However, when Patton appeared to be getting better from the accident, he had a "heart attack." The fact, however, is that after October 13 only the doctors saw Patton, holding him virtually incommunicado by forbidding any other persons to visit him.

For many years, the possibility that his own comrades had assassinated Patton has been the motive of speculation. More recently, however, the suspicions seem to have been proved true. In his book *Target Patton*,[57] military historian Robert Wilcox provides a wealth of information proving that the death of General Patton was not accidental, and pointing to OSS chief, Gen. William Donovan, a secret CFR agent, as the person who gave the order to assassinate Patton. According to Wilcox, OSS head General William Donovan ordered a highly decorated marksman called Douglas Bazata to silence Patton.

The most surprising thing about this story is that the essential facts reported by Wilcox are not new, because Bazata himself, perhaps tortured by his own conscience, already had told the story in detail, including the fact that Donovan had ordered the assassination.

On September 25, 1979, ex-OSS officer Douglas Bazata told the whole story in front of 450 invited guests, some of them ex-members of the OSS, in the Hilton Hotel in Washington, D.C. According to Bazata,

> For diverse political reasons, many extremely high-ranking persons hated Patton. I know who killed him. Because I am the one who was hired to do it. Ten thousand dollars. General William Donovan himself, director of the O.S.S, entrusted me with the mission. I set up the accident. Since he didn't die in the accident, he was kept in isolation in the hospital, where he was killed with an injection.

When asked why he had decided to go public after so many years, he answered that he "was in poor health and wanted the American people to know the truth." Bazata's confession was published in a minor, small circulation newspaper.[58]

In 1985, Ralph Epperson quoted the newspaper article in some detail in his book *The Unseen Hand*.[59] So, the fact that Patton had been assassinated by the OSS was not a deep secret since 1979. Nevertheless, the CFR-controlled mainstream media never reported it.

So much for freedom of the press in America.

Unfortunately, however, Wilcox apparently concluded that Donovan's actions had a personal motivation. He asks, "Why was Donovan so pro-Soviet?," "Might he have had some secret agenda?" But, unknowingly, at the very beginning of his book Wilcox himself provides the clue to the true motives of Patton's enemies: Patton had told some trusted aides,

> … that he was going to resign —not retire as was normal for an exiting officer in order to retain pension and benefits— but resign so he would have no army restraints. He was independently wealthy and did not need the pension or benefits. He would then be free to speak his mind and give his version of the war and what had happened to him —the truth as he saw it. And his side would be a blockbuster. He knew secrets and had revelations, he said, he was sure would "make big headlines."[60]

Of course, the conspirators realized that they could not run the risk of allowing Patton, a true American hero who gloried in the nickname "Old Blood and Guts," to go public and destroy their carefully conceived plans. Therefore, following their standard operating procedure, they ordered his assassination.

But assassinating General Patton, helping Nazi leaders escape justice and facilitating the Soviet's taking control of Eastern Europe were not the only criminal actions performed by Donovan and his OSS men. The OSS was the conspirator's tool to test PSYWAR techniques they had developed and used later to wage psychological warfare operations against the American people and other peoples around the world.

Chapter 5

The National Security Act, the CIA and the Creation of Artificial Insecurity

Since love and fear can hardly exist together, if we must choose between them, it is far safer to be feared than loved.
— Niccolo Machiavelli, *The Prince*, 1513.

On July 26, 1947, President Harry S. Truman signed into law the National Security Act establishing the National Security Council (NSC). It also created the Central Intelligence Agency as well as the Secretary of Defense, the Joints Chiefs of Staff and a separate Air Force branch of the military. This marked the official beginning of the Cold War, an artificial creation of the CFR conspirators.[1]

The NSC was allegedly created to manage the bloated foreign policy, military and intelligence apparatus of the U.S. government. Nevertheless, the National Security Act, like most important U.S. Government documents, had not been written at the White House but at the Harold Pratt House in Manhattan, headquarters of the CFR. Given the fact that at the time some American presidents were not fully under the conspirators' control, its true purpose was to create a shadow organization whose members, acting as blinders, controlled the presidents by controlling the information reaching them. It is not a coincidence that, since its creation, most National Security Council members have been secret CFR agents.

The National Security Act of 1947 and the Origins of the National Security Council

According to the official history, it was mainly dissatisfaction with Roosevelt's decision-making processes that lead to the creation of the National Security Council (NSC). Its creation, the official story goes, was a key initiative of President Harry S. Truman, who had assumed office in April 1945. Truman had long sought to unify the armed forces into one Cabinet department.

However, information now available shows a different picture. Following the conspirators' *modus operandi*, the National Security Act was the creation of CFR agents working in the shadows behind the backs of the American people to advance the conspirators' interests.

In this case two of them, Navy Secretary James V. Forrestal and his former business colleague Ferdinand Eberstadt, who had served as vice chairman of the War Production Board, were commissioned to study the effects of the unification of national security activities and to recommend a government organization that would be most effective in protecting the country.[2] The subsequent Eberstadt Report (actually a CFR Report) envisioned a National Security Council chaired by the President (or, in his absence, the vice President), which would include the four service secretaries, the secretary of state, and the chairman of a board to coordinate allocation of resources.[3] This approach, however, drew criticism from non CFR-controlled people as being incompatible with the concept of the president as chief executive under the Constitution. According to one scholar, Eberstadt was trying to modify the Presidency as an institution[4] —which was exactly what the CFR conspirators were trying to do.

As a result of the Eberstadt Report, in December 1945 President Truman sent a special message to Congress, requesting a statute to establish a single department of national defense and a single chief of staff, but without mentioning the creation of a national security council. Truman, not fully under the conspirators' control, feared that any way the president would be bound by the council consensus would infringe on his constitutional powers.

Finally, after several months of negotiations, the new national security legislation was enacted in July as the National Security Act of 1947. In addition to establishing the CIA, it created the NSC, which included the president, the secretary of state, the new secretary of defense, the secretaries of the military departments, and the chairman of the new National Security Resources Board.[5] Other officials who had been confirmed by the Senate could be added as NSC members by the president from time to time. According to the act, the responsibility of the NSC was:

> To advise the President with respect to the integration of domestic, foreign, and military policies relating to the national security so as to enable the military services and the other departments and agencies of the Government to cooperate more effectively in matters involving the national security.[6]

The National Security Act gave the National Security Council just advisory, not executive powers. Even more important, it didn't give the newly created CIA authority to carry on covert operations abroad. However, just a few months later, on December 1947, CFR agents in the National Security Council secretly wrote directive NSC 4-A, making the Director of Central Intelligence responsible for psychological warfare.

Then, less than a year after it was created, CFR agents in the NSC pushed the envelope even further and illegally assumed executive powers. On June 18, 1948, the National Security Council produced NSC 10-2, a directive that superseded NSC 4-A and was kept secret from the American government and people for many long years. NSC 10-2 authorized the CIA to conduct not only psychological but also all types of covert operations.

Every once in a while some conspiracy theorist *aficionado* airs his suspicions that the CIA has fallen under the control of an evil, internal rogue cabal, that is using it to advance their own stingy monetary interests. This idea, however, is not new. It had been mentioned before, and further reinforced by Senator Frank Church (CFR), when, during the Congressional investigation he chaired to investigate the Agency's misbehavior, he called the CIA a "rogue elephant."[7]

But, unlike most conspiracy theories about September 11th, this one is totally false. There is no rogue faction controlling the CIA. Actually, since its very creation, the whole CIA has been a rogue organization that has nothing to do with the government of this country and has never worked for the people who foot the bill: the American taxpayers.

If there is a rogue group working inside the CIA, it is a disorganized one consisting of a small group of American patriots (or naïve fools if you wish), who, after being recruited under a false flag,[8] have suddenly realized that they had been working for the Agency year after year under the wrong impression that they were doing it for the benefit of their country and the American people.[9] Actually, the true and only one "rogue elephant" who has been doing all the evil things the CIA is blamed for, is the Council on Foreign Relations.

Furthermore, there is evidence that the National Security Council, like most of the aberrations created by the CFR conspirators, is a Rockefeller baby. On December 1955, Nelson Rockefeller decided to become the next president of the U.S. and resigned to his position as President Eisenhower's Assistant of Foreign Policy and as head of the secret "Forty Committee" in charge of overseeing the CIA's covert operations.

Just after sending his resignation, he also sent a two-page memorandum to the President in which he expressed his conviction that the normal approach of the secretary of state in control of foreign policy was not adequate at a time when the U.S. had become a global power. His recommendations to fix what he saw as a problem are quite revealing: Nelson suggested replacing the different cabinet agencies of the government with a sort of super government secretly acting behind the backs of the American people, responsible to a single man, the president.[10] Obviously, Nelson's idea was to become America's first dictator.

Nelson never achieved his dream. But with the creation of the National Security Council, American presidents got dictatorial powers. The only difference with traditional dictators all around the world is that the American ones are puppets under CFR control.

U.S. Presidents as CFR's Puppets

Beginning with Woodrow Wilson and up to Barack Obama, all American presidents, perhaps with a single exception,[11] have been placed in the White House by the CFR conspirators. Once there, the conspirators have manipulated them like puppets. Probably the most obvious example of a puppet president in recent times has been George W. Bush, but it seems that Obama is trying harder to break Bush's record.

When I say "puppets," I don't mean that they know or have ever been told, "From now on you will be our puppet. Do you agree?" Absolutely not. Things don't work this way in America. We are much more sophisticated. The methodology here is slightly different.

At some point in their political careers, politicians that have been proposed by CFR talent spotters as targets for recruitment and possible candidates for the presidency, are invited to a friendly meeting[12] where a group of nice, rich, powerful people ask them a lot of questions. If this group of conspirators decides that he/she is the right person they want to have as the next puppet acting as president of the United States, a few days after the meeting a "friend" approaches the target and persuades him to run for the highest office.

Of course, by the time he attends such a meeting, any intelligent, rational person would have sensed that he has been selected from above to be the president and will have to pay a price for it. But one must keep in mind that a necessary condition for becoming a politician is having an immense ego, and that there is no best blind than the one who doesn't want to see. Consequently, a necessary condition to be tapped by the CFR conspirators to become the next president of the U.S. is having an immense, hypertrophied ego, Wilson style.[13]

So, unless he is a total cynic, very soon after having been "elected" by the CFR conspirators, the candidate, now turned into president-elect as the result of a "managed" election PSYOP,[14] convinces himself that he is the cleverest man on earth, that he had been elected by a majority of votes because the American people love him, and that he is actually the true president of the United States and can use at his own will the power associated with the presidency.

Yet, the presidency of the United States is one of the most complex and demanding jobs, and very soon the newcomer realizes that, despite his preconceptions, he knows nothing about how to govern the country. Luckily, however, there are experienced, knowledgeable, friendly people around him eager to help. These are the people who "suggest" him what to do. He ignores, however, that most of them are secret agents working for very the same conspirators who put him in the Oval Office.

Some American presidents, however, eventually discover the ruse and, usually at the end of their term, show their frustration by expressing some criticism of their puppet-masters and their anti-American policies. This was the case of Woodrow Wilson, when he realized he had been a puppet in the hands of his controller, Col. Edward Mandell House. This was also the case of Eisenhower mentioning the "military-industrial complex" in his farewell address.

This group of "experts" that has surrounded the U.S. presidents with a smoke screen of disinformation had existed for many years and had been called different names: "The Brain Trust, "The Wise Men,"[15] etc. After the passage of the National Security Act of 1947, however, this group of professional disinformers secretly working for the CFR conspirators was made official under the name of "National Security Council," whose members a sycophantic author and CFR secret agent has called, the people "running the world."[16]

The National Security Council: a Key Tool of the CFR Conspirators

The National Security Council was the first step in the creation of an aberration known as the national security state. Soon after its creation, it became an unaccountable power on its own bringing only insecurity to the American people.

The National Security Council is a key element in understanding how the CFR conspirators indirectly control the U.S. government. It is the visible head of the conspirators' fifth column infiltrated inside the U.S. government. Though they have taken an oath of allegiance to defend the U.S. Constitution, NSC members' true allegiance is to the CFR conspirators. This has been recently confirmed by one of them.

On February 8, 2009, at the 45th Munich Conference on Security Policy at the Hotel Bayerischer Hof, Obama's NSC advisor General James L. Jones,[17] stated:

> Thank you for that wonderful tribute to Henry Kissinger yesterday. Congratulations. As the most recent National Security Advisor of the United States, I take my daily orders from Dr. Kissinger, filtered down through General Brent Scowcroft and Sandy Berger, who is also here. We have a chain of command in the National Security Council that exists today.[18]

So, in his own words, General Jones destroyed the myth that the NSC (and the CIA) are tools in the hands of the President. Jones' line of command has nothing to do with the White House, but goes directly through CFR agents Kissinger, Scowcroft and Berger to the Harold Pratt House in Manhattan, the true seat of power in this country.

In 1947, CFR secret agents infiltrated into the U.S. government pushed the creation of the National Security Act, which created the National Security Council and the Central Intelligence Agency, allegedly as a tool to manage the military, intelligence, and foreign policy areas of the U.S. government. But, soon after it was created, the CFR agents infiltrated in the National Security Council changed it into a tool to control the information reaching the eyes and ears of the Presidents, thus creating a smoke screen of disinformation around them.

Since the end of the Second World War, the CFR conspirators through their secret agents in the NSC have been putting blinders on American Presidents, feeding them disinformation and "suggesting" to them what decisions they should make. This guarantees that their most important policy decisions are the ones already made at the Harold Pratt House.

To make things even easier for them, the CFR conspirators created the concept of President's plausible denial—a euphemism for President's ignorance. Soon after, they expanded the concept with the notion that "what the President doesn't know can't hurt him politically." This meant that the CFR conspirators, through their agents infiltrated in the White House, gave themselves a free hand in planning and carrying out American foreign policy with as little consultation as possible with the incumbent President.

This curtain of disinformation surrounding the U.S. presidents explains why, even the ones who were not CFR members, have unknowingly advanced the goals of the CFR conspirators. Most, if not all, of the important decisions taken by American presidents about things they knew next to nothing, have already been taken at the Harold Pratt House in Manhattan, and later carefully implanted in the president's brains. These were the cases, i.e., of Truman ordering to drop atomic bombs on two Japanese cities where no military facility was located (actually Henry Stimson, Karl Compton and other CFR members convinced Truman to order the dropping of the bombs), Kennedy making the fateful decision of changing the landing place of the Cuban invasion from Trinidad to the Bay of Pigs, which caused the failure of the operation (CFR secret agents McGeorge Bundy and Adlai Stevenson persuaded Kennedy to do so), and Nixon taking the U.S. dollar off the gold standard (CFR agent Paul Volcker persuaded him to do it).

The same thing happened to Johnson when the very same hawks in the NSC who had been pushing him hard to escalate the war in Vietnam, following the conspirators' orders, transformed themselves overnight into doves asking Johnson to end the war immediately. Johnson was so appalled by the treason that he decided not to run for reelection.

In their naiveté, however, at some time in their mandate a few American presidents have decided to stop paying attention to the CFR agents surrounding him and ignore their advice. Soon after, they have paid dearly for their mistake. The most notable case was President Kennedy.

Perhaps the only exception in this series of American presidents "elected" by the CFR conspirators is John F. Kennedy, who came to be elected president thanks to his father's money and links to the Chicago Mafia. The conspirators simply accepted him because they though he was too young and inexperienced, his only interest was chasing girls and, therefore, easy to handle. But, particularly after the Bay of Pigs, Kennedy woke up to the reality surrounding him and began seen many things he had not noticed before, and he didn't like them. Unfortunately, he underestimated the guile and evil nature of his powerful enemies.

One of the fateful steps taken by Kennedy after he was sworn as president was to scrap the NSC mechanism. Being statutory, he could not abolish the NSC unilaterally, but he simply ignored it.[19] Then, after the Bay of Pigs debacle —which, as I will show later, actually was a very successful PSYOP carried out by the CFR conspirators—, he fired CIA Director Allen Dulles, a senior CFR conspirator, and told some close friends that he wanted to split the CIA "into a thousand pieces and scatter [it] to the winds."[20]

Finally, he made what were probably his two biggest mistakes.

The first one was authorizing the Secretary of the Treasury to issue currency backed by the U.S. Treasury Department, not the Federal Reserve Bank. One of the first measures taken by President Lyndon Johnson after he was sworn was to order the recall and destruction of the bills.[21]

His second biggest mistake was that, contrary to his CFR advisors' opinion, he began taking measures to end the war in Vietnam. On October 11, 1963, he ordered McGeorge Bundy to implement plans to withdraw 1,000 U.S. military personnel by the end of the year.[22] This was believed to be the first step to a complete withdrawal of American troops from Vietnam.

After Kennedy was assassinated, his Vietnam policy of withdrawing was dismantled, and this reverse happened extremely fast. Perhaps the reason for the haste was that, just two days before Kennedy was assassinated, Dean Rusk (CFR), Robert McNamara (CFR), McGeorge Bundy (CFR) and U.S. Ambassador to South Vietnam Henry Cabot Lodge (CFR), had secretly met in Honolulu to discuss Kennedy's new policy of troops withdrawal. Then, two days after the assassination, most of those who attended the meeting in Honolulu and CIA Director John McCone (CFR) had an emergency meeting with Lyndon Johnson, after which Kennedy's policy of withdrawal was quickly reversed.

Last, but not least, Kennedy conspired with the CIA to kill his archenemy, Fidel Castro —which shows that JFK not only was a person of low moral and ethical principles, but also a fool. Trying to use the CIA to kill Castro was perhaps the most stupid thing he did in his life. So, it was a sort of poetic justice that, following the conspirators' orders, the CIA, perhaps with Castro's help, terminated Kennedy with extreme prejudice.[23]

Firing Allen Dulles and mentioning that he wanted to smash the CIA into a thousand pieces was a slap in the Rockefellers' face, and JFK knew it.[24] That was his not-so-subtle way of telling them that he was the one in command —or so he believed. Ignoring the NSC, and later creating his own Ex-Comm (Executive Committee of the NSC) during the missile crisis was another direct attack on the Rockefeller's power. Finally, just the fact that he signed Executive Order # 11110, authorizing the U.S. Treasury Department to print silver certificates, that is, real money, not fiat certificates like the ones printed by the Federal Reserve Bank, and ordering the withdrawal of troops from Vietnam, were serious transgressions the CFR conspirators would never tolerate. This explains why the one who got smashed was not the CIA, but John F. Kennedy.

The bottom line is that Kennedy was killed because he believed that he was the president of the United States and tried to act as a president is supposed to do: listening to his advisors but making his own decisions. But this was something the conspirators were not going to allow him to do.

Many answers have been provided to the question: Who killed Kennedy? They range from the logical and probable to the incredible and the bizarre —with the Warren report theory of the lone madman placed at the incredible side of the spectrum. I am not going to try to provide another answer to the enigma. As a matter of fact, I think that the relevant question is not actually who killed Kennedy, but why nobody tried to kill him at least one year before.

If you read what has been published about both John and Robert Kennedy, even including the rosy stories written by court historians like Arthur Schlesinger and friends like Ben Bradlee and Ted Sorensen, you arrive at the conclusion that the Kennedy brothers were total jerks. There is abundant information available showing the total lack of respect for the rule of law prevailing in the Kennedy administration. As author Henry Hurt pointed out, there was a wholesale abandonment of morality in Kennedy's Camelot, and it reached a point where murder was acceptable.[25]

Many people had enough reasons for wanting to kill President Kennedy. At the top of the list were the anti-Castro Cubans in the U.S., FBI director J. Edgar Hoover, some important people at the CIA, Fidel Castro, the Mafia, and the South Vietnamese, just to mention a few.

But, as several authors have shown, everything indicates that the main suspects for the assassination of President Kennedy were the Wall Street bankers and oil magnates whose interest JFK had been attacking.[26] According to Professor Donald Gibson, there is evidence showing that from an unwitting tool of the CFR conspirators, after the Bay of Pigs JFK turned into one of Wall Street's strongest enemies.[27]

Moreover, perhaps Kennedy's motives may have not being only political. There have always been bad blood between the Kennedys and the Rockefellers —the Kennedy's envied if not the Rockefeller's money, their power.[28] Yet, history has shown that the Kennedys have never been a match to the Rockefellers' cunning.

Robert Kennedy mentioned to some friends that, if elected president, he would reopen the investigation of his brother's assassination. Soon after, another lone nut killed him. A year later, Ted Kennedy had a weird accident, after which he became an alcoholic and a pathetic Rockefeller lap dog. Many years later, John F. Kennedy, Jr., the scared little boy who saluted in attention his father's casket, now turned into a successful magazine editor, mentioned to some friend his intentions to run for the presidency and, if elected, to open the case of his father's assassination. Soon after, he died when the plane he was flying malfunctioned and crashed in the waters of Martha's Vineyard.[29]

Nevertheless, JFK was not the only American president whose career has been cut short after failing to follow the CFR conspirators' orders. At some time during his tenure, Richard Nixon wrongly concluded that he was the one in command. Soon after, he was removed through a disguised coup d'ètat in which CFR agents Alexander Haig and Henry Kissinger played important roles.

Why the CIA?

There is a question that may come to mind: Why did the conspirators need a new intelligence agency, the CIA, when they already had an excellent one, the CFR?

The answer is relatively simple: they didn't need another *intelligence* agency, and did not create a new one, because, as I explained above, the CIA has never been an intelligence agency in the true sense of the word —at least, not for the CFR conspirators who created it. So, again, why did they create the CIA if not to profit from its intelligence gathering and analysis capabilities?

According to an anecdote, when Soviet leader Joseph Stalin was informed that the Vatican, after getting the news that the Red Army had surrounded Berlin with an iron fist, had declared war against Nazi German, he laughed heartily and asked: "How many divisions does the Pope have?"

Like the Vatican, the Wall Street bankers and oil magnates had enormous economic power to buy supporters and critics, but they also needed physical power to intimidate the cowards and punish the rebels. Consequently, since late in the 19th century they began using the U.S. armed forces as their military arm to enforce their policies. The long list of American military interventions all around the world, beginning with the Cuban-Spanish-American war,[30] marked the beginning of "American imperialism," —or, more properly, "Wall Street imperialism." These military interventions on behalf of the Wall Street Mafia, which have gained the U.S. so many enemies around the world, were the direct result of this raw deal for the American people.

CFR agent Donald Rumsfeld is known to often quote a line from Al Capone: "You will get more with a kind word and a gun than with a kind word alone." It seems that the tough talk of the Chicago mobster closely resembles the guiding philosophy of the Wall Street Mafia: "You will get more with a lie and an army than with a lie alone."

A perfunctory analysis of American military interventions all around the world since the mid-1800s, shows how the Wall Street and oil conspirators have used the U.S. army and navy, particularly the Marines, to carry out their Mafia-like criminal actions against other peoples and governments.[31]

U.S. Military Interventions 1890-1946 [32]

Country	Dates	Forces	Comments
SOUTH DAKOTA	1890 (-?)	Troops	300 Lakota Indians massacred.
ARGENTINA	1890	Troops	Buenos Aires interests protected.
CHILE	1891	Troops	Marines clash with nationalist rebels.
HAITI	1891	Troops	Black revolt on Navassa defeated.
IDAHO	1892	Troops	Army suppresses silver miners' strike.
HAWAII	1893 (-?)	Naval, troops	Independent kingdom annexed.
CHICAGO	1894	Troops	Breaking of rail strike, 34 killed.
NICARAGUA	1894	Troops	Month-long occupation of Bluefields.
CHINA	1894-95	Naval, troops	Marines land in Sino-Japanese War
KOREA	1894-96	Troops	Marines kept in Seoul during war.
PANAMA	1895	Troops, naval	Marines land in Colombian province.
NICARAGUA	1896	Troops	Marines land in port of Corinto.
CHINA	1898-1900	Troops	Boxer Rebellion fought.
PHILIPPINES	1898-1910 (-?)	Naval, troops	Seized from Spain, killed 600,000 .
CUBA	1898-1902 (-?)	Naval, troops	Seized from Spain.
PUERTO RICO	1898 (-?)	Naval, troops	Seized from Spain.
GUAM	1898 (-?)	Naval, troops	Seized from Spain, still use as base.
MINNESOTA	1898 (-?)	Troops	Army battles Chippewa at Leech Lake.
NICARAGUA	1898	Troops	Marines land at San Juan del Sur.
SAMOA	1899 (-?)	Troops	Battle over succession to throne.
NICARAGUA	1899	Troops	Marines land at port of Bluefields.
IDAHO	1899-1901	Troops	Army occupies Coeur d'Alene region.
OKLAHOMA	1901	Troops	Army battles Creek Indian revolt.
PANAMA	1901-14	Naval, troops	Annexed Canal Zone from Colombia.
HONDURAS	1903	Troops	Marines intervene in revolution.

DOMINICAN Rep.	1903-04	Troops	U.S. interests protected in Revolution.
KOREA	1904-05	Troops	Marines land in Russo-Japanese War.
CUBA	1906-09	Troops	Marines land in democratic election.
NICARAGUA	1907	Troops	Protectorate set-up.
HONDURAS	1907	Troops	Marines land.
PANAMA	1908	Troops	Marines intervene in election contest.
NICARAGUA	1910	Troops	Marines in Bluefields and Corinto.
HONDURAS	1911	Troops	U.S. interests protected in civil war.
CHINA	1911-41	Naval, troops	Continuous occupation with flare-ups.
CUBA	1912	Troops	U.S. interests protected in civil war.
PANAMA	1912	Troops	Marines land during heated election.
HONDURAS	1912	Troops	Marines land.
NICARAGUA	1912-33	Troops, bombing	10-year occupation, fought guerillas.
MEXICO	1913	Naval	Americans evacuated by Army.
DOMINICAN Rep.	1914	Naval	Fight with rebels over Santo Domingo.
COLORADO	1914	Troops	Breaking of miners' strike by Army.
MEXICO	1914-18	Naval, troops	Interventions against nationalists.
HAITI	1914-34	Troops, bombing	19-year occupation after revolts.
DOMINICAN Rep.	1916-24	Troops	8-year Marine occupation.
CUBA	1917-33	Troops	Military occupation.
WORLD WAR I	1917-18	Naval, troops	Ships sunk, fought Germany.
RUSSIA	1918-22	Naval, troops	Five landings to fight Bolsheviks
PANAMA	1918-20	Troops	U.S. "police duty" during unrest.
HONDURAS	1919	Troops	Marines land during elections..
YUGOSLAVIA	1919	Troops/Marines	Intervene in Dalmatia against Serbs.
GUATEMALA	1920	Troops	2-week intervention against unionists.
WEST VIRGINIA	1920-21	Troops, bombing	Army intervenes against mineworkers.
TURKEY	1922	Troops	Fought nationalists in Smyrna.
CHINA	1922-27	Naval, troops	Deployment during nationalist revolt.
HONDURAS	1924-25	Troops	Landed twice during election strife.
PANAMA	1925	Troops	Marines suppress general strike.
CHINA	1927-34	Troops	Marines stationed throughout country.
EL SALVADOR	1932	Naval	Warships send during revolt.
WASHINGTON DC	1932	Troops	Army stops WWI vet bonus protest.
WORLD WAR II	1941-45	Naval, troops,	Fought Japan, Italy and Germany.
DETROIT	1943	Troops	Army put down Black rebellion.
IRAN	1946	Nuclear threat	Soviet troops told to leave north.
YUGOSLAVIA	1946	Nuc. threat, naval	Response to shoot-down of U.S. plane.

Paradoxically, one the strongest critics of the Wall Street conspirators who used the U.S. armed forces, particularly the Marines, to advance their private interests was a military hero and a proud Marine himself: Brigadier General Smedley D. Butler.[33]

As Gen. Butler put it bluntly,

> War is a racket. It has always been. It is possibly the oldest, easily the most profitable, surely the most vicious. It is the only one international in scope. It is the only one in which the profits are reckoned in dollars and the losses in lives.
>
> A racket is best described, I believe, as something that is not what it seems to the majority of the people. Only a small "inside" group knows what is it about. It is conducted for the benefit of the very few, at the expense of the very many. Out of war a few people make huge fortunes.

> In the World War [he is referring to WWI] a mere handful garnered the profits of the conflict. At least 21,000 new millionaires and billionaires were made in the United States during the World War. That many admitted their huge blood gains in their income tax returns. How many other war millionaires falsified their tax returns no one knows.
>
> How many of these war millionaires shouldered a rifle? How many of them dug a trench? How many of them knew what it meant to go hungry in a rat-infested dugout? How many of them spent sleepless, frightened nights, ducking shells and shrapnel and machine gun bullets? How many of them parried a bayonet thrust of an enemy? How many of them were wounded or killed in battle?[34]

General Butler was right. The above list of U.S. military interventions since 1890 shows that just few parts of this planet have not experienced first hand the presence of American troops protecting the interests of Wall Street bankers and oil magnates.

But eventually the world changed, and it became more and more risky and problematic for the CFR conspirators to keep openly using the U.S. armed forces, particularly in Latin America, as the main tool to impose their will upon other peoples. The fact was acknowledged by secret CFR agent Franklin D. Roosevelt himself in one of his meetings with Winston Churchill during World War II, when he pointed out that open colonialism, as it had been practiced in the past, was no longer an appropriate option in the Caribbean.[35] This was not only because the Marines had become a worldwide symbol of American aggression and oppression, but also because a growing discontent among senior officers of the U.S. armed forces, not fully under the control of the conspirators, was making more difficult to continue openly using the American military for their nefarious purposes.

Still, the CFR conspirators needed an option short of the use of direct U.S. military action when coercion and intimidation alone cannot do the job. Consequently, perhaps following Sun Tzu's dictum that all warfare is based on deception, [36] the conspirators decided to create their own illegal private army. And the best way to create this army without alarming the American people and the world was by making it invisible. Therefore, they created it surreptitiously, keeping it hidden from public scrutiny under the cover of a legitimate U.S. government organization.

So, using their secret agents infiltrated in the U.S. government, in 1947 the conspirators forced down the throats of naive, or corrupt American politicians, the National Security Act, which created an organization they planned to use to fully exert their puppeteers' control over the American presidents: the National Security Council. And an important component of the National Security Act was the creation of a Central Intelligence Agency, which they never planned to use as an intelligence agency, but as a cover to hide their military arm, now in the form of covert operations.

The CIA: the Conspirators' Secret Military Arm

The CIA proved to be exactly the right type of organization the conspirators needed to help them accomplish their illicit purpose of conducting their pillage and plundering all around the world. In the first place, it was free, because the American taxpayers were paying for it. Secondly, thanks to the CIA's operational principles of secrecy, compartmentalization and need-to-know inherent to all intelligence services, it was relatively easy to hide its real activities from both the American public and non-CFR-controlled CIA employees who ignored the Agency's true goals.

CIA Director Allen Dulles himself recognized the fact when he wrote,

> An intelligence service is the ideal vehicle for a conspiracy. Its members can travel about at home and abroad under secret orders, and no questions are asked. Every scrap of paper in the files, its membership, its expenditure of funds, its contacts, even enemy contacts, are secret.[37]

Though Dulles was specifically talking about the German intelligence services, everything he said could be applied to the CIA or to any other intelligence service. The fact that the CIA is nothing but a conspiracy was also noticed by keen political analyst Michael Parenti. According to him,

> In most of its operations, the CIA is by definition a conspiracy, using covert operations and secret plans, many of which are of the most unsavory kind. What are covert operations if not conspiracies? At the same time, the CIA is an institution, a structural part of the national security state. In sum, the agency is an institutionalized conspiracy.[38]

But, despite their cleverness, the conspirators didn't fool everybody. Former CIA Director Admiral Stanfield Turner (not a CFR member), for one, suspected that perhaps compartmentalization had some secret, non-proper uses. In a book he wrote about his experiences as CIA Director, he said:

> I found the system of compartmentation eminently sensible. I couldn't help wondering, though, if it has been used deliberately to keep people from knowing what they properly needed to know.[39]

Nevertheless, the conspirators' ruse worked to perfection. A list of U.S. military interventions abroad from 1947 to 1990, shows that after the creation of the CIA in 1947 there is an appreciable shift from the use of open force by the U.S. military to CIA-controlled covert operations.

U.S. Interventions Abroad 1947-1990[40]

COUNTRY	Dates	Forces	Comments
URUGUAY	1947	Nuclear threat	Bombers deployed as show of strength.

GREECE	1947-49	**Covert op**	U.S. directs extreme-right in civil war.
GERMANY	1948	Air Force	Nuclear Threat. Berlin Airlift.
COLOMBIA	1948	**Covert Op**	Assassination of Gaitán and Bogotazo riots.
CHINA	1948-49	Troops/Marines	Evacuate Americans before Communist victory.
PHILIPPINES	1948-54	**Covert op**	CIA directs war against Huk Rebellion.
PUERTO RICO	1950	**Covert op**	Independence rebellion crushed in Ponce.
KOREA	1951-53	Troops, naval,	U.S./So. Korea fights China.
IRAN	1953	**Covert op**	CIA overthrows democracy, installs Shah.
VIETNAM	1954	Nuclear threat	French offered bombs to use against siege.
GUATEMALA	1954	**Covert op,**	CIA directs exile invasion
EGYPT	1956	Troops	Soviets told to keep out of Suez crisis;
LEBANON	1958	Troops, naval	Marine occupation against rebels.
IRAQ	1958	Nuclear threat	Iraq warned against invading Kuwait.
CHINA	1958	Nuclear threat	China told not to move on Taiwan isles.
PANAMA	1958	Troops	Flag protests erupt into confrontation.
VIETNAM	1960-75	Troops, naval,	Fought North Vietnam
CUBA	1961	**Covert op**	CIA-directed exile invasion, Bay of Pigs.
GERMANY	1961	Nuclear threat	Alert during Berlin Wall crisis.
LAOS	1962	**Covert op**	Military buildup during guerrilla war.
CUBA	1962	Naval	Blockade, missile crisis with Soviet Union.
IRAQ	1963	**Covert op**	CIA organizes coup that killed president
PANAMA	1964	Troops	Panamanians shot for urging canal's return.
INDONESIA	1965	**Covert op**	Million killed in CIA-assisted army coup.
DOMINICAN Rep	1965-66	Troops, bombing	Marines land during election campaign.
GUATEMALA	1966-67	**Covert op**	Green Berets intervene against rebels.
DETROIT	1967	Troops	Army battles African Americans, 43 killed.
U.S.	1968	Troops	After King shot; 21,000 soldiers in cities.
CAMBODIA	1969-75	Troops, naval	Up to 2 million killed in decade of bombing,
OMAN	1970	**Covert op**	U.S. directs Iranian marine invasion.
LAOS	1971-73	**Covert op,**	U.S. directs South Vietnamese invasion; "
SOUTH DAKOTA	1973	Troops	Army directs Wounded Knee siege of Lakotas.
MIDEAST	1973	Nuclear threat	World-wide alert during Mideast War.
CHILE	1973	**Covert op**	CIA-backed coup ousts president Allende.
CAMBODIA	1975	Troops, bombing	Gas captured ship, 28 die in copter crash.
ANGOLA	1976-92	**Covert op**	CIA assists South African-backed rebels.
IRAN	1980	Troops,	Raid to rescue Embassy hostages;
LIBYA	1981	Navy, Air Force	Two Libyan jets shot down in maneuvers.
EL SALVADOR	1981-92	**Covert op**	Advisors, overflights aid anti-rebel war,
NICARAGUA	1981-90	**Covert op**	CIA directs exile (Contra) invasions

As I mentioned above, when the CIA was created covert operations were not included among its functions and they were added surreptitiously just a few months later. Nevertheless, just five years after its creation the Agency had carried out major covert operations in forty-eight countries to influence the outcome of political and military events on behalf of its CFR masters.[41]

Ex-CIA Director Admiral Stanfield Turner observed,

> The CIA's covert activities had so increased in the 1950s and 1960s that some of them inevitably became public. Much of what leaked out, seriously alarmed the public and Congress. They did not condone all the activities in which the CIA had been involved.[42]

Turner also found out that,

> The majority of the espionage professionals, from I could see, believed

> that covert action had brought more harm and criticism to the CIA than useful return, and that it had seriously detracted from the Agency's primary role of collecting and evaluating intelligence.[43]

Admiral Turner also discovered that during the tenure of directors Allen Dulles, Richard Helms and William Colby, the CIA's espionage branch which included covert operations, had become dominant to the point that other branches feared being absorbed.[44] Turner didn't mention, though, a very important fact: Dulles, Helms, and Colby, were senior CFR secret agents infiltrated into the CIA to advance the conspirators' secret goals. Moreover, not being a trusted CFR secret agent, Admiral Turner seemingly ignored that the CIA's true primary role was not collecting and evaluating information and producing intelligence.

The NSC Illegally Authorizes the CIA to Conduct Covert Operations

Historically, the U.S. had never had an official permanent civilian central intelligence agency. The functions of intelligence and espionage were carried out by the State Department, the different branches of the armed forces, particularly the Navy, and the FBI. This explains why, after the end of the war, Truman disbanded the OSS and refused to hear Donovan's arguments favoring the creation of a central intelligence agency. It contributed to his decision the fact that rumors that Donovan was trying to create an American Gestapo had been leaked the press.

It is likely that Truman, who was malleable putty in the hands of the CFR conspirators, actually acted under pressure from J. Edgar Hoover. The FBI director, perhaps not fully acting out of patriotism, but just defending his turf, hated the OSS and strongly opposed its reincarnation in the form of a central intelligence agency.[45] And everybody, including the president, feared Hoover and his secret files he euphemistically called "biographical leverage." As head of the FBI, Hoover knew the closets where all the skeletons were hiding —sometimes literally— and kept detailed records of it.

But Hoover, who had his own skeletons in the closet,[46] finally caved in to the conspirators' pressures. So, Truman gave the green light, and the Congress passed the National Security Act of 1947 that established the National Security Council and the Central Intelligence Agency.

Like all important documents in the history of the U.S. since the beginning of the past century, the National Security Act, as well as Wilson's Fourteen Points, the League of Nations, the Federal Reserve Bank, the Federal Income Tax, the Lend Lease, the Containment Doctrine,[47] the Marshall Plan,[48] the Alliance for Progress,[49] FEMA, the nefarious Patriot Act and the Department of Homeland Security, up to Obama's Health Care plan, have been written by the CFR Conspirators at the Harold Pratt House in Manhattan and placed on the President's desk for him to sign.

Nevertheless, the National Security Act did not mention that the CIA could carry out covert operations. It was the National Security Council who on a series of secret intelligence directives bequeathed the authority to the newly created

Agency to conduct covert operations to the CIA behind the backs of the American public.

So, the first measure taken by he National Security Council, a legally created government organization pushed down the throats of the American people under the pretext of avoiding intelligence "surprises" like Pearl Harbor, was to pass, behind the backs of the American people and its representatives in the Congress, an illegal directive they had no legal power to pass —the NSC had no executive powers—, authorizing the CIA to conduct illegal covert operations.

The document that gave the beast its fangs, was National Security Directive NSC 10/2, dated June 18, 1948, written by CFR agent George Kennan. By it, a new semi-independent, highly secret organization was created within the CIA under the intentionally vague name of Office of Special Projects (OSP), and CFR agent Frank Wisner was appointed to head it. Soon after, the OSP was renamed with the even more innocuous name Office of Policy Coordination (OPC).[50] Author John Loftus found out that the Office of Policy Coordination was actually a secret CFR-controlled covert action department hidden from the American public and depending directly from Secretary of Defense James V. Forrestal, a CFR agent, and what Loftus calls "the Dulles [John Foster Dulles, a senior CFR agent] faction in the State Department."[51]

Given the fact that the conspirators didn't trust CIA's first Director Admiral Hillenkoetter (not a CFR member), they managed to take the OSP from the CIA's control and make Wisner report directly to CFR agent George Kennan at the State Department.[52] Hillenkoetter, however, was not satisfied with the deal, and asked the CIA's General Counsel Lawrence R. Houston for a legal opinion as to whether the Agency could carry out covert operations. Houston's response was that the National Security Act did not provide the CIA the legal authority to conduct covert operations.

The CFR conspirators had based their request to allow the CIA to carry covert operations in a diffuse provision of the Act, which mentioned that the CIA would carry out that type of operations as the NSC might order them "from time to time." But, after admitting the fact, Houston observed that the provision also added that such missions must be "related to intelligence" and he was of the opinion that covert operations had only the most tenuous relation to intelligence. Also, he added, Congress had specified that the CIA's main mission was to coordinate intelligence produced by other intelligence services.[53]

Houston was right. Moreover, allowing the organization in charge of collecting and evaluating information to produce usable intelligence to perform covert operations is tantamount to allow an accountant to perform an audit of his own work.

Nevertheless, disregarding all objections, CFR secret agents in the National Security Council pushed NSC 10/2, which gave the CIA *carte blanche* to carry out covert operations abroad through the OSP and later through the OPC.

NSC 10/2 determined that,

> The National Security Council, taking cognizance of the vicious covert activities of the USSR, its satellite countries and Communist groups to discredit and defeat the aims and activities of the United States and other Western powers, has determined that, in the interests of world peace and U.S. national security, the overt foreign activities of the U.S. government must be supplemented by covert operations.
>
> The Central Intelligence Agency is charged by the National Security Council with conducting espionage and counter-espionage operations abroad. It therefore seems desirable, for operational reasons, not to create a new agency for covert operations, but in time of peace to place the responsibility for them within the structure of the Central Intelligence Agency and correlate them with espionage and counter-espionage operations under the over-all control of the Director of Central Intelligence.
>
> Therefore, under the authority of Section 102(d)(5) of the national Security Act of 147, the National Security Council hereby directs that in time of peace:
>
> 4. A new office of Special Projects shall be created within the Central Intelligence Agency to plan and conduct covert operations; …
>
> . . . .
>
> 5. As used in this directive, "covert operations" are understood to be all activities (except as noted herein) which are conducted or sponsored by this government against hostile foreign states or groups or in support of friendly foreign sates or groups but which are so planned and conducted that any U.S. Government responsibility for them is not evident to unauthorized persons and that if uncovered the U.S. Government can plausibly disclaim any responsibility for them. Specifically, such operations shall include any covert activities related to: propaganda, economic warfare; preventive direct action, including sabotage, anti-sabotage, demolition and evacuation measures; subversion against hostile states, including assistance to underground resistance movements, guerrillas and refugee liberation groups, and support of indigenous anti-Communist elements in threatened countries of the free world.[54]

NSC 10/2 made no mention about assassination of foreign leaders and other people who opposed the conspirators' plans, but a letter written by a "consultant" included among the documents gives an idea of what they had in mind:

> You will recall that I mentioned that the local circumstances under which a given means might be used might suggest the technique to be used in that case. I think that gross divisions in presenting this subject might be (1) bodies left with no hope of the cause of death being determined by the most complete autopsy and chemical examination, (2) bodies left in such

> circumstances as to simulate accidental death, (3) bodies left in such circumstances as to simulate suicidal death, (4) bodies left with residua that simulate those caused by natural diseases.[55]

By creating NSC 10/2, which authorized the CIA to break the laws of this nation, the CFR agents infiltrated into the National Security Council who wrote and approved it under the pretext of protecting this country committed a major crime against America. They licensed a U.S. Government agency, whose job was to defend and protect the laws of the land as expressed in the Constitution, to break the law as they wished. NSC 10/2, actually authorized CIA officers to do whatever they wanted, except telling the truth or getting caught.

The OPC became the espionage and counter-intelligence branch of the Central Intelligence Agency. CFR agent Frank Wisner, the person the conspirators selected to run their Mafia-like organization, was given a free hand in creating a criminal organization. This initial capital sin molded the CIA's amoral ethos and has marked the behavior of the Agency all these years. But even a perfunctory look at the CIA's true origins show that its treasonous activities have never been by mistake, but by design.

Covert Operations: The CIA's True and Only Purpose

Like most important documents in the recent history of the United States, NSC 10/2 was written at the Harold Pratt House in Manhattan. It was the work of CFR agent George Kennan.[56] It mentions as a proven fact "the vicious covert activities of the USSR, its satellite countries and Communist groups to discredit and defeat the aims and activities of the United States and other Western powers." These alleged "vicious covert activities" of the Soviet Union were the justification the CFR conspirators gave to the American people, whose country was supposed to be the antithesis of the USSR, to allow the CIA to engage in vicious covert activities all around the world.

Some years later, ex-OSS officer and CFR agent Arthur Schlesinger, Jr., advanced the same idea in a 1967 article in *Foreign Affairs*, the CFR's disinformation organ. According to Schlesinger, the West was forced to act against the Soviet Union, mostly because Stalin was paranoid.

But, without falling into the Left's error of believing that the Soviet leaders were saints guided by high moral principles, there is ample evidence pointing to the fact that the Cold War, like the Soviet Union itself, was the CFR conspirator's baby, conceived and nurtured[57] as a credible threat to maintain the American people in a constant state of fear. This threat justified the arms race as the result of the confrontation with the artificially created enemy. It is also a known fact that Eastern Europe was served to Stalin on a silver plate, as a sure way to increase the fear of communism in the world.

Stanford's revisionist historian Barton J. Bernstein found evidence that, "By overextending policy and power and refusing to accept Soviet interests, American policy-makers contributed to the Cold War."[58] A similar view is expressed by H. W. Brands. According to him, "The cold war had resulted largely from the efforts of the U.S. to export capitalism across the globe."[59]

Not too different is the thesis advanced by Frank Kofsky in one of the best-documented books about the causes of the Cold War, which he attributes to a conspiracy carried out by the CFR power elite. According to him,

> Regardless of how outlandish or nonsensical most 'conspiracy theories' may be, the fact of the matter is that members of the ruling class and the power elite in the late 1940s showed themselves ready to resort to conspiratorial machinations whenever they deemed it necessary.[60]

The process by which the conspirators instilled fear in the American people by brandishing the specter of Communism was repeated in the 1990's after the unexpected implosion of the Soviet Union left the conspirators without a reason for the existence of the U.S. national security state. I have always suspected that the true reason for the first war in Iraq —a trap in which Saddam Hussein foolishly fell— was to provoke the Soviets to get into the conflict. At the time, however, the Soviet bear was already dead, and not even that direct provocation brought him back to life. Unfortunately for the American people, this failure to resuscitate Soviet Communism brought us the 9/11 events that justified the War on Terror as the makeshift replacement for the Cold War.

Frank Wisner, the man the CFR conspirators appointed to head the OPC, was a troubled, mentally unstable man,[61] with the mentality of a gangster. To fill the new positions at the OPC he needed the very best ruthless lawyers money can buy. He searched for them in Wall Street, among the lawyers and bankers who, like him, had joined the OSS gang. According to his own confession, to do this dirty work Wisner wanted amateurs, not former cops, ex-military, or ex-FBI agents.[62]

Wisner knew that professionals might easily cut through the disinformational fog and discover the true purpose of the new organization —which was not the protection of the interests of the American people. Therefore, he recruited "Patriotic, decent, well-meaning, and brave" men who, as he later admitted, "were also uniquely unsuited to the grubby, necessarily devious world of intelligence"[63] and, therefore, easy to manipulate and keep in the dark about the true purposes of the organization.

Time proved that Wisner was absolutely right. Some years later, the CIA made the mistake of hiring former FBI agent Bill Harvey, a seasoned professional. Soon after, he discovered that Kim Philby, Angleton's liaison with the British MI6, was actually a Soviet mole.[64]

Chapter 6

The CIA's "Failures"

Our failures are heralded, our successes are unknown.
—CIA's disinformation bs.

There is something puzzling about the CIA.

The main reason given to the American public for the creation of the CIA was to avoid Pearl Harbor-like "surprises." Yet, if one is to believe the CIA's critics, over and over, since its very creation, the CIA has been taken by surprise by events it didn't foresee.

The Bogotazo riots in Colombia in 1948, the Soviets launching the Sputnik in 1957, Castro grabbing power in Cuba in 1959, the Bay of Pigs debacle in 1961, the Cuban missile crisis in 1962, the coup that deposed Nikita Khrushchev in 1964, the Soviet invasion of Czechoslovakia in 1968, the attack launched by Egypt and Syria against Israel in 1973, Castro's invasion of Angola in 1975, the fall of the Shah in Iran in 1979, the fall of the Berlin Wall in 1989, the collapse of the Soviet Union in 1990, India's testing of a nuclear bomb in 1998, and the events of September 11, 2001, just to mention a few, are cases in which the CIA was apparently caught asleep at the wheel.

Nonehteless, if one studies in detail every single one of these cases where the CIA allegedly failed to alert the U.S. government about the possibility of an important event, one can find that, on the contrary, CIA analysts did their job right, but nobody paid attention. The excuse developed by the CFR conspirators to justify these failures is that, though the CIA and other intelligence agencies provided the intelligence, they failed to connect the dots.

But a simple analysis of the CIA's intelligence "failures" shows that they seamlessly dovetail with the CFR conspirators' successes. Indeed, most of the international political goals of the CFR conspirators have been reached thanks to the CIA's alleged "intelligence failures." This may be the reason why after every alleged "failure" nobody in the CIA is ever disciplined, let alone fired.[1] Consequently, one can safely reach the conclusion that people at the higher levels of the U.S. government failed to connect the dots because the lines connecting the dots pointed right to CFR treason.

Proof of this is that, as ex-CIA analyst Melvin A. Goodman has pointed out, after every "intelligence failure," some of the analysts directly responsible for the failure are given big cash bonuses and promotions[2] and the CIA's budget is increased. What Goodman does not mention, however, is that this new generation of ethically challenged intelligence analysts at the CIA are the direct product of a system of education that teaches the students that truth is a social construct and ethics is not absolute, but changes in every different situation. In that sense, this new generation of CIA intelligence analysts is not too different from the present generation of university professors and scientists who, in order to keep their grants flowing, cook the books to justify their full support to unscientific, religious theories like Darwinian evolution and anthropogenic global warming. If, as Goodman rightly points out, the politicization of intelligence is bad, the politicization of science is even worse.[3]

Yet, contrary to the disinformers' claims, far from accumulating failures, the CIA has always been one of the most successful tools used by the conspirators entrenched in the Council on Foreign Relations in the pursuit of their hidden goal: the creation of the communo-fascist global government controlled by Wall Street bankers, oil magnates and multinational corporations they disingenuously call the New World Order.

The Gang That Couldn't Shoot Straight?

Due to the fact that the Wall Street conspirators already had their own intelligence agency, the CFR, they never gave any importance to the supposedly most important CIA Directorate: Intelligence. This explains why, since its very creation, the CIA has accumulated failure after failure in the area of intelligence collection and analysis.

However, the conspirators were very careful in getting sure that the Director of the CIA, as well as the Deputy Director of Plans (and before him the chiefs of the Office of Special Projects and the Office of Policy Coordination) and his close senior collaborators, were all trusted CFR agents —thus guaranteeing an absolute control over the area that really mattered to them: covert military operations. Actually, the other directorates were just a convenient cover to hide from the American public, the U.S. government, and the rest of CIA's employees, the true activities of the Agency on behalf of its CFR creators and masters.

Many well-intentioned, dedicated CIA employees have worked their whole life for the Agency, retired, and died, without realizing that they had been recruited under a false flag. Though in their pledge of allegiance they have sworn to defend their country against its enemies, foreign and domestic, unknowingly, they have worked their whole lives protecting and advancing the interests of America's most dangerous domestic enemies, the people who are working hard to destroy this country.

This explains the true cause of most of the CIA's intelligence "failures."

Since the very beginning, the criminal Wall Street Mafia was very careful in recruiting people of their same criminal mindset to do the dirty job of covert military operations. As Stanley Lovell, a CIA recruiter for "Wild Bill" Donovan, clearly stated,

> What I have to do is to stimulate the Peck's Bad Boy beneath the surface of every American scientist and say to him, "Throw all your normal law-

> abiding concepts out the window. Here's a chance to raise merry hell. Come help me raise it."[4]

Likewise, in a letter to CIA's mad scientist Sidney Gottlieb, ex-OSS, CIA officer George Hunter White wrote about his heroic escapades:

> I was a very minor missionary, actually a heretic, but I toiled wholeheartedly in the vineyards because it was fun, fun, fun. . . . Where else could a red-blooded American boy lie, kill, cheat, steal, rape and pillage with the sanction and blessing of the all-highest?[5]

So, if as the saying goes, a conservative is just a liberal who has been mugged at gunpoint, very soon a liberal will be a conservative who has been "interrogated" by CIA thugs using waterboarding and other "enhanced interrogation techniques."

As Columbia University historian Jacques Barzun pointed out, "What is reprehensible is for the modern world to have made official the dreams and actions of little boys." Spies, he added, enjoy "permissive depravity," for,

> ... in exchange for a few dirty tricks there is also power and luxury, cash and free sex . . . the advantage of being a spy as of being a soldier is that there is always a larger reason —the reason of state— for making any little scruple or nastiness shrink into insignificance."[6]

At the time he was Allen Dulles' (CFR) deputy director for plans, Richard Bissell (CFR) said that CIA officers only paid obedience to a higher authority. What neither Bissell nor Hunter White specified, however, was that the "higher" authority they paid obedience to did not reside in heavens, but in the Harold Pratt House in Manhattan.

The Gang That *Shouldn't* Shoot Straight

If one is to believe most leftist and liberal American journalists and scholars, the CIA is inept and incompetent. Nothing, however, is farther from the truth. As a good example of this I can mention that after Gary Powers' U-2 was shot down over the Soviet Union in 1960 —most likely as the result of Pentagon-CIA sabotage— the price of shares of arms manufacturing companies rose sharply in the New York Stock Exchange, and government military-contract awards increased substantially. Just two months after the incident, the Eisenhower administration allocated the biggest military appropriations ever approved at that time, $48.3 million for fiscal 1960-61.[7]

Furthermore, the U.S. defense budget for the fiscal year that began July 1, 1962, was $56.6 billion. Of these, $15.4 was designated for purchasing new weapons, $11.5 to operations and maintenance, and $6.7 to research and development. In the decade of mid-1953 to mid-1963, the U.S. spent more than $400 billion in defense.[8] Fear has always been good for business, and everybody knows that the business of America is business.

Therefore, you should not take at face value everything you read or hear about how inept and stupid the CIA is. The problem is that everything one ever hears about the CIA is its failures, but the very nature of intelligence work precludes them from announcing their successes. (This added to the fact that one must take with extreme caution any intelligence services' claims about their successes or failures.) On the contrary, in handling most of the jobs by which it has been criticized, the CIA has not been incompetent, but just deceitful —which in the case of an intelligence service should not be taken as a criticism, but as a compliment.

If this sounds too close to a conspiracy theory, I have to confess that I don't have a problem with that. At any rate, intelligence, espionage, and counterintelligence,[9] ultimately are just key elements of a conspiracy to fool, confuse and eventually defeat the enemy. The only problem is that the CIA's true enemy happens to be the American people.

In his book *The Secret History of the CIA*,[10] Joseph Trento describes the Agency as a sort of gang that couldn't shoot straight. This vision, however, is highly misleading. Though Trento has collected a large amount of information about the CIA, most of the conclusions he arrives at are wrong. Proof of it is the assertion written on the jacket of the hardcover edition of his book: "The CIA was founded on the best of intentions." Actually, as I have shown above, the CIA was founded on the worst of intentions: to betray the American people.

The main fault of Trento's book, however, arises from a wrong methodological analysis: as you should not use carpenter's tools to do a plumber's job, one should not use a journalist's (or a historian's, for that matter) analysis tools to study an intelligence organization.

On the other hand, Trento's book is a source of useful information for the skeptic researcher who knows how to read between the lines, because he has managed to unearth a great deal of previously unknown information about the CIA. For example, just his discovery that the CIA actually began as a secret CFR operation, headed by Allen Dulles, operating from a sound proof office at the Harold Pratt House, the CFR's headquarters at 58 E 68th Street, where he "laid out a scheme to operate an intelligence service outside the government," is worth the price of the book.[11]

In his next book, however, Trento changes his tune and places Dulles' secret intelligence office at 44 Wall Street.[12] Nonetheless, disregarding the place from where he operated, it is obvious that Dulles was doing the job on behalf of his Wall Street masters. It is naive to think that a small potato like Allen Dulles could have created the CIA by himself from scratch. Most likely, behind him was the true demiurge, master spy Nelson Rockefeller.

There is a saying in the military, "Once is happenstance, twice is coincidence, three times enemy action." But intelligence, and particularly counterintelligence officers leave no room for happenstance or coincidences. For them just once is enemy action, and all coincidences are potentially deceptive. Therefore, it seems curious, to say the least, that the long chain of CIA's "failures" described by Trento, apparently the result of careless, sloppy performance by even its most senior officers, have never been analyzed from the point of view of counterintelligence, that is, as the possible result of enemy action.

On the other hand, however, one must keep in mind that what we call "CIA failures," constitute failures only if we depart from the wrong premise that, in order to protect the U.S. national security, the CIA has been fighting communism, totalitarianism, or the new artificially created new enemy: terrorism.

But perhaps the most outstanding example of CIA's inability to shoot straight has been its dismal failure on its numerous attempts to assassinate Fidel Castro.

CIA's Alleged Assassination Attempts on Fidel Castro

A 1976 Senate report shocked the American public when it disclosed that the United States had been involved in more than a dozen attempts to assassinate Fidel Castro. In 1994, the American public was shocked again with the publication of a declassified CIA document dated 23 May 1967. The document was a Secret, Eyes Only Memorandum for the Record with a report on Operation Mongoose, the CIA plots to assassinate Castro.[13] Before it was declassified, only two people had read it: Richard Helms, Director of Central Intelligence, and J. S. Earman, Inspector General.

On the other hand, Castro himself and several officers in the Castroist government have claimed on several occasions that the alleged assassination attempts on the Comandante's life over the last 35 years are from as few as 12 to as high as 638.[14]

The problem I have with believing these claims of alleged assassination attempts on Castro is that, in the first place, both the CIA and Castro are very unreliable sources of information, to say the least. Secondly, even if one accepts that only half of the alleged assassination attempts really happened, there is the unquestionable fact that none of them were successful. Even stranger is the fact that Castro was never even slightly wounded or hurt in any of the alleged attempts to his life. This defies all rational logic and the credibility of even the more gullible person.

Empirical evidence indicates that assassination attempts are relatively easy to execute, and its chance of success is higher than 50%. The relatively high success rate of assassination attempts is because the assassin(s) always have the initiative and carefully select the time, place and mode of action according to his needs. This gives the assassin a clear advantage that manifests in a high rate of success.

The assassinations of John F. Kennedy, Robert Kennedy, Martin Luther King, Jr., and John Lennon, just to mention some of the most known in recent American history, are enough proof of this. In the case of Ronald Reagan, who survived an assassination attempt, it is clear that it failed only because of the total ineptitude of the would-be assassin. Therefore, I have a problem with believing Castro's claims about so many failed assassination attempts on his life. I frankly believe that, despite the tight security ring surrounding Castro, if a professionally trained assassin had really tried to kill him, he would have been dead since many years ago.

Some authors who have studied the subject are convinced that some, if not all, of the alleged CIA-directed attempts on Castro's life failed because of his extremely good luck. On the other hand, we should not discount other reasons. As I have repeated over and over in this book, in the world of intelligence and espionage things are seldom as they seem.

Furhtermore, I have another problem with accepting at face value the CIA's claims of assassination attempts on Castro. How can you accept as truth information provided by members of an organization whose main purpose is lying and deceiving? Furthermore, how can you accept as truth documents provided by an organization that has a whole department devoted to falsify documents?

The only sources claiming that there have been assassination attempts by the CIA on Castro's life are the CIA and Castro himself. But, as any intelligence analyst will agree, an evaluation of the CIA's version of assassination attempts on Castro would be close to E-4, that is, source unreliable and accuracy of the information doubtful (See Appendix II, The Evaluation of Information). Also, it is very strange, to say the least, that the CIA, who has always made a strong effort to cast a shadow of secrecy over its undercover operations to the very point of keeping information classified more than fifty years, was so eager to provide information about such a compromising recent event.

The other source, Castro himself, is at least as unreliable as the CIA. Castro has a long, proven history of lying and deceiving.[15] An intelligence evaluation of his version of the CIA's attempts on his life would produce results very similar to the CIA's, that is, source unreliable and accuracy of the information doubtful.

Referring to the many alleged assassination attempts on Castro, Ronald Kessler stated, "the ineptitude of the operations was astonishing." I would add that it was astonishing to the point of being incredible. Actually, some members of the anti-Castro exile community in Florida have mentioned several times that their attempts to assassinate Castro failed because the CIA and the FBI either obstructed their activities or alerted Castro.

Until very recently these allegations were just rumors, because nobody had brought concrete proof of these suspicions. But on May 18th, 2010, a true insider gave his support to the allegations. During an interview for Miami's Channel 23, Félix Rodríguez, an ex-CIA operative who participated in many CIA covert operations, including the capture of Che Guevara in Bolivia, mentioned that the assassination attempts against Castro carried out by the CIA were designed to fail.

The CIA's True Role

Initially, the CIA was structurally divided into four different directorates: Intelligence, Support, Administration, and Plans, each one headed by a Deputy Director. Eventually the Directorate of Administration disappeared, and the Directorate of Science and technology was created. As everything related to the CIA, however, the name Directorate of Plans was intentionally highly misleading. It actually had to do with the armed branch of the CIA, the one devoted to covert military operations of sabotage, subversion, terrorism, and psychological warfare.

After the end of World War II, Allen Dulles served as a government consultant in matters of intelligence. In 1948, after the CIA's "failure" to forecast Colombia's Bogotazo riots of April 9, 1948, Dulles was appointed to chair a three-man commission responsible for assessing the U.S. intelligence system and the CIA's failure to predict the Bogotazo.

The Dulles Report of 1949 (also known as the "Dulles-Jackson-Correa Report") was a hatchet job on CIA Director Admiral Roscoe Hillenkoetter. It held Hillenkoetter responsible for what it considered a major and ongoing failure in intelligence coordination.[16] It is interesting to see that the common explanation for the CIA's alleged "failures" —not connecting the dots for lack of inter-agency communication— was an excuse invented less than a year after the Agency was created, and the CFR conspirators have consistently continued using it *ad nauseam*. One of the latest examples was the 9/11 Commission Report.

Hillenkoetter was a professional military man, the first CIA Director and the third Director of Central Intelligence of three short-tenured directors of a transitional organization called the Central Intelligence Group —the first two had been Admiral Sidney Souers and General Hoyt Vandenberg. When in the spring of 1947 the Central Intelligence Group was renamed Central Intelligence Agency, Admiral Hillenkoetter, not fully under the control of the CFR conspirators, became the CIA's first Director.

As a result of Dulles' biased report and his conspiratorial activities behind the curtains, supported by undersecretary of State Robert Lovett (CFR-controlled, Skull & Bones) and Robert Blum (CFR), an aide to Defense Secretary James Forrestal (CFR),[17] in October 1950 Hillenkoetter was substituted by General Walter Bedell Smith, a CFR member.[18] A year later, in 1951, Dulles was made CIA's Deputy Director for Plans, the CIA's clandestine arm in charge of covert operations.

Two years later, in 1953, CFR agent President Dwight D. Eisenhower appointed Allen Dulles Director of Central Intelligence and CIA Director. Finally, the CFR conspirators were in full command of the aberrant monster they had created: the CIA. The very same year he was appointed CIA Director, Dulles and his Wall Street masters used the CIA to overthrow Iranian nationalist leader, Prime Minister Mohammed Mossadegh.

In 1928 the Rockefeller's Standard Oil, the Royal Dutch-Shell, and the Anglo-Iranian AIOC had formed a powerful oil cartel. But Mossadegh nationalized Iran's oil production, breaking the oil cartel. This action sealed Mossadegh's fate. Some American oil companies, in which Dulles was directly involved, feared their interests had been threatened by Mossadegh's nationalist views. In 1953, Dulles used the newly created CIA's covert action to overthrow Mossadegh by a CFR planned and CIA executed coup d'ètat. The CIA had used its covert action capacity not to protect the interests of the American people, but the interests of the CFR conspirators.

The Iranian operation was so successful, that they repeated it a year later. In 1954, the CFR planned and the CIA executed the coup d'ètat that overthrew Guatemala's democratically elected head of state President Jacobo Arbenz. The reason for this was not because Arbenz threatened the American people but because, a few months after being elected, he nationalized some unused land owned by the United Fruit Company.

Allen Dulles and his brother John Foster Dulles were partners in the Wall Street law firm Sullivan & Cromwell. Among their important clients was the Rockefeller-owned United Fruit. With John Foster Dulles heading the State Department and Allen Dulles heading the CIA, they were the czars of Eisenhower's foreign policy, and they made sure that the interests of Sullivan & Cromwell clients weren't ignored.

The Guatemalan coup, which cost American taxpayers $20 million (a considerable amount of money at the time), was perhaps a setback for American interests in Latin America, because it reinforced the image of an imperial U.S. forcibly affecting the destinies of her Latin American neighbors. It was, however, a total success for CIA director Allen Dulles and his powerful CFR masters.

The Mossadegh and Arbenz operations were so successful that the CFR conspirators have repeated the same procedure again and again with good results. Some years later, they repeated it again in Chile.

After a long process of destabilization carried out by both the CIA and Fidel Castro, in September 1973 democratically elected Chilean President Salvador Allende was overthrown by a coup d'ètat. The Agency had run a powerful propaganda campaign against Allende, directed at convincing the conservative middle classes that Allende was a Stalinist would-be despot and a tool of Moscow and Castro. On his part, Castro carried out a propaganda campaign directed at convincing the left that Allende was not radical enough.

It was not a coincidence that John McCone (CFR), a former CIA Director, headed the ITT, one of the U.S. corporations actively involved in the coup. In addition, war criminal Henry Kissinger (CFR) played an active role in the coup against Allende.

The CIA has been one of the best tools used by the conspirators entrenched in the Council on Foreign Relations in their pursuit of a communo-fascist global government controlled by transnational corporations, which they call the New World Order. A simple analysis of the CIA's "failures" shows that they seamlessly match with the CFR's successes in national and international politics.

In the conduct of their nefarious businesses, the CFR conspirators have used not only their own information collection capabilities through their secret agents operating inside transnational corporations, Wall Street banks, and the State Department, but also the raw information[19] obtained through the gathering and collecting capabilities of the CIA, the NSA, and other U.S. intelligence agencies. They have, however, ignored the CIA's intelligence analysis capabilities, because, having their own intelligence analysts at the CFR they don't need the Agency's.

The CFR conspirators have never given any importance to the allegedly most important CIA Directorate: Intelligence.[20] That is precisely the area where raw information is collected and converted, through careful analysis and evaluation, into intelligence, before passing it, together with the analysts' assessments, to the country's leaders —usually in the form of an intelligence report or estimate forecasting what the opposition would do or would not do— as an objective tool to take into consideration when making foreign policy decisions.

But intelligence, like any other product of the human intellect, is very subjective. It is conformed and modeled by the assumptions of the people who create it, the intelligence analysts. Moreover, an important element in the creation of intelligence departing from raw information is the knowledge the intelligence analysts have, not only about the opposition but also of the consumers of the intelligence they produce —in the CIA's case, the executive branch of the U.S. government.

But, as I have shown above in this book, the true executive branch of the U.S. Government is not in Washington D.C., but in Manhattan. This explains why the true goals and policies of the U.S. government, under the control of the CFR conspirators, are not what it claims to be.

But the people in government, that is, the people who really control the U.S. government behind the scenes —in this case the CFR conspirators— don't share their secret goals and policies with anybody except the trusted members of the inner core of the CFR, who obviously are not intelligence analysts working for the CIA. Consequently, because of their wrong assumptions about who they are really working for, intelligence analyses and estimates produced by CIA intelligence analysts most of the time are not good for the CFR conspirators. Actually, in most cases they are highly damaging for the conspirators.

This is best exemplified by the conspirators' Team B idea.

Team B VS Team A

In 1974, secret CFR agent Albert Wohlstetter, a professor at the University of Chicago and RAND analyst, wrote an article entitled "Is There a Strategic Arms Race?"[21] in which he accused the CIA of systematically underestimating Soviet missile deployment in its National Intelligence Estimates (NIE). In his article, Wohlstetter claimed that the United States was allowing the Soviet Union to achieve military superiority by not closing an existing missile gap favoring the Soviets.[22] Soon after, many other secret CFR agents, among them Donald Rumsfeld and Paul Wolfowitz, began a concerted agitprop[23] campaign strongly criticizing the CIA's annual Estimate of the Soviet threat.[24]

Then, in 1975 some CFR agents conceived the farfetched idea of creating a group of non-CIA analysts to, based on the same raw information, independently assess the Soviet threat. When asked, CIA Director William Colby (CFR) (more on Colby below) refused to approve it. Soon after, acting under pressure from the CFR conspirators, President Gerald Ford (CFR) removed Colby from his position as CIA Director.

Just a year later, when CFR agent George H. W. Bush became the Director of Central Intelligence in 1976, the CFR secret agents infiltrated in the U.S. government renewed their request for competitive threat assessments. Despite opposition from CIA top analysts who argued against such experiment, Bush checked with Ford, obtained a go-ahead, and by May 26 began the experiment.[25]

Accordingly, a team of 16 "outside experts," gave themselves to the task of taking a look at highly classified information collected by the CIA, to evaluate it and change it into usable intelligence. Actually there were three teams: One of them studied Soviet low-altitude air defense capabilities, the other one examined Soviet intercontinental ballistic missile (ICBM) accuracy, and the third one concentrated its efforts in analyzing Soviet strategic policy and objectives. This third team, chaired by Harvard University professor and CFR agent Richard Pipes, received much publicity and is the one commonly referred to as Team B. Key advisors to Team B were Foy Kohler, Seymour Weiss, Jasper Welch, Paul Wolfowitz and Paul Nitze, all of them CFR agents.

As expected, the report produced by Team B arrived at totally different conclusions than the ones reached by CIA's NIE' analysts. According to Team B's CFR agents, the CIA's NIEs were wrong in asserting that Soviet strategic actions were primarily a response to its history of being invaded. On the contrary, Team B experts agreed that most Soviet strategic actions were offensive rather than defensive in nature —the "reds-under-the-beds" syndrome. The Team B report also found ridiculous CIA's NIE conclusion that, as the Soviet Union grew more strong and capable, its foreign policy would also become less aggressive.[26]

Team B's report also criticized the conclusions of CIA's NIEs regarding Soviet strategic weapons programs, and argued that CIA analysts had consistently underestimated the threat posed by Soviet strategic weapons programs. Moreover, they warned, the Soviet's development and deployment of new weapons and advancements in existing military technologies would drastically erase the advantages that the United States and NATO had over the Warsaw Pact. In classic CFR style, Team B's conclusions were false, but scary.

Typical of the cooking-the-facts mentality of Team B's analysts was that they resorted to a sort of convoluted reverse logic to prove their points. For example, one of their most bizarre conclusions was that the Soviets had or could have developed an entirely new anti-submarine detection system for their nuclear submarines. The reason why it had not been detected by the U.S., they reasoned, was precisely because it used a system that did not depend on sound and was, thus, undetectable by contemporary Western technology.

In an effort to deny the CIA's NIE evaluation that the prevalent economic chaos in the Soviet Union was hindering their ability to produce an efficient air defense system, the CFR agents in Team B argued that the Soviet Union was trying to deceive the American public and claimed that the Russian air defense system worked fine.

Of course, all these assumptions turned out to be false.[27] Unfortunately, when CFR disinformation agent Fareed Zakaria discovered in 2003 that the conclusions of Team B's report "were wildly off the mark," it was too late to make any use of his "discovery."[28]

Now, how come, one may ask, two different teams of qualified intelligence analysts, based on exactly the same available information, arrived at so diametrically opposed conclusions? The answer is because, as I mentioned above, being the product of the human intellect, intelligence is fully subjective. Despite claims to the contrary, there is nothing objective about it. Like beauty, intelligence is in the eye of the beholder, and the eyes of CIA's patriotic intelligence analysts were totally different from the treasonous eyes of the CFR's intelligence analysts.

But this is not the only question asking for an answer.

Many books have been written about the CIA, some of them painting it with the most dismal colors, others with the most bright and patriotic ones. To some authors, the CIA is a haven for heroes, to others, a dark cave full of traitors. How come, one may ask, based on the same information these authors have arrived at so diametrically opposed conclusions?

Logical positivist philosophers believed that most disagreements among people come out either of using two different names to designate the same thing, or of using a single name to designate two different entities. According to them, the cause for most disagreements is semantic. Though I don't fully subscribe to their theory, I have to recognize that there is some truth to it.

The reason for the otherwise unexplainable duality of the CIA is because, contrary to what most people believe, the Agency is not a single entity. Actually, behind the common façade, there are two CIAs, totally different and working hard to attain quite different goals. Therefore, both CIA critics and apologists are right. The confusion arises from the fact that, unknowingly, they are talking about two quite different CIAs.

The Two CIAs

Unbeknownst to the American public, almost since its very creation the CIA has actually been a dual organization. Like the two halves of the Viscount in Italo Calvino's novel, one of them is the evil CIA; the one controlled by the bad guys.

This is the CIA that overthrew Mossadegh, Arbenz, Nixon and Allende; the CIA that betrayed the Cuban invaders at the Bay of Pigs; the CIA that spied on Americans; the CIA that experimented with psychotropic drugs and mind control on unaware U.S. citizens; the CIA that sabotaged Powers' U-2; the CIA that assassinated Lumumba, and perhaps even John F. Kennedy and William Colby.[29]

This is the CIA that helped Nazi war criminals escape from justice and even put some of them on its payroll, the CIA that brought drugs to the ghettos, the waterboarding CIA. In synthesis, the CIA of the Directorate of Special Operations, the CIA's covert action arm.

This, which I would call CIA B, is the one working hard to advance and protect the interests of U.S. Government B, that is, the illegal invisible government of the United States under the control of a Mafia of Wall Street bankers, oil magnates and CEOs of transnational corporations agglutinated in the Council of Foreign Relations. A typical employee of CIA B was Richard Bissell (CFR), Deputy Director for Plans (covert operations).

In contrast, the other one is the good CIA where patriotic Americans anonymously do their daily job, under the false assumption that they are working for an organization whose goal is defending and protecting the American people.

This is the CIA that forecasted the failure of the Bay of Pigs invasion, the CIA that predicted that the Soviets would not deploy nuclear missiles in Cuba in 1962, the CIA that alerted the government about the upcoming 9/11 attack, but nobody paid attention, the CIA that discovered that there were no WMDs in Iraq and was unmercifully defamed. This is the CIA of the Directorate of Intelligence, the CIA working hard to accomplish the mission expressed in the National Security Act of 1947. In synthesis, this is CIA A, working for U.S. Government A, the legal government of the United States. A typical employee of CIA A was Sherman Kent (not a CFR member), Chairman of the Board of National Intelligence Estimates.

The traitorous CIA B is centered on the Director's Office and the Directorate of Special Operations,[30] while the patriotic CIA A is centered on the Directorate of Intelligence.

Unfortunately, as the result of an enormous disinformation campaign made possible thanks to the CFR conspirators' control over the mainstream media, most anti-CIA books and articles have been written about the good CIA A guys, who are usually depicted as unfaithful dissidents bordering on treason.[31] In contrast, most of the pro-CIA books and articles are about the bad CIA B guys, the traitors who are disingenuously described as all-American heroes.[32]

The conflict between the two CIAs is not new. It began just a few years after the CIA was created in 1947, increased in the late 1960s, and began to be known publicly by the mid-1970s. Yet, most authors who wrote about it erroneously saw this conflict as an internal problem, something happening *within* the CIA instead of between *two* quite different CIAs.[33]

The fact that the globalist conspirators have their own people to collect, analyze and evaluate information at their private intelligence agency, the CFR, explains why the few times they have used intelligence provided by CIA's analysts, they have treated it as raw information and have reevaluated it by their own intelligence analysts at the Harold Pratt House —which is exactly why they did during the Team A-Team B charade. Given the fact that the CFR intelligence analysts are privy to the CFR's true goals and policies, they often arrive at diametrically opposite conclusions and estimates than the true patriots at CIA A. That is the true cause for the CIA's constant "failures" in the field of intelligence forecasting.

CIA A's analysts do their job under the assumption that they work for the American people, that is, for U.S. Government A, and have the American people's interests in mind when they produce their NIEs. In contrast, CFR analysts do it from the point of view of defending the interests of U.S. Government B, the one under the full control of their Wall Street and Big Oil masters. Due to the fact, however, that most of the time the interests of the American people (government A) and the CFR conspirators (government B) do not coincide, it is not surprising that CIA NIEs and CFR NIEs differ so much.

The bottom line is that the CFR conspirators are never going to pay any attention to the CIA A's forecasting that terrorists are about to take actions damaging to the people of the United States, when most likely they themselves, in cahoots with CIA B, are the ones who have incited the terrorists to take these actions or even facilitated them in order to use them as a pretext to justify taking actions damaging to the American people. A great part of the current low morale within the CIA's ranks, and the cause for many dissidents inside the CIA leaking information damaging to the CFR conspirators, is because some CIA officers have reached the conclusion that our government is not what it purports to be.

CFR Conspirators Create CIA B

The true origins of the CIA began with the Lovett Committee, chaired by Robert Lovett, a Skull & Bones member closely linked to the CFR. Secretary of War Robert Patterson (CFR) created the Lovett Committee in October 1945. The function of this committee was "to advise the government on the post-World War II organization of the U.S. intelligence activities."

Lovett's recommendations allowed the CFR conspirators to create a government organization that would actually be a renegade organization. Hiding under a cover of national security, this renegade organization, which eventually became the CIA, would work secretly to advance the conspirators' secret goals.

As I have explained above, the Central Intelligence Agency was officially created on July 26, 1947, during the Truman administration, as part of the National Security Act. But one must keep in mind that Truman was an accidental president, brought to the White House by the sudden death of Franklin D. Roosevelt. And, contrary to Roosevelt, who was a trusted CFR secret agent, the conspirators did not fully control Truman, and they knew he would be opposed to the creation of "an American Gestapo."

However, though the CIA's overt purpose was to provide a central organization to coordinate the efforts of the different intelligence services of the U. S. government, its true, covert purpose was to act as a military arm to protect the interests of Wall Street bankers and oil magnates. This military arm was the CIA's Directorate of Plans they had already created surreptitiously.[34]

Most authors who have written books about the CIA have painted a picture of Admiral Hillenkoetter as a sort of incompetent fool, an image these authors most likely got from the Dulles' report on the Bogotazo riots. But that was not the case. The conspirators hated Admiral Hillenkoetter because, based on his wartime experience, he disliked clandestine operations and was convinced that an intelligence service could not effectively do both information gathering and analysis (the CIA's alleged main mission), and covert action —which shows that Hillenkoetter was actually a very clever man.

As Hillenkoetter pointed out, having an intelligence agency, whose only job should be collecting, analyzing, disseminating, and other jobs relating to intelligence, was incompatible with performing covert military operations. He reasoned that allowing people working in intelligence to have the capability to affect their source of information would result in them trying to modify the information in order to fit it into their intelligence predictions. For example, in order to prove that their prediction about a possible coup d'ètat in a particular country was true, the covert arm would contribute to produce the actual coup.

Moreover, something that made him even more dangerous in the eyes of the

CFR conspirators, Hillenkoetter believed that the CIA should not engage in clandestine operations because they were illegal for the simple reason that the U.S. Congress had never granted the CIA such authority.[35]

Nevertheless, using the Bogotazo "failure" as a pretext, the CFR conspirators managed to get rid of Hillenkoetter. Eventually, once their trusted secret agent Allen Dulles was in command, they brought Wisner and his Office of Police Coordination into the CIA —practically creating CIA B.

American Patriots Working for CIA A

For many years, qualified CIA intelligence analysts continued doing their job guided by professionalism and high ethical standards, under the false assumption that they were working on behalf of the American people. But that assumption made their intelligence product totally unusable to the CFR conspirators working on behalf of the Wall Street bankers and oil corporations.

In 1951, CIA director General Walter Bedell Smith created the Office of National Estimates under the direction of Harvard Professor Walter Langer, who had been a senior intelligence analyst for the OSS. His team was the one in charge of producing the National Intelligence Estimates. When Dr. Langer retired, his successor, Yale Professor Sherman Kent, continued the tradition of professionalism and objectivity established by Langer of producing estimates telling it like it was, not like the politicians wanted. As expected, neither Langer nor Kent was popular among the CFR conspirators.

The problem was solved after the creation of Team B. Since then, departing from the same batch of raw data, CFR analysts produced a totally different kind of intelligence. This explains why senior CFR agents infiltrated in the U.S. government had no use for the CIA's TEAM A's intelligence analysis capabilities.

It is known that Henry Kissinger, a key CFR agent, preferred the intelligence produced by his own intelligence analysts. He profited from the reports he got from the CIA, but only after they had been re-processed and re-evaluated by his own CFR-controlled staff.[36]

The CFR conspirators' lack of interest in CIA A's intelligence analysis capabilities explains why, since its very creation, the CIA has accumulated failure after failure in the area of intelligence, and nobody seemed to care. One reason for these failures is because nobody has paid any attention to intelligence produced by the CIA. Another reason is because, on purpose, the conspirators managed to force the CIA to accept tainted sources of information. A notable example of this is that after the end of WWII CIA's almost exclusive source of intelligence from the Soviet Union and the Soviet controlled Eastern Europe was the Gehlen organization.

Most Americans ignore that, once Germany was defeated, conspirators' agents in the CIA hired Hitler's Chief of Eastern intelligence, General Reinhard Gehlen, and his whole organization, to spy on the Soviets. The CFR agents infiltrated in the CIA trusted Gehlen so much that he was given a free hand, acting with almost no supervision. It was not until 1963 that the West German government exposed a group of Gehlen's agents as Soviet double agents, tried, and convicted for their treason.[37] But CIA officers, following orders from above pressured the West Germans to allow Gehlen to escape untouched and he quietly dropped out of sight.

But, as much as the CIA creators were not interested in CIA-produced intelligence, they made sure that the CIA Directors were trusted CFR members, and that the Deputy Director of plans (CIA's Directorate of Plans eventually changed its name to Directorate of Clandestine Services, and now is called Directorate of Operations. This is the Directorate in charge of clandestine operations, including covert action), and his close senior collaborators were, if not CFR members, at least people they can trust—thus guaranteeing an absolute control over the armed branch of the CIA; the area that really mattered to them.

Actually, the other CIA A directorates were just a necessary cover to hide the true CIA B's activities on behalf of its CFR creators and masters. However, working under the false impression that they were protecting the U.S. interests, CIA A's officers at the other directorates were working hard trying to do an honest job. They didn't realize that they had become a nuisance for the CFR agents working at the CIA B Directorate in charge of clandestine operations.

Most true patriots working at other CIA A areas, including intelligence, never suspected that the bad guys at covert action operations were working to attain different goals. Still, the accurate National Intelligence Estimates produced by CIA A's intelligence analysts, eventually became, more than a nuisance, an irritant and a source of conflicts for the CFR conspirators. Consequently, in 1973, CIA Director James Schlesinger, a CFR agent, in an effort to make the CIA intelligence analysts less independent and more responsible to the interests of U.S. Government B, terminated the Office of National Estimates and created the National Intelligence Council, a sort of official Team B more docile to the CFR master's orders.

It worked on the CFR conspirators' behalf, though, that most of he new generation of intelligence analysts who replaced the old-school ones belong to the new generation of ethically and morally challenged opportunistic people.[38] These were the ones who, without any coercion whatsoever, immediately began producing Intelligence Estimates favorable to the interests of U.S. Government B.

HUMINT VS TECHINT

Peter Beinart begins an article in which he criticizes the CIA's failure to alert the U.S. about the terrorist attacks of September 11, 2001, with a revealing question: "How could the CIA have been so stupid?"[39]

Though Beinart's premises are wrong, his analysis of the apparent causes of such dismal failure is correct: in the last years the CIA has totally ignored the importance of HUMINT (Human intelligence, that is, information collected by agents in the field), in favor of relying almost exclusively on TECHINT (Technical intelligence, that is, intelligence based on information collected by satellites, radar, computers, and other gadgets. However, not knowing the true causes of the problem, Beinart's suggestion to solve it is simplistic. According to him, the CIA needs to attract the best minds to the Company.

In his book *See No Evil*.[40] CIA's former intelligence officer Robert Baer made a similar mistake. Like Beinart, Baer points to the CIA's over-reliance on technological spying in detriment of human collection by agents in the field, but he fails to point to the true source of the problem. According to him, the CIA has become a bureaucratic, inept mess.

But both Beinart and Baer are dead wrong. Actually, one of the reasons why CIA A eventually turned from an asset into a liability for the conspirators was precisely because there were too many good minds at Langley. And good minds are too inquisitive. They discover connections, find oddities —things difficult to explain if one discards stupidity and incompetence—, strange, unexplainable things that sooner or later point to an unavoidable cause: treason.

People working at CIA A are not stupid, they are simply ignored. Proof of it is that, despite so many alleged "failures," nobody at CIA A is fired, demoted, suspended, or even reassigned,[41] and after every catastrophic intelligence "failure" the result is that the CIA budget is raised —though most of the money goes to CIA B's covert action Directorate to finance covert action operations, not to increase intelligence collection and analysis. But the truly clever guys work at CIA B. They always do exactly the job that benefits the interests of their bosses. Unfortunately, however, their true bosses are not the American people —whose only role in this tragic charade is footing the bill.

What Beinart seems to ignore is that the trend that began in 1962 after the Cuban missile crisis for increasing TECHINT to the detriment of HUMINT was exactly what the people who control the CIA needed. So, the deterioration of CIA A's information collection resources as a direct result of the reduction of HUMINT capabilities, which negatively affected its intelligence analysis and production capabilities, was not a mistake but the result of a carefully planned design, and the CFR conspirators who control the CIA had strong reasons for doing it.

Contrary to intelligence officers working in the field, TECHINT gadgets don't question inconsistencies or suspect sheer treason from their colleagues and bosses. Moreover, gadgets are easier to manipulate than people. Retired gadgets don't write embarrassing memoirs. They cannot be called to testify in Congress investigations. They don't suffer from ethical, moral or patriotic inner conflicts.

Contrary to the analysts working at Langley, herded inside physical and mental compartmented boundaries, intelligence officers collecting information in the field often get a glimpse at the whole picture —a picture that most of the time does not agree with the picture the CIA projects to the outside world. Therefore, the elimination of HUMINT in favor of TECHINT was the subtle and clever way the CFR conspirators used to restrict the vision of the best, but potentially problematic minds working at CIA A.

Moreover, intelligence officers working in the field develop a healthy skepticism about their profession. Very soon they discover that intelligence officers who reach retirement age are the ones who don't trust anybody, including (or perhaps particularly) their own bosses, colleagues and intelligence service.

To be sure, a large percent of the people working for CIA A are honorable men and women. But, because of the characteristics of compartmentation and need-to-know inherent to this type of organization, they cannot see the whole picture. Moreover, most of the ones who have remained working for CIA A are not the best minds we can afford.

In the last decades, many good minds have left CIA A in droves. The fact was pointed out a few years ago in stark clarity by Linda Robinson and Kevin Whitelaw in their February 13, 2006, *U.S. News & World Review* article, "Seeking Spies: Why the CIA is Having Such Hard Time Keeping the Best."

The reason why the people who control the CIA actually don't want the best minds, is very simple: intelligence analysts who don't know anything about the countries they are supposed to analyze, including their languages, are easier to manipulate than bright people with a thorough knowledge of the country, its culture, politics and language. To the CFR conspirators who use CIA B as a tool to advance their own, secret goals, CIA A is just as a convenient cover. Therefore, clever, educated employees only mean trouble. So, they are not interested at all in having the best minds money can buy working in some areas of CIA A, particularly in the Directorate of Intelligence. Actually, allowing CIA A's analysts to do a good job would be detrimental to the CFR conspirators' best interests.

Eventually, some of these patriotic CIA A employees smelled a rat, and became whistle blowers, mostly by publishing books about the CIA's mistakes or evil deeds. These are the cases of ex-CIA officers like Victor Marchetti,[42] Ralph McGehee,[43] Frank Snepp,[44] and a few others. I don't mention Philip Agee, a well known CIA critic, because I have the feeling that, far from being a true dissident, he has been all the time a double-agent working for the CFR conspirators who own the CIA.

There were others, like Arthur Darling and Sherman Kent, who, without going all the way to becoming dissidents, at some point may have felt that something was wrong with the CIA, but most likely never discovered the true causes for it.

Darling was a historian who worked for the CIA from 1952 to 1954, and authored *The Central Intelligence Agency: an Instrument of Government to 1950,*[45] the first official history of the CIA. The sole fact, however, that he subtitled the book "an instrument of government," shows that Darling never understood the true cause of the CIA's problems. Nevertheless, he wrote a very critical study of the early CIA in which he exposed Allen Dulles' hatchet job on Adm. Hillenkoetter. But, as soon as Dulles was appointed CIA Director in 1953, he censored it by restricting the access to the document. Darling's study was not published until 1990.[46]

The case of Sherman Kent is quite similar. Kent was the Assistant Director of National Estimates, the department that produced the National Intelligence Estimate of 19th September, 1962 —the now notorious "September Estimate"—, that predicted, based on previous intelligence, the extremely low possibility that the Soviets would place strategic nuclear missiles in Cuba in 1962. But, just a few days later, the alleged discovery of strategic nuclear missiles on Cuban soil proved the Estimate was wrong. It is known that, despite all alleged evidence to the contrary, Kent never recanted, to the point that he commented to a colleague that it was Khrushchev, not himself, the one who had being wrong. [47]

Notice that I have used the word "alleged" twice, because, contrary to the hundreds of articles, academic papers and books (most of them written by CFR agents or CFR-controlled authors) "proving" how the Soviets deployed strategic nuclear missiles on Cuban soil in 1962, this claim is simply not true. Actually, the presence of strategic nuclear missiles and their nuclear warheads in Cuba in 1962 has never been proved.[48]

In synthesis, the CIA's most acerbic critics have been the true honorable American patriots at CIA A, not the ones who praise CIA B's "successes" like messing in other countries internal affairs, overthrowing and assassinating foreign leaders, water boarding, maintaining secret prisons and performing "renditions,"[49] in support of the CFR conspirators' treasonous agenda.

Almost since the very creation of the CIA, the CFR conspirators in control of U.S. Government B have been waging a secret war against the American patriots working in CIA A. Despite the fact that most, if not all, of the treasonous and illegal actions committed against the American people and the peoples of the world have been carried out by CFR secret agents in CIA B, the ones generally maligned in the CFR-controlled mainstream media are the true patriots in CIA A. But there are recent alternative views to that picture.

In his book *Failure of Intelligence: The Decline and Fall of the CIA*, professor Melvin Goodman, a former intelligence analyst working for CIA A, wrote a whole chapter, "Intelligence: The Importance of Success," in which he unknowingly shows how most of the alleged CIA intelligence failures actually have not been attributable to CIA A, who alerted timely about the outcomes, but to CFR agents in U.S. Government B who paid no attention to the alerts.[50]

The CFR conspirators never gave a rat's ass about the intelligence produced by intelligence analysts working on CIA A. Actually, they took steps to neutralize them. And they achieved this for many years by infiltrating a clever mole in their midst.

Enemy Moles Inside the CIA

According to most books and articles written about James Jesus Angleton, the CIA's legendary Chief of Counterintelligence was convinced that the KGB had infiltrated several moles at the highest levels of the CIA. With the benefit of hindsight, it seems that Angleton was right. Enemy moles had penetrated the CIA and, paradoxically, Angleton himself was one of them.

Though based on wrong assumptions about Angleton's true secret masters, that was the conclusion reached by one of Angleton's own men, Clare Edward Petty, a member of the CIA's Special Investigations Group, a unit of the Counterintelligence Staff. After given much thinking to it, Petty concluded that Angleton was a Soviet mole.[51]

Petty was right, but just on one count: Angleton was a mole, that is, an enemy agent infiltrated at the highest levels of the CIA. But, as I will show below, he was not a Soviet mole.

Like Petty, Senator Joseph McCarthy made a similar mistake. After discovering the widespread treason prevalent at the State Department and other high levels of the U.S. Government, McCarthy concluded that, by force, the traitors had to be Communists.[52]

Petty and McCarthy were not isolated cases. Many American patriots have suspected the existence of a communist conspiracy at the higher levels of the U.S. government. Eventually, however, some of them discovered the true source of treason. At least a senior member of the John Birch Society, an organization that for many years has been blaming the Communists for many acts of treason against the American people, reached the conclusion that Communism was just a smokescreen to hide the CFR conspirators' treasonous activities. This was the case of William J. Jasper, a Senior Editor of *The New American*, the John Birch Society's organ.

In an introductory article to an issue of the magazine fully devoted "to present the truth about the Conspiracy and the Conspirators, and their goals, strategy and tactics …", Jasper mentions the case of Bella Dodd, a member of the National Committee of the Communist Party U.S.A. who left the party and became an ardent anti-Communist, as saying, "I think that the Communist conspiracy is merely a branch of the much bigger conspiracy."[53] Jasper also mentions that in his essay *The Truth in Our Time*, Robert Welch, founder of the JBS, stated, "the Communist movement is only a tool of the total conspiracy."[54]

If the actions of the CFR moles infiltrated inside the CIA, the State Department and other areas of the U.S. government have benefited America's enemies, it is not because they were pro-Nazi or pro-Soviet or are now pro-terrorists. It is because one of the CFR's main goals has always been the destruction of America as we know it. In their struggle to attain this goal, the conspirators have been using America's enemies as proxies. And there is no doubt that they have been highly successful.

Angleton's Deep Game

Undoubtedly, James Jesus Angleton was one of the most colorful figures in the world of intelligence and espionage. His life and career has been the subject of many books and articles, [55] as well as at least one spy novel.[56] Angleton's life was the classic mystery wrapped inside an enigma protected by a bodyguard of lies. It is known that privately Richard Helms called him a "strange, strange man."[57]

Nevertheless, it seems that, despite such close scrutiny by so many bright minds, the CFR's secret agent James Jesus Angleton fooled everybody. Behind this deceitful façade of mystery, intellectualism and patriotism, Angleton was not only a traitor, but also a common criminal —one more among the many hit men the CFR conspirators have used to advance their secret treasonous agendas, foreign and domestic.

In 1954, CIA Director Allen Dulles appointed Angleton as chief of the CIA's counter-intelligence section. Two years later Angleton had the greatest success of his career when he obtained a transcript of Nikita Khrushchev's 1951 secret speech to the Soviet Party Congress denouncing the atrocities committed by Joseph Stalin. After that, Angleton faded into anonymity until the CIA "family jewels" scandal brought him to light.[58]

Among the many things the "family jewels" put in evidence was that the CIA, in violation of its charter that expressly prohibited the Agency to operate on American soil, had conducted in 1967 an extensive operation, codenamed Chaos, to spy on American citizens who protested for the war in Vietnam.[59] The CIA officers in charge of Chaos were Angleton and his counterintelligence staff.[60]

This was not the first time Angleton had engaged in criminal activities on behalf of his CFR masters. In 1964, a few hours after Mary Pinchot, a 43-year-old Washington D.C. area artist was gunned down in Georgetown, Angleton broke into her house and stole her diary. Pinchot was one of President Kennedy's secret lovers, and apparently she kept a diary of the affair. The conspirator's feared that it may contain evidence linking them to the president's assassination, and they sent their trusted secret agent Angleton to accomplish the mission.

According to John Loftus and Mark Aarons, Angleton was not a hero but a villain. Among his many treacherous and criminal activities,

> Angleton laundered Nazi money, built a Vatican escape route for the fugitives of the Third Reich, and defrauded two U.S. presidents with utterly fictitious intelligence reports that helped twist American policy in the Middle East. Instead of being a friend of Israel, James Jesus Angleton was a vicious enemy of the Jews, kept under Israeli control only by the threat of blackmail.[61]

Unfortunately, however, Loftus and Aarons see these treasonous, unethical activities as a result of Angleton's own criminal actions, ignoring that he was just following orders from his CFR masters.

In October 1983, *Harper's* magazine published an intriguing, extremely well written article by Ron Rosenbaum, entitled "The Shadow of the Mole." In his article Rosenbaum —who is not only a master on the subject, but also showed that he had access to inside sources of information— told about the curious relationship developed between James Angleton and Kim Philby —the British intelligence officer who turned out to be a Soviet mole.

The most widely publicized story is that Philby, who trained Angleton in the double-cross system,[62] somehow managed to outwit his former student. Some even reasoned that Angleton's later efforts to find a mole inside the CIA were probably just an embittered reaction to his failure in detecting Philby's treachery.

The counterintelligence techniques used by Angleton in his fruitless search for the Soviet mole apparently bordered on paranoia. In his fixation to find the mole, he created an internal climate of suspicion that paralyzed CIA's A information collection capabilities. At some point many senior people at the CIA began to think that Angletonian thinking was "too convoluted" —'sick thinking' they called it— and Angleton was fired.

But Rosenbaum introduces a new, unexpected angle in his article. He believes that "James Angleton's thought was not convoluted enough." According to Rosenbaum, Philby planted in Angleton's mind the idea of the existence of a high level Soviet penetration in the CIA. But this was a false idea —a notional[63] mole. This is what Rosenbaum calls the double-double cross system.

The double-cross system, a now classical counterintelligence method, was developed by the British secret service when it captured German spies in England during WW II. On threats of execution, the spies were turned,[64] and forced to send back on their radio transmitters whatever disinformation or chicken feed the British wanted to feed the German intelligence.

But wait. According to Rosenbaum, it is also possible that Angleton had discovered Philby's treachery and, using the double-cross techniques he had learned from him, had turned the Soviet mole into an American mole. According to Rosenbaum, this is what we may properly call the double-double-double cross system.

Central to understanding Angleton's fall, is the role played by Anatoly Golitsin, a KGB counterintelligence officer who defected to the West in 1961. Golitsin, who was handed over to Angleton to run the operation, claimed that the KGB had been successful in planting a mole at the highest levels of American intelligence. This marked the beginning of Angleton's paranoid search for the mole.[65]

At some point, Golitsin warned Angleton that Soviet intelligence would attempt to prevent the CIA from discovering the mole by sending disinformation agents to obstruct the investigation. Soon after, as Golitsin had predicted, Yuri Nosenko, another KGB officer, defected to the West. Nosenko's information seemed to question Golitsin's bona fides.

From the very beginning, Angleton was convinced that Nosenko was the disinformation agent sent by the KGB to obstruct his search for the mole. However, the fact is that, even after long periods of harsh interrogation bordering on torture, Nosenko never recanted, and the CIA was never able to prove that he was a Soviet plant.

A joke told in the Soviet Union was about a factory guard who, every other Friday saw this factory worker coming out of the factory pushing a wheelbarrow packed with hay. The guard searched inside the hay, found nothing and let the guy go. This ritual repeated over several years until a time when the guard was about to retire. When the guy pushing the wheelbarrow appeared at the gate he told him: "I know you are stealing something. I am just about to retire and this is my last day here. I will not tell anybody, but, please, let me know what are you stealing." The guy smiled and answered, "Oh, I am stealing the wheelbarrows."

In the same fashion, Angleton fooled everybody with his life-long fight trying to discover a Soviet mole inside the CIA. That was the hay. But the wheelbarrow was that, as a result of his search for the mole, he paralyzed the intelligence activities of the true American patriots working in the clandestine service division of CIA A. And I have to confess that, after reading dozens of articles and books about Angleton, he also fooled me for a long time. But recently I found the key to his treachery in Colby's book *Honorable Men*.[66]

When William Colby was appointed head of the CIA's Soviet and Eastern European Division in the late fifties, he discovered that the Agency's intelligence and counterintelligence sections of CIA, mostly as a result of Angleton's activities, had been divided into two schools of thought engaged in an almost total conflict.

On the one hand, Colby found that the CIA's Clandestine Intelligence Division[67] was devoted to working on developing sources behind the Iron Curtain, interrogating defectors, and running clandestine operations, specially about Soviet military matters. On the other hand, the Counterintelligence Division, led by Angleton, was carrying on an unrelenting campaign to reveal and frustrate the KGB's operations against American intelligence, particularly its efforts to infiltrate a high-level mole inside the CIA.[68] According to Angleton, Soviet defectors should not be trusted.

After realizing the damage Angleton was causing to the Clandestine Intelligence Division, Colby's first step was to approach CIA Director Schlesinger (CFR) and ask him to curtail Angleton's power. However, Angleton had a close relationship with Dulles (CFR), Helms (CFR) and McCone (CFR),[69] and despite Colby's strong arguments Schlesinger didn't do anything. On the contrary, soon after Colby's approach to Schlesinger, Helms (CFR) told Colby that they would like to transfer him to Vietnam.[70] Soon after, Colby was appointed head of the CIA's Far East Division and sent to Vietnam during the hottest period of the war.

Was Colby's sudden transfer to Vietnam a way to put him away from the Angleton case? We can only guess, but in retrospect I think that this may have been one of the reasons for Colby's transfer.

In order to understand why Angleton's disinformation work was so important to the CFR conspirators we need to take a look at the Soviet Union itself. In the first place, the Soviet Union was an artificial creation of the Wall Street bankers and oil magnates who wanted to eliminate a potential competitor in the oil business and needed an enemy to justify their treasonous activities against the U.S. But Communism is not a productive economic system, and the Soviet Union by itself alone would never have turned into the menacing enemy they needed. Therefore, the conspirators had to resort to clever schemes to artificially keep alive the monster they had created. To this effect, they kept the Soviet threat active by giving the Soviets military materiel, advanced technology and know how, behind the backs of the American people, either directly,[71] through some programs like the Lend Lease, or indirectly, by allowing Soviet spies to "steal" it.

Despite what American history books tell, the Soviets didn't steal America's atomic secrets: the conspirators infiltrated in the U.S. government gave them to the Russians.[72] Moreover, the CFR conspirators sabotaged the Navy's efforts to launch a missile with a satellite, which allowed the Russians to launch in October 1947, the first artificial Earth satellite, the Sputnik, before the Navy's Viking rocket and Vanguard satellite.[73] Then, the conspirators used it as a way to scare the American public with the fear of the Soviets' missile and nuclear capabilities to launch a devastating attack on the U.S.

In the same fashion, the conspirators allowed Soviet spies to steal naval technology to the point that, addressing the graduating class at Annapolis Naval Academy, Secretary of the Navy John Lehman told the new officers,

> Within weeks, many of you will be looking across just hundred of feet of water at some of the most modern technology ever invented in America. Unfortunately, it is on Soviet ships.[74]

Likewise, CFR agents infiltrated in the U.S. government authorized the export of U.S.-made specialized machinery to make mini ball bearings for use in accelerometers —essential for the ICBM's guidance systems— to be exported to the Soviet Union thus making the Soviet ICBMs much more accurate.[75] They also authorized Ford Motor Company to build a heavy truck factory in the Kama River, which later produced military trucks the Vietnamese used against the U.S. military during the war.[76]

Despite all this help, however, the Soviet military machine was never a real threat to the American one. Therefore, the conspirators' propaganda machine worked hard to inflate it.

Painting the Soviets as ten-feet tall gorillas was a full time job for the CFR agents at the Pentagon. Nevertheless, honest CIA A officers at the clandestine service division kept finding solid intelligence proving that the threatening Soviet military machine was a bluff. And the main source for this intelligence was Soviet defectors who accurately described the permanent economic crisis and the overall inefficiency and chaos of the Soviet system.

However, the CIA's counterintelligence Division, under Angleton's control, maintained that those defectors were actually plants[77] under KGB control that the Soviets deliberately were sending to the CIA to feed manipulated information as part of a massive deception program. Moreover, according to Angleton, most of this disinformation consisted in painting the Soviet Union as economically and militarily weak, when it actually was strong and warmongering.[78]

The bottom line is that, despite all his cleverness, dedication and alleged paranoia, Angleton never found the Soviet moles infiltrated at the CIA. What he did, however, was to practically sabotage and put in disarray the CIA's clandestine service division.

An index indicating that Angleton was doing an important job on behalf of his CFR masters was that, when William Colby was back in Langley as CIA Director, he discovered to his utter surprise, that one of the few senior CIA officers who had escaped the purge as the result of the "family jewels" scandal, was none other than James Jesus Angleton.[79] So, Colby began shearing Angleton's long wings and not only removed from his control such functions as terrorism and CIA's liaison with the FBI but also stopped his total control over the CIA's relationship with Israel. [80]

In order to understand Colby's behavior one must keep in mind, first, that despite the fact that he had become a CFR member, he was never accepted in its inner circles. Colby was a trusted man with impeccable OSS credentials, but he had humble origins and was not part of the Old Boys club. Secondly, and this is even more important, Colby had been unexpectedly propelled to the CIA directorship almost by accident, as a result of the chaos created at CIA by the many resignations and firings from the troubled Nixon administration.

Therefore, despite the fact that he had dedicated his whole career to advance the CFR conspirators' plans, contrary to people like Dulles, Helms or Angleton, there is the possibility that Colby, like many honest CIA employees, had been recruited under a false flag. Consequently, he may have done his treasonous work unwittingly, under the false impression that he was a true American patriot working for the American people.

Showing his extreme naiveté, incredible for a man with his experience, Colby told that, after discovering the counterproductive results of Angleton's Counterintelligence Division, and finding out that, despite all of his efforts, there were no tangible positive results in the counterintelligence field, he did not suspect Angleton and his staff of engaging in improper activities. He simply, "just could not figure out what they were doing." But, "what really turned me off was the discovery that [Angleton's] counterintelligence theories[81] were actually hurting good clandestine operational officers."[82]

Apparently, it never crossed Colby's mind that, like himself, Angleton and his men —most of them perhaps unwittingly— had been doing a very good job on behalf of Angleton's treasonous CFR masters.

Chapter 7

The Cold War PSYOP

A characteristic common to all intelligence officers, East and West, is that they have a special open-mindedness. For them nothing is impossible just because it is improbable.
—Thomas Powers.

When you have eliminated the impossible, whatever remains, however improbable, must be the truth.
—Sherlock Holmes.

With the end of World War II and Germany's defeat,[1] the conspirators lost the enemy they had carefully created and nurtured: the Nazis. Consequently, they needed a new enemy to fill the vacuum and justify their aggressive political and military policies around the world. Therefore, they adjudicated that role to the Soviet Union and communism. But, first, they needed to convince the American people of the existence of the new threat.

Since early 1948, the destinies of Fidel Castro and the Council on Foreign Relations have been closely intertwined. Just a perfunctory analysis of the Castro-U.S. relations since 1948 shows that almost every American who has supported Castro has been linked, directly or indirectly, to the CFR and, despite the conspirators' efforts to hide this relationship, some people have suspected it.

U.S. Ambassador Earl E. T. Smith, for one, was convinced that Castro was a Communist, and he was allowed to grab power in Cuba in 1959 thanks to the efforts of several people in the State Department, among them William Wieland and Roy Rubbotom.[2] These two shady characters, particularly Wieland, have been consistently accused of being pro-Castro because they were Communists.

The truth, however, is that, far from being Communists, they were just following orders from above. One must keep in mind that, beginning in late 1949, the U.S. State Department fell fully under CFR control,[3] and the U.S. Secretary of State at the time Castro took power was John Foster Dulles, a senior CFR agent. Therefore, it is safe to surmise that the true protectors of Castro were not in the Kremlin but in the Pratt House in Manhattan.

The CFR Conspirators Use the CIA to Recruit Fidel Castro

On April 9, 1948, Bogotá, the capital of Colombia, was the scene of violent riots, later known as the Bogotazo.[4] The event that apparently unleashed the riots was the assassination of Colombia's populist leader Jorge Eliécer Gaitán. The rioters destroyed most of the city and several thousand people were killed. The events coincided with the celebration in Bogotá of the Ninth International Conference of

American States, which had opened its sessions on March 30, 1948, chaired by U.S. Secretary of State and Secret CFR agent General George C. Marshall.

Most books and articles about the CIA mention the Agency's first two successful covert operations: the overthrowing of Premier Mossadegh of Iran in 1953 and the overthrowing of President Arbenz of Guatemala in 1954. A few of them go further and mention the CIA's messing with the elections in Italy in 1947-1948, allegedly to avoid the Italians electing members of the Communist Party. Some of them spare a few paragraphs to mention the CIA's alleged first mistake: its failure to predict the Bogotazo riots. But there is more about the Bogotazo affair than the CIA, Castro, and their CFR masters want us to know.

The Bogotazo is a key event to understand many similar false flag operations carried out by the CIA following the CFR conspirators' orders —including the 9/11/2001 operation. Therefore, I am going to study it in some detail. As authors Loftus and Aarons rightly pointed out, "Omission from history is the hallmark of success in covert operations."[5]

In the morning of April 9, Jorge Eliécer Gaitán, a Colombian political leader, was gunned down as he was leaving his office. Fidel Castro and three other students from the University of Havana, Rafael del Pino,[6] Enrique Ovares and Alfredo Guevara (no relation to Che Guevara), had arrived in Bogotá a few days before the Conference was scheduled to start. Their overt purpose was to attend a student's congress, which had been planned to coincide with the Conference.

Castro and del Pino had contacted Gaitán, allegedly to invite him to speak at the inaugural session of the student's congress, and Gaitán had agreed to meet them early in the afternoon. That same afternoon, less than two hours before the meeting, Gaitán was shot as he was leaving his office to have lunch with a few friends. Castro and del Pino were close by when the assassination took place.

The murder of Gaitán unleashed a frenzied, senseless orgy of killing, burning, and looting that destroyed most of the center of Bogotá and virtually cut it off from the rest of the world for two days. The riots took the lives of more than a thousand people. Before the riots ended, 150 buildings had been burned down or severely damaged. The riots marked the onset of a dark period in Colombia's history called "la Violencia," (the Violence), which claimed more than 200,000 lives in the decade following the Bogotazo and has continued almost uninterrupted to the present day.

What none of the books about the CIA mention, however, is that the Bogotazo actually was the CIA's first successful large-scale psychological warfare operation (PSYOP) carried out on behalf of the CFR conspirators. In it, they tested new covert warfare, propaganda and mind control techniques later employed in operations ranging from the assassination of President Kennedy to the 9/11 PSYOP.

In addition, the Bogotazo operation was the event where the conspirators used for the first time their newly recruited secret agent: Fidel Castro.

For reasons one can only guess, CIA talent spotters at the U.S. Embassy in Havana decided to recruit Fidel Castro as an agent provocateur and send him to Bogotá, Colombia, on a sensitive mission. Apparently Castro's already impressive record as a gangster, assassin and psychopath totally lacking in moral principles convinced them that he was the right person they were looking for to perform a delicate and important job.

In the summer of 1947, while a law student at the University of Havana, Fidel Castro was accused of killing fellow student Leonel Gómez, his opponent for the nomination of president of the Law School Student Federation in the coming elections. Nevertheless, the judge decided there was not enough evidence and Castro was not indicted. On February 22, 1948, Manolo Castro (not related to Fidel), president of the University's Student Federation, was killed in a Chicago-gangster-style shoot-out at a cinema in downtown Havana. Two days later Castro was detained on charges of murder, but he was set free two days later, allegedly because of lack of evidence.

Castro's criminal activities were reported in the Cuban press, and noticed by intelligence officers at the U.S. Embassy in Havana. A confidential Dispatch to the State Department signed by Embassy Counselor Lester D. Mallory, dated April 26, 1948, states,

> He [Castro] is the student leader of the Law School of the University of Habana (lit.) and last came to the Embassy's attention in connection with the shooting of the former FEU [University Students' Association] President Manolo Castro (no relation). Fidel Castro is believed to be a member of the Union Insurreccional Revolucionaria (UIR), the band of thugs and "student" strong-arm boys which is generally considered to have been responsible for the killing of Manolo Castro in the culmination of a longstanding police and student feud.[7]

For many years some people, including myself, had suspected that the only explanation for Castro's long life of unmolested anti-American hatred just 90 miles from American shores was because he was working for the very same people he claimed to hate, and I found abundant circumstantial evidence proving it. It was not until 1995, however, that somebody provided the first direct evidence that Castro had been recruited by the U.S. intelligence services.

In a book self-published in 1995,[8] Ramón B. Conte, an eyewitness who used to do some minor contract work for the CIA as a heavy,[9] mentions in some detail how the recruitment of Fidel Castro took place in early 1948, during a meeting at the residence of Mario Lazo. Lazo was an American-educated Cuban lawyer who represented most American interests in Cuba. Conte and another CIA operative were on a stakeout in a car parked across the street in front of Lazo's house. They were armed and ready to intervene if Castro, known for his flaring temper and love for firearms, refused the offer and turned violent.

Castro attended the meeting accompanied by his friend Rafael del Pino Siero, a CIA asset who had been in the U.S. Army during WWII. Among the people who attended the secret meeting were Lazo himself, CIA officer Richard Salvatierra, CIA agent Isabel Siero Pérez,[10] former U.S. ambassador to Cuba Willard Beaulac,[11] and two other Americans. Conte only identified them as Col. Roberts and a CIA officer known as Mr. Davies.[12]

Some years after Conte published his book, I interviewed him over the phone. In the interview he added to the list of people who attended the meeting at Lazo's home an important name he failed to mention in his book: William D. Pawley.[13]

Pawley was a millionaire businessman close friend of President Eisenhower and Allen Dulles. At the time of the meeting, he was U.S. ambassador to Peru and Brazil. He had been closely linked to the U.S. intelligence services since the times of the OSS, and was one of the main organizers of the Ninth Inter-American Conference that was planned to take place in April in Bogotá.[14]

According to Conte, a week after the initial meeting, Castro and del Pino met again with CIA's Salvatierra, who had been assigned the job of Castro's controller. In this second meeting, Castro was given instructions about his first mission. It consisted in traveling to Bogotá, Colombia and, acting as an agent provocateur, participate in the assassination of Gaitán, which would be used as a pretext to provoke the riots known as the Bogotazo. The secondary goal of the operation was to plant false clues that would be used later to blame the Communists for the riots. The riots would help Secretary Marshall to use the fear of communism as a threat to convince the delegates attending the Conference that the Communist menace was real.[15]

The Bogotazo False Flag Operation and the Cold War PSYOP

Most Colombians who have studied the Bogotazo believe that the event was just a violent outburst in Colombia's national politics. But, as I will show below, they are wrong.

Actually, the Bogotazo was a false flag operation.[16] It was an important part of a psychological warfare operation that had nothing to do with Colombia's internal affairs. Indeed, a secret report about the riots made by Naval Attaché Col. W. F. Hausman, of the U.S. Office of Naval Intelligence, mentions that the riots had been initially planned to occur during the Pan American Conference in Rio de Janeiro in 1947, but the Brazilian police did a good job and dispersed the rioters before they did any harm.[17]

The Bogotazo false flag operation was the event that triggered the beginning in the Western hemisphere of a PSYOP of enormous proportions: the Cold War.

As I mentioned above, the CIA's alleged failure to forecast the Bogotazo riots was later used by CFR agent Allen Dulles as a pretext to get rid of CIA Director Adm. Hillenkoetter and eventually get control over the CIA. There is evidence, however, proving that the CIA actually informed U.S. authorities about the possibility of disturbances during the Conference but, as usual, the warnings were ignored.

In his memoirs, U.S. Ambassador to Colombia Willard Beaulac wrote,

> It was freely and apparently reliably reported that the Communists planned to demonstrate against the conference and, if possible, to cause riots and even civil war in an effort to break it up.[18]

Detailed and accurate CIA reports about the possibility of Soviet instigated insurgency in Colombia were blocked in the American Embassy in Bogotá and not forwarded to Secretary of State Marshall.[19] A CIA report filed from Colombia more than two months before the Bogotazo stated:

> January 29. — Mr. G. [most likely Antonio García], the leading Colombian Communist, who has been given the task of overthrowing the Pérez [Ospina] (Conservative) government, boasts that he can count on planes and artillery when necessary. In Bogotá, this group has allegedly stored arms and explosives in 17 houses.[20]

Now, one must keep in mind that, as I warned in the Preface of this book, out of unavoidable oversimplification, when one says "a CIA report," it actually means "a report written by somebody at CIA." We must also keep in mind that, as I have explained above in this book, the CIA has never been a homogenous organization. The only CIA department the conspirators care about and fully control is covert operations, and need-to-know and compartmentation are intrinsic to the intelligence work. Therefore, one can safely assume that the CIA officer who made the report most likely was not part of the Bogotazo PSYOP, a secret operation fully under the tight control of CFR agents at Wisner's Office of Special Projects.

After studying the Bogotazo case, the Senate Internal Security Subcommittee made these comments about the reasons why the CIA reports were not delivered in timely fashion:

> O.J. Libert, State Department aide in Bogotá, and Ambassador Willard L. Beaulac were charged by Admiral Hillenkoetter with failure to forward these messages to the State Department in Washington. Mr. Libert vetoed sending these messages to Secretary Marshall's security officers because he thought Bogotá police protection was "adequate," and he did not wish to "alarm the delegates unduly."[21]

Beaulac's activities in blocking the intelligence report, and his insistence in blaming the Communists for the riots, as well as his probable participation in the earlier meeting at Lazo's residence, are consistent with him being an active part of the Bogotazo operation. Moreover, it is safe to assume that, as a trusted CFR member, Secretary of State Marshall was also an important part of the operation, and he had been informed about it.

In his testimony of April 15, 1948, before a special Congress subcommittee investigating the CIA's "failure" to forecast the Bogotazo riots, CIA Director Adm. Hillenkoetter rebuked his critics by stating that the CIA had reported timely about the "possibility of violence and outbreak" during the Conference, and that this information had been transmitted to officials in the State Department.[22] Hillenkoetter also charged that Embassy officials in Bogotá had blocked the transmission of a CIA key report dated March 23 to the Sate Department, alerting about the possibility of disturbances during the Conference.[23]

Moreover, according to an October 14, 1948, Report of the Office of Intelligence Research of the State Department, the theory that the Communists were involved in the assassination of Gaitán is based on the allegation that they had made, far in advance, plans to sabotage the activities of the Conference of American States and to disturb the activities of several of the delegations, principally that of the U.S.[24]

An important clue to the disinformation techniques used in the Bogotazo operation is the fact that, though the CIA allegedly failed to inform Marshall about the possibility of riots, CFR secret agents in the field kept the Colombian press well informed in advance about that possibility. As Francisco Fandiño Silva, a well known Colombian journalist, later recalled, "The American Embassy informed me that it had received reports that a bomb attack was to be made against the General [Marshall]."[25]

Following the same pattern of disinformation, on March 24, Gaitán received a disingenuous warning from Ambassador Beaulac, telling him that the Communists were planning to break up the Conference and that, if they succeeded, Gaitán's Liberal Party most likely would be blamed for the events.[26]

Just a few hours after the Bogotazo riots erupted, General Marshall, CIA Director Adm. Hillenkoetter, U.S. Ambassador to Colombia Willard Beaulac, Colombia's President Dr. Mariano Ospina, Secretary of the Presidency Rafael Azula, and other important witnesses concluded that the Bogotazo was a Communist operation instigated by the Soviet Union.

Puzzled by the Agency's first intelligence "failure," CIA officer Russell Jack Smith telephoned to a contact in Secretary Marshall's office in the State Department and asked,

> Where did the Secretary get the information that the rioting in Bogotá was a communist plot?" "Oh," his contact said casually, "he just looked out of the window in his villa six or seven miles away and said, 'The communists did it.'"[27]

A few days later, on April 13, 1948, the *Philadelphia Inquirer* published an article under the title "Marshall Blames World Communism for Bogotá Revolt," providing more elements in an effort to convince the American public that the assassination of Gaitán and the Bogotazo riots had been a work of the Colombian Communists with the support of the Soviet Union.

Later efforts were made to convince the American public that the Bogotazo had been a Communist operation.

The Agent Provocateurs

On their way to Colombia, Castro and del Pino stopped first in Panama, where they were introduced to President Enrique Jiménez and del Pino gave a violent anti-American speech.[28] Argentina's president Juan Domingo Perón, who acted as a cut-out to hide the true source of the money, provided the funds for Castro and del Pino's trip. Perón's pro-Nazi activities have been extensively documented, and he was a personal friend of CFR senior agent Allen Dulles.

A few days later, the Cubans repeated their performance in Venezuela, where they meet with a group of university students and became acquainted with former President Rómulo Betancourt, who was to head Venezuela's delegation to the Conference in Bogotá.[29] Because of his nationalist, anti-imperialist stance,[30] and the fact that as a young man he had been a leader of the Communist Party, Betancourt was seen as a troublemaker and the CFR conspirators had accused him of being a Communist. Castro's meetings with Jiménez and Betancourt was another element used to boost his cover as a Communist.

As soon as Fidel Castro and Rafael del Pino Siero arrived at the Medellín, Colombia airport, the Colombian National Security Office immediately placed them under surveillance. Alberto Niño, former Colombia's Security Chief, later wrote that he had been informed that the Cubans had come as a replacement for two Soviet agents stationed in Cuba.[31] Fulfilling their role as agent provocateurs, once in Bogotá, Castro and del Pino openly distributed pro-Communist literature just a few days before the Bogotazo and kept Communist literature in their hotel room, to be later found by a Colombian detective.

Some witnesses claim that about 4:00 p.m., just a few hours after Gaitán had been assassinated, they saw a street mob, led by Fidel Castro, shouting *"A Palacio"* ["To the Palace," meaning the Presidential mansion]. According to the witnesses, Castro was carrying a rifle and boasted that he just had killed two priests. But, if he really said so, he was lying. No priests were killed during the Bogotazo.

In an effort to add credibility to the allegation that Castro was a Soviet agent, William D. Pawley, U.S. Ambassador to Brazil and a Conference delegate, declared to a U.S. Senate investigation that, while he was riding an official Embassy car the day the riots begun, he heard somebody on the radio saying,

> This is Fidel Castro from Cuba. This is a Communist revolution. The President has been killed. All the military establishments are now in our hands. The Navy has capitulated to us and this revolution has been a success.[32]

Some authors have used Pawley's words as the ultimate proof that at that early time Fidel Castro already was a Communist. Nevertheless, as I mentioned before, this goes against the evidence. In the first place, because of the possibility that, according to Conte, Pawley had attended the meeting at Lazo's home where the CFR conspirators recruited Castro. Secondly, because of Pawley's key role as a personal envoy of President Eisenhower in trying to convince Cuba's President Batista to leave the country and open the way for Castro grabbing power in Cuba in 1959. (More on this below).

Using agent provocateurs to incite rebellious people to commit terrorist acts, or even faking them, is not alien to the conspirators who control the U.S. government. In his book *Body of Secrets*,[33] James Bamford mentions Operation Northwoods, the code name for a proposed false flag operation that included sabotages, provocations and assassination attempts of U.S. citizens.

The plan, attributed to CFR member Maj. Gen. Lyman Lemnitzer —which indicates that it was most likely conceived at the Harold Pratt House—, is detailed in a declassified Joint Chiefs of Staff document from 1961, which outlined U.S. plans to covertly fabricate various pretexts that would justify an American invasion of Cuba. The plan included staging the assassination of Cubans living in the U.S., simulating an attack on the Guantánamo base, and blowing a U.S. ship in Cuban waters to create a "Remember the *Maine*" type of incident.

Bamford believes that Operation Northwoods is perhaps the most corrupt plan ever created by the U.S. government — but we must keep in mind that he wrote his book before the 9/11 false flag operation. There is no doubt, however, that the military men who created the anonymous document, consciously dishonored their uniforms, their branch of service, and their country.

More recently, it became known that Secretary of Defense Donald Rumsfeld, a CFR member, mentioned the conspirators' plan for the creation of an organization called Proactive, Preemptive Operations Group (P2OG). The P2OG's main purpose is to prod indecisive or reluctant terrorists into committing terrorist actions —even if these actions cost American lives.[34]

Planting False Clues

Since their arrival in Bogotá, Castro and del Pino devoted an inordinate amount of time to plant false clues in an effort to implicate the Colombian Communists and the Soviet Union in the coming assassination of Gaitán and the riots.

On September 22, 1949, *El Gráfico* of Caracas, published a confidential report filed by Colombian Detective number 6. The Report was originally published in the influential Bogotá daily *El Siglo*. It deals with the results of the surveillance on Castro and del Pino prior and during the Bogotazo riots.

In the Report, Detective number 6 stated that,

> He was detailed by the Chief of Detectives of the National Police, Dr. Iván Arévalo, to guard the President of the republic, Dr. Mariano Ospina Pérez, and his wife during the evening performance which they were attending a the Colón Theatre on April 3rd.
>
> At about 10:00 P.M., shortly after the third act of the play had begun, "There was a shower of leaflets from the gallery. These had been printed in Havana [speculated Detective number 6]; they lacked the Bogotá municipal tax stamp; they were definitely Communist in style and revolutionary in phraseology and contrary to the democratic principles of our country, England and the United States.
>
> With two other detectives, he proceeded to the gallery where he caught the two Cubans in the act of showering "the boxes and orchestra of the Colón Theatre with their revolutionary propaganda."

> Detective number 6 took Fidel Castro and del Pino into custody and proceeded to their lodgings —room 33 of the Hotel Claridge. There the two Cubans *voluntarily* [emphasis added] showed the detectives various papers, some of importance. There was a letter from Rómulo Betancourt "recommending both of them," *and various Communist or leftwing books* [emphasis added], including one of Betancourt "with whom they claimed to have close relationships or friendship and political affinity. [35]

According to the Report, the detectives asked for written authorization from their superiors to pick up Castro and del Pino's passports and summon them to the Bureau of Detectives of the National Police for further interrogation on their Communist activities. Strangely, the permission was denied.[36] It seems that some important people needed Castro and del Pino free to continue doing their job uninterrupted.

The very same day Gaitán was assassinated at 1:30 PM, Castro and del Pino were sitting at a café facing the building where Gaitán's office was located, waiting for an interview they were going to have with Gaitán at 3:00 PM. Castro and Gaitán had already met briefly a few days earlier.[37] The date and time of the interview was recorded in Gaitán's daily schedule. According to journalist Jules Dubois, the interview was to be held in the offices of the Newspaper *El Tiempo*.[38]

Was Castro a Communist?

Most of the authors who have tried to explain the Bogotazo as an operation carried out by Communists and Castro as a Communist himself—i.e. Nathaniel Weyl in his *Red Star Over Cuba* and Angel Aparicio Laurencio's *Antecedentes desconocidos del nueve de abril*—, have relied heavily on Alberto Niño's book.[39] Niño was the former Security Chief of Colombia, and his book has an obvious anti-Communist slant.

For example, according to Niño, "These same days arrived to Bogotá the well known Cuban Communists Fidel Alejandro Castro and Rafael del Pino."[40] Nevertheless, contrary to Niño's allegation, there is not a single bit of evidence showing that before the Bogotazo either Castro or del Pino had been linked in any way to the Cuban Communist party.

Moreover, for being an anticommunist, Niño shows a total ignorance of Communist tactics. As further proof that Castro and del Pino were Communists, he mentions that the day before the onset of the Bogotazo events, the Cubans attended a meeting at the Colombian Labor Organization where Castro gave a lecture on the techniques of the coup d'ètat. However, just a perfunctory reading of Communist literature shows that the Communists have always opposed coup d'ètats, which they consider a fascist technique.

A United Press report dated April 19,1947, details how, according to a Hotel Claridge employee, two Colombian detectives got to the hotel and, after searching the Cubans' room, found some of their personal mail which, according to a witness, they opened in his presence. The witness added that the correspondence showed that both Cubans belonged to the Cuban Communist Party.[41]

According to the report, the detectives also found, and confiscated as evidence, identification cards with photographs, identifying Castro and del Pino as first-grade agents of the Third Front of the USSR in South America.[42] Other sources mentioned that in some of the correspondence the investigators found ground plans of Colombia's Capitol and the Conference's site.[43] Security Chief Alberto Niño also mentions that, among some things seized by the police from the Cubans on April 3rd, there was a letter addressed to Fidel Castro from "Mirtha."[44]

Though essentially a love letter, it contained a revealing sentence: "I remember that you told me you were going to start a revolution in Bogotá."[45] The information in the letter seems to be confirmed by the fact that on April 8, the day before Gaitán was assassinated, Castro and del Pino had held a meeting with militants of the Colombian Labor Federation, where Castro lectured on the techniques of general strike and armed seizure of power (a.k.a. putsch or coup d'ètat).[46]

It is interesting to notice that when Castro and his men attacked the Moncada garrison in Santiago de Cuba in 1953, the Cuban Communists issued a statement published in New York's *Daily Worker*, in which they strongly criticized the action, calling it a putschist attempt.[47] It is highly revealing, however, that the Cuban Communists' used the word "putschist" —communist parlance for fascist— to criticize Castro's methods.

In 1944, during his last high school year at the Jesuit's Colegio de Belén, Castro had his first clash with the Cuban Communists, when he used Belén as a tribune to attack an educational proposal, popularly known as the Marinello Law,[48] the creation of Dr. Juan Marinello, the president of the Cuban Communist party and a senator. Castro's attack implied that Marinello's plan had been conceived following Soviet Russia's or Nazi Germany's lines. The true motive for Fidel's attack was that, if approved by Congress, the proposal would negatively affect private education in Cuba, including the Catholic Colegio de Belén.

Although Castro was just an unknown high school student at the time, the Communists took exception to his words and retaliated with a vicious attack on the young Fidel in the pages of *Hoy*, the Communist Party's official newspaper. They called Fidel a "*come gofio*" (sucker). Most likely, it was at that time when the officers at the American embassy in Havana took first notice of him.

A few years later, in 1947, when Castro was a student at the University of Havana, he ran for vice-president of the Law School. Knowing that the Communists had a strong following among the students, he began using a strong anti-American rhetoric and managed to convince some of them to support him. But, once elected, he began a militant campus campaign against them. The Communists retaliated by denouncing him as a traitor.[49] Since that early date there was no love left between Fidel Castro and the Cuban Communists.

Far from showing any Communist leanings, after the Bogotazo Castro continued pushing his fascist ideas. On July 26, 1960, in a speech commemorating the failed attack on the Moncada garrison in Santiago de Cuba, Fidel Castro declared his commitment to "liberate" the rest of Latin America.[50] What he didn't make clear, however, is that his way to achieve that goal essentially consisted in the indiscriminate application of fascist-like putschist coup d'états, including the assassination of some democratically elected presidents of the target countries.

If the available record is correct, as everything seems to indicate, Fidel Castro was not a Communist before or after the Bogotazo events. Consequently, it seems likely that Castro's recruitment in Lazo's house actually took place, and that his role as an agent provocateur during the Bogotazo was played on behalf of the people who control the CIA: the CFR conspirators.

The Bogotazo and the Assassination of Gaitán

Most authors who have studied the Bogotazo riots agree that, far from being a spontaneous uprising there were signs indicating previous preparation. Fidel Castro himself has given some credibility to these suspicions.

In an interview with Indian journalist Kurt Singer in late 1960, Castro mentioned how, when he was barely twenty, he "participated in the realization of *a plan* [emphasis added] whose goal was the liberation of Colombia."[51] The fact that he was following a plan is confirmed by the letter mentioned above in which his girlfriend Mirtha[52] tells him she is worried because, before the trip, he had told her that he was "going to start a revolution in Bogotá."[53]

Given the fact, however, that at the time 21 year old Castro lacked the experience, the resources and political stature to lead such a plan, one can conclude that it was somebody else's plan. Moreover, with the benefit of hindsight, it is safe to surmise that the plan he mentioned had been conceived by the Wall Street conspirators at the Harold Pratt House and carried out by their recently created CIA.

Indeed, there are many things pointing to the fact that the Bogotazo riots had been planned way in advance. Probably the most clear was that, a few hours before the assassination of Gaitán took place, the newspaper *El Popular*, of Barquisimeto, Venezuela, printed on its edition of April 9, 1948 (logically prepared the night before it was printed) the news of the assassination and the riots and released it to the public.

The amazing fact was noticed and mentioned by other publications. A few days later, on April 14, another Venezuelan publication, *El Gráfico de Caracas*, reproduced a photocopy of the *El Popular*'s issue with the information. On April 29, a Colombian newspaper, *El Siglo* of Bogotá, also reproduced *El Popular*'s information.[54]

Now, if one discards the possibility of extra-sensory perception, the only thing that may explain the publication of the news about the assassination of Gaitán and the Bogotazo riots, *before* they happened, is that the CIA's Mighty Wurlitzer[55] made a mistake.

Nevertheless, these are not the only strange things about the Bogotazo.

Though the rioters used improvised destructive devices to carry out their job, some observers later noticed that they worked with astounding efficiently and speed. According to some sources, many rioters wore red arm bands, the traditional symbol of Colombia's Liberal Party, but some of them were emblazoned with the hammer-and-sickle,"[56] the universal symbol of communism.

A witness who saw first hand the work of a group of about 25 rioters declared that they were disciplined and organized. The leader wore a red armband. Then, they joined three more similar groups, whose leader wore a white armband. One oof the leaders had a typed list of specific buildings to loot and destroy. During the time he joined the groups, the witness said that he didn't hear any comment criticizing General Marshall or the United States.[57]

Evidence shows that, despite the apparent chaos, the rioters acted as if following a plan. Some witnesses observed that the destruction was so organized to the point of having points in the city where gas cans that could be used to set buildings on fire had been previously stored in strategic places. [58] On the other hand, the famous Treatro Colón, the Jockey Club and the Gun Club, maximum symbols of the Colombian high class, were left untouched. Moreover, though the looters stole all private property they could carry, they left untouched the real estate records and property transactions archived in the offices of the notaries public.[59]

Even more difficult to understand is that, despite the bloodthirsty excesses of the chaotic mass of rioters, some among them seemed to be acting in coordination. For example, while some of them were preparing Molotov cocktails to destroy a building, others stormed it and, while destroying the furniture, forced everyone out in an effort not to cause unnecessary deaths.[60] Moreover, despite the fact that radio announcers frantically accused Gen. Marshall of being implicated in Gaitán's assassination, the rioters left Marshall and the Conference delegates unmolested. Actually, no Colombian or foreign public figure lost his life in the riots.[61]

A few minutes before 2 p.m., the mob got to the National Capitol, where the Conference had been in session and most of the delegates were ready to leave, and began sacking the building. But, strangely, none of the more than one hundred delegates present was harmed. The mob kept them surrounded until late in the evening, when they were rescued by military forces and escorted to their respective embassies.

The next day, Argentinean Foreign Minister Carlos Atilio Bramuglia, with the support of many delegates who feared for their lives, suggested that the Conference be cancelled. General Marshall, however, perhaps based on privileged information, strongly opposed their suggestion. Eventually, the meeting place of the Conference was moved to a school in the outskirts of the city, where it continued unmolested its deliberations which culminated with the proclamation of the Declaration of Bogotá.[62]

The use of several propaganda devices during the Bogotazo, typical of psychological warfare operations, points out to a previous careful preparation of the events. For instance, just a few minutes after Gaitán was assassinated, a leaflet was distributed in the streets of Bogotá. The printing evidenced the use of more than six different typefaces; the paper on which it was printed was dry; the margins and the printed text were neat, with no ink smudges. The text, allegedly written by the Colombian Communists, accused President Ospina of the crime.[63]

Just a few minutes after the news of the assassination of Gaitán was known, railroad stations, post and telegraph offices, and radio stations had fallen under the control of the rioters. Moreover, radio stations played an important role in the coordination of the riots. Most of the authors who have studied the Bogotazo agree that radio broadcasters played a key role in instigating the mob.[64]

Less than 20 minutes after Gaitán was assassinated many radio stations began broadcasting messages inciting violence and instructing the rioters on how to obtain weapons by assaulting hardware stores, how to prepare Molotov cocktails, and where to attack.[65] Though some legitimate announcers apparently sensed the danger that Gaitán's assassination may cause, and warned their listeners not to join the rioters and stay at home or at work,[66] others did the opposite and incited the rioters to loot, kill and destroy.

The broadcasters demonstrated a high degree of professionalism that goes contrary to the generalized opinion that everything happened in the spur of the moment. A secret report made by Naval Attaché Col. W. F. Hausman, of the U.S. Office of Naval Intelligence, to the ONI headquarters, mentions "secret radio transmissions," inciting the people to revolt.[67] According to another report, at least three clandestine radio stations, one of them mobile, began broadcasting their inflammatory messages just a few minutes after Gaitán was assassinated.[68] Moreover, most of the radio stations involved in the operation used the same technique. They broadcasted for a few minutes, and then changed their frequency before resuming broadcasting so they could not be easily located by triangulation.[69]

A recurrent message in the radio harangues was a call to kill President Ospina, whom they accused of being sold to Yankee imperialism. According to some of the radio messages, Ospina, in cahoots with General Marshall, had ordered Gaitán's assassination.[70] Surprisingly, however, the broadcasters never incited the mob to disrupt the Conference or physically attack Marshall or any other American attending the Conference.

Many witnesses reported the activity of snipers during the riots.[71] Actually, a large part of the casualties were the result of sniper activity. Due to the fact that some of the snipers were shooting from the top of high buildings and from churches' bell towers, an unfounded rumor began circulating that priests were shooting at the people.

It was widely reported that some of the rioters assaulted police stations where they stole arms and ammo. Yet, as anybody with military training may testify, sniping is not an easy ability to master. Even though firing a rifle is not too difficult, hitting a target at a distance farther away than half a block is quite a different thing, particularly if the shooter has no previous training and the rifle has not been professionally zeroed.

Therefore, the question remains. Who were the snipers? Where did they get their weapons? Who trained and deployed them?

It was not a coincidence that the Bogotazo riots erupted while the Ninth Conference was taking place. In 1945, after the end of WWII, the American military-industrial complex and its Wall Street associates were desperately looking for a way to continue producing armaments and saw Latin America as a potential market for their products. This explains why, in an effort to add the military field to Latin America's economic dependency to the United States, they kept active the military bases the U.S. has acquired south of the border with the pretext of the war against the Axis, continued training officers from Latin American countries, and moved to standardize South and Central American military equipment along U.S. lines.

To that end, the CFR conspirators infiltrated in the U.S. government emphasized Latin America's importance as a safe source of basic materials from a geographic area where foreign powers could not interfere. The plan was to use the Latin American military as their praetorian guard to protect the natural resources that, according to their reasoning, rightly belonged to the Wall Street conspirators. The first step in that direction was the signing of the Rio Pact of 1947, a military alliance between the United States and the Latin American countries (with the exception of Uruguay, which refused to sign).

Most Latin American governments had signed the Pact with the hope that the U.S. would give them the economic help they badly needed —of which corrupt politicians hoped to steal a great part— in return for their political and military cooperation. A year later, however, the economic aid had not materialized, and the politicians were not happy. Now the U.S. had asked them to meet again in Bogotá to sign new treaties.

Cardinal among them was the creation of a new tool for political and economic domination, the Organization of American States (OAS), as well as a commitment to fight the new artificially created enemy: Soviet communism. A secret memorandum dated March 22, 1948, signed by George Kennan (CFR), Director of Political Planning at the State Department, mentions that the problem of Communism would be considered at the Ninth Conference, as well as anticommunist measures that would be prepared and implemented in the interamerican system.[72]

However, given their previous experience, most leaders of the Latin American countries were not eager to help the U.S. to reach its goal. This was evidenced during the first days of the Conference by the delegates' reluctance to cave in to Marshall's pressures. Particularly concerning to the delegates was the inclusion of a dangerous loophole in the OAS proposed Charter of Article 15, which stated: "No State or group of States has the right to intervene, directly or indirectly, for any reason whatsoever, in the internal or external affairs of any State." This principle was supposed to apply not only to armed force, but also to any other form of interference or attempted threat. But the loophole specified that "measures" could be "adopted for the maintenance of peace and security in accordance with existing treaties."

With the addition of this loophole, the CFR conspirators controlling the U.S. government guaranteed their right to intervene at will in Latin America, and the Latin American delegates were not pleased. But the sight of the angry mobs in the streets, the burning of the buildings, and the indiscriminate killing, proved to be more persuasive than Marshall's arguments. The last day of the Conference, the delegates not only unanimously approved the Charter creating the OAS, but also a document condemning international communism.[73]

After they had approved the creation of the OAS, some of the scared delegates still had the audacity to ask Marshall if there was any possibility of a "Marshall Plan" for Latin America. But, adding insult to outrage, Marshall answered that it was beyond the possibilities of the United States to finance such a plan. The capital required, he added, "must come from private sources."[74]

The OAS Charter provided the legal mechanism for upholding the Monroe Doctrine. Due to the fact that the U.S. controlled the majority in the OAS, including several Latin American votes, this would guarantee their right to legally intervene militarily in the affairs of the OAS member countries. If the votes did not give the CFR conspirators the legal right to intervene, they reserved the right to do it unilaterally just the same.

An Intelligence Analysis of the Bogotazo

Most people who have studied the Bogotazo agree that the event that unleashed the riots was the assassination of populist leader Jorge Eliécer Gaitán, head of the Liberal party, by a mentally deranged young man, Juan Roa Sierra. Nevertheless, just a perfunctory analysis of the Bogotazo events from the point of view of counterintelligence shows that it was a by-the-book false flag operation of the type carried out by the OSS and later the CIA on behalf of their CFR masters.

Actually, the Bogotazo was a key part of a larger psychological warfare operation (PSYOP),[75] whose ultimate goal was to scare the American and Latin American people with the fear of Communism —an artificially created enemy to substitute the artificially created previous enemy that had just disappeared: Nazism.[76] Therefore, it was not by chance that the first mission assigned to the CIA's Office of Special Projects against what soon after became the CIA's new "main enemy," the Soviet Union,[77] was the Bogotazo false flag operation.

Propaganda and sabotage techniques used during the Bogotazo —broadcasting fake reports inciting the rioters, distribution of leaflets implicating the Communists, etc.—, seem to have been carried out following the OSS guidelines for psychological warfare operations as specified by the OSS Morale Operations Branch.[78] The main goal of the OSS Morale Operations Branch was to create unfounded panic, intimidate, demoralize, and spread confusion and distrust among enemy civilians and military forces. A secondary goal was to stimulate feelings of resentment and rebellion among occupied populations.[79] Morale Operations used "black"[80] propaganda, in which the source of the information is disguised.[81]

Adding weight to that suspicion is the fact, ignored by most authors who have studied the Bogotazo, that two weeks before the event the FBI office in Colombia had been dismantled. According to a secret document, all FBI legal attachés (FBI officers at U.S. embassies work under the cover of "legal attachés") were recalled to the U.S. and would not to be replaced.[82]

Before the creation of the CIA, the FBI was the U.S. agency in charge of espionage and counterespionage in Latin America, and it was doing a good job.

Despite his personal shortcomings, Hoover was a patriot who always worked for America. Proof of it is that the FBI was one of the few key agencies of the U.S. government the CFR conspirators were unable to penetrate. Therefore, dismantling the FBI office at the U.S. Embassy on Colombia most likely was a precautionary measure to avoid non-controlled, trained, inquisitive minds witnessing an event they would easily have discovered was a CIA dirty trick.

The role of Fidel Castro as an agent provocateur during the Bogotazo operation has been extensively documented. Unfortunately, however, most authors who have studied the subject have ignored it. Strangely, these authors have failed to notice what becomes evident once Castro's participation in the Bogotazo is seen with a critical eye.

Soon after the riots, the Colombian government asked the British Scotland Yard to investigate the events. To this effect, the British authorities sent to Colombia a team of investigators, formed by Chief-Inspector Peter Beveridge, Chief-Inspector Albert Tansil, and Sir Norman Smith, ex-Chief of the British Police in India. Despite some inexactitudes —mostly due to lack of support from the Colombian authorities, poor knowledge of the language and the country, as well as the short time provided for the investigation—, the report is an excellent source of information about the Bogotazo and the assassination of Gaitán.

When Dr. Jordán, Chief Investigator of Colombia's Justice Ministry first met the Scotland Yard investigators, he presented them with a written summary of the salient facts of his investigation as well as his tentative conclusions. According to Jordán, he was in the possession of documentation implicating the Communists in the assassination of Gaitán. But, when Dr. Jordán finally gave the documents to the British, "they proved to consist of two files, of scanty material, without opinion or nothing," proving little about the Communists' participation in the events. [83]

Despite Dr. Jordán's efforts to implicate the Communists in the assassination of Gaitán, the British investigators categorically stated that, "We are fully convinced that no political party, as such, had any part in the murder."[84] They reached that conclusion based, on the patent lack of readiness of the political parties, whether Conservative, Liberal, or Communist, to suppress or to take full political advantage of the revolt which flared up after the murder.[85] "We state, therefore, our definitive opinion, that no political Party, can have had any connection with the murder."[86]

Proof that Dr. Jordán was withholding some important information is the fact that nothing is mentioned in the dossier he gave to the Scotland Yard investigators about the active participation of two Cubans in the events. The British found later about the Cubans just by chance, through some files given to them by the Colombian Minister of Foreign Affairs containing a report by a Colombian police detective mentioning the two Cubans.[87]

Based on the detective's report, the British investigators mention that,

> Two Cubans, del Pino and Castro, *brought themselves prominently to notice* [Emphasis added] by scattering from a balcony in the Theatre Colon

> leaflets with a strong Communist tinge which denounced the retention by other Powers of Colonies in the Western Hemisphere and which culminated in an attack on American "imperialism." They did it at 10:30 p.m. on 3rd April at the time of a command performance at which the President of Colombia was present.[88]

In his Report, Detective number 6 says that the manager of the Claridge Hotel told him that, "on the night of the 9th, they [Castro and del Pino] arrived armed with rifles or shotguns and revolvers and with a good haul of loot." The manager added that Castro talked on the phone *in English* [emphasis added] that night with various people.[89]

In an effort to discredit that information, one author has mentioned the fact that at the time Castro did not speak English.[90] But del Pino, who was an American citizen and a former member of the U.S. armed forces, was fluent in English. Now, given the fact that Soviet intelligence officers are not supposed to speak English with their agents whose mother tongue is Spanish, who were Castro and del Pino talking to over the phone?

The detective added that according to a resident at the Claridge Hotel, he overheard the Cubans on the night of April 9th *speaking of the "rightness of the blow,"* and the *"complete success of the part they had been called upon to play."* [Emphasis added] He believed that the Cubans were certainly the highly paid tools of those who had planned the political murder.[91]

Granted, some may argue that the behavior described above does not agree with the conduct expected from secret agents working on a delicate mission. Nevertheless, one may have in mind that the agents were two young men with no previous training in intelligence who may have been carried out by the strong emotions of the day.

The Scotland Yard investigators made a similar mistake. Based on the information they had gathered, the British officers erroneously concluded that the behavior of the two Cubans, who, as they noticed, *made themselves noticed*, [emphasis added] "was scarcely that of men party to a secret and dangerous conspiracy of murder."[92] But the investigators missed the point. One of Castro's roles as an agent provocateur during the Bogotazo was precisely distracting the attention of the investigators from the main agents involved in the operation, to put the focus on false, accessory ones.

The Bogotazo operation was the pretext used by the CFR conspirators to initiate what is known as "the War Scare of 1948,"[93] a PSYOP that marked the true beginning of the Cold War in the Western Hemisphere. The Cold War proved to be extremely beneficial to CFR's Wall Street bankers and transnational corporations who, as they had done with Nazi Germany, now were making good money selling their goods to both parts of the Cold War conflict.

Everything indicates that the riots, which apparently were spontaneously provoked by the assassination of Gaitán, had been planned and prepared in advance, and the assassination was only a cover to hide its true causes.

Gaitán's Assassin: a Manchurian Candidate?[94]

Though his motive is still a matter of discussion, most of the people who have studied the Bogotazo events agree that Gaitán's assassin was Juan Roa Sierra, a 25-year-old drifter and loiterer who came from a poor family of workers. The scant information available about Roa tells that he was introverted, lazy, and had delusions of grandeur. Though he sometimes got odd jobs, he was kept alive by sleeping with a much older woman who provided for him. His opinions were violently right wing, but he was a person with no known political affiliation.[95]

On April 9, around 1:30 in the afternoon, on his way to have lunch with a few friends, Gaitán was about to exit the building where his office was located when somebody opened fire on him. Several witnesses have described the event, but some versions are contradictory.

According to Guillermo Pérez Sarmiento, director of the United Press in Colombia, "we heard the shots, three one right after another and the last after an interval."[96] Pérez Sarmiento continues his account of the event adding that, a few minutes later, he walked to the nearby Granada drugstore, where the police had momentarily detained the suspect, and saw him, "between two policemen; he had turned his greenish face away and seemed to be gripped by panic."[97]

Another witness, Plinio Mendoza Neira, one of Gaitán's close friends who was with him when the assassination took place, gives a similar account, "I suddenly felt that Gaitán was pulling back, trying to cover his face with his hands and trying to get back to the building. Simultaneously I heard three consecutive shots and then another one fractions of a second later."[98]

Bogotá's detective number 6 adds very important information about Roa Sierra. According to him, some time before the assassination,

> I saw del Pino standing in the door of the Colombia café, talking with a shabbily dressed individual whose photograph would later appear in the newspapers as the murderer of Gaitán. [99]

Other sources seem to confirm the detective's assertion, and indicate that Castro and del Pino had met Roa Sierra on several occasions before the assassination. According to a United Press report published in *El Tiempo* of Bogotá, "Roa was seen in the company of several people who appeared to be foreigners, a few days prior to the crime."[100]

Police officer Carlos Alberto Jiménez Díaz, who happened to be close by, grabbed the man from behind. Then, Roa turned on his heels, raised his hands and let the policeman grab the gun he was holding and disarm him.

According to the policeman, Roa offered no resistance to the arrest and he easily disarmed him.[101] Just after the policeman arrested him, Roa exclaimed: "Don't kill me, corporal."[102] Soon after, another police officer came to the scene and, to avoid the possibility of a lynching, both of them rushed through the sparse crowd to the Granada drugstore across the street. They managed to get into the drugstore before a scared employee closed the iron grating.[103]

One of the drugstore employees later mentioned that he had asked the suspect, "Why have you committed this crime, killing Dr. Gaitán?" and the suspect answered, "Oh, sir, powerful things I can't tell you," adding in a pitiful tone, "Virgin of the Carmen, save me!" Then the employee asked him, "Tel me who ordered you to kill [Gaitán], because the people are going to lynch you." To what he answered, "I can't."[104]

Probably one of the persons who more carefully have investigated the details of the crime is author Rafael Azula Barrera. According to what an eyewitness who saw Roa Sierra a few moments after the crime told him, Juan Roa Sierra was small, insignificant, pale-faced, his face angular and weak; he had been unshaven for several days and was dressed miserably with a gray trench coat and a blue tie with red stripes ... he was trying to hide behind the iron grating bars of the Granada Drugstore.[105] When asked by the police why he had fired the shots, Roa Sierra just answered "the highest motives."[106]

Azula Barrera mentions how the efforts to save him were useless. The angry crowd in front of the drugstore grew in size and the drugstore owners were forced to raise its iron grate. Then all the people present began hitting him with fury, and a few moments later he had been torn to pieces. Then the mob dragged the dying man through the street until they dropped his bloody remains in front of the Presidential Palace.

The mob killed the alleged assassin mercilessly and instantly. With terrifying speed and cruelty, they had beaten him to death and stomped his face into an unrecognizable, bloody mass, stripping him of his clothes as they dragged the body up the street.

Yet, cautions Azula Barrera, since the first moment there were doubts as to whether the man taken by the crowd was really the assassin. Just a couple of weeks after the assassination, Milton Bracker of the *New York Times* asked himself whether Roa had accomplices who stood by apparently to protect him, but actually to silence and kill him.[107]

Roa Sierra had never been in the military, nor had any training in the use of small arms, to the point that when he bought the revolver from an acquaintance, it was the latter who tested the gun firing a single shot.[108] However, according to some of the witnesses, the person who fired the shots had perfect control of the weapon. An eyewitness even mentioned the fact that the man who fired the shots used a professional stance, with his legs slightly flexed.[109]

Other close witness to the assassination later recalled that, as he entered the building to meet Gaitán, he had seen an individual close to the main door of the building where Gaitán's office was located. A few minutes later, when Gaitán was about to exit the building, the same individual he had seen before walked quickly to where Gaitán was approaching, raised his arm and fired three shots in a quick sequence. But, even though he saw the individual raise his arm and hear the shots, he didn't see the hand holding the weapon because a wall obstructed his vision.[110]

Another close witness mentioned that the individual had perfect control of himself, full of passion and great energy, and he saw hatred in his eyes. He also mentions the aggressive way he looked at them in a challenging way.[111] But, after the shots were fired, he looked around, saw a policeman, turned around and raised his arms.[112]

Another witness mentions that, as he entered the building, he saw a quiet man close to the door, whom he thought was a building employee. But, when he saw the man again on the street after the assassination, he was totally transformed, full of rage and extremely agitated.[113]

Gaitán's friend Plinio Mendoza Neira mentioned that the assassin was rather of low height, with long, uncombed hair, unshaved, and looked like twenty-five or twenty seven years of age. Mendoza adds that, as he was shooting, the man seemed very composed, not nervous at all, fully in command of the situation.[114]

Another witness, however, told a different story. "The man I saw," he said, "was full of passion, to the point that I knew he was a fanatic.[115] "His eyes were full of hatred. He didn't look like a person who had been paid to do a job. That face was animated by a wild passion."[116]

But, according to some eye-witnesses who agree with the impression that at the moment of the murder Roa was blazing with passion, they all agree that, "a moment later, he made no effort to escape and, indeed, gave the appearance of surrendering himself almost willingly."[117]

Several witnesses also mentioned something interesting. According to them, the first three shots were sort of muted, resembling more the sound of firecrackers than gunshots.[118] Other witnesses claim they saw Roa pointing his gun to Gaitán *after* the wounded leader had collapsed to the floor.

But now things get a little more complicated. According to some witnesses, there were *two* individuals implicated in the assassination of Gaitán.

A lift operator at the Nieto building, where Gaitán's office was located, mentions the presence in the scene of the assassination of a tall, dark haired, white individual with brown, popping eyes, of about 28 years of age, carrying a trench coat wrapped on his left arm. According to the lift operator, since mid March the same individual had visited the building several times stopping on the fourth floor, where Gaitán's office was located. The operator added that on the day of the assassination, around 12:30, the man went up using the stairs and down from the fourth floor using the elevator. Downstairs he joined another individual, who had been waiting for him in the alley.[119]

Another witness, who at the time had just entered the Gato Negro café, noticed two individuals. One of them called his attention because he seemed unable to control his nervousness. Five minutes later, the nervous individual exited the café to stand casually on the sidewalk. According to him, this was the man who fired at Gaitán.[120]

Another witness, Jorge Antonio Jiménez Higuera, confirmed the presence of two individuals. According to him, a few minutes after 1 p.m., he saw two individuals close to the entrance to the Nieto building. One of them made a gesture with his head, as alerting the other that Gaitán was about to exit the building. Then one of them shot Gaitán.[121] According to Higuera, the assassin was young, of short height, with light brown hair, and wore a gray-brownish suit. The other one was taller and thinner, and was older than the assassin. He was the one who had made the gesture to the assassin.[122] Another witness describes the second individual as tall, not heavy, wearing a brown suit with white stripes.[123]

Another witness mentioned how, just a moment after he heard the first shots, he saw a man fire a final shot. A few moments later, he saw a group of people hitting an individual. He told his friend, "This is not the guy. This is another one."[124] He added that he was sure this man was totally different from the one the police had initially arrested.[125]

Pascual del Vecchio, another witness who managed to get inside the drugstore where the police had brought Roa, mentions that he asked him why he had killed Gaitán, and Roa answered with a broken voice, "Bring me to the justice." He also mentions that two strange subjects had entered the drugstore and began hitting Roa furiously with a hard object. Then they dragged him to the street still hitting him. As he was telling them not to kill Roa, to allow him to confess his crime, his friend Antonio Izquierdo Toledo, Governor of Cundinamarca, told him, "Pascual, don't be a fool. They can kill you. They are part of the plot."[126]

Another person who witnessed the events mentioned that Roa seemed very scared, and didn't complain for the hits he was taken and seemed resigned about his situation.[127] Another witness mentioned that the man the police had behind the drugstore's counter had "a fixed stare, livid, speechless.[128]

According to what he had told some friends and relatives in the days previous to the assassination, Roa had been trying to get a driver's license in order to work as a driver and bodyguard for some foreigners, who had told him they were explorers looking for a gold mine in the Plains. These were the ones who gave him the money to buy the gun to protect them from possible attacks from the Indians and wild animals.[129]

Roa's mother said that some time before the events his son told her that at times he was having tremors in his whole body, a knot in the pit of his stomach, and something strange in his brain.[130] She also mentioned that, since a few months before the assassination, she had noticed that his son began behaving a little strange. He frequently laughed to himself, threw up his job and looked too thoughtful. He had fainting fits and suffered from severe headaches, saying that he felt as if corn was popping inside his head.[131] She added that, a few months before the assassination, her son had joined the Rosicrucians.

An Intelligence Analysis of Gaitán's Assassination

Two main things can be inferred from the stories told by the witnesses. First, that there were two men involved in the assassination, one, most likely Roa, short, dark skinned, poorly dressed, nervous, full or hatred, and out of control, and another one, taller, of fair complexion, well dressed, fully in control of the situation and acting like a professional killer. Secondly, that Roa, just seconds after the assassination, changed his behavior dramatically, passing without transition from an emotional violent state to one of depression and inaction —the man changed from a tiger into a mouse in a split second. But, though puzzling to the untrained eye, these apparently unexplainable things are easy to explain if one has a key: mind control.

My interpretation of the assassination of Gaitán is that Roa Sierra was a Manchurian Candidate.[132] He was a predecessor of Lee Harvey Oswald, Sirhan Sirhan, James Earl Ray, Mark David Chapman and John Hinckley, Jr., the ones who years later were used as patsies in the assassinations of President John F. Kennedy, his brother Robert, Martin Luther King, Jr., and John Lennon, as well as the one who tried to kill President Reagan —placing George H. W. Bush just a step away from becoming president.

The term Manchurian Candidate to indicate a brainwashed, mentally controlled assassin, came into use in 1959, when author Richard Condon made it the title of his best-selling novel, later made into a popular movie starring Frank Sinatra, and, more recently, a remake starring Denzel Washington. Though in the novel the person is hypno-conditioned to commit the actual crime, Roa, like Oswald and Sirhan, most likely was cast in the double role of decoy and fall guy —a "patsy"— while the true assassin committed the crime —which is the core of my Roa as Manchurian Candidate theory.

As early as September 1942 the OSS had begun experimenting with mind control, searching for a drug that would force men under interrogation, such as captured Nazi submarine crews, to reveal secrets.[133] On May 1943, OSS officers used THC acetate to obtain information from a subject. They referred to the THC acetate simply as "TD," a cryptonym for "Truth Drug."[134]

Nevertheless, it was not until 1947, after the creation of the CIA, that the Navy's Project CHATTER initiated the United States' first serious foray into truth serums. In 1949, the CIA began project BLUEBIRD using Nazi scientists to find a truth serum. Project BLUEBIRD evolved into Project ARTICHOKE and eventually into MK-ULTRA. Project MK-ULTRA was much larger in scope, focusing on mind control and the means to achieve it was not limited to drugs and psychedelics. MK-ULTRA experiments included using hypnosis, lobotomy, electroshock, sensory deprivation, ESP, drugs and sexual abuse.[135]

According to Roa's mother, Encarnación Sierra, in the weeks previous to the assassination of Gaitán his son had visited at least 9 times the office of Johan Umland Gert, a German astrologer.[136] Umland not only divined Roa's future, but also gave him money.[137] It was Umland who introduced Roa to Rosicrucianism.

Most likely, Roa either was brainwashed by Umland, who actually may had been a CIA psychiatrist specialized in mind control or had collaborated with the CIA psychiatrists in the process. Adding to my suspicion is the fact that Umland was German and that, through Project PAPERCLIP, the CIA had brought to the U.S. many Nazi scientists, including many of the ones who had been working on mind control research for the Nazis.

William Turner, an author who studied the assassination of Robert Kennedy and the possibility that his alleged assassin may have been a Manchurian Candidate acting under posthypnotic suggestion,[138] has studied the symptoms of hypno-conditioning. Cardinal among them is a dramatic personality change before the event and a state of peaceful tranquility while committing of the action, particularly evident in the subject's eyes. Then, after committing the action, signs of withdrawal from the hypnotic state appear: the individual seems disoriented, without a clear idea of what has just happened. This state is the results of posthypnotic amnesic blocks implanted by the programmer in the subject's mind.[139] If one is to believe the witnesses' accounts, Roa evidenced most of the symptoms mentioned by Turner.

Moreover, in *Mind Control: America's Secret War* the first part of DVD # 2, of *Inside the CIA: Secrets Revealed*, a documentary created by the History Channel, Sirhan B. Sirhan's uncle mentions that, a few months before the assassination of Robert Kennedy, his nephew had joined the Rosicrucians. The fact that both Sirhan and Roa had joined the Rosicrucians in the months previous to the assassinations may be just the product of a coincidence —or maybe not.

On April 16, 1943, Dr. Albert Hofman, a scientist working in a research lab for the Sandoz drug and chemical company, discovered the psychogenic properties of LSD, a substance he himself had first created in the same lab five years earlier.[140] Unknowingly, he had opened the doors to chemical mind control.

As Dr. Hofman was conducting his experiments, OSS scientists, under the direction of Dr. Winfred Overholser, head of the S. Elizabeth's Hospital in Washington, D.C., were conducing similar experiments using *cannabis indica*, popularly known as marihuana.[141] At the same time, some Nazi doctors working for the Gestapo and the SS were conducting mind control experiments on prisoners at the Dachau concentration camp.[142]

With the creation of the CIA in 1947, some of these mind-control experiments continued, and in April, 1950, CIA Director Adm. Roscoe Hillenkoetter, made them official when he approved the creation of a project code-named BLUEBIRD.[143] A few years later, BLUEBIRD was renamed ARTICHOKE. On April 1953, the CIA created MK-ULTRA, a wide scope program devoted to the study of psychological warfare, and ARTICHOKE became part of it. The person selected to direct MK-ULTRA was Dr. Sidney Gottlieb, who later reached some notoriety as the man who produced a lethal poison to assassinate Congo's Prime Minister Patrice Lumunba.

The available record strongly suggests that Roa was a patsy, the fall guy whose only role was taking the blame for the assassination. A professional hit man, using a silenced gun —which explains the low popping sound of the three first shots reported by the witnesses— carried out the assassination. Like in the case of Lee Harvey Oswald, the killing of Roa was part of the plan to avoid him being interrogated by the authorities. If Roa fired any of the shots most likely it was only the last one. Yet, even this is doubtful, because his gun was in very bad shape.

As I mentioned above, in the intelligence and espionage business there is no such thing as coincidences. Intelligence, and particularly counterintelligence officers leave no room for happenstance or coincidence. For them all coincidences are potentially deceptive and must be seen as possible enemy actions.

For example, the fact that Castro and del Pino had an appointment to meet

Gaitán just a few hours after the time he was assassinated may be the product of a coincidence. But, after knowing, first, that Castro was suspected of having being recruited by the CIA; second, that in the days previous to the riots he had called attention upon himself like an obvious agent provocateur;[144] third, that a few days before the assassination of Gaitán he and his friend del Pino had been seen in the company of the alleged killer; and, fourth, that he was close by the very moment Gaitán was killed, even the most gullible Army officer would have suspected enemy action.

One can only guess the true purpose of Castro's presence so close to the place where the assassination took place, Nevertheless, knowing Castro's psychopathic nature[145] I am inclined to think that, perhaps in violation of his orders, he was there just to enjoy the show.

By assassinating Gaitán, the CFR conspirators killed several birds with a single stone. In the first place, they got rid of a nationalist leader; a potential enemy they feared. Secondly, they used Gaitán's assassination as a tool to incite the masses to join a revolt they had prepared way in advance. Finally, by blaming the Communists and by implication the Soviet Union in the assassination and the riots, they created an excellent ideological pretext to justify the beginning of the Cold War they had carefully planned.

On the other hand, I am not going to fall into the Left's mistake of just blaming the CIA and painting the KGB and the Soviet Communists as innocent bystanders. To be sure, they had their own long list of dirty tricks performed against the peoples of the world and the Russian people as well. I don't even discard the possibility that they may have had some plans of their own to disrupt the Conference. But it seems that the assassination of Gaitán and the magnitude of the Bogotazo riots took them by surprise. Evidence of this is the state of confusion of the Colombian Communists and their inability to profit politically from the Bogotazo.[146] In this particular operation, the CFR conspirators outwitted the KGB.

New Pieces of the Puzzle

Confirming the forensic principle that every contact leaves a trace,[147] many years later an important piece of this historical puzzle appeared in the most unexpected place: a Cuban prison.

In late 1980, Gen. José Abrantes, Chief of Cuba's Ministerio del Interior (Office of Homeland Security), ordered one of his officers, Captain Carlos Cajaraville, now in exile in Florida, to interrogate a prisoner who had asked to buy his freedom in exchange for valuable information.[148] The prisoner was an American citizen named John Mepples (also known as MacMepples) Spiritto, who was doing time in a Cuban prison for having collaborated in the early 1960s with some anti-Castro guerilla groups in the Escambray Mountains in central Cuba.[149]

According to Spiritto, who claimed that he had worked for the CIA, he was sent to Colombia in 1947 as part of Operation PANTOMIME, a CIA plan to neutralize or assassinate Gaitán. Apparently, the information he provided was credible, because he was freed and given an apartment to live in the elegant Vedado section of Havana. A few years later, some Cuban counterintelligence officers, realizing the potential propaganda value of Spiritto's information, decided to exploit it. The idea was using Spiritto in a documentary film, which they titled "Pantomima," discrediting the CIA.

In the documentary Spiritto, who is fluent in Spanish, mentions how in 1947 the CIA sent him to Colombia. His orders were to buy Gaitán by making him an offer he could not refuse. It consisted in money and a teaching position at a University in Rome or Paris, in exchange for ending his political activities in Colombia. But, surprisingly, Gaitán refused the offer. Spiritto informed the failure to Thomas Elliot, his superior in Bogotá, who ordered him to work Gaitán by other means, including his physical elimination.

Two years after Spiritto's interview was filmed, Major Manuel ("Redbeard") Piñeiro, Chief of Cuba's America Department in charge of counterintelligence operations against the U.S., contacted Gaitán's daughter, Gloria, and invited her to come to Havana and watch it. Piñeiro wanted to see if Gloria's recollection of the event matched Spiritto's information.

Gloria flew to Havana, watched the film and, to her utter surprise, discovered that Spiritto's mention of how he tried to suborn her father offering him money, a teaching position in the Sorbonne in Paris or in Rome's university, and a luxury apartment in the city of his choice, perfectly matched to what her father told privately to their family in 1947—and only they were privy to it. Gloria asked Piñeiro to give her a copy of the film, but Piñeiro refused, alleging the possibility of political problems with the Colombian government.

A few years later Colombian journalist Arturo Alape, who was in Cuba trying to get an interview with Castro for a book he was writing about the Bogotazo, was allowed to see the film. Even though the Cubans didn't give him a copy of the film, Alape allegedly managed to secretly make a recording of the sound track. Eventually Alape transcribed the sound track with Spiritto's interview and gave Gloria a copy.

At the time, however, the production of the documentary had confronted some unexpected problems. Apparently the Cuban intelligence officers, who, like all intelligence officers, are trained to look for anomalies, realized that Castro was mentioned again and again in it, doing things very difficult to explain. Knowing how things work in Castro's Cuba, they decided to be on the safe side and stopped the production of the documentary.

According to Cajaraville, the Cuban intelligence officers working on the production of the documentary feared that it might not be of Castro's liking[150] —something that in Cuba has proven to be very unhealthy. Eventually, the documentary was declared off limits for reasons of national security —which shows that the Cuban intelligence officers have learned a lot from their colleagues at CIA.

Some time later, Alape was invited by a Cuban intelligence officer to visit Spiritto at his apartment in Havana. During the visit, the CIA agent recanted about all the information he previously had provided in the documentary, alleging that he simply lied in order to get out of prison. This is the excuse later offered by

Alape for not including Spiritto's testimony in his book of testimonies about the Bogotazo, in which he prominently included Castro's own version of the events, which is a total fabrication.

Nevertheless, Alape's explanation does not ring true, because he knew that Gloria Gaitán, based on the confidential information about the CIA's offer to her father, had appraised Spiritto's confession as true. A more plausible explanation is that Alape, a Castro-friendly journalist,[151] did not want to hurt Castro's feelings. Moreover, Alape's book was published by a Cuban government's publishing house, Casa de las Américas, which would not have published it if the book had contained any critical opinion about Castro. My conclusion, therefore, is that Alape either got cold feet or was intellectually dishonest and acted opportunistically.

In 1994, while Castro was visiting Colombia, Gloria met him and asked for a copy of the film, but, to her surprise, Castro flatly denied the existence of such a film. When Gloria told him that she had a copy of the film's soundtrack, they had a strong argument.[152]

But this was not the end of this real-life spy story. According to Gloria Gaitán,

> In 1993 I was contacted by Dr. Yesid Castaño, who told me that Dr. Robayo, owner of Kokorico [a restaurant], had documentation his friend Thomas Elliot, a CIA officer, had given him before dying of cancer. The information included a whole dossier with information about the planning of my father's assassination.[153]

Unfortunately, some time after Dr. Castaño contacted Gloria, Dr. Robayo was assassinated under strange circumstances, and the documents he allegedly had in his possession disappeared.

There is an important fact, however, that is missing in most of what has been published about Mepples Spiritto. According to some sources, in the early 1950s Spiritto had been working in Manhattan as part of the CIA's top-secret ARTICHOKE mind control project.[154]

With the benefit of hindsight, one can safely surmise that, after his first-hand experience on the CIA's first successful experiment in the use of a psychologically programmed patsy, Spiritto would have been an invaluable asset for working on a project like ARTICHOKE, whose goal was precisely creating psychologically programmed patsies and assassins.

Yet, things were even more complicated.

In his autobiography *Vivir para contarla*, Colombian Nobel Prize writer Gabriel García Márquez, who affirms that he witnessed the killing of Roa Sierra, told what he saw:

> Fifty years later it is still fixed in my memory the image of the man who seemed to be instigating the mob in front of the pharmacy, of whom I have not found any reference in any of the testimonies given by the witnesses. I saw him from very close by, very well dressed, with a skin like alabaster, and a millimetric control over his actions. He called my atten-

> tion so much that I kept watching him until a brand new car picked him up soon after the mob took away the assassin's cadaver and, since then, it disappeared from history's memory —even mine. Only many years after, in my times as a journalist, it occurred to me that the man might have been instrumental in the killing of a false assassin to protect the identity of the true one.[155]

Until now nobody has found who the mysterious man was, but García Márquez' suspicion that he was part of the assassination makes sense. Moreover, I have the suspicion —and it is just a hunch based on circumstantial evidence because until now I have not been able to find any direct evidence proving it— that the elegantly dressed mysterious man who accompanied Gaitán's alleged assassin Roa Sierra to Gaitán's office, and later instigated the crowd to lynch Sierra, may have been none other than James Jesus Angleton.

I base my suspicion on five things. First, the fact that Angleton fits to a large degree the physical description of the second individual mentioned by the witnesses, the one who incited the rioters to kill Roa Sierra. Moreover. He also fits the description Gaitán's secretary made of the man who in two occasions accompanied Roa during his visits to the office: a well-dressed skinny white man with bulging eyes and an aggressive manner.[156]

According to Gaitán's secretary, in the few months before the murder, Juan Roa Sierra came several times to her office room, which gave entrance to that of Dr. Gaitán, with a request to see Gaitán. She also remembered that, at least in two occasions, Juan Roa Sierra was accompanied,

> . . . by another man, thin, tolerably well dressed but of a wild appearance, with bulging eyes and an aggressive manner. On these occasions, the later, and not Juan Roa Sierra, acted as spokesman in the attempt to obtain an interview. [157]

Secondly, because this mysterious man was playing a key part in a very secret and important operation, and Angleton was one of Allen Dulles' few trusted men. One of the few photographs of James Jesus Angleton ever published,[158] shows him carrying the urn containing Dulles' ashes, an honor granted only to one of the deceased's closest friend

Third, because his mother was Mexican and Angleton, though not fully fluent in Spanish, knew enough of the language to briefly pass as a native. Angleton was the son of an American cavalry officer, James Hugh Angleton, who rode into Mexico with General Pershing in pursuit of Pancho Villa. He fell in love with a Mexican beauty he met at the border city of Nogales, Carmen Mercedes Moreno.[159] As proof of her Catholic faith, she gave her son the middle name Jesus, pronounced "Jesús," Spanish style.

In an interview with Tom Mangold, Carmen mentioned James' close ties with his maternal grandmother, Mercedes, who spoke no English. This is another evidence that Angleton was fluent to a certain degree in the Spanish language.[160]

Fourth, there is some unaccounted time in Angleton's life that, strangely, coincides with the Bogotazo events. According to what has been published, during the war Angleton, who was an OSS officer, became estranged with his wife, Cicely, and his baby son, to the point that she initiated divorce proceedings. However, in 1947, Angleton suddenly resumed communication with her and eventually they got back together.[161]

In early 1948, Angleton moved to Tucson, Arizona, to join his wife and son, where he allegedly lived with his wife in her parents' home from January through June 1948. In July, Angleton accepted a senior position at CIA as the top aide to the director of the Office of Special Operations (OSO) and the family moved to Washington, D.C.[162] The only source for this information, however, is Cicely Angleton herself, in an interview she had with Jeff Goldberg on March 3, 1989.[163]

Nevertheless, this is a little strange. According to Angleton's CIA personnel records, though he officially joined the Agency on December 30, 1947, he was granted a seven-month leave of absence to live in Tucson with his family before assuming his position at CIA.[164] Consequently, Angleton had enough time and opportunity to move secretly to Colombia under a false identity and passport, accomplish his first CIA mission there, and come back to Tucson unnoticed before moving to Washington D.C.

Finally, first at the OSS and later at CIA, Angleton had direct participation in two early secret projects on mind control: BLUEBIRD and ARTICHOKE.

In conclusion, Angleton had the motive, the ability, the means, and the opportunity to have participated in the Bogotazo operation. Even more, like most experienced criminals, he was clever enough to create an alibi, backed by a respectable, though not fully impartial witness: his wife.

I explained for the first time my theory that Roa was a Manchurian Candidate, in my novel *La madre de todas las conspiraciones*, published in 2005. In it, I mention the fact that Spiritto later worked for the CIA's project ARTICHOKE.[165] Well, the possibility that Roa may have been a Manchurian Candidate is so obvious that other people already have independently arrived at the same conclusion.

Just recently, I found in the Internet a long article by an independent researcher from Australia, Greg Parker, "Bogota Ripples, Was Sierra a 'false assassin'?", in which he offers an excellent analysis of Gaitán assassination and reaches a similar conclusion.[166] According to Parker, [Roa] "Sierra was the first CIA 'brainwashed' assassin," a Manchurian Candidate, —which is exactly my own conclusion.

The Bogotazo: Still a Mystery

The Bogotazo is key to understand how the CFR conspirators have used the CIA to advance their illegal goals of turning the U.S. into a totalitarian communo-fascist dictatorship. This explains their efforts of muddying the historical waters and blocking any intent by non-controlled researchers to discover the truth about the Bogotazo events. Proof of it is the CIA's efforts to block Paul Wolf's attempt to obtain certain CIA documents.

Wolf, a private investigator now turned into a successful attorney, has devoted long hours researching the Bogotazo and Gaitán's assassination. Eventually he reached the unavoidable conclusion that the CIA should know about Gaitán's assassination. In order to prove his hypothesis Wolf, using the powers of the Freedom of Information Act (FOIA), applied for the declassification of such documents.[167] But the CIA blocked all his efforts.

Finally, Wolf took another step, and legally demanded that such documents be made public. This, however, was just the beginning of a long legal battle. Finally, on August 12, 2002, Wolf and his lawyer appeared before a U.S. District Judge to explain his case. The CIA was represented by one of its lawyers.

Wolf's attorney explained that the Bogotazo took place during the 9th Conference of Latin American States, actually "an inception meeting in the Cold War, sorting of a putting together of an alliance within the Western Hemisphere in relation to the Cold War." He also mentioned the unexplainable fact that, despite the FOIA provisions that after 25 years classified material should be automatically declassified and available to the public, material related to the Bogotazo dated more than 50 years ago is still kept classified.

The CIA's lawyer justified the Agency's reluctance to declassify the records on the basis that, if they exist —something that the CIA neither confirm or deny—, making them public would reveal sources and methods which may be harmful to national security. This claim was repeated several times by the CIA's attorney during the viewing.

But this claim doesn't make any sense. Today, the tradecraft methods used by the CIA in 1948 have changed to the point of being irrelevant. Therefore, if one discards the methods, the only remaining motive may be that the CIA is protecting its sources, or its secret agents.

Nevertheless, after more than 50 years of the Bogotazo events, one may safely surmise that most of CIA's sources and secret agents who participated in the Bogotazo are dead. So, what key source or secret agent that played an active role in the Bogotazo, which if it were revealed would be harmful to the U.S. national security (actually to the conspirators who control the U.S. government) is still alive? Currently, the only person still alive who actively participated in the Bogotazo events is Fidel Castro.

In conclusion, everything indicates that the assassination of Gaitán and the Bogotazo were the result of a carefully planned psychological warfare operation carried out by the CIA on behalf of its CFR masters. This explains why many known key participants in the Bogotazo were linked to the CFR, the OSS or the CIA. The known ones are:

Gen. George C. Marshall (CFR), U.S. Secretary of State, Chief U.S. delegation to 9th Conference.

Gen. Matthew B. Ridgway (CFR), military advisor to U.S. delegation to 9th Conference

Averell Harriman (CFR), U.S. Secretary of Commerce.

William Wieland, protégé of Sumner Welles (CFR), probably intelligence liaison between CIA and State Dept., later Castro supporter
Roy Rubbotom, U.S. State Department, later Castro supporter
William Pawley, friend of Allen Dulles, links to CIA, attended Lazo meeting.
Willard Beaulac, U.S. ambassador to Colombia, ex-U.S. Ambassador to Cuba, suspected of attending Lazo meeting.
Norman Armour (CFR, OSS), Assistant Secretary of State, U.S. delegate to 9th Conference.
Richard Salvatierra, CIA officer, attended Lazo meeting.
John Mepples Spiritto, CIA officer, project ARTICHOKE, tried to buy Gaitán.
John C. Wiley (CFR, OSS), former U.S. Ambassador to Colombia.
Robert Lovett (Skull & Bones), U.S. Acting Secretary of State, close links to CFR.
Rafael del Pino Siero, U.S. intelligence asset, attended Lazo meeting
Fidel Castro Ruz, attended Lazo meeting.

Apart from the information I have provided above, the activities during the Bogotazo of so many people linked to the U.S. intelligence services and the CFR are a strong indication that the Bogotazo was not a random outburst of violence. Mos likely, it was a false flag operation, the key element of a carefully planned and executed major Hegelian-type PSYOP called the Cold War —the first of many to be carried out by the CIA and the CFR conspirators in their long battle against the American people and the peoples of the world in the pursuit of their goal of world domination.

The methodology used in this PSYOP closely followed the Hegelian principle of thesis-antithesis-synthesis,[168] in which the Bogotazo operation was the scary antithesis used as a threat to force the American and Latin American people into accepting the frightening new synthesis called the Cold War.

The Bogotazo marked the onset of the Cold War in the Western Hemisphere. Just a few years later CFR conspirator Nelson Rockefeller was frantically selling the idea of building nuclear shelters in every American building, and American schoolchildren were hiding under their desks rehearsing for a coming nuclear attack. The time for Americans to live under a permanent state of fear had arrived.

Chapter 8

The CFR Mole Infiltrates the Soviets

You do not like Communism. We do not like capitalism.
There is only one way out —peaceful coexistence.
—Soviet Premier Nikita Khrushchev speaking
during a visit to the U.K. in 1956.

In several extraordinarily well-documented books, professor Antony Sutton proved beyond any reasonable doubt not only that the Soviet Union was a creation of international bankers, but also how they kept the sinking ship of Soviet economy artificially afloat for several decades. He also proved how the Soviet military machine was developed thanks to the use of American military technology, not because Soviet spies were able to steal it, but because CFR conspirators inside the U.S. government gave it to the Soviets.

The American Left, which is just an illusion, a mirage created by the most reactionary Right, has simplistically explained this as the result of greed: the American military-industrial complex sells weapons to America's enemies in order to make money. But, though this may have been right to a certain extent until the 1950s, there are alternative explanations pointing to the fact that, since then, money is not by any means the conspirator's main motivation.

The Destruction of Russia and the Creation of the Soviet Union

The Soviet Union was an artificial creation of international bankers and oil magnates. Their purpose was to put Russia into an economic freezer —which they did for 60 long years— and curtail Tsar Nicholas II's intentions of turning the country into a major oil competitor in the free market.

On 13 March 1881, following the assassination of Alexander II, his son, Alexander III became Russia's Tsar and his grandson Nicholas became Tsarevich (heir). A few years later, in 1890, Alexander III began an ambitious industrialization program, which included the creation of a modern railroad net unifying the country. The result of this effort was the construction of the 5,400 mile-long Trans-Siberian railroad, the most ambitious railroad project at the time, which would transform Russia's entire economy and change the country into a modern industrial society.

Nicholas took the throne in 1894 at the age of 26 following Alexander III's unexpected death. On May 14, 1896, Nicholas was formally crowned as Russia's Tsar. Nicholas II continued his father's economic policies, particularly the railroad project.

The man in charge of the railroad plan was Count Sergei Witte, Russia's minister of finance.[1] Witte's efforts soon changed Russia's role of "breadbasket" provider to British grain-trading houses into a potentially modern industrial nation. As expected, his accomplishments were strongly opposed by the British government.[2] However, Witte's work suddenly stopped when Tsar Nicholas II was deposed as a result of the 1905 Russian "revolution."

The main problem the conspirators had with Russia, however, was not its efforts to become an industrialized nation, but that a large amount of oil had been discovered in Baku, near the Caspian Sea in Azerbaijan. At the time, the Baku oil field was considered the largest known oil deposit in the world. By the early 1880s, Russian crude production reached 10.8 million, almost a third of U.S. production.[3]

As expected, Rockefeller and his criminal associates of the American International Corporation (AIC), Andrew Mellon, J.P. Morgan and Andrew Carnegie, were deeply alarmed about the Russians challenging their ambitions of controlling the world oil supply, and they began conspiring to develop a plan to stop the Russians in their tracks.[4] They concluded that the only way to achieve their goal was to depose Tsar Nicholas II, and the only way to accomplish that was through a "revolution."

History books, mostly written by unscrupulous CFR-controlled disinformers passing as historians, have painted the Russian revolution as the result of a spontaneous uprising of the Russian exploited proletarian masses against their oppressive government.

According to this vision, Russia's disastrous participation in WWI, which had cost the lives of four million men, created widespread discontent. A growing economic crisis and food scarcities contributed to increase the problems. Demonstrations of people asking for food started in many cities. This chaotic situation created the conditions for the revolt that overthrew the tsarist government and eventually changed Russia into the Soviet Union, a new society based on the anti-capitalist, communist principles of Marxism.[5]

This vision, however, is not exactly true.

Thanks to the efforts of scholars like Antony Sutton,[6] G. Edward Griffin[7] and others, now we know that the "spontaneous" Russian "revolution" was actually a covert operation planned and carried out by international bankers and oil magnates. It would have been impossible to succeed without the money supplied by some of the most notable millionaires at that time.

Though initially he favored his father's autocratic ideas, eventually Tsar Nicholas II had initiated the implementation of a series of reforms directed to change Russia from a medieval into a modern society, which included the emancipation of the serfs, the creation of a Duma —a national assembly—, and rural communes. These reforms would have encouraged the Russian people to think about the possibility of a benign government in which the people would democratically participate.

Nevertheless, some influential Wall Street bankers and oil magnates were not happy with these changes in Russia, and conceived another plan. In order to proceed with their plan, John D. Rockefeller, together with fellow conspirators, like bankers Mellon and Morgan and steel magnate Andrew Carnegie, plus several of America's robber barons, joined their resources for up to $50 million (an enormous sum at the time), and created the American International Corporation (AIC), a powerful cartel allegedly devoted to stimulate world trade. The truth, however, is that the AIC was created to fund the overthrow of Tsar Nicholas II by a small group of professional revolutionaries: the Bolsheviks.[8]

To this effect, between 1907 and 1910 the conspirators met several times with Russian revolutionary Leon Trotsky, already living in exile in New York, and with Vladimir I. Lenin, another Russian revolutionary living in exile in Zürich. Eventually the arch-capitalists struck a deal with the arch-anti-capitalists: in exchange for financing their "revolution," the capitalists would be allowed to have a hidden hand in designing the economy of what was soon to become the Soviet Union — allegedly the staunchest anti-capitalist nation in the world.

With the help of the conspirators, Lenin returned to Russia with plenty of gold in his famous "sealed" train, and, soon after Trotsky, under the protection of President Wilson and Colonel House, followed Lenin's path with more gold. This gold made possible the Russian "revolution."

Yet, some people already knew about Lenin's activities and who were his true masters. In a speech to the House of Commons on November 5, 1919, Winston Churchill exposed in a few words the whole conspiracy:

> . . . Lenin was sent into Russia . . . in the same way that you might send a vial containing a culture of typhoid or of cholera to be poured into the water supply of a great city, and it worked with amazing accuracy. No sooner did Lenin arrive that he began beckoning a finger here and a finger there to obscure persons in sheltered retreats in New York, Glasgow, in Bern, and other countries, and he gathered together the leading spirits of a formidable sect, the most formidable sect in the world . . . With these spirits around him he set to work with demoniacal ability to tear to pieces every institution on which the Russian State depended.

What Churchill failed to mention, though, was that the ones who had disseminated the Communist plague were bankers from England, Europe and the U.S., among them the Rothschilds, Sir George Buchanan and Lord Alfred Milner (members of the Round Table, who had been instrumental in the creation of the CFR), the Warburgs, the Rockefellers and J.P. Morgan. With their investment, the conspirators had created a pseudo-enemy they controlled —to some extent. Soon after, the Soviet Union became the bogeyman the conspirators used for many years as a credible threat to manipulate and control the U.S. and other Western countries. The rest is history.

But the conspirators failed to foresee that Communism and Marxist economy are such total disasters that, since the very beginning, the monster they had created never managed to provide for its own sustenance, and was always teetering on the verge of collapse. So, while ostensibly fighting to destroy it, they had to put all their ingenuity and large amounts of money on keeping the Soviet communist monster artificially alive and kicking.

In his massive scholarly work, *Western Technology and Soviet Economic Development*, and later in his *National Suicide: Military Aid to the Soviet Union*, and finally in *The Best Enemy Money Can Buy*,[9] professor Antony Sutton extensively documented how, militarily, the Soviet Union was kept alive thanks to massive technology transfer, mostly from the United States. Moreover, this technology transfer was not the result of the good work of Soviet spies, but of the treachery of CFR agents at the highest levels of the U.S. government.

Probably the two most outstanding accomplishments of the CFR conspirators were giving the Soviets the technology for producing, first, nuclear weapons and, later, for building better intercontinental ballistic missiles.

According to the official story, Soviet spies Ethel and Julius Rosenberg stole and gave the Soviet Union in 1950 the scientific documents necessary to create an atomic bomb. This, however, is simply not true.[10] The Soviets didn't have to steal the atomic bomb secrets because CFR secret agents infiltrated into the U.S. government gave the information to them in 1943 disguised under the cover of the Lend Lease program.[11]

Actually, the Rosenbergs belonged to what Sun Tzu calls "expendable agents"[12] —stupid spies actually intended to be caught. One of the uses of expendable agents is to distract the enemy's attention from the real spies. In this case, however, the CFR conspirators at the highest levels of the U.S. government knew that the Rosenbergs were fake spies —which perhaps explains Truman's rush to destroy the evidence by ordering their unnecessary execution.

Professor Sutton has also documented in detail the second case, the willful transfer of American technology to make Soviet ICBMs more accurate.[13] According to Sutton, the threat of annihilation of the United States and the West by intercontinental Soviet nuclear missiles would have never existed,

> If President Richard Nixon and National Security adviser Henry Kissinger had heeded warnings in 1970 from its own Department of Defense and outside experts that the Soviets were lagging in missile production technology and required specific technologies from the West to MIRV[14] their fourth generation ICBMs.[15]

Sutton didn't mention, however, that both Nixon and Kissinger were secret CFR members. They failed to pay attention to the warnings not because they were ignorant or fools, but because the conspirators' plan precisely consisted in giving this advanced technology to the Soviets.

The Cold War was the conspirators' tool to justify their imperialist aggressive policies. With the support of the U.S. mainstream media, they brainwashed and scared the American people into accepting these treasonous and destructive policies. Despite the fact that communism was a total economic disaster, the Soviet Union, thanks mostly to the conspirators' constant help, unwittingly played for many years its scripted role of artificially created bogeyman.

But in the early fifties an unexpected event threatened to upturn the apple cart the conspirators so carefully had crafted: Nikita S. Khrushchev became the Soviet Union's leader, and he had some innovative ideas of his own.

Khrushchev's Peaceful Threat

The death in 1953 of Soviet dictator Joseph Stalin marked a starting point in the cooling off of the Cold War. The main actor in this radical turn in Soviet foreign policy was Soviet Premier Nikita S. Khrushchev. Suddenly, Khrushchev's mercurial versatility had replaced Stalin's inflexible dogmatism

Though over 70, Khrushchev was still tough, devious and versatile. Short, bald and portly, wearing poorly tailored suits, Khrushchev bore the well-deserved nicknames "the hangman of the Ukraine" and "the butcher of Budapest."[16] But, paradoxically, he was also the one who had led the 208 million Soviet citizens to their greatest measure of liberty and prosperity since the Bolshevik Revolution.[17]

Many American journalists who visited the Soviet Union were impressed by Khrushchev's boundless energy, inner vitality and intelligence. This blunt, aggressive little man had a peculiar sense of humor and was indefatigable and perspicacious. He was not only one of the most loyal party men, but surely among the most astute.

What he lacked in formal education he made up in sheer energy and gall. He appeared to sense in advance every major shift in policy, unerringly picking the right coattails to hang from. He was also a consummate actor. He could be gay, sad, friendly, or downright furious according to what would serve him best.[18]

The death of Stalin expanded the limits of Khrushchev's power to a point that some saw him either as the "first oligarch," or as a "dictator" with total control over Soviet events. In any case, thanks to this particular historical juncture Khrushchev found himself temporarily freed from the forces of conventional morality and rationality, and was in a privileged position to influence political events. That meant he was able to command the necessary resources to intervene decisively and unilaterally in the political process in the Soviet Union. It was a situation that encouraged the expression of his personal talents for shaping events.[19]

Nevertheless, despite all his intelligence and perspicacity, Khrushchev was mostly ignorant about the complicated realities of Soviet foreign policy, particularly in its relations with the West. When Vice-President Nixon visited the Soviet Union in mid-1959, he was reportedly impressed with the depth and stubbornness of Khrushchev's misconceptions about the United States.[20]

Even more important, it seems that, unlike Lenin and later Gorbachev, Nikita Khrushchev was not a CFR secret mole, nor was he under the control of the secret CFR agents infiltrated at the highest levels of the Soviet government.[21]

In his famous speech at the 20th Congress of the Communist Party of the Soviet Union in 1956,[22] in which he criticized Stalin, Khrushchev surprised the delegates when he expressed his belief that "peaceful coexistence" was not only possible but also essential. And added, "there are only two ways —either peaceful coexistence or the most destructive war in history. There is no third way."

Thereafter, Khrushchev believed, the struggle between Washington and Moscow must continue, but it should be a peaceful one, conducted solely in the political, economic, and social fields, not in the military. There were perhaps some personal reasons for Khrushchev's sudden change. As a Red Army officer, he had experienced first hand fighting a war that had cost the Soviet Union the lives of 20 million of its citizens and destroyed most of the country. Another war, now involving the use of nuclear weapons, would be more destructive, even to the point of totally destroying mother Russia.

Consequently, since 1956 the Soviet Union under Khrushchev's guidance radically changed its confrontational foreign policy and sought to moderate its relations with the United States. In Khrushchev's view, the threat of mutual annihilation in a nuclear war overshadowed the immediate conflict between the socialist and capitalist camps. Consequently, the Soviet Union proclaimed their commitment to a new program of peaceful coexistence with the Western capitalist powers.

Without ignoring the elements of duplicity most likely involved in Khrushchev's new doctrine, it seems that at the time the Soviet leaders were sincerely convinced that in the long run what they considered their superior economic and social system would triumph, but that would be only *if* in the short run a devastating nuclear conflagration could be averted.

As expected, the CFR conspirators were extremely alarmed with Khrushchev's new policies. Unknowingly, the Soviet Premier was threatening them with the destruction of the Soviet bogeyman they had invested so much time and money to create. Obviously, they were not going to allow an idealist fool like Nikita Khrushchev to derail their plans.

It seems likely that, in their search for a solution, they may have recalled the young Cuban who did such as an outstanding service for them acting as an agent provocateur during the Bogotazo. And that was exactly what they needed now: and agent provocateur who could infiltrate the Soviets and push them into warming up the Cold War.

But when the CFR conspirators found the whereabouts of their young Cuban agent they discovered, to their utter surprise, that he was in the most unexpected place: the Sierra Maestra mountains of Eastern Cuba, fighting an unwinnable guerrilla war against their faithful puppet, Cuban dictator Fulgencio Batista.[23]

A Spy is Born . . . or Made?

We don't know exactly when Fidel Castro sold his soul to the CFR conspirators, but there is factual evidence that, since he was very young, he was craving to become an agent for the American imperialists — that is, Wall Street bankers and oil magnates — he later claimed to hate.

While attending grade school at the Colegio Dolores in Santiago de Cuba, a 12-year-old Fidel Castro wrote a letter in macaronic English to President Roosevelt asking him for money and offering his help in locating some of Cuba's natural resources for U.S. exploitation. Below his signature, he added this revealing note: "If you want iron to make your ~~sheaps~~ ships I will show to you the bigest [lit.] (minas) [mines] of iron of the land. They are in Mayarí. Oriente, Cuba."[24]

Fidel Castro loves to portray himself as the archenemy of the United States. In speech after speech, he berates "Yankee imperialism" as the ultimate evil. However, if you pay more attention to what Castro *does* rather than what he *says* the picture changes considerably.

At some time in the early 1940s, before his "Bogotazo" adventure, a young Fidel Castro became so infatuated with American films that he decided to become a film actor, and traveled to California where he managed to get a job as an extra at the Metro Goldwin studios in Culver City. He appeared in at least two films, *Bathing Beauty*, starring Esther Williams and Red Skelton, and *Holiday in Mexico*, starring Walter Pidgeon and Ilona Massey. Both films were directed by George Sidney and included music by Xavier Cugat and his orchestra.[25] The fact that the films appeared in 1944 and 1946 indicate that Castro spent some long, unaccounted periods of time in the United States.

The information about Castro living in the U.S. and acting in Hollywood's films has been one of his best-kept secrets. He has never mentioned it, and it does not appear in any of his biographies.[26] This may indicate that he has something to hide about this period of his life he spent in the U.S. We can only guess, but there is a possibility that Castro may already had been recruited by the CFR conspirators prior to the meeting at Mario Lazo's home.

But this is not the only period of his life Castro has lived in the U.S.

On October 12, 1948, while still a law student at Havana University, Fidel Castro married Mirtha Díaz Balart. Followed the Americanized usage of the Cuban upper-middle-class, after the wedding they traveled to the United States for their honeymoon —to which President Batista, a good friend of Fidel's father, contributed a wedding gift of a thousand dollars.

A few months after the couple returned to Cuba, Castro had a violent argument at the university with a man named Camaid. To avoid problems with the Cuban authorities, he flew to the U.S. with his wife and voluntarily exiled himself in New York City for about a year and a half.[27]

Not much is known of his whereabouts during that long stay in the U.S., and he has carefully avoided any mention to that period of his life when he practically disappeared into thin air. Nobody, including close friends and relatives, seem to know what he did, where he lived or how he made a living. It is very suspicious that a man like Fidel Castro, who had always tried to be on the spotlight, had disappeared for at least two long periods of his life in the U.S.

Castro's biographer Robert E. Quirk mentions that he rented an apartment in the Bronx and enrolled in a language school to perfect his command of English. He also mentions that during this time Castro gave no evidences of his later furious anti-Americanism.[28]

I have heard rumors that during one of these unaccounted periods he lived in the U.S., Castro received some intelligence training. Some military intelligence officers who got their training in Quantico, Virginia,[29] claim that, while there, they heard rumors that Fidel Castro had been trained at the facility. Unfortunately, nobody has been able to confirm such rumors.

Fidel Castro to the Rescue

As soon as the CFR conspirators found out the whereabouts of their secret agent, they made contact with him at the Sierra Maestra Mountains and began supporting him in his fight against Batista. This support has been extensively documented.

In 1961, the Senate Internal Security Subcommittee issued a 12-volume study entitled "Communist Threat to the U.S. Through the Caribbean." The study features the testimonies of some senior U.S. government officers who firmly believed that Castro could not have been brought to power in Cuba without the continued assistance of the CFR-controlled U.S. State Department.

The subject came up again in the course of a press conference held by President Kennedy on January 24, 1962. President Kennedy was asked about the security risks involving State Department employee William A. Wieland who, according to three American ex-ambassadors in testimony before the Senate Internal Security Subcommittee, had helped Castro come to power. Though Kennedy denied that Wieland was a security risk, doubts about him persisted.[30]

As a *protégé* of CFR agent Sumner Welles, William Wieland was promoted four times in just nine months in the State Department, and later was assigned to Brazil in 1948 as a press attaché. During his stay in Brazil, the American ambassador to that country, William Pawley, filed reports on Wieland's "leftist" ideas and activities, after which Wieland was promoted again and transferred to Colombia as Vice Consul.[31]

Wieland joined the Foreign Service in a very irregular way. Evidence shows that he lied in his application forms. The fact that Wieland had no problems in advancing his career despite grave accusations about his alleged pro-Communist leanings is as a clear indication that his diplomatic position was a cover for intelligence work. Moreover, the impetuous fashion in which President Kennedy denied that Wieland was a security risk is further evidence that Wieland was not what he claimed to be. But there are more strange things about the Castro-Wieland connection.

While the American Vice Consul in Bogotá in 1948, Wieland must have known about Castro's participation in the Bogotazo riots. Both Wieland and Roy Rubbotom, Assistant Secretary of State and Wieland's chief at that time, were in Bogotá during the riots and must have known about Castro's activities.[32] There are also good reasons to believe that, during his fight against Batista, Castro received support from Wieland when Wieland was the head of the Caribbean Desk in the U.S. State Department.

A clear indication that the U.S. Government supported Castro was its haste to recognize his government after Batista left the country on January 1, 1959. This haste was surprising even to some American diplomats. According to Ambassador Earl T. Smith, the U.S. was too hasty in its recognition of the Castro government.

Usually the U.S. withholds recognition from a new government until it is formally established and operating. Normally, the U.S. does not want to be among the first nor among the last to recognize a new government. The U.S. usually waits until assurances are given that the new government will honor its international obligations. In Latin America, it was the custom for the U.S. to wait until several Latin American countries had recognized the new government. However, in January 7, 1979, just six days after former President Batista fled from Cuba and one day before Fidel Castro arrived in Havana, the U.S. officially recognized the Castro government.[33]

In his well-read newspaper column, journalist Drew Pearson revealed on May 23, 1961, that persistent rumors in the diplomatic corps indicated that the CIA had been helping to put Castro in power for years. The rumors had further stated that CIA agents, in their efforts to get rid of President Batista, had supplied arms and ammunitions to Castro during his guerrilla war in the mountains.

There are more reasons to believe that the CIA gave weapons to Castro. When he was in the Sierra Maestra Mountains fighting Batista's troops, Castro received some weapons delivered by the International Armaments Corporation. The IAC was the company that sent weapons to Guatemala under CIA's orders to overthrow Jacobo Arbenz's government. Moreover, the IAC had been created by Samuel Cummings, a former CIA operative.[34]

In addition, there is evidence that, between October 1957 and the middle of 1958, the CIA gave no less than fifty thousand dollars to Castro's men in Santiago de Cuba.[35] Moreover, rumors had it that a CIA agent, known as Robert Chapman, spent a long time in the mountains with Raúl Castro.[36]

Despite this help, however, there was a stalemate between Castro's guerrillas and Batista's army. However, in early 1957, the CFR conspirators moved their pawns and began openly supporting their secret agent's fight against Batista.

On February 24, 1957, the *New York Times* published the first of a series of three articles written by its correspondent and CFR agent Herbert L. Matthews, who had interviewed Fidel Castro in the Sierra Maestra Mountains in eastern Cuba.[37] Matthews depicted Castro as a liberal and a folk hero —a Latin American Robin Hood crusading against evil. Matthews' articles gave Castro instant international recognition.

Matthews' articles in the *NYT* were just the beginning of a barrage of favorable information about Castro. On February 4, 1958, *Look* published an extensive interview with Castro. On February 25, 1958, the *NYT* continued giving coverage to Castro and published an interview with the Cuban leader conducted by its correspondent Homer Bigart.

Some weeks later *CBS* broadcasted a special program by Taber and Hoffman entitled "The Story of Cuba's Jungle Fighters." On May 27, *Life* magazine published a long, illustrated article about Fidel and his struggle against Batista. A much longer Spanish version, directed to Latin America, appeared two days later in *Life en Español.*

As 1958 advanced and the situation in Cuba tilted toward Fidel Castro and his guerrilla fighters, outside Cuba things also seemed to be going Fidel's way. In the United States, both the government and the press were becoming more and more favorably disposed towards Fidel Castro and his men. Thanks mainly to the selling of Fidel Castro by the CFR-controlled American mainstream media, people all over the world were being conditioned to see Castro's guerrillas as legendary liberators of an oppressed people. Thus, Castro's road to power was conveniently paved by the CFR-controlled American government and media.

Others who contributed enormously to Castro's success were CFR agents infiltrated in the State Department. When Ambassador Earl T. Smith was preparing to assume his new post as Chief of Mission in Havana, no one in the State Department ever told him about Castro's involvement in the Bogotazo. Rubbotom and Wieland arranged to have Smith briefed on Castro's virtues, not by the exiting ambassador, as it was the common practice, but by Herbert Matthews, whom they portrayed as an expert in Cuban affairs. Nor was Ambassador Smith told that both Rubbotom and Wieland were in Colombia during the Bogotazo.[38]

It is customary in the U.S. diplomatic service, when an ambassador returns from his post abroad, to be questioned by the State Department as to his latest views and his estimate of the situation. This process is called debriefing. After Ambassador Smith resigned in January 10, 1959, he was never debriefed. His predecessor, Ambassador Gardner, testified that he was also not debriefed at the end of his mission in Cuba.[39]

U. S. Ambassador Smith commented that, during his mission in Havana, the pro-Castro leanings of the CIA station chief at the embassy were so evident that from time to time he asked him in jest if he was not a *Fidelista.*[40] Testifying before the Senate Internal Security Committee on August 30, 1960, Smith affirmed that the chief of the CIA section in the American Embassy in Havana was pro-Castro, and that the number 2 CIA man in the embassy encouraged a revolt of Cuban navy officers against president Batista in September, 1957.[41]

Ambassador Smith went further and accused the United States government, i.e. certain members of the Congress, the CIA, the State Department, as well as some segments of the press, of being directly responsible for Castro coming to power. "Castro never won a military victory," declared Smith. "The fact that the U.S. was no longer supporting Batista had a devastating psychological effect upon the Cuban armed forces and upon the leaders of the labor movement. The U.S. actions were responsible for the rise of Castro to power."[42]

Fulgencio Batista, the Cuban dictator, was the direct result of the CFR conspirators' activities behind the backs of the Cuban people. In 1933, U.S. Ambassador to Cuba Sumner Welles (CFR) had pushed Batista, an unknown sergeant in the Cuban army, to power through a coup d'ètat.[43] Eventually Batista became Cuba's president, and he actively participated in Cuba's politics until he retired and moved to Daytona Beach in Florida. Some years later, however, he came back to Cuba and repeated his tune by grabbing power through a coup d'ètat. While in power, he was subservient to the conspirators' interests in the island.

However, by late 1958 the CFR conspirators decided that it was time to substitute their puppet Batista with a new puppet: Fidel Castro. To this effect, they sent their agent William Pawley to Cuba on a delicate mission: convincing Batista to leave the country and allow Castro to take power in Cuba.[44]

Millionaire William Pawley, former U.S. Ambassador to Peru and Brazil, was a personal friend of President Eisenhower and CIA Director Allen Dulles. He had owned several successful businesses in Cuba and was a personal friend of President Batista. Moreover, he is suspected of having attended the secret meeting at Mario Lazo's home where Castro had been recruited for his Bogotazo job. Also, Pawley was in Bogotá during the Bogotazo riots, where he played an important role, though perhaps unknowingly, on behalf of the CFR conspirators.

Once in Havana, Pawley had a three-hour long interview with the Cuban President. Yet, despite all his persuasive arguments, he failed to convince Batista to quit and leave the country. The Cuban President told him that he had lost all faith in officials of the U.S. State Department. Pawley returned to Washington and informed President Eisenhower that his mission had failed. [45]

Therefore, on December 14, 1958, the CFR agents at the State Department formally intervened to oust Batista and bring in their secret agent Fidel Castro. To this effect, they instructed U.S. Ambassador in Cuba Earl T. Smith to inform President Batista that the U.S. no longer supported him and he should leave Cuba as soon as possible.[46]

Two hours after midnight on the New Year's Eve of 1959, Batista fled the Island, leaving the door open for Castro's grabbing power in Cuba. The CFR conspirators' had achieved their secret goal.

On April 1959, during his first visit to the United States after taking power in Cuba, Castro received a lot of coverage in the American media. What the mainstream media barely mentioned, was that Castro visited the headquarters of the Council on Foreign Relations in New York, where he spoke on "Cuba and the United States."[47] And the mainstream media also failed to mention that, while in New York, Castro was the guest of honor at the Rockefeller mansion, where he was met by retired Chase Manhattan Bank and main CFR conspirator David Rockefeller and a select group of his globalist cronies and members of the mainstream media they control.

Nor did the U.S. mainstream media cover Castro's meeting of over an hour with a friendly, persuasive, and fluently Spanish-speaking CIA officer. According to some witnesses, the CIA man emerged in a state of ecstasy over Castro's receptivity, responsiveness and understanding. The subject of the conversation still remains a secret.[48]

Just a few weeks after he returned from this trip to the U.S., Castro began implementing a carefully designed two-pronged plan of his CFR masters: its goal was the destabilization of Latin America and the penetration of the Soviet leadership by an agent provocateur who would push the Soviets into unnecessary military adventures all around the globe.

In order to survive, the military-industrial-academic complex needs long, non-winnable wars and revolutions, and Dr. Castro was ready to give them the medicine it craved for. To this effect, as soon as he grabbed power in Cuba Castro began sending military expeditions to Santo Domingo, Panama, Venezuela, and other Latin American countries as well as aggressively approaching the Soviets.

The fact was acknowledged by Peter Collier and David Horowitz. According to them,

> Far from being driven reluctantly into waiting Soviet arms, Fidel actively *provoked* and escalated the confrontation with Washington in *order* to force a cautious, apprehensive and recalcitrant Kremlin to grant that embrace.[49] [Emphasis in original]

Castro's betrayal of the Soviets began as early as 1959, when he first approached them purporting to be a very different person than the one he actually was. One of the first things he did after he took power in Cuba was establishing contact with the Soviets.

In early 1960, Soviet deputy Prime-Minister Anastas Mikoyan was visiting Mexico as the head of a Soviet industrial exhibition. Castro sent to Mexico some of his close associates to meet Mikoyan and convince him to visit Cuba. After some initial hesitation, Mikoyan traveled to Havana on February 4, 1960, and thus became the first Soviet leader to visit Cuba to see for himself the curious revolutionary phenomenon taking place in the sunny Caribbean Island. Favorably impressed by the newborn revolution, he signed the first Soviet-Cuban trade agreement on February 13 of that year.

Seemingly, Mikoyan was the first Soviet leader to fall under Castro's mesmerizing powers. According to several witnesses, Fidel charmed Mikoyan. The shrewd Armenian, considered the best horse trader in the Soviet Central Committee, became such a Castro advocate that Cubans joked he was Fidel's secret agent in Russia.

Initially, the Soviet leadership received Castro's aggressive approaches with extreme suspicion. Castro's Catholic background, and the fact that the Cuban communists distrusted him, only added to their caution.[50] Moreover, given the way Castro was openly provoking the U.S., the Soviets leaders believed that, either he eventually would accommodate to U.S. pressures, or the Americans would overthrow him. Finally, to test the waters, the Soviets sent senior KGB officer Alexei Alekseev to Cuba. His goal was to recruit Castro, but CIA-trained Castro ended up by recruiting Alekseev.

The participation of CFR agents in the U.S. government in the creation of a new artificial enemy 90 miles from American shores has been extensively documented. Actually, the same CFR agents in the State Department and the CIA who had accused Castro of being a Communist during the Bogotazo, changed their tune while Castro was in the Sierra Maestra Mountains fighting Batista.

According to the new CFR party line, Castro was not, and had never been, a

Communist. But a few months after Castro took power they did an about face and began showing "evidence" that Castro was, and had always been, a Communist and a secret agent of international communism. To top this all, Castro himself began telling everybody that he was a Communist.

With the benefit of hindsight, it is evident that the CFR agents were doing a big effort in trying to sell their Trojan Horse[51] to the Russians. But no one knew better than the Soviets that Fidel Castro was not a Communist. Most likely, the information the KGB had gathered about him showed not only that Castro had never joined the Cuban Communist party or any of the Communist front organizations, but also that the Cuban Communists hated him. Moreover, he was not a crypto-Communist, nor had he ever being recruited by the Soviet intelligence services. So, why were the Americans so eager to prove that he was a Communist?

In the typical wilderness-of-mirrors,[52] convoluted reasoning of counterintelligence officers, Angleton and other CFR agents inside CIA must have assumed that the Soviets were going to conclude that the American efforts to sell Castro as a Communist were too crude to be a deception exercise and, therefore, that Castro actually was what he pretended to be.

After Mikoyan returned from his visit to Cuba, he told his colleagues at the Central Committee about his favorable impression of what he had seen in the island. It was only then that the Soviets considered a careful rapprochement with Castro. Three months later, on May 8, 1959, full diplomatic relations were established and from then on Moscow's newspapers began printing almost every day enchanted articles about the sunny Caribbean island rediscovered by the Armenian Columbus. Every official speech included flattering remarks about the Cuban revolution. In the meantime, Soviet "theoretical" writers were at pains trying to classify Castro's strange revolution from the point of view of Marxism-Leninism.

Soviet oil began to enter Cuba in April 1960, and in May, with the reestablishment of diplomatic relations with the Soviet Union, the policy of non-recognition established by President Batista in 1952 was reversed. Events now began to move precipitously; but their nature and speed were attributed to anti-Castro American initiatives and Cuban reactions thereto. The CFR conspirators were forcing Khrushchev's hand.

On July 7, 1960, Castro seized the American-owned oil refineries in Cuba that refused to refine Russian crude oil. Giving Castro a strong push into Soviet hands, President Eisenhower cut U. S. imports of Cuban sugar by 700,000 tons. Two days later Khrushchev delivered a speech in which he agreed to buy more Cuban sugar, at a price above the prevailing rate on the world market.

Still, the long-term perspectives of Castro's rapprochement with the Russians were not very promising. Khrushchev was convinced that the U.S., which had never tolerated hostile neighbors, would not permit the creation of a Communist outpost ninety miles from her borders. What might be a clear advantage for the Kremlin could only be a handicap for a young socialist revolution trying to rebuild the economy of its country on a diversified basis.

By the end of 1960 the Castro government's control over all major branches of the Cuban economy was practically an accomplished fact. However, despite Castro's advances, Khrushchev was not buying. And he was not buying because, among other things, he and other Soviet leaders suspected that Castro was a U.S. agent playing the Americans' game.

According to Nikita Khrushchev's son Sergei, now an American citizen living in the U.S., when Castro took power in Cuba the Soviet leaders did not know who he really was. Sergei recalls that, on an occasion he was visiting his father at the Kremlin, he overheard him talking with other Soviet leaders about Castro. According to Sergei Khrushchev, "They were sure Castro was a CIA agent and was working together with the United States."[53]

But then, an event took place that changed the whole picture: the U.S. invasion at the Bay of Pigs.

The Bay of Pigs PSYOP

In the morning of April 17, 1961, just three months after John F. Kennedy had been inaugurated as American president, 1400 Cuban exiles sent by the United States were wading toward disaster at a beach called Playa Girón, in a bay south of the central part of the Cuba —the Bay of Pigs. The first news about the invasion that appeared in the Soviet press reflected the general consensus that Castro's revolution was living its very last hours in the face of an American direct invasion.[54] Soon after, the Soviet leaders watched in disbelief how President Kennedy, with the power to command enough military force to destroy the world, did nothing as Fidel Castro's troops repelled the attack and captured prisoners off the beach.

CIA officials had been privately assuring the Eisenhower and the Kennedy administrations that Cuba would soon become another Guatemala. However, as early as March 1960, Castro had already begun telling the world that Cuba *would not* be another Guatemala.[55] CFR agents inside CIA must have been quite efficient informing Castro, for it was precisely in March when President Eisenhower approved the invasion plan.[56]

The original invasion plan, on which the Joint Chiefs of Staff and the CIA had agreed, involved a one-shot confrontation of Castro's already formidable armed forces with a vest-pocket-sized force of Cuban exiles trained in regular WWII combat techniques rather than in guerrilla operations and political subversion. The plan amounted to asking the fifteen hundred patriots landed at the Bay of Pigs to seize control of the Island from over a hundred thousand relatively well trained, well armed Castroite soldiers and militia.[57]

It was clear beforehand that, in the event that the invasion failed, Castro's prestige and strength were going to be greatly enhanced. Undersecretary of State Chester Bowles, who had heard of the plan, expressed precisely those concerns to Secretary of State Rusk.[58] With the benefit of hindsight, however, the evidence indicates that the whole operation had been planned to fail.

In the first place, the American government supplied the Cubans with obsolete aircraft and decrepit ships allegedly chosen with the idea that such equipment would not be identified with the ones used by American regular forces. That justification is unconvincing, because the Americans would never be able to hide their massive participation in the invasion, even if it was indirect.

Secondly, when President Kennedy approved the initial plan he had promised that the American forces would provide the air cover to the invasion. Two U.S. carriers were to stand by, within short range, their decks loaded with armed fighter planes, to secure the vital air cover for the invasion. Confident in this assurance from the highest American levels of government that air support would be provided, the invaders disembarked.

Castro hurriedly sent his tanks and infantry, and the invasion force fought valiantly while waiting for the U.S. air support to arrive. But that very Sunday evening, following the advice of his CFR advisors, President Kennedy made the fateful decision to prohibit the U.S. planes from providing the vital air cover. Without that support, the invasion was doomed to fail.[59]

Several authors have popularized the notion that the failure of the invasion was not due to President Kennedy's order proscribing U.S. air cover, but because of lack of Cuban popular support to the invaders, a key assumption in the CIA's invasion plans.[60] The invasion failed, they conclude, because the people stood for Castro instead of turning to back the invaders as expected.

These authors seem to forget, however, that because of the gross error of alerting Castro two days in advance by way of an ill planned and ineffective air attack on his planes on April 16, the Cuban dictator was put on alert. After the air raid, Castro moved quickly, sending all potential enemies to jail to avoid any internal uprising.

The most important thing these authors seem to ignore is that people usually support a *winning* invasion, not a failed one, and just a few hours after the invasion began it was evident that it had failed. As a matter of fact, in the first hours of the invasion some peasants of the region, including a few of Castro's militiamen, voluntarily joined the invading forces. Therefore, the invasion did not fail for lack of popular Cuban support; it failed because Kennedy's CFR advisors convinced him not to provide air support to the invasion.

A few months after the failed invasion attempt intriguing details on why the Bay of Pigs operation had failed began appearing through the dust clouds of official excuses, explanations and disinformation evidencing a massive cover-up. The controversy raged for several months over whether or not air cover was originally planned and later withdrawn from the invasion. Then, in the last months of 1961, Ambassador Whiting Willauer provided disturbing first-hand information in a testimony he gave to a U.S. Senate committee.

According to Willauer, a specialist in this type of military operations, on December 10, 1960, he was recalled from his ambassadorial post in Honduras and charged with planning an invasion of Cuba in conjunction with the Joint Chiefs of Staff and the CIA. In his initial plan, air cover, both for low-level and high-level support, was to be provided by Cuban-flown B-26 bombers and by carrier-based Navy jets.[61]

Willauer's job began before President Kennedy took office in the White House.

He held the title of Special Assistant to Secretary of State Christian Herter, a CFR agent. After Kennedy's inauguration, CFR agent Dean Rusk asked Willauer to continue in this capacity. However, within two weeks, he was left out of the loop, his CIA contacts were ordered to avoid him and he was completely ignored in the State Department. For 30 days, his immediate superior, CFR secret agent Chester Bowles, refused to see him. He was never debriefed by a successor for the useful information he could have passed on. After nearly two months in "isolation," Willauer received, on April 16, 1961, the day before the Bay of Pigs invasion, a telephone call dismissing him from the State Department [62]

Though the story was largely ignored by the CFR-controlled American mainstream press, the disturbing information provided by Willauer about the Bay of Pigs invasion was extremely important. But the invaders Castro has captured didn't need to hear Willauer's explanation. At the trial in Havana, some of the 1,179 captives of the failed operation had arrived at the same conclusion and reportedly said that false intelligence, presumably by the U.S., led them to disaster.[63] Some of them commented that the U.S. had betrayed them. They didn't know however, that it was not the U.S., but CFR agents infiltrated in the U.S. government the ones who had betrayed them.

Nevertheless, the Bay of Pigs invaders were not the only ones who had been betrayed. At the time of the invasion, a strong anti-Castro urban underground movement already existed in most large Cuban cities. Plans for an uprising, coordinated with the invasion, had already been laid out, but were so mismanaged in their execution as to indicate deliberate sabotage. To be successful, even with air cover, such a small force had to be supported by uprisings all over Cuba.

But the uprisings never occurred. And they failed to materialize because the leaders of the underground movement were left in the dark about the landing date and did not know whether the Bay of Pigs operation was a real or a diversionary invasion. The CIA's short wave broadcast station (Radio Swan) failed to broadcast the prearranged signals to trigger the waiting underground into action. Instead, the station broadcasted a series of conflicting and false reports of uprisings in Cuba.[64]

In 1960 CFR agent Richard M. Bissell, Jr., a CIA Deputy Director, was made responsible for the unification of the exiled anti-Castro Cubans under a single leadership movement called the "Cuban Revolutionary Council."[65] Just before the invasion began, the coordinators of the Cuban Revolutionary Council, based in the U.S., and of nearly 100 underground anti-Castro organizations in Cuba, together with the invasion leaders, were rounded up by CIA agents and held incommunicado at a secluded spot in the Opa-locka military base near Miami. They were not alerted that the invasion had started until it had already failed and were in that way prevented from alerting their contacts in Cuba.[66]

In October 1959, Huber Matos, a Rebel Army major in charge of Camagüey province, was accused of treason and condemned to 20 years hard labor. The prosecution of Huber Matos stirred strong opposition among several anti-Communist leaders in Castro's own Rebel Army. Some months after Matos was sentenced, several anti-Communist clandestine groups became active in the cities and in the countryside. By mid 1961, the Escambray Mountains in the central part of Cuba were teeming with anti-Castro guerrilla rebels. For a while, the Escambray guerrillas were a virtual focus of anti-Castro resistance, and they were desperately asking for military supplies.

Nevertheless, the CIA apparently had decided some months before the Bay of Pigs invasion that the guerrillas were not useful to advance the secret CFR objectives. At the beginning of the operations, the CIA sabotaged the guerrillas by supplying them with 30.06 caliber ammunition, but with M-3's grease guns that fired .45 caliber bullets. In other areas, the CIA supplied .45-caliber ammunition to accompany Browning Automatic Rifles that shoot 30.06 caliber bullets. Finally, a few months before the invasion, the CIA stopped sending supplies and urged the rebel leaders to stop fighting and wait for the invasion that was about to take place. In this way, the CIA paralyzed the ongoing guerrilla campaign and the spontaneous opposition against Castro's regime, bringing about the guerrilla's defeat.[67]

The Bay of Pigs invasion presented to any skeptical counterintelligence officer with an incredible collection of mistakes —perhaps too many to be the product of a coincidence.

First of all, the operation was one of the worst kept secrets in the recent military history of the United States. The CIA plans were exposed in the press more than a month before the actual invasion began. The leak started when Professor Ronald Hilton, editor of Stanford's authoritative *Hispanic American Report*, called attention to the anti-Castro bases in Guatemala. In due course the *New York Times*, *Time* magazine, *UPI* and *AP* were leading a coordinated press barrage about the coming invasion.

On April 15, 1961, rebel planes struck Havana and Santiago de Cuba. Some authors have rightly pointed out that the ineffective air strike two days before the invasion had only the effect of alerting Castro about the coming invasion.[68] This, however, does not seem to be the case. Early in November 1960, just six months before the invasion, Castro had carefully inspected the Bay of Pigs area —the very same place where the invasion later took place. Was this a coincidence?[69]

Among the most incredible blunders, the following were paramount: In an effort to avoid identifying the invasion force with the U.S., the CIA armed the 1400 men with weapons requiring 30 different types of ammunition. The invaders made the big mistake of placing most of the ammunition and communication equipment in a single ship, the *Houston*. By another strange coincidence (coincidence is *not* a scientific term) the *Houston* was singled out as a priority target by Castro himself and sunk at the very beginning of the landing, and the vital communication and ammunition cargo in it was lost.

An aerial photograph of the Bay of Pigs taken from a U-2 plane at an altitude of more than 70,000 feet shows coral reefs clearly visible off the beaches. It is known that the photographs were used for intelligence purposes in the invasion operation. It is therefore difficult to explain how the photo analysts didn't detect the dangerous reefs and alert the invaders.[70] The invaders discovered the coral reef only after the bottoms of most of their landing crafts had been destroyed by it.

The town of Trinidad, where in case of failure the invaders could easily have gained access to the Escambray Mountains to reorganize and begin a guerilla warfare operation, was the original landing site. But the Bay of Pigs was surrounded by a swamp, with no ways of escape. Moreover, the choice of the Bay of Pigs for the landing was strange, because, unlike Trinidad, the region was known to be a hotbed of pro-Castroism. Author Hugh Thomas manifested his surprise with his remark, "It would have been hard indeed to have found a region in Cuba in which a rebellion could have been less easily inspired among the local people."[71]

On June 11, 1961, a New York congressman and Chairman of the Republican National Committee charged that the Bay of Pigs invasion had failed because Kennedy rescinded and revoked the Eisenhower plan to have the invaders protected by American air power. Almost two years later, in January 1963, Robert Kennedy denied the accusation in interviews with the *Miami Herald* and *U.S. News and World Report*. According to Robert Kennedy, his brother never withdrew U.S. air cover.[72] Admiral Arleigh Burke (not a CFR agent), however, believed that the invasion very nearly succeeded and probably would have if the President had not cancelled the second air strike. The invasion might have worked even without air support of any kind, the admiral argued, if the first strike had not been scheduled two days in advance of the landing, eliminating the element of surprise.

However, recent information shows the CFR's hands behind every single "mistake" that caused the failure of the Bay of Pigs invasion. Actually, CFR agents were the ones who manipulated Kennedy to make the fateful decisions.

In the first place, the Bay of Pigs invasion was not Eisenhower's plan at all. Actually, CFR's senior agent and CIA Director Allen Dulles brought the invasion plan to Eisenhower. As a CFR puppet, Eisenhower didn't oppose it, but didn't back it either. He washed his hands and told Dulles that he didn't want to know about it.

On April 4, 1961, both Dulles and CIA Deputy Director for Plans Richard Bissell (CFR) briefed the President about the upcoming invasion. They were so enthusiastic about the operation that Dulles told President Kennedy he was certain that "our Guatemalan operation would succeed," adding that the prospects for the invasion's plan to succeed were even better than they were for that one.[73] Kennedy assumed that Dulles' and Bissell's optimism about the success of the Cuban invasion was because the operation had "the Agency's full authority behind them."[74] Kennedy ignored, however, that both Dulles and Bissell had never informed the analysts working in CIA's Intelligence Directorate about the upcoming invasion.[75]

When they were done, Kennedy asked his advisers their opinion about going on with the plan. JFK's advisers Dean Rusk, Robert McNamara, Douglas Dillon, Lyman Lemnitzer, Thomas Mann, Adolf Berle and Arthur Schlesinger, Jr., all of them CFR agents, approved the continuation of the invasion plan.[76]

Other authors blame President Kennedy for giving the fateful order that changed the invasion's landing point. They don't tell, however, that Kennedy ordered the tragic change because CFR agent Dean Rusk persuaded him that the political risks of landing near a town where women and children might be hurt made the plan unacceptable. McGeorge Bundy (CFR), Adlai Stevenson (CFR), and John McCloy (CFR) supported Rusk's views. A few days later, during the April 4 briefing, CIA's Richard Bissell (CFR), outlined an alternative plan for the invasion, with the Bay of Pigs instead of Trinidad as the landing place. The CFR conspirators' trap had been set.

Granted, it is true that Kennedy ordered the cancellation of the rest of the planned air strikes previous to the invasion. As a result, some of Castro's fighter planes were left untouched. These were the planes that shot down the invaders' planes and sank their ships, thus guaranteeing that the Bay of Pigs invasion failed. But Kennedy cancelled the air strikes only after McGeorge Bundy (CFR), Dean Rusk (CFR), and Adlai Stevenson (CFR), persuaded him to do so.

In less than 72 hours Castro's forces defeated the CIA-trained and backed brigade; about 114 men were killed, and more than 1,100 men were captured and held until the United States traded $53 million in food and medicines for their freedom. It was an outstanding military victory for Castro.

Even more important, the U.S. failed invasion gave Castro a legitimacy he could not have won any other way. No other American act could have helped him more. In addition, the invasion struck a mortal blow to the anti-Castro underground movement in Cuba and, soon after, to the anti-Castro guerrillas in the Escambray Mountains. Furthermore, Bissell had united all anti-Castro groups in the U.S., into a single organization. The invasion's failure decapitated it with a single blow.

Moreover, since the image of the opposition to Castro had always been an American one, with Cubans in the U.S. appearing to participate in a subordinate capacity, the harsh treatment given to the anti-Castro underground seemed to be justified by the circumstances. All opposition to the regime had been identified in the Cuban people's mind as American-inspired and counter-revolutionary, thus playing right into Castro's hands.

The bottom line is that, contrary to common wisdom, far from being a failure the Bay of Pigs PSYOP was a total success. Its main goals: boosting Castro's bona fides vis-à-vis the Soviets, and strengthening Castro's iron grip over the Island, were fully accomplished. After their success, the CFR conspirators were now dangling[77] Castro as a succulent bait for the Soviets to bite.

Further proof that the CFR conspirators who control the CIA planned the invasion to fail is that they knew it beforehand. In this case, we also have the smoking gun showing that the CIA knew five months before the Bay of Pigs invasion that it was going to fail.

A declassified 300-page document with an internal CIA history shows that on November 15, 1960, five months before the Bay of Pigs invasion, a CIA task force code-named Western Hemisphere Branch Four (WH/4), in charge of plotting to overthrow Fidel Castro, met to prepare a memo for CFR agent and CIA deputy director of Plans, Richard Bissell. The memo would be used to help CFR agent and CIA Director Allen Dulles brief President-elect John F. Kennedy on foreign affairs. Present at the WH/4 meeting were not only Bissell, but also Dean Rusk, who was then Secretary of State; Robert S. McNamara, Secretary of Defense, and McGeorge Bundy, the President's special assistant for national security affairs —

all of them CFR agents.[78]

The memo concluded that the invasion was unachievable as a covert paramilitary operation without the direct support of U.S. military forces.[79] The document was found in June 2005, among several declassified documents in a box marked "Miscellaneous" at the National Security Archive

An interesting detail that shows the conspirators' hands behind the curtains is that the document mentions the key role played by William Pawley in the Bay of Pigs PSYOP. This is the same Pawley who attended the meeting at Mario Lazo's home where Castro was initially recruited; the same Pawley who was in Bogotá during the Bogotazo riots and later claimed he had listened to Castro on the radio saying that he was a Communist. This is the same person who, in late 1958, was sent to Cuba to inform Batista that the U.S. no longer supported him and that he had to go.[80] Again, coincidence is not a scientific concept.

Though the finding of the document is new, its existence was known since a long time ago. In 1987, Jack Pfeiffer, CIA's former chief historian, sued the CIA to release what he knew was a view of the Bay of Pigs quite different from the official one. He suspected that despite CIA's Inspector General Lyman Kirkpatrick had ordered to destroy the document some copies may still remain. He was right.[81]

But Pfeiffer was wrong when he reached the conclusion that Kirkpatrick had destroyed the records and blamed Bissell for the disaster because of personal motives —according to Pfeiffer, Kirkpatrick ambitioned Bissell's position and wanted to discredit him for that reason. Nevertheless, knowing that Bissell was a CFR agent, and that Kirkpatrick most likely was a CFR asset, we may safely surmise that everything was part of a CFR cover-up intended to distort the historical record.

National Security Archive director and professional disinformer Peter Kornbluh mentioned that the WH/4 analysis was so sound that it eerily foreshadowed a scathing and sometimes controversial report written by CIA Inspector General Lyman Kirkpatrick in the summer of 1961.[82] Kirkpatrick, however, blamed the Bay of Pigs fiasco on the usual human frailties the CFR disinformers commonly use as a excuse to hide treason: arrogance, ignorance and incompetence.

Nevertheless, thanks to this document, we know that this is not true. The fact that in mid-November 1960 the WH/4 concluded that the goal that a 1,500-3,000 man force could secure a beachhead with an airstrip was "unachievable" except with direct Pentagon participation, and five months later become "achievable" with only 1,200 men and as a sole CIA covert operation without U.S. military support, was not the product of arrogance, ignorance or incompetence.[83] It was sheer treason.

In conclusion, the failed Bay of Pigs invasion had far-reaching implications. As professor Peter H. Smith rightly pointed out,

> It boosted Castro's political stature in Cuba, Latin America, and the developing world. And it helped him drive his revolution toward the Soviet Union; it was in December 1961, not before, that Castro declared his lifelong allegiance to Marxist-Leninism.[84]

Not surprisingly, boosting Castro's political stature and driving him toward the Soviet Union were exactly the CFR conspirator's goals. Consequently the Bay of Pigs operation was a total success for the conspirators.

Chapter 9

Agent Castro Warms Up the Cold War

The duty of every revolutionary is to make the revolution.
—Fidel Castro, Second Havana Declaration, 1962.

After the successful Bay of Pigs PSYOP, Castro continued pushing the Soviets into accepting him as a new member of the communist camp.

On April 16, 1961, just a few hours before the onset of the failed Bay of Pigs invasion, Castro made an impassioned speech at the funeral of the victims of the initial air strike, in which he declared that he was building a socialist society in Cuba. On December 2, 1961, he gave another turn to the screw. On a long televised speech he went a step further and declared to his amazed audience that he had always been a Marxist-Leninist at heart and would remain such until the last day of his life.[1]

Castro's non-communist affiliation had been so widely taken for granted internationally, particularly in the U.S., that his speech caused a commotion. Castro himself had previously confessed he had never read past the first pages of *Das Kapital* or any other Marxist literature. We may safely surmise that Soviet leaders and intelligence analysts received his speech with extreme suspicion. Evidently, Fidel Castro was trying to create for himself, a posteriori, a false biography. That is what in intelligence parlance is known as a "legend."[2]

The Soviets Swallow the Dangling Bait

Most scholars who have analyzed Castro's untimely decision to declare his revolution Marxist believe that it was Castro's personal choice. They also see it as a logical reaction to "Yankee imperialism," which they see as the main culprit for the alleged dismal economic conditions in Cuba. However, as I will show below in this book, during the last years Batista was in power Cuba experienced an economic boom unseen in all its previous history as a democratic republic. So, if a poor economy was not the reason, what were Castro's true motives?

Adding still further to the mystery and complexity of the enigma was the fact that the pro-Soviet Cuban communist party never liked Castro and never opposed Batista. On the contrary, they opposed all of the anti-Batista movements, including that of Fidel Castro.[3]

How could Cuba become a Communist state when the Cuban Communists themselves opposed the revolution that produced that state? If Castro was a communist, why was the Communist party initially so critical of his military operations? If he represented interests hostile to the United States, why did a responsible journalist from the *New York Times* describe him as sympathetic to the Americans? If Castro was a Communist, why did a CIA officer, testifying before a congressional subcommittee, declare in late 1959, the year Castro took power in Cuba, that the available evidence did not warrant such a conclusion?[4]

Castro was frantically trying to sell the Soviets an image of his anti-Americanism, but the facts pointed to the contrary. The available evidence indicated that, contrary to conventional wisdom, Castro, like most anti-Castro Cubans in Miami, was an admirer of the American Way of Life. His favorite sports were basketball and baseball. He only watched American cowboy films, and most of the women with whom he had been romantically involved were of the same profile: upper class, Americanized, English-speaking, most of them blondes.[5]

In retrospect, it seems clear that Castro was following a pre-conceived plan, but it was not *Castro's* plan at all. Actually he was just carrying out a plan carefully designed by his CFR masters to infiltrate the Soviets —but the ever suspicious Soviet leaders still were not buying.

As late as 1954, the overthrow of Arbenz's nationalist government in Guatemala by the CIA brought only a mild reaction from the Kremlin. The Soviet leaders had never considered Latin America as a prime political target, much less "ripe for revolution." Instead, they had set out to expand Soviet presence in the area by attempting to project an image of international respectability. Their immediate goal was to show the world that the Soviet Union was a great economic power possessing a well-developed industrial machine with advanced technology capable of accomplishing great feats in space and willing — through the development of normal trade and cultural relations— to share peacefully these accomplishments with other nations.

Khrushchev's goal, faithful to his new policy of peaceful coexistence, was to prove the effectiveness of Communism as a political and economic formula in the eyes of the developing nations, or, as he liked to say, "To demonstrate before the world the superiority of Communism over Capitalism."

If one follows closely the Soviet policy toward Latin America, certain conclusions become evident. First of all, the area did not have top priority for the Soviets during most of this period. Second, until 1960 they had had only modest success in their attempts. The turn of events in Cuba gave them an unexpected opportunity to extend Soviet influence, but it was not clear that they wanted to assume the responsibilities —either economic or political — foisted upon them by the unexpected events.

Before 1959, Soviet objectives in Latin America had been twofold. On the one side, the Kremlin's short-term political objectives had been focused at increasing the number of countries extending diplomatic recognition to the USSR and developing its trade relations with the countries of the area. On the other side, and sometimes in direct conflict with the former, a close look at the party literature at the time shows that the Soviet's longer-run objectives had remained what they always had been: to gain, under the name of the Marxist ideology, influence and control on the Latin American republics of the hemisphere.

In the first months of 1959, after Castro's victory over Batista, Nikita Khrushchev was already working in the preparatory phase of his carefully planned visit to the United States. His greatest desire at that crucial moment was to see all Communist parties throughout the world promoting his newly created concept of peaceful coexistence. Of course, there was nothing intrinsically wrong in the Cuban Communist Party's participation in a patriotic struggle to rid Cuba of a corrupt dictator. Yet, the last thing Khrushchev needed was for the Cuban Communists to undertake a revolutionary course that might give the Americans motive to doubt his good intentions.

For Khrushchev, Castro was just another case of a bourgeois nationalistic leader with a radical posture and confused ideas who would eventually accommodate himself to the United States. Both the Soviet leaders and the Cuban Communists feared that if Castro followed Arbenz's example, he would share his fate. Therefore, their caution was more than justified.

Most scholars who have studied the initial years of Castro's revolution agree that Washington's erroneous policies pushed Castro into Moscow's arms. John F. Kennedy himself provided a typical example of this type of thinking. According to him, if the U.S. had offered the "fiery young rebel a warmer welcome in his hour of triumph, especially on his trip to this country," perhaps he might not have "gone over" to the Soviet side.[6]

This, however, is true on one count only. Obviously, the U.S. government's policies (all of them conceived at the Harold Pratt House) pushed Castro to the Soviet Union, but it was not by mistake, but the result of a carefully conceived plan. Proving the forensic axiom that every contact leaves a trace, in this case I have found the smoking gun.

On March 2001, coinciding with a meeting of professional CFR disinformers in Havana working hard on muddying the historical waters about the Bay of Pigs invasion, the CIA choose to declassify a batch of "documents"[7] and gave copies of them to the so-called National Security Archive. Among them there is one apparently irrelevant, but a very important key to decode the whole Castro PSYOP.

One of the most fascinating features of intelligence work is that sometimes a single and seemingly unimportant piece of information can set a whole bunch of apparently unrelated facts into a meaningful pattern. Intelligence officers believe that if you can find that elusive piece of information you can rewrite large parts of history from a surprisingly different point of view. This document is an example that confirms this theory.

The document is a top secret telegram dated November 24, 1959, 11 months after Castro grabbed power in Cuba, sent by British Ambassador in the U.S., Sir H. Caccia, to the Foreign Office in London. According to Sir Caccia, "I had to see Allen Dulles this morning on another matter and took the opportunity to discuss Cuba on a strictly personal matter."

Then Mr. Caccia informs about Dulles' opinion about how long the Castro government will remain in power and who are his opponents in Cuba, and how Dulles mentioned, *on passant*, what most likely was the true motive of his visit. In the fourth paragraph of the telegram, Sir Caccia mentions,

> From his own point of view, he [Dulles] said that he greatly hoped that we would decide not to go ahead with the Hunter [planes] deal. His main reason was that this might lead the Cubans to ask for Soviet bloc arms. He had not cleared this with the State Department, but it was, of course, a fact that in the case of Guatemala it had been the shipment of Soviet arms that had brought the opposition elements together and created the occasion for what was done. The same might be true in the case of Cuba, and the presence, for instance, of MIGs would have a tremendous effect, not only in the United States, but with other Latin-American countries, quite apart from Trujillo.[8]

Dulles' explanation to the British Ambassador about his motives were smoke and mirrors. The really important thing about his visit is contained in the first two sentences. He is asking the British not to sell arms to Castro so he will be "forced" to ask the Soviets for arms.

Now, the sole fact that the Director of the CIA took part of his busy schedule to pay a visit to the British Ambassador to talk to him about inconsequential subjects is very revealing. The reason is because the senior CFR conspirator and master spy wanted to leave no trace about this very important matter. But the unavoidable conclusion is that the CFR conspirators were pushing Castro into the Soviet's arms. And, by influencing the British not to sell arms to Castro, they gave him the pretext to approach the Soviets without arousing their suspicion.

It is not by chance that, just three months after Allen Dulles' visit to the British embassy, Soviet vice-Premier Anastas Mikoyan visited the Island in the first official visit of a high level Soviet official to Cuba. During the visit Castro used all his extraordinary powers of persuasion to convince the Armenian that he was what he purported to be.

Knowing Soviet behavior, however, one may safely surmise that the Soviet leaders may have been extremely concerned with the turn of events in Cuba. And their concern was genuine, because it was difficult to believe that Castro had been forced to trade with the Soviet Union, much less approach them politically. Perhaps the United States was not supporting the revolution as it might have, but it is questionable whether Castro had explored all the possible avenues of support. For example, why didn't he ever try to negotiate trade agreements with Canada, Great Britain, or West Germany?

Cuba and the Soviet Union signed their first trade agreement on February 13, 1960. Castro consciously chose the support of the Soviet Union, a support he had been pushing for a long time. He was gratuitously delivering the Soviets on a silver plate what they had never dreamed of having: an ally in what the Americans had always considered their own backyard.

But this was very unusual. A parade of Communist leaders all over the Americas had been preaching communism for more than thirty years, and not one of them had been ever able to gain political power. Now Fidel Castro, who was not a Communist, was presenting the Russians with the gift of a power base ninety miles from the Unites States. The Russians had ample reasons for being suspicious. Why was Castro delivering Cuba over to Communism? How could he become a Communist when the Cuban Communists themselves opposed the revolution that brought him to power?

But the temptation was too big. Despite all the warning signs, the Soviet leaders swallowed the dangling bait line, hook and sinker. And the event that ultimately convinced them that Castro was what he purported to be was his unexpected victory at the Bay of Pigs. Because the invasion was on his birthday, Nikita Khrushchev mentioned to his Kremlin colleague that this invasion was a birthday present from the United States.[9]

Somebody with a cooler head should have warned the Soviet leader about never accepting gifts from the Greeks —particularly when the gift was a Horse![10]

The CFR's Agent Provocateur Strikes Again

Once the Soviets reluctantly accepted Castro as a new member of the international Communist movement, Khrushchev expected the Cuban leader to back his new policy of peaceful coexistence. But, to Khrushchev's utmost surprise, Castro openly disagreed.

Faithful to his role as agent provocateur, Castro expressed his opinion that, although the Cubans were committed to avoid nuclear war, they would not allow its threat to weaken their determination to fight against world imperialism. In Castro's view, Third World countries could not afford to wait for the eventual peaceful triumph of socialism. Their life and death battles must not be fought in the future, but now.

By the end of 1961 already a great concern about Castro and the Cubans had been raised in Moscow, not only among KGB intelligence analysts, but also among Soviet leaders as well. First of all, Cuba under Castro had become a real economic embarrassment to the Soviets, who had made a great mistake in trying to undertake the development of a country whose tastes, needs, and economy had been modeled on American patterns. Cuba, which was intended to be a showcase of the Soviet model of development in America, was in fact quickly turning into a showcase of Soviet inefficiency, mainly because of the Cuban leader's inability to make good use of Soviet aid.

Furthermore, Cuba was becoming an ideological source of distress due to the propagation of Castro's "heretical" ideas and his propensity to preach to the Soviets about how to conduct things. Castro's behavior was creating a new focus of dissent in a field already engaged in internal quarrels. In addition, his front line position on the Latin American anti-imperialist struggle put a question mark on Khrushchev's doctrine of peaceful coexistence, and played right into the Soviet Union's enemies.

These concerns grew in January 1962 when Castro went a step further by raising some highly critical questions about the ideological purity of the Soviet commitment to peaceful coexistence. In a communiqué issued from Havana during a meeting of the International Organization of Journalists, Castro outlined his dissenting view of peaceful coexistence:

> The policy of peaceful coexistence is coexistence between states. This does not mean coexistence of classes. This policy does not mean coexistence between exploitation and the exploited. It is impossible for peaceful coexistence to exist between the exploited masses of Latin America and the Yankee monopolies. . . . As long as imperialism exists, international class war will exist between the exploited masses and the monopolies.[11]

The pro-Soviet old-guard Cuban Communists and Nikita Khrushchev were rightfully worried about Castro's radical theories and extremely concerned with the secret training of revolutionaries in Cuba for military adventures against Cuba's neighbors.[12] Yet, having mistakenly come to Castro's rescue —if only for the initial bait of exploiting the political propaganda opportunities offered by the U.S.-Cuban dispute— Khrushchev found himself with an unsolicited client on his hands which he could not disavow, at least overtly, without great embarrassment and loss of prestige.[13]

The Soviet leader had impaled himself in the horns of a dilemma: abandoning Cuba would mean jeopardizing Soviet pretensions of leadership of the communist camp; but allowing Cuba to exist would probably have the same result, because Castro had his own aspirations of control over the international communist movement.

Castro's guerrilla activities were also a big source of concern for the Soviet leader. On the one hand, even if Castro was real, the Soviet Union simply could not afford to have a bunch of Castros in Latin America. A Castro-style takeover of Bolivia, Guatemala or the Dominican Republic would suck up Russia's resources like quicksand, and the resulting fiasco could only hurt the Soviet Union and Khrushchev's prestige. The Soviet Premier was not interested at all in Pyrrhic victories. On the other hand, perhaps Khrushchev's initial suspicions about Castro might have been true, and Castro was not what he purported to be. If this were the case, Castro might be acting as an agent provocateur, pushing the Soviet Union into unwanted, risky military adventures.

Then, on February 4, 1962, agent Castro gave another turn to the screw when he ended his speech proclaiming the Second Declaration of Havana with the incendiary phrase, "The duty of every revolutionary is to make the revolution."

Evidently, the sequel to the Soviet commitment to Castro's Cuba had been a calamitous failure.[14] As seen from the Kremlin, Castro was unpredictable, volatile, undisciplined, and often nonsensical. His wholesale executions, mass arrests, and terrorist adventures against his Latin American neighbors, together with the sight of hundreds of thousands of Cubans attempting to flee his rule, raised the very Stalinist specter Khrushchev was trying to dispel. Moreover, Castro was making a mess out of the Cuban economy and neglected to pay attention to "suggestions" coming from Moscow.

Therefore, even though Khrushchev never fully accepted the possibility that Castro might have been a U.S. mole, he decided that the most sensible thing he could do was to overthrow Castro and replace him with an old-time Cuban Communist, obedient to the Soviet Union.[15]

Initially, Khrushchev thought about getting rid of Fidel by applying direct military force, using the large Soviet military presence in Cuba. Nevertheless, given the Soviet role vis-à-vis the Third World and the Chinese, he couldn't resort to direct action or threaten him with force. It was less easy, however, to resist the temptation to proceed to overthrow him by covert means, with the help of the KGB's section of Special Operations.

Khrushchev Tries to Get Rid of Castro, But Fails

The first Soviet plan to overthrow Fidel Castro was handed over to the Soviet Ambassador in Havana, Sergei Mikhailovich Kudryavtsev. He was an experienced KGB colonel who had been expelled from Canada accused of heading a Soviet spy ring.[16] Since his arrival in Havana in 1960, Kudryavtsev had been a conspicuous figure in Cuban politics. Unlike many Soviet envoys, he never bothered to conceal his power or limit himself to behind-the-scenes activities.

Khrushchev's plan consisted in eliminating Castro and replacing him with Aníbal Escalante, a trusted member of the pro-Soviet Cuban communist party. Following Khrushchev's plan, Kudryavtsev and his KGB men at the Soviet embassy, in coordination with some senior Cuban communists, began plotting to overthrow Castro.

Castro discovered the plot since its very beginning in early 1962, but he let it go on for a while, playing a cat and mouse game with the Russians. Finally, at the end of May, he moved swiftly, detaining the plotters and neutralizing Kudryavtsev and his KGB operatives. On May 30, 1960, Ambassador Kudryavtsev left Havana for good.

Some time later Castro confessed that he "had expelled Kudryavtsev" for having engaged in "open and excessive political activities."[17] However, since Soviet ambassadors do not carry out personal policies —particularly when they are also high-rank, seasoned intelligence officers—,[18] it seems likely that Kudryavtsev had enjoyed the full confidence of the Soviet leadership in performing the difficult task of taming Castro.

When Nikita Khrushchev received the news of the failed coup he became furious. He now tried to find a way to get rid, once and for all, of his Cuban "Communist." But, if Castro was in his hands, he was no less in Castro's hands. After the purging of Escalante and several of the "old line" Cuban communists, some members of the Cuban communist party, out of fear, were following Fidel's line and had become an instrument of his policies rather than Moscow's. In addition, Castro not only had expelled the Soviet Ambassador, but had also handpicked the new Soviet Ambassador: Alexander Alexeev,[19] a Soviet intelligence officer Castro had already "turned."[20]

This state of affairs highly irritated Khrushchev. Still, the Soviet Premier could not afford to openly destabilize the Castro government. Any direct Russian action against Cuba would have led to serious political and ideological consequences for the Soviet Union.

In such circumstances the sensible course for Khrushchev was to cut his losses and get out of the game, particularly considering that the Soviet lines of supply to Cuba were long and extremely vulnerable. Nevewrtheless, leaving Cuba voluntarily would have been tantamount to an admission of failure and would have involved substantial loss of face. If, however, Castro could be eliminated as a result of American "aggression," then Khrushchev and the USSR could retreat from Cuba, their honor relatively untarnished. After an American invasion of the island the failure of Communism in Cuba could be blamed not on deficiencies in Soviet-style communist management of Cuban affairs, but on "Yankee Imperialism."[21]

Therefore, after the Kudryavtsev-Escalante coup d'ètat failed miserably, Khrushchev conceived another plan.

This plan was simple: it consisted in provoking President Kennedy to invade Cuba and overthrow Castro. The provocation would consist in deploying "nuclear missiles" —actually dummies— on Cuban soil. After Kennedy had invaded Cuba, he would have found himself with empty hands because he would have had no Soviet nuclear missiles to show to the American public. This would have made Kennedy the laughing stock of the world and placed the U.S. in a very embarrassing and difficult position before the world and its own conscience, as the big, powerful nation that unjustifiably attacks a very small, innocent one.

Thus, President Kennedy would unknowingly have helped Khrushchev in doing the dirty work of getting rid of Castro. With an American invasion of Cuba Khrushchev would have solved his Castroist problem and made good use of the U.S. loss of face. In the end, he would have inherited Castroism, but without the troublesome Castro,[22] very similar to the way some years later Castro inherited Guevarismo, without the troublesome Che Guevara.

The whole story of how Khrushchev conceived and implemented his second plan to get rid of Castro, and why it failed, is studied in detail in my book *The Nuclear Deception: Nikita Khrushchev and the Cuban Missile Crisis*.[23]

I am fully aware of claims, made 30 years after the crisis, that nuclear warheads were on the island, and that more were bound for Cuba on Soviet ships. But CIA reports during the crisis consistently denied the presence of nuclear warheads in Cuba. Moreover, American planes, flying low over the missile sites and Soviets ships, never detected any of the radiation that would be expected from nuclear warheads.

The main force behind a concerted effort to prove that nuclear warheads were in Cuba was CFR agent Robert Strange McNamara. McNamara found support for his theories from none other than his former executive action target, Fidel Castro, and from a group of Russians, among them, Sergei Mikoyan (son of Anastas Mikoyan), an old KGB hand.

It is difficult to believe, however, as some researchers claim, that there were nuclear warheads in Cuba and that Soviet field officers in the island had been authorized to use tactical nuclear warheads without further authorization from Moscow. Premier Khrushchev knew that just a single nuclear warhead fired by Russian troops in Cuba would have triggered the beginning of World War III, a war unlike any other in history. Doing that would have been tantamount to geopolitical nuclear suicide for the Soviet Union. But, as author Philip Knightley has pointed out, all stories told by spies should be treated with extreme skepticism,

> Even the 'now it can be told' variety, in which spies who have kept silent for forty years finally reveal the great triumphs of their agencies turn out to be, at best, exaggerations and, at worst, myths and legends.[24]

The problem with accepting the fact that there were no nuclear warheads on Cuban soil, or on their way to the island, is that it blows away all the grand theories developed and supported by CFR disinformation agents and tacitly accepted by the CFR-controlled American mainstream media and academia. Yet, giving credibility to past non-existing dangers provide credibility to present non-existing ones.

Some researchers honestly believe the theory —some of them even claim to have seen the actual Soviet documents— which prove that nuclear warheads were actually in Cuba. These researchers are wedded to the theory that "facts explain events" which, in the last resort, depends on the way in which you choose your facts. They seem to forget that facts are just information, and information is not true intelligence until it has been appraised and validated. As a rule, a counterintelligence analyst believes that only information that has been taken from the enemy and turned over is bona fide intelligence. But if the enemy had intended it to be turned over, it is disinformation.

Intelligence officers think that intelligence could be distinguished from deception by judging how well it fits in with the rest of the intelligence reports. If it neatly dovetails with other validated reports, it is assumed to be valid intelligence. The case for the nuclear warheads on Cuban soil, however, has big holes. It doesn't fit with the rest of the available data. It presupposes, among other things, that Nikita Khrushchev, the Soviet military, and Soviet intelligence were inept fools. That image is probably good for polishing some egos at home, but nobody, particularly in the world's intelligence services, is going to buy it.

Khrushchev claimed in his memoirs that his main concern in sending missiles to Cuba was Castro's fear of an American invasion. He also said that the idea came to him while he was visiting Bulgaria in April 1962 and thought about the U.S. missiles just across the Black Sea in Turkey. Therefore, he decided to give the Americans a dose of their own medicine.

But Khrushchev was not crazy, nor was he a masochist. So, it is highly improbable that he had decided to give nuclear missiles to trigger happy Castro just a few days after Khrushchev had tried and failed to overthrow him and Castro had indecorously kicked the Soviet Ambassador and his KGB thugs out of Cuba.

Nevertheless, even if this was not the case, simple logic dictates that no great power is going to give missiles to any newcomer who just asks for them. The

USSR installed missiles where it wanted, and nowhere else.

Moreover, neither before 1962, nor after, the Soviets deployed nuclear warheads beyond their borders. It was not until many years later, only after they had developed reliable security devices to control its arming, that the Soviets allowed a limited number of nuclear warheads to cross their borders, but always kept them secure under strict control of KGB *spetsnatz* troops. Why, then, would the Soviets place nuclear missiles so close to trigger-happy Fidel Castro?

In 1962 Khrushchev had practically unlimited powers and the authority to use the missiles as he saw fit, not only at home, but also in foreign affairs. So, he ordered that missiles be sent to Cuba, but without the nuclear warheads —which he never sent, *and never intended to send to the island.* Moreover, there is a strong possibility that the missiles themselves, like the ones Khrushchev was displaying at the time in Moscow's parades, were empty dummies.[25] The fact that Kennedy didn't order the Navy to verify on site that the objects covered with tarps leaving the Island on Soviet ships were actual missiles indicates that his NSC advisors knew it.

Nikita Khrushchev never understood why Kennedy had acted in such an irrational and foolish way, by not attacking Cuba and, thereby, allowing Castro to stay in power. He ignored that the American President had acted following the advice of his advisers, most of them CFR secret agents.

The Cuban missile crisis was a further irritant to Khrushchev's already risky political situation. Though the state of the Soviet economy was the main factor in his demotion in October 1964, undoubtedly his Cuban misadventure contributed to his fall. A year after Khrushchev's *faux pas*, he received an important visitor: David Rockefeller. A few days after David's kiss of death, CFR moles in the Kremlin deposed Premier Khrushchev.

Castro's Good Job on Behalf of his CFR Masters

With Nikita Khrushchev out of the picture and new leaders in the Kremlin, mostly under the control of the CFR conspirators, Castro continued unmolested doing his job as an agent provocateur for his CFR masters.

By 1967, Castro's criticism of peaceful coexistence had become strident and was no longer limited to philosophical considerations. In Castro's view, peaceful coexistence had become a primary issue of contention in the socialist's camp policy. The military struggle against imperialism should not be limited by concerns about peaceful coexistence.

It is interesting to note that, as it happens most of the time, for some strange reason Castro's views were very close to the views held by the American military-industrial-complex and Wall Street financial interests, which saw Khrushchev's doctrine of peaceful coexistence as a direct threat to their economic interests and, therefore, opposed it tooth and nail.

Following Castro's warmongering line, in May of that year Castro's own Cuban Communist Party issued the following statement:

> If the concept of peaceful coexistence between states with different social systems does not guarantee the integrity, sovereignty, and indepen-

dence of all countries alike, large and small, it is essentially opposed to the premises of Proletarian Internationalism. What kind of peace are the Vietnamese enjoying? What kind of coexistence is the U. S. practicing in that country?[26]

In early 1968, the UN General Assembly opened discussions on a multilateral agreement to curb the spread of nuclear weapons. The discussions resulted in a Non-Proliferation Treaty. Since it opened for signatures in 1968, 113 countries, including all the nuclear-weapons states, signed the treaty. But, during the Non-Proliferation Treaty discussions, Cuban UN delegate Raúl Roa Kourí clearly expressed Castro's position when he asserted that "Cuba would never give up its inalienable right to defend itself using weapons of any kind, despite any international agreement."[27] In the same fashion, Castro had earlier refused to sign the Tlatelolco agreement of 1967.

Shortly after the missile crisis of October 1962, the heads of state of seven Latin American countries called for hemispheric consultations to create a nuclear-free zone in Latin America. The agreement was finally signed in Tlatelolco, Mexico, in February of 1967. Cuba was among the countries invited to participate, but the Castro government refused, stating that it would not participate in the negotiation of an agreement to denuclearize Latin America because the U.S. deployed nuclear weapons and maintained nuclear bases in Latin America.[28]

Castro's posture in relation with the Tlatelolco agreement was in sharp contrast to the policy of the Soviet Union. In retrospect, it seems that his reticence to sign both agreements was not the product of a passing mood, but of a carefully designed plan conceived at the Harold Pratt House to keep the Cold War as hot as possible. It was a harbinger of things to come.

The Latin American Guerrillas and Other PSYOPs

Since the very first day Fidel Castro grabbed power in Cuba in 1959, he unleashed an unrelenting attack against the Latin American and other peoples of the world. This played right into the hands of his CFR masters, who used it as a pretext to increase the U.S. intervention and control over the threatened economies of these countries.

On April 26, 1959, just a few months after his victory over Batista's troops, Castro sent a hit team of about eighty-four Cubans and Panamanians to Panama, to kill President Ernesto de la Guardia and spark a revolution. Within a few hours of landing, the invasion was crushed. Most observers agreed that the Castro government was behind the attack, but Castro denied the charges.[29]

The unsuccessful Panama expedition is a good clue to Castro's true political thinking. The Panamanian government was not a dictatorship, and its president had been elected by popular vote, therefore the attack had no ideological justification —that is, if Castro is really the leftist he claims to be. Moreover, adding insult to injury, at the time of the attack Castro was visiting Washington in an attempt to allay American fears of his totalitarian leanings.

Subsequently, both Castro and Che Guevara denied official Cuban participation in the affair and condemned it as the work of "a group of adventurers headed by a *barbudo* [bearded guy] who had never been in the Sierra Maestra . . . [who] managed to fire the enthusiasm of a group of boys to carry out the adventure." Guevara went further and claimed that the Cuban leadership had "worked with the Panamanian Government to destroy it."[30]

A few hours after landing in Panama and allegedly after having received an appeal from Castro to call off the expedition, the invaders surrendered to an Organization of American States investigating team. Though the Panamanian government never charged the Castro regime with responsibility for the invasion, most people believe Castro's hidden hand was behind it. With the benefit of hindsight it made sense, because the invasion followed Castro's *modus operandi* for that type of operation.

Just a month after the Panama affair, another group secretly departed from Cuba and headed for Costa Rica in an operation to kill Nicaraguan President/Dictator Luis Somoza. Somoza was a sworn enemy of Fidel Castro. On the first of June 1959, two planes full of invaders left Costa Rica and headed for Nicaragua. They planned to coordinate their attack with the landing of several yachts filled with more armed revolutionaries. Somoza complained to the Organization of American States, and implied that the yachts had sailed from Cuba, but offered no evidence to support his charges. The invasion was suppressed in a few hours, and Castro denied any involvement in the attack.

Less than two weeks later, on June 14, 1959, Castro sent a similar group to the Dominican Republic to kill President Trujillo. Castro's hostility to Trujillo dated back to his days at the University of Havana, when in 1947 he joined an expedition of several hundred men trying to assassinate Trujillo. Castro's hatred for Trujillo was intensified when the Dominican president gave political asylum to Batista and a large number of anti-Castro Cuban exiles.

Fidel Castro's personal involvement in this expedition is undeniable. On June 14, some 200 Dominican exiles who had been undergoing military training in Cuba, and ten Cubans, all commanded by one of Castro's Rebel Army officers, left Cuba in a plane and two small ships and headed for the northern coast of the Dominican Republic. Again, the plan followed Castro's *modus operandi*. The guerrillas were to establish a *foco* —a small, armed, mobile guerrilla band— in the mountains, while revolutionaries in the cities would rally mass demonstrations and strikes. But the invasion soon ended in total failure, and Trujillo's army soldiers left no survivors to tell the story.

However, in the case of the Dominican adventure, more than just suspicions points to Castro's involvement in personally preparing and arranging the operation. It seems that, in his enthusiasm, he forgot all prudence and made an appeal for open support to the invasion, which he hastened to disavow the next day.

On June 16, two days after the attack was launched, Castro appeared on TV and asked for support for the Dominican invaders.[31] However, when Trujillo's government protested to the OAS, Castro recanted and denied his participation in the invasion. Making good use of his arts as an unashamed dissembler, Castro declared: "Our strategy is to repeal aggression, not to attack, but to defend ourselves and our territory."[32]

Both the Nicaraguan and Dominican operations ended in failure, and Castro denied that he personally had authorized the ventures. Nevertheless, given Castro's propensity to carry out this type of covert operation and his total control over Cuban events, one has to conclude that he was fully behind the attempts.[33]

Just a couple of months later, in mid-August, 1959, Castro struck again. This time an expeditionary force moved against Haiti. Its main goal was to assassinate François "Papa Doc" Duvalier, the dictatorial president of Haiti, another of Castro's preferred targets. According to official declarations of the Duvalier government, the invading force was composed of some thirty men, all of them Cubans. The group was led by an Algerian who had served with Castro in the Sierra Maestra, and was financed by Louis Déjoie, a former Haitian senator and avowed enemy of Duvalier. Later it was known that Che Guevara, following Castro's direct orders, had organized the expedition.

Like the expeditions on Panama and Dominican Republic, the Haitian adventure ended in total disaster, and most of the attackers were killed. Castro never responded to or denied the Duvalier's government charges of his complicity in the affair.[34]

On July 26, 1960, in a speech commemorating the failed attack on the Moncada garrison in Santiago de Cuba, Fidel Castro declared his commitment to "liberate" the rest of Latin America.[35] His idea of "liberation," however, resembled more the fascist technique of coup d'ètat than communist proletarian revolutions.

For example, there is evidence that Castro tried to kill the democratically elected president of Panama, Roberto Chiari. According to an FBI report dated October 25, 1962, one of Castro's hit men, named Humberto Rodríguez Díaz, in complicity with a former Cuban ambassador to Panama, planned an attempt on the life of the Panamanian president.[36]

Later on, in the spring of 1963, Castro shipped several tons of weapons and ammunition to a Venezuelan revolutionary underground.[37] Castro's obsession with killing President Rómulo Betancourt, who initially was his supporter, has been extensively documented.

It is highly revealing that Castro's actions against Venezuela were not directed against a tyrannical, undemocratic regime. On the contrary, they were directed at avoiding the establishment of democracy. The immediate goal of the Castro-backed revolutionaries was to disrupt the 1963 presidential elections. As Castro and the Venezuelan guerrillas saw it, if these elections were disrupted and the military provoked into seizing power, the way of democratic reform would be completely discredited in Venezuela. But Betancourt and the democratic reformers were committed to holding the elections, and Castro lost interest.

That same year Bogotá's newspapers published reports that planes that had landed at Colombia's Guajira peninsula carrying a group of assassins from Cuba had been sent by Fidel Castro. Their mission was to kill President León Valencia and overthrow his government. President Valencia himself officially corroborated the information on October 17, 1963, when he notified all diplomatic missions in Bogotá that he held Castro responsible for the action.

A few months later, on February 26, 1964, coinciding with a planned visit of President Valencia to Cali, another plot to kill him was uncovered. Next year President Valencia pointed to Castro as the instigator behind both assassination attempts.[38]

On July 19, 1979, Nicaraguan dictator Luis Somoza was overthrown by the Castro-backed Frente Sandinista de Liberación Nacional (FSLN, Sandinista Front for National Liberation), and fled the country to become a political exile in Paraguay. Just a few months later, Somoza and his bodyguards were assassinated on a street of Asunción by a Sandinista hit team using machine guns and bazookas. Some members of Castro's intelligence services boasted at the time that the assassination team had been trained in Cuba.[39]

Nevertheless, Castro's subversive activities on behalf of his CFR masters were not limited to Latin America. Once in power, he began supporting all kinds of terrorist groups, particularly anti-American ones, and created the America Department, an intelligence organization whose main objective was supporting anti-American terrorist activities in Latin America and the U.S.[40]

In 1966, Castro hosted in Havana the Tricontinental Conference, a Cuba-based international organization for promoting revolution by violent means. More than 500 representatives from virtually every terrorist group in the world attended the conference. A secretariat to the organization was created at the America Department, to select what groups to support and to promote subversion and chaos in Latin America and the U.S. The MININT (Ministerio del Interior) created several training camps, where would be terrorists were trained in urban guerrilla warfare, kidnappings, assassinations, and other types of terrorist activities.

Many terrorists groups received their training there, among them the Uruguayan Tupamaros, the Argentinian Montoneros and ERP, the Colombian FARC, M-19, and ELN, the Chilean MIR and Frente Patriótico Manuel Rodríguez, the Peruvian MRTA (Tupac Amaru Revolutionary Movement, who attacked the U.S. Embassy in Lima in 1984 and the residence of the U.S. Ambassador in 1985), the Basque ETA (which had a General Headquarters in Havana), the Irish IRA, and the Sandinista, Guatemalan and Salvadoran guerrillas.

In addition, Castro also supported American terrorist groups like the Black Panthers, the Weathermen, the Puerto Rican FALN (Armed Forces of National Liberation), who between 1974 and 1985 organized 120 terrorist bombings in the U.S., and the Macheteros,[41] responsible for hijacking a Wells Fargo armored truck in Connecticut in September 1983 and robbing $7.2 million —most of which found its way to Havana. Both the FALN and the Macheteros were organized by Castro's intelligence services and some of them received their terrorist training in Cuba.[42]

It has been extensively documented that members of the Black Panther organization were trained in Cuba in terrorist operations. In the mid-seventies, the CIA reported that close to 300 Palestinians were undergoing training in Cuban camps.

It is also known that Ilich Ramírez Sánchez, the infamous "Carlos, the Jackal," attended the Tricontinental Conference in Havana in 1966 and was trained in Cuba in urban guerrilla tactics, explosives, sabotage, and other terrorist activities.[43] In November 2000, several Ibero-American heads of state attending the Tenth Ibero-American Summit in Panama passed a resolution condemning ETA's terrorist acts. Yet, they were surprised when Castro refused to join them.[44]

Fidel Castro and the 9/11 False Flag Operation

As expected, Fidel Castro, acting as an agent provocateur on behalf of his CFR masters, played his role in the 9/11/2001 false flag operation that was used as a pretext to begin the war on terror.

In late 2000, Castro began working frantically creating a strong alliance of anti-American Muslim countries. Visits to Cuba of Muslim leaders of all levels, as well as visits of members of the Castroist government to anti-American Muslim countries, increased considerably.

In July of 2001, Hojjatoleslam Hajj Seyed Hassan Khamenei, grandson of Iran's Ayatollah Khomenei —leader and founder of the Islamic republic of Iran— visited Cuba for the celebration of the triumph of Castro's revolution.[45] According to official Cuban reports, Fidel Castro himself, accompanied by his distinguished guest, led the combative march of 1.2 million Cubans along Havana's seaside Malecón Avenue celebrating another anniversary of the victory of Castro's revolution. But the march's main purpose was to make three key demands to the U.S.: an end to the blockade (Castro's jargon for the embargo), the release of the five Castro spies detained in a Miami jail, and *the end of U.S. acts of terrorism against Cuba*.[46] [Emphasis added]

Finally, in May of 2001, Castro made a long trip in which he visited several anti- American Muslim countries, among them Algeria, Iran, Malaysia, Qatar, Syria and Libya.[47] Iran, Libya, and Syria, together with Cuba, Iraq, North Korea and Sudan, had been listed as terrorist states since 1993 in the U.S. Department of State yearly report "Patterns of Global Terrorism."

According to the report,

> Cuba continued to provide safe haven to several terrorists and U.S. fugitives in 1999. A number of Basque ETA terrorists who gained sanctuary in Cuba some years ago continued to live in Cuba, as did several U.S. terrorist fugitives.
>
> Castro also maintained ties to other states sponsors of terrorism and Latin American insurgents. Colombia's two largest terrorist organizations, the Revolutionary Armed Forces of Colombia (FARC) and the National Liberation Army (ELN), both maintained a permanent presence on the island. In late 1999, Cuba hosted a series of meetings between Colombian Government officials and ELN leaders.[48]

In Algeria, Castro was received by Algerian President Abdelaziz Bouteflika.

One source close to the Cuban delegation commented privately that the official communiqués always gave the impression that more things were actually discussed in the exchanges with "an old friend of many revolutionary conspiracies" than it was reported in the press. Political analysts in Havana mentioned the possibility that, despite what was said publicly in Algiers, the two leaders examined topics related to the Cuban interest in strengthening the Non-Aligned Movement and the so-called Group of 77, as the official Cuban press affirmed in evaluating the tour, and also about how to stop the worldwide spread of United States influence.

Upon his arrival in Iran, the second stage of his journey, Castro was prodigal in praising Iranian Islamism. Afterwards, he made an emphatic declaration: "I have not come to speak of trade, but of politics and of culture." Observers noted attentively an affirmation by president Mohammed Khatami: "The cooperation between Iran and Cuba will be able to confront the hegemony and the injustice of the great arrogance [of the United States]." Speaking at Tehran University on May 10, 2001, Castro vowed, "the imperialist king will finally fall."[49]

During Castro's meeting with Iranian Supreme leader Ayatollah Ali Khamenei, the Iranian leader proposed an "Irano-Cuban cooperation" against the U.S. Referring to "U.S. hegemony," Khamenei said that Tehran considered the "American regime as an arrogant power, seeking a unipolar world, to which we seriously object."[50] "The U.S. is weak and extremely vulnerable today," Khamenei stressed, adding that "U.S. grandeur can be broken, and if this takes place, it will be a service rendered to mankind and even the American people," adding that their resistance against U.S. hegemony "is based on our Islamic beliefs, since in Islam resistance against injustice is considered a value."[51]

For his part, Castro said that he was not "afraid of America, and the Cuban nation, 40 years after its revolution, is now stronger than ever." "Iran and Cuba," Castro added, "in cooperation with each other, can bring America to its knees. The U.S. regime is very weak, and we are witnessing this weakness from close up."[52]

In his visit to Qatar, Castro was received by the Sheik Hamad bin Kalifa al-Thani, the emir of Qatar, who had visited Cuba last September. From Qatar, Castro flew to Damascus, responding to an invitation by Syrian leader Bashar al-Assad, who received him at the airport. It was reported that, while in Syria, Castro held private and official talks with his Syrian counterpart, in which they examined how to strengthen bilateral ties.[53] During his visit, Castro again publicly praised the importance of Islamism in the modern world. In his visit to Libya, the next step of his trip, Castro was received by Colonel Muammar al-Qaddafi, who gave his friend Fidel a tour of the house the Americans bombarded in 1986. After visiting the house, Castro mentioned that, as in his own case, the U.S. has used explosives, biological weapons and every means possible to destroy Qaddafi, but has failed.[54]

However, before visiting Syria and Qatar, Castro made a stop in Quala Lumpur, Malaysia, to pay a visit to his friend Mahatir Mohamad, whom he praised as an "excellent leader." During his visit to Malaysia, Castro repeated his new-coined mantra that he is a "great admirer of [the Islamic] religion."

In an article for *WorldNetDaily*, Toby Westerman mentions a conversation he had, on condition of anonymity, with a former intelligence officer for the Lebanese army now living in the U.S. In his report, the officer, whom he refers to simply as Jack, cited Cuba as a "fertilizer ingredient" for Islamic terrorism.[55] There is more than a grain of truth in Jack's remarks.

As an agent provocateur, Castro loves playing the "catalyzer" (or fertilizer) role, and he has played it to perfection in innumerable occasions. He has been the catalyzer in the creation of anti-American guerrillas in Latin America. Without his expert intervention, neither the Sandinistas in Nicaragua nor the New Jewel Movement in Grenada would have achieved power. His hidden catalyzing hand was also present in the work of many terrorist groups in Europe and the U.S.

The main purpose of his visit to the Muslim countries mentioned above was to act as an agent provocateur, inciting fanatic Muslims to commit terrorist acts against America. Patsies play an important role in most false flag operations, and Castro has been a true master in supplying them to the CFR conspirators.

The Castro-Chávez PSYOP

The available record shows that, far from debilitating the conspirators' control over Latin America, more than fifty years of Castro's direct intervention in the region has reinforced it.

As professor Peter H. Smith, a specialist in Latin America politics, rightly pointed out,

> In retrospect, the historical record reveals three basic points: first, the United States exercised a strong and continuous degree of hegemony over the Western Hemisphere from the 1950s to the 1990s; second, within this overall pattern, U.S. hegemony suffered a slight decline from the 1960s to the 1980s; and third, still within his patterns, U.S. hegemony climbed to an all-time high between the mid-1980s and the mid-1990s.[56]

It was precisely between the 1950s and the 1980s when Castro-controlled guerrillas devastated the region. So, how come U.S. hegemony in the region just slightly faltered? The reason for this is that it actually "seemed" to decline, for the only reason that the conspirator's didn't need to send the Marines too often to scare nationalist leaders they can't buy: Fidel Castro was doing it for them. By destroying most pro-Soviet communist parties in Latin America, Castro was doing an excellent job on behalf of his CFR masters.

An intelligence field in which Fidel Castro has shown his mastery is in recruiting gullible fools under the false flag of fighting American imperialism and using them as proxies to do his dirty job on behalf of his CFR masters. Some of them, like Che Guevara, eventually smelled a rat, and he had to be terminated with extreme prejudice. Others, however, became very useful fools. One the most useful fools Castro has ever recruited is Venezuela's Hugo Chávez.

Hugo Chávez is the typical Latin American gorilla, a knuckle-dragging military man, abundant in muscle and lacking in brains. In 2000, with the secret help of Castro and the CIA, he managed to grab power in Venezuela. Immediately, following Castro's advice, he began a process of destruction of his country very similar to what Castro has done in Cuba and the CFR conspirators are currently doing in Latin America.

In 2002 opposition against Chávez grew to the point that a group of the military attempted to overthrow him, but rumors circulated that the CIA alerted Chávez about the upcoming coup. The CIA strongly denied it, but on November 24, 2004, State Department Deputy Spokesman Adam Ereli pointed out, citing a 2002 report of the Office of Inspector General on U.S. policy toward Venezuela in the run-up to the coup, that the U.S. Government had alerted the Government of Venezuela of possible coup attempts and a credible assassination threat.[57]

In 2004, tired of seeing how Chávez's disastrous policies were destroying the country, some democratic sectors of the Venezuelan people called for a referendum. As if on cue, senior CFR agent Jimmy Carter flew to Venezuela representing his own Carter Center to monitor the election.[58]

Polls conducted by the very reliable American firm of Penn, Schoen, and Berland showed Chávez losing by a large margin, but Chávez claimed victory by a small margin. Widespread cases of irregularities and evidence of fraud were reported, but Carter saved the day by legitimizing Chávez's fraudulent victory.

After the event, there was speculation that Carter blessed Chávez's stolen election to prevent further violence. However, one should keep in mind that Carter was actually protecting the interest of his CFR masters, and Chávez's role as Latin American bogeyman is vital in the conspirators' plans for the region.

The Castro-Chávez PSYOP against the peoples of Latin America is just the continuation of the Castro PSYOP after the diminishing power of Castro's influence in the region. Both of them show the typical use of Hegelian dialectics.

As a result of a the Castro PSYOP, the CFR conspirators fanned the fear of Castro-communism to push Latin American dominant classes into the arms of what they considered the lesser of two evils, the U.S. under their control. This explains why, despite all of Castro's apparently anti-American activities, the U.S. hegemony in the region climbed to an all-time high between the 1980s and the mid-1990s.

Even after the fall of the Soviet Union, Castro kept doing a good job. Then, his health began deteriorating until he got so sick that many people augured his imminent death. But, surprisingly, he began recuperating. Nevertheless, Castro realized that he didn't have the stamina to continue doing full time his job on behalf of his CFR masters, so he passed the torch to his agent Hugo Chávez. This does not mean that he told Chávez what he was really doing, but Castro has proved to be a master in manipulating people for his own benefit.

Further proof that, wittingly of unwittingly, Chávez is playing the CFR conspirator's game is that in an interview with Ignacio Ramonet, the editor of the French monthly *Le Monde diplomatique*, Castro told him that he had saved Chávez's life in April, 2002, when a group in the military tried to overthrow him with a coup d'ètat. According to Castro, he personally persuaded the anti-Chávez military to liberate Chávez and reinstall him in power.[59]

Some liberal "progressives" have strongly criticized the CIA because it didn't alert Chávez about the upcoming coup they knew about. What they don't mention, however, is that the CIA helped Col. Hugo Chávez in 1992 when he gave the coup d'ètat that brought him to power in Venezuela.[60]

Currently, with the support of sub-agent Hugo Chávez, Castro keeps carrying out an important PSYOP against the peoples of Latin America on behalf of his CFR masters. The goal of this operation, similar to the Bogotazo, but on a continental scale, is to scare the hell out of the ruling classes in Latin America with the fear of Castro-Chavism.

A large portion of the nationalist Latin American ruling class fear the growing economic penetration and political influence of Wall Street and American transnational corporations in their countries, and were reluctant to accept the new free trade agreements with the U.S.

The ruling classes of most Latin American countries are intimidated by Castro-Chavism's ability to mobilize anti-government violence and by Chávez' use of oil as a blackmail tool. Moreover, some of them simply don't want to appear supporting policies favored by American "imperialism."

They seem to ignore, however, that the CFR conspirators have been using to their advantage the fear of Castro-Chavism as a strong factor to force the Latin American leaders they have not been able to buy or coerce into accepting noxious policies like the North American Free Trade Agreement (NAFTA), the Central America Free Trade Agreement (CAFTA), and the coming Free Trade Area of the Americas (FTAA), as the lesser of two evils.

The Central America Free Trade Agreement (CAFTA) and the Free Trade Area of the Americas (FTAA), are just previous steps towards the creation, first, of the North American Union that will comprise Canada, the U.S. and Mexico and, later, of the American Union, which will extend from Alaska to Patagonia. The American Union, under the total control of Wall Street bankers and oil magnates through their international financial organizations —and, if necessary, with the help of the U.S. military— will bring the destruction of the economies of the Latin America countries, the extinction of the middle classes, the enrichment of a few and the impoverishing of workers and farmers . . . exactly as Castro has done in the Cuba.

Playing a key role in this process is the International Monetary Fund (IMF), an institution created and controlled by CFR-controlled Wall Street bankers. In an article entitled "Neo-Bolsheviks of the I.M.F.," Russian economist Georgi Arbatov made the best description of what the IMF really is. According to Arbatov, IMF officials are,

> Neo-Bolsheviks who love expropriating other people's money, imposing undemocratic and alien rules of economic and political con-

duct and stifling economic freedom.[61]

Arbatov is right on the mark. The IMF has been the main cause of the economic disaster of all countries who have fallen under its economic control. No wonder the economic measures imposed by the IMF have been dubbed "shock treatment." Like the psychiatric treatment of the same name, patients not killed during the treatment suffer its terrible consequences the rest of their lives.

Chapter 10

PSYOPs Against the American People I

None are more hopelessly enslaved than those who falsely believe they are free.
—Johann von Goethe.

The conspirators' ultimate goal has always been to take full political control of America. To this effect, they have used their innumerable secret agents in both parties, the government, the judiciary, the mainstream media, the educational system, the intelligence agencies and the military, to implement and carry out carefully planned psychological warfare operations (PSYOPs). As I explained above in the Introduction, the methodology used is based on the Hegelian dialectics principle of thesis-antithesis-synthesis.

These PSYOPs are both long term, like the Cold War, the War on Drugs, the War on Terror, and the two-party PSYOP, and short term, like the gay marriage PSYOP implemented to keep George W. Bush in the White House for a second term and the Obama PSYOP used to put Barack Obama in the White House.

Usually, long-term PSYOPs begin with a false flag operation playing the role of the scaring antitheses. These were the cases of the Bogotazo, which marked the beginning of the Cold War PSYOP, and the 9/11 events, used as a pretext to initiate the currently ongoing PSYOP called the War on Terror.

Though the name "false flag operation" used to designate a PSYOP in the form of a self-inflicted attack you blame on somebody else you want to destroy is relatively new, the operation itself is very old. Most known examples are Nero burning Rome and blaming the Christians; American jingoist warmongers blowing up the *Maine* battleship in Havana's bay and blaming the Spaniards as a justification for the war against Spain and their imperialist expansion; Hitler burning the Reichstag and blaming the Communists to justify his grab for power in Germany, and the Nazis attacking a German radio station in Gleiwitz and blaming the Poles in order to justify the invasion of Poland.

More recent examples are the Bogotazo riots, used as a pretext to begin the Cold War; the Gulf of Tonkin incident, used as a pretext to escalate the Vietnam war;[1] and the 9/11 events, used as a pretext to initiate the War on Terror —a handy substitute after the unexpected collapse of the Soviet Union brought an end to the Cold War.

Another type of PSYOP is the one I would call the Br'er Rabbit PSYOP ("Pleeze, don' thro' me in dat briar patch!"). An early example of this type of PSYOP was when the banking monopolists pretended to be against the creation of the Federal Reserve in 1913, knowing that the American people would be in favor of anything they were against. As expected, most Americans supported the creation of the Federal Reserve Act.[2]

Current examples of this type of PSYOPs are the U.S. military's "don't ask, don't tell" policy regarding gays, and the U.S. embargo on Castro's Cuba. Contrary to what brainwashed Americans believe, far from damaging the alleged victims, both measures benefit the people they are supposed to hurt.

The "don't ask don't tell" policy gay leaders complain so much about,[3] is actually a measure taken to protect gays in the military by making them invisible. I have the feeling that, particularly after the Army was decimated as the result of the forced inoculation of a lethal vaccine –the so called "Gulf War syndrome"–, the number of gays in the U.S. military has increased dramatically, much more above the percentage of gays in the U.S. population. But we don't know how much, precisely because the "don't ask don't tell" policy does not allow us to have reliable statistics.

In the same fashion, the U.S. imposed the so-called "embargo" on Castro's Cuba —which, despite the fact that Castro calls it a "blockade," has proved to be totally ineffective to overthrow the regime. Nevertheless, the embargo was actually a handy pretext given to Castro so he can justify the Island's total social, human and economic disaster (which, as I will show, below is actually a total success from the point of view of Castro and his CFR masters) by blaming the U.S. for it. Proof of it is that, despite its lack of effectivity —currently, the U.S. is one of Cuba's main commercial partners—, the embargo has been maintained active year after year for several decades by U.S. presidents of both factions of the Repucratic party.[4]

Perhaps with the exception of the old generation of anti-Castro Cubans who were effectively brainwashed by the CIA, most Cubans inside and outside the Island have reached the conclusion that the embargo only benefits Castro. Nevertheless, in order to protect their secret agent the "embargo" is maintained by CFR agents in the U.S. government.

Another example of this type of PSYOP is oil corporations complaining about the Left for protesting against the construction of new refineries and new oil extraction fields, while at the same time bankrolling the Left for doing so. What the people ignore is that the oil companies are united in a cartel, that is, an illegal association of producers and suppliers to artificially maintain high prices and eliminate competition. Actually, the less oil they produce at lower production costs the higher the oil prices and their profits.

However, though false flag operations are old, Hegelian-type PSYOPs are a relatively new phenomenon. They are essentially based on the principle of artificially creating a big threat in order to convince the people to accept the real threat as the lesser of two evils. But some of them involve the use of a notional[5] threat, that is, a non-existing threat that has been implanted in the mind of the target population using modern propaganda and indoctrination techniques —essentially mass brainwashing.

The idea of using a notional threat instead of a real one is very useful, because the conspirators could never eliminate a non-existing threat, and can extend the conflict as long as they need it.

A War in the Peoples' Minds

After the end of WWII, globalist conspirators at the Royal Institute of International Affairs in London and the Council on Foreign Relations in New York, devoted all their creative energy to devise a plan for the implementation of a new totalitarian communo-fascist society under their control —what they call the New World Order.

Contrary to their assertions, however, the New World Order is not new at all. Actually, it is a very old idea. Essentially, the New World Order is a sort of neo-feudalism[6] incorporating some characteristics of totalitarian fascist and communist regimes as well as modern techniques of mass mind control.

The New World Order would be fully implemented once the conspirators have accomplished their goal of reducing by any means necessary the population of this planet to no more than 15 percent of the current levels. After the conspirators reach that goal, they will lower the economic means of the surviving serfs to pre-industrial levels of consumption. In contrast, the very few masters will live in the opulence, enjoying all the benefits of the post-industrial revolution.

How they plan to accomplish that? One way may have been using bare force, in the Hitler, Stalin or Castro fashion. Nevertheless, as I explained above in this book, the conspirators have no armies, so they concluded that the only way to conquer the enemy was by conquering their minds. That way they would accept without complaining the reduction of their standards of living to pre-industrial levels of consumption, or even being killed, as necessary steps that need to be taken, as the lesser of two evils, in order for planet earth to survive.

Obviously, convincing people to willingly accept their own economic and physical destruction, and even cooperate with it, is not an easy task. So, to achieve their goal, the conspirators resorted to the most modern techniques of psychological mind control, most of them developed and successfully tested during WWII.

Probably the best-known scientist who sold his soul to the conspirators was British Fabian Bertrand Russell. In his 1951 book *The Impact of Science on Society*, Russell saw education as a perfect modern tool of mass brainwashing and mind control through propaganda. He explained in detail the future techniques of mind control:

> Physiology and psychology afford fields for scientific technique which still await development. Two great men, Pavlov and Freud, have laid the foundation. I do not accept the view that they are in any essential conflict, but what structure will be built on their foundations is still in doubt. I think the subject which will be of most importance politically is mass psychology. . . . Its importance has been enormously increased by the growth of modern methods of propaganda. Of these the most influential

> is what is called "education." Religion plays a part, though a diminishing one; the press, the cinema, and the radio play an increasing part. . . . It may be hoped that in time anybody will be able to persuade anybody of anything if he can catch the patient young and is provided by the State with money and equipment.
>
> The subject will make great strides when it is taken up by scientists under a scientific dictatorship. . . .The social psychologists of the future will have a number of classes of school children on whom they will try different methods of producing an unshakable conviction that snow is black. Various results will soon be arrived at. First, that the influence of home is obstructive. Second, that not much can be done unless indoctrination begins before the age of ten. Third, that verses set to music and repeatedly intoned are very effective. Fourth, that the opinion that snow is white must be held to show a morbid taste for eccentricity. But I anticipate. It is for future scientists to make these maxims precise and discover exactly how much it costs per head to make children believe that snow is black, and how much less it would cost to make them believe it is dark gray.[7]

Yet, Russell warned the conspirators about the risk of allowing these powerful techniques to fall into the hands of the populace,

> Although this science will be diligently studied, it will be rigidly confined to the governing class. The populace will not be allowed to know how its convictions were generated. When the technique has been perfected, every government that has been in charge of education for a generation will be able to control its subjects securely without the need of armies or policemen.[8]

Another important scientist who contributed to the developing of mind-control techniques was Aldous Huxley. Speaking in 1961 at the California Medical School in San Francisco, he forecasted,

> There will be in the next generation or so a pharmacological method of making people love their servitude and producing dictatorship without tears, so to speak. Producing a kind of painless concentration camp for entire societies so that people will in fact have their liberties taken away from them but will rather enjoy it, because they will be distracted from any desire to rebel by propaganda, or brainwashing, or brainwashing enhanced by pharmacological methods. And this seems to be the final revolution.[9]

In his 1949 novel *1984*, George Orwell described a future totalitarian society, very similar to what the conspirators have in mind, in which mind control is reached through constant repetition of messages from a TV set people are forced to keep on most of the day. What never crossed Orwell's mind, however, was that some day people would voluntarily have similar devices at home, pay for them, and even enjoy the continuous flow of mesmerizing propaganda. Currently, in the average American home television is turned on seven hours a day. Reality always surpasses fiction.

This war in the people's minds, which began in Woodrow Wilson's times and is still going on, has been so subtle and effective that most of the victims have totally missed it. Some have blamed the gradual disintegration of America's economy, culture and values on different causes: party politics, greed, ignorance, communist ideology, etc. Just a few, however, have seen the true nature of this underground war in the people's minds. One of them was Senator Jesse Helms. Speaking before the Senate on December 15, 1987, Senator Helms pointed right to the true nature as well as the source of the attack:

> This campaign against the American people —against traditional American culture and values— is systematic psychological warfare. It is orchestrated by a vast array of interests comprising not only the Eastern establishment but also the radical left. Among this group we find the Department of State, the Department of Commerce, the money center banks and multinational corporations, the media, the educational establishment, the entertainment industry, and the large tax-exempt foundations.[10]

Sun Tzu's dictum, "All warfare is based on deception,"[11] is even more true in the field of psychological warfare. Actually, psychological warfare *is* deception.

In his book *Deception: The Invisible War Between the KGB and the CIA*, Edward Jay Epstein mentions Angleton's theory of deception. According to Angleton, in order for a deception operation to be successful, first, the target has to be in a state of mind that he wanted to accept as intelligence any disinformation he gets from his own leaders. This may not happen unless the target's prevailing preconceptions fits in with the opponent's interests. Secondly, the target has to be in a state of mind that he is so confident about the disinformation he receives from his leaders that he is unwilling to consider evidence, or even theories, that he is or can be duped. This kind of blanket denial amounts to a conceit, which Angleton believed could be cultivated in an adversary.[12]

According to some sources, in 1933, Lavrenti Beria, a professor of Psychopolitics at the Lenin University in Moscow, addressed some American students with an inspirational lecture. Among other things, professor Beria mentioned,

> Psychopolitics is an important if less known division of Geopolitics. It is less known because it must necessarily deal with highly educated personnel, the very top strata of "mental healing." . . . By psychopolitics our chief goals are effectively carried forward. To produce a maximum of chaos in the culture of the enemy is our first most important step. Our

> fruits are grown in chaos, distrust, economic depression and scientific turmoil.[13]

We don't know if the Beria quote is genuine.[14] What we know for sure, however, is that the CFR-controlled OSS was the first organization in the U.S. to elaborate a coherent theory of psychological warfare. According to it, the techniques of "engineering of consent," used in peacetime advertising and propaganda, could be effectively used in psychological warfare.[15] Following this trend, Assistant Secretary of War John J. McCloy, a trusted CFR agent, established in 1944 a small, highly secret Psychological Branch within the War Department General Staff G-2 (Intelligence) organization.[16]

One of the key points of a successful deception operation is to hide the true source of the attack. Therefore, in order to understand the true nature of the current psychological warfare attack on the American people we need to know who the enemy is and what its motivations are. As Sun Tzu said, only if you know the enemy and know yourself you will win a hundred battles.[17]

In this book, I have pointed to the Council on Foreign Relations as the headquarters of the enemy forces. The CFR is basically a creation of the Rockefellers and a few international bankers. Unfortunately, the people who have discovered their treasonous conspiratorial actions have seen them as the result of greed. According to them, the creation of a New World Order is just the conspirators' way to reach their ultimate goal: maximum power and wealth.

But this theory does not explain their backing of apparently liberal causes like the New Age, the gay movement, women's liberation, women's reproductive rights, Darwinism, evolution, environmentalism and global warming, just to mention a few. In order to understand this apparent contradiction, we need to know what really are the conspirators, true, secret goals.

Since the beginning of the past century the already billionaire Rockefellers, changed the main focus of their conspiratorial activities from making money into reaching quite different goals. At some point in their lives they got possessed by an irrational fear: they were convinced that the planet was overpopulated and that the masses were consuming too much of the earth's natural resources which, by law, belonged to them —or so they believe. Therefore, they concluded that, in order for this planet to survive, the earth's population must be dramatically curtailed, and the survivors reduced to pre-industrial levels of consumption.

The ultimate goal of the so-called New World Order, a Rockefellers' idea, is basically that: the creation of a global society under their total control after having eliminated no less than 85 percent of the population of the planet, and the remaining survivors divided into two social classes, the very poor and the very rich. Consequently, they put all their creative efforts, first, into finding efficient ways to kill most of the rest of us and, secondly, on how to reduce our present levels of consumption to pre-industrial levels. And this had to be done with the full consent and help of the ones who were to die or become dirty poor.

Surprisingly, thanks to the use of effective psychological warfare operations based on the most advanced techniques of mind manipulation and control, they are reaching their intended goals. Like turkeys raised for Thanks Giving dinner, most Americans are willingly putting their heads on the chopping block to make the butcher's job easier.

PSYOPs Do Exist

In late-1947, President Truman approved NSC-4/A. This document put the newly created CIA in control, through its Office of Policy Coordination, of planning and executing psychological warfare operations. The overt purpose of these psychological warfare operations was to wage the Cold War against America's main enemy: communism and the Soviet Union.

Nevertheless, as I have shown above in this book, the main enemy of the conspirators who created the CIA has always been the American people. Consequently, it is obvious that the true target of these psychological warfare operations is the American people.

On April 20, 1950, Truman gave a speech in which he announced a new "Campaign of Truth" as an antidote to Soviet propaganda.[18] Most of this Campaign for Truth, however, consisted in a campaign of lies to instill fear in the Americans' minds, painting the Soviet Union as an 800-pound gorilla with an itchy finger on the nuclear button.

Ultimately, the conspirators' two main goals are the elimination of 85 percent of the world's population and the reduction of the survivors to pre-industrial levels of consumption. Once we realize what the two main goals of the conspirators really are, it becomes evident that all the big themes overtly and covertly promoted by the conspirators since the 1960s are conducive to reaching two goals: population elimination and consumption reduction.

The massive practice of abortion and extended use of anticonceptives, the promotion of homosexuality, the artificial creation of wars, terrorism and violent conflicts, the instigation of fratricidal and religious wars, the control and restriction of alimentary sources in Africa and Latin America, the prohibition of the use of DDT in Africa and other underdeveloped countries —which resulted in less productive crops, the reappearance of malaria and the death of millions of people—, the creation and dissemination of bacteriological warfare agents (most likely the AIDS virus was one of them), are directly linked to this goal of population reduction.

On the other hand, the bankrolling of the religious left to promote environmentalism, sustainability[19] and New Age religious beliefs, as well as the promotion of scientific fallacies like anthropogenic global warming, the opposition to the exploitation of new oil reserves, and the creation of new oil refineries and nuclear plants, directed at the destruction of the energy base in which the industrial revolution is based. Without that energy base, a drastic reduction in consumption to pre-industrial, medieval levels will occur automatically.

Curtailing these energy resources is the first step in the implementation of the neo-feudal society the conspirators envision for the rest of us. It is highly revealing that both American "progressive" leftists and the most reactionary members of the

Council on Foreign Relations see Castro's Cuba, a country in which the conspirators have successfully tested the coming neo-feudal society, as the model to follow. (More on this in chapter 12).

Two key elements in this conspiracy of enormous proportions, whose ultimate goal is the elimination of most of the world's population, are Darwinism and gun control. Darwinism is the key element of a PSYOP whose goal is discrediting and eventually destroying the Christian religions. Christianity sees life as a gift from God, therefore it creates moral dilemmas and ethical barriers in the minds of the would-be mass executioners.

Darwinism will play the role of eradicating from the minds of the executioners all moral and ethical barriers that Christianity has erected against the killing of human beings. Obviously, it is morally easier to kill evolved pieces of inanimate matter than human beings whose life, according to Christians, is sacred because it is a gift bestowed to them by their God.[20]

Granted, the idea that life is a gift bestowed to us by our Creator is still a religious belief without any scientific base whatsoever. But nobody can deny that it has more socially redeeming value than the religious belief that life is just an accident of nature —unless your secret goal is destroying several billion human lives.

In the same fashion, the registration and eventual confiscation of guns, and the total prohibition of its possession by citizens, makes it very difficult for the targets of democide to defend themselves. History has shown that it is a lot easier to kill unarmed people than armed ones. Gun confiscation was the first step the mass killers took in Nazi Germany, Communist Russia, China and Castro's Cuba before committing democide.[21]

If the horrors of Nazi Germany were not a historic fact, most readers may think that this possibility is too terrible to be even considered. Nevertheless, we should not forget that history has a tendency to repeat itself, and the new generations usually forget past experiences and keep repeating the same mistakes. Proof of it that many people, including some of the descendants of Nazi victims, honestly believe that gun control is a good measure for governments to take.

Nedless to say, the many psychological warfare operations devised, planned and carried out by the conspirators to reach their goals are kept wrapped under the most total secrecy. As I have mentioned above in this book, secrecy is the main tool used by the conspirators to successfully advance their plans. Yet, a few times they have been careless, have made mistakes, and the study in which a particular PSYOP is based has been revealed.[22] I will study below some of the main ones, but this is an incomplete list. Currently there are so many PSYOPs running on simultaneously against the American people that it would take a whole book to study all of them.

The War-for-Eugenics PSYOP

In November 1967, a strange book with an enigmatic title was published: *Report From Iron Mountain: On the Possibility or Desirability of Peace.*[23] The book purported to be a report written by a "Special Study Group" commissioned by an unknown governmental department that wanted to remain anonymous —or so they claimed. The 15 members of the study group, which also remained anonymous, addressed it to that secret department.

The group, whose members had been selected because of their high level of experience, expertise and scholarship, worked for close to two and a half years in producing the Report. According to Leonard Lewin, the person who published it, the Report was leaked to him by one of its members, who identified himself as "John Doe."

The name "Iron Mountain" refers to the location where the first and the last meetings of the Study Group took place. It is highly revealing that Iron Mountain, in upstate New York near the Hudson River, is not far from the Rockefeller Family's compound at the Pocantico Hills.

Moreover, deep below Iron Mountain, the Rockefellers built a huge underground bunker to be used as an emergency nuclear shelter to survive a nuclear Armageddon.[24] The bunker is also the emergency headquarters for Shell, Manufacturers Hanover, Standard Oil of New Jersey, and other Wall Street firms and multinational corporations.

Some people believe that the Report is actually a study produced by the Hudson Institute, located at Croton-on-Hudson, not far from the Iron Mountain and that it was commissioned by Secretary of Defense Robert Strange McNamara, a trusted CFR agent. The Hudson Institute is one of the CFR's think tanks. It was founded by Herman Kahn, another CFR secret agent.

In essence, the Report concluded that the return of slavery as an institution might be useful, that poverty is both desirable and necessary, and that calculating the optimum number of deaths by planned warfare is a legitimate function of government. But, after studying different ways to have population growth under control, they concluded that there is no better substitute than war to reach that goal.

On the other hand, as the present bogus war on terror has shown, turning a non-existing threat into a real one is not an easy task, and wars are not easy to maintain indefinitely. Consequently, as a second best option the Report advises the use of environmental pollution as a credible global threat to keep the masses in check, even if the deliberate poisoning of the environment is required to make it credible. This way the sheeple would willingly accept the reduction of their standard of living, higher taxes and increased government control of their lives as the lesser of two evils.

Soon after the Report was published, the conspirators'-controlled mainstream press launched a coordinated damage-control campaign to disinform the public. The essence of this campaign consisted in telling the people that the Report was nothing but a joke, a well-written parody having nothing to do with reality.

CFR secret agent Walt W. Rostow, President Kennedy's NSC adviser, declared that the Report was a hoax. The *Washington Post*, owned by CFR agent Katharine Graham, called it "a delightful satire." CFR agent Herman Kahn, director of the Hudson Institute, denied its authenticity. CFR-controlled *Time* magazine called the Report a skillful hoax.[25] According to CFR honcho Henry Kissinger, "Whoever wrote it is an idiot."[26]

There is some evidence, however, indicating that the Report was the real McCoy. The same year it was initially published, Harvard professor John Kenneth Galbraith, a CFR member, blew the whistle in an article he wrote under his pen name of Hershchel McLandress. It was published on November 26 in the book review section of the *Washington Post.*

According to Galbraith, he knew that the Report was authentic because he had been invited to participate in it. Also, despite the fact that he was unable to officially be part of the group, he was consulted from time to time about different aspects of the discussions, and had been asked to keep the project secret.[27]

Another indication that points to the CFR conspirators as the true creators of the Report is that, after explaining in detail "the shortcomings of war a mechanism for population control,"[28] —despite the profusion of wars world population continues to grow— they suggest ecological measures as a possible substitute.

A few years later, in 1970, CFR agent George Kennan published an article in *Foreign Affairs* entitled "To Prevent a World Wasteland –A Proposal." [29] Essentially Kennan proposed phasing out the military threat and phasing in the new eco-threat.

That very same year, Nelson Rockefeller published his book *Our Environment Can Be Saved*, in which he invoked international political implications as a justification for pre-empting environmental disaster. According to Nelson, preventing the coming "environmental crisis" should "become an area of increased cooperation between nations." He also recommended that the U.S. should "help coordinate international planning for environmental controls."[30]

More recently, CFR agent Al Gore published his *Earth in the Balance*,[31] to promote, based on bogus science, the very same ideas expressed in the *Iron Mountain* report. *Earth in the Balance* essentially delineates a transition program from an economy of war to one of pseudo-peace where the main enemy would be the eco-threat.[32]

Today, after so many unnecessary wars promoted by the CFR conspirators have caused the death of millions of people, it is difficult to believe that the Report was just a Hoax. However, its content is so damaging to the conspirators that the disinformation campaign created to discredit it is still going on. In 1995, the CFR-controlled *Wall Street Journal* published a front-page story (dis)informing its readers by trying to convince them that the *Report From Iron Mountain* was a hoax perpetrated by Leonard Lewin. Actually, in 1972 Lewin himself confessed in the *New York Times Book Review* his role in the "hoax." According to him, he wrote it "to caricature the bankruptcy of the think-tank system mentality."[33] But, was it?

In October 3, 1962, a few days before the onset of the Cuban missile crisis, CFR's secret agent Fidel Castro sent one of his trusted men to New York on a secret mission. He was to activate a terrorist team to accomplish Castro's orders to blow up a big portion of Manhattan, including the Statue of Liberty, Macy's department store, several subway stations, the 42nd street bus terminal and Grand Central station, as well as several refineries along the New Jersey shore, including the Humble Oil and Refining Company in Linden. To this effect they had stored a huge cache of explosives in the store of one of the team's members.[34]

But the saboteurs' plan was too ambitious and included too many people, and soon Hoover's FBI, not under CFR control, got word of it and detained the main conspirators. Had their plan worked out the way it had been conceived, it would undoubtedly have ignited American public opinion and prompted retaliation against Cuba. Had it occurred during the tense days of the crisis it may have been taken for a Russian preemptive attack on the United States and may have triggered a spasm-like retaliatory strike on the Soviet Union, with unpredictable consequences —most likely causing the deaths of several million people around the world.

Fortunately, the plan failed. Still, Fidel Castro is a very resourceful man —no wonder the CFR conspirators have been using him for so many years. After his failed attempt to create a provocation that may have brought a nuclear confrontation between the superpowers, Castro pulled another deadly ace from his sleeve.

It is a well-known fact that at the apex of the crisis, on October 27, 1962, an American U-2 reconnaissance plane was shot down on the eastern part of Cuba by a Soviet surface-to-air missile. Several explanations, some of them conflicting among each other, have been given to explain that bizarre event, but most people agree that the missile was fired in violation of orders from Khrushchev and the Soviet high command.

Following Castro's orders, and disregarding Soviet advice, in the morning of Saturday, October 27, antiaircraft batteries manned by the Cuban army began firing at American low-flying reconnaissance planes, damaging at least one. As Castro himself told Tad Szulc, "I am absolutely certain that if the low-level flights had been resumed we would have shot down one, two, or three of these planes. . . With so many batteries firing, we would have shot down some planes. I don't know whether this would have started nuclear war."[35]

Some years later, declassified documents show that, on October 26, Castro already had demanded an assurance from Khrushchev that, if the U.S. invaded Cuba, the Soviet Union would launch a nuclear attack against the United States. In a clear reference to the use of nuclear weapons against the United States, Castro urged Khrushchev to consider the "elimination of such a danger," and added, "there is, I believe, no other choice."[36]

It is evident that, whatever he really had in mind, Castro was trying to precipitate a nuclear confrontation between the Soviet Union and the United States. We know that, perhaps triggered by Castro's insane letter, Khrushchev got cold feet and ordered the dismantling of what looked like strategic missile bases in Cuba and sent everything back to the Soviet Union. But this is not the end of the story.

In late 2009, the *New York Times* published an incredible story, which shows that, twenty years after his failed attempts during the missile crisis, Castro was still doing his best to spoil our day. According to a newly released document, in the early 1980s Castro tried again to convince the Soviets to launch a nuclear strike against the United States.[37] According to Andrian A. Danilov, a Soviet general staff officer from 1964 to the 1990s who wrote the Soviet Union's reference guide on strategic nuclear planning, in the early 1980s Castro "pressed hard for a tougher Soviet line against the U.S. up to and including possible nuclear attacks."[38] According to another source, in 1981 Castro told the Soviet leaders to "seriously consider re-establishing the nuclear missile bases in Cuba dismantled after the missile crisis."[39]

Of lately, Castro has begun talking again about his dreams of nuclear Armageddon. On July 5, 2010, Cuba's state-run media published Castro's prediction that nuclear war will soon break out as the result of an U.S. conflict with Iran. A few days later, a happy, smiling Castro explained in greater detail his prediction on a taped interview aired on July 12 on Cuban television.

According to Castro, nuclear war could break out if the U.S. tries to militarily enforce sanctions against Iran for its nuclear program. "When they launch war, they're going to launch it there. It cannot help but be nuclear," he said. "I believe the danger of war is growing a lot. They are playing with fire."[40]

Some questions come to mind: Has Castro been acting on his own, or following orders from his CFR eugenicist masters? Where were the Rockefellers on the two occasions Castro tried to provoke a nuclear Armageddon? Were they hiding in their nuclear shelter under the Pocantico Hills?

Having nuclear-trigger-happy Fidel Castro as a friend perhaps explains Nelson Rockefeller's obsession with nuclear shelters. After a visit to India in 1973, Jawaharlal Nehru told some friends, "Governor Rockefeller is a very strange man. All he wants to talk about is bomb shelters."[41]

India's Prime Minister was not off the mark. After Nelson became the Governor of New York, he ordered the building, and paid with his own money, of a nuclear shelter for the Executive Mansion, another for his apartment building on Fifth Avenue in Manhattan,[42] as well as the one I mentioned above in the Rockefeller's compound in upstate New York at the Pocantico Hills. He also ordered the building of a gigantic nuclear shelter in Albany, for an "alternative seat of government," in case of nuclear attack.[43] All these shelters were kept ready at all times, with canned food and water replaced periodically to ensure freshness.

The Albany shelter was actually a bunker designed to withstand a direct nuclear blast and its radioactive residue,[44] and was connected to the NORAD alert system through a sophisticated communications setup second only to the ones used by the Pentagon. May it be that Nelson planned to accomplish his dream of becoming the U.S. president with a little help from his friend Fidel?

The *Report From Iron Mountain* concluded that, though peace may be possible, it was not desirable. Moreover, though war still was the best tool for population control ever devised by man, it proved not powerful enough to control the masses craving to improve their standard of living through consumption of goods. Consequently, new creative ways had to be developed to curb the people's consumption. The Report suggested finding credible threats to justify the draconian measures they had in mind.

After much consideration, the authors of the Report concluded that environmental pollution would be a credible threat to scare the masses to the point of voluntarily accepting the lowering of their standards of living —even if they had to help nature a little by deliberately poisoning the environment in order to add credibility to their predictions.[45]

The Anti-Christian PSYOP

A few years ago, while I was researching on the web, I found a curious article that mentioned a study almost unknown to the American people. The most interesting thing about it is that the author of the article —a blogger who wrote it under the pseudonym "Mr. End," because he "feared reprisals"— calls himself a leftist.[46]

According to Mr. End, in 1968 the [Rockefeller created and controlled] U.S. Department of Education[47] commissioned the Stanford Research Institute (SRI) to take a look to the future and tell them what they saw. But the SRI futurologists didn't stop there. They took a step further and studied the changes in Western society that could conduct to a desirable future, that is, not only what was coming but also what, according to them, would have been good to come.

The resulting study was published by the SRI in 1982 under the title *Changing Images of Man*.[48] Among the prestigious academic reviewers who read the manuscript were: Joseph Campbell, Rene Dubs, Irvine Lasso, Margaret Mead, Carl Rogers and B.F. Skinner.[49]

A back cover note explains that *Changing Images of Man* was "Prepared by the Center for the Study of Social Policy/SRI International," adding,

> Stanford Research Institute (now SRI International) released a report in 1974 that has become a classic in the "alternative futures" literature. It has been adopted as a text in non-traditional courses at more than a dozen universities and reprinted repeatedly by SRI.
>
> *Changing Images of Man* explores the reasons why changes may have to take place in the fundamental conceptual premises, laws, attitudes and ethics once suitable for guiding the development of the United States and other highly industrialized nations if a humane (and "workable") future is to be achievable. It discusses the evidence that such changes may be occurring and the possibility that an evolutionary transformation may be underway that is at least as profound as the transition in Europe when the Medieval Age gave way to the rise of science and the Industrial Revolution.

Yet, there is more than meets the eye behind such an academically ascetic note. To see it, though, we need to take a closer look at the "academic" organization that produced the study.

The Stanford Research Institute was founded in 1946 as a research institution (think-tank) associated with Stanford University in California. However, there are some spooky elements behind the academic façade.

According to some sources, the original idea for the creation of the SRI occurred during one of the super-secret meetings at the Bohemian Grove,[50] a mysterious secret society whose members join once a year in the woods near the Russian river in northern California. Since its creation, the SRI has been fully devoted to the investigation of sophisticated war-related technologies, some of them bordering science fiction, for its main clients, the Pentagon and the CIA. Thanks to such special clients, the SRI's budget is higher than the RAND Corporation, one of the most known U.S. think tanks, and some years even higher than the budget for the whole Stanford University.

For many years, the Central Intelligence Agency has been one of the main SRI clients. The SRI has produced studies on behalf of the CIA in the fields of modification of human behavior, remote viewing, brainwashing techniques and mass mind control. All these studies neatly fall into the field of what is known as psychological warfare.

The anonymous blogger believes that *Changing Images of Man* is the golden dream of a conspiracy theorist. The study describes in detail a master plan of a vast social engineering program to be carried out by the highest levels of the U.S. military-industrial complex.

And he continues his analysis expressing his idea that a conspiracy theorist from the Right would see this book as a factual proof of a long-term project whose essence is a satanic conspiracy to control the world. "But us, particularly those in the political left who don't pay attention to these theories, should step down from our ivory towers from which we disdainfully see those 'ignorant fundamentalists' and re-examine how the political elites work." For example, this document evidently represents an attempt to undermine Christianity. It is clear that Christianity is not "useful" for the creation of the "desirable future" mentioned in the book's Introduction.[51] By the way, the book does not mention to whom the future they envision would be desirable, but it is obvious that the future they have in mind is desirable only to the globalist CFR conspirators.

Mr. End emphasizes the fact that, according to the report, Christianity needs to be transformed into something very different, and it is evident that this transformation is already happening. Actually, as he points out, the plan described in *Changing Images of Man* is so obvious that the strangest thing is that so few in the left have mentioned it before him. Of course, Mr. End ignores that the American Left is a mirage; an illusion created and bankrolled by the most reactionary Right.[52] (More on this below in Chapter 11).

The anonymous blogger did not exaggerate. *Changing Images of Man* is not the product of a small group of people secretly planning marketing strategies to sell their product and defeat the competition. On the contrary, it is a master plan that recommends the implementation at national level, and later global, of a political and social system —a mixture of fascism and communism— that better suits their interests.

The Introduction gives the reader a hint that the study is not the typical scientific analysis of a problem, but rather a manual for action. According to the authors,

> ... an essential requirement for realizing any of the more desirable alternatives would likely require fundamental changes in the way our industrial culture is organized. Laws, attitudes, ethics —even the very way we conceptualize the nature of humankind— may require reform if they are to "fit with" and appropriately guide the complex interrelated political and social systems that have come to dominate modern life. As the inimitable Pogo said in the comics, "We have met the enemy and he is us."[53]

The conspirators have reached the conclusion that democracy, much less representative democracy, is not useful anymore, and that the ability of capitalism —that is, mom and pop true capitalism, not the monopoly capitalism they love— to sustain the present life styles of most citizens in the middle class has reached its end. So, what a better transition to a neo-feudal, post-capitalist system than one where the middle class not only accept, but also beg for the elimination of its economic and social status in order to begin a new gilded age for mankind?

The program for the social and mental transformation of the masses developed by the SRI experts does not oversight any aspect. For example, in the Introduction the report mentions the need "to explore more deeply the enormous significance that emerging changes in psychosexual norms and premises have for the future society."[54] The producers of the document also mention their belief hat Christianity is one of the mayor obstacles for the creation of a new "ecological thinking."

So, if some Christian leaders for many years have been convinced that there is a conspiracy to destroy Christianity —see, i.e., the special issue of December 2005 of *Whistleblower* magazine devoted to the subject of criminalizing Christianity—, it is simply because the conspiracy actually exists.

A few pages below, the report analyzes several religions that would be desirable as a substitute for Christianity. Obviously, to them neither Christianity, nor Judaism or Islam have anything good to offer. After this, the authors of the report begin making a subtle apology of an almost forgotten religion, which in fact is an ancient Christian minority, called Gnosticism.

Before continuing with this analysis of the SRI report, it is important to know that the conspirators do not support any political ideology or profess any religious belief. If sometimes they have supported fascism, communism, Darwinism or atheism, it is just because at that particular time they had used it to carry out their secret agenda. Actually, when the need comes, they change ideologies like snakes shed their skin. Therefore, if now they have decided to promote Gnosticism it is just because they believe it is an ideology suitable to be used as a spearhead against Christianity. But, why Gnosticism?

Gnosticism was the name adopted by a religious mixture of Christianity and pagan mysticism that flourished in the first centuries of the Christian era in the Mediterranean and the Middle East. Gnosticism was a synthesis of ancient Babylonian, Hindu, Egyptian and Zoroastrian beliefs. Contrary to Christians,

Gnostics believed that every human being had a God within. In the Middle Ages the Catholic Church declared gnosticism a heresy and destroyed it.

But Gnosticism didn't die. It went underground, and has been kept alive enmeshed in the beliefs of Freemasons, Rosicrucians and Sufis.

Gnostics believed that the material world was not only a distraction and an illusion, but also that it was essentially evil. This explains why the conspirators chose Gnosticism as the religion for the upcoming serfs of the future society they envision. Gnosticism is the religious belief that will lead the masses to accept like sheep without complaints the moral and material misery of the coming communo-fascist society the conspirators call the New World Order.

Proof that the covert promotion of Gnosticism was advancing at full steam is the success, pushed by a massive propaganda campaign, of novels like *The Da Vinci Code*. A similar role is played by the popular series of Harry Potter novels, whose main goal is to inoculate impressionable young minds with the malignant memes[55] of irrationality, occultism and black magic.

On the other hand, after the conspirators' managed to sneak in a Muslim in the White House, it seems that they changed their tune, and decided to use Islam instead of Gnosticism as their main tool to destroy Christianity. Let's wait and see.

In his insightful analysis of the SRI report, Mr. End who, as I mentioned above, does not consider himself a religious or a conservative person, affirmed that, after studying this document he reached the conclusion that the Christians who have qualified this report as diabolical are not too far from the truth. Neither is he far from the truth.

Changing Images of Man is a sort of modern version of the secret document produced in January 20th, 1942, at the Swansee Conference where, following Hitler's orders, Reinhard Heydrich, Adolf Eichman, and other Nazi leaders scientifically planned the killing of 11 million human beings. While the Swansee Conference was taking place, the Rockefellers and some of their Wall Street friends, among them Prescott Bush and Allen Dulles, were busy making deals with their Nazi partners, IG Farben and Schering AG, makers of the Zyklon B gas used in the extermination chambers.

The only difference between the two plans is that, while the Swansee Conference participants used a precise technical language, the writers of *Changing Images of Man* intentionally used a cryptic language, difficult to understand by the non-initiated. Nevertheless, despite the semantic barriers used to confuse the non-initiates, the plan to eliminate a large part of the inhabitants of this planet and reduce the rest to medieval levels of subsistence is easily recognizable.

The Gay Movement PSYOP

In 1989 a book with a provocative title: *After the Ball: How America Will Conquer Its Fear and Hatred of Gays in the 90's*,[56] appeared in the bookstalls of every bookstore in the United States, though most likely was read only by gays and gay-friendly people —precisely the public it intended to reach. The authors' mini-bios in the book are revealing: Marshall Kirk is a researcher in neuropsychiatry. Hunter

Madsen is an expert on public persuasion tactics and social marketing.

Despite the innocuous title, the book is an extraordinarily well-designed war tool: it was a master plan for a psychological warfare operation against the American people. And the authors were so sure that it was going to work that they used the future tense *will* instead of *might* conquer in the title of their book. They were right. After 20 years, their goals have been reached and surpassed far beyond the author's best expectations.

The authors begin the Introduction with a lapidary phrase: "The gay revolution has failed."[57] And it has failed, they believed, because gays have used the wrong tactics. They have been too honest, too candid in trying to gain acceptance. In order to win, they advise, they should use cunning, disinformation and deception instead.

But fortune, in the form of a terrible disease, AIDS, miraculously provided them with an excellent opportunity to win the battle for the straights' feeble minds. According to the book's authors, AIDS brought gays an unprecedented public recognition and sympathy. "AIDS give us a chance, however brief, to establish ourselves as a victimized minority legitimately deserving America's special protection and care."[58]

Then they clearly explain what their plan is all about,

> The campaign we outline in this book, though complex, depends centrally upon a program of unabashed propaganda, firmly grounded in long-established principles of psychology and advertising. Some readers will be disappointed with the seemingly tame idea of a propaganda campaign; they rather "storm the barricades," . . . Alas —in a way we, too, would like to storm some barricades, but such tactics have proven themselves impractical —ineffective or even harmful— and *their day is past*.[59] [Emphasis in the original]

Halfway through the book, the authors fully reveal their game, calling what they have in mind by the right name. And what they have in mind is not a simple change in attitudes, but a total conversion. By this, "we actually mean something far more profoundly threatening the American Way of Life, without which no truly sweeping social change can occur." Essentially, they plan to change "the average American's emotions, mind, and will, *through a planned psychological attack*, in the form of propaganda fed to the nation via the media."[60] [Emphasis mine] In addition, they clarify even more what they have in mind,

> We have in mind a strategy as calculated and powerful as that which gays are *accused* of pursuing by their enemies —or, if you prefer, a plan as manipulative as that which our enemies themselves employ. It's time to learn from Madison Avenue, to roll out the big guns. *Gays must launch a large-scale campaign —we've called it the Waging Peace campaign— to reach straights through the mainstream media*. We're talking about

> propaganda.[61] [Emphasis in the original]

What they are describing is nothing but a carefully planned psychological warfare operation to wage a secret war against their enemies, straights, very similar to the one the CFR conspirators have been waging against their main enemy, the American people. And a war it is. In February 1988, a "war conference" of 175 gay activists convened in Warrenton, Virginia, representing gay organizations from across the country. The conference established a four-point agenda for the advancement of the gay movement, giving first priority to "a nation-wide media campaign to promote a positive image of gays and lesbians.[62]

Further on in the book the authors of *After the Ball* proceed to describe their PSYOP plan in detail. In a sub-chapter significantly entitled "Pushing the Right Buttons: Halting, Derailing, or Reversing the Engine of Prejudice," they delineate, after explaining how in the past gays have tinkered ineptly with the engine of prejudice, the right steps to fight the problem. They are, 1. Desensitization, 2. Jamming, and 3. Conversion.

According to them,

> To desensitize straights to gayness, inundate them in a continuous flood of gay-related advertising, presented in the least offensive fashion possible. If straights can't shut off the shower, they may at least eventually get used to get wet.[63]

As the name implies, jamming,

> Involves the insertion into the engine of a pre-existing, *incompatible* emotional response, gridlocking its mechanism as thoroughly as though one has sprinkled fine sand into the working of an old-fashion pocket watch.
>
> . . .
>
> Jamming succeeds insofar as it inserts even a slight *frisson* of doubt and shame into the previously unalloyed, self-righteous pleasure. The approach can be quite useful and effective —*if* our message can get the massive exposure upon which all else depends.[64] [Emphasis in the original]

The third step, conversion, is much deeper in scope. Desensitization's goal is to lower the anti-gay threshold of the average American to a level of sheer indifference, and jamming attempts at counteracting negative feelings with those of shame. But what they have in mind is something much more powerful. According to the authors,

> Both desensitization and jamming, though very useful, are mere preludes to our highest —though necessarily very long-range— goal, which is Conversion. It isn't enough that antigay bigots should become confused about

> us, or even indifferent to us —we are safest, in the long run, if we actually make them like us. Conversion aims at just this.[65]

As I mentioned above, 20 years after the book was published the authors' goals have been reached and surpassed far beyond their most optimistic expectations. However, as they cautioned several times in the book, none of this would have worked without a massive exposure by flooding the mainstream media.[66] But we also know that the mainstream American media is fully under the control of the CFR conspirators. Without their support, the gay movement would have amounted to nothing. How can we explain that the most reactionary sector of American society has secretly supported the allegedly "progressive" gay movement?

The answer is very simple: homosexuals don't procreate. Therefore, the promotion of homosexuality is just another eugenics tool in the conspirators' plan to depopulate the planet.

The collaboration of the gay movement leaders and the CFR conspirators is evidenced by the extraordinary support the gay movement receives from the CFR-controlled media, associate corporations, and non-profit foundations. But there is even further proof. The authors of *After the Ball* openly advise this collaboration as a strategy to advance their interests. In one of the sub-chapters, appropriately entitled "Four Strategy: Political Conspiracies," they mention how gay activists, "have concentrated their efforts on politics, meaning efforts to secure gay rights by conspiring with liberal elites within the legal and legislative system."[67]

But the authors also mention that gay activists have been collaborating not only with the leftist but also with the rightist elite, "The goal here has been to forge a little *entente* or conspiracy with the power elite, to jump ahead of public sentiment or ignore it altogether."[68] [Emphasis in the original] This, however, the authors see as "impractical in the short run and imprudent in the long."

There are some key characteristics of the gay movement, however, about which the authors of *After the Ball* have been disingenuous simply by totally ignoring them.

In the first place, the gay movement is actually a political movement, not a social one. As the authors of *After the Ball* advice, "wherever possible come out."[69] But there is nothing sexual in coming out. Actually, coming out is a political statement, and this proves the fact that the gay movement is actually a political movement cleverly disguised as a social one.[70]

By the way, "outing" closet homosexuals is a coercion tool the Nazis used to scare their opponents. Not surprising, it is also used by American militant gays.

Secondly, though gay leaders and propagandists use the terms "gay" and "homosexual" as synonyms, the terms in fact denote two very different things. The confusion is not the product of chance, but of a carefully designed disinformation campaign developed by the American gay movement, who has used it as a smokescreen to hide its true nature. Evidence, however, shows that gay and homosexual are not synonyms. As a matter of fact, the terms denote two very different phenomena, and the distinction is not merely linguistic.

A homosexual is a person who willingly has sex with persons of his/her own sex. The term gay, on the contrary, is political, and does not refer to any specific sexual practice. It denotes a militant homosexual, a member of an action organization, actively engaged in activities to advance a particular agenda in the political sphere whose ultimate goal is to take political control of the state apparatus by revolutionary, violent means, to radically change society. This is exactly what gays did in Nazi Germany and in Castro's Cuba. This is what writer Yukio Mishima and his gay paramilitary group tried to do in Japan through a coup d'ètat in 1970. Fortunately for Japan and the world, he failed in his attempt.

Contrary to the widespread image of homosexuals as effeminate, the core of the men who call themselves "gays" belong to the "butch" type of virile, macho homosexuals. For the "butch," macho gays, young attractive boys are the most desirable option for sexual pleasure, while effeminate homosexuals, heterosexual males and feminine women are regarded in this order as progressively inferior.

Nevertheless, though most gays are actually homosexuals, not all homosexuals are necessarily gays. Actually, despite he fact that as a result of cultural imperialism most homosexuals in Latin America and Spain now call themselves "gays," the concept is alien to the Hispanic culture. The reason for this is that in Latin America and Spain homosexuality had never been politicized.

Moreover, the term gay properly includes all types of people, homosexuals or not, who, one way or another, out of conviction, fear or opportunism, actively support and advance the gay political agenda. Accordingly, Bill Clinton, who has always actively supported the gay movement's agenda, can be appropriately called gay. For the same reason, Camille Paglia, a known lesbian who does not support the gay agenda, could not be properly called gay.

In the same fashion, millions of homosexuals around the world, particularly in Third World countries, do not support the gay agenda and have no intention of making a political statement by coming out of a closet they have never been in to openly proclaim their homosexuality. Consequently, they cannot be properly called gays. Gay, therefore, is a political term, while homosexual is a sociological one. The fact that most gays are homosexuals does not mean that the terms are synonyms.

Though most people, including some homosexuals, erroneously use the terms as synonyms, the distinction between gays and homosexuals is of cardinal importance to understand the essence of the gay phenomenon. As a matter of fact, the American gay movement is fully aware of the distinction, and uses the terms as synonyms for its own ideological purposes, as a way to distort reality. The fact that gay and homosexual are not synonyms is perhaps the best-kept secret of the gay movement.

Thirdly, the true reason for the authors' advice to "portray gays as victims, not as aggressive challengers,"[71] is because, far from being victims, gays usually have been victimizers.[72] Actually, every time gays have gained political power, the first ones who have suffered the focus of their hatred have been effeminate homosexuals. This happened in Nazi Germany and again in Castro's Cuba. It will happen in the U.S. if some day militant gays get political control over this country.

Once this cardinal distinction between gays and homosexuals is understood, it is relatively easy to understand why in the early seventies, while the Castro government was harassing, torturing, and killing effeminate homosexuals by the hundreds and interning them in concentration camps, many American gays joined the Venceremos Brigade and traveled to Cuba, allegedly to work in the sugar crop but actually to give support to the Castro regime. American Gays, who are essentially anti-homosexual, had no objections to the harassment, torture and killing of efeminate homosexuals in Castro's concentration camps.[73]

As fellow travelers, gay movement members have profited enormously from their secret alliance with the CFR conspirators, and have paid the favor by helping the conspirators perform their dirty game. The most recent payment was the gay marriage PSYOP that helped George W. Bush stay in the White House for a second term.

The Gay Marriage PSYOP

One of the most unexplainable things about American gays is their desire to get married in a country where less and less heterosexual couples are getting married and the institution of marriage is in decline. Another is that this incontrollable desire usually flashes a few months before a major election, and quietly fades after it. The answer to the mystery is that gay marriage is just another PSYOP.

This does not mean that most gay couples who married or wanted to do it were consciously supporting the PSYOP. On the contrary, I think that most of them are well intentioned and sincerely believed they are trying to exercise a right that had been denied to them.[74] Nevertheless, like in all psychological warfare operations, the brainwashing works not only in the minds of the target population, but also in the minds of the ones who unwittingly are part of the PSYOP. Like Roa Sierra, Oswald, and the Muslims who participated in the 9/11 operation, most of the gays who rushed to San Francisco's City Hall to get married played the role of patsies —the necessary useful fools.

One of the main reasons offered by gays for their incontrollable desire to be legally married is that currently they are discriminated because they don't have the rights to health care and other benefits that married heterosexual couples have. However, this argument doesn't hold water, because a growing number of companies are currently giving non-married homosexual couples the same rights as married heterosexual couples. On the contrary, for some unexplainable reasons, these very same companies keep discriminating against non-married heterosexual couples and don't extend those benefits to them.

Actually, the ones really discriminated are hundreds of thousands of non-married heterosexual couples who don't receive the benefits given both to married heterosexual couples and unmarried homosexual couples, but they don't run to City Hall to get married. Actually, they may be happy for not paying the marriage tax penalty[75] —another reason why it is difficult to understand the gay couples' incontrollable impulse to getting married

In 2004, the CFR conspirators changed their plans to appoint Hillary Clinton as the next president of the United States and decided to keep George W. Bush in the White House for 4 more years. But Bush's disastrous policies had won the dissatisfaction of most of his conservative base in the Republican Party, particularly among Southern Christians. Then, as if on cue, San Francisco gays fell their pre-election uncontrollable urge to get married, and all hell broke loose —its flames conveniently fanned by the mainstream media and some CFR-controlled evangelical pastors.

As the typical result of this Hegelian-type PSYOP, the scared conservatives were duped, and reluctantly chose Bush again as the lesser of two evils.[76] Soon after, the frantic gay-marriage advocates calmed down and dug in back in their holes like cicadas waiting for the next presidential election. A few months later somebody discovered that San Francisco's pro-gay mayor Gavin Newsom, the man who supported the whole charade, had been a contributor to Bush's 2000 presidential campaign.

By the way, I am not the only one who has suspected something fishy about Mr. Newsom's decision in February 2000 to open City Hall to thousands of gay weddings. Actually, it became a subject of considerable debate among Democrats. Some in the party were suggesting even before the election that Mr. Newsom had played into President Bush's game plan by inviting a showdown on the divisive same-sex-marriage issue.

Most of these talks were kept behind closed doors. Nevertheless, when Senator Dianne Feinstein, a fellow Democrat and Newsom supporter, answered a question about the subject at a news conference outside her San Francisco home, the prickly discussion spilled into the open and the cat was out of the bag.

After Bush had been reelected in 2004, Feinstein was asked her opinion about the same-sex marriages in 2004, and she immediately blamed San Francisco's mayor Gavin Newsom for the Democrat's defeat. According to Senator Feinstein, "I believe it did energize a very conservative vote. It gave them a position to rally around. The whole issue has been too much, too fast, too soon."[77]

Feinstein was not an isolated case. Representative Barney Frank of Massachusetts, an openly gay member of Congress, also disagreed with Newsom. Mr. Frank was opposed to the San Francisco weddings from the start and told it to Mr. Newsom before the ceremonies began. He urged the mayor to follow the Massachusetts path, which involved winning approval for the marriages in court before issuing licenses.

Mr. Frank concluded that mayor Newsom had helped to galvanize Mr. Bush's conservative supporters in those states by playing into people's fears of same-sex weddings. "The thing that agitated people were the mass weddings," he said, adding, "It was a mistake in San Francisco compounded by people in Oregon, New Mexico and New York. What it did was provoke a lot of fears."[78]

The self-described "radical anti-capitalist queer group" Gay Shame went a step further, and attacked Newsom, both physically and verbally, for his gay marriage decision. The first time, they attacked him with pipes and sticks during the Gay Pride parade. Later they expressed their disgust with both Newsom and the

San Francisco gay community, calling them "sell-outs" for backing Newsom's opening of gays to marriage —which they called "the central institution of that misogynist, racist system of domination and oppression known as heterosexuality."[79] Though their actions may be questionable, from their point of view their logic is unbeatable.

Playing his scripted part on the gay marriage PSYOP, as the 2004 election approached, George W. Bush began distancing himself from the gay community —despite the fact that he got an estimated 25% of the gay vote in 2000— while, at the same time, embracing the four million southern evangelicals, most of whom didn't vote for him in 2000 and made the election a cliffhanger.

In an article she wrote for *Salon.com*, Joan Walsh summarized the angry reaction to the gay marriage event by some gays and Democrats who were not part of the PSYOP,

> Newsom's decision to allow 4,000-plus gay couples to marry in February, before he was stopped by the courts, irritated many fellow Democrats, who feared he'd handed a perfect wedge issue to President Bush. Some party leaders even blamed Newsom for last winter's sudden speedup of a constitutional amendment to ban gay marriage, which seemed to gather momentum from his bold local gambit.[80]

Chapter 11

PSYOPs Against the American People II

Let us never tolerate outrageous conspiracy theories regarding the attacks of September 11.
—President George W. Bush.

The Environmental PSYOP

There are several things about the environmental movement, particularly its cornerstone, human-made global warming, which indicate that it has nothing to do with science, but that it is just a psychological warfare operation based on lies, disinformation and propaganda.

The so-called "climategate,"[1] which has been called the biggest scientific scandal of this generation, revealed the inside workings of the global warming PSYOP. The thousands of e-mails, allegedly "stolen" from the University of East Anglia and posted online by an unknown hacker, provided compelling evidence that much of what is being touted as scientific fact are actually erroneous, fraudulent, and perhaps criminal actions. Using phony research, most of the participating "scientists" conspired to advance the globalist conspirators' secret agenda in exchange for government and foundation grants.[2]

Several e-mails contained, among other topics, discussions about how to best portray distorted data sets. The "scientists" caught with their hands in the cookie jar now claim their comments have been taken out of context, but it has become obvious that the e-mails are evidence enough to invalidate all the research. Moreover, the e-mails show how the "scientists" involved in the scam secretly discussed ways to manipulate the scientific peer review process so that skeptics and critics could not get their articles and papers published in scientific journals.[3]

In one of the e-mails, Phil Jones, director of the East Anglia's Climatic Research Unit, shamelessly asks some of his colleagues to delete certain messages that had been requested under the freedom-of-information act. In another, Jones mentions an effort to "hide the decline" in the world's temperatures in a graph they had put together for the cover of a report for policymakers. The graph, which proved to be a total fabrication, shows a steady rise in the planet's temperatures in the last decades.[4]

In a highly biased editorial, *U.S.A. Today* had the audacity to claim that,

> By hiding and distorting information, the climate scientists have delivered what global warming skeptics could not: hard evidence that some researchers are cooking the books. But poor judgment at one research

> center does not equal global conspiracy. The overwhelming scientific consensus remains that the Earth is warming, largely because of human activity, with calamitous consequences ...[5]

Well, if this is not a conspiracy close to the one described by Michael Crichton in his novel *State of Fear*,[6] then we have to re-define the term "conspiracy."

Moreover, "consensus" has never been a scientific term. On the contrary, one of the main principles of the scientific method, in which all Western science is based, is the possibility that a theory can be proven false. If this principle is ignored, the theory in question can be termed philosophic, aesthetic or religious, but never scientific.

Nevertheless, the world's mainstream media has largely ignored the climategate scandal and, despite the growing polemic, the international climate change summit at Copenhagen went on unmolested, pushing population control policies and world government under the pretext of protecting the environment —which was the true purpose of the whole charade.[7]

Nevertheless, the most important thing about "climategate," ignored in most of the discussion, is that it has revealed a *modus operandi*, used over and over by the conspirators and their secret agents to carry out their disinformation work. If some day hackers manage to get into the files of other scientific communities and post their private communications online, climategate would not be too much different from a darwinismgate, evolutiongate, stemcellgate, overpopulationgate, or any other of the currently ongoing PSYOPs.

There is nothing new, however about this *modus operandi*. As early as 1975 Rear Admiral, U.S. Navy (ret.) Chester Ward, a CFR insider turned critic, described it in detail. According to Admiral Ward,

> Once the ruling members of the CFR have decided that the U.S. Government should adopt a particular policy, the very substantial research facilities of CFR are put to work to develop arguments, intellectual and emotional, to support the new policy, and to confound and discredit, intellectually and politically, any opposition. The most articulate theoreticians and ideologists prepare related articles, aided by the research, to sell the new policy and to make it appear inevitable and irresistible. By following the evolution of this propaganda in the most prestigious scholarly journal of the world, *Foreign Affairs,* anyone can determine years in advance what the future defense and foreign policies of the United States will be. If a certain proposition is repeated often enough in that journal, then the U.S. Administration in power —be it Republican or Democratic— begins to *act as if* that proposition or assumption were an established fact. [Emphasis in the original][8]

Currently, the discredit of the world's scientific community, including organizations like the United Nations' Intergovernmental Panel on Climate Change and the Nobel Prize organization, is so widespread that just the fact that any official scientific organization backs a new "scientific" theory should be motive enough to suspect its true scientific value. But it doesn't matter. Despite a widespread global skepticism about the scientific value of the global warming theory, the CFR conspirators keep pushing their agenda and using it as a justification for global control.

Granted, no sane person on this planet can deny that we need to curb pollution and take care of the environment. What should make us suspicious, however, is that the same organizations responsible for creating the present levels of pollution, that is, big oil and transnational corporations, are the ones secretly bankrolling the environmental movement.

For example, the evident inaction of "green," anti-big oil organizations in relation to the BP oil spill is strange, to say the least. As oil geopolitics analyst William Engdahl pointed out,

> That deafening silence of leading green or ecology organizations such as Greenpeace, Nature Conservancy, Sierra Club and others may well be tied to a money trail that leads right back to the oil industry, notably to BP. Leading environmental organizations have gotten significant financial payoffs in recent years from BP in order that the oil company could remake itself with an "environment-friendly face," as in "beyond petroleum" the company's new branding.[9]

Therefore, if one discards the possibility that the big corporations may be financing their enemies, the logical conclusion is that the environmentalists are helping the corporations they claim to hate. Actually, just the most perfunctory analysis shows that environmental legislation hurts small businesses more than it does big corporations.

Moreover, most of the environmental laws proposed give multi-national corporations more competitive advantage and so helps them to get bigger and bigger. Since just by being bigger corporations have the greatest capacity for environmental damage, environmentalists, wittingly or unwittingly, are contributing to the deterioration of the environment.

Further proof that the "environmentally correct," "progressive" left is just a tool of the reactionary conspirators is that some harmful forms of environmental pollution are never mentioned in their complaints. The most important ones among these sources of pollution are noise, as well as electric and electromagnetic radiation (e.g., high-voltage lines and cell phone transmission towers). Much less they mention chemtrails (scientifically called "stratospheric aerosol geoengineering"), unless to ridicule the people who show proof of is existence. The reason for this selective blindness is because stopping these types of pollution does not bring any benefit to the energy monopolies, nor helps the conspirators' plans for the creation of a New World Order.

There is strong evidence indicating that the environmental movement is an artificial creation of the CFR conspirators. As early as 1970, *Foreign Affairs*, the CFR's official publication, published an article by senior CFR agent and mouthpiece George Kennan entitled "To Prevent a World Wasteland —a Proposal,"[10] in which the main points of the environmental movement were delineated. According to Kennan, the only way to prevent the world from turning into a wasteland was by creating a global super-agency to regulate environmental issues at the expense of reducing or eliminating national sovereignty.[11]

However, nothing evidences more the control of the most reactionary right over the American "progressive" left than its fight against nuclear energy.

In 1966, CFR agent McGeorge Bundy was appointed president of the Rockefeller-controlled Ford Foundation. A few years later, he established the Energy Policy Project, an important new project for the Foundation. In 1974, seizing the opportunity provided by an artificially created oil crisis, the Project produced a study titled *A Time to Choose: America's Energy Future*.[12] As expected, its main recommendation was a reduction in oil consumption.

The study strongly attacked nuclear energy, proposing instead the use of inefficient alternative sources or of energy, like solar, wind and recycled waste. Soon after, the conspirators-controlled mainstream media began a barrage of bad propaganda against nuclear power. As a result, about 40 planned nuclear power plants which were to be built in the U.S. were cancelled.

Then, on April 1, 1979, a nuclear reactor in Three Mile Island, Pennsylvania, had a strange accident. The mainstream press seized the accident to fan the fears of nuclear power. Key in this effort to scare the American people was the release of *The China Syndrome*, a film starring ultra-leftist Jane Fonda, which depicted in scary detail an accident very similar to the one which allegedly happened at Three Mile Island —whose dangerousness was highly exaggerated by the mainstream media. By a strange coincidence, the film had been released just 12 days before the Three Mile Island accident.

Since then, the American Left took the banner of the anti-nuclear fight and has been active in demonizing any attempts to build new nuclear plants in the United States. As expected, the Rockefellers and their Big Oil friends were delighted and, as a way of payment, their "charitable" foundations have been generously bankrolling their allies in the Left.[13]

Recently, Obama mentioned his willingness to open offshore areas to oil drilling[14] and reactivate the building of nuclear power plants in the U.S.[15] Unfortunately, a strange accident on a British Petroleum oil extraction platform in the Gulf of Mexico made him rethink his willingness to authorize offshore drilling.

On the other hand, knowing that Obama is a CFR puppet, I advise my readers not to hold their breath. Unless we break the stronghold Wall Street bankers and oil magnates exert over the U.S. government, neither Obama nor any other CFR-controlled puppet president will allow new oil exploitation, much less the construction of new nuclear power plants.

Just a perfunctory analysis shows that the true purpose of the environmental movement has never been to save the planet. On the contrary, its true purpose is to help the conspirators achieve two of their main goals: the drastic reduction of the current levels of population, and the reduction of the survivors to pre-industrial levels of consumption. According to CFR agent Lester R. Brown of the Worldwatch Institute, a Rockefeller supported organization, since the end of World War II,

> … atmospheric carbon dioxide (CO2) levels have increased by 13 percent, setting the stage for hotter summers. The protective ozone layer in the stratosphere has been depleted by 2 percent worldwide and far more over Antarctica. Dead lakes and dying forests[16] have become a natural accompaniment of industrialization.[17]

Mr. Brown argues that all environmental problems (real or imaginary) are the direct result of overpopulation and high levels of consumption. Consequently, the only way to solve the "problem" is to drastically reduce the world's population and reduce the rest of *us* (not *them*, of course) to pre-industrial levels of consumption.

If one is to believe Christopher Flavin, a globalwarmer[18] "scientist," "Coping effectively with global warming will force societies to move rapidly into uncharted terrain, *reversing powerful trends that have dominated the industrial age.*"[19] [Emphasis added]. Flavin was concerned that "a Soviet consumer society with automobiles and larger houses could well push carbon emissions above their current level."[20] He concluded that, "the planet will never be able to support a population of 8 billion people generating carbon emissions at the rate, say of Western Europe today."[21]

More recently, the Environmental Protection Agency declared carbon dioxide a health hazard. This was a first step in the implementation of carbon dioxide regulations on emissions from steel mills, power plants, cement factories and other factories that constitute the very base of the U.S. industrial production. These regulations will result in raising energy costs that will negatively affect the already weak U.S. economy.[22]

Anyway, using scientific arguments to uncover the lies of a bunch of unscrupulous, opportunistic liars and disinformers passing as scientists[23] is self-defeating and an exercise in frustration. Therefore, I am not going to focus on the scientific (or unscientific) aspects of these theories, much of which already has been written, but in their disinformational, propaganda aspects characteristic of a PSYOP.

During the San Fermín festival in Pamplona, Spain, a few fighting bulls are set out free to run along the streets of the old city quarter on their way to the bull ring. As it has become a tradition since 1924, a group of daredevils run in front of the bulls. As their only protection, the runners are allowed to carry several rolled-up newspapers to fend off the bulls. If one of the bulls comes too close to a runner, he throws a newspaper in another direction, and the bull follows the newspaper instead of the runner.

Global cooling,[24] acid rain, the ozone hole, the greenhouse effect, and global warming (now conveniently changed into "climate change"), have been the newspapers thrown past the people's eyes to divert them from the true cause of the problem. Once a "scientific" theory is discredited, they create another bogus one out of the blue as a new rolled out newspaper to throw past the eyes of the public to divert their attention from the true source of the problem by sending them on the wrong path.

Bringing scientific facts to show the "errors" of the supporters of global warming would be tantamount to acting like a bull following the rolled-up newspaper, because global warming has absolutely nothing to do with science but with intelligence and espionage. In his treatise *The Art of War*, Sun Tzu states that all warfare is based on deception. Nevertheless, as I have mentioned above, psychological warfare operations are not simply based on deception; they *are* deception.

Global warming is actually a psychological warfare operation waged against the peoples of the world. Its goal is to convince the people to voluntarily accept the lowering of their standards of living to pre-industrial levels of consumption and willingly become medieval serfs for the NWO masters.

There is strong evidence proving that the global warming theory is nothing but a psychological warfare operation. This evidence is the way the conspirators-controlled globalwarmers have implanted in the mind of a large majority of the people in the world the idea that an inert gas, vital in the maintenance of life in this planet, is actually a dangerous, poisonous pollutant.

I remember an illustration in my high school biology textbook depicting the carbon cycle, also called the life cycle. On the left, the illustration showed humans and animals, inhaling oxygen and exhaling carbon dioxide, and on the right there were trees and other plants inhaling carbon dioxide and exhaling oxygen. The graphic illustrated the process by which carbon compounds are interconverted in the environment, mainly involving the incorporation of carbon dioxide into living tissue by photosynthesis, and are returned to the atmosphere through respiration, the decay of dead organisms, and the burning of fuels.

The fact is that, despite the prevailing consensus among prestigious "scientists," carbon dioxide is not a pollutant and it is not harmful to humans. On the contrary, it is a colorless, non-toxic gas and a valuable plant food. Actually, CO2 is the friendliest gas in our atmosphere. A warm climate with abundant carbon dioxide in the atmosphere would be beneficial for all types of life on planet earth. No wonder the conspirators hate it so much.

In the 1950s, before he changed his opinion, atomic scientist and geochemist Harrison Brown, mentor of John Holdren, Obama's science Czar, suggested the possibility of forcing higher levels of carbon dioxide into the atmosphere to increase food production.[25]

CO2 remains as a trace gas because photosynthesis converts it to O2 (Oxygen) almost immediately. In order to sustain life in this planet, we need mega-tons of CO2 to be put daily into our atmosphere to grow our food. The world's food supply depends on the CO2 emissions of SUVs, volcanoes, fires, plant-rot and termites[26] to supply this essential greenhouse gas at sufficient levels to ward off famine.

Currently, the concentration level of carbon dioxide in the world's atmosphere is at 385 parts per million —greenhouses require 4 to 5 times that level to get good green plant production. In order to be harmful to humans it would need to be no less than 6,000 ppm. Actually, carbon dioxide in the atmosphere does not control climate and the minimal effect of man's CO2 emissions is wholly beneficial.

The average level of carbon dioxide in nuclear submarines after several days of constant immersion is known to rise as high as 4,000 parts per million. But, as retired Army meteorologist Gunnar C. Carlson has pointed out, despite of this high level of CO2, no crew has ever been poisoned by carbon dioxide in nuclear submarines.[27]

As I mentioned above, Bertrand Russell wrote that with the adequate brainwashing techniques the social psychologists of the future would be able to implant in the minds of the school children the unshakable conviction that snow is black.[28] The fact that most Americans currently believe that CO2 is a poisonous gas proves that Russell was right.

Another indication that global warming is actually brainwashing as the result of a psychological warfare operation is the conspirators' use of semantic deception. This is evidenced in newly coined phrases like "carbon footprint," "carbon emissions," "carbon tax," "carbon offsets," "carbon allowances," and the like. In the conspirator's disingenuous lingo, carbon stands for CO2, that is, carbon dioxide.

But carbon dioxide, CO2, is not "carbon," the same way that water, H2O, is not "hydrogen." Though carbon is one of the three molecules present in CO2 —a combination of one carbon molecule *and* two oxygen molecules—, carbon dioxide is a totally different thing: an inert gas that has nothing to do with carbon or oxygen.

However, by using the word "carbon" as a synonym for "carbon dioxide," and repeating it over and over until firmly implanting it in the people's minds, the brainwashing conspirators have subliminally turned an inert gas into a pollutant. The word "carbon," comes from the Latin *carbo*, *carbon*, meaning 'coal, charcoal.' Coal and charcoal are black, dirty substances linked in the people's minds to pollution. Consequently, if "carbon dioxide" is actually "carbon," it by force must be a dirty, poisonous, dangerous pollutant.

Actually, nothing could be farther from the truth. Humans exhale carbon dioxide that plants breathe and eventually exhale, but only after transforming it into oxygen, which humans breathe. Both carbon dioxide and oxygen are basic elements of life on this planet. But, through years of constant brainwashing, the conspirators have changed CO2, a gas of life, into a gas of death.

Some pseudo-conservative critics of Obama, who call him a Communist despite his close links to Wall Street bankers, affirm that his secret goal is wealth redistribution, that is, taking the wealth from the U.S. and other rich countries and redistributing it among poor countries. Of course, this is pure nonsense. The true purpose of the CFR conspirators who control Obama is not redistributing wealth, but destroying other people's wealth, particularly middle-class wealth. They don't want to raise the economic level of third world countries at the expense of lowering the economic level of the developed ones, but to lower the economic level of the developed countries to the level of the poor ones.[29]

What they have in mind is equality in poverty and misery, not in wealth. Why? Because once we become dirty poor and live in pre-industrial levels of consumption without reproducing beyond the enforced preset levels, we will not consume the earth's resources that rightfully belong to *them* —our rich, all-powerful masters and their large families. And you bet that they would take care that all the international laws they are pushing would contain exceptions for them —like the possibility of buying carbon offsets. This explains why, while they are conspiring behind our backs to turn the rest of us into medieval serfs, the self-appointed masters of the world are showing the world how they are already living in post-industrial levels of hyper-consumption. Despite their claims, they have no plans to stop flying in their private jets, sailing in their multi-million yachts, riding in their flashy limos, devouring caviar wedges and drinking plenty of champagne.

One of the two main phobias that have haunted the Rockefeller family for long years is the fear of losing their fortune —one of the Rockefeller sisters, Winifred, feared losing her fortune and living in poverty so much that she committed suicide in 1951 at her home in Deer Park, Greenwich, Connecticut, after killing her two daughters. The other is the fear that the growing masses of population would deprive them of the natural resources of the planet that, by birthright, belong to them and their billionaire friends. But, since the 1950s, when the fear of losing their fortunes became a more remote possibility, the fear of growing population levels became their first concern, to the point of turning into an obsession.

Just a perfunctory study of the way the "philanthropic" foundations controlled by the Rockefellers and their friends channel their funds, show that most of their efforts are devoted to financing organizations whose main goal, overt or covert, is population control through eugenics. We must also keep in mind their ability to instigate wars and revolutions, and to artificially create plagues and famine, the most effective way to control population growth.

However, even after they had devoted much money and effort for more than half a century to curb population, they reached the conclusion that population growth was uncontrollable unless they were to take much more drastic measures to stop it. So, after conducting long and rigorous "scientific" studies, they concluded that, in order to guarantee their survival at the levels of luxury and superabundance they are used to, they had to eliminate no less than 85 percent of the planet's population and reduce the survivors to pre-industrial levels of consumption. And the only way to accomplish it was by the implementation of a worldwide communo-fascist form of government that they call the New World Order.

After the end of WWII, population in the Western world increased dramatically, a phenomenon later known as the "baby boom." This was the result of a series of factors like better diet, access to pure drinking water, modern drugs and medical procedures, and overall improved hygiene. Between 1957 and 1990, the birth rate exceeded so much the death rate that the world's population almost doubled.

The members of the world's elites became extremely concerned. Secret studies made by elite organizations like the Bilderberg Group, the Club of Rome and others ringed the alarm. Studies like *The Population Bomb,*[30] *The Limits to Growth*[31] and *The Global 2000 Report to the President*,[32] a Report to President Carter, agreed that overpopulation was the biggest threat to civilization.

Further proof that one of the true goals of the global warming charade is actually population control is that one of the main measures proposed in the international climate change summit at Copenhagen in December, 2009, was to adopt the Chinese government's policy of just one child per family.

Now, let's suppose for the sake of argument that for the next three years we have two feet of snow in Miami in August, the sea levels are actually receding, and the levels of CO2 in the atmosphere have decreased. Faced with the unavoidable reality of a global cooling,[33] the global warming hoax would not be longer sustainable. Would that mean that the globalwarmers would recant and admit they were wrong?

Of course not. They would never admit they were wrong because they never believed themselves the lie they tell us.

But don't worry about. They already have found the new rolled-up newspaper to throw in on the bull's path: it is called the "Great Pacific Garbage Patch," an enormous island of trash, mostly plastic, floating in the middle of the Pacific Ocean.[34]

Aside from the fact that all the catastrophic effects they now attribute to global warming could be easily translated to this new horrific danger threatening the planet, nobody could deny that this one is human-made. So, be prepared for a fast switch.

Anthropogenic Global Warming?

The main point of contention about the global warming argument (now conveniently transmogrified into climate change) is not that the climate is changing, because it has always been changing since the beginning of recorded history. What most people don't accept is that it is human-made —the key argument advanced by the globalwarmers.

But perhaps there is a kernel of truth in the theory that at least some of the current climate changes the earth is experiencing is caused by humans, though not by the ones driving SUVs, smoking Havana cigars or eating too much red meat. Most likely global warming is actually a self-fulfilling prophecy, and the true global-warmers, apart from Gaia herself,[35] are the CFR conspirators themselves.

It is known that in the 1960s and 1970s the Soviet Union developed an efficient climate modification technology for military purposes. In a speech delivered on January 1960 to the Presidium of the Communist Party of the Soviet Union, Premier Nikita Khrushchev said, "Our scientists have created a new weapon so powerful that it could erase all life on this planet. It is a fantastic weapon." Tom Bearden, a scientist who has studied the subject, has published several interesting articles devoted to the use of climate manipulation used by the Soviet military in asymmetrical warfare.[36]

But the Soviets are not alone. On April 28 1997, U.S. Secretary of Defense William Cohen confirmed the existence of climatological warfare when he declared that some states have create eco-terrorism weapons that "can alter the climate, set off earthquakes, volcanoes remotely through the use of electromagnetic waves."[37]

This technology, known as "scalar technology," is based on the discoveries made at the beginning of the 20th century by Nikola Tesla, and kept secret until a few years ago. The mysterious HAARP facility in Alaska, based on Tesla's scalar technology, has been active for many years. Some scientists believe that it may have been related to some strange weather and phenomena —like the huge hurricanes that affected the U.S. in 2005, the year hurricane Katrina devastated New Orleans, and the heat waves in France in 2003 and in Russia in 2010.

On January 12, 2010, Haiti suffered a strangely localized strong earthquake that destroyed most of the country's capital, Port-au-Prince, which some think was artificially provoked.[38] Just a few hours after the earthquake, before any humanitarian help was sent to the Haiti, the U.S. armed forces took control of the country, and have kept that control since.[39] A few weeks later it became known that Haiti's mineral resources not only include gold and other strategic minerals, but also huge oil reserves.[40] May it have been just the product of a coincidence that just a few months before the earthquake the UN had designated CFR agent Bill Clinton as special envoy for Haiti?[41]

In his 1970 book *Between Two Ages: America's Role in the Technetronic Era*, senior CFR agent Zbigniew Brzezinski forecasted that in the near future the governments of some technologically advanced countries might resort to climate warfare to attack other countries. This will include the artificial alteration of the climate to create droughts, intense cold or heat waves, floods, powerful storms, earthquakes and tsunamis. And the beauty of it, shamelessly expressed Brzezinski, is that the enemy would not know that he was under attack.

According to Brzezinski,

> Technology will make available, to the leaders of major nations, techniques for conducting secret warfare, of which only a bare minimum of the security forces need be appraised. . . . Technology of weather modification could be employed to produce prolonged periods of drought or storm.[42]

When Brzezinski made his forecast, he was not theorizing. He was actually referring to an already existing technology the U.S. had secretly developed. In August 1996, the U.S. Air Force published a secret report entitled "Weather as a Force Multiplier: Owning the Weather in 2025," in which the possibilities of climate warfare are studied in detail. [43] Another indication that climate modification for military purposes is a reality is that on March 3, 2005, Texas senator Kay Bailey Hutchinson introduced a bill with a highly revealing title: The Weather Modification and Research Technology Transfer Authorization Act of 2005.

An objection could be made that, if the technology for climate control already exists, how come the conspirator's global warming seems to have turned out to be a global cooling? There are several explanations for this. In the first place, there are many factors affecting the earth's climate, like solar activity and undersea volcanoes, which are out of the conspirator's control. Secondly, scalar technology is still experimental, and some of their attempts may have failed or backfired.

Even more important, given the fact that other countries have already developed climate warfare capabilities we should not discard the possibility that we have actually been at war for many years, though our government has not informed us about it.

The Two Party PSYOP

A very important long-term ongoing PSYOP against the American people is the one whose goal is to make gullible, brainwashed Americans believe that the Democratic and Republican parties are opposing entities with different ideologies and just by changing the puppets in Washington D.C. things will change for the better. However, as George Wallace once rightly said: "There's not a dime's worth of difference between the Democrat and Republican Parties." Currently, there is not even a penny's worth of difference.

Wallace's words were confirmed by the scholar that better studied the CFR's inner workings: Georgetown University professor Carroll Quigley. In his book *Tragedy and Hope*, Quigley told the truth about the American two-party system:

> The argument that the two parties should represent opposed ideals and policies, one, perhaps, of the Right and the other of the Left, is a foolish idea, acceptable only to doctrinaire and academic thinkers.
>
> Instead, the two parties should be almost identical, so that the American people can "throw the rascals out" at any election, without leading to any profound or extensive shifts in policy. . . [E]ither party in office becomes, in time, corrupt, tired, unenterprising, and vigorless. Then it should be possible to replace it, every four years if necessary, by the other party, which will be none of those things, but will still pursue, with new vigor, approximately the same basic policies.[44]

The process of fusion of the two parties has continued uninterrupted until our days, when it has become evident except to the more brainwashed or ill-intentioned Americans that the two parties are actually the same one, which I call the Repucratic party. The only difference, if any, is that one of them is the party of the enemy and the other one is the party of treason. Which one?

Well, if you are a true liberal who loves this country, the Republican is the party of the enemy, and the Democrat is the party of treason. On the other hand, if you are a true conservative who loves this country the Democrat is the party of the enemy and the Republican is the party of treason.

Despite this fact, however, it seems that just a few years ago the CFR conspirators still were not satisfied. In 2004, secret CFR agent Peter G. Peterson wrote a book under the highly deceptive title: *Running on Empty: How the Democratic and Republican Parties are Bankrupting Our Future and What Americans Can Do About It.*[45] According to Peterson, the two parties were too polarized. His solution: make them even more "bipartisan."[46] As I mentioned above in this book, in the conspirators' lingo, "bipartisan" actually means, "CFR-controlled."

Many professional brainwashers go every day and do their work conditioning the American people like rats in a psychologist's labyrinth. With their constant efforts, they guarantee that Americans will never feel the curiosity to take a look above the labyrinth's boundaries the conspirators have set for them.

Among the main brainwashers actively participating in this ongoing two-party PSYOP are Noam Chomsky, Amy Goodman, Daniel Schorr, Keith Olbermann, Michael Moore and other disinformers of the Left. Their main goal is to keep lefties and liberals convinced that evil Republicans are responsible for everything that is wrong in America, and the only solution to the problem is replacing them with Democrats. They are not different from Rush Limbaugh, Sean Hannity, Mark Levin, Bill O'Reilly, Ann Coulter, David Horowitz and Michelle Malkin, just to mention a few of the more important ones whose job is exactly the same, but in reverse. According to these disinformers of the Right, stupid Democrats are responsible for everything wrong in this country, and just by replacing them with clever Republicans everything will be okay.

I have not included Glenn Beck in the above list because I am still trying to make up my mind about him. Currently I think that he is either a well intentioned, though naïve and misinformed person, or a new type of sophisticated disinformer, potentially more dangerous than Rush Limbaugh.[47] At any rate, his role in destroying Texas gubernatorial candidate Debra Medina by calling her a "truther"[48] is not a good sign, to say the least. On the other hand, if Beck despises "truthers" so much, does that mean that he is a liar?

Also, I did not include Michael Savage in the list despite of the fact that he is the third most listened "conservative" talk radio host because he is not a brainwasher, and his only commitment seems to be with truth. Moreover, very recently Dr. Savage has begun openly and directly criticizing the NWO conspirators — which tells much about his intellectual honesty and integrity.

Probably the most influential among these professional disinformers is talk radio host Rush Limbaugh. I will use Limbaugh as an example not because he is the only faux conservative, but because he is the most important agent in the two-party PSYOP. But most of the information and analysis I will show below also applies to the rest of the disinformers of the Right and the Left I mentioned above.

Rush Limbaugh has always despised the "black helicopter crowd," implying that only those afflicted by a peculiar mental disease could believe or contemplate such claims. He openly mocked these beliefs in his so-called "Kook Test":

> Do you believe that David Rockefeller, Henry Kissinger and other famous members of the New World Order provide daily instructions to

> agents of the FBI, CIA, BATF, and the National Organization of Women? Do you believe that the feminist movement was the brainchild of David Rockefeller for the purpose of having men and women at war with each other on a daily basis so as to distract them from the real conspiracy of the CFR? If you have answered even one of these questions "yes," then you are a kook and have passed the test.[49]

He has been very careful, however, in hiding from his listeners the fact that in his *Memoirs* David Rockefeller himself confirmed that the Rockefeller family is "part of a secret cabal working against the best interest of the United States." David also wrote that he and his family are internationalists "conspiring with others around the world to build a more integrated global political and economic structure —one world, if you will." Moreover, he added: "If that's the charge, I stand guilty, and I am proud of it."[50]

Talk radio is a relatively new phenomenon. Actually, the talk radio brainwashers' job is a complement to the excellent brainwashing job that has been carried out for many long years by the American mainstream media and the system of government education —the one disingenuously called "public education."

How can we positively identify a professional brainwasher? It is relatively easy. Look for these two signs: constant repetition and inconsistency.

One of the favored brainwashing techniques used by professional disinformers —which also allow us to identify them— is constant repetition. They repeat a few key concepts over and over until they are embedded in the target's unconscious mind. Once it is done, the target will think that the ideas are his, without realizing that they have been implanted in his mind.

This technique was successfully used by Hitler through radio and by Castro through television. And constant repetition is one of the main characteristics of both Limbaugh's and Hannity's radio shows. Just listening to any of them for half an hour you will hear the words "conservatives," "Republicans," "liberals," and "Democrats," repeated over and over dozens of times. Another word repeated over and over is "administration," as in "the Obama administration" or "the Bush administration." To these professional brainwashers everything is just a matter of partisan politics, and the only parties they mention in their programs are the two factions of the Repucratic Party.

Another clear sign that we are facing a professional disinformer is lack of consistency. Disagreement is part of the democratic, civilized way of living. The expression of contradictory points of view by different individuals is a strong evidence of freedom and a very healthy feature of a democratic republic. Moreover, we need to acknowledge the fact that sometimes people change their opinions with the passage of time.

What is not acceptable, however, are contradictory points of view expressed *by the same individual at the same time.* It is precisely because of their inconsistency why most people don't like politicians. Inconsistency is the mark of the opportunist and the liar. It is also the mark of the professional disinformer.

It seems that the worldview of Limbaugh and the rest of the disinformers like him is reduced to the narrow field of partisan politics (bipartisan politics actually means Council of Foreign Relations-controlled politics). Anything else that cannot be explained by partisan politics apparently is irrelevant to Rush.

He never tries to explain why, despite all the partisan rhetoric, when it gets into power the new "administration" never even tries to undo the bad things made by the previous "administration." On the contrary, what we see is a seamless continuation of the same disastrous anti-American policies.

Moreover, what you never hear in any of Limbaugh programs are the words "New World Order," "North American Union," or "Council on Foreign Relations." And when a caller begins questioning the government's actions during 9/11, Limbaugh cuts him short and calls the person a leftist loony.

It is interesting to notice that, though Limbaugh, Hannity and other disinformers of the Right call themselves conservatives, they evidence the belief in one of the most obnoxious characteristics of the liberal's ideology: situational ethics, which is just a fancy name for moral relativism.

True conservatives are not supposed to believe in moral relativism. To them, some actions are right or wrong disregarding the political affiliation of the perpetrator. However, to faux conservatives like Limbaugh, Hannity and most of their listeners, an action is right or wrong depending on the political affiliation of the person who carries it out.

Both Limbaugh and Hannity practically ignored the existence of Ron Paul during the past presidential campaign, and only mentioned Dr. Paul to criticize him. Also, Constitution Party candidate Chuck Baldwin was nonexistent to them. On the other hand, they gave lots of coverage to John McCain, who played the same treasonous role Gore and Kerry played in previous presidential campaigns. By the way, it is not a coincidence that the three of them, Gore, Kerry, and McCain, are proud members of the Council on Foreign relations.

When George W. Bush's treasonous activities against this country became so blatantly obvious that it was becoming impossible to ignore them —his attitude towards illegal immigration was probably the most notorious—,[51] even some of the minor brainwashers like Sean Hannity began criticizing him a little bit. But not Rush Limbaugh. He was adamant. Everything that meant even the slightest criticism of W. Bush was and still is anathema for him.

A recent Department of Homeland Security Report titled "Right-wing Extremism: Current Economic and Political Climate Fueling Resurgence in Radicalization and Recruitment,"[52] dated April 7, 2009, worried some Americans. Though the Report was never classified as secret, it is obvious that it was not intended for public consumption.

The Report[53] warns members of the DHS against the possibility of violence by "right-wing extremists," who are identified as people concerned about illegal immigration, abortion rights, increasing federal power, restrictions on firearms, abortion, and the loss of U.S. sovereignty. Moreover, it singled out returning war veterans, that is, Americans who have risked their lives under the belief that they were defending their country, as threats to their homeland.

According to the Report, worsening economic woes, potential new legislative restrictions on firearms and

> ... the return of military veterans facing significant challenges reintegrating into their communities could lead to the potential emergence of terrorist groups or lone wolf extremists capable of carrying out violent attacks.[54]

The DHS Report is actually a sort of follow up on a previous Report by the Missouri Information Analysis Center. It linked conservative groups, like followers of presidential candidates Ron Paul, Chuck Baldwin, Bob Barr, the so-called patriot movement, and people who oppose the North American Union and the New World Order, to domestic terrorism.[55] It is not a coincidence that the MIAC Report was compiled with the assistance of the Department of Homeland Security.

The most important thing about the Report, however, is not the people it mentions, but the ones it doesn't. Like in Sherlock Holmes' famous novel, the dog that didn't bark is an important clue to decipher the mystery. In this case, it is also a useful tool to identify some prominent disinformers.

For example, it is an important clue that Rush Limbaugh is not mentioned in these Reports. Allegedly, Limbaugh is a right wing conservative, and apparently he had turned into the Obama Administration's Public Enemy number one, to the point that Obama himself openly criticized him several times.

Limbaugh even reached the cover of *Newsweek* magazine, who depicted him as a right-wing extremist. Nevertheless, despite all of this, he is not mentioned in the DHS Report. Nor is mentioned Limbaugh's alter ego, Sean Hannity, also the target of Obama's criticisms. Why these important omissions?

Very simple: because, despite their claims to the contrary, neither Limbaugh, or Hannity, or most of the "conservative Republican" critics of the Obama administration represent a real threat to the globalist conspirators' plans. The conspirators only fear true American patriots like Ron Paul, Chuck Baldwin, Bob Barr and returning military veterans —the ones who some day may decide to tip the apple cart in this country.

Actually, Rush Limbaugh and Sean Hannity on the "conservative" side of the Repucratic coin, as well as Amy Goodman and Daniel Schorr on the "liberal," Democratic one, play an important role in this ongoing psychological warfare operation currently being waged by the globalist conspirators against the American people.

A measure of the importance of the role these professional disinformers play in this ongoing two-party PSYOP was revealed some months ago, when Obama himself had to come to the rescue of none other than his archenemy Rush Limbaugh.

As the saying goes, you can only fool some of the people some of the time, and some of Limbaugh's listeners apparently smelled a rat. Finally, they had realized that both Bush and the Republican Party had betrayed them and were defecting in droves to join the tea party and other non-controlled political groups.

Most of Limbaugh listeners apparently have lost their capacity for thinking by themselves —no wonder they proudly call themselves "ditto-heads." Nevertheless, during the final months of Bush's ignominious regime, more and more well-informed true conservative listeners were given Limbaugh a hard time. They were expressing their concern for unchecked federal spending policies and even questioning Bush's treasonous behavior on immigration, only to be summarily cut off the air by Limbaugh.

The fact that many of his listeners were defecting may have shown on Limbaugh's diminishing ratings, something that must have worried the CFR conspirators. Consequently, they sent their puppet Barack Hussein Obama to rescue their puppet Rush Limbaugh by openly criticizing him and elevating Limbaugh to leader of the opposition.[56]

Immediately, perhaps based on the belief that the enemy of my enemy by force has to be my friend, the anti-Obama listeners came back to the Limbaugh's program to get their daily doses of disinformation. Most likely, they ignore the fact that the false enemy of my enemy is not necessarily my friend. The conspirators' strategy worked to perfection: after Obama criticized him, Limbaugh's ratings surged. Rush himself recognized the fact when he admitted that recent efforts by the Obama administration to demonize him actually helped his show by raising his audience 32 percent.[57]

I have brought the case of Rush Limbaugh not because I have any particular grudge against him. On the contrary, being radio my first profession and the one I still love, I greatly admire him professionally. Rush Limbaugh was the man who created conservative talk radio from scratch.

Living in California, I mostly used to listen to Public Radio (which in my mind I had dubbed "Radio Moscow"), until one day that I discovered Rush on a local AM station (which in my mind I immediately dubbed "Radio Berlin") and I became one of his listeners. But this was the time when Bill Clinton was in the White House, and Rush was very convincing. As soon as W. Bush became president, however, Rush lost most of his edge.

Initially Rush Limbaugh was a true watchdog, playing the critical role the mainstream media had deserted. But at some time in his successful career, Rush became part of the mainstream media —when you can claim to have more than ten million listeners, you *are* mainstream media, like it or not— and the CFR conspirators don't like having loose cannons in the mainstream media.

I am not going to speculate why Limbaugh and many others like him betrayed the American people by choosing to work as brainwashers for the CFR conspirators instead of serving their country. I remember, however, that a few years ago Rush had a problem, must likely a set up, related to overuse of prescription drugs.[58] Some time later, he signed an eight-year contract for 400 million dollars.[59] As the saying goes in Latin America: *"A los periodistas se les pega o se les paga"* —"Journalists: you either hit them or buy them"—, and, contrary to what most Americans may think, here in the U.S. things are not too different.

The War on Terror PSYOP

The Cold War was a war against communism, but, because communism is an ideology, you would never win a war against communism. In the same fashion, the War on Terror is a war against terrorism but, given the fact that terrorism is just a method of warfare, you cannot win a war against a method. Consequently, the conspirators decided that, like the Cold War, the War on Terror would be a long war impossible to win.

As the Bogotazo false flag operation marked the onset of the Cold War PSYOP, the 9/11 false flag operation marked the beginning of the War on Terror PSYOP. The similarities between the two operations show that they were planned and executed following exactly the same methodology. (See Appendix III, False Flag Operations: Bogotazo and 9/11/2001.)

Much has been written about the impossibility that the version offered by the U.S. government about the 9/11 events may be true. Even more has been written about the possibility that the U.S. Government had a direct participation in allowing the events to happen. Consequently, I am not going to repeat the story here. What I will do, however, is to prove, from the point of intelligence analysis, that the possibility that the 9/11 events occurred according to the government's version is very low.

For this I need to begin by evaluating the information to change it into usable intelligence. Actually, the definition of intelligence from the point of view of intelligence and espionage is very simple: intelligence is just information that has been evaluated. It has to do with the analysis of the accuracy of a piece of information, as well as the reliability of its source.

With minor differences, the methodology used by intelligence analysts around the world to properly evaluate information, known as appraisal or assessment, is indicated by a conventional letter-number system. According to this system, the reliability of the source may range from A, completely reliable, to E, totally unreliable. On the other hand, the accuracy of the information may range from 1, that is, most likely true, to 5, improbable.

The evaluation of information must take into consideration both the reliability of the source and the credibility of the information itself. Though independent, however, these two aspects cannot be totally separated from each other. Thus, information judged to be "probably true" obtained from a source considered "usually reliable," is designated as B2." (See Appendix II, The Evaluation of Information).

In order to properly evaluate the 9/11 events, one must keep in mind that all the initial information given to the American people originated from a single source: the U.S. government. With the single exception of Congresswoman Cynthia MacKinney, who since the very beginning questioned the U.S. Government's version of the events, nobody in the two branches of the Repucratic Party questioned it.[60]

But the U.S. Government, like all governments in the world, is made out of politicians, and politicians have never been a source of truthful information.[61] Moreover, it is a proven fact that currently the U.S. Government is fully under the control of the Council on Foreign Relations' conspirators, whose openly expressed goal is the destruction of the U.S. as a sovereign country and the creation of a New World Order. Consequently, I will qualify the only source of the 9/11 information, that is, CFR secret agents infiltrated in the U.S. Government, with a D: Not usually reliable.

Now I will take a look at the accuracy of the information itself.

The main characteristic of truthful information is that it perfectly dovetails with previous information that has been proved to be true. Of course, there is a first time for everything, and the fact that an event has never happened is no sure indication that it will not happen. In the analysis of historical events, however, we have the added advantage that we can add to the evaluation of the information the occurrence of similar events in which the information has proved to be true not only previously, but also *after* the event in question.

Consequently, the evaluation of the information itself in the case of historical events is a process involving a check against intelligence already in hand about similar events before *and* after the one we are evaluating. It involves an educated guess as to the accuracy of the information related to the event based on how well it fits with previous *and* past intelligence.

In the case of the 9/11 events, the evidence shows, first, that never *before* or *after* 9/11/2001, a skyscraper with a steel structure has collapsed as a result of any type of fire. Secondly, never *before* or *after* 9/11/2001, a skyscraper —with a steel structure or not— has collapsed on its own footprint except as the result of a controlled demolition. This is precisely why companies who do controlled demolitions are paid large amounts of money to do their highly specialized job.

If buildings, particularly buildings with a steel structure, could normally fall on their own footprint when demolished, these companies would be superfluous — but they are not. Nevertheless, CFR agents in the U.S. Government want us to believe that, exceptionally, on September 11, 2001, not one, or two, but *three* skyscrapers with steel structure collapsed on their own footprint as the result of fires.

The case of WTC 7, a 47-story skyscraper that was not affected by the plane crashes and mysteriously collapsed on its own footprint late in the afternoon, is very difficult to explain even resorting to any farfetched theory. This perhaps explains why it is not mentioned in the CFR-controlled 9/11 Commission's Report.

Therefore, extrapolating from other verifiable information, any serious intelligence analyst would conclude that the accuracy of the information itself provided by CFR agents in the U.S. Government could be fairly qualified as a 5, that is, improbable. Steel-structure skyscrapers collapsing on their own footprint as a result of fire is something that never happened before September 11, 2001 and, 9 years later, it has not happened again.

Consequently, an intelligence appraisal of the 9/11 events would produce something close to a D5: that is, source not usually reliable, accuracy of the information improbable. For the same reasons, based on previous analysis, any intelligence service in the world would have easily qualified the evaluation of the information about the 9/11 events provided by CFR agents in the U.S. Government as a sloppy, disingenuous attempt to pass disinformation disguised as true intelligence. This includes the whitewash Report produced by the CFR-controlled 9/11 Commission.

Moreover, the fact that the 9/11 events served as a God-given pretext to carry out policies decided way in advance is a true index that, most likely, it was not a God-given event but a CFR-given one. As some conspirators' agents shamelessly declared, never put a good crisis to waste —particularly an artificially created crisis.

The fact that the above methodology to evaluate information and turn it into usable intelligence is still currently employed by CIA analysts may perhaps explain why some CIA employees are highly critical of the government's explanation of the 9/11 events, and dissention is growing inside the Agency. However, contrary to what some professional disinformers want us to believe, CIA dissenters are not lefties, much less America's enemies.[62] Actually, they have, perhaps unknowingly, become dangerous enemies of America's true secret enemies.

Most intelligence agencies around the world use a similar system to evaluate information in order to change it into usable intelligence. This may explain the radical about-face taken by the Russian government —one of the few governments in the world currently not fully under the control of the NWO conspirators— in its relations with the U.S. The Russian leaders may have logically concluded that, if the U.S. Government can inflict something so terrible as 9/11 on its own people,[63] there are no limits to what they can do to other peoples. Consequently, the Russian leaders are preparing themselves to protect their country and its people from the CFR madmen.

Moreover, young Russians are finally discovering that the people behind the 9/11 events are the direct descendants of the ones who conspired at the beginning of the past century to implement and maintain for 60 years the communo-fascist nightmare that almost destroyed their country, and they are not happy about it.

In an article originally published in his well-read blog *Mat Rodina* and reproduced in *Pravda* online, Stanislav Mishin clearly stated,

> It must be said, that like the breaking of a great dam, the American descent into Marxism is happening with breath taking speed, against the back drop of a passive, hapless sheeple, excuse me dear reader, I meant people.
>
> True, the situation has been well prepared on and off for the past century, especially the past twenty years. The initial testing grounds was conducted upon our Holy Russia and a bloody test it was. But we Russians would not just roll over and give up our freedoms and our souls, no matter how much money Wall Street poured into the fists of the Marxists.
>
> Those lessons were taken and used to properly prepare the American populace for the surrender of their freedoms and souls, to the whims of their elites and betters.[64]

Mishin is not alone. As I mentioned above, a few years ago Russian economist Georgi Arbatov reached a similar conclusion in an article he titled "Neo-Bolsheviks of the I.M.F." According to Arbatov, IMF officials, like the Bolsheviks, love taking other people's money, imposing undemocratic rules and stifling economic freedom."[65]

The IMF, the World Bank, and the rest of the international organizations controlled by the Wall Street conspirators have been the main cause of the economic disaster of all countries who have fallen under their economic control. No wonder the economic measures imposed by the IMF on many countries have been dubbed "shock treatment." Like in the psychiatric treatment of the same name, patients not killed during the treatment, suffer its terrible consequences for the rest of their lives.

Paradoxically, it seems that the Russians currently know more about what is really going on in the U.S. than most Americans. There is an explanation for this. In the first place, because, contrary to Americans who still seem to be living in a dream, the Russian people experienced for 60 years the results of a communo-fascist totalitarian dictatorship in their country. Secondly, because currently the Russian people are not the target of a psychological warfare operation to make them believe that snow is black.[66]

The Obama PSYOP

Paraphrasing Winston Churchill's famous dictum, I would say that the election of Barack Hussein Obama as president of the United States is a riddle, wrapped in a mystery inside an enigma, protected by a bodyguard of lies behind a dark curtain of disinformation, which we cannot decipher. . . . But, perhaps there is a key.

Every passing day, the Obama administration seems more and more like a new Clinton administration in disguise. Even worse, it looks like the director's cut of a remake of the Bush administration.

It has now become evident that Barack Obama is an artificial product created through some very clever market research. His electoral victory was a PSYOP[67] most likely conceived at one of the conspirators' psychological warfare think tanks like the Tavistock Institute in London or the Stanford Research Institute in Palo Alto, California. Its goal was to distract the people's attention while increasing even more the CFR control over the U.S. presidency, the government, and the country.

The fast ascent like a shooting star of this unknown non-entity to the highest levels of the American political sky reveals some interesting things. In the first place, it shows that he was sold to the American public using the same marketing techniques used to sell the phony products shown on infomercials: people were told that they needed Obama right here, right now. In apocalyptic messages, they were persuaded by the controlled mainstream press[68] to believe that he, and only he, was the only answer to the coming catastrophe, the Armageddon, the end of the world . . . or else.

The problem, however, is that, like most Chinese-made cheap gadgets, just after a few weeks of using it, the CFR-made Obama product has shown that it cannot perform the job it was supposed to do and is breaking apart.

However, before Obama appeared out of the blue, the conspirators already had a reliable product they had tested, packaged and already in the marketing stage: Hillary Clinton. So, Why Obama?

Contrary to what most gullible Americans believe, we the people do not elect our presidents: the conspirators do it for us. Once they decide who will be the next president, they use the mainstream media they fully control to brainwash us to believe we elected him with our votes.

Like on a TV wrestling show, they create a false conflict between the two candidates fully under their control —most of them CFR members. Recent examples of these electoral charades were the cases of Gore and Kerry, both of them CFR members, running against CFR member George W. Bush, and CFR member John McCain running against CFR-controlled Barack Obama.

For many years, the place where the U.S. presidents were "tapped" (a Skull & Bones practice) was during one of the secret meetings at the Bohemian Grove in northern California. This was the place, i.e., where Nixon and Reagan were tapped. However, as the conspirators became more globalists, they translated their president tapping sessions to the international organizations they control, like the Bilderberg Group and the World Economic Forum. That was the place where both Bill and Hillary Clinton were tapped. George W. Bush was never "tapped" because, apart from being a Skull & Bones member, he got his job thanks to his father, a senior CFR conspirator.

In 1991 David Rockefeller invited a young, almost unknown Governor for Arkansas to attend the Bilderberg meeting in Baden-Baden Germany. Just a year later Bill Clinton was in the White House.

Most likely, Hillary was tapped and told that she would be the next U.S. president, during one of the secret meetings of the Bilderberg or the one at the World Economic Forum she attended in early 1998 at Davos, Switzerland. On that occasion, the globalist conspirators cheered her as a world leader. Evidence that she was absolutely sure that the presidency was in her pocket is that, even after it became evident that she would not win the Democratic presidential nomination, she refused to concede her defeat.

Now, it is known that most people who have made the mistake of crossing the Clintons have seen their lives quickly shortened. Bill, and particularly Hillary, are first class haters. Proof of it is that, in her anger, she went to the point of publicly saying that the reason she was not quitting was because, like Robert Kennedy, Obama may be assassinated.

Defending her decision to stay in the race against Obama, Hillary dismissed calls to drop out by saying,

> My husband did not wrap up the nomination in 1992 until he won the California primary somewhere in the middle of June, right? We all remember Bobby Kennedy was assassinated in June in California.[69]

Then, suddenly, she conceded her defeat, made a strong effort to overcome her wrath, and became a reluctant Obama supporter. What happened?

In early June 2008, the Bilderberg Group had an impromptu, non-scheduled urgent meeting at the Westfields Marriot hotel in Chantilly, Virginia. Attendees included senior globalist conspirators David Rockefeller and Henry Kissinger.

The Westfields Marriot hotel is located close to the Dulles airport. Though the mainstream media never informed the American public about this, everything indicates that both Hillary and Obama managed to disappear from the media's eye and sneaked in to the Bilderberg' meeting for most of the weekend.[70]

Nobody knows what happened at the secret meeting, but, after attending it, Hillary gave an about face and began supporting Obama. The rest is history.

But the question remains, why Obama?

Like in the Winston Churchill quotation of a radio broadcast he made in October 1939, which I liberally recreated above, where he said that the Soviet Union was a riddle wrapped in a mystery inside an enigma, perhaps there is a key.

A perfunctory analysis of the composition of the Obama administration shows that he is close to breaking the record number of CFR agents in previous U.S. administrations. The list I have compiled below is not exhaustive, but it will give you an accurate idea of who really controls the Obama administration.

Prominent Obama advisors during his campaign were Zbigniew Brzezinski, Anthony Lake, Eric Schwartz, Lawrence Korb, Madeleine Albright, William Daley, Bruce Reidel and Daniel Tarullo, all of them CFR agents.

Among the CFR agents in the Obama administration are Secretary of Treasury Timothy Geithner, Middle East Envoy George Mitchell, Special Envoy Richard Holbrooke, David Cohen, Secretary of Defense Robert Gates, Director of National Intelligence Admiral Dennis Blair, Surgeon General Sanjay Gupta, Ambassador to the United Nations Susan Rice, National Security Council member Ivo Daalder, State Department Special Envoy Dennis Ross, Assistant Secretary of State, Asia & Pacific, Kurt M. Campbell, Deputy Secretary of State, James Steinberg, White House Military Office Louis Caldera, National Security Advisor General James L. Jones, State Department Special Envoy Richard Haas, Deputy National Security Advisor Thomas Donilon, Policy National Security Working Group member Stephen Flynn, Secretary of Veterans Affairs Eric Shinseki, and Chairman of the Economic Recovery Committee Paul Volker.

Geithner's informal group of advisors include CFR agents E. Gerald Corrigan, Paul Volker, Alan Greenspan and Peter G. Peterson, among others. Geithner's first job after college was with senior CFR member Henry Kissinger at Kissinger Associates. CFR Brent Scowcroft has been an unofficial advisor to Obama and was mentor to Defense Secretary Robert Gates, also a CFR agent.

Among the many "Czars" Obama appointed to oversee different aspects of "his" policy are CFR agents Richard Holbrooke, Alan Bersin, Paul Volcker, Todd Stern, George Mitchell, John Holdren, Ashton Carter and Gary Samore.

Though there is no proof that Obama's Secretary of State Hillary Clinton is a

CFR member (the CFR has secret members), she has attended several meetings of the Bilderberg and the World Economic Forum. Moreover, she is married to CFR and Trilateral Commission member Bill Clinton.

Last, but not least, Michelle Obama is a member of the Chicago CFR branch.

Consequently, it is obvious that Barack Hussein Obama, though not an overt CFR member, is just another CFR puppet.

Everything indicates that Barack Hussein Obama is not the person that was sold to the American public —actually, we have no clear idea about who he really is, where he came from, or what his ideas are. It is evident that he cannot produce any coherent argument when he is not following his CFR-controlled teleprompter. It is obvious that he knows nothing about the content of any of the dangerous executive orders he has signed or the projects he has sent to Congress for approval —all of them most likely conceived at the Harold Pratt House.

Nothing exemplifies this more than the so-called "ObamaCare."

During a conference call with leftist bloggers hosted by Obama, in which he urged them to press Congress to pass H.R. 3200, the National Health Care Act, "his" health plan, Obama confessed that he was not familiar with a provision in the Bill mentioned by one of the callers.[71] Now, if he was not familiar with a bill some people have dubbed "ObamaCare," who wrote it? Well, actually there is nothing "Obamian" in "ObamaCare." Obama's National Health Care is actually a clone on steroids of "HillaryCare," the failed Clinton programs of 1993.

However, a close reading of the Bill, which *our* elected representatives did not have the time to read, shows that key elements of eugenics, like euthanasia, anti-conceptives and the facilitation of abortion, are present in the program. Given the fact, however, that these are key elements in population control of the poor, one can safely surmise that ObamaCare is actually a Rockefeller plan conceived to fulfill their eugenicist obsession with world depopulation.[72] And I would bet that the "ObamaCare" program was written at the Harold Pratt House, not for the benefit of the American people, but to engross even more the big pockets of Big Pharma, the insurance companies and the disease profession (the one disingenuously called the *health* profession).

But greed is not the main motivation behind this plan. Its true, secret goal is population control through eugenics, something the Rockefellers love so much.

Proof that ObamaCare has nothing to do with improving the health of the American people is that, almost simultaneously with its approval, the Department of Airport Security has begun the installation of full body scanners in major U.S. airports. The scanners are a health risk, known for causing or triggering many ailments, some of them fatal.

Some of Obama's close collaborators have consistently repeated Mao's dictum that power comes out of the barrel of a gun. This explains why they were so interested in creating an army of their own. Unfortunately they have already created it under the cover of Obama's health care plan.

The reason why the conspirators' puppet has invested so much time and effort to pass it, is because, hidden among the thousand plus pages of the ObamaCare plan there is a sub-plan that has nothing to do with health, but with violence and death. Like the giant Polyphemus, the American people have been blinded by years of psychological warfare. In the same fashion, like Odysseus holding on to the belly of a ram to fool Polyphemus, ObamaCare hides under its dark belly the creation of a private army to fight loyal American citizens, including the ones in the U.S. armed forces.

Subtitle C, Sections 5201 to 5210 –Increasing the Supply of the Health Care Workforce— of a law few people seems to have read, established a Ready Reserve Corps.[73] It consists of a commissioned Regular Corps and Ready Reserve Corps that will be militarily trained but not sworn to uphold the Constitution. This army, the "national security force" he mentioned during his campaign, will be under the command of Obama himself.[74] Now, knowing the Obama is just a puppet of the CFR conspirators, this means that their intention is creating a new army in case they have to fight the constitutional U.S. army.

The strategy is not new. Hitler used the SA to threaten the regular army. Then, after he had consolidated his power, he used the newly created SS to get rid of the SA. In the same fashion, after Castro took power in Cuba in 1959, he used his Rebel Army to get rid of other competing groups who had fought Batista's dictatorship. But, as soon as he had consolidated his power, he created the Popular Militia, mostly controlled by members of the Cuban communist party, to get rid of the Rebel Army.

The overt purpose for this new CFR army is to stand by in case it is needed for a national health emergency. The covert purpose is to wage war against American patriots. As William Norman Grigg rightly pointed out, "The Homeland Security state is unambiguously preparing for war with the public —in fact, it has been doing so for a long time."[75]

Still, the question remains, Why Barack Hussein Obama? Did the conspirators appoint him to turn a possible rebellion into a race war? Did they appoint Obama because, due to his inability to offer proof that he really is a natural born American citizen, they can blackmail him with their knowledge that they can get rid of him any time they want?

Obviously, the conspirators know Obama better than we do. But to us, the American people, Barack Hussein Obama still is a riddle, wrapped in a mystery, inside an enigma, protected by a bodyguard of lies behind a dark curtain of disinformation. Despite this, however, some things about his character, revealed by his actions, not his words, are beginning to surface, and most people don't like what they see.

Professor James Petras, an honest leftist, called Obama's electoral victory "The Election of the Greatest Con-Man in recent History." As Petras rightly pointed out,

> What was evident from even a cursory analysis of his key campaign advisers and public commitments to Wall Street speculators, civilian militarists, zealous Zionists and corporate lawyers was hidden from the electorate, by Obama's people friendly imagery and smooth, eloquent deliv-

> erance of a message of 'hope'. He effectively gained the confidence, dollars and votes of tens of millions of voters by promising 'change' (implying higher taxes for the rich, ending the Iraq war and national health care reform) when in fact his campaign advisers (and subsequent strategic appointments) pointed to a continuation of the economic and military policies of the Bush Administration.
>
> Within 3 weeks of his election he appointed all the political dregs who brought on the unending wars of the past two decades, the economic policy makers responsible for the financial crash and the deepening recession castigating tens of millions of Americans today and for the foreseeable future. We can affirm that the election of Obama does indeed mark a historic moment in American history: The victory of the greatest con-man and his accomplices and backers in recent history.[76]

I think that We the People are running out of time. If, out of passivity or ignorance, the American people allow the conspirators to fulfill their evil plans, Barack Hussein Obama may well become the last president of the United States as a republic and a sovereign nation. Moreover, I am convinced that for this crucial phase of their plan, the globalist conspirators need in the White House a person they can fully control. A power-thirsty psychopath with a criminal mind; a Hitler, a Stalin, a Castro. A person who cannot sway or hesitate when the time comes for him to implement the drastic measures that this final phase of the conspirators' evil plan will require.

Is Obama the type of person I have described above? He doesn't seem to me, but we will know very soon. I hope it will not be too late.

Some leftists and "progressives" have begun calling Barack Obama "the first post-America president" —whatever that means. If that is true, the post-America these people have in mind is not too different from the distorted America that began with Lincoln's abuses of power, continued with Wilson and Roosevelt, and culminated with the frontal attack on the individual liberties of American citizens shamelessly carried out by George W. Bush.

It is evident that the new puppet the CFR puppeteers have installed in the White House is continuing exactly the same policies advanced by the previous puppet, but at an accelerated pace.[77] Unfortunately, most Americans don't realize that we are facing a new paradigm, and this is not politics as usual anymore. What we need to solve America's problems is not a post-American president but a post-CFR-controlled American republic, as the Founding Fathers intended it to be.

American conservatives are extremely concerned about the recent turn of events in this country. During the time Barack Obama has been in the White House, our new dictator —the power to sign executive orders, that is *diktats*, have turned American presidents into dictators— has launched an aggressive program to get control over some private corporations that is equivalent to a nationalization. If fascism is by definition the corporations controlling the state, and communism is the state controlling the corporations, it is evident that he is turning this country into a communist dictatorship

Nevertheless, American liberals are no less concerned about the turn of events. Not only does Obama's foreign policy seem the continuation of Bush's fascist one, but he has surrounded himself with a coterie of agents of the most reactionary segment of the American oligarchy: Wall Street bankers and members of the Council on Foreign Relations. No wonder most of the neofascist warmongering neocons are very pleased with him.

Consequently, most people on both sides of the political spectrum are confused. Just a few weeks after he moved to the White House, it has become evident that, like Bush, teleprompter-reading Obama is a puppet. But, whose puppet? A puppet of the Left, or of the Right? Does his masters' goal is changing America into a communist totalitarian dictatorship or into a fascist totalitarian dictatorship? Well, probably both.

Most of the confusion arises from the wrong idea most people have about fascism and communism. The most prevalent one is that, if you visualize a horizontal line and place democracy at the center of the political spectrum, communism will be at the extreme left and fascism at the extreme right. That explains why most people see communism as an ideology of the left and fascism as an ideology of the right. But, as I will show below, this vision is wrong.

In reality, the political spectrum is closer to a circle than a line. If we visualize it that way, we will see that both extremes, communism and fascism, are very close to each other. The reason for this is because both of them are nothing more than different forms of socialism.

Benito Mussolini, the Italian Fascist dictator, always saw himself as a man of the left, working to defend the working class and opposed to capitalism and free markets. Even the Nazis saw themselves as leftists. Don't forget that the Nazi party was an offshoot of the German Workers Party, a leftist organization.

Some Nazi leaders were well aware of the similarities between Fascism and Communism, and used them on their behalf. In his speech "Heil Moskau!" of 21 November 1927, Goebbels urged Germans to leave the Communist Party and join the Nazis.[78] The Nazi Propaganda Minister and PSYOP guru knew very well that it was not difficult to turn a Communist into a Fascist. He was right. As he predicted, many Communists left their party and joined the Nazis.

On the other hand, contrary to the most extended belief, Communism is actually the creation of the most reactionary right —a false flag operation concocted by the international bankers and oil magnates to better exploit the workers.

Moses Mordecai Marx Levi, a.k.a. Karl Marx, published his *Communist Manifesto* in 1848. But the Manifesto borrowed so heavily from Clinton Roosevelt's book *The Science of Government Founded on Natural Law*, published in 1841, which Marx found at the Reading Room of the British Museum, that it seemed close to a plagiarism. This is why Dr. Emanuel M. Josephson, one of the few authors who have studied the subject in detail, titled his book on Clinton Roosevelt *Roosevelt's Communist Manifesto*.

Josephson was absolutely right. Both Roosevelt's *Science* and Marx's *Mani-*

festo agree on the prerequisites for the implementation of the new communist society:

1. Abolition of private property
2. Heavy progressive income tax
3. Abolition of all rights of inheritance
4. Confiscation of property of all emigrants and rebels
5. Creation of a Central Bank
6. Government control of Communications & Transportation
7. Government ownership of factories and agriculture
8. Government control of labor
9. Corporate farms, regional planning
10. Government control of education
11. Abolition of religion
12. Abolition of the family as basic social unit

Marx's *Communist Manifesto* was commissioned by the Communist League in London. The League, formerly known as the League of the Just (or the League of Just Men), was an offshoot of the Parisian Outlaws League (which evolved from the Jacobin movement). The League was made up of rich and powerful men from different countries that had conspired to create much of the turmoil that engulfed Europe in 1848 —very similar to the turmoil we are experiencing these days.

It seems, however, that it was not by chance that Marx found Roosevelt's book. In 1849, both Clinton Roosevelt and Horace Greeley, owner of the *New York Tribune*, the country's first national newspaper, provided funds for the Communist League in London to pay for the publication of Marx's *Communist Manifesto*. Moreover, Greeley put Marx on his newspapers' payroll.[79]

The fact that Communism is actually the creation of international bankers explains why the Rockefellers have always been in love with Castro and every other fascist and communist dictator in the world. It may also explain why Obama is pushing America in the way of communo-fascism with the full support of Wall Street bankers.

Yet, only brainwashed Americans who still see the present situation as a political battle between conservative Republicans and liberal Democrats have a reason to be surprised, because there is nothing to be surprised about. Obama is just the logical conclusion of a process that began a long time ago, in the early 1900s. Its secret goal was turning the American Republic, and eventually the world, into a communo-fascist totalitarian dictatorship under the control of a few international bankers. This would be a totalitarian dictatorship very similar to the one Fidel Castro has successfully tested in Cuba for over half a century on behalf of the Wall Street conspirators (more on this below). This new global dictatorship is what the conspirators call the New World Order.

If some Americans are concerned because Obama is going the communist way, it is because they have been brainwashed in the public schools to believe they live in a Democracy under a capitalist economic system. The reality, however, is quite different. Actually, the United States of America has been a communist country since 1913. This was when "Colonel" Edward Mandell House instructed his puppet Woodrow Wilson to create the Federal Reserve System and the Internal Revenue System (originally named the Bureau of Internal Revenue) following ideas taken from Roosevelt's *Science of Government* and Marx's *Communist Manifesto.*

As I explained above in this book, Edward Mandell House was an enigmatic character and a secret agent of the Wall Street bankers and oil magnates. In 1911, he wrote a book, *Philip Dru: Administrator. A Story of Tomorrow*, which was published under a pseudonym in 1912. The book was actually a political manifesto thinly disguised as a novel.

In House's book, Dru, his fictitious hero, masterminds a rebellion to seize control of the government and makes himself a dictator —though he calls his position "administrator." Once in power, he abolishes protective tariffs, sets up a system for social security, imposes a graduated income tax, and develops a banking system that presages the Federal Reserve. Finally, he unites the Great Powers of the world in a league for collective security similar to the League of Nations and the UN.

Dru's goal was the implementation of "Socialism as dreamed by Karl Marx," but with a "spiritual element" —very similar to what in recent times has been called "communism with a human face" and also "friendly fascism."

Is Barack Obama a modern Philip Dru? Everything indicates that he is, and it seems that I am not the only one who suspects it.

In an address to the United States Senate in three parts, June 29, June 30 and July 1, 1992, "On the Threshold of the New World Order: The Wilsonian Vision and American Foreign Policy in the 1990's and Beyond," then Senator Joseph R. Biden said,

> When the peace conference convened at Versailles in 1919, Woodrow Wilson presented, to a world desperately eager to hear it, America's second vision of a new order. The first American vision —the Founders' vision— had concerned the establishment of a just new order within nations through institutions of democracy. The second American vision — Wilson's vision— concerned the establishment of a just new order among nations through institutions of cooperation.
>
> . . .
>
> Modern-day conservatives who are instinctively frightened by the Wilsonian vision have propounded a mythical image of Woodrow Wilson as a dangerously naive idealist. Idealist he was. But there was no naiveté in the Wilsonian vision. As history soon proved the danger lay in a failure to implement what Wilson proposed.
>
> . . .
>
> How is it, then, that the United States failed so conspicuously and so

> fatefully to join the League of Nations that Woodrow Wilson himself had designed and advanced as the ultimate protection against future cynicism and future cataclysm?
>
> . . .
>
> With that turn of history, the League of Nations was doomed and a new world was born, but not a new world order.
>
> . . .
>
> Now, as the century nears it close, the near-universal repudiation of the totalitarian idea has removed the last great obstacle to the Wilsonian vision.

CFR agent Joseph Biden did not explain, however, how this "near-universal repudiation of the totalitarian idea" could bring about the totalitarian "Wilsonian vision" of Edward Mandell House. Apparently, Biden ignores, or wants us to ignore, that Wilson had no ideas of his own. All of them had been implanted in his brain by his controller, Col. House. Wilson himself publicly admitted it when he said, "Mr. House is my second personality. He is my independent self. His thoughts and mine are one."[80]

In his book *The Strangest Friendship in History: Woodrow Wilson and Colonel House*, author George Sylvester Viereck mentioned that it was House, not Wilson, the one who made the slate for the Cabinet. House also formulated the first policies of the Administration, and practically directed the foreign affairs of the United States.[81]

Biden also forgot to mention that Col. House was an agent of a group of international bankers and a founding father of the treasonous Council on Foreign Relations. This is the same organization of which Biden is a proud member.

Some people see globalization as an attempt to extend corporate monopoly control over the entire globe, over every national economy, over every local economy, over every life. But that's not the whole truth. Actually, globalization is just a tool for the implementation on a global scale of a process of destruction of industrial civilization, resulting in a sort of neo-feudalism, with only two social classes: the super rich and the super poor.

Strangely, this world without sovereign nations, where the super poor will be forced to live just above subsistence (sustainable) levels, is not too different from the aberration Fidel Castro has implemented in Cuba. Paradoxically, most "progressive" Americans are known for their regressive admiration of Castro's policies —which are nothing but a testing ground for the corporate monopoly conspiracy they claim to oppose.

In the same fashion, some liberals see imperialism as an expansionist form of capitalism, though they usually make the distinction that they are not talking about mom and pop stores competing among each other, but about the big financial institutions and the transnational corporations. Like Lenin, they see imperialism as a superior phase of capitalism. According to them, you cannot talk about imperialism without talking about capitalism.

But they are dead wrong. Actually, you can talk about imperialism without talking about capitalism, because imperialism, the direct product of monopoly capitalism, is not capitalism at all, but another form of socialism —the political system liberal progressives love so much. In fact, most of the evils attributed to capitalism are not of its own, but the result of socialist, anticapitalist features surreptitiously infiltrated inside capitalism by the monopoly globalists.

One of the most useful and beneficial characteristics of capitalism is competition. Yet, contrary to what most people may think, the person who said, "Competition is a sin," was not Marx, Lenin, or Mao, but John D. Rockefeller. Therefore, it is evident that monopoly capitalism is nothing but socialism in disguise.

During a speech on July 2, 2008 at Colorado Springs, Obama apparently bypassed his teleprompter and spoke his mind,

> We cannot continue to rely on our military in order to achieve the national security objectives that we've set. We've got to have a civilian national security force that's just as powerful, just as strong, just as well funded.[82]

In his campaign document entitled "The Blueprint for Change: Barack Obama's Plan For America," "National Security," the section expanding the idea of a civilian national security force runs only a close second in size and complexity to the section on "Education."[83]

You don't need to be a rocket scientist to reach the conclusion that "a civilian national security force that's just as powerful, just as strong, just as well-funded" as the U.S. military, will also be as well armed as the U.S. military. Therefore, the only reason for creating such a paramilitary force would be to eventually militarily oppose the U.S. military in case some units refuse to obey Obama's orders.

Some people on the left of the political spectrum see all the bad things happening in America as the result of a conspiracy of Republicans and the Right — which they equate with evil. They were rightly calling the attention to the growing parallel between George W. Bush and the Nazi leader. Doctored photos of president Bush dressed in Nazi military dress and sporting a Hitler-like moustache proliferated on the Web.

Now the moustache is appearing on Obama's doctored photos. Actually, the similarities between the two characters seem to grow by the day. Proof that his critics are not too off the target is the fact that Obama's civilian national security force is too close for comfort to the SA's brown shirts paramilitary troops that helped Hitler come to power in Germany.

Chapter 12

Castro's Cuba: A Testing Ground for the New World Order?

The standard of living of the average American has to decline. . . I don't think you can escape that.
—Paul Volcker.

So long as the rulers are comfortable, what reason have they to improve the lot of their serfs?
—Bertrand Russell.

It is highly revealing to discover that both "progressive" American leftists and the most rightist reactionary members of the Council on Foreign Relations have publicly expressed many times their opinion that Castro's Cuba is the social and economic model to follow. If you don't know what the New World Order is all about, just a glance at Castro's Cuba will give you a close idea of what the conspirators have in mind for the survivors of the coming artificially produced cataclysm that will kill most of the population of this planet.

Castro's Cuba has proved to be an economic, social, ethical and human disaster, but it is also an example of the future feudal communo-fascist totalitarian regime the globalist conspirators call the New World Order.

The Cuban Economy Before Castro

American Liberals usually approach the issue of Third World revolution from a simplistic point of view: The real cause, they claim, is not external subversion but injustice, poverty and deprivation. If Latin America were not racked with injustice, they argue, there would be no cause for revolution.

Liberals, however, seem to ignore the cold, hard facts. While economic and social conditions remained more or less the same in Latin America, since Fidel Castro came to power in Cuba in 1959 rebellious attempts in the region increased ten-fold. This may be just a matter of coincidence, but there are indications that such is not the case. Castro's direct efforts to create subversion and unrest in the region, beginning just a few days after he took power in Cuba in 1959, have been extensively documented in detail.

On the other hand, no one can claim that injustice, poverty and deprivation in Latin America are now a thing of the past. But, since economic realities in Cuba after the fall of the Soviet Union forced Castro to reduce to a minimum his subversion attempts, the region, notwithstanding some isolated outbursts, no longer seems ripe for revolution. What happened then? The truth is that, though social injustice, poverty and deprivation are still there and growing, Castro's subversive efforts almost disappeared, and with them the idea of a Latin American Castroist revolution.

Moreover, nobody can seriously deny that injustice, poverty and deprivation in Castro's Cuba since he grabbed power in 1959 has been and still is higher than in most Latin American countries. But, while many Latin American countries have seen their governments destabilized by Castro-backed guerrilla movements, the Castro government, free from Castro's own destabilizing efforts, has shown 50 years of continuous stability almost unprecedented in the region.

The most widely accepted theory explaining the Cuban revolution is that its main cause was the horrible economic condition in the Island. However, there is something in these theories trying to explain *a posteriori* the causes of the Cuban revolution that do not ring true. Contrary to the view spread by Castro-friendly authors, when Castro grabbed power in Cuba in 1959 the economic indexes for the Island were the highest in the world among the non-industrial countries. Actually, in economic development Cuba was right behind the eight or ten leading industrial countries of the world.

If one is to believe French philosopher Jean-Paul Sartre, Cuba before 1959 was a vast sugar plantation; a Caribbean gulag where the American slave masters exploited an undernourished and sick people. According to the French philosopher's vision, Cuba was a country whose blood had been slowly sucked out by the American imperialist octopus.[1] The facts, however, show a very different picture.

Granted, the claim that Cuba from 1902 to 1934 was an American protectorate and economic colony is not a leftist exaggeration, but this situation changed dramatically after the end of WWII. According to estimates of the International Monetary Fund, in 1957 Cuba ranked fourth in per capita income among the 20 Latin American republics. In 1957, the average Cuban had an annual income of $361 annually. This compared with $409 annually for Argentina, $281 for Brazil, $234 for Mexico, and $88 for Paraguay. The average for Latin America as a whole was $284. The 1957 per capita income of Cuba was about one-sixth of the United States, 90% that of Italy, significantly higher than that of Japan, and six times that of India. All these estimates are in dollars of 1957-purchase power. In a 1956 report on Cuba, the U.S. Department of Commerce concluded, "Cuban national income has reached levels which give the Cuban people one of the highest standards of living in the Americas."[2]

Pre-Castro economic development in Cuba was sound, and it had been fast. Contrary to the image found in most American books sympathetic to Castro, the fact is that the Cuban economy experienced a constant boom during Batista's administration. The economy Castro inherited was a growing, not a declining one, and much of that growth was not only the direct result of American investment and of the development of export markets for the Cuban economy but also to the growing power of Cuban capital.

Around 1956 the Cuban economy under President Batista began an upward swing, and 1957 —the year that Castro began fighting his guerrilla war in the mountains— was one of the best years for the Cuban economy since the creation of the Republic at the beginning of the century. During 1957, Cuba's economic activity reached the highest level registered since World War II, and the average income per capita soared to $400.00, one of the highest in Latin America.[3]

In terms of purchasing power, the average Cuban worker was one of the highest paid in the world. According to statistics published in 1958 by the International Labor Organization, from a comparative standpoint the American worker earned an average of $4.06 per diem, the Cuban worker earned $3.00 per diem, while the West German worker earned $2.73 per diem (approx. 8% less than the Cuban worker). The statistics also show that the Cuban agricultural worker's average wage was 3 pesos (the Cuban peso was then at par with the U.S. dollar) for an 8-hour working day. But when these wages are adjusted to reflect their real value as determined by their purchasing power, we have the following results: United States: $4.06; Cuba: $3.00; Denmark: $2.86; West Germany: $2.73; Belgium: $2.70; France $1.74.

In 1958, Cuba occupied the first place in Latin America on number of TV sets per capita, with 1 set per 18 inhabitants, followed by Venezuela with 1 set per 32, Argentina with 1 set per 60 and Mexico with 1 set per 70. Moreover, Cuba was the second country in America to broadcast black and white TV programs, and the first in Latin America to broadcast color TV (1957). The year before Castro took power in Cuba, the country had 160 commercial radio stations. Also, Cuba was the second in radio receivers per capita, with 1 per 5.6, only below Uruguay with 4.6.

In consumption of fresh fish Cuba was number one in America, with 5.6 pounds per capita, followed by the United States with 5.4 pounds. In 1958, Cuba occupied the third place in caloric consumption in Latin America, with 2,682 calories per capita, only below Argentina with 3,106 and Uruguay with 2,991.

Louis A. Pérez, Jr., is a scholar who has studied in detail the growing similarities between the American and the Cuban culture and society. As he pointed out, "In almost every important way Cuba was integrated directly into North American marketing strategies."[4] And added,

> In habits, in tastes, in attitudes, in other ways too numerous to fully appreciate, with consequences impossible to measure, Cubans participated daily in North American cultural transactions. They became like North Americans . . ."[5]

Universal health care is touted by Castro apologists as one of the most significant advances of the regime. In reality, the Castro government inherited an already advanced health sector. In 1957, a year before Castro took power, Cuba's 128 physicians and dentist per 1000 population was at the level of the Netherlands and ahead of the United States and the United Kingdom.

In 1957, Cuba's infant mortality rate (one of the most accurate indexes for overall health conditions in a country) was only 32 per 1000 live births, the lowest in Latin America and the 13th lowest worldwide, ranking ahead of France, Belgium, West Germany, Israel, Japan, Austria, Italy, Spain and Portugal.

Today Cuba stands 24th worldwide, and this omits mention of the staggering abortion rate of 0.71 abortions per live birth in 1991, which reduces infant mortality by terminating high-risk pregnancies. Cuba had the sad distinction of having more than doubled the abortion rate of any industrialized country in that year.

Before Castro, Cuba ranked fourth among Latin American countries in educational development. Its literacy rate was 76% then and 96% now. This improvement looks less impressive when compared to other countries in Latin America similar to Cuba in the 1950's, such as Panama and Costa Rica, which have shown similar gains without massive government subsidization. Moreover, most other Latin countries (including the poorest among them) also have registered impressive literacy gains over the last 40 years: Haiti from 11% to 45%; Guatemala, 30% to 56%; El Salvador, 42% to 72%; Dominican Republic, 43% to 82%; Brazil, 49% to 83%; Ecuador, 56% to 90%; and Colombia, Panama, Costa Rica, Paraguay, Chile and Argentina all now in the 90-96% bracket.

The standard of living and mind-set of average Cubans was so close to their American neighbors, that the Island was used by Madison Avenue marketing and advertising firms as a testing ground for the products they were promoting. In order to test their marketability, some of these products, like some beer brands, the kitchen cleanser Ajax, and other household products, were launched in the Cuban market several months before launching them in the American markets.

In the mid-fifties, SEARS opened a big store in Havana and, soon after, began selling its products through its catalogs to the whole island. By that time the leading American telecommunication companies used Cuba to test their new microwave technology and, upon leaving, left a network that in some aspects was better than any in the United States at the time.[6] The nickel processing plant under construction in Nipe bay, left unfinished when Castro nationalized it, was the most technologically advanced in the world at the time.

On the other hand, while Americans exerted a considerable control over the Cuban economy, there was a growing trend toward more and more control by Cubans over their country's economy and resources. In 1959, Cubans owned most branches of the Cuban economy, probably with the exception of the railroad, power and telephone companies, and large sugar mills. According to United Nations sources, in 1958 Cubans owned 86% of the total capital invested in the Island while foreign investments, having declined steadily since 1933, amounted to only 14%.

The sugar industry, the main Cuban source of income, presented a similar picture. Total sugar production by foreign interests had declined from 78% in 1939 to 38% in 1958. A similar decline in foreign influence was evidenced in bank deposits. Deposits in foreign banks of money earned in Cuba represented 83.2% of total deposits in 1939, but by 1955 they had declined to 38%.

Before 1959 Cuba was the second exporter of sugar in the world and the major exporter of sugar to the U.S. However, soon after Castro took power in Cuba, he systematically destroyed the Cuban sugar industry under the pretext of diversifying the agriculture. It is a strange coincidence, however, that this destruction of the Cuban sugar industry coincided with the introduction of synthetic sweeteners in the U.S.

Moreover, during the WWII years, Cuba began successfully producing ethanol from sugar cane. A mixture of ethanol and gasoline was sold in Cuba under the brand name of "carburante nacional."

American ethanol is corn-based. That means it takes seven gallons of fuel to produce eight gallons of corn-based ethanol. In contrast, it takes only two gallons of fuel to produce eight gallons of sugar cane-based ethanol.

That's the reason why Brazil's sugar cane based ethanol program has been so successful. Nevertheless, the U.S. ethanol program is not an energy program at all. Actually, it is a corporate welfare program designed to benefit big agribusiness corporations.

It is interesting, though, that despite oil scarcities, Castro never tried to produce sugar cane ethanol for fuel, and kept the Island totally dependent initially on Soviet and now Venezuelan oil. As a loyal agent of the Rockefellers, most likely Castro did not want to commit the capital sin of competing with the big oil and agribusiness corporations.

To be sure, there were economic differences in Cuba, but they were not much different from the ones we find today in the U.S., Japan, or Germany. Moreover, I would venture to say that, as a result of some characteristics of the Hispanic culture and Cuban character, those economic differences were less marked than in other countries.

According to Fidel Castro and his close associates, Batista was little more than a pimp, selling off their country to degenerate foreigners.[7] The truth, however, is that notwithstanding Batista's excesses (he was a sort of Nixon on steroids) and the graft and corruption prevalent among his close associates, when Castro took power in Cuba in 1959 the Island was experiencing an economic bonanza. The 1950s proved to be extremely good years for the Cuban economy. All the national economics indexes were growing at an accelerated pace.

By the time, Walt Whitman Rostow, an economist and political theorist as well as a trusted CFR agent, wrote a book that immediately called the attention of the CFR conspirators: *The Stages of Economic Growth: A Non-Communist Manifesto*.[8] Even a cursory look at the book shows that, of all Latin American countries, Cuba was the only one ready to jump from a third world undeveloped economy to a fully developed one. Cuba would have become the Japan of the Caribbean.

As you may guess, that was not in the conspirators' overall plan for Latin America. So they developed a special plan to avoid the birth of an economic power just 90 miles south of the American shores. Fortunately for them, they had their trusted secret agent Fidel Castro at hand to help them carry it out.

Cuba as a Testing Ground

Pro-Castroists who visit Cuba refuse to see the unavoidable reality of Castroism. Hundreds of American gays were visiting Cuba at the very same time Castro was imprisoning effeminate homosexuals and sending them to the infamous UMAPs,[9] but they saw nothing, heard nothing, and ignored what they could not avoid knowing.

Many American intellectuals have been visiting Cuba while Castro is sending Cuban writers, artists and poets to prison, but they prefer to believe the stories concocted by the jailers and torturers. Many politically correct tenured radicals have been visiting the Island under the tenuous cover of academic research. Still, they refuse to see that Castro, an old, white rich male, has created in Cuba the most racist, sexist, homophobic, phallocentric and logocentric society in the Western hemisphere,[10] but they keep hiding the fact from their students while proceeding with the deconstruction of Western thought.

Many leftist American Jews know that Castro harassed the Cuban Jews and that the incidents that occurred in Cuba during the Mariel boatlift were reminiscent of the early persecutions of the Jews in Nazi Germany, but they choose to ignore the subject. Most American feminists love Castro, but they prefer to ignore Castro's discrimination and crimes against women who are rotting in Cuban prisons for political reasons.

Many black American revolutionaries were visiting Cuba to enjoy the marvels of a discrimination-free society, but, after they discovered that the facts were quite different from the myth, they managed to keep the secret to themselves. Today, the new American Uncle Toms keep traveling to Cuba to pay their respects to their beloved white slave master, ignoring the fact that many black Cuban dissidents are dying in Castro's prisons of hunger strikes as an act of protest against tyranny. Many religious organizations claim that they are helping the Cuban people to overcome the American embargo, but the result is that they actually have joined Castro in his efforts to destroy religious freedom in Cuba.

Over the years, these people have shown a high capacity for deception and especially for self-deception. As the Spanish saying goes, there are none so blind as those who will not see. But there is the possibility that the real explanation for these people's behavior would be even more worrisome: they see exactly what is happening to Cuba and the Cuban people, and they are delighted.[11] To them Castro's Cuba is a sign of things to come: a successful example of the New World Order.[12]

Castro has devastated the country economically and physically,[13] killed a large part of the Cuban people, and destroyed morally[14] and materially the ones who have managed to survive his wrath. Yet, the worst part of it is that this destruction has not been by mistake but by design. Following his CFR masters' orders, Castro's ultimate goal has always been the destruction of Cuba and its people.[15]

As we saw above, Cuban society was very close to the American one. This explains why, since the early fifties, many American marketing companies were using the Island as a probing ground to test their products before launching them in the U.S. Seemingly, the use of Cuba as a testing ground for American products, services and ideas, did not end when Castro took power in 1959. Castro's Cuba is a large-scale experiment in social engineering, a test run of the New World Order[16] before its worldwide implementation.

This perhaps explains why some people in the State Department, the CIA, the American mainstream press and the Council on Foreign Relations, helped Castro to come to power in Cuba. It may also explain why the CFR conspirators convinced President Kennedy to change the original invasion plans and sent the Cuban patriots to a sure death at the Bay of Pigs. It may also explain why Castro, unchallenged by the U. S., has been in power in Cuba for more than half a century creating anti-American havoc all around the world.

In 1995 Castro visited the U.S. to address the U.N. General Assembly during its 50th anniversary celebration. He was the guest of honor at the Rockefeller family mansion in New York. To avoid confrontation with protesters, the invitation was moved to the Harold Pratt House, headquarters of the Council on Foreign Relations, on East 68th Street in Manhattan. There, Castro was met by retired Chase Manhattan Bank Chairman David Rockefeller and the best and the brightest of the internationalist crowd.[17]

The Council on Foreign Relations, the brainchild of the Rockefellers, is probably the major force behind the creation and implementation of the New World Order. The CFR has been working frantically for many years to help prepare for a "peaceful, democratic transition after Castro"—CFR lingo for "Castroism after Castro."[18]

There are several telltale signs characterizing the New World Order. An important economic feature of it is sustainable development, a nebulous term frequently used by CFR conspirators. Though it is almost impossible to find a definition of sustainable development, at least we have one of what is *not* sustainable. At the opening session of the Rio Conference (Earth Summit II) in 1992, CFR agent Maurice Strong[19] stated,

> It is clear that current life styles and consumption patterns of the affluent middle class involving high meat intake, consumption of large amounts of frozen and convenience foods, use of fossil foods, appliances, home and work place air conditioning,[20] suburban housing are *not* sustainable. . . . A shift is necessary toward life-styles less geared to environmental damaging consumption patterns. . . . Isn't the only hope of the planet that the industrialized civilizations collapse? Isn't our responsibility to bring that about?

Strong's idea of sustainable development accurately depicts Cuba after 50 years of Castroism. However, Maurice Strong is not an isolated case. World Bank President James Wolfensohn, (CFR), praised Castro for doing "a great job" in providing for the social welfare of the Cuban people. The Bank's 2001 edition of *World Development Indicators* showed Cuba topping virtually all other poor countries in health and education statistics. Wolfensohn pointed to Cuba *as a model to follow*.[21]

The World Bank was created in 1944, but in 1968 Robert McNamara became its president and he turned it into a New Age/New World Order tool. Wolfensohn is a former board member of the Rockefeller Foundation and a friend of Maurice Strong.

Some years ago, one of Castro's mouthpieces, Juan Valdés, head of the Latin American Department of the Cuban Center of American Studies, explained in some detail the philosophy of his boss, the Cuban misery specialist.[22] According to him, the goal of the Cuban system is not to give the same things capitalism gives — more houses, more cars, more suits, more videocassettes—, but to place the people on the same egalitarian level.

In that sense, Valdés added, the rationing card [in force since 1962] should not be seen as a fault of Cuba's economic system, but as a political and economic success. The reason for this is that rationing "places the population at the same subsistence level, unifying them in that egalitarian base."[23] Valdés never mentioned, though, that Castro and the cleptocracy surrounding him live way above the subsistence level of poverty imposed on the Cuban people.

In another publication, Valdés explained in detail Cuba's goal, "We are never going to have a consumer society." Then, after making clear that this is "a Cuban position that has found opposition inside the socialist camp," Valdés added, "We believe that socialism should not be oriented toward giving [the people] the same things capitalism gives; more houses, more cars, more clothes, more video recorders."[24] Valdés' statement, made before he was purged from the CAS, is further proof that Castroism has nothing to do with Marxism or communism.

Due to its intrinsic faults, communism was a social and economic failure. Nevertheless, the communists' goal was never the destruction of their countries. Soviet leaders, particularly Nikita Khrushchev, always tried to turn the Soviet Union into an economically advanced country. Not even Stalin would have uttered such a statement as Valdés. But what we are witnessing in Cuba today is not a failure as a result of unsound policies, but the success of the deliberate planned destruction of a country and its people.

Brazilian journalist Gonzalo Guimaraens observed, ". . . contrary to what most people may think, misery is imposed on the island-prison as a philosophical option and a way of living, not merely as a result of a disastrous economic situation." This philosophical option is championed by Castro, blessed by liberation theologists, and praised by some members of the Cuban Catholic Church.[25]

After the fall of the Soviet Union in 1991, Castro imposed on the Cuban people a system of economic austerity he called the "special period" very similar to the shock treatment of austerity measures the IMF has imposed in many countries. The so-called "special period" is still going on in Cuba after 20 years and apparently, it will never end.

With the benefit of hindsight it is obvious that Cuba's special economic period has been a successful test run for the so-called "austerity measures" the NWO conspirators are now planning to force upon the people of most Western nations. The measures are so draconian that some authors call them "austerity Fascism."[26]

Castro's Cuba: a CFR Conspirators' Paradise

If one is to believe some New Age followers, consumption is sinful, and the only way for humans to live in harmony with Gaia is to live at a subsistence level. Therefore, sustainability without development is the goal. Of course, there is an element of hypocrisy behind this whole idea, because most New Age active supporters of sustainability are strong consumers of Gaia's resources and among the heaviest polluters of the planet. Al Gore is a typical example of this type of hypocrite.

According to Leonardo Boff, a Brazilian ex-Catholic priest who created a sort of New Age Liberation Theology, the true goal is not a socialism of abundance, but a socialism of poverty. Castro's Cuba is the materialization of Boff's dream. No wonder he and his buddy Frei Betto see in Cuba the signs of the kingdom of God. Looking ahead to Elián González's[27] life in Castro's Cuba, *CBS* correspondent Randall Pinkston affirmed that, though Cubans are not free to speak, they appear untroubled by the lack of modern conveniences. In small cities like the once prosperous Cárdenas, Elián's hometown, thanks to 40 years of Castroism there is no running water indoors, there are open drainages, and taxis have metamorphosed into horse drawn carts.

Another important component of the New World Order is population control. Jacques Cousteau, a New Ager friendly to Castro, declared to the UNESCO *Courier*, "The United Nations' goal is to reduce population selectively by encouraging abortion, forced sterilization, and control human reproduction, and regards two-thirds of the human population as excess baggage, with 350,000 people to be eliminated per day."[28]

The Castroist experiment has been very successful in birth control. Castro's Cuba is one of the world nations with the highest percentage of abortions. According to Cuban statistics, from 1968 to 1997 more than 3 million abortions were performed in Cuba, a country of 12 million inhabitants.[29] CFR agent Ted Turner, another friend of Castro, is a strong population control advocate. In 1997, he donated $1 billion to the UN, provided most of the money be used for birth control.

In order to guarantee its long-term success, the New World Order requires the conversion of schools from sources of education to centers of ideological indoctrination. This provides both for the transformation of teachers into "agents of social change" for the New World Order and for a dumbed down populace. The system, now under full-scale implementation in the U.S., was field-tested since the early 1960s in Castro's Cuba, when traditional teachers and textbooks were replaced with politically correct new ones. Some important people in the U.S. are convinced that the Castroist educational system is second to none.

During an April 2000 summit in Havana, UN Secretary General Kofi Annan insisted that Castro's regime has "set an example we can all learn from." In February 2001, a high-level delegation of the Council on Foreign Relations led by David Rockefeller visited Cuba and held a long meeting with Castro. After the meeting, CFR chairman Peter Peterson praised the Cuban leadership's passionate commitment to providing high education and health standards for its people. "I suspect that Cuba is among the best educated countries in the entire hemisphere," he added.[30]

The globalist conspirators see workforce training (school-to-work) as an essential part of their plan for a global economy. This plan not only short-circuits the children's future career plans and opportunities and provides a slave-like workforce, but also guarantees dumbed down citizens incapable of fighting for their rights. Under the name "*la escuela al campo*," school-to-work has been successfully tested in Cuba.

As soon as they reach middle-school level, Cuba children are sent to schools in the countryside where, totally separated from parental supervision and guidance, not only work from morning to evening cultivating products for export, but are also exposed to all types of bad influences. Venereal diseases are rampant among Cuban teenagers, and abortions are a common experience for Cuban girls attending the school-to-work mandatory programs. Part of the time is also devoted to military instruction. As expected, time devoted to true instruction is kept at a minimum. Any similarity with Obama's plans for a civilian workforce is not the product of a coincidence.

The education Cuban children receive in Castro's Cuba is geared to create a new type of human being: the New Man. This all-encompassing structure to indoctrinate children is implicit in the 1976 Castroist Cuban Constitution, and is enforced by law. Parents cannot deviate from this structure.[31] "Beginning in preschool, children are taught songs and poems praising the revolution and Castro, establishing a personality cult around his figure. Moreover, belief in God is discouraged. They are taught instead, to believe in Castro."[32]

Shortly after birth, children are registered at the MININT (Cuba's Office of Homeland Security) and given a "Minor's ID," actually a small booklet, which they must carry at all times until they are reach 16, when an adult ID is issued. The ID card records information on the political conduct of the child. The children are often forced —without parental authorization— to participate in political activities. As they enter secondary education at age 11, they are sent without the parent's consent to schools in the countryside where they provide free labor for the government rather than attend classes.

In the process of teaching, it is important to determine whether the learning objectives are cognitive, attitudinal, or performance based. Performance-based objectives have to do with some ability the students have to learn, such as soldering, driving, fixing a mechanical apparatus or learning a foreign language. Cognitive objectives have to do with conveying information, concepts, and principles. They involve thinking skills. Attitudinal objectives have to do with people's values and beliefs and how to change them.

The educational approach in Cuban schools is fully attitudinal. It employs group discussions, team projects, team teaching, group seminars, and collaborative learning. This approach is best suited for the goal of the Castroist government, which is not teaching facts, concepts and principles in the pursuit of truth, but ideological indoctrination and behavior modification. Therefore, if you find some similarities between education in Cuba and Clinton's Goals 2000, Bush's No Child Left Behind, and other similar indoctrination plans created by the American New World Order advocates, it is not by chance, but because these theories have already been successfully tested in Castro's Cuba.

An essential pre-requisite for the New World Order is the creation of a new world religion. Basically, the conspirators need to solve the problem of the Judeo-Christian religion —a major obstacle to their success. Accordingly, Christians and Jews have to somehow be neutralized or, if possible, unwittingly recruited to support their agenda. To this end, the UN, with funding from sources such as the Rockefeller Foundation, created in 1948 the World Council of Churches. This marked the beginning of the modern ecumenical era.

On October 1962, a rebel faction in the Catholic Church forced the hand of the Pope, and the Second Vatican Council opened the door for the Church's support of the new world religion. Ecumenism, ostensibly an effort to unify different Christian churches, has been the conspirator's springboard for interfaithism, which actually means the acceptance of all religions and cults as equal. It is no surprise, then, that the U.S. National Council of Churches, the Geneva-based World Council of Churches, and its affiliate, Pastors for Peace, all of them part of the World Council of Churches, have been for long years fanatically supporting the Caribbean tyrant and his NWO experiment.

On October 12, 1999, an international ecumenical delegation, including Rev. Konrad Kaiser, general secretary of the World Council of Churches, visited Cuba and had a series of meetings with Castro. The Caribbean tyrant described Jesus as "a great social revolutionary." When told how Luther challenged the Catholic Church of his time, Castro said that he often felt like Luther must have felt. [33] Kaiser declared that the ecumenical movement "shares a concern for justice that has a great deal in common with the life and struggle of the Cuban people."[34]

Though sustainable development, population control, and a new world religion are important elements of the New World Order, the conspirators foresee the possibility of some opposition from certain "religious fanatics," "white supremacists," and "nationalist extremists." Therefore, in order to assure a smooth transition to the New World Order under the military control of the United Nations, strict gun control laws are needed to take the guns from the hands of the citizens.[35] Cuba has been a successful probing ground to test the implementation of such policy.

After the victory of the popular uprising against the Batista dictatorship in 1959, most Cuban citizens were carrying, openly and concealed, all types of weapons, from pistols and revolvers to assault rifles and sub-machine guns. Most of the people involved in the war against Batista were very young; therefore, many of the citizens carrying guns were teenagers. Public schools doubled as centers for militia training, and they kept at hand all types of guns and ammo. Surprisingly, those were probably the most peaceful times in Cuba's recent history. Criminality was at its lowest, and violence involving guns was almost unknown. At the time, I never heard of a case of school violence involving guns.

But, by mid 1963, when Castro felt himself strong in power, people were asked to register their guns. A few months later, a law was passed confiscating guns from the hands of private citizens. Soon after, criminal actions involving guns increased considerably, particularly criminal actions committed by the Castro government against unarmed Cuban citizens. Contrary to what most people believe, the major cause of violent death in the past century was not war, terrorism, or criminality, but *democide*, that is, governments killing their own citizens.[36]

Like all totalitarian tyrants and their supporters, Fidel Castro is a firm believer in gun control. As in all countries where stiff gun control laws have been enacted, the pretext used in Cuba was to curb criminality. But, as history has shown over and over, criminals don't destroy countries, governments do. Nazi Germany, Soviet Russia, Communist China, and Castro's Cuba, just to mention a few, are countries where stiff gun control laws were passed. Yet, as soon as the gun control laws were in place, people were witness to thousands of their fellow citizens killed by guns in the hands of government thugs. In fact, the disarmament of its citizens was a precondition for enabling their governments to kill them with total impunity.

Like his UN counterparts, Castro is a *selective* gun hater. He hates guns, but only the ones in the hands of the citizens. His selective hatred for guns is justified; unarmed citizens are easier to kill than armed ones. No wonder Castro is the hero of population control advocates.

In his book *Dirty Truths*, Michael Parenti rightly points out that the fight against terrorism is actually a fight against countries who don't want to open their doors to the exploitation of U.S. investors, telling them: come on in, it's all yours. It actually mean, in our country,

> There are no occupational safety laws, no corporate taxes, no environmental standards, no limit to what you can carve out of our land at outrageously low prices, no minimum wage, no real labor unions. And if the workers or peasants get out of line, our police and military … will take care of them, for there are no constitutional protections either. You give us oligarchs a generous cut and the rest is all yours.[37]

Unfortunately, however, Parenti fails to mention that his depiction of this hypothetical corrupt country sold to the U.S. transnational corporations under the excuse of a war against terrorism is an accurate description of Cuba under Castro's tyrannical rule. No wonder Parenti's "progressive" friends on the left, as well as the most reactionary people on the right, see Castro's Cuba as the model to follow.

Actually, Castro's Cuba is a CFR conspirator's wet dream. A country where powerful worker's unions had gained enormous rights for its members has been turned into a gigantic *maquiladora*, where workers have no rights at all.

Cuban workers working for foreign firms in Cuba are not paid directly in dollars. Following instructions specified in their contracts, foreign firms operating in Cuba pay in dollars to some of Castro's personal enterprises, which, in turn, pay the Cuban workers in devaluated pesos. For every dollar the Castro regime receives, it pays the poor Cuban worker the equivalent of five cents to the dollar while keeping the other 95 cents to engross Castro's Swiss bank accounts.

In the 1970s, Castro discovered the potential of exploiting the highly qualified Cuban work force, and created overseas civilian programs, mostly involving construction workers. This program drained the Cuban domestic economy at a moment it could least afford to export construction workers and supplies. Notwithstanding the negative effects on the Cuban economy, Castro continued with the program because it generates the hard currency that he and his cronies highly desire. The initial program opened the door for exporting other types of Cuban qualified workers, mostly health and education professionals. The Cuban media has frequently reported the success of these programs in laudatory terms.

Cubans working abroad have to sign a "Return-to-Cuba-Contract" in which they are forced to give 75 percent of the salaries received abroad to the Castro government. Before receiving a government authorization for working abroad, workers must prove that they have no ties to Cuban exiles or dissident groups in Cuba, have never solicited a U.S. visa, and don't have family members abroad. The reason for this is because Castro does not want his slaves to escape, and losing the average $100 to $300 monthly per person that many Cuban exiles in the U.S. send to their relatives in Cuba. This way, the "Marxist" *Comandante*, in cahoots with his global monopolist partners, steals the surplus value of the Cuban workers and keeps the lion's share of their money. That's a very creative brand of modern slavery Castro has implemented in his Cuban plantation.

The continued praise the Castroist regime gets from the CFR conspirators promoters of the New World Order gives substance to my theory that the destruction of Cuba and its people by the Castro government has not been by mistake but by design. As I mentioned above, in 1959, the year Castro grabbed power in Cuba, the country already had fulfilled all the preconditions for an economic takeoff and was in what economist W. W. Rostow, a CFR agent, calls the "take off stage" in the road to becoming an industrialized country.[38] But half a century of Castroism have sent the country back to the lowest economic levels of Latin America —and the promoters of the experiment-in-progress in the once prosperous Caribbean island are overjoyed.

Fidel Castro himself provided further proof that he is actually an agent of change working for the New World Order conspirators. On October 12, 1979, Castro gave a surprisingly short speech at the 34th UN General Assembly. After giving his usual anti-American diatribe, the Comandante en Jefe stated, "We want a New World Order based on justice, equality and peace to replace the unfair and unequal system that prevails today . . ."[39]

As you may have guessed, the New World Order Castro and his CFR friends want to implement worldwide would be very similar to today's Cuba. This perhaps explains why the U.S. government, through a parade of Republican and Democrat administrations controlled by the CFR conspirators, has managed to avoid overthrowing Castro's tyranny during these 50 long years. Moreover, the U.S. poorly disguised support for the Castro regime, and the attempts to perpetuate Castroism in Cuba after the death of the tyrant, has not been the result of political mistakes, but of a carefully designed plan.

Chapter 13

The End of the CIA and the Beginning of the New World Order

I do solemnly swear that I will support and defend the Constitution of the United States against all enemies foreign and domestic; that I will bear true faith and allegiance to the same; that I take this obligation freely, without any mental reservation or purpose of evasion; that I will well and faithfully discharge the duties of the office on which I am about to enter; so help me God.

—U.S. Military Oath.

There are only two things we should fight for. One is the defense of our homes and the other is the Bill of Rights. War for any other reason is simply a racket.

—Marine Corps Major General Smedley Butler.

As I have explained above, the main reason why the CFR conspirators were interested in the creation of the CIA was to have their own covert, secret armed forces without having to pay for it. The use of the CIA both as a scapegoat to blame the Agency for all the intelligence "failures" and, more recently, as a tool for producing disingenuous intelligence analyses used to justify their anti-American foreign policies, most likely have been added bonuses the conspirators didn't think about initially.

Using the Fabian infiltration tactics they have polished to perfection, the CFR conspirators effectively infiltrated and controlled, first, the American mainstream press and, later, the Republican and the Democratic parties. Using the pretext of the War and Peace Studies program, they infiltrated the State Department and have controlled it since the 1930s.

When Senator Joseph McCarthy discovered several traitors infiltrated at the highest levels of the State Department, he immediately thought they were Communists, because he mistakenly believed that only Soviet-controlled agents would commit such treasonous deeds. But, to his utter surprise, CFR agents in the U.S. government and the CFR-controlled mainstream media went out as a single man to get McCarthy, until they destroyed him. McCarthy, like most Americans today, was looking for treason in the wrong direction. The traitors at the State Department were not communists, but CFR agents passing as Soviet spies.[1]

However, there was still a big stumbling block in the conspirators' path to totalitarian control: the U.S. military. Continuing a long tradition, American military men were true patriots, who took very seriously their oath to defend and protect the Constitution against all enemies, foreign and domestic. Consequently, the conspirators resorted to their Fabian ways of gradual infiltration to capture the U.S. military from the inside.

The CFR Conspirators Take Control of the U.S. Military

At the time of the creation of the OSS until the end of WWII, the CFR conspirators had no full control over the U.S. armed forces. Though they had managed to infiltrate some of their secret agents at the highest levels of the U.S. military, like generals Dwight Eisenhower,[2] George Marshall and Matthew Ridgway, they found strong opposition to their treacherous activities among other military leaders, like generals George Patton,[3] Douglas MacArthur,[4] George Strong, Omar Bradley, James Doolittle, Curtis LeMay, Patrick Hurley and Albert Wedemeyer.

Yet, as the good Fabians they are, the CFR conspirators are experts in the art of infiltration. In 1962, they started an innocuously called Military Fellows Program for military interns who spend one year at the Harold Pratt House. The patriotically and ethically challenged interns who demonstrate their willingness to advance their careers by betraying their country and becoming CFR agents, are recruited and their careers rapidly advance.

The CFR's Military Fellows Program is a sure way to indoctrinate potential agents that already have been discovered by CFR talent spotters. Once their qualification for the job have been firmly established, the candidates are recruited as CFR secret agents —the best agent is the one who doesn't know, or doesn't want to know, that he has been recruited— and put to work on behalf of the CFR's secret goals. As part of the plan, they are pushed up above the ranks until they reach key positions in the U.S. military apparatus. Currently, most of these secret CFR agents infiltrated in the military are occupying positions of power in the U.S. armed forces.

The process is not new. Both Dwight Eisenhower and Alexander Haig, just to mention two notable examples, were the product of these pushed promotions. The conspirators have been doing it successfully for many decades and make no bones about it. On one occasion, when Haig was leaving for a trip to Cambodia to meet with Premier Lon Nol, Kissinger escorted him to a staff car, where reporters and a retinue of aides waited. As Haig bent to get into the automobile, Kissinger stopped him and began polishing the single star on his shoulder. "Al, if you're a good boy, I'll get you another one," he said.[5]

In his rapid promotion, Haig jumped over hundreds of other officers. He was the only four-star general who got his promotion without having been a divisional commander. Soon after, President Ford appointed Haig to be supreme commander of NATO. Nevertheless, rumors had it that he was a "political general" who had reached his grade thanks to his connections with Kissinger.[6]

Since 1962, however, with the introduction of their Military Fellows Program, the conspirators made this process more systematic. CFR agents already in key positions of their respective branches assign young officers to spend a full year at the Harold Pratt House in Manhattan, headquarters of the Council on Foreign Relations. The alleged purpose of the program, as described by the CFR, is "to allow the fellows to broaden their interest and knowledge of foreign policy by following their own intellectual pursuits and participating in Council activities." During the year, they produce studies in the field of diplomacy and foreign affairs.

Given the fact that the U.S. military's role is not to make policy, but to follow the orders emanating from the executive branch of the U.S. government, this emphasis in studying policy is puzzling, to say the least. It goes without saying, though, that any military fellow who during his year at the CFR shows his allegiance to the U.S. Constitution, his respect for the sovereignty of this country, or his opposition to globalization and the New World Order —the basic tenants of the CFR's ideology— is automatically blackballed, and his career will not see any advance. In contrast, the ones who demonstrate their allegiance to the CFR masters find fast promotion to general or admiral rather routine. The most reliable among them are even invited to join the CFR as members.[7]

For example, one of them, Air Force Colonel Robert Ginsburgh, spent 1963-64 at the Harold Pratt House and was accepted as a CFR member in 1965. Soon after, he was promoted to Brigadier General and then to Major General. After retiring from active duty from the U.S. military in 1980, he continued in active duty serving the CFR conspirators as a member of its nominating committee choosing officers for the Military Fellows Program. Other members of this committee who were also CFR agents, have been retired General Lyman Lemnitzer —infamous for his role in Operation Northwoods, an aberration most likely concocted at the Harold Pratt House— and retired Admiral John M. Lee.[8]

The CFR conspirators, however, did not confine their infiltration and recruitment of agents in the U.S. military to the Military Fellows program alone. They have systematically reached out to recruit pliable senior officers by inviting each year other already high-rank military personnel to join the CFR.[9] Very few, if any, have refused the offer.

Another tactic employed by the CFR conspirators consist in infiltrating their secret agents in the military by positioning them as leaders of the military academies. Since 1945, many superintendents at West Point, as well as the U.S. Air Force Academy and the U.S. Naval Academy, have been trusted CFR agents.

The CFR's Fifth Column Inside the U.S. Armed Forces

The results of this CFR effort of systematic infiltration of the U.S. military has brought results far beyond their expectations: as of 2006, there were 124[10] senior officers of the three branches of the U.S. armed forces with confirmed membership in the CFR. Today, most likely the number is higher.

U.S. Armed Forces officers members of the CFR (2006):[11]

Abbot, Charles S. "Steve" (Admiral) - former Deputy Commander of U.S. European Command; a Rhodes Scholar

Abizaid, John P. (Gen.) - Commander of Central Command (CENTCOM)

Allen, Lew Jr. (Gen.) - former Air Force Chief of Staff (1978-1982); director of National Security Agency (1973-1977)

Baker, John R. (Lt. Gen.) - former Vice Commander of Air Mobility Command (2002-2005)

Barry, John L. (retired Maj. Gen., Air Force) - Director of Plans and Programs for Air Force Materiel Command

Bell, Burwell B. (Gen., Army) - Commander, U.S. Forces Korea; former Commander of U.S. Army Europe (USAREUR)

Bowman, Frank Lee (Adm.) - retired in 2005

Boyd, Charles Graham (Gen.) - former Air Force general; President and CEO of American Executives for National Security

Bradford, Zeb B. Jr. (Brig. Gen., Army) - retired Army officer

Burns, William F. (Maj. Gen., Army) - former Director of Arms Control and Disarmament Agency (1988-1989)

Cambria, Salvatore F. (Brig. Gen., Army) - former Commander, Special Operations Command South, U.S. Southern Command

Carl, Maria L. (Lt. Col., Air Force) - Chief of Public Affairs at Patrick AFB (Cape Canaveral, Florida)

Carson, Charles William Jr. (Gen., USAF) - former commander of 12th Air Force, Tactical Air Command

Caulfield, Matthew P. (Brig. Gen., USMC) - retired Marine general

Cerjan, Paul G. (Lt. Gen., Army) - Vice President of KBR Worldwide Military Affairs; former President of National Defense Univ.

Cheney, Stephen A. (Brig. Gen., USMC, retired) - Chief Operating Officer for Business Executives for National Security

Christman, Daniel William (Lt. Gen.) - former Superintendent of U.S. Military Academy at West Point (1996-2001)

Clark, Wesley K. (Gen.) - former NATO commander under Clinton; a Rhodes Scholar

Cortez, Christopher (Maj. Gen., USMC, retired) - former Commanding General, Marine Corps Recruiting Command

Crowe, William J. (Adm.) - former Ambassador to Great Britain (1994-1997); former Chairman of Joint Chiefs of Staff (1985-1989)

Dunn, Michael M. (Lt. Gen., USAF) - former President of National Defense University

Dur, Philip A. (Rear Admiral) - VP for Program Operations at Northrop Grumman; former Attache to France

Dalton, James E. (Gen., USAF) - former director of the Joint Staff; former Vice President of Logicon, Inc.

Dawkins, Peter M. (Brig. Gen.) - Army officer who won the Heisman Trophy in 1958; a Rhodes Scholar

Doty, Grant R. (Lt. Col., Army) - an Army officer

Duffie, David A. (Captain, Navy) - a Navy officer

Eberhart, Ralph E. (Gen., USAF) - former Commander of Northern Command and NORAD (2000-2004)

Finelli, Francis A. (Lt. Col., Army, retired) - a Managing Director of the Carlyle Group

Flynn, George J. (Brig. Gen., USMC) - Chief of Staff, U.S. Special Operations Command under George W. Bush.

Fogleman, Ronald R. (Gen.) - former Air Force Chief of Staff (1994-1997)

Foglesong, Robert H. (Gen.) - former U.S. Air Force Europe (USAFE) Commander; retired in 2006.

Foley, S. Robert Jr. (Adm.) - former Commander, U.S. Pacific Fleet (1982-1985); former Commander of Seventh Fleet

Fowler, Jeffrey L. (Rear Adm.) - Commander, U.S. Navy Recruiting Command.

Gard, Robert G. Jr. (Lt. Gen., Army) - former President of National Defense University (1977-1981)
Gerstein, Daniel M. (Col.) - Executive Officer to the Under Secretary of the Army George W. Bush.
Golden, James R. (Brig. Gen., Army) - former executive at Tenneco; former Head of the Dept. of Social Sciences at West Point
Gordon, John A. (Gen., USAF) - former deputy director of CIA (1997-2000); former administrator of National Nuclear Security Administration and Under Secretary of Energy for Nuclear Security (2000-2002)
Gregson, Wallace C. Jr. (Lt. Gen., USMC) - Commander, U.S. Marine Forces Pacific
Hackett, Craig D. (Maj. Gen., Army) - Commander, U.S. Army Security Assistance Command at Fort Belvoir, Virginia
Haig, Alexander M. Jr. - former Secretary of State (1981-1982); former NATO commander
Hailston, Earl B. (Gen., USMC) - former commander of U.S. Marine Forces, Central Command (CENTCOM)
Hamel, Michael A. (Lt. Gen., USAF) - Commander of Space and Missile Systems Center, Air Force Space Command
Hayden, Michael V. (Gen., USAF) - current CIA Director; former Director of National Security Agency (1999-2005)
Haynes, Fred (Maj. Gen., USMC) - former Commanding General of Marine Corps Base at Camp Lejeune (1974-1975)
Hayward, Thomas B. (Adm.) - former Chief of Naval Operations (1978-1982)
Henry, Peter A. (Colonel, Army) - former Chief of Staff of Multinational Security Transition Command in Iraq and former Deputy Commander of Civilian Police Assistance Training Team in Baghdad, Iraq.
Hill, James T. (Gen., Army) - former commander of U.S. Southern Command (2002-2004)
Hosmer, Bradley C. (Lt. Gen., USAF) - former Superintendent of U.S. Air Force Academy (1991-1994)
Inman, Bobby R. (Adm.) - former Director of National Security Agency (1977-1981); former deputy director of CIA (1981-1982)
Jebb, Cindy R. (Col., Army) - Deputy Head of Dept. of Social Sciences at West Point
Johnson, Jay L. (Adm.) - former Chief of Naval Operations (1996-2000)
Jones, David C. (Gen.) - former Chairman of JCS (1978-1982)
Jones, James L. (Gen.) – former Commandant of the Marine Corps (1999-2003)
Jumper, John P. (Gen.) - former Air Force Chief of Staff (2001-2005)
Keane, John M. (retired Gen., Army) - appeared in a Bilderberg meeting in 2005
Kelley, Paul X. (Gen.) - former Commandant of the Marine Corps (1983-1987)
Kern, Paul J. (Gen.) - senior counselor of The Cohen Group; former commander of U.S. Army Materiel Command (2001-2004)
Klimp, Jack Wilbur (retired Lt. Gen., USMC) - former Commander of Task Force Mogadishu in 1993
Klotz, Frank G. (Lt. Gen.) - Vice Commander of Air Force Space Command (2005-present); a Rhodes Scholar
Knowlton, William Allen (Maj. Gen.) - former Superintendent of U.S. Military Academy at West Point (1970-1974)
Kramek, Robert E. (Adm.) - former Commandant of the Coast Guard (1994-1998)
Krepinevich, Andrew F. (Lt. Col., Army) - Executive Director of the Center for Strategic and Budgetary Assessments

Krulak, Charles Chandler (Gen.) - former Commandant of Marine Corps (1995-1999)

Larsen, Randall J. (Col., Air Force) – Founder and CEO, Homeland Security Associates, LLC; former AF officer.

Larson, Charles R. (Adm.) – former Superintendent of U.S. Naval Academy under Reagan and Clinton.

Lennox, William J. Jr. (Lt. Gen.) – former Superintendent of U.S. Military Academy at West Point (2001-2006)

Loranger, Donald Eugene (Maj. Gen., USAF) – former Vice Commander of the 8th Air Force (1994-1996)

Lynch, Thomas F. III (Colonel, Army) – Commander, U.S. Army Forces Central Command at Qatar

Marquet, L. David (Captain, Navy) - former Commander of Submarine Squadron Three

McCaffrey, Barry R. (Gen.) - former Commander of U.S. Southern Command (1994-1996); Clinton's "drug czar"

McCarthy, James P. (Gen., Air Force) - former Deputy Commander of European Command

McChrystal, Stanley A. (Maj. Gen., Army) - Vice Chief of Operations, Joint Staff at the Pentagon

McClure, Robert L. (Col., Army) - former Chief of Army War Plans at the Pentagon; retired in 2004

McMaster, Herbert Raymond (Col., Army) - currently a commander of 3rd Armored Cavalry Regiment

McPeak, Merrill A. (Gen.) - former Air Force Chief of Staff (1990-1994)

Meigs, Montgomery C. (Gen.) - former United States Army Europe (USAEUR) Commander

Meyer, Edward C. (Gen.) - former Army Chief of Staff (1979-1983)

Miller, Christopher D. (Brig. Gen., USAF) - Commander of 509th Bomb Wing, a Rhodes Scholar

Mize, David M. (Maj. Gen., USMC) - former Commanding General of Camp Lejeune

Moorman, Thomas S. Jr. (Gen.) - former Air Force Vice Chief of Staff (1994-1997)

Moseley, Teed Michael (Gen.) - Air Force Chief of Staff (2005-present)

Mundy, Carl E. Jr. (Gen.) - former Commandant of the Marine Corps (1991-1995)

Munsch, Stuart B. (Captain, Navy) - a Rhodes Scholar; former Commander of USS Albuquerque

Murray, Douglas J. (Col., USAF) - Head of Department of Political Science at Air Force Academy

Myers, Richard B. (Gen.) - former Chairman of Joint Chiefs of Staff (2001-2005)

Nash, William L. (Maj. Gen.) - former commander of U.S. Army 1st Armored Division (1995-1997)

Odom, William E. (Gen.) - former Director of National Security Agency (1985-1988)

Owens, William A. (Adm.) - former Vice Chairman of Joint Chiefs of Staff (1994-1996)

Petraeus, David H. (Lt. Gen., Army) - Commander of Multi-National Security Transition Command in Iraq; former Commander of 101st Airborne Division

Pilling, Donald L. (Adm.) - former Vice Chief of Naval Operations (1997-2000); former Commander of U.S. Sixth Fleet

Powell, Colin L. (Gen.) - former Secretary of State (2001-2005); former Chairman of Joint Chiefs of Staff (1989-1993)

Prueher, Joseph Wilson (Adm.) - former Ambassador to Red China (1999-2001); former Commander of U.S. Pacific Command
Pursley, Robert E. (Lt. Gen., USAF) - former commander of U.S. Forces in Japan (1972-1974)
Pustay, John S. (Lt. Gen., USAF) - former president of National Defense University (1981-1983)
Reimer, Dennis Joe (Gen.) - former Army Chief of Staff (1995-1999)
Resnicoff, Arnold E. (Captain, Navy) - former Navy Chaplain and rabbi
Richardson, William R. (Gen.) - former U.S. Army TRADOC commander under Reagan
Roggero, Frederick F. (Brig. Gen., USAF) - Deputy Director of Operations at the Air Mobility Command Headquarters
Rokke, Ervin J. (Lt. Gen., USAF) - former president of National Defense University (1994-1997)
Rondeau, Ann E. (Vice Admiral) - Director of Navy Staff; former Commander of Naval Training Center Great Lakes
Route, Ronald A. (Vice Adm., Navy) - Navy Inspector General; former President of Naval War College (2003-2004)
Ryan, Michael E. (Gen.) - former Air Force Chief of Staff (1997-2001)
Schwartz, Norton A. (Gen., USAF) - Commander of U.S. Transportation Command (2005-present)
Scowcroft, Brent (Lt. Gen., Air Force) - former National Security Advisor (1989-1993, 1975-1977)
Sewall, John O.B. (Maj. Gen., Army) - former Vice Director for Strategic Plans and Policy (J-5) on the Joint Staff
Shalikashvili, John M. (Gen., Army) - former Chairman of Joint Chiefs of Staff (1993-1997)
Shinseki, Eric (Gen.) - former Army Chief of Staff (1999-2003)
Smith, Perry M. (Maj. Gen., USAF) - former Commandant of National War College (1983-1986)
Smith, W. Y. (Gen., USAF) - former Deputy Commander of U.S. European Command (1981-1983)
Stavridis, James G. (Vice Admiral) - Senior Military Assistant to the Secretary of Defense Rumsfeld
Train, Harry D. II (Adm.) - former Supreme Allied Commander Atlantic (1978-1982); former Commander of Sixth Fleet (1976-1978)
Trainor, Bernard E. (Gen., USMC) - military correspondent and propagandist for the New York Times and NBC
Turner, Stansfield (Adm.) - former CIA Director (1977-1981); Rhodes Scholar
Usher, William R. (Maj. Gen.) - former Air Force general
Vessey, John W. (Gen.) - former Chairman of Joint Chiefs of Staff (1982-1985)
Vuono, Carl E. (Gen.) - former Army Chief of Staff (1987-1991)
Warner, Volney James (Brig. Gen., Army) - head of J-5 (Strategy and Analysis), Joint Forces Command
Welch, Jasper A. Jr. (Gen.) - former Air Force general
Welch, Larry D. (Gen.) - former Air Force Chief of Staff (1986-1990)
Wilkerson, Thomas Lloyd (Maj. Gen., USMC) - former Commander of Marine Forces Reserve
Winfield, W. Montague (Maj. Gen., Army) - Commander of U.S. Army Cadet Command
Woerner, Fred F. (Gen.) - former Commander of U.S. Southern Command (1987-1989)

Wortzel, Larry M. (Col., Army) - Army Attaché at the American Embassy in Beijing (1995-1997)
Zinni, Anthony Charles (Gen., USMC) - former CENTCOM commander (1997-2000)

Is the list above just a collection of 124 "good old boys" that have sold their souls to the CFR conspirators in order to get their stars? We can only guess. What we know for sure, however, is that the "bad boys" who honor their oath of allegiance to the U.S. Constitution and don't play the CFR conspirators' game do not advance their careers, and some of them are even demoted. This was the case, i.e., of three-star general John Riggs, who lost a star as a result of publicly criticizing Rumsfeld's CFR party line.[12]

Faithful to Two Flags?

Speaking in 1991 at one of the secret Bilderberg conciliabula in Baden-Baden, Germany, CFR key conspirator David Rockefeller proudly mentioned his treasonous work undermining the constitutional principles of this country,

> . . . the world is now more sophisticated and prepared to march towards a world government. The supranational sovereignty of an intellectual elite and world bankers is surely preferable to the national auto-determination practiced in past centuries.[13]

It is highly disturbing, to say the least, that 124 high-rank active-duty and retired officers of the U.S. military are publicly showing their divided loyalties by being active members of an organization whose openly expressed ultimate goal is nothing less than the elimination of the United States of America as a sovereign nation.

Moreover, it is very difficult to understand why a select group of senior officers of the U.S. armed forces, who voluntarily took without mental reservations an oath to serve and protect the U.S. Constitution against all enemies, foreign and domestic, belong to an organization whose most senior members have openly expressed their goal of abolishing the U.S. Constitution and destroying this country's sovereignty.

The public record shows that the Council on Foreign Relations is one of the most anti-American organizations in the world. Senior CFR members have openly expressed on uncountable occasions their intentions to erode and dismantle the U.S. Constitution and destroy the U.S. sovereignty. They plan to accomplish this by, first, fusing the U.S. with Mexico and Canada into the North American Union and, finally, creating the American Union from Alaska to Patagonia under the political and military control of a global government they call the New World Order —which, of course, the CFR conspirators plan to control.

Moreover, how can one explain that so many senior officers belong to an organization whose senior members despise the U.S. military? Henry Kissinger, a senior CFR member and one of its most outspoken mouthpieces, expressed in stark clarity the conspirators' opinion of the American military men who, unwittingly, have been exposing their lives to advance the conspirators' anti-American global agenda. According to investigative journalists Woodward and Bernstein, Kissinger, in the presence of CFR member Gen. Alexander Haig, pointedly referred to military men as "dumb, stupid animals to be used" as pawns for foreign policy.[14]

But Kissinger is not the only CFR agent who despises American soldiers. In an article about some generals who criticized CFR secret agent and secretary of defense Donald Rumsfeld, author David Margolick, exposed Rumsfeld's lack of respect for the senior officers under his command and how he humiliated them on multiple occasions.[15]

Arthur Schlesinger, Jr., another CFR secret agent, put it bluntly when he wrote, "In Defense of the World Order . . . U.S. soldiers would have to kill and die."[16] After the Fort Hood killings of November 2009, one could properly add, "even when they are in a military base in U.S. territory."

The mainstream media has carefully avoided asking the key question about the Fort Hood killings: how the fanatic assassin managed to kill and maim so many soldiers inside a U.S. military base? The answer is because the CFR conspirators infiltrated into the U.S. government fear American soldiers so much that they don't allow them to carry weapons in the country they are supposedly dying to defend. Not even when they are inside a military base.

In their book *An Enormous Crime*, authors William Hendon and Elizabeth Stewart documented the existence of American prisoners of war in Vietnam left behind after the end of the war. The book also shows abundant evidence of how the U.S. government, through different administrations of both factions of the Repucratic Party, has managed to hide the fact from the American public.[17]

Nevertheless, the book is short off the mark in reflecting the magnitude of the treason the CFR conspirators in the U.S. Government have committed against the American military. Granted, leaving in the lurch American POWs in Vietnam was an enormous crime. But, then, what can we call the killing and disabling of dozens of thousand of military men and women who participated in the Gulf War by forcing them to take vaccines containing the poisonous substances that caused the Gulf War syndrome?[18] What can we call the cover-up to hide this horrendous crime from the American people?

The CFR Conspirators Destroy the CIA They Don't Need Anymore

After having successfully infiltrated the U.S. armed forces, as the above CFR membership list of senior officers shows, the conspirators may have reasoned, why do they need a surrogate army when they now have the real thing? If they now control the U.S. army, why do they need the CIA?[19] The true reason why the CIA is fading into oblivion is because the conspirators don't need the Agency anymore.

Granted, the CIA still has its own super secret Special Operations Group fully devoted to forcibly intervene in the political affairs of foreign states by the assassination of their leaders and the promotion of coup d'ètats. But most of its operations ended in failure. After the 9/11 events, CIA director George Tenet made an effort to revitalize the SOG, but some key senior CFR agents had other plans.[20]

The conspirators, through their senior agents vice-president Dick Cheney and defense secretary Donald Rumsfeld, created, as part of this new idea of a small, more efficient army, a new U.S. agency inside the Pentagon, the Office of Special Plans, to totally bypass the CIA.[21] By early 2003, the Defense Department already had in its Special Operations Command 44,000 commandos from the Army, Navy and Air Force. They are as well trained in covert warfare as the CIA's operatives.[22]

Most authors who have studied the subject, saw Donald Rumsfeld as the intellectual creator of this so-called Revolution in Military Affairs. But, given the fact that Rumsfeld is a total ignoramus in military matters,[23] where did he get the idea of a small gang-like army of Special Forces and global SWAT teams for special operations fighting non-declared wars? At the Harold Pratt House, of course.

Rumsfeld's vision of a leaner and meaner Army is nothing more than the CFR's own vision of the CIA's secret operations branch, now on steroids. It fits to a T what the CIA has been doing for its CFR masters since its creation in 1947.

The conspirators' idea of the new army, as embraced by Rumsfeld, is not too different from the one shown in the CBS series *The Team:*[24] a small army of Special Forces, acting as global SWAT teams of rogue adventurers poorly disguised as military men. Their role is waging non-declared illegal wars around the world on behalf of CFR bankers and oil magnates, without congressional approval and behind the backs of the American people.

The new CFR puppet in the White House has increased the use of these global SWAT teams. By June 2010, they were operating in 74 countries, compared to about 60 at the beginning of last year.[25] Even more disturbing is the fact that these gangsta-like units are increasingly operating outside war zones, resulting in a large number of civilian casualties.

The idea of a "Revolution in Military Affairs" originated in 1994 in a paper entitled 'The Revolution in Military Affairs and Conflict Short of War," produced by the Strategic Studies Institute (SSI) of the U.S. Army War College at the Carlisle Barracks, Pennsylvania.[26] In the paper, authors, Steven Metz and James Kievit, stated,

> Many American strategic thinkers believe that we are in the beginning stages of a historical revolution in military affairs (RMA). This will not only change the nature of warfare, but also alter the global geopolitical balance.[27]

According to the authors, this revolution is not only strategic. It is also fundamentally technological. It involves,

> Sensor technology, robotics, nonlethal weapons, and intelligence meshes will be used in combating terrorism, counteracting narcotrafficking, and peace operations. These technologies, along with stimulator training and unmanned aerial vehicles, will also be useful in insurgency and counterinsurgency.[28]

This is simply the translation to the military field of the same idea of preponderance of TECHINT over HUMINT the conspirators already implemented in the CIA. The motives are perhaps the same: the CFR conspirators don't trust American military men and women. Obviously, robots, contrary to real people, will never reach the conclusion that, as Kissinger acknowledged,[29] they are been used as cannon fodder to advance secret anti-American agendas.

As I mentioned above, an April 2008 Department of Homeland Security confidential report, entitled "Right-wing Extremism: Current Economic and Political Climate Fueling Resurgence in Radicalization and Recruitment,"[30] reveals that the CFR conspirators fear the U.S. military more than Islamic terrorists. The Report warned members of the DHS about the possibility of violence by unnamed "right-wing extremists," which are identified as people concerned about illegal immigration, abortion rights, increasing federal power, restrictions on firearms, abortion and the loss of U.S. sovereignty. Moreover, it singles out returning war veterans, that is, people who have risked their lives under the belief that they are defending the security of their country, as particular threats to their homeland.

According to the Report, worsening economic woes, potential new legislative restrictions on firearms and "the return of military veterans facing significant challenges reintegrating into their communities could lead to the potential emergence of terrorist groups or lone wolf extremists capable of carrying out violent attacks."[31]

The authors of the "Revolution in Military Affairs" paper recognize the fact that, "The use of new technology may also run counter to basic American values," and that, "Deception, while frequently of great military or political value, is thought of as somehow 'un-American.'"[32]

The authors conclude that the majority of Americans may find the use of many of the emerging technologies "morally difficult." Therefore, they suggest that the military might consider that American values and attitudes thus create significant constraints on full use of emerging technologies, at least in anything "short of a perceived war for national survival.[33] Obviously, American military men and women holding traditional American values and ethics are a big obstacle to the conspirators' plans.

The authors write that to achieve a "Revolution in Military Affairs," the Army must fully recognize that psychological technology is of much greater importance than strike technology. As the authors of the paper point out,

> Ways must be found to use emerging technology, including advanced artificial intelligence and information dissemination systems, to help military strategists develop, implement, and continually improve methods of influencing opinion, mobilizing public support, and sometimes demobilizing it.[34]

What the authors of the report fail to mention, however, is that the psychological warfare techniques they advise could be used by any totalitarian government against its own people, including the U.S. government against political opponents —like the ones the OHS report mentioned above qualifies as "extremists." On the other hand, the OHS Report is an indication that, despite the concerted efforts of the religious right and disinformers like Rush Limbaugh and Sean Hannity, more and more enlisted men and women are realizing that they have been recruited under a false flag. Consequently, they are reaching the conclusion that they are not fighting for their country, but for the defense of the interests of Wall Street bankers, oil magnates and CEOs of transnational corporations.

The "Support *Our* Army" Myth

Professional pseudo-conservative disinformers like Rush Limbaugh, Sean Hannity and Mark Levin, repeat over and over the mantra of their full support of our military. But, is the current U.S. military actually "ours"? Are the men in the U.S. military currently exposing life and limb in the defense of the American people and the Constitution of the United States of America as expressed in their oath of allegiance?

Most people seem to forget that, as the Greek philosopher Heraclitus of Ephesus cryptically expressed many centuries ago, you cannot step twice in the same river —meaning that, even though the river's name may be the same, its water is not, because it is continually flowing. One can surely apply this wisdom to the analysis of any institution, including the U.S. military.

The U.S. military most Americans have in their minds is still the one who, despite betrayal at the highest levels of the U.S. government, fought with honor the German Nazis and the Japanese in WWII. That was a true people's army; an army of citizens-soldiers risking their lives to fight for what they believed was a noble cause. But there are indications that the real motive why the CFR conspirators and their secret agent Franklin Delano Roosevelt pushed America into an unwanted war was not to liberate Europe or to save the Jews, but to protect their interests in Germany and save their criminal Nazi friends from justice.

As I mentioned above in this book, General George S. Patton apparently reached a similar conclusion when he found out that the U.S. High Command had sabotaged his Third Army and betrayed the American soldiers causing the unnecessary death of one third of all American casualties in WWII.

In a recent article entitled "Can Christians Serve in the New World Order Army?," Chuck Baldwin, presidential candidate for the Constitution Party and one of the persons qualified as "extremists" in the OHS report, pointed out, "Many patriotic Americans, including many retired and former military personnel, are increasingly chagrined at the direction the U.S. armed forces are taking."[35]

Baldwin's article analyzes the issue so well that I am going to quote him in some detail. According to Baldwin,

> Another disconcerting element of modern military service is the reality that today's American military is more and more used as the tool of the globalists to forge an international New World Order. For instance, both Republican and Democratic Presidential administrations will send U.S.

> military personnel (including the National Guard) to guard the borders of foreign countries, but never ask them to protect our own borders. Sending the National Guard overseas, especially, strains the principles of constitutional government.
>
> Using U.S. troops as international "peacekeepers" only serves the interests of the international New World Order; it has nothing to do with protecting the lives and property of the American people. In fact, an argument could be made that every war the United States has fought since World War II has been unconstitutionally waged: for the purpose of fulfilling the globalist aspirations of world leaders and not for the defense of the United States. Accordingly, many Christian parents are hesitant to give their children to modern military service.
>
> ....
>
> It is also obvious, however, that the powers that be are quickly "remaking" (to use Barack Obama's word) our military and law enforcement agencies into an image never desired or designed by America's Founding Fathers. Thus, the conflict between good men and bad policies will only worsen. And many will continue to question the wisdom of giving their sons and daughters to modern military service.
>
> On the other hand, an argument could be made that it is at such a time as this that good men are all the more needed in the U.S. military and in law enforcement. That is a very valid argument, by the way: as long as those good men realize what they will be required to risk when their superiors order them to surrender allegiance to the Constitution or to sacred principle. But then again, we are all required to share in that risk, are we not?[36]

A letter to the editor sent by a reader to *U.S.A. Today* reflects a similar opinion:

> It is surprising that throughout the article on American servicemembers who are returned in body bags at Dover, Del., the relatives do not express outrage because their government lied to them and their families about the bogus war on terrorism. I and thousands of others were also lied to when we ended up unjustifiably in Vietnam. . . . These families and the rest of America should look beyond the crisp military uniforms and their stirring image of the U.S. flag. This ritual is a subterfuge designed to keep patriotic emotions afloat while stifling critical thinking that might question the reasons these men and women had to die for less than a noble cause.[37]

As the OHS report clearly shows, the CFR conspirators fear that some of these good men mentioned by Baldwin will refuse to follow illegal orders. The writers of the Revolution in Military Affairs confide that, through the use of combat robots and other sophisticated technology, a small group of men can efficiently do the job the U.S. military may refuse to do. This idea may have sound like celestial music to the CFR conspirators' ears. No wonder they ordered their agents Rumsfeld and Cheney to pursue it.

In another of his thoughtful articles,[38] Baldwin quotes an outstanding address given by Lieutenant Colonel (ret.) Guy Cunningham[39] on the Independence Day weekend of 2007 in Pensacola, Florida. In it, he mentioned the results of the 29 Palms Survey (conducted in 1994),[40] in which more than 20% of combat-trained Marines who answered the survey stated that they would fire upon American citizens in order to confiscate their firearms if ordered to do so and, if required, would swear allegiance to the United Nations. Obviously, this is not the same American military that fought the Nazis in WWII. Cunningham also said he feared that if those same questions were asked to the Marines today, the percentage would be even higher.

Lt. Col. Cunningham is not the only one concerned about the current role of the U.S. Military. In a response to a warmongering article by CFR agent Robert Kagan,[41] Angelo Codevilla wrote,

> Mr. Kagan asks, "Who among us . . . is prepared to rise to the challenge of global activism?" I would ask in return: who among those who pretend to lead the United States in the world is prepared to serve in the armed forces and submit his body to the blood tax? Today only one-third of Congressmen and fewer than a tenth of executive appointees, professors, journalists, and executives of major corporations have ever served in the armed forces. Nor their families serve. Nor, by and large, are they personally acquainted with those sectors of society that contribute to the armed forces and those whose personal remoteness embolden them to play global chess.[42]

Codevilla is absolutely right. As Brig. Gen. Smedley Butler forcefully expressed long ago,[43] the Wall Street Mafia use *our* military as cannon fodder to defend and protect *their* global interests from *their* enemies, foreign and domestic.[44] Actually, there is nothing those warmongering unconditional supporters of the U.S. military would not do to help our military men and women accomplish their mission —except telling their own children to join them.

In the early 1990s, the CFR conspirators felt that their infiltration of the U.S. armed forces had reached a point of almost total control. It was then when they began using again the U.S. military power openly and directly, without hiding it anymore behind the cover of the CIA. Consequently, the Agency has outlived its usefulness for the conspirators and the days of the CIA are counted. Save for using it as a fall guy if anything goes wrong, the conspirators don't need the Agency anymore.

After the creation of the position of Director of National Intelligence, established by the Intelligence Reform and Terrorism Prevention Act of 2004, the U.S. intelligence is in worse shape than ever before —under Rumsfeld tenure, almost 80% of the intelligence budget was going to the Department of Defense, not to the

CIA or other intelligence agencies. The reason for this, and why the U.S. intelligence cannot be fixed, is because a more efficient U.S. intelligence apparatus will soon discover that most actions against the U.S. have actually been incited or carried out by CFR agents infiltrated in the U.S. government, and this is something the CFR conspirators don't want the American people to know.

In his speech I mentioned above, Lt. Col. Cunningham referred to the stranglehold that the Council on Foreign Relations holds over the U.S. military, estimating that "75% of military admirals and generals with two stars or more have been trained by the CFR."[45] Cunningham is right on the mark. As the table below shows,[46] with almost full control of the military the CFR conspirators are not using CIA any more.

Country	Dates	Forces	Comments
Liberia	1990	Troops	Foreigners evacuated during civil war.
Saudi Arabia	1990-91	Troops, Air Force	Iraq countered after invading Kuwait.
Iraq	1990-?	Troops, naval	Blockade of Iraqi and Jordanian ports.
Kuwait	1991	Navy, troops	Kuwait royal family returned to throne.
Somalia	1992-94	Troops, naval	U.S.-led United Nations occupation.
Yugoslavia	1992-94	Naval -NATO	blockade of Serbia and Montenegro.
Bosnia	1993-?	Air Force	No-fly zone patrolled, bombed Serbs.
Haiti	1994	Troops, Navy	Blockade against military government;
Zaire (Congo)	1996-97	Troops	Marines at Rwandan Hutu refugee camps,
Liberia	1997	Troops	Evacuation of foreigners.
Albania	1997	Troops	Evacuation of foreigners.
Sudan	1998	Air Force	Attack on pharmaceutical plant
Afghanistan	1998	Air Force	Attack on former CIA training camps
Iraq	1998-?	Air Force	Four days of intensive air strikes
Yugoslavia	1999	Air Force	Heavy NATO air strikes
Yemen	2000	Navy	USS Cole, docked in Aden, bombed.
Macedonia	2001	Troops	NATO forces deployed.
Afghanistan	2001-?	Troops, Air Force	Massive U.S. mobilization.
Yemen	2002	Missiles	Predator drone missile attack on Al Qaeda,
Philippines	2002-?	Troops, Navy	Combat missions, Sulu Archipelago.
Colombia	2003-?	Troops	U.S. special forces sent
Iraq	2003-?	Troops, Navy	Saddam regime toppled in Baghdad.
Liberia	2003	Troops	Involvement in peacekeeping force.
Haiti	2004-05	Troops, Navy	Marines land to support ousted president.
Pakistan	2005-?	**Covert op**	Air strikes & Special Forces raids
Somalia	2006-?	Navy, **covert op**	Special Forces advise Ethiopian invasion
Syria	2008	Troops	Special Forces in helicopter raid

After the Gulf war, where a large part of commissioned and non-commissioned officers of the fighting army was lost thanks to the Gulf War Syndrome — a direct result of forced vaccinations— the conspirators substituted most of them with people of their confidence. Now they have almost total control of the U.S. fighting armed forces. Proof of it is that currently the commanding officers of the two main theaters of operations, Lt. Gen. David H. Petraeus in Iraq and, until recently, Maj. Gen. Stanley A. McChrystal[47] in Afghanistan, are trusted CFR agents.

Epilogue

What Can We Do to Win This War?

All warfare is based on deception.
—Sun Tzu.

A genuine man goes to the roots. To be a radical is no more than that: to go to the roots.
—José Martí.

There are a thousand hacking at the branches of evil to one who is striking at the root.
—Henry David Thoreau.

If an unfriendly foreign power had carried out against the American people the treasonous actions carried out by the Wall Street bankers, Oil magnates and CEOs of transnational corporations entrenched at the Council on Foreign Relations and the organizations they control, we might well have considered it an act of war.

Just recently, the conspirators-controlled mainstream press announced the U.S. Justice Department's claims that it had broken a Russian spy ring. According to the report,

> Ten alleged members of a "long-term, deep-cover" Russian spy ring have been arrested on the U.S. East Coast, the Justice Department said yesterday. The suspects, who are accused of seeking to infiltrate U.S. policy-making circles, face charges including conspiring to act as illegal Russian agents and to commit money laundering.[1]

Well, conspiring to infiltrate U.S. policy-making circles with their secret agents is exactly what the CFR conspirators have been doing for many years, and nobody in the Justice Department or the mainstream press seems to care. This attack has become so evident that Professor Robert Weissberg, who analyzed the phenomenon, has used the term "alien rule" to describe it.[2] According to Weissberg,

> After auditioning countless political terms, I finally realized that the Obama administration and its congressional collaborators almost resemble a foreign occupying force, a coterie of politically and culturally non-indigenous leaders whose rule contravenes local values rooted in our national tradition. It is as if the United States has been occupied by a foreign power, and this transcends policy objections.[3]

Unfortunately, Weissberg fails to see that most key members of the Obama and Bush administrations and their congressional collaborators are members of the Council on Foreign Relations. Our current leaders are just malleable tools in the hands of the Wall Street bankers, oil magnates and CEOs of transnational corporations agglutinated at the CFR. For almost a century, this small group of conspirators has been waging a quiet, non-declared war of attrition against the American people, and it seems that they are now ready for the final, decisive battle. Unfortunately, as the last two presidential elections evidenced, the brainwashed American people keeps reacting against the puppet presidents by electing other puppets while leaving the puppet masters untouched.

The fact, however, that both Republicans and Democrats are trying to destroy the Tea Party —the Democrats by confrontation and the Republicans by infiltration— shows that both of them are scared. And what scares them most is that the Tea Party's anti-incumbent philosophy actually means the end of the two-party charade, a key tool in the ongoing PSYWAR against the American people.

We should remember that it was Carroll Quigley, a true CFR insider, the one who told the truth about the American two-party system. In his book *Tragedy and Hope*, Quigley explained how the two parties, one representing the Right and the other the Left, are just a clever scheme devised by the CFR conspirators to fool the gullible American people.[4]

Currently, some Republicans who apparently love their party more than their country are trying to convince the voters that electing Republicans will make a difference. This is exactly what the Democrats did less than two years ago, and many of them are not happy with the results. Having Obama in the White House has proved to be not too different from having George W. Bush.

According to an often-quoted dictum, doing the same over and over and expecting different results is a clear symptom of insanity. Unfortunately, some professional brainwashers who call themselves "conservatives" are working hard trying to convince the voters that by putting the Republican Party back in power things will change for the better.

We should recall, though, that after taking control of Congress in 2006 some members of the Democratic faction of the Repucratic Party were talking about a "new direction" in American domestic and foreign policy. Moreover, Obama's campaign main theme was that of "change."

But, just a few months after he became president, Obama showed no intention to change the course of American politics. Actually, he is enthusiastically following the same direction as George W. Bush. As Chuck Baldwin rightly pointed out,

> The Republican and Democrat parties seldom actually reverse the course set by their predecessors; they merely adjust the rhetoric (and maybe the speed), but the overall course toward socialism and globalism never changes.[5]

Mr. Baldwin is absolutely right. Substituting the CFR puppets of the party in power with CFR puppets from the other party will not bring any change. Consequently, if we want to win this decisive battle and eventually this war against us, we need to stop acting as usual and become radicals in the sense pointed out by Martí and Thoreau.

As Cuban patriot José Martí rightly pointed out, the word radical comes from the Latin word for "root." Therefore, a radical is a person who tries to go to the root of the problem. Unfortunately, as Henry David Thoreau observed, for every thousand hacking at the branches of evil there is just one striking at the root. The American Republic is in grave danger, and we are past the time for Band Aid cures.[6] In order to produce major changes we need to find the true source of the problem and strike at it hard.

Most Republicans, who see themselves as conservatives, apparently believe that they are the only ones who have a direct connection with the Founding Fathers of this country. They seem to forget, however, that the men who created this country were not conservatives, but revolutionaries. Moreover, they were radicals who wanted to transform a society they saw as unjust and intolerable.

The term radical is usually used as an equivalent to the term extremist. This is the way it is used by disinformers Limbaugh and Hannity, and by the Department of Homeland Security Report I mentioned above in this book. In it Ron Paul, Chuck Baldwin, Bob Barr, Alex Jones and other patriotic Americans are accused of being "extremists."[7] But they are not extremists. They are just radicals. They want to solve the problem we face by attacking the root of the problem.

In the film *Aliens*, the humans under attack finally realize that taking out one by one the aliens infesting the base is an exercise in frustration, because they reproduce faster than they can zap them. Then a member of the group realizes that in order to solve the problem they must take out the alien queen.

In the same fashion, taking out the CIA, FEMA, or the OHS will not solve the problem. Actually, we will not solve the problem, unless we get rid of the alien queen. This alien queen is the one who hatched not only the CIA, but also the Fed, the IRS, the NSC, the NSA, the FEMA, the OHS and the rest of the aberrations working hard to destroy the freedoms guaranteed by our Constitution. Getting rid of Obama will not solve the problem, because the alien queen is currently hatching dozens of eggs that will provide replacements with new generations of Obamas, Kissingers, Brzezinskis, Carters, Clintons, Cheneys and Bushes. And the alien queen's nest is at the Harold Pratt House in Manhattan, headquarters of the Council on Foreign Relations.

Is the U.S. Becoming a Totalitarian Dictatorship?

Since the very moment an American president violated the Constitution by signing an executive order the United States became a de facto dictatorship. A dictatorship is a form of government where laws are enacted by *diktats*, that is, executive orders signed by the chief of state —a dictator— without the approval of the other branches of government, much less the people governed.

This is exactly what American presidents have been doing for more than a century. Therefore, they are nothing but dictators. But there is a big difference between a dictatorship and a totalitarian dictatorship, and I know it first hand, because I have lived in a democratic republic, a dictatorship and a totalitarian dictatorship —exactly in that order.

On March 10, 1952, General Fulgencio Batista staged a coup d'ètat in the Republic of Cuba and overthrew the democratically elected President Carlos Prío Socarrás. Despite a few initial protests, some people welcomed the strong arm that was supposed to put an end to corruption and graft in Cuban politics. However, soon after, Batista became even more corrupt than Prío. Nevertheless, the economy experienced a boom, and most Cubans simply ignored the fact that the government had changed from a democracy to a dictatorship.

Except for a few short periods in which Batista temporarily cancelled constitutional rights in an effort to fight Castro's terrorism and subversion, there was not a big difference between both forms of government. Freedom of the press continued to a great extent, the judicial power kept its independence, and Cubans moved freely inside and out of the island. Save for a few minor incidents, government critics freely expressed their opinions and went unmolested. With the exception of a few dozen Cubans closely linked to the Prío government, very few Cubans took the way of exile while dictator Batista was in power.

But, in January 1959, Fidel Castro overthrew Batista and took power in Cuba. Then, in March 1960, with the pretext of fighting terrorism and subversion, Castro cancelled the Constitution, eliminated habeas corpus, and very rapidly began curtailing most of the freedoms Cubans took for granted. A few years later, it became evident to anybody with eyes to see that the country had become a totalitarian dictatorship.

In the 1980s. CIA Director William J. Casey came up with the idea of developing a checklist that would provide clues to detect the emergence of a totalitarian state in any country.[8] Casey's theory was that, while all totalitarian states are not alike, their similarities were more important than their differences. There are features common to all of them, argued Casey. The most important are control of the press, rigged elections, the description of honorable political opponents as "enemies of the state," and the violent destruction of political enemies.

If we could identify these features, reasoned Casey, we would be better able to measure whether a state was moving toward totalitarianism and, if so, how far along the road to totalitarianism that state had traveled. Casey ordered the CIA to produce a report listing these totalitarian characteristics

The country Casey had in mind at the time was Nicaragua, but the Report produced by the CIA could be applied to any country, including the current United States. According to the CIA report,

> A key feature of any totalitarian state is the conviction by its leaders and supporters that the revolution is supreme.
>
> They must protect the revolution at all costs. The protection and success of the revolution is so important that nothing —absolutely noth-

> ing— must be allowed to stand in its way.
>
> If established laws become an inconvenience they have to be circumvented, ignored, changed or broken.
>
> If a loyal member of the team becomes a problem, demote him, banish him to the hinterlands, oust him. If it is necessary, destroy him politically or even physically.
>
> If their political opponents are gaining support, do whatever it takes to stop them, however distasteful that action might be.
>
> If caught doing these nasty things, they could say in their defense that they had no choice. The Revolution made them do it.
>
> Totalitarian leaders equate themselves with the revolution. Whatever protects them is justifiable because of their revolution; whatever threatens them personally is intolerable, because they are the revolution.[9]

Based on my personal experience of living in Castro's Cuba, I would add other warning signs of the beginning of a totalitarian dictatorship. They are:

Closing, walling, and positioning armed guards on borders to avoid citizens escape the country.

Stiff gun control laws conducting first to registration and eventual confiscation of all types of guns in the hands of the civilian population.

Proliferation of paramilitary organizations (i.e., Bush's OHS, Obama's health army).

Creation of new repressive agencies (like FEMA, Office of Homeland Security, etc.)

Creation of block organizations to spy on citizens (Ashcroft's failed TIPS program).

Full 24/7 surveillance of citizens.

Suspension of Constitutional guarantees, including habeas corpus.

Using the Army for policing civilian population (no Posse Comitatus).

Unannounced, surprising changes of currency, followed by imposing limits on the amount of money citizens are allowed to convert to the new currency.

Limitation of the amount of currency citizens can keep at home.

Confiscation of jewelry and precious metals owned by private citizens.

Implementation of a national ID citizens must carry at all times.

Issuing of new, special passports required for traveling abroad.

Increasing difficulties for citizens to travel abroad.

Total control by the government over the mass media, particularly the Internet.

Banning of private schools and prohibition of home schooling.

Creation of government live-in schools to totally separate children from their families.

Closing of most Christian churches and Jewish synagogues. Only the most pliable to the government's policies may remain.

Banning of any type of meetings not specifically authorized by the government.

Secretly banning some books, films and videos without telling the public which ones. Possessing any of these becomes a crime.

Self-censorship. Widespread fear to openly express one's ideas, much less criticize the government.

Implementation of pre-crime laws.

Confiscation of land from small farmers.

Implementation of strict food rationing.

Prohibition to grow any type of food or possession of farm animals by private citizens.

Strict prohibition of hunting and fishing.

Harsh laws passed against dissidents. Some of them are interned in concentration camps, their property is confiscated, and their citizenship is revoked.

Mysterious disappearance of government critics. Some of the most vocal ones suffer strange "accidents."

Building of concentration camps for the "reeducation" of political dissidents. Soon after they are filled with "dissidents," most of them white, religious "extremists." Some time later homosexuals, Jews and blacks join them. Finally, people of all types, coming from the poorest sectors of society —the former middle class—, are interned in the camps.

Harsh treatment, beating and even torture of prisoners become prevalent in the camps.

Just a perfunctory analysis of America today shows that we are dangerously advancing the perilous road to totalitarianism.

A September 30, 1954 Report on the Activities of the Central Intelligence Agency stated:

> It is now clear that we are facing an implacable enemy whose avowed objective is world domination by whatever means. Hitherto acceptable norms of human conduct do not apply. If the United States is to survive, long-standing American concepts of "fair play" must be reconsidered. We must develop effective espionage and counterespionage services and must learn to subvert, sabotage and destroy our enemies by cleverer, more sophisticated and more effective methods than those used against us.[10]

Though the enemy the creators of the CIA Report had in mind was the Soviet Union, their suggestion is fully applicable to the enemy the CFR conspirators are facing today: the American people. Until now, however, the war against we the people has been mostly a psychological one. Therefore, in order to defeat the enemy in this battle of the mind we need to develop a psychological warfare counter-offensive.

Ballots or Bullets?

As soon as the press announced Barack Obama's electoral victory, millions of patriotic Americans rushed to gun stores and bought thousands of guns and millions of rounds of ammo in preparation for the coming rebellion against the government. They ignore, however, that the war already began almost a century ago. However, as I have shown above in this book, this is not a shooting, but a psychological war. Its battlegrounds are not physical but mental. Its most potent weapons are not nuclear, chemical or biological, but deception, propaganda, disinformation, lies and manipulation, and it has worked to perfection.

As Sun Tzu wisely advised, only the ones who know the enemy like themselves will be victorious in all battles. Unfortunately, however, most Americans still ignore who their real enemy is.

Even the ones who are aware of the problems we face remind me of the story of the blind men trying to describe an elephant by touch alone. The result is that, according to the part they are touching, the cause of the problem is global warming, illegal immigration, war-for-oil, capitalist greed, gun control, etc. But they are deceiving themselves. The New World Order beast has only two legs: depopulation through eugenics and misery and poverty through deindustrialization.[11]

Nevertheless, thanks to the efforts of professional disinformers like Rush Limbaugh, Sean Hannity and Mark Levin, many Republicans apparently believe that just by changing the Democrats in Washington D.C, everything would be okay. They ignore that the Obama administration is just the seamless continuation of the Bush II administration, which was the seamless continuation of the Clinton administration, which was the seamless continuation of the Bush I administration . . . *ad nauseam*. Obama's aloof golfing and vacationing after the BP oil spill is eerily reminiscent of Bush' reaction of total inaction at the school in Florida after he was told of the attack on 9/11.

Further proof that Barack Obama could easily be dubbed Bushama —as some people already have done— is that Naomi Wolf's book *The End of America: Letter of Warning to a Young Patriot*,[12] is one of the harshest indictments of Obama. Curiously, the subject of her book, published in 2007, was not Obama, but George W. Bush. It speaks in favor of her intellectual honesty that Wolf recently joined the Tea Party movement and, to the utter consternation of her unprincipled liberal friends, has been strongly criticizing Obama.

"Liberal" Democrats blamed Bush for curtailing our liberties after September 11, 2001. They seem to forget, however, that Bush's Patriot Act was just a version on steroids of Clinton's Anti-Terrorism and Effective Death Penalty Act of 1996, passed one year after the Oklahoma City bombing. The Act gave the attorney general the power to use the U.S. armed forces against American citizens, nullifying the Posse Comitatus Act of 1878, as well as selectively suspending habeas corpus, the keystone of Anglo-American liberty.

In the same fashion, "conservative" Republicans are blaming Obama for his accelerated run to change America into a communist tyranny. Apparently they ignore that just by putting into effect a long list of laws passed by executive orders signed by the Bushes, Clinton, Reagan and other CFR-controlled president-dictators before them, Obama can legally turn America overnight into a communo-fascist totalitarian dictatorship.

Just a cursory look at a few of these executive orders shows that its intent was never to safeguard, but to enslave the American people:

E.O. 10995 – ... provides for the seizure of all communications media in the United States.

E.O.10997 – ... provides for the seizure of all electric power, petroleum, gas, fuels and minerals, both public and private.

E.O.10998 – ... provides for the seizure of all food supplies and resources, public and private, and all farms, lands, and equipment.

E.O. 10999 – ... provides for the seizure of all means of transportation, including personal cars, trucks or vehicles of any kind and total control over all highways, seaports, and waterways.

E.O. 11000 – ... provides for the forced conscription of American citizens for work forces under federal supervision, including splitting up of families if the government has to.

E.O. 11001 – ... provides for government seizure of health, education and welfare functions.

E.O. 11002 – ... designates the postmaster general to operate a national registration of all persons. [Under this order, you must report to your local post office to be separated and assigned to a new area. That's how families would be broken].

E.O.11003 – ... provides for the government to take over all airports and aircraft, commercial, public and private.

E.O.11004 – ... provides for the Housing and Finance Authority to relocate communities, designate areas to be abandoned and establish new locations for populations.

E.O.11005 – ... provides for the government to take over railroads, inland waterways, and public storage facilities.

E.O. 11051 – ... gives the office of Emergency Planning complete authorization to put the above orders into effect in time of increased international tension or economic or financial crisis.

E.O. 12148 – ... puts FEMA in charge of national security emergencies, such as: national disasters, social unrest, insurrection, or national financial crisis.

In a recent article, Professor Thomas Sowell raised his concern that the U.S. may be on a course to become a tyranny.[13] However, I think that Professor Sowell is wrong. The U.S. is not becoming a tyranny like Francois Duvalier's in Haiti or Idi Amin's in Uganda. Actually, the U.S. is on a slippery slope to becoming something even worse: a totalitarian dictatorship.

Can we, the American people, still stop this madness by just the force of ballots? I surely don't know, but we should try and give the conspirators a run for their money.

Currently, many members of Congress are CFR members and most of the rest have been co-opted and are controlled through money, compromise or outright coercion. Consequently, we need to begin by getting rid of them. As Charles Reese, of the *Orlando Sentinel,* rightly pointed out,

> To put it into perspective just remember that 100 percent of the power of the federal government comes from the U.S. Constitution. If it's not in the Constitution, it's not authorized.
>
> Then read your Constitution. All 100 percent of the power of the federal government is invested solely in 545 individual human beings. That's all. Of 260 million Americans, only 545 of them wield 100 percent of the power of the federal government.
>
> That's 435 members of the U.S. House, 100 senators, one president and nine Supreme Court justices. Anything involving government that is wrong is 100 percent their fault.[14]

Therefore, in order to begin the process of restoring order to this madhouse, we must begin by cleaning the Augean Congress stables and get rid of just 535 corrupt politicians who don't deserve our respect, much less our vote. And it is not complicated at all. The rules of thumb are relatively simple:

In the first place, don't give your vote to any candidate who is a member of the Council on Foreign Relations or the Trilateral Commission, or has attended the secret meetings of the Bohemian Grove, the World Economic Forum, the Bilderberg Group or any other organization of the many working to destroy U.S. sovereignty and implement a global government. Moreover, don't give your vote to any candidate running for the Republican of Democratic parties. With very few exceptions, all of them have become corrupt and currently are obedient puppets of the CFR conspirators. Actually, don't give your vote to any candidate just because he is running for a particular party, but because of his/her personal qualities —the main one would be a commitment to follow, respect and protect the Constitution against all enemies, foreign and domestic.

Secondly, don't give your vote to any incumbent. The patriots who created this country fought against a monarchy. We don't need career politicians for life, who see their positions as personal entitlements and don't feel the need to protect the interests of the American people but of the corporations and other special interest groups that contribute to their campaigns.[15]

Third, if you don't find any suitable candidate for a particular position, run for office yourself. Particularly run for key positions where we need true American patriots, such as sheriffs and judges. If you don't have any political experience, that's an asset, not a liability. For their own benefit, don't vote to reelect any politicians, even if they have done the best job one can conceive. Once they do their job for a maximum of four years, they should go back to be simple citizens — exactly as they were before being elected. Doing otherwise we run the risk that, sooner or later, they will become corrupt and will be bought by the CFR conspirators.

Finally, treat politicians the same way you treat a waiter in a restaurant or an employee in a supermarket: with respect, but not with deference. Politicians are our servants, not our masters, therefore, treat them as such. Remind them every time you talk to them, that we have elected them not because they are smarter than we are, but just because we want them to act as our representatives in government, and must do whatever we tell them to do.

Demand —don't beg— that they do represent us as they are supposed to do. If they stop doing that, stop treating them with respect. They deserve our respect only if they respect us. This rule applies from the president down to the lowest ranking government employee.

Don't buy the lie that you have to respect the office of the president. Presidents are not kings. There is no throne in the Oval Office. Presidential executive orders are illegal. They are not mentioned in the Constitution. Therefore, all executive orders must be repelled. Presidents-cum-dictators who violate the Constitution by signing *diktats* in the form of executive orders do not deserve our respect. On the contrary, we should despise them and let them know our feelings.

Why Do They Hate *Us*?

The majority of the upper middle classes around the world love America —particularly the American way of life as it is depicted in Hollywood films. Nevertheless, there is also a growing sector of the working classes in the world who hates the U.S. Just a perfunctory analysis of the reasons for this hatred, however, shows that it is mostly because of American imperialism. These people think that, with the pretext of fighting, first, communism and, now, terrorism, as well as allegedly opposing antidemocratic regimes, America has been kicking asses indiscriminately all around the world for more than a century.

Despite the fact that most Americans don't see their country as an empire, the facts show a different picture. Since the nineteenth century when the *USS Maine* battleship mysteriously exploded in Havana's bay, this country has been continuously expanding its territory and its political control over client states through more than 700 military bases all around the world.[17]

The idea that America is an empire may be strange to both American conservatives and liberals, because it goes contrary to the guiding principles of our Founding Fathers idea of an American Republic. Irving Kristol expressed this sentiment when he wrote, "One of these days, the American people are going to awake to the fact that we have become an imperial nation, even though public opinion and all of our political traditions are hostile to the idea."[18]

Still, most Americans don't get it, and that explains why they keep asking themselves: "Why do they hate us?" The theory was inadvertently articulated in a *Wall Street Journal* editorial piece after 9/11 in which Arab business leaders were asked why they hate us. Their answer was, we hate you because you are blocking democracy, supporting brutal terrorist regimes, preventing economic development and enforcing poverty in Arab countries.

But all the answers to that question, including "because we are there," are wrong. And they are wrong because the question has been improperly formulated, and you cannot get a right answer to a question when the question itself is wrong. The right question should not be "Why do they hate *us*?" but "Why do they hate *us* instead of hating *them*?"

As I mentioned above, the main reason because they hate us is American imperialism. But I have lived for 28 years in this country. During these years I have met Americans of all walks of life, and I am still waiting to meet the first American imperialist. Probably I have not lived in the right places, but the fact is that true American imperialists are a tiny minority, mostly composed of Wall Street bankers, oil magnates, CEOs of corporations, senior members of the military-industrial-academic complex, and the corrupt, opportunist politicians they have co-opted.

As Constitution scholar Edwin Vieira, Jr., rightly pointed out, the so called American "empire" is not America at all, but

> … the twisted, unconstitutional, unholy perversion of America that has been temporarily imposed upon WE THE PEOPLE by the globalists in our midst in aid of their own megalomaniac schemes for world hegemony.[19]

This small group of imperialist, corporatist conspirators agglutinated at the Council on Foreign Relations and other similar organizations, not only secretly control America, but also the governments and major organizations of the world. This include the UN, the CIA the WTO, the WHO, the FDA, universities, the Federal Reserve, most of the world's militaries, mass media, and religious organizations, and that is just a partial list.

Jeffrey Grupp's *Corporatism: The Secret Government of the New World Order,*[20] shows that corporatism is the real underlying issue from which literally all major human problems now and in the past derive from. The other issues people usually blame for the causes of humanity's problems (politicians, war, human nature, greed, religion, the educational system, etc.), are just symptoms of the real problem, which is corporatism. In his book, Professor Grupp proves that the United States is a corporatist nation on its way to become similar to the fascist and communist totalitarian horror-states described in books such as Orwell's *1984* and Zamiatin's *We*.

Corporatism shows that in the near future America will be a full-fledged prison nation that will ultimately merge into the corporatist global prison planet that Hitler was initially attempting to set up, and which is now called the New World Order. Consequently, given the fact that fascism is the political system in which the corporations control the state, and communism is the one in which the state controls the corporations, a sure way to avoid the horrors of both fascism and communism would be to abolish corporations and their hidden ideological hands, the so-called "philanthropic" foundations.

Moreover, there is growing evidence that most international corporations, who have joined the New Agers in blaming us for destroying Gaia, are actually the ones involved in a concerted effort to destroy us human beings living in this planet.[21] Consequently, if these international corporations want to destroy us, it would be a simple act of legitimate defense to do our best to destroy them.

Back in 1956 Charlie Wilson, then chairman of General Motors Corporation, said, "What is good for General Motors is good for America." At the time, General Motors, like other similar corporations, was a true American corporation. It operated mostly in the U.S. territory, employed American workers, and paid them decent salaries.

Today, however,neither GM nor any of the big "American" corporations is American anymore. Even though some of them still keep their headquarters in the U.S., they have become true transnational corporations. They have fired well-paid American workers, closed their factories here, and are manufacturing their products abroad, using low-paid foreign workers or outright quasi-slave work.

Consequently, today more than ever, it adds insult to injury that members of the U.S. armed forces are dying abroad protecting the interests of transnational corporations who are mostly contributing to the destruction of America. Marine Corps Major General Smedley Butler rightly pointed out the dynamics of corporate empire when he spoke these words to the American Legion in 1933, "There are only two things we should fight for. One is the defense of our homes and the other is the Bill of Rights. War for any other reason is simply a racket."

Unfortunately, we have been fighting all these years to defend and protect the interests of a bunch of oil magnates, Wall Street bankers and CEOs of transnational corporations who hate America and despise the U.S. Constitution. These are the only imperialists in this country, not the American people. So, again, why do people all around the world hate *us*, the American people, instead of hating *them*, that tiny minority of people who don't represent the American people?

The answer to the question could very well be that it is because, thanks to decades of brainwashing as the result of a psychological war that has obliterated and destroyed our spirit and consciousness, *we,* the American people, have lost our will to govern ourselves and have allowed *them* to do it instead. Apparently, a large part of Americans now seem to agree with David Rockefeller's idea that the supra-national sovereignty of an intellectual elite and world bankers is surely preferable to the national auto-determination of the people practiced in past centuries.[22]

Fortunately, however, not all Americans agree with that idea. So, there is still hope.

The Conspirators' Final Push for the New World Order

The disinformers of both the right and the left keep repeating over and over that Barack Obama's socialist secret agenda is actually redistribution of wealth, by taking money from the rich and giving it to the poor. But this is another myth created by the brainwashing conspirators.

In the first place, Obama has no agenda of his own. He is just an obedient puppet following the conspirators' orders. Consequently, any secret agenda pushed by Mr. Obama is actually the CFR conspirators' agenda, and we know that it is a very simple one. Its two main goals are the elimination of no less than the 85 percent of the world's population and the reduction of the survivors to pre-industrial levels of consumption in a neo-feudal society they call the New World Order. In other words, their true, ultimate goals are depopulation and deindustrialization.

Secondly, the redistribution of wealth the conspirators have in mind for Obama to carry out is not the one the "progressive" left has in mind. Instead of taking from the rich to give to the poor, it consists in taking from the middle classes and giving to the hyper rich until the middle class is destroyed and only the dirty poor remains —exactly as Castro did in Cuba. A first glimpse at this redistribution of wealth was Wall Street firms getting multi-billion dollar bailouts and its executive's cashing multi-million dollar bonuses while American workers were getting pink slips and losing their homes.

Though the conspirators' goals in Cuba and the U.S. are the same, necessarily its implementation needs to be different. The reason for this is that in Cuba Castro first took power by the force of arms, and in America, the conspirators have taken power by infiltration and psychological warfare operations directed at conquering the people's minds. Once in power, Castro imposed the drastic changes at gunpoint. In America the conspirators are trying to impose them by propaganda and mind control, though there are strong indications that they have realized that the only way to finish its implementation is at gunpoint.

In Cuba, Castro dictated laws imposing the changes. Here in America indirect measures disguised as laws to protect the environment, the people's health and the like will impose the changes. For example, Cubans are prohibited to fish to supplement their meager sources of food. Here in America they will pass laws prohibiting fishing on rivers and lakes under the pretext of protecting the rivers and lakes from pollution and the fish from extinction.

In Cuba free access to the Internet was prohibited, without requiring any explanation from the government. Here it would be prohibited under the pretext of national security and to protect the country against terrorist cyber attacks.

In Cuba Castro successfully confiscated all guns in private hands, disarming the citizens and guaranteeing his full totalitarian control over the Cuban people. But Americans are not Cubans. As soon as Obama's victory was announced hundreds of thousands American citizens ran to the gun stores to prepare themselves for the coming war against the federal government.

They ignore, however, that they already have been under attack for many years, not from a conventional but from a psychological war. Unfortunately, most

Americans are not prepared to fight this type of war. Therefore, guns will be banned thanks to Obamacare under the excuse that they pose a health risk.

In his book *Brotherhood of Darkness*,[23] Dr. Stanley Montieth has quoted three concepts that are essential to understand the problem the American people currently face. The first concept is: "An understanding of the forces that have shaped the events of the twentieth century is predicated not on facts to be learned, but rather on secrets to be discovered" The second concept is: "Men and women become accomplices to those evil they fail to oppose." The third concept is: "The price that good people pay for their apathy and indifference to public affairs is that they are ruled by evil men."[24]

The ignorance of these concepts may well make the difference between freedom and slavery in America. Ignore them at your own risk.

PSYWAR and Mind Viruses

The main type of weapon the CFR conspirators have used in this PSYWAR against the American people is the meme. Memes are powerful ideas that take control over your mind. While some of them are good, some of them are bad.

British author Richard Dawkins introduced the concept of "meme" (pronounced like "gene") in his 1976 book *The Selfish Gene*.[25] According to Dawkins, ideas propagate the same way as viruses do. Consequently, memes are sort of viruses of the mind, which propagate highly contagious diseases in the form of ideas —not necessarily bad. Examples of malignant memes —not provided by Dawkins, who is a "progressive" liberal believer in Darwinism— are Nazism, Communism, Darwinism, New Age, eugenics, gun control and global warming. Moreover, as Dawkins pointed out, memes do not need to be true to be powerful.

The U.S. military has its bacteriological warfare labs, like the one in Fort Detrick, Maryland, fully devoted to the production of lethal viruses. In the same fashion, the CFR conspirators have their psychological warfare labs, like the Tavistock Institute, the Stanford Research Institute, the RAND Corporation and the Hudson Institute, where they create mind viruses in the form of malignant memes.

Therefore, if memes act like viruses, and the two main ways to avoid being contaminated by viruses are immunization and isolation, these prophylactic measures can be applied to memes as well. The best vaccination against malignant memes is to read, watch and listen critically. If you feel yourself agreeing hundred percent with everything a talk radio host, journalist or author says or writes, that is a sure symptom that you have been contaminated by mind viruses.

The other proven and effective way to avoid contagion is isolation. Viruses are usually transmitted by carriers called vectors. A vector is any animal capable of transmitting the causative agent of human disease. Most common vectors are flies, mosquitoes, fleas, ticks mites, rats and bats.

The main vectors involved in the transmission of the malignant memes created in the conspirators' think tanks are the mainstream media, schools —particularly government schools, the ones disingenuously called "public schools—, universities, churches, and political parties.

As I mentioned at the beginning of this book, like Ninja assassins, the main weapon used by the conspirators to commit their crimes with impunity has been their invisibility. Therefore, in order to win this battle of the mind we need to become shadow warriors ourselves by becoming invisible to our enemies. Given the conspirators' ability to infiltrate large organizations, the best defensive tactic is to create a multitude of small cells they cannot penetrate.

This type of small cell already exists: it is called your family, and its headquarters is your home. This is the only organization the conspirators cannot fully infiltrate and control. They know it, and this explains their concerted efforts to destroy the family as a social unit.

In the case of education, the only sure way to avoid contagion is by not sending your children to government schools. Given the fact, however, that even private schools can be — and actually most of them already are— contaminated, the only true solution is home schooling. But even the most drastic measure, no schooling at all, is much better than sending your children to public schools.

In relation to churches, if you discover that your pastor or priest has become an agent for big government disinformation,[26] stop going to church and worship at home. Even better, create a small church at home and invite a few friends and neighbors to join you by attending your religious services.

The two main political parties have been infiltrated and currently are under the full control of the CFR conspirators. Creating a new party or organization would not help, because eventually the conspirators would manage to infiltrate it the way they have already infiltrated the Tea Party movement.

Even the best and well-intentioned candidates running for the Republican or Democratic Party are not good, because, if elected, they will be neutralized by the party's machinery or co-opted by the conspirators. Moreover, by giving your vote to a Republican or Democratic candidate you are helping to legitimize a corrupt, illegitimate organization. Consequently, the best solution is to create an organization they can't penetrate. It is called the "no party at all." Become an independent, and give your vote only to independent candidates.

In the case of the mainstream media, the best solution is to stop reading mainstream newspapers and magazines and getting rid of the idiot box as well. That is exactly what I did about eighteen years ago, when I reached the conclusion that it was much better to be non-informed than disinformed, and I am extremely pleased with the results.[27]

In the case of the printed mainstream press, I mean not reading it daily. I usually read some of the press when it is several weeks old and it has lost most of its brainwashing power. For example, if I had read the article "Carbon's New Math," about the grave dangers of global warming, when it was published in the October 2007 issue of *National Geographic* magazine,[28] I would have been scared to death. But when I read it a few weeks ago after I bought the magazine for 25 cents at a Salvation Army store, it made me laugh. After the passage of time, an article like this becomes history instead of news; it loses most of its manipulative, brainwashing impact, and you see it as what it really is: pure unscientific, manipulative propaganda.

Contrary to the mainstream media, the web is an excellent source of non-manipulated information —provided you know how to use it. In the first place because, due to its inherent characteristics, the Internet is like a Hydra with innumerable heads the conspirators cannot control. The Internet is an offshoot of the Arpanet, a military communications decentralized nodular network designed to survive a full-scale nuclear attack on the U.S. Consequently, after the conspirators concluded that they cannot control the Internet, they will try to find a way to eliminate it.[29] Therefore, let's enjoy it while we can.

Another reason why the Web is a good source of information is because, contrary to the traditional media, you have the capability to actively interact with it. It loses its effectiveness, though, if you don't read it critically or read it passively like a printed newspaper or magazine.

The Internet broke the conspirators' monopolistic iron grip over the media. Successes of grassroots organizations like the 9/11 Truth, Ron Paul's Campaign for Liberty, and the Tea Party movement have been made possible only because of the Internet. It has also enormously accelerated the dissemination of information. After more than half a century of the Pearl Harbor events, still most Americans believe the official lie. Thanks to the Internet, however, just less than ten years after the 9/11 false flag operation took place, about a hundred million Americans don't believe the cock-and-bull story given by the government as an explanation.

Now, if you cannot live without sending your children to school, listening to your brainwashing pastor or talk radio disinformers, watching TV, and reading the mainstream press, then you deserve to live as a medieval serf under the boot of the New World Order masters. Ultimately, people have the governments they deserve. Unfortunately, when people realize that the only thing left is to vote with their feet it is always too late.

So, is everything lost? Have we lost this psychological war against us? Surprisingly, we have not. Actually, we have a fair possibility of winning it —provided we discover who the true enemy is, where the attack is coming from, and how to counterattack in kind. The reason for my confidence in our victory is because there are indications that the conspirators are scared.

We must keep in mind that, contrary to professional revolutionaries like Lenin, Hitler, Mao or Castro, most of the conspirators at the CFR's inner core are physical cowards, who have never fought in the wars they have artificially created. Even more important, despite all their power and money the conspirators are not all-powerful gods.

Granted, the conspirators are very strong, but they are not so strong that all resistance is futile. Their plans are not perfect and sometimes fail miserably. As political analyst Adrian Salbuchi rightly pointed out,

> They have many weak points: internal dissent, serious miscalculations, omissions, mistakes, errors, oversights, sloth, ignorance, at times stupidity, pride that always comes before the fall. At times they often seem to shoot themselves on the foot.[30]

For example, Obama's health care plan —whose main purpose is creating a Nazi-like, CFR-controlled army of thugs to oppose American patriots— failed miserably as a Hegelian PSYOP. Its antithesis was an artificially created flu epidemic that was going to be used to terrorize the American public into accepting the health plan as the lesser of two evils. The main reason why the PSYOP failed was because a large part of the American people never believed the threat. Many of them even refused to take the vaccines that allegedly were going to save them from certain death.

The Global warming PSYOP has also failed miserably. It is becoming obvious that Gaia betrayed the conspirators. Their failure is the direct result of plain stupidity. If, instead of global warming, they had focused their campaign since the very beginning on climate change, that would have fooled us, because it is evident that, like always, we are approaching a big global climate change, though not caused by human activity. Nevertheless, they made the mistake of believing their own lies, and got caught in their own trap.

The fact that the conspirators' plans are failing, and that they are scared of the growing dissidence among their ranks —the rats are the first ones to escape from a sinking ship— was acknowledged by none other than Zbigniew Brzezinski. Speaking at a recent Council on Foreign Relations meeting in Montreal, he warned that a "global political awakening," in combination with infighting amongst the elite, was threatening to derail the move towards a one-world government.[31]

The lesson we can learn about this people's victory is that the best way to fight a mind war is by refusing to let the enemy's memes get control of your mind. Still, no war has ever been won on the defensive. In order to win, you have to attack the enemy with all you have.

How can we do it? We the people need to become vectors in the dissemination of true information to counteract the conspirator's malignant memes.

As I have shown above, it is very simple and anybody can do it. The only requirement is the will to live as free men.

Patrick Henry's most often quoted line is "give me liberty or give me death." Actually, people who value life more than liberty *are* already slaves. If we need to face hard times, we will do it, but in our own terms, as free men, not as slaves on terms dictated by the NWO conspirators.

The current artificially created economic crisis, which is just beginning and will develop into the Greatest Depression, is the direct result of the fact that Americans don't consume enough. And they don't consume enough because they don't make enough money. And they don't make enough money because they don't have good-paying jobs. And they have lost their jobs because the CFR-controlled transnational corporations have moved the jobs abroad to increase their profits and destroy America. And CFR agents infiltrated in the mainstream press and both the Republican and Democratic parties sold the whole scheme to the gullible American people under the pretext of "free trade."[32] As I have mentioned several times above in this book, America is a country betrayed by its ruling class.

But we should not blame the Wall Street bankers or the transnational corporations for this disastrous state of things. There is no law forcing us to buy here in America the products they make abroad. Every time you buy a cheap product made in China at COSTCO, Wallmart or any other of the big corporate stores to save a few bucks, you are hammering another nail in America's coffin.

Usually, revolutions are carried out by small groups of well-armed people who decisively impose their will at gunpoint upon a majority of unarmed people. If the American people fail to stop the CFR conspirators, it will be the first case in the history of mankind that a group of unarmed cowards conquer and enslave a large majority of armed warriors.

Therefore, if America disappears as a sovereign country, we are the only ones to blame. People have the governments they deserve. The ball is now in our court. Either we hit it back and refuse to become the conspirators' serfs, or lower our heads and accept the yoke.

Ronald Reagan's[33] first words when he met Soviet leader Mikhail Gorbachev in Geneva in 1987 were: "Let me tell you why we mistrust you and why we despise your system." If today, just 25 years later, a large portion of Americans mistrust their government and despise their leaders it is because the conspirators who control our government are trying to change America into a new Soviet Union.

President Ronald Reagan helped the Russian people to get their freedom back. We need another Ronald Reagan to help us recover our freedom.

In the late 19th century, Cuban patriots waged a successful war against Spain's tyranny. The Cuban soldiers, poorly dressed, most of them barefooted and lacking in armament and food, faced a powerful, well-trained army. The Cubans' weapon of choice in this asymmetrical war was the *machete*. However, few months after the war began, it was a common occurrence to see the heavily armed Spanish soldiers fleeing a *machete* charge conducted by Maj. Gen. Antonio Maceo and his courageous men.

Maceo's idea of freedom is revealed in his words, "You don't beg for your freedom. You win it with the cutting edge of your *machete*. Begging for rights is only proper of cowards, incapable of exerting them." Maceo knew it very well; he was a descendant of slaves.

People who value security more than freedom have already become slaves. Ultimately, slavery is a state of mind.[34]

Appendix I

A Chronology of Treason

Muchos pocos hacen un mucho.
[Mony a mickle maks a muckle.]
—Miguel de Cervantes, *Don Quixote.*

Behind every act of treason committed against the American people, there is always one or more members of the Council on Foreign Relations. Enumerating all these acts of treason would make this list too long, but just a minor cut to the fruit will reveal its rotten entrails.

- (1891) Cecil Rhodes establishes a secret society called the Circle of Initiates. Like most secret organizations, it had one individual or a very small group at the center.
- (1909) Lord Milner, an agent of the Rothschilds and main trustee of the Cecil Rhodes fortune, creates an outer circle to the Circle of Initiates. He names it the Association of Helpers, also called the Round Table Group.
- (1913) President Woodrow Wilson and his advisor, "Colonel" Edward Mandell House, illegally create the Federal Reserve Bank and the Internal Revenue Service. Both organizations are private corporations under the guise of U.S. Government institutions.
- (1919) The Round Table is later transformed by "Colonel" Edward Mandell House, John Maynard Keynes, Arnold Toynbee, John Foster Dulles and others into a publicly acknowledged, formal council know as the Institute of International Affairs.
- (1919) President Wilson, "Colonel" House," and a group of Wall Street, create the League of Nations, as a first step for the establishment of a world government. The U.S. Senate refuses to approve the League, and it crumbles.
- (1921) The conspirators decide to break down the Institute of International Affairs into an American branch, the Council on Foreign Relations, and a British branch, the Royal Institute of International Affairs.
- (1922) The Council on Foreign Relations begins the publication of its official organ, the magazine *Foreign Affairs*. A few years after, the magazine becomes a sort of crystal ball, forecasting the direction where the U.S. and the world are heading.
- (1924) A panic in the Wall Street stock market, followed by a full crash, causes a severe economic crisis, later known as "The Great Depression." The crisis affects first the United States, and, soon after, Latin America and the whole industrialized world. Some people suspect that the bankers who own the Federal Reserve Bank artificially created the crisis.
- (1941) Secretary of War Henry Stimson (CFR) tells President Roosevelt (CFR) to maneuver the Japanese to fire the first shot so they look as the aggressors. Then Roosevelt uses the Pearl Harbor attack as a pretext to push the American people into war in Europe and Asia.
- (1942-1945) While American soldiers are dying in Europe fighting Nazi Germany,

Prescott Bush (CFR), Henry Ford (CFR), Nelson Rockefeller (CFR), and Allen Dulles (CFR), keep cutting business deals with German corporations, helping that way the Nazi war machine.

- (1945) The U.S. delegation to the San Francisco Conference, where the creation of the United Nations Organization is discussed, includes 47 CFR members, among them Adlai Stevenson, John Foster Dulles, Nelson Rockefeller, and Alger Hiss. The Charter of the U.N.O. they approved had been previously written at the Harold Pratt House in Manhattan, headquarters of the Council on Foreign Relations.
- (1945) Following advice from Secretary of State Edward Stettinius (CFR), Secretary of War Henry Stimson (CFR), and General George Marshall (CFR), President Truman (not a CFR member) orders dropping atomic bombs on Hiroshima and Nagasaki. Nagasaki, where no military installation was located, was the site of the largest Christian community in Japan.
- (1945) At the end of the war, the Rockefellers (CFR), with the help of their agent Allen Dulles (CFR), allow many Nazi officers (Eichmann, Mengele, Priebke, Kutschmann, etc.) to escape to America via Argentina, recruits ex-Nazi officers to work for the CIA and, through Operation PAPERCLIP, bring Nazi scientists to America.
- (1946) John D. Rockefeller, Jr. (CFR), donates a piece of land in Manhattan, appraised at $8.5 million dollars, for the construction of the UN building.
- (1947) Writing under the pseudonym "X," George Kennan (CFR) publishes an article in *Foreign Affairs*, explaining his theory of "containment." It means just containing the expansion of Soviet Communism, not fighting to destroy it. Immediately, President Truman makes Containment the core of his Truman Doctrine.
- (1947) President Truman signs a law creating the National Security Council and the Central Intelligence Agency.
- (1948) George Marshall (CFR) and Dean Acheson (CFR) press President Truman to stop providing military supplies to Chiang Kai-shek, thus allowing for the communist takeover of China.
- (1949) The American Committee on a United Europe is created. Gen. William Donovan (CFR) is its chairman; Allen Dulles (CFR) vice-chairman; George S. Franklin (CFR) secretary.
- (1949) Headed by Frank Wisner (CFR), Allen Dulles (CFR), and Richard Helms (CFR), the CIA begins Operation Mockingbird. Its goal is to recruit under the false flag of fighting communism American media news organizations and journalists as agents to disseminate disinformation. Some years later, the CIA admits having recruited more than 400 influential journalists and at least 25 organizations of the U.S. mainstream media.
- (1950) Testifying before the Senate Foreign Relations Committee on February 17, James Warburg (CFR), son of CFR founder Paul Warburg, prophesies: "We shall have world government whether or not you like it —by conquest or consent."
- (1950) Following the Containment doctrine, Dean Acheson (CFR) and Dean Rusk (CFR) arrange the no-win undeclared war in Korea and the removal of General Douglas McArthur. Gen. McArthur (not a CFR member) had a plan to win the war.
- (1950) Senator Joseph McCarthy exposes the treasonous activities of State Department officials Alger Hiss (CFR), and Owen Lattimore (CFR), accusing them of being Communists. He also accuses General George Marshall (CFR) of treason. President Eisenhower (CFR), Secretary of State Dean Acheson (CFR), and journalist Edward Murrow (CFR), join forces in defending the traitors

and vilifying McCarthy.

- (1953) Soviet Prime Minister Nikita Khrushchev declares his doctrine of peaceful coexistence, by which the fight between capitalism and communism must continue in the field of ideas but not in the military one. The fact causes consternation among the ranks of the American military-industrial complex and Wall Street bankers.
- (1956) J. Edgar Hoover, Director of the Federal Bureau of Investigations (FBI), receives hundreds of letters from concerned citizens and members of Congress, accusing the Council on Foreign Relations of treason and promoting communism through its agents infiltrated in the U.S. government. Hoover orders to begin an investigation. Soon after, President Eisenhower (CFR) dictates an order prohibiting the FBI to investigate federal government employees.
- (1957) Journalist Herbert Matthews (CFR) interviews Fidel Castro in Cuba's Sierra Maestra Mountains. In the interview, published in the *New York Times*, Matthews describes Castro as a Cuban Robin Hood, a tropical Simon Bolívar, and a lover of democracy and justice. The *New York Times'* Chairman of the Board was Arthur Hay Sulzberger (CFR), and the publisher Orvil Dryfoos (CFR).
- (1958) John Foster Dulles (CFR) and Allen Dulles (CFR), of the Eisenhower administration, betray Cuba's President Batista by confiscating arms he had bought and paid in advance to fight Castro's insurgency. The fact demoralizes the Cuban Army and allows for Castro to grab power in Cuba.
- (1958) While State Department official William Wieland (a protégé of CFR founder Sumner Welles) undermines President Batista's government, the CIA's chief of station in Havana and the American consul in Santiago de Cuba, also a CIA officer, provide Castro with plenty of money as well as weapons and ammo smuggled from the U.S. military base in Guantánamo.
- (1958) Following the advice of Secretary of State John Foster Dulles (CFR), and his brother, CIA director Allen Dulles (CFR), President Eisenhower (CFR) sends William Pawley (a close friend of Allen Dulles) to Havana. Pawley informs Batista that the U.S. no longer supports him, and suggests him to surrender power and leave the country.
- (1959) President Batista leaves Cuba on January 1st. Soon after, Castro assumes control of power over the island. Breaking with a long tradition, the U.S. is the first country to recognize the new government.
- (1959) Castro makes his first official visit to the U.S. During his visit, he gives a speech at the Harold Pratt House, headquarters of the Council on Foreign Relations. The event passes unreported by the American mainstream press.
- (1960) To the conspirators' surprise, millionaire Joseph P. Kennedy, with the help of his friends in the Chicago Mafia, buys thousands of votes and gets his son John F. Kennedy (not a CFR member) elected President of the United States.
- (1960) In his farewell speech, President Eisenhower alerts the nation about the existence of a military-industrial complex in the United States.
- (1960) On the 50th anniversary of the UN, Castro travels to New York, where he gives a long speech. Later he is the honor guest of a reception at the Rockefellers mansion in Manhattan. To avoid a confrontation with people who protest in front of the mansion, the event is moved to the Harold Pratt House, headquarters of the CFR. There, Castro has a long and friendly private exchange with David Rockefeller (CFR) and other Wall Street bankers.
- (1960) The French freighter *La Coubre*, loaded with arms, ammo and explosives, explodes in Havana's harbor. The mysterious explosion kills several people. The next day Castro goes on TV and accuses the U.S., and specifically the

CIA, of terrorism. Then, he dictates some antiterrorist measures, including the elimination of habeas corpus and other rights guaranteed by the Cuban Constitution. He also orders to create the Ministry of State Security and the Committees for the Defense of the Revolution —a national red of informers in every city block.

- (1960) President Kennedy inherits from Eisenhower a plan for an invasion of Cuba by anti-Castro exiles. The designated landing point is the city of Trinidad.
- (1961) Following the advice of McGeorge Bundy (CFR), Adlai Stevenson (CFR), and John McCloy (CFR), President Kennedy orders a change in the invasion's landing point. On April 4, CIA's Richard Bissell (CFR) outlines an alternative plan for the invasion, with the Bay of Pigs, instead of Trinidad as the landing place. Surrounded by swamps, the Bay of Pigs was a mousetrap.
- (1961) On April 16, McGeorge Bundy (CFR), Dean Rusk (CFR), and Adlai Stevenson (CFR), persuade President Kennedy to cancel the rest of the planned air strikes previous to the invasion. As a result, Castro's fighter planes shoot down the invaders' planes and sink their ships, thus guaranteeing that the Bay of Pigs invasion fails. The failure of the Bay of Pigs invasion consolidates the Cuban tyrant in power.
- (1961) As a result of the Bay of Pigs debacle, President Kennedy fires CIA director Allen Dulles (CFR), and appoints John MacCone (CFR) as CIA Director. Kennedy tells some close friends he wants to "splinter the CIA into a thousand pieces and scatter it to the wind."
- (1962) In his book *The Fourth Floor*, former U.S. Ambassador to Cuba Earl T. Smith (not a CFR member), exposes how a group of State Department officers, particularly William Wieland and Roy Rubbotton, conspired to bring Castro to power in Cuba.
- (1962) General Lyman Lemnitzer (CFR) creates Operation Northwods, which contemplates the killing of Cuban and American citizens, allegedly as a pretext to begin military operations against Cuba.
- (1962) President Kennedy ignores the advice of several senior military officers, (none of them CFR members), and refuses to seize the opportunity provided by the missile crisis to invade the island and get rid of Castro. The fact creates discomfort among the military.
- (1963) President Kennedy signs Executive Order 11110, returning to the U.S. Treasury the power to print currency independently of the Federal Reserve Bank. Four billion dollars in U.S. Treasury notes are printed, and they have just begun to circulate when Kennedy is assassinated. The first thing President Johnson does after he is sworn into office is to recall the bills and destroy them.
- (1963) A whitewashing commission is created to investigate President Kennedy's assassination. Four of its seven members, Allen Dulles, John McCloy, John Sherman Cooper and Gerald Ford, are CFR members. The Commission concludes that Oswald was the assassin, and he acted alone. However, a large majority of the American public is convinced that Kennedy was the victim of a government conspiracy.
- (1964) October. Two years after the end of the missile crisis, Nelson Rockefeller (CFR, Trilateral), visits the Soviet Union and has a secret meeting with Soviet Premier Nikita Khrushchev. On October 15, less than a week after Rockefeller leaves the country, Khrushchev is deposed.
- (1964) Robert McNamara (CFR), and Dean Rusk (CFR), invent the Gulf of Tonkin incident, claiming that North Vietnamese PTs attacked the destroyers *Maddox* and *Turner Joy*. The attack never happened, but it gives Johnson the pretext

to escalate the war that eventually cost the lives of thousands of Americans.

- (1965) Dean Rusk (CFR), Robert McNamara (CFR), and Henry Cabot Lodge (CFR), push the U.S. fully into the Vietnam conflict—and then draw up rules tying American soldiers' hands to their backs, making victory impossible.
- (1966) In a speech at the closing session of the Tricontinental Conference in Havana, Castro proclaims the Second Havana Declaration. The main thesis of the Declaration, which is a call for violent revolution in the world, is a direct criticism to Khrushchev's doctrine of peaceful coexistence.
- (1967) In the closing address to the First Latin American Conference of Solidarity (OLAS), Castro delineates Cuba's new internationalist (globalist) foreign policy.
- (1968) On January 8, as part of a Discussion Group on Intelligence and Foreign Policy, senior CIA officer Richard Bissell (CFR) gives a secret lecture on "covert action" at the Harold Pratt House. Among the participants are Douglas Dillon (CFR), Thomas Hugues (CFR), Joseph Kraft (CFR), Robert Amory (CFR), Allen Dulles (CFR), Theodore Sorensen (CFR), and thirteen other senior CFR members.
- (1968) Richard Nixon (CFR) and his National Security Advisor Henry Kissinger (CFR) continue their treacherous policies, which lead to the Communist takeover of South Vietnam, Cambodia, and Laos.
- (1970) Harvard Professor Zbigniew Brzezinski (CFR) writes *Between Two Ages*. The book shows that Brzezinski's thinking closely parallels that of CFR founder "Colonel" Edward Mandell House. David Rockefeller loves the book so much that he offers Brzezinski the direction of his new pet project: the Trilateral Commission.
- (1970) The newly created Trilateral Commission publishes a report that recommends that, in order for "globalization" to succeed, American manufacturing jobs have to be sent abroad and American workers' wages have to decline.
- (1971) The CFR conspirators realize that the war they created in Vietnam has become a liability. So, they use Daniel Ellsberg (CFR), to bring the Pentagon Papers to the CFR-controlled *New York Times*. The publication of *The Pentagon Papers* helps create strong anti-war feelings among the American people.
- (1974) Henry Kissinger (CFR) writes National Security Study Memorandum 200. It delineates a genocidal policy of depopulating much of the African continent, to allow U.S. transnational corporations, not Africans, exploit the continent's natural resources.
- (1975) More than 40,000 of Castro's troops invade Angola. Other African countries falling under the control of Castro's troops are Ethiopia, Congo, and Guinea-Bissau. Thousands of Africans die as the result of Castro's military intervention.
- (1975) November 24. In an official statement, the United States acknowledges for the first time the presence of Cuban troops in Angola. Soon after, U.S. Ambassador to the UN Andrew Young (CFR) declares that the Castroite troops are a stabilizing force in Africa.
- (1976) January. During a short visit to Venezuela, Henry Kissinger tells President Carlos Andrés Pérez in a private conversation: "Our intelligence services have grown so bad that we only found out that Cubans were being sent to Angola after they were already there."
- (1976) CFR agents inside the U.S. State Department pass the Clark Amendment, named after Senator Dick Clark (CFR). The Amendment forbids the U.S. to give any help to Jonas Savimbi's UNITA group in its fight against the Castroite troops.
- (1977) A few months after the Castroite troops gain control of Angola, the country becomes one of the main commercial partners of the U.S. in Africa. 95 per-

cent of Angola's oil is exported to the West. Half of the production of the Gulf Oil in Angola ends up in American refineries. The consortium De Beers controls the diamond mines.

- (1979) On October 12th, Fidel Castro gives a speech at the UN 34th General Assembly, in which he calls for a "New World Order."
- (1979) Following the advise of Zbigniew Brzezinski (CFR, Trilateral)), Cyrus Vance (CFR), and Warren Christopher (CFR), Jimmy Carter (CFR, Trilateral) undermines U.S. allies in Iran and Nicaragua.
- (1981) Under President Reagan (not a CFR member), George Schultz (CFR), William J. Casey (CFR), and Malcom Baldridge (CFR), arrange U.S. foreign aid to communist Romania, communist Poland, and the USSR; they also obstruct the fight of anti-Communists in El Salvador.
- (1985) Several Latin American countries default on their payments of the interests of their debts to Wall Street banks. As a result, a devastating economic crisis erupts in most of Latin America. Castro suggests a bailout of the banks.
- (1986) President George H.W. Bush authorizes American companies to provide Saddam Hussein with samples of anthrax and botulinum, allegedly for medical research.
- (1986) Culminating a deal initiated by ex-President Jimmy Carter (CFR, Trilateral), President Bill Clinton (CFR, Trilateral), gives North Korea $5 billion worth of oil, and authorizes American companies to give the Kim Jong regime two nuclear reactors and $2 billion to develop them —allegedly for non-military use.
- (1990) In an *Atlantic Montly* article of September 1990, "The Roots of Muslim Rage," Bernard Lewis (CFR) coins the term "clash of civilizations."
- (1990) Incited by the U.S. Government, Sadam Hussein launches a military attack against Kuwait, giving President George H.W. Bush (CFR) the pretext for the Gulf War.
- (1990) On September 11th, President George H.W. Bush (CFR) delivers a speech to the Congress, titled "Toward a New World Order."
- (1990) During a recess in the meetings at the World Economic Forum, in Davos, Switzerland, millionaire Maurice Strong (CFR, Trilateral) declares that the goal of a group of billionaires like him is the collapse of industrial civilization. Then, Strong gives his own depiction of a sustainable society under the coming New World Order. It is very similar to Cuba after 55 years under Castro's rule.
- (1991) The CFR's Annual Report affirms: "Obviously, the stage is being set —in Europe, in the Soviet Union, in the Middle East, and elsewhere— for a new world order."
- (1992) The Head of the Earth Summit, Maurice Strong (CFR, Trilateral) declares in Rio de Janeiro that the only hope for the planet is the collapse of industrial civilization.
- (1993) On May 4, CFR president Leslie Gelb declares "the Council can find, nurture and begin to put people in the kinds of jobs this country needs. And that's going to be one of the major enterprises of the Council under me."
- (1993) Writing in the Los Angeles Times about the U.S. Congress approval of the NAFTA agreement, Henry Kissinger (CFR) states: "What Congress will have before it is not a conventional trade agreement but the architecture of a new international system . . . a first step toward a new world order."
- (1993) The Summer issue of CFR's organ *Foreign Affairs* publishes an article by Professor Samuel P. Huntington (CFR), warning about the coming clash of civilizations, particularly between the Judeo-Christian and Muslim worlds.

- (1996) The subject "Threat of Islamic Fundamentalists" is discussed in one of the meetings of the World Economic Forum in Davos, Switzerland.
- (1997) Zbigniew Brzezinski (CFR, Trilateral), writes *The Grand Chessboard*, a book in which he warns about the coming terrorist threat. He cites a historical example of why a catastrophic event is needed to galvanize Americans against terrorism: "The public supported America's engagement in World War II largely because of the shock effect of the Japanese attack on Pearl Harbor."
- (1997) A group of so-called "neo-cons," among them Richard Cheney (CFR), Paul Wolfowitz (CFR), Norman Podhoretz (CFR), Richard Perle (CFR), Lewis "Scooter" Libby (CFR), John Bolton (CFR), Elliot Abrams (CFR), and Robert Kagan (CFR), create the Project for a New American Century, which promotes a new era of American imperialism. In one of their initial documents they mention the need of a Pearl Harbor-like catastrophic, catalyzing event to galvanize public opinion in support of their plans.
- (1999) Henry Kissinger (CFR), Ellsworth Bunker (CFR), and Sol Linowitz (CFR), arrange for the Panama Canal giveaway —and give $400 million dollars to the Chinese totalitarian dictatorship to take it.
- (1999) Following orders from President Clinton (CFR, Trilateral), and with the support of Secretary of State Madeleine Albright (CFR), Gen. Wesley Clark (CFR) sends NATO troops to invade Kosovo, allowing the killings of hundreds of Serbian Christians by Muslims. The war directly benefits the Kosovo Liberation Army, a Muslim terrorist group with ties to Osama bin Laden.
- (2001) A delegation of Wall Street bankers, presided by David Rockefeller (CFR, Trilateral), visits Cuba, where they have a long meeting with Fidel Castro. After the meeting, CFR director Peter Peterson makes comments to the press in which he praises Castro for the high levels of education and public health in Cuba. And he adds: "I believe that Cuba is one of the best educated countries in the Western Hemisphere."
- (2001) A CFR study commission produces a report entitled "U.S.-Cuban Relations in the 21st Century: A Follow Up Report." The document is a frenzied, desperate attempt to save the collapsing Castroite regime and maintain Castroism after Castro. It is approved despite strong complaints by some of the commission members, who refuse to sign it.
- (2001) In visits to Cuba, World Bank President James Wolfensohn (CFR), and UN Secretary General Kofi Annan, express their conviction that Castro's Cuba is an example to follow.
- (2001) September 11. President George W. Bush (CFR) and his close advisors, among them Vice-president Richard Cheney (CFR), and Secretary of State Condoleezza Rice (CFR), allow the September 11th attacks to happen. Then, Bush declares a long war on terrorism. Soon after, he creates the Office of Homeland Security and dictates new laws canceling habeas corpus and several other constitutional rights.
- (2002) President George W. Bush (CFR) appoints Henry Kissinger (CFR), to chair a Commission to investigate the failure to detect and stop the 9/11 attacks. Faced with widespread negative reaction, Kissinger declines. Finally, Bush appoints a new Commission, chaired by Thomas Kean (CFR), with Lee Hamilton (CFR) as vice chair, and members Jaime Gorelick (CFR) and Philip Zelikov (CFR). The Commission produces a whitewash report in which everything is explained as the result of honest mistakes and lack of interagency communication.
- (2002) Thanks to the new NAFTA free trade agreements, the transnational agribusiness

Archer Daniels Midland (CFR corporate member) exports to Mexico a yearly average of 6 million tons of corn, most of it genetically modified. This unfair competition throws thousands of Mexican small farmers into poverty.

- (2002) Ben Bernanke, the new President of the Federal Reserve Bank, admits that the Bank artificially created the Great Depression of 1929 –1934.
- (2003) Under false pretenses, President George W. Bush (CFR) orders the invasion of Iraq. Kissinger's (CFR) protégé, Paul Bremer (CFR), is appointed first colonial administrator of the country. Then, closely following the Korea and Vietnam cases, Bush draws up rules tying American soldiers' hands in their backs, thus making victory impossible. Very soon after, Iraq becomes a Vietnam-type quagmire.
- (2004) The Venezuelan people call for a referendum to recall Hugo Chávez. Ex-President Jimmy Carter (CFR, Trilateral) offers his help to oversee the voting. Despite widespread cheating, Carter gives his approval to the election, legitimizing Chávez and consolidating him in power.
- (2004) President George W. Bush (CFR) opens the southern border of the U.S. to a veritable invasion of Mexican workers. The poor illegal immigrants, whose only intention is finding a way to a better living through hard work, ignore that they are pawns in a secret CFR plan to destroy the sovereignty, as well as the economy, of both Mexico and the United States.
- (2005) The leaders of the governments of Mexico, the United States and Canada meet again to reinforce the Security and Prosperity Partnership of North America agreement. The focus on their agenda is the erasing of national borders.
- (2005) A CFR Study Commission, which includes William Weld (CFR), Doris Meissner (CFR), and Robert Pastor (CFR), produces a document entitled "Building a North American Community." It details a 5-year plan for the establishment of a common security perimeter around Canada, the United States, and Mexico, and the eventual fusion of the three countries into a single one, the North American Union, with a common currency, the Amero.
- (2006) The Iraq Study Group, co-chaired by former secretary of state James Baker (CFR) and former congressman Lee Hamilton (CFR), is created. Its purpose is "to conduct a forward-looking, independent assessment of the current and prospective situation on the ground in Iraq." Other members of the Iraq Study Group include: Lawrence Eagleburger (CFR), Vernon Jordan (CFR), Sandra O'Connor (CFR), William Perry (CFR), and Charles Robb (CFR)
- (2006) President Bush (CFR) appoints Robert Gates (CFR) to substitute Donald Rumsfeld (CFR) as Secretary of defense.
- (2006) Lawrence Eagleburger (CFR) replaces Robert Gates (CFR) as a co-chair of the Iraq Study Group.
- (2007) In a CFR-sponsored online debate, Michael Levi (CFR) and Graham Allison (CFR) discuss the possibility of a detonation of a nuclear device in a major American city.
- (2008) Zbigniew Brzezinski's protégé Barack Obama becomes president of the United States. Soon after, he appoints dozens of CFR members to occupy key positions in his administration.
- (2009) Senators John Rockefeller (CFR) and Olympia Snowe (CFR), introduce the Cybersecutiry Act of 2009, that would give the President the power to control the Internet.
- (2010) May. Some of the most notorious members of the "billionaires club" — CFR members David Rockefeller, Bill Gates, George Soros, Patty Stonesifer, Peter G. Peterson and Michael Bloomberg — join Oprah Winfrey, Ted

Turner, Warren Buffet and other eugenicists in a secret meeting where they discuss the most efficient ways to eliminate one billion human beings.

- (2010) Senators Joe Lieberman (CFR) and Jay Rockefeller (CFR), push to pass the Protecting the Cyberspace as a National Asset Act, a law that would give the federal government the power to shut down the Internet.
- (2010) Between 12 and 30 million Mexican illegals have invaded the country and now reside in the U.S. Mexican radical revolutionary groups such as the National Council of La Raza are openly calling for the "reconquista" of the Southwestern United States. La Raza's director, Raul H. Yzaguirre, is a secret CFR agent.
- (2010) June 3-6. The Bilderberger Group meet in Sitges, Spain, to assess the implementation of the globalists' plans for the creation of a New World Order. The list of American attendees include Bill Gates, Roger Altman, Martin Feldstein, Philip Gordon, Richard Holbrooke, Henry Kissinger, Craig Mundie, Peter Orszag, Charlie Rose, Robert Rubin, James Steinberg, and Paul Volcker, all of them CFR agents.

(2010) August. The CFR-controlled Bill and Melinda Gates Foundation gives a $6.5 million grant to the National Council of La Raza.

Since the end of WWII, the number of CFR members in key government positions has been growing continuously. In the last 50 years, most U.S. Secretaries of State and CIA Directors have been CFR members. The number of senior members of the Armed forces that have CFR membership is growing. The most important people in the mainstream press are CFR members. CFR-controlled "philanthropic" foundations, like the Rockefeller, Ford, MacArthur and Carnegie, bankroll every anti-American group in this country, and many abroad.

Appendix II

The Evaluation of Information: Intelligence, the 9/11/2001 Events, and the Cuban Missile Crisis of 1962

According to the Joint Chiefs of Staff's *Dictionary of Military and Associated Terms*, *intelligence* is the final product resulting from the collection, processing, integration, analysis, and interpretation of available information.[1] So, even though the term intelligence comprises something much more complex, we may safely accept the shorter definition that intelligence is just information after it has been properly evaluated.

In its advisory report to the U.S. Government, the 1955 task force on Intelligence Activities of the second Herbert Hoover Commission stated that: "Intelligence deals with all the things which should be known in advance of initiating a course of action."[2] A true expert gave a similar definition more than 2000 years ago. According to Sun Tzu, "the reason why the enlightened prince and the wise general conquer the enemy whenever they move and their achievement surpass those of ordinary men is foreknowledge [intelligence]."[3]

Though the definition of intelligence is very simple and straightforward, most authors dealing with the subject confuse it. Some of them consistently use the terms information and intelligence as synonyms, when it is obvious that they are not. Others even have used the term "raw intelligence" as a synonym for information, but, as we will see below, contrary to information (which might contain misinformation and disinformation), intelligence is a very elaborated product; there is nothing raw in it. Now, how is information evaluated?

The evaluation of information, also known as appraisal or assessment, is the process by which a piece of information is analyzed in terms of credibility, reliability, pertinence and accuracy, in order to change it into intelligence. The evaluation of information is accomplished at several stages within the intelligence cycle[4] with progressively different contexts.

The evaluation or appraisal of a particular item of information is indicated by a conventional letter-number system.

Reliability of the Source	**Accuracy of the Information**
A Completely reliable	1 Confirmed by other reliable sources
B Usually reliable	2 Probably true
C Fairly reliable	3 Possibly true
D Not usually reliable	4 Doubtful
E Unreliable	5 Improbable
F Reliability cannot be judged	6 Accuracy cannot be judged

The evaluation simultaneously takes into consideration both the reliability of the source based on its previous performance, and the credibility of the information itself. The process involves a check against intelligence already in hand and an educated guess as to the accuracy of the new information based on how well it dovetails with previous intelligence.[5] Though independent, the two aspects cannot be totally separated from each other. The authoritativeness of the source, which may not necessarily coincide with its reliability, can never be ignored, though it is sometimes overrated in the light of the credibility of the information — something that has to do with the expectations of the people involved in the evaluation process. But people, including intelligence analysts, tend to believe what they suspect or expect to be true, or what better fits their personal needs, so there is always an element of bias in any evaluation of information.

It must be emphasized that both evaluations must be entirely independent of each other, and they are indicated in accordance with the system shown above. Thus, information judged to be "probably true" received from a source considered to be "usually reliable" is designated as "B2."

One must keep in mind that the question of what is authoritative and what is not is very relative. A highly authoritative source may produce credible information, but the intelligence officer must always ask himself the question "Why?" The higher the authoritativeness of the source, the higher the possibility that it may be biased or had been compromised and, therefore, the higher the danger of disinformation. Highly authoritative sources from totalitarian governments may not always tell the truth, to say the least, but highly authoritative sources from democratic countries may not be very reliable either. There is evidence that the CIA has been involved in recruiting scholars at the most prestigious American universities, and journalists in the most influential American media. Also, there is suspicion that the KGB, the Mossad, and even the Cuban intelligence services, among others, have done a good job penetrating American universities and media.

From the point of view of intelligence and espionage, a stolen document is often more valuable than a gratuitously conveyed secret one from whatever source, since it diminishes, though not totally eliminates, the risk of deliberately misleading information. The "why?" however, applies not only to the danger of planted disinformation. It must also be asked about the source, even of one whose *bona fides* is beyond question. The danger here is of an intelligence service believing what it wants to believe —a problem that has affected all the world's intelligence services at one time or another. The problem of the bias of the evaluator is one that is unavoidable in intelligence; it extends even to information of fullest credibility from the most reliable sources.

Bias in evaluation can never be fully eliminated in an intelligence service and, more importantly, in high government circles. Moreover, creating evaluators to evaluate the evaluators can only compound it. Within the intelligence establishment, the only effective safeguard lies in the individual competence and quality of its members. Even more important is their intellectual honesty and personal courage to face pressures from above.

One must always bear in mind that no source can ever be regarded as infallible and no single bit of information can ever be regarded as totally accurate. Whatever the case, the chances for error, misinterpretation, misunderstanding and deceit are too high to blindly trust any information.

Super patriots, doctrinaire partisans, court historians, bureaucratic climbers, people of provincial outlook, enemy moles —all of them are potential dangers to sound information evaluation. Perspective, perspicacity, worldliness, a soundly philosophical outlook, the knowledge and sense of history, and perhaps a bit of skepticism and a sense of humor — these are the qualities of an intelligence analyst that minimize error in the interpretation and evaluation of information.

The 9/11, 2001, Events

All the initial information the American people received about the 9/11 events came from a single source: the American government. With the single exception of Congresswoman Cynthia MacKinney, who since the very beginning questioned the U.S. Government's version of the events, nobody in the two branches of the Repucratic Party questioned it. The American mainstream media as a whole accepted the Government's version of the events and became an obedient mouthpiece parroting it over and over *ad nauseam*. Actually, the only dissenting source of information about 9/11 has been the Internet and books published by minor independent presses.

However, the U.S. Government, like all governments around the world, is made out of politicians, and politicians have never been a source of truthful information.[6] Moreover, the current U.S. Government is fully under the control of the CFR conspirators, whose goal is to destroy the US and implement a totalitarian New World Order. Consequently, I will qualify the only source of the 9/11 information, that is, secret CFR agents in the US Government, with a D: Not usually reliable.

Now I will take a look at the accuracy of the information itself.

Probably the main characteristic of truthful information is that in the past similar information has proved to be true. Of course, there is a first time for everything, and the fact that a similar event has never happened prior to the present one is no sure indication that it cannot happen. But, in the analysis of historical events, we have the added advantage that we can add to the evaluation of the information the occurrence of similar events in which the information has proved to be true or not, *after* the one in question.

Consequently, the evaluation of the information itself in the case of historical events is a process involving a check against intelligence already in hand about similar events before and after the event in question. It also involves an educated guess as to the accuracy of the information related to the event based on how well it fits with this intelligence.

In the case of the 9/11 events, the evidence shows that, first, never before or after 9/11/2001, has a skyscraper with a steel structure collapsed due to a fire. Secondly, never before or after 9/11/2001, a skyscraper has collapsed on its own footprint except as the result of controlled demolition. This is why companies who do controlled demolition are paid large amounts of money to do their job.

If buildings, particularly buildings with a steel structure, could usually fall on their own footprint when demolished, these companies would be superfluous — but they are not. But CFR agents in the U.S. Government want us to believe that, exceptionally, on September 11 2001, not one, or two, but three skyscrapers with steel structure collapsed on their own footprint as the result of fires.

Therefore, extrapolating from other verifiable information, any serious intelligence analyst would conclude that the accuracy of the information itself provided by the CFR agents in the U.S. Government could be fairly qualified as a 5, that is, improbable.

Consequently, an intelligence appraisal of the 9/11 events will produce a D5: that is, source not usually reliable, accuracy of the information improbable. For the same reasons, based on the evaluation of the information about the 9/11 events provided by the CFR agents in the U.S. Government, any intelligence service in the world can easily decode it as a sloppy, disingenuous attempt to pass disinformation disguised as true intelligence.

Moreover, the fact that the 9/11 events served as a God-given pretext to carry out policies decided way in advance is a true index that perhaps it actually was not a God-given but a CFR-given one. As some conspirators' agents have shamelessly declared, never put a good crisis to waste —particularly an artificially created crisis.

The Cuban Missile Crisis of 1962

Similarly to the alleged CIA failure to anticipate the 9/11 events, much has been written about the CIA's failure to predict the deployment of Soviet strategic nuclear missiles on Cuban soil in 1962. This failure has been directly attributed to the CIA's September Estimate.

On several occasions, President Kennedy had asked the intelligence community for an evaluation of the Soviet military buildup in Cuba, but apparently no official within the government, probably with the exception of John McCone, had anticipated the Russian move. On each of the four times that the U.S. intelligence community emitted its National Intelligence Estimate,[7] with official reports on Cuba and the Caribbean, they had advised the President that the Russians would not make offensive weapons available to Castro. The last NIE, dated the 19th of September, just before the crisis erupted —the now notorious September Estimate— provided similar conclusions. Based on the appraisal of the information made by Sherman Kent and his analysts, the United States Intelligence Board (USIB) concluded without reservations that Soviet emplacement of offensive missiles in Cuba was highly unlikely.

Following the methodology to evaluate information I have described above, the estimate pointed out that the Soviet Union had not taken this kind of step with any of its satellites in the past. In fact, the Soviets had never placed strategic nuclear weapons outside its own territorial borders, not in the loyal Communist Eastern

Europeans nations, nor in communist China.[8] Both U.S. military and civil leaders had believed all along that the Soviet Union would never risk such action, especially after the repeated reassurances, both public and private, the Soviets had given them.[9]

However, just a few days after the estimate was issued, American U-2 planes took photos in which the CIA photo-interpreters found what they considered strong evidence of the presence of Soviet medium-range strategic nuclear missiles on Cuban soil. What went wrong?

Well, actually nothing went wrong.

The fact that never before, and never after the Cuban missile crisis the Soviets deployed nuclear missiles beyond their borders is a strong indication that the predictions of Sherman Kent and his analysts in their evaluation of the situation in Cuba was confirmed by the facts. They forecasted that the Soviets would never place nuclear missiles in Cuba, and they sure didn't. The only thing that would have proved the Estimate wrong would have been the actual proof of the presence of nuclear warheads in Cuba in 1962. This would have been the smoking gun. But, contrary to repeated unsubstantiated claims to the contrary, as of today, the presence of nuclear warheads in Cuba in 1962 has never been proved.[10]

And no smoking gun has ever been found for the simple reason that it was never there. Consequently, the September Estimate could not have been more accurate. Sherman Kent and the rest of the people at the USIB proved their worth to the American intelligence community.[11] Unfortunately, they didn't know that, by doing the right thing on behalf of the American people, they were damaging the interest of their (unknown) true masters, the CFR conspirators.

In a *post mortem* analysis of the alleged causes of the Estimate's "failure," Assistant Director for National Estimates Sherman Kent, Chairman of the Board of National Estimates, reluctantly admitted that they had come down on the wrong side. Yet, he could not restrain himself from pointing out what he considered the "incredible wrongness of the Soviet decision to put missiles in Cuba."[12] Of course, Kent was absolutely right in believing that, if Khrushchev actually did what he seemed to have done, he was dead wrong. Even more, something that perhaps Kent might have thought, but didn't put in writing, by doing what he apparently had done, the Soviet Premier would have proved to be a stupid, incompetent fool and a madman. However, as any book about the Soviet Premier can show, this was not the case. Nikita Khrushchev was a lot of things, some of them not pretty, but he was not a kook.

Now, an elementary rule of tradecraft states that when there is an unexpected, unexplainable change in the opponent's behavior, the first thing to suspect is deception.

According to the CIA's own prescribed tradecraft practices, as stated in the document *A compendium of Analytic Tradecraft Notes*,[13] there are warning signs to detect enemy deception which address the likelihood that a country or organization is engaged in a disinformation attempt. The first set of warnings has to do with the likelihood that a country may be engaged in an attempt to distort the analyst's perceptions: (I have added between brackets the known facts which prove that every single one of the six warning signs was present during the Cuban missile crisis and were later ignored by CFR agents at both the NSC and the CIA.)

1. **Means**. The country being assessed has the experience and means to undertake sophisticated deception operations. [*Maskirovka,* a common Soviet practice. During WWII, the Soviets had built a huge factory near the Ural Mountains fully devoted to the production of decoys and dummies.]

2. **Opportunity**: When the country is known to have knowledge of the periodicity and acuity of technical collection vehicles that pass over an area it wishes to protect, analysts have to be aware that the resultant information may be incomplete if not also deliberately distorted. [After studying Power's U-2 after it was shot down in the USSR, the Soviets knew about the plane's extraordinary capabilities for detection.]

3. **Motive**. A motive to deceive is believed to be present. [In the case of Khrushchev, his motive may have been his desire to get rid of the unreliable Castro. But he also may have wanted the Americans to do, unwittingly, the dirty job for him.]

The second set of warnings focuses on anomalies in the information available to the analysts. These warning signs include:

4. **Suspicious gaps in collection**. The analysts are not receiving the range and volume of information they would expect if there were no deliberate tampering with sources and collection platforms. [The US information collection activities on the Soviet Union stopped after Powers' U-2 plane was shot down.]

5. **Contradictions to a carefully researched pattern**. The new information does not match with the opponent's previously observed priorities and practices. [The Soviets never had deployed nuclear weapons beyond their borders.]

5. **Suspicious confirmation**. A new stream of information from clandestine sources or technical collection seems to reinforce the rationale for the action. [I.e., information provided by Penkovsky, a suspected Soviet plant, reinforced the alleged existence of nuclear missiles in Cuba.][14]

The author of the *Notes* was Jack Davis, a retired officer who spent 40 years as practitioner, teacher, and critic of intelligence analysis. Though the *Notes* were published in 1997, they summarized tradecraft practices that have been standard operating procedures in the CIA for many years, including during the Cuban missile crisis. Therefore, the gross failures in tradecraft by the CIA analysts, and the CIA officer's inability to detect the Soviets' deception efforts, cannot by any stretch of the imagination be attributed to "errors," but to a willful desire by CFR agents in the U.S. government to mislead president Kennedy.

It is difficult to explain why so many senior CIA officers committed such an obvious breach in their established tradecraft practices. Nevertheless, I have a theory, but explaining it would take too long and is beyond the scope of this book. Therefore, if you want to know it you may have to read my book *The Nuclear Deception: Nikita Khrushchev and the Cuban Missile Crisis*, available at Amazon.com.

Finally, why did President Kennedy fail to seize the opportunity to get rid of his supposed archenemy? Why didn't he authorize the U.S. Navy to board the Soviets ships allegedly bringing out of Cuba the missiles and their nuclear warheads, and verify it? Did Kennedy know something we don't? These are the real questions to be answered to solve this historical riddle called the Cuban missile crisis.

Who Controls the Past ...

Some of the readers familiar with the subject of the Cuban missile crisis may object that, contrary to what I have expressed above, there is an abundance of books proving beyond any reasonable doubt that there were missiles and their nuclear warheads in Cuba in 1962. However, a serious analysis of these books shows that most of what they claim is in contradiction with the facts.

The reason for this hemorrhage of books trying to pass as fact non-confirmed assumptions is because, faithful to Orwell's *1984* dictum, "Who controls the present controls the past. Who controls the past controls the future," the CFR conspirators give much importance and spend an inordinate amount of time muddying the historical waters. For example, for many years the most widely accepted interpretation of the Pearl Harbor events was CFR member Roberta Wohlstetter's *Pearl Harbor: Warning and Decision*.[15] In it, after accepting that the U.S. government knew of the incoming attack, using a recurrent CFR excuse she attributed the inability to act to a failure in inter-agency communication.

In the same fashion, the most accepted interpretation of the Cuban missile crisis was the one advanced by CFR member Graham T. Allyson in his book *Essence of Decision*.[16] We now know that Wohlstetter's and Allyson's interpretation of the events is totally false, and perhaps not by mistake, but by design.

As with the case of Pearl Harbor, after the Cuban missile crisis many professional disinformers passing as serious scholars have published a spate of terror-ridden books trying to convince us about how close we were to the nuclear brink during the crisis. In these books the nuclear warheads allegedly present in Cuba in 1962 have miraculously reproduced like rabbits jumping from a magician's hat and the Russian officers in the field had their itchy fingers close to the firing button. This, however, has nothing to do with the reality of the events. Unfortunately, most people still believe the fairy tale concocted by the CFR conspirators.

If things have changed in relation to the 9/11 events, it is because of the Internet, a medium the CFR conspirators cannot control, and its ability to advertise critical books published by small, non-controlled publishing houses. Now, why do the CFR conspirators devote so much time to fixing the past? The answer is simple: because by giving credibility to past artificially created, non-existing threats they add credibility to present and future, artificially created, nonexistent ones.[17] As James Jesus Angleton once said, "The past telescopes into the future."[18]

Appendix III

Hegelian-type PSYOPS
(Thesis, antithesis, synthesis)

Cold War PSYOP – War on Terror PSYOP
False Flag Operations: Bogotazo and 9/11/2001

Operational Traits	Bogotazo, April 9, 1948	WTC, Pentagon, 9/11/2001
Use of patsies	Patsy (Gaitán's assassin).	Patsies (Muslims on planes).
Warnings ignored	CIA warnings are ignored.	CIA warnings are ignored.
Previous knowledge	Venezuelan newspaper publishes news before riots.	S.F. Mayor Willie Brown is told in advance not to fly that day.
False clues	Marxist books found in Castro's hotel room. Castro drops communist leaflets.	Copy of Koran found at Boston airport. Hijacker's passport found in WTC wreckage.
Buildings destroyed	Bogotá buildings previously rigged with flammable materials.	WTC towers previously rigged with explosives.
Dirty Tricks	Fake radio reports.	Fake bin Laden videos.
Post-mortem Analysis	CFR agent Dulles produce disingenuous report.	CFR-controlled Commission produces whitewash report.
Motive (enemy disappears)	Nazi Germany falls. Bogotazo used as pretext to begin Cold War.	Soviet Union falls. 9/11 used as pretext to begin War on Terror.
Doctrine (ideological justification)	CFR's George Kennan's Containment Theory.	CFR's Samuel Huntington's Clash of Civilizations.
Beginning of	Long, unwinnable war against international communism.	Long, unwinnable war against international terrorism.
New enemy	Communist radicals.	Muslim fanatics.
CFR' secret agents	Marshall, Dulles, Pawley, Castro.	Bush, Cheney, neocons, Castro.
Agent provocateur	Fidel Castro.	Fidel Castro.
Previous trail	Castro visits Latin American Countries inciting anti-American feelings.	Castro visits several Muslim countries inciting anti-American feelings.
PSYOP's goal	Scare the American people with fear of communism.	Scare the American people with fear of terrorism.

NOTES

Preface

1. As I will show below in this book, the American Left and the American right, particularly the Democratic and Republican parties, are just the two sides of the same coin.

2. Ron Paul made the comments about "an ideological battle" and a "conspiracy of ideas" during a 2008 Republican Presidential Candidates debate.

3. Currently, the United States of America is a quite different country from the American Republic conceived by the Founding Fathers.

4. Agent provocateur (a.k.a. provocation agent): A person who penetrates a target organization to provoke and incite its members to do foolish things that go beyond their initial intentions and commit unlawful acts far beyond their original aims. (a.k.a., "tree-shaker" in CIA parlance) The agent provocateur's mission is to associate himself with a certain target group or suspected person with whom he must pretend to sympathize. Usually, his goal is to incite the target (a person or an organization) into some action that will bring about apprehension, punishment or discredit to the person or the organization. For an excellent description of the job of an agent provocateur, see, William Norman Grigg, "The Manufactured Menace From Michigan, Take Two," *LewRockwell.com*, April 3, 2010, http://www.lewrockwell.com/grigg/grigg-w138.html.

5. Disinformation: false information that is intended to mislead, especially propaganda issued by a government organization directed to an opposing or rival organization or the media. The term originated in the 1950s, formed on the pattern of the Russian word *dezinformatsia* as used by the KGB. See, Richard H. Shultz and Roy Godson, *Dezinformatsia: The Strategy of Soviet Disinformation* (New York: Berkley Books: 1986). On the othar hand, a more mundane synonym for disinformation would be bullshit. See, i.e., Harry G. Frankfurt, *On Bullshit* (Princeton, NJ: Princeton University Press, 2005).

6. Of lately, some people have expressed their belief that conspiracy theory should properly be called the study of parapolitics or deep politics. Though perhaps they have a point, I think that the concept of conspiracy theory is much wider in scope han these terms.

7. Attributed to Jeffrey Outlaw Shallit, a pro-evolution computer scientists and mathematician.

8. Medford Evans, *The Assassination of Joe McCarthy* (Boston: Western Islands, 1970), p. 113.

9. *Project for the New American Century*, "Rebuilding America's Defenses: Strategy, Forces and Resources For a New Century," September, 2000, p. 51.

10. On the other hand, perhaps it is just an example of what an author calls "the revelation of the method," a sort of in-your-face technique. See, Michael A. Hoffman, II, *Secret Societies and Psychological Warfare* (Coeur d'Alene, Idaho: Independent History and Research, 2001), pp. 51-53.

11. Alex Callinicos, The Grand Strategy of the American Empire," *International Socialism Journal* No. 97 (Winter 2002), http://pubs.socialistreviewindex.org.uk/isj97/callinicos.htm.

12. James Petras, *Rulers and Ruled in the U.S. Empire: Bankers, Zionists and Militants* (Atlanta, Georgia: Clarity Press, 2007).

13. Agent: 1. A person who is recruited, trained, controlled, and employed to obtain and report information for intelligence or counterintelligence purposes from inside a target organization. Agents are the only members of the espionage system whose mission is actually spying. As a rule, intelligence services only rarely, if ever, employ fellow citizens as agents. The term, therefore, must never be confused with its lay use, as in "FBI agent" or "secret agent." In the interests of security, an agent acts independently from other agents and is

under the control of a principal or a case officer. 2. Euphemism for a spy who is in your side.

14. At a pragmatical level, the Soviets shared an almost identical view of the world with the American ultra-conservatives — as exposed in the theories advanced by Dan Smoot, Phyllis Schlafly, and John A. Stormer, among others — which see a small group of men secretly meeting and carefully planning (conspiring) to manipulate society toward certain goals. In that sense Soviet leaders were not far from what Richard Hofstadter calls "the paranoid style" in American politics. See Richard Hofstadter, *The Paranoid Style in American Politics* (New York: Knopf, 1965). For a detailed account of conspiracy theories in America see George Johnson, *Architects of Fear* (Los Angeles: Jeremy P. Tarcher, 1983); also Carl Oglesby, *The Yankee and Cowboy War* (Kansas City: Andrews and McMeel), 1976; and William P. Hoar, *Architects of Conspiracy* (Boston: Western Islands, 1984) A wealth of information —though tongue-in-cheek — about conspiracy theories is found in Robert Shea and Robert Anton Wilson, *The Illuminatus! Trilogy* (New York: Dell, 1975) On the other hand, G. William Domhoff cautions about the other side of the spectrum, that fails to see conspiracies even where there are, and which he calls "the compulsive style in American Social Science." This compulsive style is "narrow, restrictive, highly phobic about flights of fancy, and usually partial to the status quo." See G. William Domhoff, *The Higher Circles.* (New York: Vintage, 1971), pp. 302-303.

15. Cousteau's words may have carried some authority, because they appeared in the UNESCO's *Courier* on November, 1991.

16. In the field of inteligence and espionage, professional spies are called intelligence officers. Agents are the persons, usually foreigners who betray their own countries, recruited by intelligence officers.

17. During an interview, ex-CIA officer Tyler Drumheller told ABC, "In an organization of professional liars, we have to be honest with each other." Drumheller quoted in Rowan Scarborough, *Sabotage: America's Enemies Within the CIA* (Washington, D.C.: Regnery, 2007), p. 100.

18. Jefferson Mack, *Running a Ring of Spies: Spycraft and Black Operation in the Real World of Espionage* (Boulder, Colorado: Paladin Press, 1996), p. 51.

19. See, for example, Ronald Kessler, *Inside the CIA* (New York: Pocket Books, 1992); Joseph Trento, *The Secret History of the CIA* (Roseville, California: Forum, 2001), and Ralph Weber (ed.), *Spymasters: Ten CIA Officers in Their Own Words* (Wilmington, Delaware: SR Books, 1989), just to mention a few of the critical ones. Other obvious CIA-promoted, pedestrian books are T.J. Waters, *Class 11: Inside the CIA's First Post-9/11 Spy Class* (New York: Dutton, 2006), and Ishmael Jones (pseud.) *The Human Factor: Inside CIA's Dysfunctional Intelligence Culture* (New York: Encounter Books, 2008)

20. Vladislav M. Zubok, "Spy VS. Spy,"*Cold War International History Electronic Bulletin*, No. 4 (Fall 1994)

21. In the field of intelligence an espionage, "intelligence" means the product resulting from the collection, processing, integration, analysis, and interpretation of available information after it has been properly evaluated. As a matter of fact, the official American definition of intelligence as used by the CIA and other intelligence services is "evaluated information." See The Evaluation of Information on Appendix II of this book.

22. For a critical analysis of the National Security Archive see, Servando Gonzalez, *The Nuclear Deception: Nikita Khrushchev and the Cuban Missile Crisis* (Oakland, California: Spooks Books, 2002).

23. As a critic of the *ad causam* methodology when applied to the analysis of intelligence events, I will not fall in my own trap by using it in this book, which deals mostly with spies and espionage. Consequently, I am consciously using the *ad hominem* methodology as a valid, ethical, scholarly alternative. If some of the scholars I critically mention in this

book feel upset because of my treatment, I would like to make it clear that I have no personal animosity against any of them. They should not expect, however, to delve into the spy world and be dealt with as scholars. If some of them feel hurt and complain about my treatment, it will be further proof that they are too naïve to be involved with spies. If they cannot stand the heat, they should stay out of the kitchen.

Conversely, in the case of the spies I mention in this book, no disclaimer is needed. My approach is standard operating procedure in the trade, and they, as practitioners of the second oldest profession, not only are used to it but take it for granted. Moreover, they don't feel any professional respect for people who don't treat them the way they expect to be treated: aas professional liars and dissemblers

24. Tradecraft: the basic techniques, the *modus operandi* of a particular intelligence service in the conduct of its espionage activities. According to CIA veteran William Hood, tradecraft , though mysterious to outsiders, is just a " little more than a compound of common sense, experience, and certain almost universally accepted security practices. . ." William Hood, *Mole* (New York: Ballantine, 1982), p. xiv.

25. Sun Tzu, *The Art of War* - translated by Samuel B. Griffin (London: Oxford University Press, 1963), p. 66.

26. Compartmentation is based on the principle that a large, multifaceted project can be broken down into subparts that can be researched and developed independently. Compartmentation implies the concept of need-to-know, by which only the information related to a specific subpart of an operation is relayed only to the persons working on it. The result is that only a few high-level people know what the whole projectis is all about. Therefore, if there is a leak, the chance for the entire operation to being compromised is reduced.

27. The sole existence of a phenomenon such as Fidel Castro proves that historical materialism has always been on the wrong track.

28. E. H. Carr, *What is History* (Cambridge: Uiversity of Cmbridge Press, 1961).

29 For a strong criticism of the prevalent theories about the presence of strategic missiles and their nuclear war.heads in Cuba in 1962 see Servando Gonzalez, *The Nuclear Deception: Nikita Khushchev and the Cuban Missile Crisis* (Oakland, California: Spooks Books, 2002).

30. Spook: CIA slang for spy, intelligence officer, counterespionage officer or, in general, any espionage agent. Though the term initially had some pejorative connotations, it seems that CIA officers have learned to live with it, and occasionally they call themselves spooks. Some people believe that the term spook comes from the CIA's close links to Yale's Skull & Bones secret society, an importat source of CIA officers.

31. Psychological Warfare Operation, also known as PSYOP: The systematic use of propaganda and other psychological actions in intelligence operations. having the primary purpose of influencing the opinion, emotions, attitudes, and behavior of hostile, non-cooperative, neutral of even friendly groups, in such as a way to support the achievement of some intelligence objectives by the opposing group carrying out the PSYOP.

32. Michael A. Hoffman, II, *Secret Societies and Psychological Warfare* (Coeur d'Alene, Idaho: Independent History and Research, 2001), pp. 51-53.

33. *Ibid.*, p. 53.

Introduction

1. David Schuman, *American Government: The Rules of the Game* (New York: Random House, 1989).

2. Classical liberalism, the political philosophy that seeks to promote individual liberty and progress, traces its origins to the writings of John Locke.

3. Schuman, *op. cit.*

4. The term humanism is intentionally misleading. Though "humanism" evokes the idea of humanitarianism, that is, being kind and helpful to people and treating them humanly, it has nothing to do with it. Nor does it have anything to do with the Humanities; the study of art, music, literature, and other fields of human culture. Actually, Humanism is a new anti-Christian, godless religion that places Man at the center of everything and makes it the measure of all things.

5. Gertrude Himmelfarb, *One Nation, Two Cultures,* (New York: Knopf, 1999).

6. Robert H. Bork (ed.), *A Country I Do Not Recognize: The Legal Assault On American Values* (Palo Alto, California: Hoover Institution Press, 2005).

7. John D. Rockefeller III, *The Second American Revolution* (New York: Harper & Row. 1973).

8. Arthur S. Miller, *The Secret Constitution and the Need for Constitutional Change* (New York: Greenwood Press, 1987).

9. See, Dennis L. Cuddy, *The Road to Socialism and the New World Order* (Highland City, Florida: Florida Por Familiy Forum, 2000).

10. See, *Daily Mail Report*, "Apple admits child labour was used to build iPods and iPhones in Chinese factories," *DailyMail.co.uk*, , Febrary 27, 2010, http://www.dailymail.co.uk/news/worldnews/article-1254221/Apple-admits-using-child-labour-build-iPods-iPhones-Chinese-factories.html#.

11. Richard N. Gardner, "The Hard Road to World Order," *Foreign Affairs*, Volume 52, Number 3 (April 1974).

12. Chester Ward and Philis Schalaffly , *Kissinger on the Couch* (New Rochelle, N.Y.: Arlington House, 1975), pp. 144, 150.

13. Lawrence P. MacDonald, Introduction to Gary Allen, *The Rockefeller File* (Seal Beach, California: '76 Press, 1976), pp. 3-4.

14. German philosopher Georg Wilhelm Friedrich Hegel (1770-1831) made change the cornerstone of his philosophical system, which he called Dialectics. According to Hegel, an idea or principle — which he called the thesis— is challenged by its opposite —the antithesis. Eventually, from this conflict emerges a new idea or principle that is a synthesis of both.

15. See, Christopher Simpson, *Science of Coercion: Communication Research and Psychological Warfare 1945-1960* (New York: Oxford University Press, 1994), pp. 11-12.

16. Most books about espionage confuse counterintelligence and counterespionage. The primary objective of counterintelligence, often referred to as "negative intelligence", is to block the efforts of foreign secret services or governments to penetrate and obtain secret or confidential information of our own intelligence service. The activities of counterintelligence are concerned with identifying and counteracting the threat to security posed by individuals engaged in espionage inside our intelligence service and recruiting them, or doubling, to act against their masters. Counterespionage, on the contrary, is mostly police work designed to detect, destroy, neutralize, or prevent espionage activities through identification, penetration, manipulation, deception, repression and eventual capture of individuals, groups, or organizations conducting or suspected of conducing espionage activities. Traditionally, in the U.S. the CIA has carried out counterintelligence activities while counterespionage has been mostly a FBI work.

17. Mole: A penetration agent. A mole is a spy who has dug his way deep into the organization of a rival intelligence service. Some authors distinguish between genuine, conceptual, and notional moles. A genuine mole is the one who actually had penetrated an enemy intelligence service following the orders of another intelligence service who "planted" him; a conceptual mole is the one who exist just as a suspicion, or as a possibility. A notional one —the most destructive type of mole, because it is impossible to discover and neutralize— is a mole who is not actually "planted" in the enemy service, but in the minds

of its people. Moles are an essential element in disinformation and deception operations, where feedback is vital.

18. For an interesting view of how fiction and reality intermingles in the spy world, see Frederick P. Hitz, *The Great Game: The Myths and Reality of Espionage* (New York: Vintage Books, 2004).

19. David Wise, *Mole* (New York: Random House, 1992), p. 29.

Chapter 1

1. David Wise and Thomas B. Ross whose book *The Invisible Government* (New York: Bantam, 1962)

2. Joseph Trento, *Prelude to Terror: The Rogue CIA and the Legacy of America's Private Intelligence Network* (New York: Carroll and Graf, 2005), p. ix.

3. Ron Paul's words quoted at: http://rawstory.com/2010/01/ron-paul-cia/.

4. Emanuel Josephson, *Rockefeller "Internationalist": The Man Who Misrules the World* (New York: Chedney Press, 1952).

5. *Ibid.*, p. 237.

6. *Ibid.*, p. 245.

7. Dan Smoot, *The Invisible Government* (Boston: Western Islands, 1962)

8. *Ibid.*, p. 3.

9. John Stormer, *None Dare Call it Treason* (Florissant, Missouri: Liberty Bell Press, 1964).

10. Gary Allen, *None Dare Call it Conspiracy* (Rossmoor, California: Concord Press, 1972).

11. Phoebe Courtney, *The CFR, Part II* (Littleton, Colorado: The Independent American, 1975).

12. Allen, *op. cit.*, p. 13.

13 For a short, but insightful analysis of the invisible government of the United States, see Richard J. Boyland, "The Secret Shadow Government: A Structural Analysis," wwwworldnewsstand.net/history/.

ShadowGovt.htm.

14. Just recently George Clooney joined the CFR. Other Hollywood stars who have joined the CFR are Khris Khristofferson, Angelina Jolie, Michael Douglas, Richard Dreyfuss and Warren Beatty.

15. Nelson Rockefeller's biographer Joseph Persico mentions that, to his utter surprise, political journalist Richard Reeves found out that, after Nelson Rockefeller's twenty years in politics, his associates had produced "no books, no memoirs, no nothing. Think about it. It's unique." Joseph E. Persico, *The Imperial Rockefeller: A Biography of Nelson A, Rockefeller* (New York: Simon and Schuster, 1982), p. 14.

16. David Rockefeller, addressing the Bilderberg Group in Baden-Baden, Germany, June 1991.

17. For more information on the Bilderberg Group see, Daniel Stulin, *The True Story of the Bilderberg Group*, Jim Tucker, *Bilderberg Diary,* and H. Paul Jeffers, *The Bilderberg Conspiracy*.

18. For more information on the Trilateral Commission see, Holy Sklar, *Trilateralism*, Jim Marrs, *Rule by Secrecy*, and Antony Sutton *Trilaterals Over Washington.*

19. Dr. Locard's principle quoted in Zakaria Erzinclioglu, *Every Contact Leaves a Trace: Scientific Detection in the Twentieth Century* (London: Carlton, 2001), p. 10.

20. *Ibid.*, p. 12.

21. According to some source, Senator Allan Cranston found it hard "to suppress a shudder," when he heard the claim that a large part of the Los Angeles County police officers were members of the John Birch Society. Unfortunately, however, he never tried to know

how many U.S. Congress members were also CFR members. Cranston story in William Turer, *The Assassination of Robert F. Kennedy* (New York: Thunder's Mouth, 1993), p. 60.

22. On the evening of October 15, 1962, CIA deputy director Ray Cline informed JFK's national security adviser McGeorge Bundy (CFR) that U-2 planes had discovered what appeared to be Soviet medium-range nuclear missiles bases on Cuban soil. But Bundy didn't tell the President immediately. Instead he told the news to his associates at the CFR. A few minutes later, while the President was kept in the dark, CFR members Dean Rusk, Paul Nitze and Robert McNamara were informed about the findings. See, Walter Isaacson and Evan Thomas, *The Wise Men: Six Friends and the World They Made* (New York: Touchstone, 1986) P. 619.

23. The minutes of the Bissell report to a select group CFR members on January 8, 1968, are reproduced in Victor Marchetti and John D. Marks, *The CIA and the Cult of Intelligence* (New York: Dell, 1974), pp. 358-376.

24. The Fabian Society is an elite group of British intellectuals who formed a semi-secret organization for the purpose of bringing socialism to the world. But, contrary to the Communists, who wanted to establish socialism quickly trough violent revolution, the Fabians preferred to do it slowly and surreptitiously, through propaganda and legislation, after having infiltrated the government, the armed forces, the media, and the educational system. The symbol of the Fabian Society is the wolf in sheep's clothing.

25. Antonio Gramsci was an Italian Communist who died in prison in 1937. While in prison, he analyzed Western culture and concluded that the only way that Communists could finally impose their totalitarian will over the West was not by violent revolution, as classic Marxism predicated. So, concluded Gramsci, instead of grabbing by force the economic infrastructure of society and then changing its cultural superstructure, the best way to do it was by first taking over its superstructure — the educational, cultural and religious institutions — and then taking over the economic infrastructure. This would require years of stealthful infiltration.

If you find Gramci's method familiar it is because it is exactly what the CFR conspirators have been doing in America since the beginning of the 20th century, and we need to recognize that it has worked to perfection. Currently, particularly after the years of the Bushes, the Clintons, and now Barack Obama in the White House — all of them willful CFR puppets — the results cannot be more evident.

26. Critics of the Left, who strongly criticized Bill Clinton and George W. Bush and the ones of the Left that are now criticizing Barak Obama for "his" disastrous policies, actually are throwing the public on the wrong track. Wittingly or unwittingly they are playing the CFR conspirators' game.

27. There is a new edition of Prouty's *The Secret Team* available on bookstores online, but apparently it is not a faithful rendering of the original edition. But you can read the original edition of Prouty's book at: http://www.ratical.org/ratville/JFK/ST/ST.html. It is a highly revealing book worth reading.

28. Arthur M. Schlesinger, Jr., *The Imperial Presidency*, (Boston: Houghton Mifflin Company, 1973).

29. Harry S Truman, *The Washington Post*, December 22, 1963.

30. For a strong evidence indicating that far from losing the election because Bush stole it, Gore was part of the charade, watch the Introduction to the *TruthLies* documentary series at: http://www.truthlies.tv/exclusive.html.

31. On Kerry as a CFR mole infiltrated into the left, see my "Sheep Dipping CFR Style: The Kerry and Ellsberg Cases," http://www.amigospais-guaracabuya.org/oagsg023.php.

32. See Servando Gonzalez, "Why Obama? The Plot Thickens," http://www.nolanchart.com/article6391.html.

33. False flag recruiting: the recruiting of an agent by an intelligence service passing as

a different one. A technique by which an informant, defector in place or agent is recruited through the disguise of telling him he will be working for the "good guys" —another country or service different from the one who is actually making the recruitment. More recently, the term false flag has also been used to indicate an operation whose perpetrator has acted disguised under a false identity.

34. Phyllis Schlaffly and Chester Ward, *Kissinger on the Couch* (New Rochelle, N.Y.: Arlington House, 1975), p. 150.

35. Forrestal quoted in Phoebe Courtney, *The CFR: Part II* (Littleton, Colorado: The Independent American, 1975), p. 24.

36. René A. Wormser, *Foundations: Their Power and Influence* (Tennessee: Covenant House Books, c1993), p. 207.

37. See, Scott McLemee, "The Quigley Cult". *George Magazine*, Dec. 1996, p. 96.

38. "Acceptance Speech", Democratic National Convention, New York, NY, July 16, 1992.

39. Carroll Quigley, *Tragedy and Hope: A History of the World in Our Time* (New York: Macmillan, 1966), pp. 950, 955.

40. David Rockefeller, *Memoirs* (New York: Random House, 2002), p. 405.

41. Quoted in Dennis L. Cuddy, *The Globalists: The Power Elite Exposed* (Oklahoma City, Oklahoma: Hearthstone Publishing, 2001), p. 21.

42. Somebody asked Louisiana's populist politician Huey Long if he thought the U.S.A. could fall to fascism. Long, known for his wit, gave an interesting response: "Yes, but in America we'll call it anti-fascism." Speaker of the House Nancy Pelosi calling fascists Americans who are complaining at the current fascist takeover of this country by the CFR-controlled puppet Barack Obama prove that Long was right.

43. Ralph W. McGehee, *Deadly Deceits: My 25 Years in the CIA* (New York, Sheridan Square Publications, 1983).

44. *Ibid.*, p. xi.

45. *Ibid.*, p. 192.

46. Paul David Collins, "Unholy Matrimony: The Tie Between the Cult of Intelligence and the Cult of Oligarchy," Conspiracy Archive, Sept. 9th, 2006, http://www.conspiracy archive.com/Commentary/CIA.htm.

47. The RIIA later changed its name to Chatham House.

48. Henry Makow, "Gloria Steinem: How the CIA Used Feminism to Destabilize Society," *NewsWithViews.com* (July 1, 2002), http://www.newswithviews.com/NWO/newworld22.htm.

49. Richard Poe, "Chinagate: The Third-Way Scandal," in Christopher Ruddy and Carl Limbacher Jr., (eds.), *Bitter Legacy: NewsMax.com Reveals the Untold Story of the Clinton-Gore Years* (West Palm Beach, Florida: NewsMax.com, 2001), p. 83.

50. See, i.e., Johanna Neuman ,"What did the CIA lie to Congress about, and where was Cheney?," Los Angeles Times, July 10, 2009, http://latimesblogs.latimes.com/washington/2009/07/what-did-the-cia-lie-to-congress-about-and-where-was-cheney.html.

51. Limited hangout. Intelligence jargon for a favorite and frequently used gimmick of the clandestine professionals. When their veil of secrecy is shredded and they can no longer rely on a cover story, they resort to admitting —sometimes even volunteering— some of the truth while still managing to withhold the key and damaging facts of the cause. Usually used to misinform the people of their own country, not the opponents.

Chapter 2

1. Peter Grose, *Continuing the Inquiry* (New York, Council on Foreign Relations, 1996), p. 1.

2. Evolutionary biologist and theorist Richard Dawkins coined the term meme (pronounced like "gene") in his 1976 book *The Selfish Gene*, (New York, New York: Oxford

University Press, 1976) According to Dawkins, a meme is any unit of cultural information, such as a practice or idea, that is transmitted verbally or by repeated action from one mind to another similar to the transmission of viruses. Based on that, some people have called memes "mind viruses."

3. Controller: intelligence lingo for a case officer; the person in the field directly responsible for an operation, usually of a covert nature, including, but not limited to, the running of all types of agents. A case officer must be good in handling people, by creating a psychological dependence on him. His agents most feel that they can fully rely on him, as he is the only link with the organization they are risking so much for — including betraying their own countries.

4. *Ibid.*, p. xx.

5. Grose, *op. cit.*., p. 1.

6. James Perloff, *The Shadows of Power: The Council on Foreign Relations and the American Decline* (Appleton, Wisconsin: Western Islands, 1988), p.32.

7. Lawrence E. Gelfand, *The Inquiry: American Preparations for Peace, 1917-1919* (New Haven: Yale University Press, 1963), pp., 340-342.

8. *Ibid.*, pp. 44, 317.

9. *Ibid.*, p. 41.

10. *Ibid.*, p. 316.

11. *Ibid.*, p. 5.

12. *Ibid.*, p. 121.

13. *Ibid.*, p. 87.

14. See, *Fact Book on Intelligence*, Office of Public Affairs, Central Intelligence Agency, April 1983, p. 16.

15. Grose, *op. cit.*, p. 1.

16. A partial list of the initial members appeared in Edward Mandell House and Charles Seymour, *What Really Happened in Paris* (New York: Charles Scribner's Sons, 1921), p. 7.

17. Rhodes quoted in Carroll Quigley, *Tragedy and Hope: A History of the World in Our Time* (New York: Macmillan, 1966), p. 62.

18. *Ibid.*, p. 950,

19. Cristopher Andrew, *For the Presidents Eyes Only: Secret Intelligence and the American Presidency from Washington to Bush* (New York: Haper Perennial, 1996), p. 60.

20. James Perloff, *The Shadows of Power: The Council on Foreign Relations and the American Decline* (Appleton, Wisconsin: Western Islands, 1988), p.32.

21. Grose, *op. cit.*, p. 4.

22. *Ibid.*, p. 5.

23. Godfrey Hodgson, *Woodrow Wilson's Right Hand: The Life of Colonel Edward Mandell House* (New Haven, Connecticut: Yale University Press, 2006), p. 150.

24. Contrary to common belief, the Federal Reserve Bank is a private corporation that has nothing to do with the Federal Government of the United States. The true owners of the Fed are not the American people, but a select group of international bankers: Rothschild Bank of London, Warburg Bank of Hamburg, Rothschild Bank of Berlin, Lehman Brothers of New York, Lazard Brothers of Paris, Kuhn Loeb Bank of New York, Israel Moses Seif Bank of Italy, Goldman Sachs of New York, Warburg Bank of Amsterdam and Chase Manhattan Bank of New York.

25. Talent spotter: An intelligence officer or operative whose function is detecting and evaluating individuals who might be of value for an intelligence service as potential recruits for intelligence work.

26. Target: anything containing information that is not only secret, but also accessible only by means of espionage. A target must be something physical. It cannot be the mind of a person, but it can be the person itself. When the target is a person is also called the "person of interest."

27. Ray Stannard Baker, *Woodrow Wilson: Life and Letters; Vol. Three, Governor 1910-1913* (Garden City, New York: Doubleday, 19341), p. 294.

28. Gelfand, *op. cit.*, p. 6.

29. Thomas J. Nock, *To End All Wars: Woodrow Wilson and the Quest for a New World Order* (Princeton, New Jersey: Princeton University Press, 1992), p. 13.

30. The "War on Terror," is a contradiction in terms. As one general remarked, you cannot fight a technique. The WWII equivalent would have been to declare war on the *blitzkrieg* instead of on the Nazis. On the other hand, given the fact that the conspirators want long, unwinnable wars as a pretext for imperialist expansion and repression at home, the war on terror is exactly what they need.

31. *National Security Strategy of the United States*, The White House, September 20, 2002. Further proof that the so-called war on terror was planned way before September 11, 201, is that the "National Security Strategy" is based on two papers dating back to the early 1990s: one is a 1992 internal government document entitled "Defense Planning Guidance," authored by then Secretary of Defense Dick Cheney (CFR) and his deputy Paul Wolfowitz (CFR), which contemplated the use of military force against any nation the conspirators perceived to be hostile against their interests. The other one is the report "Rebuilding America's Defenses," released in September 2000 by the Project for the New American Century, a neocon think tank composed almost exclusively of CFR members.

32. From this perspective, all grants received by academics, writers, journalists, etc., from CFR-controlled foundations such as Ford, Rockefeller, MacArthur and Carnegie, as well as substantial monetary advancements paid to politicians for books to be published by CFR-controlled publishing houses, can be considered compromising leverage for agent recruitment.

33. Curtis B. Dall, *F.D.R.: My Exploited Father-In-Law* (Washington, D.C.: Action Associates, 1970), p. 108. Actually, due to the fact that, like spies, closet homosexuals live a double life, they have always heavily populated the spying profession. The cases of the famous British defectors Donald Burgess and Donald MacLean is well known, but the presence of homosexuals among CIA officers has been practically ignored both by the Agency's admirers and its detractors. For example, Carmel Offie, a sort of CIA's ugly duckling and a pioneer out-of-the-closet gay who played an important role in the OSS and the early days of the CIA, is not mentioned in most books about the Agency.

34. See, Godfrey Hodgson, *Woodrow Wilson's Right Hand: The Life of Colonel Edward M. House* (New Haven, Connecticut, Yale University Press, 2006), p. 56.

35. President Woodrow Wilson quoted by Charles Seymour, *The Intimate Papers of Colonel House*, 4 vols. (New York: Houghton Mifflin, 1926), vol. I, pp. 114.

36. George Sylvester Viereck, *The Strangest Friendship in History: Woodrow Wilson and Colonel House* (New York: Liveright, 1932), pp. 18-19, 33.

37. See, Hodgson, *op. cit.*, p. 160.

38. *Ibid.*, p. 215.

39. *Ibid.*, p. 217.

40. *Ibid.*, p. 217.

41. Woodrow Wilson, *The New Freedom* (New York: Doubleday, 1914), pp. 13-14.

42 I did not mention in this list the two Bushes, because both of them are part of the conspiracy.

43. Curtis B. Dall, *F.D.R.: My Exploited Father in Law* (Washington, D.C.: Action Associates, 1970).

44. *Ibid.*, pp. 104-105.

45. *Ibid.*, pp. 104-105.

46. See Servando Gonzalez, "Obama: Transparency, Invisibility, or Treason?," *NolanChart.com*, February 19, 2009, http://www.nolanchart.com/article6009.html.

47. George Sylvester Viereck, *The Strangest Friendship in History: Woodrow Wilson and Colonel House* (New York: Liveright, 1932).
48. *Colonel House's Papers*, Sterling Library, Yale University.
49. The fact that Alexander Haig orchestrated Nixon's resignation is mentioned by Henry Kissinger in his *Years of Upheaval* (Boston: Little, Brown, 1979), pp. 107-110.
50. Peter Collier and David Horowitz, *The Rockefellers: An American Dynasty* (New York: Signet, 1976), p. 4.
51. *Ibid.*, p. 8.
52. *Ibid.*
53. Daniel Yergin, *The Prize: The Epic Quest for Oil, Money, and Power* (New York: Pocket Books, 1993), p. 43.
54. *Ibid.*, pp. 43, 10.
55. See, Collier and Horowitz, *op. cit.*, p. 23.
56. See, Myer Kutz, *Rockefeller Power* (New York: Pinnacle, 1974), p. 36.
57. Gary Allen, *The Rockefeller File* (Seal Beach, California: '76 Press, 1976), p. 23.
58. Ida Tarbell, "The Standard Oil Company', in Earl Latham (ed.), *John D. Rockefeller: Robber Baron or Industrial Statesman?* (Boston: D.C. Heath and Company, 1949.), p. 33.
59. See, Appendix II, "The Evaluation of Information."
60. Yergin, *op. cit.*, p. 75.
61. *Ibid*, p. 54.
62. See, Collier and Horowitz, *op. cit.*, p. 22.
63. Tarbell, *op. cit.*, p. 10.
64. Yergin, *op. cit.*, p. 102.
65. Tarbell, *op. cit.*, pp. 30-31.
66. Matthew Josephson , "The Robber Barons," in Earl Latham (ed.), *John D. Rockefeller: Robber Baron or Industrial Statesman?* (Boston: D.C. Heath and Company, 1949.), p. 36.
67. *Ibid.*, p. 40.
68. *Ibid.*, p. 43.
69. Lewis Galantière, "John D.: An Academy Portrait," in Earl Latham (ed.), *John D. Rockefeller: Robber Baron or Industrial Statesman?* (Boston: D.C. Heath and Company, 1949.), p. 86.
70. Ferdinand Lundberg, *The Rockefeller Syndrome* (New York: Zebra Books, 1976), pp. 134-135.
71. Lundberg, *op. cit.*, p. 142.
72. William Manchester, *Rockefeller Family Portrait,* quoted in Gary Allen, *The Rockefeller File* (Seal Beach, California: '76 Press, 1976), p. 23.]
73. Matthew Josephson, *op. cit.*, p. 43.
74. Collier & Horowitz, *op. cit.*, p. 5., Kutz, *op. cit.*, p. 36.
75. Lewis Galantière, "John D.: An Academy Portrait," in Earl Latham (ed.), *John D. Rockefeller: Robber Baron or Industrial Statesman?* (Boston: D.C. Heath and Company, 1949.), p. 86.
76. Emanuel Josephson, *Rockefeller "Internationalist": The Man Who Misrules the World* (New York: Chedney Press, 1952), p. 18.
77. Kutz, *op. cit.* p. 36.
78. Galantière, *op. cit.*, p. 85.
79. Fitzhugh Green, *American Propaganda Abroad* (New York: Hyppocrene, 1988), p. 99.
80. Both Castro and the CIA collaborated in destabilizing the Allende government —the CIA by painting him as a radical leftist and Castro by openly criticizing him for not being radical enough. Moreover, if recently surfaced information is true, Allende did not commit suicide: his Cuban security chief, General Patricio de la Guardia, killed him, following Castro's direct orders. See my article "Fidel Castro: Asesino de Allende?," http://

www.servandogonzalez.org.

81. See, John Loftus and Mark Aarons, *The Secret War Against the Jews* (New York: St. Martin's Press, 1994), pp. 64-73.

82. Charles Higham, *Trading With the Enemy: An Exposé of the Nazi-American Money plot 1933-1949* (New York: Delacorte Press, 1983).

83. *Ibid.* For the whole story, see Chapter 3, "The Secrets of Standard Oil."

84. For the full story see, Stephen Schlesinger, "Cryptanalysis for Peacetime: Codebreaking at the Birth and Structure of the United Nation," *Cryptologia* 19 (July 1995), pp. 217-235.

Chapter 3

1. Cover story: 1. A fictitious, but plausible story used to explain the visible evidences of a clandestine operation. 2. A relatively plausible justification used to explain an operation that goes wrong. 3. A plausible story played by an intelligence officer used to conceal his real mission. Also called a legend.

2. See, Grose, *op. cit.*

3. On page 58 of his book *The Rockefeller File* (Seal Beach, California: '76 Press, 1976), Gary Allen quotes from page 42 of the CFR 1952 Annual Report mentioning the fact that, because of their government jobs, some Council members are obliged to suspend or curtail their membership for some time. He also mentions that, during the investigation of the CFR by the Reece Congressional Committee in 1953, it was discovered that the CFR had secret members. Two of them whose cover was eventually blown were pro-communist industrialist Cyrus Eaton and Senator William Fulbright.

I suspect that currently one of the most important secret CFR members is Barack Hussein Obama. My suspicion arises not only from the fact that at this final phase of the conspiracy nobody can reach the position of President of the United States without being a CFR trusted member, but also because Obama's actions exactly follow the CFR's party line.

4. *Rebuilding America's Defenses: Strategy, Forces and Resources For a New Century*, A Report of the Project for the New American Century, September 2000. You may download the document at: www.newamericancentury.org/RebuildingAmericasDefenses.pdf.

5. Carter's recruitment process is told in some detail in Brzezinski's book *Power and Principle: Memoirs of the National Security Adviser 1977-1981* (New York: Farrar, Straus, Giroux, 1983), p. 5.

6. Information about Brzezinski recruiting Obama in Webster Griffin Tarpley, *Obama: The Postmodern Coup – Making of a Manchurian Candidate* (Joshua Tree, California: Progressive Press, 2008), p. 65.

Tarpley also mentions that in the 1920s and 1930s Columbia University was the American university most friendly to the fascist ideas of Italy's Benito Mussolini — which perhaps is another clue to Obama's fascist proclivities. It is interesting to note that Fidel Castro's infatuation with Fascism began when he was a student at the Jesuit's Belén High School in Havana.

7. Tarpley, *op. cit.*, p. 65.

8. Westbrook Pegler, "U.S. Fascism Spawned in 1912," *Los Angeles Examiner*, August 26, 1954, pp. 1, 25.

9. Westbrook Pegler, "A Guide for Revolution," *Los Angeles Examiner*, September 13, 1954, pp. 1, 21.

10. Edward Mandell House, *Philip Dru, Administrator* (Appleton, Wisconsin: RWU Press, 1998). The book was anonymously published in 1912, and again in 1919. Then it became almost impossible to find until this new edition, made possible by some of House's

critics, was published in 1998 by the Robert Welch University Press.

11. "Beware the Obama 'Evil Eye'," *The Drudge Report*, drudgereport.com, June 30, 2009.

12 .Any similarity with the election of Philip Dru in House's novel and the election of Barack Obama is not the product of a coincidence. See my article "Barack Obama: Administrator: A History of Today at http://www.nolanchart.com/article6230.html.

13. Democrats believe that conservatives control the mainstream press, while Republicans claim that Democrats control it. Actually, both are right. CFR Liberals control the press, but it is *owned* by CFR Conservatives, which proves that there is not a dime's worth of difference between both sides of the Repucratic party coin.

14. Peter Grose, *Continuing the Inquiry* (New York, Council on Foreign Relations, 1996), p. 11.

15. *Ibid.*, p. 10.

16. Carroll Quigley, *Tragedy and Hope: A History of the World in Our Time* (New York: Macmillan, 1966), pp. 1247-1248.

17. Cut-out. An individual, also an agent himself, who acts as an intermediary between a case officer and his agent.

18. Juan Lopez, *Democracy Delayed: The Case of Castro's Cuba* (Baltimore, Maryland: The John Hopkins University Press, 2002).

19. Currently they have found a way of literally making money out of thin air in the form of carbon dioxide taxes. More on this below in this book.

20. For an insightful study of the Fed, see G. Edward Griffin, *The Creature from Jekyll Island: A Second Look at the Federal Reserve* (Westlake Village, California: American Opinion, 1994).

21. Krauthammer mentioning that some people were coming out of the closet on the word "empire" quoted in Emily Eakin, "All Roads Lead To DC," *The New York Times*, the Week in Review, March 31, 2002.

22. See, Robert Kagan, "The Benevolent Empire," *Foreign Policy*, Summer 1998, pp. 24-35.; Charles Krauthammer, "The Unipolar Era," in Andrew J. Bacevich, ed., *The Imperial Tense: Prospects and Problems of American Empire* (Chicago: Ivan R. Dee, 2003), pp. 47-65.

23. For a description of how the Wall Street Mafia controls the media, see Denis W. Mazzoco, *Networks of Power: Corporate TV's Threat to Democracy* (Boston, Massachusetts: South End, 1994); Michael Parenti, *Inventing Reality: The Politics of Mass Media* (New York: ST. Martin's Press, 1986). Also, James R. Bennett, *Control of the Media in the United States: An Annotated Bibliography* (New York: Garland, 1992)

24. See Antony Sutton, *Wall Street and the Rise of Hitler* (Seal Beach, California: '76 Press, 1976); also Charles Higham, *Trading With The Enemy: An Exposé of the Nazi-American Money Plot, 1933-1949* (New York: Delacorte Press, 1983).

25. During an interview with Ian Punett on Coast-to-Coast a.m. (August 2, 2009), market analyst Bob Chapman, mentioned that members of the Wall St. Mafia are basically sociopaths.

26. Operation Keelhaul at the end of WWII, Operation Phoenix in Vietnam, the killing of thousands of civilians during the invasion of Panama, and the unnecessary killing of thousands of surrounded Iraqi soldiers in the so-called "highway of death" during the Gulf War, are some of the most notorious war crimes committed by this criminal Mafia, but not the only ones.

27. Zbigniew Brzezinski, *Between Two Ages: America's Role in the Technetronic Era* (New York: Viking, 1976).

28. Herman Kahn, *On Thermonuclear War* (Princeton. N.J.: Princeton University Press, 1960).

29. In a review in 1961 in *Scientific American* on Kahn's *On Thermonuclear War*, the book that introduced many of the basic concepts of deterrence, James R Newman wrote: "Is there really a Herman Kahn? It is hard to believe . . . No one could write like this. No one could think like this . . . This is a moral tract on mass murder: how to plan it, how to commit

it, how to get away with it, how to justify it."

30. For a different view of LeMay's life and career, see Warren Kozak, *LeMay: The Life and Wars of General Curtis LeMay* (Washington, DC: Regnery, 2009).

31. But LeMay, the ultimate anti-PC (political correct), had his final revenge. Despite all the PC anti-smoking disinformational campaigns, the cigar-smoking general died at 84.

32. Christopher Hitchens, *The Trial of Henry Kissinger* (London: Verso, 2002).

33. *Ibid.*, p. xxiv.

34. See, Josh Katz, "On This Day: Aldo Moro Kidnapped by the Italian Red Brigades," http://www.findingdulcinea.com/news/on-this-day/March-April-08/On-this-Day—Aldo-Moro-Kidnapped-by-the-Italian-Red-Brigades.html. Also, Malcolm Moore, "US envoy admits role in Aldo Moro killing," *The Telegraph*, March 11, 2008, http://www.telegraph.co.uk/news/worldnews/1581425/US-envoy-admits-role-in-Aldo-Moro-killing.html. For the links between the CIA and the Red Brigades see, Andrew Gavin Marshall, "Operation Gladio: CIA Network of "Stay Behind" Secret Armies: The "Sacrifice" of Aldo Moro," http://www.globalresearch.ca/index.php?context=va&aid=9556.

35. Christopher Hitchens, *op. cit.*, p. xxv)

36. See, i.e., Todd Brewster, "Yes, Mr. President," *Vanity Fair*, April 2007, pp. 208-223, 272-274. By the way, the title of the article pushes the disinformational notion that National Security members are yes men unconditionally serving American presidents, which, as I have shown everywhere in this book, is a lie. Actually, American presidents are the ones who have become yes men of their CFR masters.

37. Wilhelm Marbes, "The Psychology of Treason," *Studies in Intelligence*, vol. 30, no. 2 (Summer 1986), (originally classified "Secret," in H. Bradford Westerfield (ed.), *Inside CIA's Private World* (New Haven: Yale University Press, 1995), pp. 70-82.

38. In the CIA's lingo, the "Agency" is a synonym for the CIA.

39. Wilhelm Marbes, *op. cit.*, p. 70.

40. *Ibid.*, p. 79.

41. Reference to the American psychologist in Thomas B. Allen and Norman Polmar, *Merchants of Treason* (New York: Dell, 1988), pp. 65-66.

42. Marbes, *op. cit.*, p. 80.

43. Since Wilson, perhaps with the single exception of JFK, all American presidents have been previously appointed by the CFR conspirators. The electoral process is just a charade to fool the American people into the wrong belief that they had elected the president.

44. Servando Gonzalez, "Obama: Transparency, Invisibility or Treason?," *NolanChart*, February 13, 2008, http://www.nolanchart.com/article6009.html.

45. I don't discard the possibility, however, that, like Russian matrioshka dolls, the CFR's nucleus may be the cover of another, even more secret organization. Studying it, however, would fall far beyond the scope of this book. Therefore, at least for myself and for the time being, the buck stops here. If you want to get into the true, deeper sources of evil, I suggest you to begin by reading Dr. Stanley Montieth's *Brotherhood of Darkness*.

46. Currently, however, thanks to the bandwagon effect, the fact that a person is or is not a CFR member is becoming irrelevant.

47. Like all intelligence agencies, the technique used by CFR recruiters is based on the MICE principle. MICE is an acronym for Money, Ideology, Compromise, Ego, the classical human weaknesses exploited to convince or force an unwilling target for recruitment into treachery and espionage.

48. *Congressional Record*, vol. 54, February 9, 1917, p. 2947.

49. Carl Jensen, *Censored: The News That Didn't Make the News —And Why* (New York: Seven Stories Press, 1995).

50. See, Servando Gonzalez, "Kiss Your Internet Goodbye," *NewsWithViews.com*, April

6, 2003, http://www.newswithviews.com/public_comm/public_commentary7.htm.

51. See, Steve Aquino, "Should Obama Control the Internet? A new bill would give the President emergency authority to halt web traffic and access private data," *Mother Jones*, April 2, 2009, http://motherjones.com/politics/2009/04/should-obama-control-internet.

52. See Carl Bernstein, "The CIA and the Media," *Rolling Stone*, October 20, 1997.

53. Blown back: False information planted by an intelligence service in a foreign country which is later picked up as true by news services of the same country who planted it and reproduced as fact, creating a vicious disinformation circle. It is known of several cases in which disinformation planted by the CIA abroad has been "blown back" into the U.S. as truth. Also known as domestic fallout.

54. See, Frank J. Donner, *The Age of Surveillance* (New York: Alfred A. Knopf, 1980), p. 270.

55 .Frances Stonor, *The Cultural Cold War: The CIA and the World of Arts and Letters* (New York: The New Press, 2000).

56. For a good analysis of the CIA's job in the American universities see, Diamond, Sigmund. *Compromised Campus: The Collaboration of Universities with the Intelligence Community, 1945-1955* (New York: Oxford University Press, 1992).

57. Systematic vote fraud in the U.S. has been extensively documented. See, i.e., John Sullivan, "In Considering Electronic Voting, Giuliani Faces the Fraud Factor," *The New York Times,* August 36, 1995, p. A11; "Voting Early and Often, *The Wall Street Journal*, December 19, 1994, p. A14; also Ivars Peterson, "Making Votes Count," *Science News*, October 30, 1993, p. 282.

58. It has become evident that the conspirators have recruited Sarah Palin. Currently they are using her as a Judas goat to guide the Tea Party sheeple right into the Republican slaughterhouse.

59. See, Caleb Marquis, "Farrakhan On President Obama: 'Selected Before Elected'," *ScooptheMagazine.com*, 24 March 2010, http://www.scoopthemagazine.com/writers-block/1950-farrakhan-on-president-obama.

60. Sniegoski quoted in Paul Craig Roberts, "U.S. Economy Imploding as Obama Follows Failed NeoCon Policies" *The Market Oracle*, February 10, 2009, http://www.marketoracle.co.uk/Article8796.html. See also, Stephen J. Sniegoski, "Obama and the Neocon Middle East War Agenda," *AntiWar.com*, March 21, 2009, http://www.antiwar.com/orig/sniegoski.php?articleid=1434.

61. See, David Horowitz, "Obama Deranged Syndrome," *National Review Online*, http://article.nationalreview.com/380283/obma-rderangement-syndrome/david-horowitz. See also, David Horowitz, "How Conservatives Should Celebrate the Inauguration," *Front Page Magazine*, January 20, 2009, http://97.74.65.51/reaadArticle.aspx?ARTID=33761.

62. See, Arthur Herman, *Joseph McCarthy: Reexamining the Life and Legacy of America's Most Hated Senator* (New York: The Free Press, 2000); also, M. Stanton Evans, *Blacklisted By History: The Untold Story of Senator Joe McCarthy and His Fight Against America's Enemies* (New York: Crown Forum, 2007).

63. Earl T. Smith, *The Fourth Floor* (New York: Random House, 1962).

64. The now well known Venona intercepts —top-secret cables sent between Moscow and the Soviet embassy in Washington, D.C.— proved beyond any doubt that most of the people McCarthy accused of treason were collaborating with the Soviets. Venona was the name of a secret operation that in 1946 broke the Soviet codes and snooped on their traffic. What the Venona intercepts didn't show, however, was that these traitors were passing information to the Soviets on behalf of their true masters, the CFR conspirators.

65 .According to some rumors, in May 1957, while convalescing from a bout of hepatitis at the Bethesda Naval Hospital in Maryland, persons unknown quietly administered Senator Joseph McCarthy lethal doses of poisonous carbon tetrachloride. He died soon after.

66. See, Carroll Quigley, *Tragedy and Hope: A History of the World in Our Time* (New

York: Macmillan, 1966), p. 950.

67. Robert Welch, *The Politician* (Privately printed edition, 1963).

68. Far from being a doctrine to liberate the workers from capitalist exploitation, Communism is a false ideology conceived by international bankers and monopoly capitalists to better exploit the workers.

69. Of recently, Glenn Beck has made the mistake of believing that these people are evil because they are "progressives." He is wrong. This blurry ideology they call progressivism is just a cover to fool some gullible Americans, particularly most of the ones who proudly call themselves "progressives." Proof of it is that, trough their actions, "progressives" have proved to be very regressive. For example, Berkeley's "progressives" have always supported the worst and longest tyranny in Latin America.

70. Asset: Any resource—person, group, relationship, instrument, installation, or supply—at the disposition of an intelligence organization for use in an operational or support role. Often used with a qualifying term such as agent asset or propaganda asset. The term is normally applied to a person who is contributing to an intelligence agency's clandestine mission, but is not a fully controlled agent.

71. Lawrence H. Shoup and William Minter, *Imperial Brain Trust: The Council on Foreign Relations & United States Foreign Policy* (New York: Monthly Review Press, 1977), p. 119.

72. James Perloff, *The Shadows of Power: The Council on Foreign Relations and the American Decline* (Appleton, Wisconsin: Western Islands, 1988), p. 64.

73. Joel Mowbray, *Dangerous Diplomacy: How the State Department Threatens America's Security* (Washington, D.C.: Regnery, 2003).

Chapter 4

1. Christy Macy and Susan Kaplan, *Documents: A shocking collection of memoranda, letters, and telexes from the secret files of the American Intelligence Community* (New York: Penguin Books, 1980).

2. *Ibid.*, p. 10.

3. Jeffrey T. Richelson, *A Century of Spies: Intelligence in the Twentieth Century* (New York: Oxford University Press, 1995).

4. *Ibid.*, p. 131.

5. Black: Said of any operation whose true source is hidden or falsely attributed to another source. In the case of propaganda, "black" also means that the content is mostly fake or forged.

6. R. Harris Smith, *OSS: The Secret History of America's First Intelligence Service* (Berkeley: University of California Press, 1972) p. 1.

7. Arthur M. Schlesinger, Jr., *The Imperial Presidency* (Boston: Houghton Mifflin Company, 1973).

8. Information of FDR as a CFR puppet in Curtis D. Ball, *My Exploited Father-in-law* (Washington, D.C.:Action Associates, 1970), pp. 23-24, 92, 185.

9. See, i.e., Stewart Alsop and Thomas Braden, *Sub Rosa: The OSS and American Espionage* (New York: Harcourt, Brace and World, 1964); Corey Ford, *Donovan of the OSS* (Boston: Little, Brown, 1970); Anthony Cave Brown, *The Last Hero: Wild Bill Donovan* (New York: Times Books, 1982); Bradley F. Smith, *The Shadow Warriors: O.S.S. and the Origins of the C.I.A.* (New York: Basic Books, 1983).

10. David Wise and Thomas B. Ross, *The Espionage Establishment* (New York: Random House, 1967), p. 4.

11. Smith, *OSS: The Secret History of America's First Intelligence Service* (Berkeley: University of California Press, 1972), p. 34.

12. Bradley F. Smith, *The Shadow Warriors* (London: André Deutsch, 1983), ch. 3.

13. Robert Alcorn, *No Banners, No Bands* (New York: D. McKay, 1965), p. 182.

14. John Prados, *Safe for democracy: The Secret Wars of the CIA* (Chicago: Ivan R. Dee, 2006), p. 43.

15. *Ibid.*

16. *Ibid.*.

17. Smith, *OSS: The Secret History of America's First Intelligence Service* (Berkeley: University of California Press, 1972)

18. *Ibid*, p. 6.

19. Robert Alcorn, *No Banners, No Bands* (New York: D. McKay, 1965), p. 182.

20. Flap. 1. A scandal, commotion, controversy, publicity or blow-up of some kind. A flap is usually the political and public fallout of a blown operation. 2. Also called "security flap" or "quiet flap." In intelligence jargon, an investigation made when a leak is suspected. It must be conducted with extreme discretion, so as not to alert any suspects. The quiet approach also means that persons caught red-handed are fired, but often permitted to go free rather than make a public appearance in court to answer criminal charges.

21. Smith, *op. cit.,* p. 6.

22. *Ibid.*, p. 7. In a footnote Smith mentions that the captain eventually joined the CIA and became a ranking Far Easter intelligence analyst for the Company.

23. *Ibid.*, p. 6.

24. *Ibid*, p. 88.

25. Philip Knightly, *The Second Oldest Profession: The Spy as Patriot, Bureaucrat, Fantasist and Whore* (London: Pan Books, 1986), p. 221.

26. John Ranelagh, *The Agency: The Rise and Decline of the CIA* (New York: Touchstone, 1987), pp. 95-96.

27. *Ibid*, p. 96.

28. Smith, *op. cit.*, p. 10.

29. *Ibid*, p. 7.

30. *Ibid*, p. 6.

31. Allen W. Dulles, *The Secret Surrender* (New York: Harper and Row, 1966), pp. 88, 113.

32. Smith, *op. cit.* p. 9.

33. Actually, this was not a difficult mission for the OSS. Most OSS officers had links to corporations that traded with the Nazis or had cartel agreements with German companies. For a detailed study of how the OSS helped Nazis to avoid punishment, see, Thomas M. Bower, *The Pledge Betrayed: America and Britain and the Degasification of Post-War Germany* (New York: Doubleday, 1982), especially Part 4.

34. Lyman Kirkpatrick, *The Real CIA* (New York: MacMillan, 1968), p. 15.

35. Charles Higham, *Trading With The Enemy: An Exposé of the Nazi-American Money Plot, 1933-1949* (New York: Delacorte Press, 1983), p. 59.

36. *Ibid*, p. 59.

37. Smith, *op. cit.*, pp. 15-16.

38. *Ibid*, p. 15.

39. Higham, *op. cit.*, p. 216.

40. Smith, *op. cit.*, p. 10.

41. *Ibid.*, p. 11.

42. Robert Wilcox, *Target Patton: The Plot to Assassinate General George S. Patton* (Washington, D.C.: Regnery, 2008), pp. 139-140.

43. *Ibid.*, p. 11. For detailed information about the OSS penetrated by leftists and Communists, see Smith, pp. 9-15.

44. *Ibid*, p. 15.

45. Robert Wilcox, *Target Patton: The Plot to Assassinate General George S. Patton* (Washington, D.C.: Regnery, 2008).

46. *Ibid.*, p. 71.

47. *Ibid.*, p. 94.

48. *Ibid.*, p. 11.

49. See, Higham, *op. cit.*, p. 212.

50. Charles Higham, *Trading Wit the Enemy: An Exposé of the Nazi-American Money Plot 1933-1949* (New York: Delacorte, 1983).

51. Antony Sutton, *Wall Street and the Rise of Hitler* (Seal Beach, California: '76 Press, 1976).

52. Jim Marrs, *The Rise of the Fourth Reich: The Secret Societies That Threaten to Take Over America* (New York: William Morrow, 2008).

53. The story of Patton's odyssey in *Daniel Yergin, The Prize: The Epic Quest for Oil, Money and Power* (New York: Pocket Books, 1993), pp. 385-388. Also in Cushman Cunningham, *The Secret Empire* (North Fort Myers, Florida: Leela Publishing, n.d.), pp. 110-111.

54. Wilcox, op.cit., p. 4.

55. A few months later, following advice from Secretary of State Edward Stettinius, Secretary of War Henry Stimson, and General George Marshall, all of them CFR agents, President Truman ordered dropping atomic bombs on Hiroshima and Nagasaki. The justification for this atrocity was because it would save American lives. But it is difficult to accept that the same people who caused the death of close to three quarter of a million of Americans lives by stopping Patton, had now acted to prevent the death of American soldiers.

56. Yergin, *op. cit.*, p. 387.

57. Robert Wilcox, *Target Patton: The Plot to Assassinate General George S. Patton* (Washington, D.C.: Regnery, 2008).

58. See, *The Spotlight*, October 15, 1979, p. 16.

59. A. Ralph Epperson, *The Unseen Hand: An Introduction to the Conspiratorial View of History* (Tucson Arizona: Publius Press, 1985), p. 301.

60. Wilcox, op. Cit., p. 12, quoting Patton's diaries, August 29, 1945.

Chapter 5

1. It is interesting to know that a few non-CFR- controlled Republicans in Congress opposed the legislation, which was promoted by liberal "progressive" Democrats, mostly because it gave too much power to the president. With the passage of time, however, they were co-opted, and now "conservative" Republicans are the strongest supporters of the imperial presidency, particularly when there is a Republican in the White House. See, William Greider, *Who Will Tell the People: The Betrayal of American Democracy* (New York: Simon & Schuster, 1992), pp. 365-366.

2. See, David I. Walsh, Letter to James V. Forrestal, 15 May 1945 in Ferdinand Eberstadt, *Unification of the War and Navy Departments and Postwar Organization for National Security*, U.S. Congress, 79th Congress, 1st session, Senate, Committee on Naval Affairs, Senate Committee Print (Washington: Government Printing Office, 1945) iii–iv. 136; Demetrios Caraley, *The Politics of Military Unification: A Study of Conflict and the Policy Process*, (New York: Columbia University Press, 1966); also, Jeffrey M. Dorwart, *Eberstadt and Forrestal: A National Security Partnership, 1909-1949*, (College Station, Texas: Texas A&M University Press, 1991).

3. See Charles A. Stevenson, "Underlying Assumptions of the National Security Act of 1947," in *Joint Force Quarterly*, Issue 48, 1st Quarter 2008, p. 130.

4. Paul Y. Hammond, "The National Security Council as a Device for Interdepartmental Coordination: An Interpretation and Appraisal," *American Political Science Review*, December 1960, 899.

5. Influenced by insights from Bernard Baruch, another CFR hand, Eberstadt consid-

ered the NSRB as the key mechanism to unify a larger corporate political-economic organization by coordinating military, industry, labor, and business in a national security program — actually the officialization of the already existing military-industrial complex later mentioned by President Eisenhower in his farewell speech.

6. National Security Act of 1947, P.L. 80-253, § 101(a), 61 Stat.

7. Ronald Kessler, *Inside the CIA* (New York: Pocket Books, 1992), p. 85.

8. False flag recruiting: the recruiting of an agent by an intelligence service passing as a different one. A technique by which an informant, defector in place or agent is recruited through the disguise of telling him he will be working for the "good guys" —another country or service different from the one who is actually making the recruitment.

Usually, after a talent spotter detects a prospect for recruitment, he learns as much as he can about the target's political sympathies. Then an agent or intelligence officer approaches him pretending he is working for the country or organization for whom the target is sympathetic, while in reality he is working for another. (Talent spotter: 1. An intelligence officer or operative whose function is to detect and assess individuals who might be of value for an intelligence service and potential recruits for intelligence work. 2. A deep-cover agent who recruits agents to work against their own country or organization.)

The Israeli Mossad operatives are experts in false flag recruitment. Being able to produce agents who can pass for just about any nationality under the sun, the Mossad has worked some remarkable operations with false flag recruitment.

9. These are, i.e., the ones wrongly accused of treason by Rowan Scarborough in his book *Sabotage: America's Enemies Within the CIA* (Washington, D.C.: Regnery, 2007).

10. Nelson's memorandum to Eisenhower in Loftus and Aaron, *op. cit.*, p. 279.

11. The exception was John F. Kennedy, whose father Joseph P. Kennedy, to the utter surprise of the Rockefellers and their CFR co-conspirators, used his money and Mafia contacts to put his son in the White House.

12. For some time these meetings were conducted at the secret gatherings of the Bohemian Grove in northern California —the place where both Nixon and Reagan were given the tap in the shoulder in the Skull & Bones tradition. For information about the Bohemian Grove see, G. William Domhoff, *The Bohemian Grove and Other Retreats: A Study in Ruling-class Cohesiveness* (New York: Harper Torch, 1974. Of lately, they mostly take place at the secret Bilderberg conciliabula. This was, i.e., where Hillary Clinton was informed that they had changed their minds and, contrary to what they had promised her, the next president of the U.S. would be Barack Obama. See, Joseph Watson, "Hillary & Obama In Secret Bilderberg Rendezvous," *PrisonPlanet.com*, June 6, 2008. For more information on the Bilderberg and their power see Daniel Stulin, *The True Story of the Bilderberg Group* (Walterville, Oregon: TrineDay, 2007).

13. On Wilson's inflated ego, see Thomas J. Nock, *To End All Wars: Woodrow Wilson and the Quest for a New World Order* (Princeton, New Jersey: Princeton University Press, 1992), p. 13.

14. For the election of Obama as a result of a PSYOP see, Webster Griffin Tarpley, *Obama: The Postmodern Coup – Making of a Manchurian Candidate* (Joshua Tree, California: Progressive Press, 2008), pp. 8, 12.

15. Walter Isaacson and Evan Thomas (1986) *The Wise Men: Six Friends and the World They Made: Acheson, Bohlen, Harriman, Kennan, Lovett, and McCloy* (New York: Simon & Schuster, 1986).

16. See, i.e., David Rothkopff, *Running the World: The Inside Story of the National Security Council and the Architects of American Power* (New York: Public Affairs, 2005), an obscene book written by a CFR member, oozing admiration for the bunch of traitors who have been systematically working to destroy America. He failed to mention, however, that the gang he admires so much is running the world on behalf of its CFR masters.

17. General James L. Jones does not appear in some of the lists of CFR members, but his actions clearly show where his true allegiance is.

18. Jones statement in http://www.infowars.com/nsc-advisor-jones-i-take-my-daily-orders-from-dr-kissinger/, March 23, 2009.

19. Lyman B. Kirkpatrick, Jr., *The Real CIA* (New York: McMillan, 1968), p. 261.

20. Kennedy's words about the CIA quoted in Taylor Branch and George Crile, "The Kennedy Vendetta," *Harper's*, August 1975, p. 50.

21. G. Edward Griffin, a true expert in these matters, does not agree with this. In his seminal book *The Creature From Jekyll Island: A Second Look at the Federal Reserve* (Westlake Village, California: American Opinion, 1994). Griffin mentions that JFK, a graduate of the Fabian London School of Economics, was an early advocate of socialism and how he advanced those ideas (Griffin, pp. 109-110). To support this assertion, he quotes a speech delivered by JFK in September of 1963 at an IMF/World Bank meeting in which he praised the virtues of redistribution of wealth and social planning (Griffin, p. 109).

But we need to keep in mind that, like his doctoral dissertation and the book published under his name, most likely JFK, like most U.S. presidents before and after him, was actually reading a text written at the Harold Pratt House. Despite the fact that he had been trained at the Fabian-founded London School of Economics where he studied under the guidance of Harold Laski, JFK was more interested in chasing girls and smoking pot than in ideology. This, however, seems to have changed in the last months of his presidency, with unexpected results.

Griffin also mentions that the bills either were never printed or, if printed, never circulated (Griffin, p. 569). Some people affirm, however, that some of these bills actually circulated, and photocopies of them have been posted in the Internet. But, even if Griffin is right about the bills —and most likely he is— there is the fact that, despite Kennedy himself stating that he was a CFR member, his name does not appear in any of the CFR membership lists.

22. See, National Security Memorandum No. 263, October 11, 1963.

23. Termination with extreme prejudice: CIA euphemism for assassination.

24. As Professor Donald Gibson pointed out, by the early 1960s the Council on Foreign Relations, Morgan and Rockefeller interests, and the intelligence community were so extensively interbred as to be virtually a single entity. Donald Gibson, *Battling Wall Street: The Kennedy Presidency* (New York: Sheridan Square Press, 1994), p. 72.

25. Henry Hurt, *Reasonable Doubt* (New York: Holt, Rinehart and Winston, 1985), p. 324.

26. See, i.e., Jim Marrs, *Crossfire: The Plot That Killed Kennedy* (New York: Carroll & Graf, 1989).

27. See, Donald Gibson, *Battling Wall Street: The Kennedy Presidency* (New York: Sheridan Square Press, 1994).

28. A measure of the Rockefellers' power is the fact that they threatened the richest man in America, whose only interest in life had been making money and producing poorly designed software, with dismembering his huge corporation and scattering it to the wind. Soon after, the scared guy saw the light and not only joined the CFR, but also founded a non-profit corporation to help the Rockies reach one of their cherished goals: depopulating Africa. For a measure of the power of the Rockefellers see, Myer Kutz, *Rockefeller Power* (New York: Pinnacle, 1967).

29. See, Sherman H. Skolnick, "What Happened to America's Golden Boy?," http://www.apfn.org/skolnicksreport/goldenboy.html; also Barry Chamish, "JFK Jr., Ten Years After," and Michael Green, "The Assassination of JFK, Jr. Far Right Draws First Blood in the 'War on Terror.'" For a detailed study of how the conspirators have used airplane "accidents" to get rid of their enemies see Skolnick's "The Secret History of Airplane Sabotage," http://www.apfn.org/skolnicksreport/shistory.html.

30. I have used the name traditionally favored in Cuba to designate the war, because, contrary to what appears in most American history textbooks, when the early imperialist conspirators decided to create the Maine incident as a pretext to enter the war, the Cuban patriots had already been fighting the Spaniards for long years. Actually, the 1898 war was the third of the wars the Cubans had waged against colonialist Spain.

31. A good source for discovering the true cause of most of U.S. interventions around the world is William Engdahl's *A Century of War: Anglo-American Oil Politics and the New World Order* (London: Pluto Press, 2004). See also, Daniel Yergin, *The Prize: The Epic Quest for Oil, Money, and Power* (New York: Pocket Books, 1993).

32. Zoltan Grossman, "From Wounded Knee to Iraq: A Century of U.S Military Interventions." (http://academic.evergreen.edu/g/grossmaz/interventions.html). For the sake of clarity, I have slightly modified Dr. Grossman's list.

33. Butler joined the Marine Corps when the Spanish American War broke out. During his 34 years of Marine Corps service, Butler was awarded two Congressional Medals of Honor, the first one for the capture of Veracruz, Mexico, in 1914, and the second one for the capture of Ft. Riviere, Haiti in 1917. In addition, he was awarded numerous medals for heroism including the Marine Corps Brevet Medal (the highest Marine medal at its time for officers). He was one of only 19 people to be twice awarded the Congressional Medal of Honor.

34. General Smedley D. Butler, *War is a Racket* (Los Angeles: Feral House, 2003), p. 23.

35. Trevor Monroe, *The Politics of Constitutional Decolonization* (Kinston: University of the Wrest Indies, 1947), p. 27.

36. Written in China 500 B.C, Sun Tzu's, *The Art of War* is considered a sort of Bible of intelligence and espionage. The book contains principles still relevant today.

37. Dulles quoted in David Wise and Thomas B. Ross, *The Espionage Establishment* (New York: Random House, 19670), p. 290.

38. Michael Parenti, *Dirty Truths* (San Francisco: City Lights, 1996) pp. 185-186.

39. Stanfield Turner, *Secret and Democracy: The CIA in Transition* (Boston: Houghton Mifflin, 1985), p.46.

40. Source, Zoltan Grossman, "From Wounded Knee to Iraq: A Century of U.S Military Interventions." (http://academic.evergreen.edu/g/grossmaz/interventions.html) For the sake of clarity, I have slightly modified Dr. Grossman's list and added some interventions. The list, however, does not fully reflect all U.S. interventions during this period because the ones the conspirators have made through proxies, i.e., Castro, are not included in it.

41. See, *Final Report of the Select Committee to Study Governmental Operations with Respect to Intelligence Activities, United States Senate*, Book I, Chapter VIII, April 26, 1976.

42. Turner, *op. cit.*, p. 76.

43. Turner, *ibid.*, pp. 84-85.

44. Turner, *ibid.*, p. 186.

45. The FBI's fight against the CIA continued during Hoover's long tenure as FBI director and has somehow continued after his death. This fight has been extensively documented by several authors, particularly Mark Riebling in his *Wedge: From Pearl Harbor to 9/11: How the Secret War Between the FBI and the CIA has Endangered National Security* (New York: Touchstone, 1994). What Riebling misses, though, is that Hoover's fight was never directed against CIA A, which he ignored, but against CIA B, probably one of America's worst domestic enemies.

46. Unconfirmed rumors about Hoover's homosexuality have been around for many years. The fact that he never married and did not date women, as well as his too close friendship with Clyde Tolson, his chief deputy, have brought credibility to it. Rumors about

the existence of some photos of Hoover dressed in drag were never confirmed. On the other hand, Hoover's supporters have contested the rumors by bringing the fact that he hated effeminate homosexuals and didn't admit then in the FBI. But history shows that gays usually harass and persecute effeminate homosexuals.

47. The Containment Doctrine was first expressed by CFR agent George Kennan in the famous article he wrote for *Foreign Affairs* under the synonym "X," and later polished by the CFR's "Wise Men." See Evan Thomas, *The Very Best Men: The Daring Early Years of the CIA* (New York: Simon and Schuster, 2006), pp. 9, 29.

48. The Marshall Plan was actually written by CFR secret agent Richard Bissell. See, Evan Thomas, *op. cit.*, p. 10.

49. Though generally attributed to JFK, actually the first person who mentioned the Alliance was CFR secret agent Fidel Castro. On May 2, 1959, during a session of the Economic Assembly of the Latin American States, Castro suggested that, in order to avoid problems in Latin America, the U.S. should help the Latin American countries economically. See, Herbert Matthews, *Fidel Castro* (New York: Simon and Schuster, 1969), pp. 166-167. Next month, during a speech at New York's Central Park, he called for an American "Marshall Plan" for Latin America in order to avoid communism. See, *Hispanic American Report*, Vol. XII, (No. 4, 1959), p. 205.

50. Evan Thomas, *The Very Best Men: The Daring Early Years of the CIA* (New York: Simon and Schuster, 2006), pp. 9, 29.

51. John Loftus, *The Belarus Secret* (New York: Alfred A. Knopf, 1982), p. 69.

52. Thomas, p. 30.

53. For Hillenkoetter's and Houston's objections to CIA's covert operations see, John Prados, *Safe for Democracy: The Secret Wars of the CIA* (Chicago: Ivan R. Dee, 2006), p. 38.

54. Christy Macy and Susan Kaplan, *Documents: A shocking collection of Memoranda, letters, and telexes from the secret files of the American intelligence community* (New York: Penguin, 1980), pp. 157-161.

55. Christy Macy and Susan Kaplan, *Documents: A shocking collection of Memoranda, letters, and telexes from the secret files of the American intelligence community* (New York: Penguin, 1980), p. 162.

56. Evan Thomas, *The Very Best Men: The Daring Early Years of the CIA* (New York: Simon and Schuster, 2006), pp. 9, 29.

57. In a series of well-researched books, professor Antony Sutton proved beyond any reasonable doubt that the CFR conspirators created the Soviet Union's military machine. See Sutton's massive *Western Technology and Soviet Economic Development* (Three volumes) (Stanford, California: Hoover Institution Press,1968-1973), also his *Wall Street and the Bolshevik Revolution* (New Rochelle, New York: Arlington House, 1974) and The Best Enemy Money Can Buy (Billings, Montana: Liberty House Press, 1986).

58. Barton J. Bernstein, "American Foreign Policy and the Origins of the Cold War," in Barton J. Bernstein, ed., *Politics and Policies of the Truman Administration* (Chicago: Quadrangle, 1970), pp. 16-17.

59. H.W. Brands, *The Devil We Knew: Americans and the Cold War* (New York: Oxford University Press, 1993), p. vi.

60. Frank Kofsky, *Harry S. Truman and the War Scare of 1948* (New York: St. Martin's Press, 1993), p. 308.

61. After retiring from CIA Wisner committed suicide. See, Evan Thomas, *The Very Best Men: The Daring Early Years of the CIA* (New York: Simon and Schuster, 2006), pp. 319-320.

62. *Ibid.*, p. 15.

63. *Ibid.*, p. 11.

64. See Ranelagh, *op. cit.*, pp. 151-152.

Chapter 6

1. The only exception is Allen Dulles, and we know what happened to President Kennedy for firing him.

2. For recent examples of how unethical CIA analysts have wittingly cooked the books to produced erroneous intelligence estimates to please their bosses, see Melvin A. Goodman, *Failure of Intelligence: The Decline and Fall of the CIA* (Lanham, Maryland: Rowman and Littlefield, 2008), pp. 93, 136, 183.

3. See, i.e., John Tierney, "Politics in the Guise of Science," *The New York Times*, February 24, 2009, pp. D1-D2.

4. Alan W. Scheflin and Edward M. Opton, Jr., *The Mind Manipulators* (New York: Paddington Press, 1978) p. 241.

5. Captain George White in a letter to Dr. Sidney Gottlieb, who ran the technical division for the CIA.

6. Jacques Barzun, "Meditations on the Literature of Spying," *The American Scholar* (Spring 1965).

7. See V. Cherniavsky, "U.S. Intelligence and the Monopolies," *International Affairs* (January 1965).

8. *U.S. News and World Report*, October 8, 1962, p. 50.

9. A proof that most authors who have delved into the field of intelligence and espionage lack a true knowledge of the spy trade is that many of them, even writing in the CIA's official publications, confuse counterintelligence and counterespionage. See, i.e., H. Bradford Westerleys introductory note to Richards J. Heuer, Jr. article on page 379, in H. Bradford Wersterfied, (ed.), *Inside CIA's Private World* (New Haven, Connecticut: Yale University Press, 1995).

Counterintelligence (CI), is a term often referred to as "negative intelligence," since its primary objective is to block the efforts of foreign secret services or governments to penetrate and obtain secret or confidential information of our own intelligence service. The activities of counterintelligence are concerned with identifying and counteracting the threat to security posed by hostile intelligence services or organizations, or by individuals engaged in espionage inside our intelligence service, mostly without making the opposition aware that the threat has been neutralized.

The goal of all CI operations is a form of penetration in which the intervening factor of an agent is turned against his controllers and kept in place feeding them disinformation disguised a true intelligence. On the contrary, Counterespionage (CE), is an activity of intelligence designed to detect, destroy, neutralize, or prevent espionage activities through identification, penetration, manipulation, deception, and repression of individuals, groups, or organizations conducting or suspected of conducing espionage activities.

The goal of all CE operations is a form of penetration in which the intervening factor of an agent is removed. This occurs when an enemy network is captured intact and in its entirety. Such cases are rare and are most often the result of plain luck, but this doesn't stop CE officers from forever trying to achieve it.

10. Joseph J. Trento, *The Secret History of the CIA* (Roseville, California: Forum, 2001.)

11. *Ibid.*, p. 44.

12. Joseph J. Trento, *Prelude to Terror* (New York: Carroll & Graf, 2005), p. 1.

13. See, *CIA Targets Fidel : Secret 1967 CIA Inspector General's Report on Plots to Asassinae Fidel Castro* (Melbourne, Victoria: Ocean Press, 1996).

14. If one is to believe Castro's own claims, the CIA has tried to kill him no less than 638 times, but I have the feeling that this figure is a little exagerated. See, i.e, the documentary film *638 Ways to Kill Castro* (Newbuty Park, California: Silver River Productions, 2007). Also, *CIA Targets Fidel* (Melbourne, Victoria: Ocean Press, 1996).

15. See, Servando Gonzalez, *The Secret Fidel Castro: Deconstructing the Symbol* (Oakland, California: Spooks Books, 2001), pp. 203-207.

16. By the way, in his study of the first years of the CIA, *The Central Intelligence Agency: An Instrument of Government to 1950* (University Park, Pennsylvania: The Pennsylvania State University Press, 1990), Arthur B. Darling, the Agency's first official historian and a scholar of honor and integrity, heavily criticized the Dulles-jackson-Correa report. When Allen Dulles became CIA Director in 1953 he restricted access to Darling's study, which was not made public until 1990.

17. Forrestal eventually became one of the CFR's strongest critics, but at the time of the Hillenkoetter affair he was still under the control of the conspirators.

18. In honor to truth, at that time even some CFR members were not fully under the control of the CFR conspirators. I think General Bedell Smith may have been one of them.

19. Sometimes erroneously called "raw intelligence." But, by definition, intelligence is an elaborated product. There is nothing raw in it. Actually, the most accepted definition of intelligence is "information (raw data) that has been evaluated and validated. Consequently, "raw intelligence" is a contradiction in terms.

20. See, i.e., Rowan Scarborough, *Sabotage: America's Enemies Within the CIA* (Washington, D.C.: Regnery, 2007), pp., 14, 18-19, 22-24. Also, Ralph W. McGehee, *Deadly Deceits: My 25 Years in the CIA* (New York, Sheridan Square Publications, 1983), pp. 190, 192.

21. Albert Wohlstetter, "Is There a Strategic Arms Race?," *Foreign Policy*, No. 15 (Summer, 1974).

22. See, Anne Hessing Cahn, "Team B: The trillion-dollar experiment," *Bulletin of the Atomic Scientists* 49 (April 1993), pp. 22–27; also Tom Barry, "Remembering Team B," *International Relations Center*, (February 12, 2004) http://rightweb.irc-online.org/analysis/2004/0402teamb.php.

23. Agitprop. Agitation and propaganda. Though mainly used by the Soviets in reference to Communist and Front Group activities, the term was first used in the early thirties by *Newsweek* magazine.

24. Actually, the polemic dates back to an internal CIA struggle that began soon after the Agency's creation, exemplified by the 1949 debate between Sherman Kent and Willmore Kendall. See Jack Davis, "The Kent-Kendall Debate of 1949." *Studies in Intelligence* 35, no. 2 (Summer 1991), pp. 37-50; *Studies in Intelligence* 36, no. 5 (1992), pp. 91-103.

24. Anne Hessing Cahn, "Team B: The trillion-dollar experiment," *Bulletin of the Atomic Scientists* 49 (April 1993), pp. 22–27.

25. *Ibid.*

26. As Soviet Union grew more strong and capable, its foreign policy would also become less aggressive.Team B Report. Page 15.

27. See, Fred Kaplan, "Can the CIA Be Saved?" *Slate* (July 9, 2004), http://www.slate.com/id/2103650.

28. Fareed Zakaria, "Exaggerating The Threats," *Newsweek* (16 June 2003)

29. In their book *Government by Gunplay: Assassination Conspiracy Theories from Dallas to Today* (New York: New American Library, 1976), Sidney Blumenthal and Harvey Yazijian (eds.) argue that the U.S. government has used murder regularly and systematically as a way to advance its agenda, killing the likes of JFK, Dr. King, the Black Panthers leaders, and others. Unfortunately Blumentahl, a key adviser to both Bill and Hillary Clinton, failed to mention the long list of assassinations attributed to the Clintons.

30. This does not mean, however, that all CIA officers working for CIA B are traitors. On the contrary, most of them are true patriots under the wrong assumption that they are working, fighting, and risking their lives for the defense of their country. For a notable example of a true patriot unknowingly working for CIA B, see, Gary Berntsen, *Jawbreaker:*

The Attack on Bin Laden and Al-Qaeda: A Personal Account by the CIA's Key Field Comander, (New York: Three Rivers Press, 2005). The book shows how CFR-controlled people in the CIA and the U.S. military allowed Bin Laden to escape from the battlefield at Tora Bora, Afghanistan.

31. A good example of this type of books is Rowan Scarborough, *Sabotage: America's Enemies Within the CIA* (Washington, D.C.: Regnery, 2007). According to CIA insider E. Howard Hunt, Regnery has been for many years subsidized by the CIA.

32. Probably the most notorious of this type of books is Evan Thomas' *The Very Best Men: The Daring Years of the CIA* (New York: Simon & Schuster, 2006)

33. See, i.e., Edward Jay Epstein, "The War Within the CIA," *Commentary* (August 1978; William Colby, *Honorable Men: My Life in the CIA* (New York: Simon & Schuster, 1978); Seymour Hersh, "Angleton," *The New York Times Magazine*, June 25, 1978; and David Martin, *Wilderness of Mirrors* (New York: Harper & Row, 1982)

34. In 1973 the Directorate of Plans became the Directorate of Operations. As everything related to the CIA, this is an intentionally misleading name. The Directorate of Plans had nothing to do with intelligence plans. It was the CIA's department of dirty tricks, that is, covert operations, the only branch of the CIA that really interested its creators.

35. Info on Hillenkoetter in Melvin A, Goodman, *Failure of Intelligence: The Decline and Fall of the CIA* (Lanham, Maryland: Rowan and Littlefield, 2008), pp. 35-36.

36. See, Phillip Knightley, *The Second Oldest Profession: The Spy as Bureaucrat, Fantasist and Whore* (London: Pan Books, 1986), p. 338.

37. Jeffrey T. Richelson, *A Century of Spies: Intelligence in the Twentieth Century* (New York: Oxford University Press, 1995), p. 273, also Mary Ellen Reese, General Reinhard Gehlen: The CIA Connection (Fairfax, Virginia: George Mason University Press, 1990), pp. 145-147, 153-154.

38. For a good description of how this process took place, and even a list of names of some of the newcomers, see Melvin A, Goodman, *Failure of Intelligence: The Decline and Fall of the CIA* (Lanham, Maryland: Rowan and Littlefield, 2008), pp. 16-20.

39. Peter Beinart, "How could the CIA have been so stupid?,"*The New Republic*, November 12, 2001, p. 6.

40. Robert Baer, *See No Evil: The True Story of a Ground Soldier in the CIA's War on Terrorism* (New York: Random House, 2003).

41. See, i.e., Theodore Draper, "Is the CIA Necessary," *The New York Review of Books*, August 14, 1997.

42. Victor Marchetti and John D. Marks, *The CIA and the Cult of Intelligence* (New York: Dell, 1974).

43. Ralph McGehee, *Deadly Deceits: My 25 Years in the CIA* (New York: Sheridan Square, 1983).

44. Frank Snepp, *Decent Interval* (Harmondsworht, Middx: Penguin, 1980.

45. Arthur B. Darling, *The Central Intelligence Agency: an Instrument of Government to 1950* (The Pennsylvania State University press: University Park, Penn., 1990).

46. *Ibid.*, pp. xx-xxi, xxv.

47. See, Raymond L. Garthoff, "U.S. Intelligence in the Cuban Missile Crisis," in Blight and Welch, (eds.), *Intelligence in the Cuba Missile Crisis* (London: Frank Cass, 1998), p. 21.

48. For a different, truly revisionist view of the story, see my book *The Nuclear Deception: Nikita Khrushchev and the Cuban Missile Crisis* (Oakland, California: Spooks Books, 2002).

49. Rendition: CIA's euphemism for kidnapping suspects and illegally moving them to countries where they can be tortured or killed.

50. See Melvin A. Goodman, *Failure of Intelligence: The Decline and Fall of the CIA* (Lanham, Maryland: Rowman & Littlefield, 2008), pp. 63-88.

51. David Wise, *Molehunt: The Search for Traitors That Shattered the CIA* (New York:

Random House, 1992), pp. 255-237.

52. See Arthur Herman, *Joseph McCarthy: Reexamining the Life and Legacy of America's Most Hated Senator* (New York: The Free Press, 2000). Also, Jon Basil Utley, "Senator Joseph McCarthy's Charges 'now accepted as fact,'" www.biblebelievers.org.au/jmc.htm

53. William F. Jasper, "Conspiracy: Where's the Proof?," *The New American*, Vol. 12, No. 19 (September 16, 1996), pp. 5-10.

54. *Ibid.*, p. 10.

55. Ron Rosenbaum, "The Shadow of the Mole,"*Harper's*, October, 1983; Seymour Hersh, "Angleton: The Cult of Counterintelligence," *The New York Times Magazine*, June 25, 1978; Edward Jay Epstein, *Deception: The Invisible War Between the KGB and the CIA* (New York: Simon and Schuster, 1989); David C. Martin, *Wilderness of Mirrors* (New York: Ballantine, 1980); Tom Mangold, *Cold Warrior: James Jesus Angleton: The CIA's Master Spy Hunter* (New York: Simon & Schuster, 1991); William Hood, *Mole* (New York: Norton, 1982) and David Wise, *Molehunt: The Secret Search for Traitors That Shattered the CIA* (New York: Random House, 1992), just to mention a few.

56. Aaron Lathan, *Orchids for Mother* (Boston: Litle, Brown, 1977)

57. Martin, *op. cit.*, p. 204.

58. You may download the whole "family jewels" archive consisting of almost 700 pages of responses from CIA employees to a 1973 directive from Director of Central Intelligence James Schlesinger asking them to report activities they thought might be inconsistent with the Agency's charter at: http://community.theblackvault.com/articles/entry/The-Family-Jewels-Collection-CIA-.

59. As an index of how things have changed in America, it is interesting to notice that currently the CIA, the FBI, the NSA and the Office of Homeland Security are conducting much more large spying operations against the American people and nobody, particularly the mainstream press, seems to care. The CIA people in charge of Chaos were Angleton and his counterintelligence staff. See, John Ranelagh, *The Agency: The Rise and Decline of the CIA* (New York: Simon & Schuster, 1987), p. 534.

60. *Ibid.*

61. John Loftus and Mark Aaron, *The Secret War Against the Jews: How Western Espionage Betrayed the Jewish People* (New York: St. Martin's Press, 1994),p. 82.

62. The double-cross system: The use of double agents turned against the service which originally controlled them and used for large-scale deception of the enemy. See, J.C. Masterman, *The Double Cross System in the War of 1939 to 1945* (New Haven, Con.: Yale University Press, 1972).

63. The term notional comes from medieval philosophy, and refers to the class of entities that exist only in the mind.

64. Turned: Intelligence jargon for an officer or agent working for another intelligence service or organization who has been convinced to change sides and continue active in the conflict. An agent so persuaded is said to be "turned." Once turned the agent becomes a double agent.

65. The whole story is told in detail in David Wise, *Molehunt: The Secret Search for Traitors That Shatered the CIA* (New York: Random House, 1972).

66. William Colby, *Honorable Men: My Life in the CIA* (New York: Simon & Schuster, 1978).

67. The reader should not confuse "clandestine" with "covert." Clandestine operations comprise all passive operations, like spying, whose goal is to obtain information from the enemy through illegal means. In contrast, the goal of covert operations (i.e., assassination, propaganda, sabotage) is to actively influence the enemy's behavior. That's why the Soviets called covert operations "active measures."

68. *Ibid.*, p. 243.

69. Wise, *Molehunt*, p. 240.
70. Colby, *Op. Cit.*, pp. 245-246.
71. See Sutton's massive *Western Technology and Soviet Economic Development* (Three volumes), also his *Wall Stret and the Bolshevik Revolution* .
72. George Racey Jordan with Richard L. Stokes, *From Major Jordan's Diaries* (New York: Hartcourt Brace, 1952). The books is currently out of print, but you can read it online at: http://www.sweetliberty.org/issues/wars/jordan/01.html.
73. For CFR conspirators sabotaging the Navy's efforts to launch a Viking rocket with a Vanguard satellite in order to allow the Russians to launch their Sputnik first, see, http://www.archives.gov/education/lessons/sputnik-memo/.
74. Lehman quoted in G. Edward Griffin, *op. cit.*, p. 303.
75. On mini ball bearings and accelerometers to be exported to the Soviet Union, see, U.S. Senate, *Proposed Export of Ball-Bearing Machines to U.S.S.R.* (Washington, D.C., 1961). Also, Antony Sutton, *The Best Enemy Money Can Buy* (Billings, Montana: Liberty House, 1986), Chapter 7.
76. Ford Motor Company built a heavy truck factory in the Kama river, who later produced military trucks the Vietnamese used against the U.S. military in the Vietnam war. See, Sutton, *The Best Enemy Money Can Buy*, Chapter 2, American Trucks in Korea and Vietnam —For the Other Side.
77. Plant: an agent or intelligence officer sent to an enemy service posing as a defector, in order to pass false information. 2. A person infiltrated into an organization with intention of exploiting a known or perceived weakness, and/or to obtain classified and potentially damaging information about it.
78. Colby, *op. cit.*, pp. 243-244.
79. *Ibid.*, p. 334.
80. *Ibid.*, pp. 335, 364.
81. Angleton cleverly disguised his treachery behind a cloud of deceptive and abstruse concepts like, "the more valuable the intelligence the greater the potential for deception," and "the greater the truth, the bigger the lie." See David C. Martin, *Wilderness of Mirrors* (New York: Ballantine, 1980), p. 20.
82. Colby, *op. cit.*, p. 364.

Chapter 7

1. For an excellent analysis of how Germany lost the war but the conspirators saved the Nazis, see, Jim Marrs, *The Rise of the Fourth Reich: The Secret Societies That Threaten to Take Over America*. New York: William Morrow, 2008.
2. See, Earl T. Smith, *The Fourth Floor* (New York: Random House, 1962).
3. The operation by which the CFR infiltrated and eventually took control of the U.S. Department of State is described in detail in Lawrence H. Shoup and William Minter, *Imperial Brain Trust: The Council on Foreign Relations & United States Foreign Policy* (New York: Monthly Review Press, 1977), pp. 148-156.
4. I have not taken into consideration for this study Castro's versions of the event (he has given several), particularly the one he gave to Arturo Alape, because Castro has proved to be a very unreliable source of information.
5. John Loftus and Mark Aarons, *The Secret War Against the Jews: How Western Espionage Bedtrayed the Jewish People* (New York: St. Martin's Press, 1994), p. 8.
6. Though del Pino claimed to be a University student, he was a student of the Escuela de Artes y Oficios [School of Arts and Trades], which was not a part of the University of Havana.
7. Confidential Despatch No. 336, April 26, 1948. Embassy, Habana. http://www.icdc.com~paulwolf/gaitan/archives/mallory26april1948.htm.

8. See, Ramón B. Conte, *Historia oculta de los crímenes de Fidel Castro* (Self-published, n.p., 1995), pp. 15-30.

9. Heavy, a.k.a. slag. CIA vernacular for assets of girth and muscle the Agency uses in situations where brute force is more important that wit. Heavies also serve as bodyguards for CIA top officers.

10. In his book *Inside the Company: CIA Diary* (New York: Bantam, 1989), p. 396, CIA defector Philip Agee identifies Isabel Siero Pérez, del Pino's aunt, as a CIA's Miami station agent.

11. Both in his book and in a phone interview I made with him, Conte mentions a Mr. William Bolieu. After much research, however, I have been unable to find any information about such a person. So, I concluded that he was actually talking about Willard Beaulac, later to be appointed U.S. Ambassasdor to Colombia.

12. Ramón B. Conte, *Op. Cit.*, pp. 17-18.

13. You may listen to Conte's interview (in Spanish) at my website: www.servandogonzalez.org.

14. Information on Pawley in Mario Lazo, *Dagger in the Heart: American Policy Failures in Cuba* (New York: Twin Circle, 1968), pp. 144-145, 170-171.

15. CFR member George Marshall already had experience in the creation of the Communist menace: he was instrumental in the implementation of a plan developed by the CFR conspirators by which Chiang Kai-Shek was betrayed and China was given in a silver plate to Mao Tse-tung and his "agrarian reformers."

16. False flag operation: an operation designed to be untraceable to the sponsor due to misrepresentation or disguise. Usually, false clues are planted to implicate another group or country as the perpetrator of the operation.

17. See, Hausman's Report mentioned in Gonzalo Sánchez, (ed.), *Grandes potencias: El 9 de abril y la violencia* (Bogotá: Planeta, 2000), p. 47.

18. Willard L. Beaulac, *Career Ambassador* (New York: Macmillan, 1951), p. 236.

19. Parts of these CIA Reports were later released by CIA Director Adm. Hillenkoeter to a Congressional committee of inquiry and published in the press.

20. Senate Internal Security Scommittee, *Communist Threat to the United States Through the Caribbean*, Hearings, Part II, August 3, 1959, Appendix, "Communist Anti-American Riots — Mob Violence as an Instrument of Red Diplomacy" (staf report), p. 116.

21. *Ibid.*, p. 116.

22. Jack Davis, "The Bogotazo," *Studies in Intelligence* Vol. 13, (Fall 1969).

23. *Ibid.*

24. "Communist Involvement in the Colombian Riots of April 9, 1948," Office of Intelligence Research (OIR), Report 4696, U.S. Sate Department, October 14, 1948.

25. Francisco Fandiño Silva, *La Penetración Soviética en América y el 9 de abril*, (Bogotá: Nuevos Tiempos, 1949).

26. See, *U.S. News & World Report*, April 23, 1948, pp. 13-14.

27. Russell Jack Smith *The Unknown CIA: My Three Decades with the Agency* (Washington, D.C.: Pergamon-Brasseys, 1989), p. 38.

28. Confidential Despatch No. 336, April 26, 1948. Embassy, Habana. http://www.icdc.com/~paulwolf/gaitan/archives/mallory26april1948.htm.

29. Jules Dubois, *Fiddel Castro: Rebel - Liberator or Dictator?* (New York: Bobbs-Merrill, 1959) , p. 18.

30. It seems that far from being a Communist, Betancourt was more close to the ideology of the Caribbean Legion, an organization of non-communist left wingers counting among them President Figueres of Costa Rica and Cuba's Prío Socarrás. See, Nathaniel Weyl, *Red Star Over Cuba* (New York: Hillman/MacFadden, 1960), p. 69.

31. Alberto Niño H., *Antecedentes y secretos del 9 de abril* (Bogotá: Editorial Pax, 1949), p. 77. Niño was the former Security Chief of Colombia.

32. Activities of Wieland, Rubbotom and Castro in Bogotá, Colombia, in Hearings, *Communist Threat to the U.S. Through the Caribbean*, Senate Internal Subcommittee, 86th-87th Congress, Parts 1-12, pp. 725, 756, 806; also in Mario Lazo, *Dagger in the Heart* (New York: Twin Circle, 1968), pp. 144-145ß.

33. James Bamford, *Body of Secrets* (New York: Random House, 2001).

34. For info on Rumsfeld's Proactive, Preemptive Operations Group (P2OG) see, Chris Floyd, "The Pentagon Plan to Provoke Terrorist Attacks," *Counterpunch.com*, November 1, 2002, http://www.counterpunch.org/floyd1101.html; also, Frank Morales, "The Provocateur State: Is the CIA Behind the Iraqi 'Insurgents' – and Global Terrorism,? *GlobalResearch.com*, May 10, 2005, http://www.globalresearch.ca/index.php?context=va&aid=67.

35. Weyl, *op. cit.*, pp 74-75.

36. *Ibid.*, p. 75.

37. Richard E. Sharpless, *Gaitán of Colombia: A Political Biography* (Pittsburgh: University of Pitsburh Press, 1978), p. 173.

38. Dubois, *op. cit.*, p. 19.

39. Alberto Niño, *op. cit.*

40. *Ibid.*, p. 54.

41. Lacides Orozco, "Two Cubans Distribute Arms," Bogotá, Colombia, April 19 (1948), *UPI*, quoted in Weyl, *op. cit.*, p. 92-93.

42. *Ibid.*, p. 92.

43. Francisco Fandiño Silva, *La penetración Soviética en América y el 9 de Abril* (Bogotá, Nuevos Tiempos, 1949), p. 77.

44. Most likely, Mirtha Díaz Balart, Castro's fiancée to whom he married later that year.

45. Niño, op. cit, p. 77.

46. *Ibid.*

47. The *Daily Worker*, New York, August 5, 1953.

48. Richard Pattee, "The Role of the Roman Catholic Church," in Robert Freeman Smith, ed., *Background to Revolution* (New York: Alfred A. Knopf, 1966), p. 110.

49. Jules Dubois, *Fiddel Castro: Rebel — Liberator or Dictator?* (New York: Bobbs-Merrill, 1959), p. 17.

50. Castro's speech quoted in Andrés Suárez, *Cuba: Castroism and Comunism* (Cambridge, Mass.: The M.I.T. Press, 1967), p. 94.

51 Castro's interview was published in English the *Illustrated Weekly of India*, and later translated into Spa.nish in the prestigious newspaper *El Tiempo* of Bogotá. See, Angel Aparicio Laurencio, *Antecedentes desconocidos del nueve de abril* (Madrid: Ediciones Universal, 1973), p. 21.

52. A few months later, Castro married Mirtha Díaz Balart.

53. Niño, *op. cit*, p. 77.

54 .Information about *El Popular* in Aparicio Laurencio, *op. cit.*, p. 39.

55. Mighty Wurlitzer. CIA's lingo fo a system or method of inserting a "news" piece in a small or cooperative newspaper or magazine, in hoping that larger papers, and eventually the big wire news services, would pick up this item of black information and disseminate it around the world. The supposed source, or originating paper, is quickly forgotten as the planted story works its way out to the front pages of the world's major papers.

56. See, Davis, *op. cit.*

57. Gonzalo Sánchez, (ed.), *Grandes potencias: El 9 de abril y la violencia* (Bogotá: Planeta, 2000), p. 352.

58. Witnesses observations mentioned in the secret report made by Naval Attaché Col. W. F. Hausman, of the U.S. Office of Naval Intelligence. Quoted in Gonzalo Sánchez, (ed.), *Grandes potencias: El 9 de abril y la violencia* (Bogotá: Planeta, 2000) p. 47.

59. Braun, *op. cit.*, p. 168.

60. The strange fact was mentioned in an article apeared in *El Tiempo* of Bogotá on April 16, 1948.

61. Herbert Braun, *The ssassination of Gaitán: Public Life and Urban Violence in Colombia* (Madison, Wisconsin: The University of Wisconsin Press, 1985), p. 168.

62. Arturo Abella, *Así fue el 9 de abril* (Bogotá: Ediciones Aquí Bogotá, 1973), pp. 54-55.

63. Rafael Azula Barrera, *De la revolución al orden nuevo* (Bogotá: Editorial Kelly, 1956), pp. 390-391.

64. See, i.e., Sánchez, *op. cit.*, pp. 345-347; Alape, *op. cit.*, p. 269; Laurencio, *op. cit.* p. 38; and Abella, *op. cit.*p. 23.

65. Abella, *op. cit.*, p. 23.

66. See, i.e., Alfonso López Michelsen, *Cuestiones Colombianas* (México, D.F.: Impresiones Modernas, 1955), p. 350.

67. Hausman's Report mentioned in Sánchez, op. cit, p. 53.

68. *Ibid.*, p. 348.

69. *Ibid.*, p. 349.

70. Abella, *op. cit.*, p. 36.

71. See, ibid., pp. 31-32;

72. Kennan's memorandum mentioned in Gonzalo Sánchez, (ed.), *Grandes potencias: El 9 de abril y la violencia* (Bogotá: Planeta, 2000), p. 50.

73. See, *The Final Act of Bogotá*, Foreign relations of the United States (FRUS), 1948, Volume IX. http://www.icdc.com/~paulwolf/gaitan/finalactofbogota.htm. The Bogotazo operation was esentially a false flag operation, the antithesis part of PSYOP based on the Hegelian principle of thesis, antithesis, sinthesis.

74. Marshall quoted in Peter H. Smith, *Talons of the Eagle: Dynamics of U.S. – Latin American Relations* (New York: Oxford University Press, 1996), p. 148.

75. Psychological warfare operations, also called PSYOPs, are operations to convey selected information and indicators to foreign audiences to influence their emotions, motives, objective reasoning, and ultimately the behavior of foreign governments, organizations, groups, and individuals. The purpose of psychological operations is to induce or reinforce foreign attitudes and behavior favorable to the originator's objectives.

The Joint Chiefs of Staff has defined psychological operations (PSYOPs) as those that: "include psychological warfare, and, in addition, encompass those political, military, economic, and ideological actions planned, and conducted to create in neutral or friendly foreign groups the emotions, attitudes, or behavior to support achievement of national objectives." Another Dept. of Defense publication develops "the concept of 'strategic psychological operations' as aimed at influencing, and shaping decision-makers' power to govern, or control their followers."

Though, by definition, PSYOPs are directed against foreign audiences, the American people is among the groups being targeted by the conspirators, and efectively controlled thorugh PSYOPs. But the CFR could not accomplish their goals without the complicity of the mainstream news media, which they absolutely control. They do this by using psychological operations. The RAND Corp. and the Stanford Research Institute are two of the institutions the CFR conspirators have used it to develop their PSYOPs against the American people.

76. The Bogotazo also helped the CFR conspirators to reach a secondary, perhaps initially unintended goal: getting rid of CIA Director Adm. Hillenkoetter, a man they didn't fully control. Eventually they replaced him with their trusted secret agent Allen W. Dulles.

77. Jefrey T. Richelson, *A Century of Spies: Intelligence in the Twentieth Century* (New York: Oxford University Press, 1959), p. 217.

78. See, OSS Sabotage Instructions, May 7, 1943, and Simple Sabotage Intractions, C. 1945. http://www.icdc.com/~paulwolf/oss/ossso.htm#sabotage.

79. For more informatin about the OSS' Morale Operations Branch, see, http://

www.icdc.com/~paulwolf/oss/ossmo.htm.

80. Black: Said of any operation whose true source is hidden or falsely attributed to another source. In the case of propaganda, "black" also means that the content is mostly fake or forged.

81. Black propaganda could be either true or false. For morale operations purposes, the truth or falsity is irrelevant. It is the effect on the target's mind what matters.

82. FBI office dismantled, in Secret, No Distribution, Memo of March 6, 1947, http://www.icdc.com/~paulwolf/gaitan/acheson6mar1947.htm

83. Sir Norman Smith, Scotland Yard Report, p. 6, http://www.icdc.com/~paulwolf/gaitan/scotlandyard.htm.

84. *Ibid.*, p. 7.

85. *Ibid.*

86. *Ibid.*, p. 8.

87. *Ibid.*, pp. 13-14.

88. *Ibid.*, p. 4.

89. *Ibid.*, p. 15.

90. Aparicio Laurencio, *op. cit.*, p. 36.

91. Smith, *op. cit.*, p. 15.

92. *Ibid.*, p. 16.

93. One of the best sources of the War Scare is Frank Kofsky's, *Harry S. Truman and the War Scare of 1948* (New York: St. Martin's Press, 1993)

94. Manchurian Candidate. A person who has been psychologically conditioned to unwittingly commit a crime after post-hypnotic conditioning.

95 .Weyl, *op. cit.*, p. 84.

96. Niño, *op. cit.*, p. 77.

97. Fandiño Silva, *op. cit.*, p. 17.

98. Azula Barrera, *op. cit.*, pp. 374-375.

99. Weyl, *op. cit.*, p. 76. If true, this conversation between del Pino and Gaitán's assassin took place just and hour and a half before the assassination took place.

100. U.P. report quoted in Weyl, *op. cit.*, p. 77.

101. *Ibid.*, p. 250.

102. *Ibid.*, p. 249.

103. Braun, *op. cit.*, pp. 134-135.

104. Alape, *op. cit.*, pp. 251-252.

105. Azula Barrera, *op. cit.*, pp. 379.

106. *Ibid.*

107. Bracker mentioned in Weyl, *op. cit.*, p.84.

108. Arturo Alape, *El Bogotazo: Memorias del olvido* (La Habana: Casa de las Américas, 1983), pp. 600-601. In his book, written 35 years after the Bogotazo, Alape includes more than forty interviews of people who were witnesses or actively participated in the Bogotazo events, including Fidel Castro. I have not quoted any part of Castro's interview in this book simply because the Cuban dictator is not a reliable source of information.

109. *Ibid.*, p. 226.

110. *Ibid.*, p. 223.

111. *Ibid.*, p. 231, 224.

112. *Ibid.*, p. 224.

113. *Ibid.*, p. 232.

114. *Ibid.*, p. 231.

115. *Ibid.*

116. Abela, *op. cit.*, p. 57.

117. Smith, ScotlandYard Report, p. 11.

118. Alape, *op. cit.*, pp. 224, 226.
119. *Ibid.*, 233-234.
120. *Ibid.*, p. 237.
121. *Ibid.*, pp. 237-238.
122. *Ibid.*, p. 241.
123. *Ibid.*
124. *Ibid.*, pp. 239-240.
125. *Ibid.*, p. 254.
126. *Ibid.*, p. 259.
127. *Ibid.*, p. 257.
128. *Ibid.*, p. 260.
129. *Ibid.*, pp. 603-604.
130. *Ibid.*, p. 598.
131. Smith, Scotland Yard Report, p. 8.
132. See, John Marks, *The Search for the Manchurian Candidate: The CIA and Mind Control* (New York: McGraw-Hill, 1980).
133. Mark Riebling, "Tinker, Tailor, Stoner, Spy," Osprey Production, 1944, http://home.di.net/lawserv/leary.html.
134. *Ibid.*
135. These subjects are described in detail in Marks, *op. cit.*
136. Abela, *op. cit.*, p. 19.
137. Guillermo Tovar, "Nueva visión del crimen de Jorge Eliécer Gaitán que partió en dos la historia del país," *Colombia.com*, April 10, 2006, http://www.colombia.com/entretenimiento/noticias/DetalleNoticia3951.asp.
138. William Tuner, *The Asassination of Robert Kennedy: The Conspiracy and Coverup* (New York: Thunder's Mouth, 1993).
139. *Ibid.*, p. 196-198.
140. Marks, *Ibid.*, p. 3.
141 *Ibid.*, p. 6.
142. *Ibid.*, p. 4.
143. Like all CIA code names, its real purpose is to disinform about the true subject of the program, therefore, it has no significance at all.
144. Smith, *op.cit.*, p. 12.
145. See, Servando Gonzalez, *The Secret Fidel Castro: Decostructing the Symbol* (Oakland, California: Spooks Books, 2001), pp. 309-315.
146. The fact that neither the Communist nor any other political party took any advantage of the revolt or had any part whatsoever in Gaitán's assassination is mentioned several times in the Scotland Yard Report. See, Smith, *op. cit.*, pp. 5-6,
147. Dr. Locard's principle quoted in Zakaria Erzinclioglu, *Every Contact Leaves a Trace: Scientific Detection in the Twentieth Century* (London: Carlton, 2001), p. 10.
148. Gerardo Reyes y Pablo Alfonso, "Castro ocultó estimonio sobre asesinato de Gaitán," *El Nuevo Herald*, October 22, 2000.
149. Information about Spiritto in Daniel Semper Pizano, "La solución al enigma es novelesca, y podría estar cercana," *El Tiempo* (Bogotá), October 11, 2000; also in "Confesión del agente norteamericano involucrado en el asesinato de Jorge Eliécer Gaitán," August 19, 2000, http://www.vermail.net/justicia/confes/htm.
150. Gerardo Reyes y Pablo Alfonso, "Castro ocultó testimonio sobre asesinato de Gaitán," *El Nuevo Herald*, October 22, 2000.
151. Alape calls himself a "historian," but his book about the Bogotazo is just a collection of testimonies, accepted at face value, without the slightest attempt at analisis or interpretation.

152. Daniel Semper Pizano, "La solución al enigma es novelesca, y podría estar cercana," *El Tiempo* (Bogotá), October 11, 2000.

153. *Ibid.*

154. H.P. Albarelli, Jr., "William Morgan: Patriot or Traitor?," *WorldNetDaily*, (April 21, 2002), http://www.worldnetdaily.com/news/article.asp?AFRTICLE_ID=27312.

155. García Márquez story in Juan Carlos Gaitán Villegas, "El misteriosos elegante del 9 de abril," *El Tiempo*, Bogotá, February 26, 2003.

156. Angleton's physical description in Tom Mangold, *Cold Warrior: James Jesus Angleton: The CIA's Master Spy Hunter* (New York: Touchstone, 1991), p. 31.

157. Smith, Scotland Yard Report, pp. 9-10.

158. According to Tom Mangold, Angleton "was rarely photographed in public." Mangold, *op. cit.*, p. 31.

159. *Ibid.*

160. *Ibid.*, pp. 32, 359.

161. *Ibid.*, p. 43-44.

162. *Ibid.*, p. 44.

163. *Ibid.*, p. 361.

164. *Ibid.*

165. Servando González, *La madre de todas las conspiraciones: una novela de ideas subversivas* (Oakland, California: El Gato Tuerto, 2005), p. 178.

166. Greg Parker, "Bogota Ripples, Was Sierra a 'false assassin'?," *The Education Forum* (Australia), September 30, 2006, http://educationforum.ipbhost.com/index.php?showtopic=8067&mode=threaded&pid=170004.

167. See, Paul Wolf, "Dclassifying Colombia's Greatest Mystery: Notes From a Talk at CITCA Meeting in Chapel Hill, NC," June 13, 2001, http://www.blythe.org/nytransfer-subs/2001-South_America/Declassifying _Colombia's_Greatest_Mystery.html.

168. German philosopher Georg Wilhelm Friedrich Hegel (1770-1831) made change the cornerstone of his philosophical system, which he called Dialectics. According to Hegel, an idea or principle — which he called the thesis— is challenged by its opposite —the antithesis. Eventually, from this conflict emerges a new idea or priciple which is a synthesis of both.

Chapter 8

1. William Engdahl's *A Century of War: Anglo-American Oil Politics and the New World Order* (London: Pluto Press, 2004), p. 32.

2 *Ibid*, p. 33.

3. Daniel Yergin, *The Prize: The Epic Quest for Oil, Money and Power*, Part I (New York: Pocket Books, 1991), p. 59.

4. John Christian Ryter, "The Secret Life of AIC," *NewsWithViews.com*, March 31, 2009.

5. It seems, however, that Clinton Roosevelt discovered the principles of communism a few years before Marx.

6. Antony C. Sutton, *Wall Street and the Bolshevik Revolution* (New Rochelle, New York: Arlington House, 1974).

7. G Edward Griffin, *The Creature From Jekyll Island: A Second Look at the Federal Reserve* (Appleton, Wisconsin: American Opinion, 1994).

8. Ryter, *op. cit.*

9. Antony C. Sutton, *The Best Enemy Money Can Buy* (Billings, Montana: Liberty House, 1986).

10. Most likely the Rosenbergs, true Communist fanatics, ignored that their true role was to disinform the American people by paying with their lives.

11. For a detailed account of the treachery see George Racey Jordan, *From Major Jordan's Diaries* (Boston: Western Islands, 1965), pp. 72-106. Major Jordan's accusations seem to have been substantiated many years later in a novel written in 1980 by Franklin Roosevelt's son James Roosevelt. See, James Roosevelt *A Family Matter* (New York: Simon & Schuster, 1980).

12. Sun Tzu, *The Art of War* [translated by Samuel B. Griffith] (London: Oxford University Press, 1963), p. 146.

13. Sutton, *The Best Enemy Money Can Buy*, pp. 101-111.

14. MIRV, the capability of an intercontinental missile to fire more than a single warhead.

15. Sutton, *op. cit.*, p. 101.

16. Khrushchev personally implemented and executed Stalin's plan for the mass starvation and liquidation of six to eight million people in the Ukraine in the early 1930s. He was the chief executioner for the bloody Moscow kangaroo purge trials in 1936. In 1937-38, during a second two-year reign of terror in the Ukraine, he supervised the slaughter of another 400,000 people. In the post-Ukraine purge, he had an active role in the liquidation or exile of hundreds of thousands in the gulags. See, U.S. Congress, House Committee on Un-American Activities, *Crimes of Khrushchev*, Part II, p. 2, Part I, pp. 7, 1.

17. *Time*, September 21, 1959.

18. Khrushchev's character described in William Randolph Hearst, Jr., B. Considine and F. Coniff, *Khrushchev and the Russian Challenge* (New York: Avon, 1961), pp. 39, 42, 92, 59, 65, 229.

19. See, F.I. Greenstein, "The Impact of Personality in Politics: An Attempt to Clear Away Underbrush," *American Political Science Review*, No. 61, 1967, pp. 629-641. On the principle of strategic intervention see T. Kotarbinsky, *Praxiology:* An Introduction to the Science of Efficient Action (New York: Pergamon, 1965).

20. Richard P. Stebbins, *The United States in World Affairs, 1959* (New York:Vintage, 1960), p. 125.

21. I have strong suspicions that the pro-Castro faction in the Kremlin (Mihail Suslov, Boris Ponomarev, Piotr Shelest, Alexandr Shelepin and Andrei Grechko), as well as KGB boss Yuri Andropov and his protegé Mikhail Gorbachev, were CFR moles.

22. Allen Dulles appointed Angleton in 1954 as chief of the CIA's counter-intelligence section. Two years later Angleton had the greatest success in his career when he obtained a transcript of Khrushchev's speech. The feat boosted Angleton's career at CIA. Now, having in mind that in intelligence and espionage things are seldom what they seem, I would not discount the possibility that the story about Angleton fetching Khruschev's speech may not be true, and was created precisely to boost Angleton's career at CIA to better cover his true work as a conspirators' mole infiltrated in CIA A.

23. I warn the reader that this last paragraph is pure speculation. Most likely the conspirators had always been in contact with Castro. But I think that my guess is not too far off the truth. Anyway, future researchers may find out some day what really happened.

24. The letter was found among the retained files of the American Embassy at Havana, and is now archived in the records of the foreign service posts of the Department of Sate, National Archives, Washington, D.C., record group 84. A facsimile of the letter was published in the *American Archivist* (Vol. 50, Spring 1987, pp. 284-288. I have reproduced a facsimile of the letter in my *The Secret Fidel Castro: Deconstructing the Symbol* (Oakland, California: Spooks Books, 2001), pp. 356-360.

25. See, Alvaro Sanjurjo Torreón, "Fidel Castro, de extra a astro," *Números*, n. 314. The information appears in James Robert Parish and Gregory W. Mank, *The Best of MGM: The Golden Years 1928-1959* (Des Moines, Iowa: Nostalgia Books, 1981), and in the CD-ROM *The Motion Picture Guide* (New York: Cine Books, 1996).

26. This information appeared for the first time in my book *The Secret Fidel Castro: Deconstructing the Symbol* (Oakland, California: Spooks Books, 2001), p. 228.

27. Incident with Camaid and Fidel's self-imposed exile in New York in Manuel Dorta-Duque, *Alejandro (alias) Fidel* (Hato Rey, Puerto Rico: Ediciones Joyuda, 1981), p. 14.

28. Robert E. Quirk, *Fidel Castro* (New York: W.W. Norton, 1993), p. 27.

29. Before it created its training facilities at Camp Peary (a.k.a. "The Farm"), the early CIA used the FBI training facilities at Quantico.

30. *The New York Times*, January 25, 1962. In the course of the conference, reporter Sara McClendon asked the President about the Wieland case. Kennedy was evidently upset by the question, and emphatically denied that Wieland constituted a security risk.

31. Hearings, *Communist Threat to the U.S. Through the Caribbean*, Senate Internal Subcommittee, 86th-87th Congress, Parts 1-12, p. 736.

32. *Ibid.*, pp. 725, 756, 806.

33. Earl T. Smith, *The Fourth Floor (*New York: Random House, 1962), p. 196; also in *Communist Threat, op. cit.*, p. 683.

34. See, Alexandra Obrenovich, *Who is Responsible?* (New York: Carlton Press, 1962) Also, rumors ran that a CIA agent, known as Robert Chapman, spent a long time in the mountains with Raúl Castro.

35. Tad Szulc, *Fidel: A Critical Portrait* (New York: William Morrow, 1986), p. 427.

36. CIA agent with Raúl Castro, evidence of Bruce McColm to the author.

37. Accusations that the *New York Times* has acted as a CIA disinformation tool also in Daniel Schorr, *Cleaning the Air* (New York: Houghton Mifflin, 1977).

38. Earl T. Smith, *The Fourth Floor* (New York: Random House, 1962), pp. 67-68.

39. *Ibid.*, p. 231.

40. *Ibid.*, p. 33.

41. Wise and Ross, *The Invisible Government*, p. 266.

42. Smith, *op. cit..*, pp. 135, 47.

43. For a revealing study of CFR agent Sumner Welles' machinations in Cuba see, Luis Aguilar, *Cuba 1933: Prologue to Revolution* (Ithaca, New York: Cornell University Press, 1972.

44. The whole story is told in detail in Mario Lazo, *Dagger in the Heart: American Policy Failures in Cuba* (New York: Twin Circle, 1968), pp. 169-178.

45. *Ibid.*, p. 175.

46. The story is told in detail by Ambassador Smith himself. See, Earlt E. T. Smith, *The Fourth Floor: An Account of the Castro Communist Revolution* (Washington, D.C.: Selous Foundation Press, 1987) pp. 169-174.

47. Lawrence Shoup and William Minter, *Imperial Brain Trust* (New York: Monthly Review Press, 1977) p. 42; also in Dan Smoot, *The Invisible Government* (Boston: Western Islands, 1962), p. 19. Castro's visit to the CFR is one of the best kept secrets of his visit to the U.S. It is not mentioned in any other book about Castro.

48. Philip Bonsal, *Cuba, Castro, and the United States* (Pittsburgh: University of Pittsburgh Press, 1971), p. 64.

49. Peter Collier and David Horowitz, *Deconstructing the Left: From Vietnam to the Persian Gulf* (Studio City, California: Second Thoughts, 1991), p. 98.

50. For many years I was convinced that I had been the first to mention the possibility that Castro was actually a CIA mole infiltrated into the Soviet camp. I mentioned it first in my book *Historia herética de la revolución fidelista* (San Francisco: El Gato Tuerto, 1986), pp. 87, 104-110. I later expanded this thesis in a long article I published in the internet in 1995, "Fidel Castro Spermole;" http://www.intelinet.org/sg_site/intelligence/sg_supermole.html. I mentioned again this possibility in my book *The Secret Fidel Castro: Deconstructing the Symbol* (Oakland, California: Spooks Books, 2001), and I studied it in greater detail in my 2008 article "Fidel Castro: ¿agente de la CIA?," http://www.intelinet.org/sg_site/intelligence/sg_castro_cia.html

It was not until a few years ago, however, that I discovered to my utter surprise that I was not the first who had thought about the possibility of Castro being a CIA secret secret agent; somebody already suspected it way before it crossed my mind: Nikita S. Khrusuchev. On a speech he gave at Kansas State University, Khrushchev's son Sergei, now an American citizen, mentioned that when he was a teenager he overheard his father and other Soviet leaders mentioning the fact that they didn't know who Castro really was, but they suspected that he was a CIA agent working for the United States. See, Carrie Linin, "(Sergei) Khrushchev Oulines Missile Crisis," *The Collegian*, Kansas State University, http://www.spub.ksu.edu/issues/v099b/sp/n116/cam-cuban-linin.html.

51. One of Castro's most known nicknames is *"El Caballo"* (The Horse). See, Georgie Anne Geyer, *Guerrilla Prince* (Boston: Little, Brown & Company, 1991), p. 205.

52. In an intertextual link to T.S. Elliot poem "Gerontion," James Jesus Angleton used to call counterintelligence "a wilderness of mirrors."

53. Sergei Khrushchev's on Castro in Carrie Linin, "Khrushchev Outlines Missile Crisis," *The Collegian*, Kansas State University.

54. Soviet consensus about Fidel's revolution living its last hours, Prof. Mikhail Berstram in conversation with the author at his office in Stanford University.

55. Castro's warnings in Tad Szulc and Meyer, *The Cuban Invasion* (New York: Praeger, 1962), p. 74.

56. Eisenhower's approval of invasion plan in ibid., p. 77.

57. Invasion plan in Bonsal, *op. cit.*, p. 183.

58. Bowles concerns to Rusk in David Halberstam, *The Best and the Brightest* (Greenwich, Conn.: Fawcett Crest Books, 1972), p. 85.

59. Details of invasion's failure in *U.S. News and World Report*, September 17, 1962.

60. CIA's assumptions about popular support for the invaders in Daniel M. Rohrer, Mark G. Arnold, and Roger L. Conner, *By Weight of Arms: American Military Policy* (Skokie, Illinois: National Textbook Co., 1969), pp. 44-45.

61. Willauer's testimony in *Communist Threat to the U.S.Through the Caribbean*, 86th Congress, 1st Sess., Part. 3, Nov. 5, 1959, pp. 874-875.

62. Willauer "frozen out" and dismissed from State Department in ibid., pp. 875-878.

63. Prisoners' report of false intelligence in *The New York Times,* April 1, 1962, p. 40.

64. Radio Swan's false reports in *St. Louis Post Dispatch*, April 22, p. 1961.

65. Bissell reunifies anti-Castro Cubans, in "Inside Story of the Cuban Fiasco," *U.S. News and World Report,* May 15, 1961.

66. Invasion leaders held incommunicado in *National Review*, August 13, 1963, p. 106.

67. For an interesting testimony on how the CIA left the anti-Castro guerrillas in the lurch, see Air Force Colonel Fred D. Stevens, "J.F.K. Muzzled Me," *The Miami Herald,* December 1, 1961.

68. Air strike alerting Castro in Peter Wyden, *The Bay of Pigs* (New York: Simon and Schuster, 1979), p. 219.

69. Castro inspecting area in *ibid.*, p. 104.

70. Failure to detect coral reefs, in *ibid.*, p. 219.

71. Hugh Thomas, *The Cuban Revolution* (New York: Harper & Row, 1977), p. 585.

72. Robert Kennedy denied accusation in Wise and Ross, *The Invisible Government*, pp. 201-202.

73. Theodore Sorensen, *Kennedy* (New York: Haroer & Row, 1965), p. 296.

74. Arthur Schlessinger, Jr., *A Thousand Days* (London: André Deutsch, 1965), p.

75. Christopher Andrew, *For the President's Eyes Only: Secret Intelligence and the American Presidency from Washington to Bush* (New York: Harper Perennial, 1996), p. 261.

76. David Atlee Phillips, *The Night Watch* (New York: Ballantine, 1977), p. 129.

77. Dangle. An intelligence officer who is intentionally put into the path of an enemy

agent in hopes that he will draw his attention. The idea is that the enemy agent eventually may try to recruit the dangle. Given the fact, however, that the basic rule of thumb of the intelligence job is to suspect anyone who takes the initiative in making an intelligence contact, "dangles" make red lights flash and are usually not recruited.

78. CFR agents present at the WH/4 meeting in Robert Pear, "The Pointing of Fingers at the Bay of Pigs," *The New York Times*, December 30, 1987, p. B-6.

79. Carol Rosenberg, "Bay of Pigs U.S. Invades Cuba Failure on Many Levels," *The Miami Herald*, August 11, 2005.

80. As it has become too common among people who know too much, Pawley eventualy committed suicide under strange circumstances.

81. See, "New Look at an Old Failure. An Ex-Cia Historian Fights to Air His Version of the Bay of Pigs," *TIME* magazine, June 1, 1987, p. 29. See also, Robert Pear, "The Pointing of Fingers at the Bay of Pigs," *The New York Times*, December 30, 1987, p. B-6.

82. Rosenberg, *Ibid.*

83. Keep in mind that these were the comon excuses the CFR disinformes used before they discover the new catch-all excuse: failure to connect the dots!

84. Peter H. Smikth, *Talons of the Eagle: Dynamics of U.S. – Latin American Relations* (New York: Oxford University Press, 1996), p. 167.

Chapter 9

1. For an excellent analysis of Castro's "I am a Marxist" speech, see Loree Wilkerson, *Fidel Castro's Political Programs from Reformism to "Marxism-Leninism* Gainesville, Fl.: University of Florida Press, 1965).

2. Legend. A false biography or cover story, supplied mostly to illegals and sleepers, enabling them to live undetected within a foreign country. A legend may include a false trail created to cover a false or notional biography.

3. The pro-Soviet Cuban Communists never had much faith in what Castro was to do in Cuba, affirmed former President Carlos Prío Socarrás. During the two years of war against Batista, Castro's 26th of July Movement never received a single bullet nor a single *peso* from the Cuban Communists. Prío Socarrás quoted in Daniel James, *Cuba: The First Soviet Satellite in the Americas* (New York: Avon, 1961), p. 29.

4. CIA officer's testimony about Castro not being a Communist in *Communist Threat to the U.S.Through the Caribbean*, 86th Congress, 1st Sess., Part. 3, Nov. 5, 1959, pp. 162-164.

5. Castro as U.S. admirer in Geyer, *Guerrilla Prince*, p. 71.

6. John F. Kennedy, *The Strategy of Peace* (New York: Harper, 1960), p. 133.

7. Most of them could not be properly called documents, but highly edited photocopies of alleged documents that cannot be authenticated by any forensic means.

8. Top Secret Telegram from British Ambassador in Washington D.C., Sir. Harold Caccia, to Foreign Office, 7.06 p.m., November 24, 1959. See, George Gedda, "JFK Warned of a 'Chain Reaction,'" AP, March 22, 2001, http://www.cubanet.org/CNews/y01/mar01/22e4.htm.

9. Khrushchev seeing the Bay of Pigs invasion as birthday present, mentioned by his son Sergei Khrushchev in a speech he gave at Kansas State University, see Carrie Linin, "Khrushchev Outlines Missile Crisis," *The Collegian*, Kansas State University.

10. As I mentioned above, one of Castro's most known nicknames is *"El Caballo"* (The Horse).

11. Andrés Suárez, *Cuba: Castroism and Communism, 1959-66* (Boston: MIT Press, 1967), p. 144.

12. See M. Michael Kline, "Castro's Challenge to Latin American Communism," in Jaime Suchlicki, ed., *Cuba, Castro, and Revolution* (Coral Gables, Florida: University of Miami Press), p. 1972.

13. See Leon Goure and Julian Weinkle, "Soviet-Cuban Relations: The Growing Integration," in Jaime Suchlicki, ed., *Cuba, Castro, and Revolution* (Coral Gables, Florida: University of Miami Press, 1972), p. 149.

14. A 1983 RAND study estimated the Soviet "burden of empire" in the Third World to have increased from roughly $18 billion in 1971 to $ 41 billion in 1981. Most of that money had been drained because of Cuba. See, Charles Wolf et. al., *The Costs of the Soviet Empire* (Santa Monica, California: The Rand Corporation, 1983), p. 9. There was also evidence of great disenchantment in the Soviet government not only about its involvement in Cuba, but also in Central America, Angola and Ethiopia, all of them Castro motivated misadventures.

15. Richard Lowenthal, "The Logic of One-Party Rule," in Abraham Brumberg, ed., *Russia Under Khrushchev* (New York: Praeger, 1962), p. 36. Some people have brought out the Brezhnev doctrine of irreversibility of Communism to argue that Khrushchev would never have tried to get rid of Castro. But the Brezhnev doctrine should not be overgeneralized. It is not certain that other leaders before Brezhnev and Kosygin would have responded in the same way to Castro's challenges. Stalin obviously felt no hesitation on cutting Tito off completely from Soviet support—even if that meant forcing Yugoslavia into the capitalist camp. Similarly, Khrushchev—despite the lessons of Yugoslavia—did not hesitate to withdraw support from China in an equally hostile and abrupt manner when the Marxist leadership dared to challenge his control of the international revolutionary movement.

16. Information about Kudryavtsev in Barron, *KGB*,. 26-27, also in Christopher Andrew and Vasili Mitrokhin, *The World Was Going Our Way: The KGB and the Battle for the Third World* (New York: Basic Books, 2005), p. 37.

17. On Kudryavtsev's expulsion see *The New York Times*, June 5, 1962, 3; also in Lisa Howard, "Castro's Overture," *War/Peace Report*, September 1983, p. 4.

18. In his authoritative book *KGB,* Barron respectfully calls Kudryavtsev "the old master of subversion." See, John Barron, *KGB: The Secret Work of Soviet Secret Agents* (London: Corgi, 1979), p. 20.

19. Castro selecting new Soviet Ambassador in Arkady N. Shevchenko, *Breaking with Moscow* (New York: Ballantine, 1985), p. 187.

20. Turned: Said of an officer or agent working for another intelligence service or organization who has been convinced to change sides and continue active in the conflict. An agent so persuaded is said to be "turned." Once turned the agent becomes a double agent.

21. For an appealing argument about what the Soviet Union would have gained with an American invasion of Cuba see John N. Plank, "Monroe's Doctrine -and Castro's," *The New York Times Magazine*, October 7, 1962.

22. Khrushchev was given to play these type of games. In 1960 he set a trap for the Americans by not revealing how much he knew about the U-2 shot down over Soviet territory on May 1. He waited several days until the Eisenhower administration hanged on its own rope by categorically denying that the plane was on a spy mission. Then, Khrushchev announced that the pilot of the U-2 was alive and healthy and in Soviet hands. He had not mentioned this previously, he explained, in order to see what lies the Americans would tell.

23. Servando Gonzalez, *The Nuclear Deception: Nikita Khrushchev and the Cuban Missile Crisis* (Oakland, California: Spooks Books, 2002).

24. Philip Knightley, *The Second Oldest Profession* (New York: W. W. Norton, 1986), p. 7.

25. There are indications that, as late as 1960, even some units of the newly created Soviet Strategic Rocket Forces were not receiving real missiles, but dummies. See Viktor Suvorov (pseud.) *Inside the Soviet Army* (New York: Berkley Books, 1983), p. 69.

26. *Granma Weekly Review*, May 21, 1967.

27. *Granma*, May 14, 1968, p. 4.

28. Fidel Castro "Cuba no firma desnuclearización mientras E.U. sea una amenaza atómica," *Revolución*, August 27, 1965, pp. 1-2.

29. Tad Szulc, "Exporting the Cuban Revolution," in John Plank, ed., *Cuba and the United States* (Washington, D.C.: Brookings Institution, 1967), p. 79.

30. Richard Gott, *Guerrilla Movements in Latin America* (New York: Anchor Books, 1972), p. 13.

31. *Hoy*, June 16 and 17, 1959.

32. Andrés Suárez, *Cuba: Castroism and Communism, 1959-66* (Boston: MIT Press, 1967), p. 68.

33. Mario Lazo, *op. cit.*, p. 195.

34. Geoffrey Warner, "Latin America," in Geoffrey Barraclough, ed., *Survey of International Affairs 1959-1960* (London: Oxford University Press, 1964), pp. 478-479.

35. Quoted in Andrés Suárez, *op. cit.*, p. 94.

36. FBI report of agent William Stevens, File # 105-655, 24 October 1962, in Gus Russo, *Live by the Sword* (Baltimore: Bancroft Press, 1998), p. 223.

37. "Communist Activities in Latin America," *Report of the Subcommittee on Inter-American Affairs*, U. S. House of Representatives Committee on Foreign Affairs (July 1967), p. 7.

38. Paul D. Bethel, *The Losers* (New Rochelle, N.Y.: Arlington House,1969), pp. 424-425.

39. Recently surfaced confidential information from secret sources in Cuba seem to confirm their claims. Apparently, the notorious Ilich Sánchez Ramírez (aka "Carlos" and "the Jackal") was one of Castro's hit men, and had an active role in the assassination of Somoza. When Carlos had his operations center in Paris in the 1960s, he received Cuban logistic and economic support. His Cuban handler was Armando Pérez Orta, an officer of the Cuban intelligence services operating under the pseudonym "Archimedes."

40. Ernesto Betancourt, "Castro's Terrorist Connection," *No Castro.com*, October 2001, www.nocastro.com/Terrorism/castro-terrorist2.htm.

41. *Ibid.* For a comprehensive overview of Castro's terrorist activities, see, Eugene Pons, "Castro and Terrorism: A Chronology 1959-1967," Institute for Cuban & Cuban-American Studies, Occasional Paper Series, September 2001, with a Foreword by Jaime Suchlicki.

42. *Ibid.*

43. Pons, *op.cit.*

44. The *Miami Herald*, November 11, 2000.

45. "Ayatollah Khomeini's grandson visits Cuba," *Granma Internacional Digital*, August 2, 2001, www.granma.cu/ingles/julio5/30ayat-i.html.

46. Mireya Castañeda, "The people of Cuba march for justice,"*Granma Internacional Digital*, July 26, 2001, www.granma.cu/ingles/julio4/marcha-I.html.

47. "Fidel meets with Portuguese authorities before returning from extensive tour," *Granma Internacional Digital*, www.granma. cu/ingles/mayo/21portu-i.html. Curiously, just a few hours after the events of September 11, 2001, *Granma Internacional Digital* purged its databases of all the information related to Castro's links with the anti-American muslim world.

48. See, i.e., "Patterns of Global Terrorism: 1999," www.state.gov/www/global/terrorism/1999report/intro.html.

49. *AFP*, May 10, 2001.

50. "Fidel Castro and the Ayatollah Khamanei," *Agency France Press*, May 10, 2001, www.neoliberalismo.com/iran_cuba.htm.

51. *Ibid.* Apparently Khamenei's sources of intelligence were very good, because a few weeks before the attacks the Mossad informed the FBI and the CIA that it had picked up indications of a "large-scale target" in the U.S. and that Americans would be "very vulnerable." See Richard A. Serrano and John-Thor Dahlburg, "Officials Told of 'Major Assault' Plans," The *Los Angeles Times*, September 20, 2001. It seems that the Mossad picked up the information from an intercepted message between U.S. terrorists. They were ignored.

52. *Ibid.*

53. "A Tribute to the Syrian Symbol of Struggle," *Granma Internacional Digital*, May 16, 2001, www.granma.cu/ingles/mayo3/20siria-i.html.

54. "Fidel Visits the House Bombed by the United States, Causing the Death of Qadaffi's Daughter," *Granma Internacional Digital*, May 17, 2001, www.granma.cu/ingles/mayo3/2lilia-i.html.

55. Toby Westerman, "Bin Laden Using U.S. Radio Broadcasts?," *WorldNetDaily*, November 8, 2001, www.worldnetdaily.com/news/ articles.asp?ARTICLE_ID=25242.

56. Peter H. Smith, *Talons of the Eagle: Dynamics of U.S.-Latin American Relations* (New York: Oxford University Press, 1996), p. 224.

57. See, http://www.state.gov/r/pa/prs/dpb/2004/38758.htm.

58. See, Steven F. Hayward, "The Carter-Chavez Connection," *Front Page Magazine*, August 26, 2004, http://97.74.65.51/readArticle.aspx?ARTID=11657.

59. See, Carlos Alberto Montaner, "Lo que el golpe unió lo desunirá la muerte," *El Nuevo Herald*, April 23, 2006.

60. The whole story is told in Captain (ret.) Ed Geary's book, *The Venezuelan Conspiracy: The True Story of the CIA and U.S. Coast Guard's Covert Mission to Overthrow the Government of Venezuela.*

61. Georgi Arbatov — "Neo-Bolsheviks of the I.M.F.," *The New York Times*, May 7, 1992, p. A27.

Chapter 10

1. Despite of the fact that the incident never happened, CFR agents in the Congress passed the Gulf of Tonkin Resolution, which Attorney General Nicholas Katzenbach (CFR) accepted as a "functional equivalent" of a congressional declaration of war. This gave Johnson a tacit approval for a full-scale US involvement in the war. See, Jonathan Kwitny, *Endless Enemies: The Making of and Unfriendly World* (New York: Penguin, 1986), pp. 357-358.

2. See, Jeffrey Grup, "The New World Order Wants the New World Order to Fail: Order Out of Atacking the New World Order," *InfoWars.com*, June 7, 2009, http://www.infowars.com/the-new-world-orders-wants-the-new-worldorder-to-fail-order-out-of-atacking-the-new-world-order/.

3. Given the fact, however, that most gays claim to be militant pacifist leftists who hate violence, war, and despise the military, it is difficult to understand their desire to join the U.S. military. Unless they have a secret agenda.

4. Spanish ex-president José María Aznar has mentioned that, during a private conversation he had with Castro in 1998, the Cuban tyrant himself told him that he "needed the embargo for this and the coming generation." See, "Aznar exige el fin del embargo a Cuba para favorecer la democracia en la isla," *Público.es*, April 11, 2010, http://www.publico.es/209092/aznar/exige/embargo/cuba/favorecer/democracia. More recently, U.S. Secretary of State Hillary Clinton reached the conclusion that Cuba's leaders do not want to normalise ties with the U.S. because then they would lose their excuse for the state of the country. See, "Hillary Clinton scorns 'entrenched' Cuba," *BBCNews*, April 10, 2010, http://news.bbc.co.uk/2/hi/americas/8612765.stm.

5. The term notional comes from medieval philosophy, and refers to the class of entities that exist only in the mind.

6. The idea is not new. On April 3, 1902, *The Independent* published an article by W. J. Ghent, former editor of *The American Fabian*, entitled "The Next Step: A Benevolent Feudalism," in which he explains in detail his idea of the coming society.

7. Bertrand Russell, *The Impact of Science on Society*, (London: George Allen & Unwin, 1952), p. 40.

8. Ibid.

9. Huxley quoted in http://encyclopedia.stateuniversity.com/pages/915/Aldous-Leonard-Huxley.html.

10. Senator Helms quoted in Gary H. Kah, *En Route to Global Occupation* (Lafayete, Louisiana: Huntington House, 1991), p. 48.

11. Sun Tzu, *The Art of War* [translated by Samuel B. Griffin] (London: Oxford University Press, 1963), p. 66.

12. Angleton on Deception in Edward Jay Epstein, *Deception: The Invisible War Between the KGB and the CIA* (New York: Simon and Schuster, 1989), pp. 108-109.

13. Lavrenti Beria, *Brain-Washing: A Synthesis of the Russian Textbook of Psychopolitics* (Los Angeles: The American St. Hill Organization, 1955).

14. There is some controversy about the true source of the book. See, i.e., Massino Introvigne, "L. Ron Hubbard, Kenneth Goff, and the 'Brain-Washing Manual" of 1955, CESNUR, Centro Studi sulle Nuove Religioni, http://www.cesnur.org/2005/brainwash _13.htm.

15. Paddock, Alfred H., Jr., *U.S. Army Special Warfare: Its Origins. Psychological and Unconventional Warfare, 1941-1952* (Washington, D.C.: National Defense University Press, 1982), p. 6. For a thorough study on the use of mass media on mass control see, Noam Chomsky (with Edward S. Herman), *Manufacturing Consent: The Political Economy of the Mass Media* (New York: Pantheon, 1988).

16. See, Edward Lilly, "The Psychological Strategy Board and Its Predecessors. Foreign Policy Coordination 1938-1953," in Gaetano Vincitorio (ed.), *Studies in Modern History* (New York: St. Johns University Press, 1968), p. 346.

17. Ibid., p. 84.

18. See, John Prados, *Keepers of the Keys: A History of the National Security Council From Truman to Bush* (New York: William Morrow, 1991), p. 52.

19. This does not mean, however, that I particularly disagree with the concepts of sustainability and environmentalism. Actually, long before I heard of these concepts, I was protecting the environment as much as I could and making an effort to live a sustainable life without dilapidating natural resources. The problem I have is that I discovered that the same people who popularized unsustainable life styles and enormously contributed to the destruction of the environment are now secretly bankrolling the environmentalists. So, it is not that I disagree with the message but that I suspect the messengers' true intentions.

20. This explains the Nazis' acceptance of Darwinism as a sort of official doctrine. See, Richard Weikart, *From Darwin to Hitler: Evolutionary Ethics, Eugenics and Racism in Germany* (New York: Palgrave Macmillan, 2004).

21. Democide is a term coined by political scientist R. J. Rummel in his book *Death by Government* (New Brunswick, N.J.: Transaction Publishers, 1994). According to him, democide is "the murder of any person or people by a government, including genocide, politicide, and mass murder."

22. Another possibility would be, however, that the conspirators are not exposing some parts of their game because they make mistakes. Actually, they may be using a psychological device, practiced by secret societies all around the world, called "the revelation of the method." By openly letting you know that their arguments are false, but also that you are impotent to stop them, they reduce you to a deeper state of powerlessness where you conclude that there is nothing you can do to stop them and resistance is futile.

23. Leonard C. Lewin, *Report From Iron Mountain: On the Possibility and Desirability of Peace* (New York: The Free Press, 1996).

24. See, Alan B. Jones, *How the World Really Works* (Paradise, California: ABJ Press, 1996), pp. 132-133.

25. See, G. Edward Griffin, *The Creature From Jekyll Island: A Second Look at the Federal Reserve* (Appleton, Wisconsin: American Opinion, 1994), p. 524.

26. Kissinger quoted in Leonard Lewin, "Report From Iron Mountain," *The New York Times Book Review*, March 19, 1972.

27. Griffin, Ibid., p. 524.

28. Lewin, op. cit., p. 86.

29. George Kennan, "To Prevent a World Wasteland -A Proposal," *Foreign Affairs*, April 1970.

30. Nelson Rockefeler, *Our Environment Can Be Saved* (New York: Doubleday, 1970), pp. 152-153.

31. Al Gore, *Earth in Balance* (Boston, MA: Houghton Mifflin, 1992).

32. Gore's *Earth in Balance* as a continuation of *Iron Mountain*'s ideas in Tal Brooke, *One World* (Berkeley, California: End Run, 2000), p. 71.

33. Victor Navaski, Introduction to Leonard C. Lewin, *Report From Iron Mountain: On the Possibility and Desirability of Peace* (New York: The Free Press, 1996), pp. v, xiii.

34. Andrew Tully, *White Tie and Dagger (New York: Pocket Books, 1968), pp. 74-78.* Tully mistakenly believes the plot was a Soviet idea, but it was Castro's. The plot is also reported in Andres Oppenheimer, *Castro's Final Hour* (New York: Simon and Schuster, 1992).

35. Daniel Ellsberg, "The Day Castro Almost Started World War III," *The New York Times*, October 31, 1987, p. A7.

36. Dino A. Brugioni, *Eyeball To Eyeball* (New York: Random House, 1991), p. 461. Castro's letter to Khrushchev of October 26 is part of a set of documents obtained by the Cold War International History Project, Woodrow Wilson International Center, Harvard Collection.

37. See, William J. Broad, "Details Emerge of Cold War Nuclear Threat by Cuba," *The New York Times*, September 22, 2009, p. D4.

38. Ibid.

39. Christopher Andrew and Vasili Mitrokhin, *The World Was Going Our Way: The KGB and the Battle for the Third World* (New Yordk: Basic Books, 2005), p. 126.

40. Jeff Franks, "Fidel Castro Appears on TV, Fears Nuclear War," *The Star Online*, July 13, 2010, http://thestar.com.my/news/story.asp?file=/2010/7/13/worldupdates/2010-07-13T063521Z_01_NOOTR_RTRMDNC_0_-500737-1&sec=Worldupdates.

41. Nehru quoted in *Newsday*, December 12, 1973.

42. Michael Kramer and Sam Roberts, *"I Never Wanted To Be Vice-President of Anything!": An Investigate Biography of Nelson Rockefeller* (York: Basic Books, 1976), P. 219.

43. Phil Tracy, "The Albany Bunker," *The Village Voice*, February 15, 1973.

44. *Ibid.*

45. Lewin, *op. cit.*, pp. 66-67, 70-71.

46. Unfortunately, the site where I found the blogger's article has disappeared. See, http://dreamsend2.wordpress.com/2007/08/17/whassup-wseaword/. However, Mr. End is mentioned in http://rigorousintuition.ca/board/viewtopic.php?p=147639&sid= 379fd35e 9521995022e7387fd5971d48.

47. For an analysis of how the John D. Rockefeller and other conspirators created in 1902 the General Education Board as a precursor of the Department of Education, see Emanuel A. Josephson, *Rockefeller "Internationalist"* (New York: Chedney Press, 1952), pp. 125-146, 441.

48. O.W. Markley and Willis W. Harman, (eds.), *Changing Images of Man* (New York: Pergamon, 1982). You may download a facsimile copy of the book at: www.bibliotecapleyades.net/archivos_pdf/changing_images.pdf. The Pergamon edition is basically the same as *Changing Images of Man*, Research Report No. 4, issued May 1974 by the Center for the Study of Social Policy, SRI International.

49. *Ibid.*, p. xv.

50. For one of the few studies about the Bohemian Grove see, G. William Domhoff, *The*

Bohemian Grove and Other Retreats: *A Study in Ruling-class Cohesiveness* (New York: Harper & Row, 1974. Also, Kelly McGinley, "World Leaders Meet Secretly in Sonoma Valley, CA.," NewsWithViews.com, August 14, 2005. Also, Alex Jones has published several articles on the Bohemian Grove and a documentary on DVD. See, *Dark Secrets: Inside the Bohemian Grove*, http://www.infowars.com/bg1.html. The Bohemian Grove has been accused of many things ranging from conspiratorial activities and practicing druid rituals to Satanism, child molestation, human sacrifices and homosexuality. Richard Nixon, who attended at least one of the meetings, mentioned that, "The Bohemian Grove, which I attend from time to time ... it is the most faggy goddamned thing you could ever imagine." See, "Nixon Tape Discusses Homosexuality at the Bohemian Grove," *PrisonPlanet.com*, March 26, 204.

51. Markley and Harman, *op. cit.*, p. vvii.

52. The American Left has always been indirectly bankrolled by the most reactionary elements of the Right, using their non-profit, "philantropic" foundations as cut-outs to hide from public scrutiny the true source of the money. See, i.e., Evan Gahr, "Looking at Philanthropy: The Gift of Giving: Paymasters of the PC Brigades," *The Wall Street Journal*, Jan. 27, 1995; Bob Feldman, "Alternative Media Censorship: Sponsored by CIA's Ford Foundation?," *Disinfo.com*, September 18, 2002, http://old.disinfo.com/archive/pages/article/id2709/pg1/index.html; Joyce Price, "Media Give Liberal Causes Millions More, Study Says," *The Washington Times*, Nov. 14. 1993; Marshall Robinson, "The Ford Foundation: Sowing the Seeds of a Revolution," *Environment*, v. 35 n. 3 (April 1993), 10-20; Goldie Blumenstyk, "New Head of Ford Fund's Education Program is Champion of Women and Minority Students," *The Chronicle of Higher Education*, v. 39 n. 16 (Dec 9, 1992), A27; Daniel Brandt, "Philanthropists at War," *NameBase NewsLine*, No. 15 (October-December, 1996). The fact perhaps explains why the American Left is perhaps one of the most reactionary Lefts in the world. Of course, they see themselves as "progressives." I call them "regressives."

53. *Ibid.*, p. xviii.

54. *Ibid.*, p. xx.

55. Meme (pronounced like "gene"): a term coined by evolutionary biologist and atheist Richard Dawkins in his 1976 book *The Selfish Gene* (Oxford: Oxford University Press, 1976). According to Dawkins, a meme is any unit of cultural information, such as a practice or idea, that is transmitted verbally or by repeated action from one mind to another similar to the transmission of viruses. Consequently, some people have called memes "mind viruses." More important, according to Dawkins, a meme does not need to be true to gain a widespread acceptance –i.e., Nazism. One could add evolution and Darwinism.

56. Marshall Kirk and Hunter Madsen, *After the Ball: How America Will Conquer Its Fear and Hatred of Gays in the 90's* (NewYork: Plume, 1989).

57. *Ibid.*, p. xv.

58. Ibid., pp. xxvi-xxvii. On the other hand, there is the possibility that other forces, not fortune alone, played the important element they needed to advance their gay agenda. According to some researchers, AIDS was a virus artificially created to decimate Africa's population through bacteriological warfare.

59. *Ibid.*, p. xxviii.

60. *Ibid.*, p. 153.

61. *Ibid.*, p. 161.

62. *Ibid.*, p. 163.

63. *Ibid.*, p. 149.

64. *Ibid.*, pp. 150, 153.

65. *Ibid.*, p. 153. Any similarities with the ultimate goal of the totalitarian Big Brother in Orwell's *1984* are most likely not the product of a coincidence.

66. *Ibid.*, pp. 153, 157.

67. *Ibid.*, pp. 170-171.

68. *Ibid.*, p. 171.

69. *Ibid.*, p. 167.

70. For a history of the gay movement as a political movement, see Barry D. Adam, *The Rise of the Gay and Lesbian Movement* (Boston: Twayne, 1987), pp.12-16.

71. Kirk and Madsen, *op. cit.*, p. 183.

72. See, Camille Paglia, "The Dangers of the Gay Agenda," *Salon.com*, Novemeber 1998, http://www.salon.com/col/pagl/1998/10/28pagl.html.

73. American gays joining Venceremos Brigade in Dennis Altman, *Homosexual Oppression and Liberation* (New York: Avon, 1971), p. 218.

74. Personally, I don't think the government, much less the federal government, should have any role whatsoever in deciding which citizens have the right to marry and which don't.

75. See, Sheri and Bob Stritof, "The Marriage Tax Penalty," http://marriage.about.com/od/finances/a/marriagepenalty.htm. Also, Martin Vaughan, "Married Couples Pay More Than Unmarried Under Health Bill," *The Wall Street Journal*, Jan 6, 2020, http://online.wsj.com/article/SB126281943134818675.html.

76. In the case of George W. Bush, personal sympathies may have played a role in the gay marriage charade. Bush's sexual preferences have been the subject of many articles in the Internet. See, i.e., Sherman H. Skolnick, "The Overthrown of the American Republic," Part 47, February 2, 2004. According to Skolnick, "Since puberty, Bush has been the homosexual lover of Victor Ashe, former Mayor of Knoxville, Tennessee." See also, Alan Stang, *Not Holier Than Thou: How Queer is Bush?* (Houston: Patton House: 2007).

77. Maria Lagos et.al., "Sen. Feinstein's lesson on Prop. 8," *SFGate.com*, November 6, 2008, http://articles.sfgate.com/2008-11-06/bay-area/17128173_1_same-sex-marriage-san-francisco-police-chief-earl-sanders.

78. See, Dean E. Murphy, "Mayor Gavin Newsom says he has no apologies for opening San Francisco City Hall to same-sex weddings. But some fellow Democrats, including a gay congressman, say his doing so helped the Bush campaign," November 5, 204. http://corporateswine.net/newsom.html.

79. See, Joan Walsh, "Will the Real Gavin Newsom Please Stand Up," *Opinion Editorials.com.*, July 23, 2004, http://www.opinioneditorials.com/guestcontributors/stillwell_20040330.html. But the Gay Shame radicals obviously missed the point that the secret goal of the conspirators who conceived the idea of gay marriage is precisely the destruction of the institition of marriage.

80. See, Joan Walsh, "Gavin Newsom's Mean Streets," *Salon.com*, July 23, 2004, http://dir.salon.com/ story/news/feature/2004/07/23/newsom/index.html.

Chapter 11

1. The so-called "Climategate" scandal began in November 2009 when a hacker published in the Internet thousands of emails and other documents from the University of East Anglia's Climatic Research Unit. By the way, what the hacker brought to light was not new, just that had been ignored by the mainstream media. See. i.e., Henry Lamb, "The Other 'Green" in Global Warming," *WorldNetDaily.com*, February 3, 2007, http://www.wnd.com/index.php/%3C/b%3E//www.shopnetdaily.com/store/index.php/index.php?fa =PAGE.printable&pageId=39997.

2. See, Jim Kouri, "Climate Change Hoax Ignored by Obama, Gore & the Elite Media," *NewsWithViews.com*, December 6, 2009, http://www.newswithviews.com/NWV-News/news174.htm.

3. *Ibid.*

4. See "'Climategate' Gives Ammo to Global Warming Skeptics," editorial, *USA To-*

day, December 20, 2009, p. 12A.

5. *Ibid.*

6. In his novel *State of Fear*, Michael Crichton describes a conspiracy in which, in order to get grants to fund their studies advancing gobal warming, enviromental "scientists" falsify data, misrepresent facts and threaten critics.

7. See, "Hacked climate emails include calls for 'Earth Government' as foundation of new world order, splitting of America," Infowars, November 24, 2009, http://www.infowars.com/hacked-climate-emails-include-calls-for-earth-government-as-foundation-of-new-world-order-splitting-of-america/

8. Phyllis Schlafly and Chester Ward, *Kissinger on the Couch* (New Rochelle, N.Y.: Arlington House, 1975), p. 151.

9. F. William Engdahl, "Gul Oil Spill 'Could Go Years' If Not Dealt With," www.engdahl.oilgeopolitics.net/print/Gulf%20Oil%20Spill.pdf.

10 George Kennan, "To Prevent a World Wasteland —a Proposal," *Foreign Affairs*, April, 1970. As I mentioned above in this book, George Kennan was the one who, in a *Foreign Affairs* article, launched the idea of containment. He is the same George Kennan who in 1948 wrote NSC 10/2, that illegally allowed the CIA to conduct covert operations. One may erroneously conclude, however, that Kennan was an intellectual genius. Nothing further from the truth. Like Henry Kissinger and Samuel P. Huntington, Kennan was just a mouthpiece for expressing and making public the conspirators' ideas they had implanted in his mind at the secret CFR conciliabula.

11. See, Larry Abraham and Franklin Sanders, *The Greening* (Atlanta, Georgia: Soundview, 1993), p. 290.

12. Ford Foundation Eergy Policy Project, *A Time to Choose America's Energy Future* (Cambridge, Mass.: Ballinger, 1974).

13. This, of course, is not surprising. Paradoxically, the American Left has always been secretly bankrolled by the most reactionary elements of the Right. On the Right bankrolling the Left see, Henry Lamb, "The Other 'Green' in Global Warming, *WorldNetDaily.com*, February 3, 2007, http://www.wnd.com/index.php/index.php?fa=PAGE; Bob Feldman, "Alternative Media Censorship: Sponsored by CIA's Ford Foundation?," http://www.questionsquestions.net/gatekeepers.html; also, Evan Gahr, "Looking at Philanthropy. The Gift of Giving: Paymasters of the PC Brigades," *The Wall Street Journal,* January 27, 1995; Joyce Price, "Media Give Liberal Causes Millions More, Study Says," *The Washington Times*, Nov. 14. 1993; Marshall Robinson, "The Ford Foundation: Sowing the Seeds of a Revolution," *Environment*, v. 35 n. 3 (April 1993) 10-20; Goldie Blumenstyk, "New Head of Ford Fund's Education Program is Champion of Women and Minority Students," *The Chronicle of Higher Education*, v. 39 n. 16 (Dec 9, 1992), A27; Daniel Brandt, "Philanthropists at War," *NameBase NewsLine*, No. 15 (October-December, 1996). The fact perhaps explains why the American Left is one of the most reactionary Lefts in the world. Of course, they see themselves as "progressives."

14. "Obama to Open Offshore Aeas to Oil Drilling," *The New York Times*, March 31, 2010, p. 1.

15. "Obama ups nuclear investment for climate fight," *Reuters*, Februrary 16, 2010, http://www.reuters.com/article/idUSTRE61F33V20100216.

16. If it is true that some forests are dying, it is no less true that some new forests are appearing. See, i.e., Elisabeth Rosenthal, "New Jungles Prompt a Debate on Saving Primeval Rain Forests," *The New York Times*, January 30, 2009, pp. 1, A10.

17. Lester R. Brown, "The Illusion of Progress," in Lester R. Brown et. al., *State of the Wortld 1990: A Worldwatch Institute Report on Progress Toward a Sustainable Society* (New York: W.W. Norton, 1990), p. 3.

18. It is interesting to notice that, even though the words "truthers" and "birthers" —

derogatory, ad-hominem terms created to discredit the people who wanted to investigate dubious aspects of the US government— are frequently used, the mainstream media never mention the "globalwarmers," "evolutioners," "Darwiners," "ecologers," "sustanabiliters", "eugenicers," "newworldorderers," or any other type of lyers.

19. See, Christopher Flavin, "Slowing Global Warming," in Lester R. Brown et. al., *op. cit.*, p. 18. Army meteorologist Gunnar C. Carlson is a former chief meteorologist in the Pentagon and Atmospheric Science Laboratory at White Sands Missile Range in New Mexico.

20. *Ibid.*, p. 20.

21. *Ibid.*, p. 21.

22. See, Julie Schmit, "EPA's CO2 Ruling Could Raise Energy Costs," *USA Today*, December 8, 2009, p. 4B.

23. If any reader thiks that I am using too harsh words to qualify these unscrupulous pseudo-scientisist, please read Monckton's article and you'll see that I am falling short of the mark. See, Christopher Monckton, "They Are Criminals," *Pajamas Media*, November 23, 2009, http://pajamasmedia.com/blog/viscount-monckton-on-global-warminggate-they-are-criminals-pjm-exclusive/. The Viscount Monckton of Brenchley is a British politician, business consultant, and policy advisor.

24. In the mid-1970s, the same "scientists" that now are scaring us with a catastrophic global warming were scaring the people with the coming of a catastrophic global cooling. On April 28, 1975, the cover article of *Newsweek* warned about a coming global cooling. On August 14, 1976, *The New York Time*s reported "many signs that the Earth may be headed for another ice age." Gary Sutton, co-founder of Teledesic and CEO of several other companies, wrote that in 2002 he stood in a room of the Smithsonian, where "an entire wall charted the cooling of our globe over the last 60 million years." See, Gary Sutton, "The Fiction Of Climate Science," *Forbes. Com*, April 12, 2009, http://www.forbes.com/2009/12/03/climate-science-gore-intelligent-technology-sutton.html.

25. See, Jerome R. Corsi, "Science Czar's Guru Called For More Carbon," *WorldNetDaily.com*, December 7, 2009, http://www.worldnetdaily.com/index.php?pageId=118304.

26. Termites are a major source of CO2 in this planet.

27. See, Marvin Tessneer, "Military Meteorologist is Global Warming Skeptic," *The Las Cruces Bulletin*, October 23, 2009, p. A13.

28. Bertrand Russell, *The Impact of Science in Society*, (London: George Allen & Unwin, 1952), p. 40.

29. See, i.e., Brian Winter, "Poor Blame Rich at Climate Talks," *USA Today*, December 10, 2009, p. 6A.

30. Paul Ehrlich, *The Population Bomb* (New York: Ballantine, 1968).

31. Donella H. Meadows et. al., *The Limits to Growth*: *A Report of the Club of Rome's Project on the Predicament of Mankind* (New York: Universe Books, 1972)

32. *The Global 2000 Report to the President* (New York: Pergamon, 1980).

33. Robert Felix, *Not by Fire But by Ice*: *The Next Ice Age Now* (Bellevue, WA: Sugarhouse Publishing, 2007).

34. See, Lindsey Hoshaw, "Afloat in the Ocean, Expanding Islands of Trash," *The New York Times*, November 10, 2009, p. D2.

35. Adding insult to injury, we have the fact that Gaia, the benevolent Mother Goddess the globalwarmers are trying to protect from this plague called humans, is the main producer of CO2 and all types of pollutants product of volcanic activity, as well as destruction by flooding, fires by lightning strikes, hurricanes, tornadoes and earthquakes. Consequently, instead of trying to kill us, humans, in order to save their beloved Gaia, they should try to protect us from the criminal, destructive actions of Gaia.

36. Tom Bearden, "Scalar Electromagnetics and Weather Control: Anomalous Weather

Worldwide," BibliotecaPleyades.net, May 1988, http://www.bibliotecapleyades.net/bearden/bearden13.htm. Also, Tom Bearden, "Weird Weather Warfare & 'Energetic Weapons,'" BibliotecaPleyades.net, http://www.bibliotecapleyades.net/ciencia/secret_projects2/project138.htm.

37. Departent of Defense News Briefing by Secreatry of Defense William S. Cohen at the Conference on Terrorism, Weapons of Mass Destruction, and U.S. Strategy, University of Georgia, Athen, April 28, 1997.

38. See, Russian Navy: The US Created the Earthquake in Haitit, http://socioecohistory.wordpress.com/2010/01/27/russian-navy-the-u-s-created-the-earthquake-in-haiti/.

39. See, "The Militarization of Emergency Aid to Haiti: Is it a Humanitarian Operation or an Invasion?," http://socioecohistory.wordpress.com/2010/01/19/the-militarization-of-emergency-aid-to-haiti-is-it-a-humanitarian-operation-or-an-invasion/.

40. See, "Massive Reserves Of Gold And Oil In Haiti?," http://thisistheendoftheworldasweknowit.com/archives/massive-reserves-of-gold-and-oil-in-haiti.

41. AP: "U.N. Names Bill Clinton Special Envoy to Haiti," *USAToday.com*, April 19, 2009, http://www.usatoday.com/news/world/2009-05-18-clinton-haiti_N.htm.

42. Zbigniew Brzezinski, *Between Two Ages: America's Role in the Technetronic Era* (New York: Viking, 1976), p. 57.

43. The study was available in .pdf format at the web site of the Federation of American Scientiststs, at www.fas.org/irp/agency/army/mipb/2002_04.pdf, but now the link points to a different document.

44. Carroll Quigley, *op. cit.*, pp. 1247-1248.

45. Peter G. Peterson, *Running on Empty: How the Democratic and Republican Parties are Bankrupting Our Future and What Americans Can Do About It* (New York: Farar, Straux and Giroux, 2004).

46. *Ibid.*, pp. 147, 191, 216. In June of 2003, Peterson had published in *The New York Times Magazine* an article on the same lines, entitled "Deficits and Dysfunction: How the Republican and Democratic Parties Are Robbing Our Future."

47. I hope I am wrong about Beck, because I personally like him and the fact that he has brought humor to the field of political criticism.

48. For a good analysis of Beck's treatment of Debra Medina, see, Alex Wallenwein, "Is Glenn Beck Obama's 'Female Canine Companion'?", *NolanChart.com*, February 13, 2010, http://www.nolanchart.com/article7374.html.

49. Just recently, however, Limbaugh has begun mentioning the existence of a "ruling class" in America, which he identifies with the Left. Is Rush becoming a kook?

50. David Rockefeller, *Memoirs* (New York: Random House, 2002), p. 405.

51. Republicans now seem very concerned about Obama's policy of open borders to illegals. They apparently forgot that Obama is just following Bush's and Clinton's policies —which actually have been dictated at the Harold Pratt House as part of a plan to accelerate the creation of the North American Union and the destruction of the U.S. as a sovereign nation. Proof that the whole illegal immigration problem is a CFR creation is that Raul Yzaguirre, president of the National Council of La Raza —one of the most rabid pro-illegal immigration organizations— is a proud CFR member.

52. US Department of Homeland Security, Office of Intelligence and Analysis, Assesment, "Right-wing Extremism: Current Economic and Political Climate Fueling Resurgence in Radicalization and Recruitment," April 7, 2009.

53. You may download a .pdf copy at www.fas.org/irp/eprint/rightwing.pdf.

54. *Ibid.*

55. See, Kurt Nimmo, "Secret State Police Report: Ron Paul, Bob Barr, Chuck Baldwin,

Libertarians are Terrorists," Infowars.com. March 11, 2009, http://www.infowars.com/secret-state-police-report-ron-paul-bob-barr-chuck-baldwin-libertarians-are-terrorists/.

56. See, Tim Shipman, "Barack Obama picks a fight with Rush Limbaugh as bipartisan spirit crumbles," *Telegraph.co.uk*, January 24, 2009, http://www.telegraph.co.uk/news/worldnews/northamerica/usa/barackobama/4331839/Barack-Obama-picks-a-fight-with-Rush-Limbaugh-as-bipartisan-spirit-crumbles.html.

57. See, Joe Kovacs, "The Right Stuff," *WorldNetDaily*, March 11, 2009, http://www.wnd.com/index.php?fa=PAGE.view&pageId=91390.

58. See, Damian Sofsian, Conservative Radio Host's Prescription Drug Addiction Story, *EzineArticles.com*, http://ezinearticles.com/?Conservative-Radio-Hosts-Prescription-Drug-Addiction-Story&id=74378.

59. See, "Right Wing Radio Host Rush Limbaugh sign 200 Million Dollar deal," *M&G News*, July 2, 2008, http://www.monstersandcritics.com/news/usa/news/article_1414676.php/Right_wing_radio_host_Rush_Limbaugh_signs_ 400_million_ dollar_deal.

60. The American mainstream media as a whole accepted the U.S. Government's version of the events and became an obedient mouthpiece parroting it over and over *ad nauseam*.

61. See, i.e., David Wise, *The Politics of Lying* (New York: Random House, 1973).

62. Some CIA dissenters are maliciously described as traitors in Rowan Scarborough's, *Sabotage: America's Enemies Within the CIA* (Washington, D.C.: Regnery, 2007).

63. In the Summer of 2001, Russian intelligence notified the CIA that 25 terrorist pilots had been specifically trained for suicide missions. In August, Russian President Putin told Russian intelligence to warn the U.S. government "in the strongest possible terms" of an imminent attack on airports and government buildings," *MS-NBC* interview, Sept., 15, 2001.

64. Stanislav Mishin, "American capitalism gone with a whimper," *Pravda online*, April 27, 2009. http://english.pravda.ru/opinion/columnists/107459-american_capitalism-0.

65. *The New York. Times*, 7 May 1992, p. A27.

66. As British Fabian philosopher Bertrand Russell clearly expressed in his 1951 book, *The Impact of Science on Society*, "The social psychologists of the future will have a number of classes of school children on whom they will try different methods of producing an unshakable conviction that snow is black." If this proves to be too costly, speculated Russell, scientists should find out "how much less it would cost to make them believe it is dark gray." See also, Jeffrey Steinberg, "From Cybernetics to Littleton — Techniques in Mind Control," *The Schiller Institute*, April 2000, http://www.schillerinstitute.org/new_viol/cybmindcontrol_js0400.html.

67. See, Webster Griffin Tarpley, *Obama: The Postmodern Coup* (Joshua Tree, California: Progressive Press, 2008), pp. 4, 8, 12.

68. SeeTom Henegan, "Obama-Bush-Cheney-U.S. Media PSYOP," May 24, 2009, http://blogs.myspace.com/tom_heneghan_intel.

69. Geoff Earle, "Hillary Raises Assassination Issue: Defends Long-Running Campaign," *the New York Post*, May 23, 2009, p. 1.

70. Paul Joseph Watson, "Hillary & Obama in Secret Bilderberg Rendezvous," *PrisonPlanet.com*, http://www.prisonplanet.com/articles/june2008/060608_hillary_obama.htm.

71. See, "Morning Bell: Obama Admits He's "Not Familiar" With House Bill," *The Heritage Foundation*, posted July 21st, 2009, http://www.heritage.org/2009/07/21/morning-bell-obama-admits-hes-not-familiar-with-house-bill/.

72. See, i.e., "Why the Population Bomb is a Rockefeller Baby," *Ramparts* magazine,

May, 1970.

73. See, Laurie Roth "Obama Wants His Private Army," NewsWithViews.com, April 2, 2010, http://www.newswithviews.com/Roth/laurie208.htm.

74. Nancy Matthis, "Obama Just Got His Private Army," *InfoWars.com*, March 27, 2010, http://www.infowars.com/obama-just-got-his-private-army. See also, Chelsea Schilling, "ObamaCare prescription: Emergency health army," *WorldNetDaily.com*, March 25, 2010, http://www.worldnetdaily.com/index.php?pageId=132001.

75. William Norman Grigg, "Casus Belli," March 29, 2010, http://freedominourtime.blogspot.com/2010/03/causus-belli.html.

76. James Petras, "A Historic Moment: The Election of the Greatest Con-Man in Recent History," *AtlanticFreePress*, December 8, 2009, http://www.atlanticfreepress.com/news/1/6590-a-historic-moment-the-election-of-the-greatest-con-man-in-recent-history-.html.

77 .A political observer has commented that Obama's foreign policy essentially amounts to a Kissinger-style realpolitik with a Smiley face. See, Lionel Beehner, "Catchphrase Diplomacy. Just words: 'Tough love,' 'smart power'.", *USA Today*, September 2, 2009, p. 9A.

78. *Der Angriff.* Aufsatze aus der Kampfzeit, Munich: Zentralverlag der NSDAP., 1935, pp. 236-238.

79. Some people believe that both Clinton Roosevelt's *Science* and Karl Marx's *Manifesto* were plagiarized from yet an earlier eighteenth century collection of writings by Adam Weishaupt, and that Roosevelt simply picked up the torch and passed it on to Marx, but that's another story.

80. Wilson quoted by Charles Seymour, *The Intimate Papers of Colonel House* (New Yor: Houghton Mifflin, 1926), vol. I, pp. 114-115.

81. See, George Sylvester Viereck, *The Strangest Friendsship in History: Woodrow Wilson and Colonel House* (New York: Liveright, 1932), pp. 18-19, 33.

82. "Obama on 'civilian national security force'. Transcript of senator's controversial remarks in Colorado July 2," *WorldNetDaily.com*, July 18, 2008, http://www.wnd.com/index.php?fa=PAGE.view&pageId=69960.

83. Yoy may download the whole document at: obama.3cdn.net 2778abe561ba550d40_f7m6bsa2i.pdf.

Chapter 12

1. Jean Paul Sartre, *Sartre on Cuba* (New York: Ballantine, 1961).

2. U.S. Department of Commerce, *Investment in Cuba*. (Washington D.C.: Government Printing Office, 1956), p. 184.

3. Department of Economic and Social Affairs, *Economic Survey of Latin America 1957* (New York: United Nations, 1959), p. 177.

4. *Ibid,* p. 307.

5. Louis A. Pérez, Jr., *On Becoming Cuban* (Chapel Hill: University of North Carolina Press, 1999), p. 53. Pérez's book studies in detail the growing similarities between the American and the Cuban culture and society in the post-war.

6. K. S. Karol, *Guerrillas in Power* (New York: Hill and Wang, 1970), p. 324.

7. See, i.e., Jon Lee Anderson, *Che Guevara* (New York: Grove Press, 1997), p. 170.

8. W. W. Rostow, *The Stages of Economic Growth: A Non-Communist Manifesto* (Cambridge: Cambridge University Press, 1960)

9. UMAP, acronym for *Unidades Militares de Auxilio a la Producción* [Military Units to Help Production], a deceptive name for concentration camps for effeminate homosexu-

als, Jehovah Witness, and other political dissidents interned to do hard labor.

10. That is, if one is to follow their own politically correct definition of a racist, sexist, homophobic, phallocentric and logocentric society, terms that ultimately are but covert expressions of American cultural imperialism of the Left. It seems, however, that the politically correct tenured radicals apply these hate terms only to the bad guys, and they are convinced that Castro is one of the good guys.

11. See, i.e., Ramón Ferreira, "La miseria cubana está de moda," ["Cuban Misery is Fashionable"] *El Nuevo Herald*, March 8, 2001. According to Ferreira, to these people Cuba's poverty "is cool."

12. For example, California New Agers are exhilarated about the possibility of continuous power black-outs all over the state. No wonder they are so happy when they travel to Cuba: during the last 30 years, black-outs have been a common occurrence in Castro's Cuba.

13. Some novels and short stories written by Cuban authors describe the destruction of Cuba and its people much better than any scholarly work. See, among others, José Antonio Ponte, *In the Cold of the Malecón* (San Francisco: City Lights, 2000); Daína Chaviano, *El hombre, la hembra y el hambre* (Barcelona: Planeta, 1998); Teresa Dovalpage, *A Girl Like Che Guevara*; Mirta Valdés, ed., *Cubana: Contemporary Fiction by Cuban Women* (Boston: Beacon Press, 1998); and Zoe Valdés, *La nada cotidiana* (Buenos Aires: Emecé, 1997). For a perceptive description of the day-to-day misery of the average Cuban, see Corinne Cumerlato and Denis Rousseau, *L'Ille du docteur Castro* (Paris: Editions Stock, 2000); also Catherine Moses, *Real Life in Castro's Cuba* (Wilmington, Delaware: SR Books, 2000).

A recent visitor to Cuba wrote his impressions, "I was appalled by what I saw in Cuba. When you walk the streets you see faces that are as devastated as the buildings. People look depressed, beaten down. They stare into the distance, as if in trance, as they wait for buses or in endless food lines, or when they sit on the sea wall, staring intently toward the horizon, toward Miami." Tony Mendoza, "Cuba Today: Instant Antiquity," *The Chronicle of Higher Education*, October 24, 1997, pp. B8-B9. The initial sequences of Win Wender's documentary film *Buenavista Social Club* shows images very similar to the ones described by Mendoza.

14. Christopher Hunt, an American writer who visited Cuba in 1996, wrote that, during his grass-roots journey from Havana to Santiago to Bayamo to Holguín to Camagüey to Sancti Spíritus to Santa Clara to Varadero, what he left behind was a trail of bribe-takers, prostitutes, would-be pimps, black marketeers, bootleggers, bolita gamblers, money-changers, sex tourists, snitches and men who asked him for his socks. See Orlando Alomá, "In Fidel's Footsteps: A Tourist Views Cuba," *The Miami Herald*, January 11, 1998.

15. A Cuban woman said with tears in her eyes, "I don't know why Fidel hates us so much. Why does he just keep trying to crush us?," Catherine Moses, *op. cit.*, p. 84.

16 The evidence indicates that the New World Order is but a refurbished version of Nazism. The strong ideological similarity between the Nazi and the New Age movements is because Nazism was an early version of the New Age movement. Hitler himself was a believer in occultism and oriental religions, he was a "veggie," hated smokers, and the Nazis believed that mother earth was a living organism and pioneered the ecological movement. See, i.e., Janet Biehl and Peter Staudenmaier, *Ecofascism: Lessons From the German Experience* (San Francisco: AK Press, 1995); also Luc Perry, *The New Ecological Order* (Chicago: University of Chicago Press, 1995).

Though fascism is always associated with nationalism, it seems that a new variety of fascism is emerging: international socialism, that is, fascism on a global scale controlled by transnational corporations with the United Nations as its law enforcer. International socialists, however, are not using the traditional *coup d'état* tactics traditional fascists have customarily used to grab power, but the more subtle strategy developed by the British Fabians and Italian Marxist Antonio Gramsci.

17. See, Miguel A. Faría, Jr., "In Bed With Castro," *NewsMax.com*, June 6, 2000.

18 .See, Irving Louis Horowitz, "An Appeasement Policy for Castro's Cuba?," *The Miami Herald*, December 6, 2000. In another article, professor Horowitz states that the CFR has become "the fulcrum and spearhead of the Cuba Lobby—those seeking the establishment of normal diplomatic and social relations with Communist Cuba." See, "Humanitarian Capitulation: U.S.-Cuba Relations According to the Council on Foreign Relations," *Center for a Free Cuba*, www.cubacenter.org/media/archives/2000/fall/humanitarian.html.

19. Rockefeller wrote the foreword and Strong wrote the introduction for the Trilateral Commission's book *Beyond Interdependence: The Meshing of the World's Economy and the Earth's Ecology*.

20. Of course, this does not apply to *them*. A journalist who attended the Earth Summit chaired by Strong, noticed that the whole conference site had air conditioning blasting while all the doors were open. See "U.N to Rule Over America?: Geoff Metcalf Interviews Journalist, Author William Jasper on World Tyranny," *WorldNetDaily*, July 15, 2001.

21. See, Jim Lobe, "Learn From Cuba: World Bank Says," *Inter Press Service Finance*, April 30, 2001.

22. The philosophy of the Cuban tyrant and misery specialist is very close to the philosophy of his American New Age counterparts. For example, the true purpose of the creation of commuter lanes in California's highways was not to optimize traffic, but to annoy drivers by creating traffic jams and eventually discourage them from driving.

23. "1917-1987: Socialismo em Debate," *Instituto Cajamar*, Sao Paulo, 1988, pp. 133-134. Valdés also quoted in Gonzalo Guimaraens, "Cuba comunista: el miserabilismo como escuela de ateísmo," ["Communist Cuba: Misery as a School of Atheism"] *Diario Las Américas*, April 7, 2001.

24. *Ibid*., p. 133.

25. *Ibid*.

26. See, i.e., Paul Joseph Watson, "Austerity Fascism Is Coming And It Will Be Brutal," *PrisonPlanet.com*, June 8, 2010, http://www.prisonplanet.com/austerity-fascism-is-coming-and-it-will-be-brutal.html,

27. Elián González was the 6-year-old Cuban boy who arrived at American shores on Thanksgiving Day, 1999. A few months later he was kidnapped at gun point by Janet Reno's thugs and sent back to Cuba.

28. UNESCO *Courier*, November, 1991.

29. Claudia Márquez, "Más de tres millones de abortos en 30 años," *El Nuevo Herald*, September 23, 2000.

30. Pascal Fletcher "U.S. Policy Experts Encouraged by Talks in Cuba," *Reuters* (Havana), February 18, 2001.

31. See, Agustín Blázquez and James Sutton, "Education in Elián's Cuba: What Americans Don't Know," *ABIP*, March 19, 2000. See also, Damaris Ocaña, "Study, Work, Rifle: Cuba's Educational System Presses Revolutionary Message Along With ABC's," *The Miami Herald*, August 6, 2000.

32. Blázquez and Sutton, *Ibid*.

33. "WCC Leaders Meet Fidel Castro," *Persecution News*, October 15, 1999.

34. "Fidel Castro Meets With World Council of Churches," *World News*, October 15, 1999.

35. See, Diane Sabom, "U.N. Wants to Rule New World Order." A sculpture in front of the U.N. building in Manhattan depicts an oversized revolver with its barrel tied in a knot, to emphasize their dislike for guns. The fact, however, that the sculture depicts a revolver —not a missile, a fighter plane, or a military rifle— subliminaly shows the U.N.'s true target for gun control: private citizens.

36. See James F. Dunnigan, *Dirty Little Secrets of the Twentieth Century* (New York: William Morrow, 1999), pp. 282-285.

37. Michael Parenti, *Dirty Truths* (San Francisco: City Lights, 1996), p. 80.

38. Walt Whitman Rostow, *The Stages of Economic Growth* (Cambridge: Cambridge University Press, 1960).

39. "Castro Speaks, Meets Officials at U.N., Departs for Home," Havana Domestic Service, http://lanic.utexas.edu/la/cb/cuba/castro/1979/19791012.

Chapter 13

1. It would be unfair, however, to blame MacCarthy for his mistake. Professor Carroll Quigley, probably the scholar who better has studied the conspiracy, pointed out that the conspirators operate, to some extent, "in the way the radical Right believes the Communists act." See, Carroll Quigley, *Tragedy and Hope: A History of the World in Our Time* (New York: Macmillan, 1966), p. 950.

2. See Robert Welch, *The Politician* (Privately printed edition, 1963), pp. 7-11. Welch's is the best, and most likely only, study of how the CFR conspirators recruited an unknown and ambitious young Army officer named Dwight Eisenhower and pushed his military career from an unknown lieutenant colonel in 1940 to a full general in early 1943, until making him in less than four years the Supreme Commander of the U.S. armed forces and later the president of the United States.

3. For a detailed account of how the CFR conspirators used their secret agent William Donovan to get rid of Gen. Patton, see Robert Wilcox, *Target Patton: The Plot to Assassinate General Goerge S. Patton* (Washington, D,C,: Regnery, 2008).

4. For an account of how CFR secret agents Dean Acheson, George Marshall, Lauchlin Currie, Owen Lattimore and Harry Truman destroyed Gen. MacArthur's career, see Robert H.C. Welch, Jr., *May God Forgive Us* (Chicago: Henry Regnery, 1952). Perhaps based on George Orwell's known dictum that who controls the past controls the future, the CFR conspirators devote an inordinate amount of time and effort rewriting history. An outstanding example is Lance Morrow's article "George C. Marshall: The Last Great American," *Smithsonian*, August 1997, devoted to glorify an inglorious military bureaucrat and treasonous secret CFR agent. Another is an article by David Halberstam, "Command Performance," *Smithsonian*, November 2007, whose sole aim is to denigrate General MacArthur and glorify CFR's secret agent Matthew Ridgway.

5. Kissinger-Haig anecdote in Bob Woodward and Carl Bernstein, *The Final Days* (New York: Touchstone, 1994), pp. 194-195.

6. See, William Safire, *The New York Times*, November 24, 1980.

7. See John F. McManus, *Changing Comands: The Betrayal of America's Military* (Appleton, Winsconsin: The John Birch Society, 1995), pp.150-151.

8. *Ibid.*, p. 151.

9. *Ibid.*, p. 154.

10. Given the fact that the CFR has secret members, this number is most likely higher.

11. Source: Council on Foreign Relations 2006 Annual Report. http://www.stopthe northamericanunion.com/CFRMembers.html.

12. David Margolick, "The Night of the Generals," *Vanity Fair*, April 2007, pp. 276.

13. David Rockefeller, addressing the Bilderberg Group in Baden-Baden, Germany, June 1991.

14. Kissinger calling U.S. military men and women "dumb, sutpid animals," in Bob Woodward and Carl Bernstein, *The Final Days* (New York: Touchstone, 1994), pp. 194-195.

15. Margolick, *ibid.*

16. Schlessinger on U.S. soldiers in *Foreign Affairs*, July-August, 1995.

17. William Hendon and Elizabeth Stewart, *An Enormous Crime* (New York: Thomas Dunne Books, 2007).

18. See, Meryl Nass, MD, "Anthrax Vaccine Causes Gulf War Syndrome," http://

www.anthraxvaccine.org/AnthraxGWS.htm.

19. A Web joker rightly dubbed George W. Bush's plans for a permamnent war on terror "Enron with an Army." The description perfectly fits the CFR's idea of a new, lean military serving the conspirators' aims of global domination: Wall Stret with an army.

20. See, Douglas Waller, "The CIA's Secret Army," *TIME* magazine, February 3, 2003, pp. 22, 24.

21. See Robert Dreyfuss and Jason Vest, "The Lie Factory," *Mother Jones*, Jan.-Feb. 2004.

22. Waller, *op. cit.*, p. 28.

23. Lieutenant General Greg Newbold, Major General Paul Eaton, General John Riggs, Major General Charles Swannack, Jr., Major General John Batiste, and Lieutenant General Paul Van Ripper, none of them CFR members, had a very low opinion of Rumsfeld's knowledge of military matters. In a PBS program *Frontline*, Van Ripper went to the point of publicly stating that he considered Rumsfeld arrogant, disdainful of others, lawless, and ignorant. See David Margolick, "The Night of the Generals," *Vanity Fair*, April 2007, pp. 246-251, 274-280.

24. *The Team* was most likely part of a PSYOP to lower even more the moral and ethical threshhold of the American people into accepting that kind of illegal U.S. government actions as a normal thing.

25. See, Karen DeYoung and Greg Jaffe, "U.S. 'secret war' expands globally as Special Operations forces take larger role," *The Washington Post*, June 4, 2010, http://www.washingtonpost.com/wp-dyn/content/article/2010/06/03/AR2010060304965.html.

26. Steven Metz and James Kievit, "The Revolution in Military Affairs and Conflict Short of War," Strategic Studies Institute (SSI), U.S. Army War College, Carlisle Barracks, PA 17103-5050, USA, U.S. Government Printing Office, 1994-504-111/00089.

27. *Ibid.*, p. v.

28. *Ibid.*

29. Woodward and Bernstein, *op. cit.*

30. Though the DHS Report is dated April 7, 2008, the creation date of the .pdf file shows that it was actually written on January 23, 2007, that is, during the Bush regime. See, Servando Gonzalez, "The American Gestapo and the Dog that Didn't Bark," *NolanChart .com*, April 27, 2009, http://www.nolanchart.com/article6346.html.

31. This opens the door to using post-traumatic stress syndrome and other mental problems, real or imagined, as a pretext to deny ex-military men and women their right to carry guns in their own country, even inside military units.

32. Metz and Kievit, op. cit, p. 15.

33. *Ibid.*, p. 16.

34. *Ibid.*, p. 31.

35. Chuck Baldwin, "Can Christians Serve in the New World Order Army?" *NewsWith Views*, May 7, 2009, http://www.newswithviews.com/baldwin/baldwin510.htm.

36. *Ibid.*

37. Clifford J. Hutchins, Rochester, Was., Letter to the Editor, *USA Today*, July 23, 209, p. 8A.

38. Chuck Baldwin, "The Age of Despotism," July 7, 2009, http:www.chuckbaldwinlive.com/c2009/cbarchive_20090707.html.

39. Comander Cunningham was a Green Beret who served in the same Special Forces company alongside his father and two brothers: an infantryman with the 101st Airborne Division, a Navy pilot, a mission commander and analyst.

40. The Joint Combat Arms Survey (Part A.; DD Form 3208, revised 2-96, 70mm) was given to U.S. Navy SEAL platoons and U.S. Marine combat veterans. It was first administered on September 15, 1993. It circulated widely within the Department of the Navy. Some

people suspect that the reason it was administered only to the Navy is because the Navy, including the Marines, was not subject to USC Title 10 Posse Comitatus prohibitions against using federal military forces for domestic law enforcement.

41. Robert Kagan, "What to Do About Foreign Policy," in Neal Kozoly, (ed.), *What to Do About?* (New York: Regan Books, 1995), pp. 158-168.

42. Angelo Codevilla's response to Robert Kagan's article, in Neal Kozoly, (ed.), *What to Do About?* (New York: Regan Books, 1995), p. 173.

43. General Smedley D. Butler, *War is a Racket* (Los Angeles: Feral House, 2003.

44. For an unflattering, critical view of the role the U.S. military is currently playing, written by two ex-miliatry men, see, Fred Reed, "Psychopathy Legitimized," *LewRockwell.com*, July 23, 2010, http://www.lewrockwell.com/reed/reed182.html; also, William J. Astore and Tom Engelhardt, "Stop Calling Them Heroes," *AntiWar.com*, July 23, 2010, http://original.antiwar.com/engelhardt/2010/07/22/stop-calling-them-heroes/.

45. Baldwin, *op. cit.*

46. Zoltan Grossman, "From Wounded Knee to Iraq: A Century of U.S Military Interventions." (http://academic.evergreen.edu/g/grossmaz/interventions.html.

47. The publication of Michael Hastings' article "The Runaway General" in *Rolling Stone* magazine in which Gen. McChrystal (CFR) strongly criticized Obama, Biden, and other "wimps in the White House" caused a commotion in political and military circles. But the notion that the *Rolling Stone*'s reporter fooled McChrystal is preposterous. Most likely, it was McChrystal who fooled Hastings. Actually, McChrystal's unexplainable *faux pas*, which a *New York Times*' editorial qualified as "puzzling and disturbing," might be the first step of another carefully planned PSYOP against the American people. Let's wait and see.

Epilogue

1. Lucian Kim and Ilya Arkhipov, "U.S. Espionage Claims Recall Cold War `Spy Mania,' Russia Says," *Bloomberg*, Jun 29, 2010, http://www.bloomberg.com/news/2010-06-29/u-s-espionage-claims-recall-cold-war-spy-mania-russian-government-says.html.

2. Robert Weissberg, "A Stranger in Our Midst," *American Thinker*, April 29, 2010, http://www.americanthinker.com/2010/04/a_stranger_in_our_midst.html.

3. *Ibid.*

4. Carroll Quigley, *Tragedy and Hope: A History of the World in Our Time* (New York: Macmillan, 1966), pp. 1247-1248.

5. Chuck Baldwin, "Open Gays In The Military And Amnesty For Illegals," March 26, 2010, \t "_blank" http://chuckbaldwinlive.com/home/?p=1027.

6. A typical Band Aid cure would be voting for Republicans to get rid of the Democrats. See, Devvy Kidd, "Re-electing the Band Aid Brigade," Devvy.com, May 18, 2010, http://www.devvy.com/new_site/band_aid_brigade_051810.html.

7. US Department of Homeland Security, Office of Intelligence and Analysis, Assessment, "Right-wing Extremism: Current Economic and Political Climate Fueling Resurgence in Radicalization and Recruitment," April 7, 2009.

8. Casey's theory in Herbert E. Meyer, "Totalitarian impulses," *The Washington Times*, February 13, 1998.

9. *Ibid.*

10. Report of the Special Study Group [Doolittle Committee] on the Covert Activities of the Central Intelligence Agency, September 30, 1954, in William M. Leary (ed.) *The Central Intelligence Agency: History and Documents* (University, Alabama: The University of Alabama Press, 1984), p. 144.

11. Proof that the decline of the American economy is part of a plan, is that in the late 1970s, then-Federal Reserve Chairman, Paul Volcker —a member of the CFR and the Tri-

lateral Commission, who once worked for the Rockefeller's Chase Manhattan Bank— clearly stated, "The standard [of living] of the average American has to decline."

12. Naomi Wolf, *The End of America: Letter of Warning to a Young Patriot* (White River Junction, Vermont: Chelsea Green, 2007.

13. See, "Is U.S. Now On Slippery Slope To Tyranny?," *Investors.com*, June 21, 2010, http://www.investors.com/NewsAndAnalysis/Article/537967/201006211813/Is-US-Now-On-Slippery-Slope-To-Tyranny-.aspx.

14. Charley Reese, "Looking For Someone to Blame? Congress is a Good Place to Start, *The Orlando Sentinel*, March 7, 1995, p. A-8.

15. For an interesting opinion about the subject, visit www.tenurecorrupts.com.

16. Charley Reese, *Ibid.*

17. See Ivan Eland, *The Empire Has no Clothes: U.S. Foreign Policy Exposed* (Oakland, CA: The Independent Institute, 2004).

18. Irving Kristol, " The Emerging American Imperium," *The Wall Street Journal*, August 18, 1997.

19. Edwin Vieira, Jr., "Balking the Enemy's Plans," http://www.newswithviews. com/Vieira/edwin228.htm, May 26, 2010.

20. Jeffrey Grupp, *Corporatism: The Secret Government of the New World Order* (Joshua Tree, California: Progressive Press, 2009).

21. See, Mike Adams, "Corporate Atrocities Against Nature May Ultimately Destroy Human Civilization, *NaturalNews.com*, June 18, 2010, http://www.naturalnews.com/z029023_corporations_crimes_against_nature.html.

22. See, David Rockefeller's speech at the Bilderberg meeting in Baden-Baden, Germany, 1991.

23. Stanley Montieth, *Brotherhood of Darkness* (Oklahoma City, Oklahoma: Hearthstone, 2000).

24. *Ibid.*, pp. 9-10.

25. Dawkins, Richard (1989). *The Selfish Gene* (2 ed.). Oxford: Oxford University Press. p. 192.

26. For a strong criticism of how many protestant pastors have become vehicles of disinformation, see Chuck Baldwin, "Saving Souls-Losing Freedom," *NewsWithViews*, April 20, 2010, http://www.newswithviews.com/baldwin/baldwin581.htm; also Chuck Baldwin, "Spiritual Wickedness in High Places," *NewsWithViews*, February 17, 2010, http://www.newswithviews.com/baldwin/baldwin570.htm.

27. Currently I don't even own a TV set, and I have not watched TV for many years. Actually, the last time I watched TV for a few minutes was when I got a phone call from a friend on September 11, 2001, and he told me about the events happening in New York City. When I managed to get close to a TV set to watch what was going on I suffered two shocks: the first one when I saw the first tower collapse on its own footprint in a typical controlled demolition style. My second shock was when I saw Dan Rather. I had not seen him for so many years that I was shocked when I saw how old he had become.

28. Bill McKibben, "Carbon's New Math: To Deal With Global Warming, the First Step is to Do The Numbers, *National Geographic*, October, 2007, pp., 33-37.

29. See my 2003 article "Kiss Your Internet Good-bye," *NewsWithViews*, April 6, 2003, http:// www.newswithviews.com/public_comm/public_commentary7.htm.,

30. Adrian Salbuchi, "The Global Power Elite is NOT That Strong!", *YouTube.com*, May 28, 2010, http://www.youtube.com/watch?v=l1_5UfSJQaA.

31. See, Paul Joseph Watson, "Brzezinski Decries Global Political Awakening During CFR Speech," *Prison Planet.com*, Wednesday, May 19, 2010, http://www.prisonplanet.com/brzezinski-decries-global-political-awakening-during-cfr-speech.html.

32. Probably the best analysis of the betrayal of the American people by its ruling class

is Patrick J. Buchanan's, *The Great Betrayal* (Boston: Little, Brown & Company, 1998). Buchanan rightly blames the deindustrialization of America on the U.S government and the transnational corporations that control it.

33. Despite their personal flaws, JFK and Reagan were true American patriots who loved this country. This explains why the CFR conspirators tried to get rid of both of them.

34. See, Servando Gonzalez, "Slavery is a state of mind," *NewsWithViews*, March 11, 2003, http://www.newswithviews.com/public_comm/public_commentary6.htm.

Appendix I

1. Quoted in Michael Warner, "Wanted: A Definition of 'Intelligence.' Understanding Our Craft," CIA's Center for the Study of Intelligence, https://www.cia.gov/library/center-for-the-study-of-intelligence/csi-publications/csi-studies/studies/ vol46no3/article02.html.

The author of the article reminds the reader that intelligence is an elusive concept, and there are many different definitions of the term. In the same fashion, the concept of information, the raw material out of which intelligence is produced, is even more elusive, to the point that there is no agreement among scientists about its true nature. The fact explains why Claude Shannon, the creator of the information theory, decided to call it "communication theory" instead. See, Claude Shannon, "A Mathematical Theory of Communication," *Bell System Technical Journal* No. 27 (July and October, 1948).

2 . Quoted in Allen Dulles, *The Craft of Intelligence* (New York: Signet, 1965) , p. 11.

3. Sun Tzu, *The Art of War* - translated by Samuel B. Griffin (London: Oxford University Press, 1963), p. 144.

4. Intelligence Cycle: The process by which information is acquired, converted into intelligence, and made available to policymakers. There are usually five steps which constitute the intelligence cycle: planning and direction, collection, processing, analysis and evaluation, and dissemination.

5 According to communication theory, the amount of information is directly proportional to the unexpectedness of the message. This also applies to the field of intelligence and espionage, but one must keep in mind that information is not true intelligence under it has been evaluated.

6. See, i.e, David Wise, *The Politics of Lying* (New York: Random House, 1973).

7. In 1950 the CIA created the Office of National Estimates, to produce high-level national intelligence estimates, in an effort to forecasts possible Soviet behavior.

8. See, Robert Kennedy, *Thirteen Days* (New York: W.W. Norton, 1971), p. 6; Hugh Sidey, *John F. Kennedy, President* (Greenwich, Conn.: Crest Books, 1963), p. 298; Klauss Knorr, "Failure in National Intelligence Estimates, The Case of the Cuban Missiles," *World Politics*, Vol. XVI No. 3 (April, 1964); and Arnold Horelick, "The Cuban Missile Crisis. An analysis of Soviet Calculations and Behavior," *World Politics,* Vol. XVI No. 3, April 1964.

9. On the apparent failure of the U.S. intelligence community to predict the deployment of the Russian missiles in Cuba, see *Investigation of the Preparedness Program*, Interim Report on the Cuban Military Buildup by the Preparedness Investigating Committee, Committee on armed Services, U.S. Senate, 88 Congress, 1st Session, Washington, 1963. The Report is usually called the Stennis Report because Senator Stennis was chairman of the subcommittee.

10. During an interview at the Kennedy Library in 1970, somebody asked Deputy Secretary of Defense Roswell Gilpatric about the presence of nuclear warheads in Cuba in 1962. Gilpatrick's answer was clear: "We never had any positive evidence" [that Soviet warheads were in Cuba]. "If you ask my own belief, I don't think that there were." ... "I think there were plans for flying them in, but I don't think they were actually matched up ... with the launchers." Quoted in Seymour Hersh, *The Dark Side of Camelot* (Boston: Little,

Brown and Company), p. 355.

11. Men of strong convictions, some of the authors of the September estimate, notably CIA officers Sherman Kent, Abbot Smith and John Huizenga, never recanted. Faced with their apparent failure, their conclusion was that it had been Khrushchev, not the Estimate, who had been wrong. Information on Kent, Abbot and Huizenga in Raymond L. Garthoff, "US Intelligence in the Cuban Missile Crisis," in James Blight and David Welch, *Intelligence in the Cuba Missile Crisis*, (London: Frank Cass, 1998), p. 21.

12. Sherman Kent, "A Crucial Estimate Relived," *Studies in Intelligence*, Spring 1964.

13. See, Central Intelligence Agency, *A compendium of Analytic Tradecraft Notes*, Washington, D.C. February 1997.

14. *Ibid.*

15. Roberta Wohlstetter's *Pearl Harbor: Warning and Decision* (Stanford, California: Stanford University Press, 1962).

16. Graham T. Allyson, *Essence of Decision: Explaining the Cuban Missile Crisis* (New York : Little, Brown, 1971).

17. See, i.e., Webster Griffin Tarpley, *9/11: Synthetic Terror Made in USA* (Joshua Tree, California: Progressive Press, 2006).

18. See, Ron Rosenbaum, "Day I Was Stopped From C.I.A. Approach Now Appears Karmic," *The New York Observer*, January 29, 2006.

Bibliography

Aarons, Mark, and John Loftus, *Unholy Trinity*. New York: St. Martin's Griffin, 1998.

Abraham, Larry and Franklin Sanders, *The Greening*. Atlanta, Georgia: Soundview, 1993.

Alape, Sergio, *El Bogotazo: memorias del olvido*. La Habana: Casa de las Américas, 1983.

Alexander, Robert J., *Communism in Latin America*. New Brunswick, N.J.: Rutgers University Press, 1957.

Allen, Gary, *None Dare Call it Conspiracy*. Rossmoor, California: Concord Press, 1972.

——, *The Rockefeller File*. Seal Beach, California: '76 Press, 1976.

——, *Kissinger*. Seal Beach, California: '76 Press, 1976.

——, *Say "No!" to the New World Order*. Rossmoor, California: Concord Press, 1987.

Allen, Robert Loring, *Soviet Influence in Latin America: The Role of Economic Relations*. Washington, D.C.: Public Affairs Press, 1959.

Alsop, Stewart and Thomas Braden, *Sub Rosa: The OSS and American Espionage*. New York: Harcourt, Brace and World, 1964.

Bamford, James, *Body of Secrets*. New York: Random House, 2001.

Barnet, Richard J. *Intervention and Revolution*. New York: World, 1968.

Bayard, James, *The Real Story on Cuba*. Derby, Conn.: Monarch, 1963.

Bennett, James R., *Control of the Media in the United States: An Annotated Bibliography*. New York: Garland, 1992.

Berman, Morris, *Dark Ages America*. New York: W. W. Norton, 2006.

Bethel, Paul D., *The Losers*. New Rochelle, N.Y.: Arlington House,1969.

Biehl, Janet and Peter Staudenmaier, *Ecofascism: Lessons From the German Experience*. San Francisco: AK Press, 1995..

Boca, Angelo Del, and Mario Giovana, *Fascism Today*. New York: Pantheon, 1969.

Bonsal, Philip W., *Cuba, Castro and the United States*. Pittsburgh. Penn.: University of Pittsburgh Press, 1971.

Bovard, James, *The Bush Betrayal*. New York: Palgrave Macmillan, 2004.

Braun, Herbert, *The Assassination of Gaitán: Public Life and Urban Violence in Colombia*. Madison, Wisconsin: The University of Wisconsin Press, 1985.

Brzezinski, Zbigniew, *Between Two Ages: America's Role in the Technetronic Era*. New York: Viking, 1976.

Buchanan, Patrick J., *The Great Betrayal*. New York: Little, Brown and Company, 1998.

Bullock, Alan. *Hitler: A Study in Tyranny*. Abr. ed. New York: Harper & Row, 1971.

Butler, Gen. Smedley D., *War is a Racket*. Los Angeles: Feral House, 2003.

Carr, Joseph P., *The Twisted Cross*. Lafayette, Louisiana: Huntington House, 1985.

Chossudovsky, Michel, *The Globalization of Poverty and the New World Order*. Shanty Bay, Ontario, Canada: Center for Research on Globalization, 2003.

Colby, Gerard, *Thy Will Be Done*. New York: HarperCollins, 1976.

Colby, William, *Honorable Men: My Life in the CIA*. New York: Simon & Schuster, 1978.

Coleman, John,, *Diplomacy by Deception*. Carson City, Nevada: Bridger House, 1993.

——, *The Conspirators' Hierarchy: The Committee of 300*. Carson City, Nevada: WIR,1997.
Conte, Ramón B. *Historia oculta de los crímenes de Fidel Castro*. Miami: n. p., 1995.
Courtney, Phoebe, *The CFR, Part II*. Littleton, Colorado: The Independent American, 1975.
Cuddy, Dennis L., *Secret Reacords Revealed*. Oklahoma City, Oklahoma: Hearthstone, 1999.
——, *The Road to Socialism and the New World Order*. Highland City, Florida: Florida Por Familiy Forum, 2000.
——, *The Globalists: The Power Elite Exposed*. Oklahoma City, Oklahoma: Hearthstone Publishing, 2001.
Cunningham, Cushman, *The Secret Empire*. North Fort Myers, Florida: Leela Publishing, n.d.
Dall, Curtis D., *My Exploited Father-in-law*. Washington, D.C.:Action Associates, 1970.
Darling, Arthur B., *The Central Intelligence Agency: an Instrument of Government to 1950*. The Pennsylvania State University press: University Park, Penn., 1990.
Devlin, Kevin, *The Soviet-Cuban Confrontation: Economic Reality and Political Judo*. Research Department of Radio Free Europe, 1 April, 1968.
Diamond, Sigmund, *Compromised Campus: The Collaboration of Universities with the Intelligence Community, 1945-1955*. New York: Oxford University Press, 1992.
Domhoff, G. William, *The Bohemian Grove and Other Retreats: A Study in Ruling-class Cohesiveness*. New York: Harper Torch, 1974.
———, *The Higher Circles*. New York: Vintage, 1971.
Donner, Frank J., *The Age of Surveillance*. New York: Alfred A. Knopf, 1980.
Eckstein, Susan, *Back From the Future: Cuba Under Castro*. Princeton, N.J.: Princeton Univresity Press, 1994.
Eland, Ivan, *The Empire Has no Clothes: U.S. Foreign Policy Exposed*. Oakland, CA : The Independent Institute, 2004.
Engdahl, William, *A Century of War*. London: Pluto Press, 2004.
Epperson, A. Ralph, *The Unseen Hand: An Introduction to the Conspiratorial View of History*. Tucson Arizona: Publius Press, 1985.
Epstein, Edward Jay, *Deception: The Invisible War Between the KGB and the CIA*. New York: Simon and Schuster, 1989.
———, Edward Jay. *Counterplot. Inquest. Legend. The Assassination Chronicles*. New York: Carroll & Graf, 1992.
Estulin, Daniel, *The True Story of the Bilderberg Group*. Walterville, Oregon: TrineDay, 2007.
Evans, Stanton Medford, *The Liberal Establishment*. New York: The Devin-Adair Co., 1965.
——, *The Usurpers*. Boston: Western Islands, 1968.
——, *The Assassination of Joe McCarthy*. Boston: Western Islands, 1970.
Facts on File, *Cuba, The U.S. and Russia, 1960-63*. New York: Facts on File, 1964.
Fitzsimmons, Louise, *The Kennedy Doctrine*. New York: Random House, 1972.

Flynn, Ted, *Hope of the Wicked*. Sterling, Virginia: MaxKol, 2000.

Gelfand, Lawrence E., *The Inquiry: American Preparations for Peace, 1917-1919*. New Haven: Yale University Press, 1963.

Gerassi, John, *The Great Fear in Latin America*. New York: Collier, 1965.

Goldenberg, Boris, *The Cuban Revolution and Latin America*. New York: Praeger, 1965.

Gonzalez, Servando, *The Nuclear Deception: Nikita Khushchev and the Cuban Missile Crisis*. Oakland, California: Spooks Books, 2002.

——, *The Secret Fidel Castro: Deconstructing the Symbol*. Oakland, California: Spooks Books, 2001.

Goodman, Melvin A., *Failure of Intelligence: The Decline and Fall of the CIA*. Lanham, Maryland: Rowan and Littlefield, 2008.

Gott, Richard, *Guerrilla Movements in Latin America*. New York: Anchor Books, 1972.

Gouré, Leon, and Morris Rothenberg, *Soviet Penetration in Latin America*. Miami: University of Miami Press, 1975.

Grant, George, (ed.), *Gays in the Military*. Franklin, Tennessee: Legacy Communic ations, 1993.

Gregor, A. James, *The Fascist Persuasion in Radical Politics*. Princeton, N.J.: Princeton University Press, 1974.

Gregory, Oswald J., and Anthony J. Estrover, eds. *The Soviet Union and Latin America*. New York: Praeger, 1970.

Greider, William, *Who Will Tell the People: The Betrayal of American Democracy*. New York: Simon & Schuster, 1992.

Griffin, G. Edward, *The Creature from Jekyll Island: A Second Look at the Federal Reserve*. Westlake Village, California: American Opinion, 1994.

Grose, Peter, *Continuing the Inquiry*. New York: Council on Foreign Relations, 1996.

Grupp, Jeffrey, *Corporatism: The Secret Government of the New World Order*. Joshua Tree, California: Progressive Press, 2009.

Gurudas (pseud.), *Treason: The New World Order*. San Rafael, California: Cassandra Press, 1996.

Herman, Arthur, *Joseph McCarthy: Reexamining the Life and Legacy of America's Most Hated Senator*. New York: The Free Press, 2000.

Hersh, Burton, *The Old Boys*. St. Petersburg, Florida: Tree Farm, 2002.

Hersh, Seymour. *The Dark Side of Camelot*. New York: Little Brown, 1997.

Higham, Charles, *Trading With the Enemy: An Exposé of the Nazi-American Money plot 1933-1949*. New York: Delacorte Press, 1983.

Hoffman, II, Michael A., *Secret Societies and Psychological Warfare*. Coeur d'Alene, Idaho: Independent History and Research, 2001.

House, Edward Mandell, *Philip Dru, Administrator*. Appleton, Wisconsin: RWU Press, 1998.

Isaacson, Walter, and Evan Thomas, *The Wise Men: Six Friends and the World They Made*. New York: Touchstone, 1986.

Jefreys-Jones, Rhodri, *The CIA and American Democracy*. New Haven, Connecticut: Yale University Press, 1998.

Jones, Alan B., *How the World Really Works*. Paradise, California: ABJ Press, 1996.

Josephson, Emanuel, *Rockefeller "Internationalist": The Man Who Misrules the World*. New York: Chedney Press, 1952.

——, *The Truth About Rockefeller*. New York, Chedney Press, 1964.
Kah, Gary H., *En Route to Global Occupation*. Lafayete, Louisiana: Huntington House, 1991.
Kessler, Ronald, *Inside the CIA*. New York: Pocket Books, 1992.
Laqueur, Walter, *Fascism: Past, Present, Future*. New York: Oxford University Press, 1996.
Lazo, Mario, *Dagger in the Heart: American Policy Failures in Cuba*. New York: Twin Circle, 1968.
Lewin, Leonard C., *Report From Iron Mountain: On the Possibility and Desirability of Peace*. New York: The Free Press, 1996.
Lively, Scott, and Kevin Abrams, *The Pink Swastika*. Salem, Oregon: Founders Publishing, 1997
Loftus, John and Mark Aarons, *The Secret War Against the Jews*. New York: St. Martin's Press, 1994.
Lundberg, Ferdinand, *The Rockefeller Syndrome*. New York: Zebra Books, 1976.
Manrara, Luis V. *Cuba Disproves the Myth that Poverty is the Cause of Communism*. Miami: The Truth About Cuba Committee, 1963.
Marchetti, Victor, and John D. Marks, *The CIA and the Cult of Intelligence*. New York: Dell, 1974.
Martin, David C., *Wilderness of Mirrors*. New York: Ballantine, 1980.
Marks, John, *The Search for the Manchurian Candidate: The CIA and Mind Control*. New York: McGraw-Hill, 1980.
Marrs, Jim, *Rule by Secrecy*. New York: HarperCollins, 2000.
——, *The Teerror Conspiracy*. New York: Disinformation, 2006.
——, *The Rise of the Fourth Reich*. New York: William Morrow, 2008.
Mazzoco, Denis W., *Networks of Power: Corporate TV's Threat to Democracy*. Boston, Massachusetts: South End, 1994.;
McGehee, Ralph W., *Deadly Deceits: My 25 Years in the CIA*. New York, Sheridan Square Publications, 1983.
McManus, John F., *Changing Comands: The Betrayal of America's Military*. Appleton, Winsconsin: The John Birch Society, 1995.
Montieth, Stanley, *Brotherhood of Darkness*. Oklahoma City, Oklahoma: Hearthstone, 2000.
Newman, Philip C. *Cuba Before Castro, An Economic Appraisal*. Ridgewood, N.J.: Foreign Studies Institute, 1965.
Oswald, J. Gregory, and Anthony J. Strover, eds., *The Soviet Union and Latin America*. New York: Praeger, 1970.
Parenti, Michael, *Dirty Truths*. City Lights: San Francisco, 1996..
——, *Inventing Reality: The Politics of Mass Media*. New York: ST. Martin's Press, 1986.
Pauwels, Louis, and Jacques Bergier, *The Morning of the Magicians*. New York: Avon, 1960.
Perloff, James, *The Shadows of Power: The Council on Foreign Relations and the American Decline*. Appleton, Wisconsin: Western Islands, 1988.
Perry, Luc, *The New Ecological Order*. Chicago: University of Chicago Press, 1995.
Persico, Joseph E., *The Imperial Rockefeller: A Biography of Nelson A. Rockefeller*.

New York: Simon and Schuster, 1982.

Prados, John, *Safe for democracy: The Secret Wars of the CIA*. Chicago: Ivan R. Dee, 2006.

Quigley, Carroll, *Tragedy and Hope: A History of the World in Our Time*. New York: Macmillan, 1966.

Ranelagh, John, *The Agency: The Rise and Decline of the CIA*. New York: Touchstone, 1987.

Russo, Gus, *Live by the Sword*. Baltimore: Bancroft Press, 1998.

Scheflin, Alan W. and Edward M. Opton, Jr., *The Mind Manipulators*. New York: Paddington Press, 1978.

Schlaffly, Phyllis and Chester Ward, *Kissinger on the Couch*. New Rochelle, N.Y.: Arlington House, 1975.

Schlesinger, Jr., Arthur M., *The Imperial Presidency*. Boston: Houghton Mifflin Company, 1973.

——, *A Thousand Days*. London: André Deutsch, 1965.

Shoup, Lawrence H. and William Minter, *Imperial Brain Trust: The Council on Foreign Relations & United States Foreign Policy*. New York: Monthly Review Press, 1977.

Shultz, Richard H. and Roy Godson, *Dezinformatsia: The Strategy of Soviet Disinformation*, New York: Berkley Books: 1986..

Simpson, Christopher, *Science of Coercion: Communication Research and Psychological Warfare 1945-1960*. New York: Oxford University Press, 1994.

Smith, Earl T., *The Fourth Floor*. New York: Random House, 1962.

Sklar, Holly, (ed.), *Trilateralism*. Boston: South End, 1980.

Smith, R. Harris, *OSS: The Secret History of America's First Intelligence Service*. Berkeley: University of California Press, 1972.

Smith, Russell Jack, *The Unknown CIA: My Three Decades with the Agency*. Washington, D.C.: Pergamon-Brasseys, 1989.,

Smoot, Dan, *The Invisible Government*. Boston: Western Islands, 1962.

Stang, Alan, *Not Holier Than Thou: How Queer is Bush?* Houston: Patton House: 2007.

Stockwell, John, *In Search of Enemies*. New York: W. W. Norton, 1978.

Stonor, Frances, *The Cultural Cold War: The CIA and the World of Arts and Letters*. New York: The New Press, 2000.

Stormer, John, *None Dare Call it Treason*. Florissant, Missouri: Liberty Bell Press, 1992.

Stulin, Daniel, *The True Story of the Bilderberg Group*. Walterville, Oregon: TrineDay, 2007.

Sutton, Antony C., *The Best Enemy Money Can Buy*. Billings, Montana: Liberty House, 1986.

——, *Wall Street and the Bolshevik Revolution*. New Rochelle, New York: Arlington House,

——, *Wall Street and the Rise of Hitler*. Seal Beach, California: '76 Press, 1976.

Tarpley, Webster Griffin, *9/11: Synthetic Terror Made in USA*. Joshua Tree, California: Progressive Press, 2006.

——, *Obama: The Postmodern Coup – Making of a Manchurian Candidate*. Joshua Tree, California: Progressive Press, 2008.

Thornton, Thomas P., *The Third World in Soviet Perspective*. Princeton, N.J.: Princeton Univ. Press, 1964.

Tzu, Sun, *The Art of War* - translated by Samuel B. Griffin. London: Oxford University Press, 1963.

Walton, Richard J., *Cold War and Counter-Revolution: The Foreign Policy of John F. Kennedy*. New York: The Viking Press, 1972.

Welch, Robert, *The Politician*. Privately printed edition, 1963.

Wilcox, Robert, *Target Patton: The Plot to Assassinate General George S. Patton*. Washington, D.C.: Regnery, 2008.

William Hood, *Mole*. New York: Ballantine, 1982.

Williams, Lindsey, *The Energy Non Crisis*. Wheatridge, Colorado: Worth Publishing, 1982.

Wise, David and Thomas B. Ross, *The Espionage Establishment*. New York: Random House, 1967.

Wise, David, *Mole*. New York: Random House, 1992.

——, *Molehunt: The Search for Traitors That Shattered the CIA*. New York: Random House, 1992.

——, *The Politics of Lying*. New York: Random House, 1973.

Wise, David, and Thomas B. Ross, *The Invisible Government*. New York: Bantam, 1962.

Wolf, Naomi, *The End of America: Letter of Warning to a Young Patriot*. White River Junction, Vermont: Chelsea Green, 2007.

Wormser, René A., *Foundations: Their Power and Influence*. Tennessee: Covenant House Books, c1993.

Wyden, Peter, *The Bay of Pigs*. New York: Simon and Schuster, 1979.

Yergin, Daniel, *The Prize: The Epic Quest for Oil, Money, and Power*. New York: Pocket Books, 1993.

Index

CPSIA information can be obtained at www.ICGtesting.com
Printed in the USA
BVOW02s0921060715

407282BV00001B/35/P